THE LOST CARAVEL

For my
good friend
Gavan Daws,
percipient biographer
of half-known lives,
who will, I hope, experience
no horror on reading this
attempt to reconstruct the past
with such insubstantial clues
as the colour of people's eyes...
Robert Langdon
Canberra, 30 May 1975.

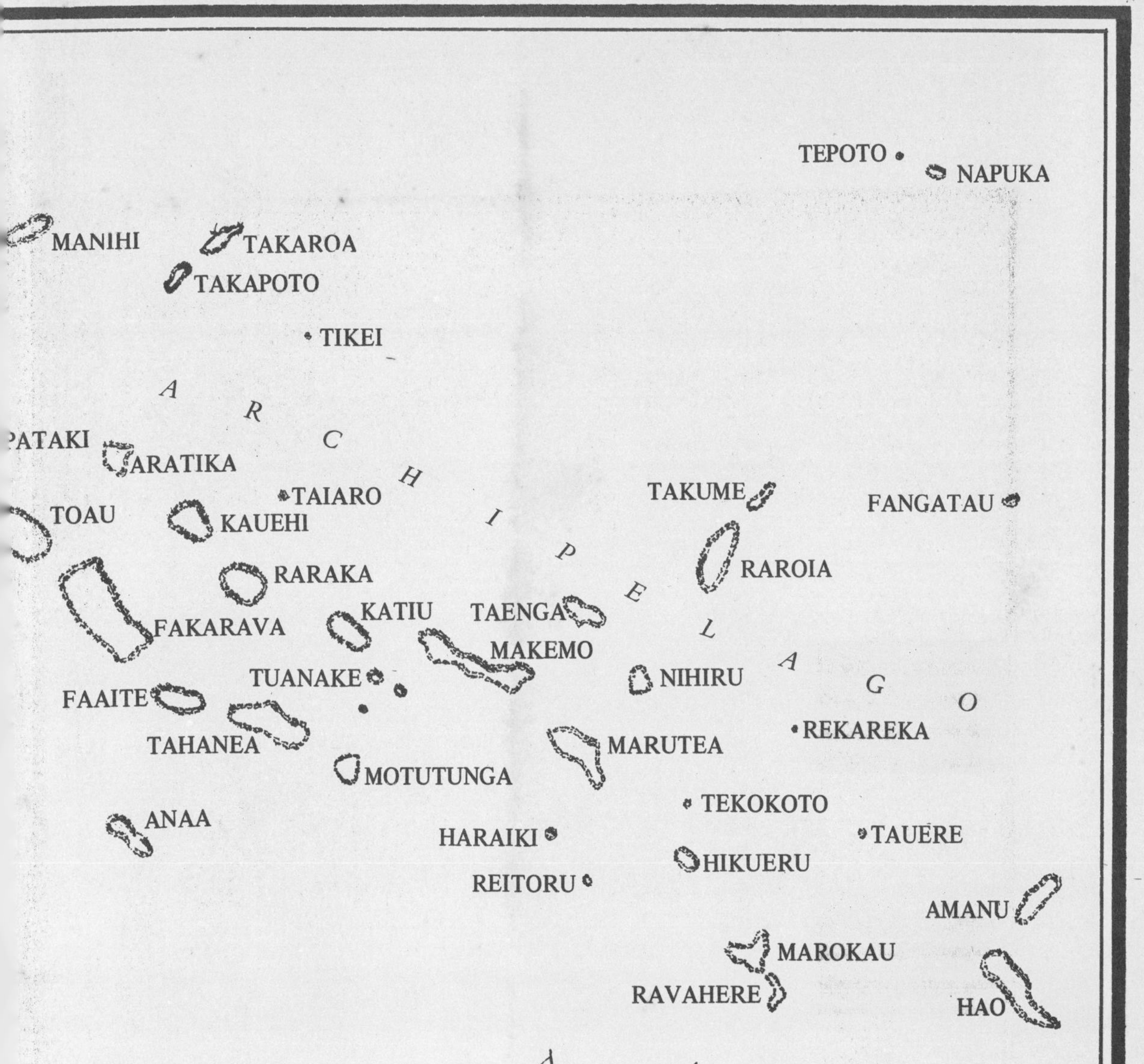

TEPOTO
NAPUKA
MANIHI
TAKAROA
TAKAPOTO
TIKEI
A R C H I P E L A G O
ATAKI
ARATIKA
TAIARO
TOAU
KAUEHI
TAKUME
FANGATAU
RARAKA
RAROIA
KATIU
TAENGA
FAKARAVA
MAKEMO
TUANAKE
NIHIRU
FAAITE
TAHANEA
REKAREKA
MARUTEA
MOTUTUNGA
TEKOKOTO
ANAA
HARAIKI
TAUERE
HIKUERU
REITORU
AMANU
MAROKAU
RAVAHERE
HAO
NENGONENGO
N
PARAOA
MANUHANGI
HEREHERETUE

John Collins

THE LOST CARAVEL

Robert Langdon

Pacific Publications

Sydney

National Library of Australia Card Number and ISBN 0 85807 021 9.

Designed, typeset, printed and published in Australia
by Pacific Publications (Aust) Pty Ltd,
29 Alberta Street, Sydney, Australia.

To
my wife Iva
and
daughter Louise
who patiently shared
their lives
with castaways
while
'The Lost Caravel'
made its
long voyage
into port

Contents

Plates

Maps

Illustrations in text

NOTE: All translations in this book from Spanish and French sources are by the author, except where published translations are cited. In translation, the old name Paumotu has been rendered as Tuamotu.

The attraction of Pacific prehistory is that of a series of fascinating 'whodunits', the attempted solution of which gives many people interest and pleasure. Long may the attempts continue!

Andrew Sharp in *Ancient Voyagers in Polynesia*.

1

The four cannon of Amanu

SCATTERED over some five hundred thousand square miles of ocean in the eastern South Pacific is a collection of seventy-six islands, chiefly atolls, known as the Tuamotu Archipelago.[1] At the eastern end of the archipelago, the atolls are few and far between, and are only a few miles in circuit, being scarcely more than salt water ponds. In the west, where the atolls are more numerous, they are sometimes as much as 100 miles around, and are seldom more than twenty or thirty miles apart.

In structure, all the atolls, large and small, are monotonously similar. Basically, they are coral reefs, usually oval or circular in shape, enclosing a lagoon. On the reefs are islets of varying size—sometimes several miles long—known as *motu*. The islets are formed of coral sand and other detritus, which occasionally provides a foothold for a few hardy trees and plants such as coconuts, pandanus palms and puka puka trees. Most of the *motu* are not more than a quarter of a mile across, and are usually much less. They are rarely more than twenty feet high even at low tide, although those bearing coconuts seem from a distance to be somewhat higher.[2]

Because the atolls are so low, with many of their reefs awash, they are extremely hazardous to navigators. Roggeveen, the Dutch explorer, who lost one of his ships among them in 1722, named them The Labyrinth.[3] Bougainville, the French explorer, who sighted some of them in 1768, called them collectively the Dangerous Archipelago.[4] And the ubiquitous Captain Cook spoke of them as 'half drowned islands' and 'this cluster of low over-flowed Isles', and emphasised the need to proceed among them with the utmost caution, especially at night.[5]

The Tuamotus have the distinction of being further from any continent than any other island group or individual island. They are all considerably further from South America than isolated Pitcairn, the *Bounty* island, which is 3,300 miles distant; while even the westernmost atoll is further removed from Australia than Tahiti and the other high islands of the Society group. Yet here is a paradox. Although the Tuamotus are so remote, the first Pacific island to be seen by European eyes was tiny, isolated Pukapuka on the north-eastern fringe of the archipelago.[6] This was in 1521 when Magellan, the first European mariner to enter the Pacific, made his epic crossing of that ocean. On the other hand, because of the dangers of navigation, and the insignificance of the archipelago to commerce, it was not until 1835, when HMS *Beagle* passed through the Tuamotus with the celebrated Charles Darwin on board, that the last two of the seventy-six islands of the group were 'officially' discovered and finally added to European charts.[7]

Even today, however, the charts of the Tuamotus leave much to be desired. Despite vast improvements in mapping techniques, particularly since the advent of aerial photography, the archipelago is still imperfectly surveyed, and the charts are apt to be defective regarding coastal details, orientation and even the position of the islands.[8] Some of the modern charts are still based on surveys by the early explorers. The British Admiralty chart of Hao, for example, still relies on a 'sketch survey' made by Captain F. W. Beechey in HMS *Blossom* in 1826 and soundings of Captain Edward Belcher of HMS *Sulphur* in 1840.[9] Similarly, the US Naval Oceanographic Office charts of Rangiroa, Tikehau and other atolls depend for their accuracy on work done by members of the United States Exploring Expedition in 1839.[10] But these almost archaic charts are not to be despised. Some of the atolls have not been surveyed at all, and the largest maps one can find of them are those measuring a few millimetres across on the hydrographic charts of the Tuamotus as a whole.[11]

It was because of deficiencies in the charts such as these that a Frenchman, Captain François Hervé, chanced to make an extraordinary discovery at Amanu Atoll in 1929. Hervé, a member of an old seafaring family, was one of the few Europeans of modern times to spend a large part of his life in the Tuamotus and to know those islands intimately. Born in France in 1875, he served in the merchant marine in China and the Atlantic before going to Tahiti in 1904 to become a schooner-skipper in the Tahiti-Tuamotus trade. Some six years later, Hervé and his wife became traders at Apataki, one of the largest atolls in the northwestern Tuamotus. Using two small motor vessels, *Torea* and *Kiwi*, Hervé gathered copra for dispatch to Tahiti from the Polynesian communities of Apataki and the surrounding islands. It was a hard, isolated life with irregular mails and supplies, no medical assistance, rustic Polynesian neighbours, and extremely few European visitors. However, Hervé had plenty to keep him occupied. Without knowing of the experiments in Japan of the celebrated Mikimoto, he became interested in trying to cultivate artificial pearls. In a laboratory on stilts built out over Apataki's lagoon, Hervé studied the anatomy and reproductiveness of the pearl oyster, and its reaction to various conditions. Although his efforts to cultivate pearls commercially never came to anything, the knowledge he gained eventually won him the appointment of inspector of pearlshell fisheries in the Tuamotus. Later, in 1925, the Governor of French Oceania invited him to act as administrator of the archipelago for three months.

Hervé's acting appointment actually lasted for eleven years, and he worked in it as hard as any man ever entrusted with the post. Twice a year in the government schooner *Mouette*, Hervé made extensive tours of the archipelago, sitting in judgment on court cases, patching up differences among the islanders, introducing new notions of hygiene and improving water supplies. When the occasion demanded and opportunity offered, he also tried his hand at surveying and chart-making, in an effort to improve on the faulty charts, which, over the years, had led many an unsuspecting schooner-skipper to lose his ship on some misplaced island or poorly recorded reef.[12]

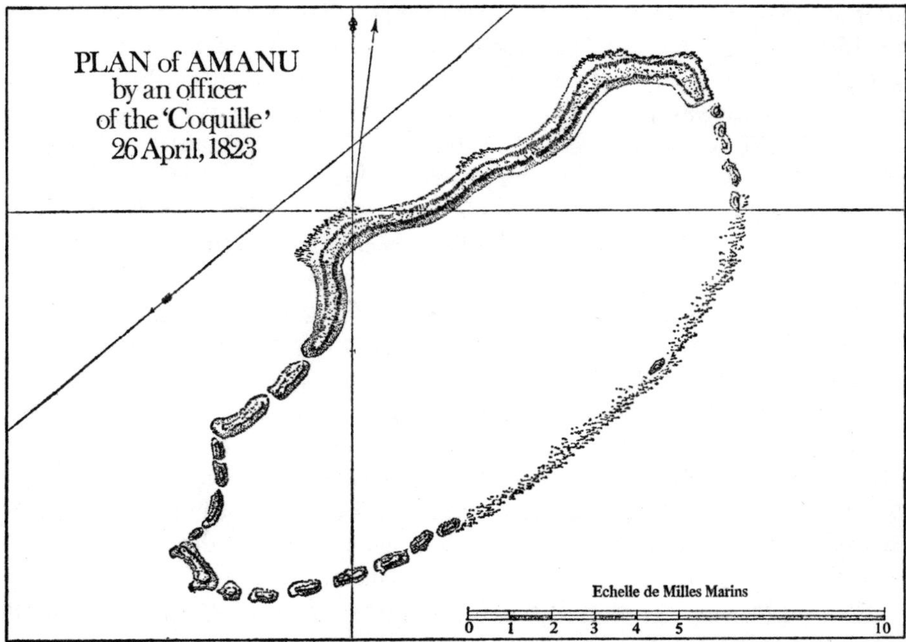

So it was that in 1929 Hervé came to make a chart of Amanu Atoll, one of the last of the large islands at the eastern end of the archipelago. Pearlers and traders from Tahiti, 500 miles to the west, had been visiting Amanu occasionally for just over a hundred years.[13] Yet the only detailed chart of the atoll available in 1929 was one made in the French exploring ship *Coquille* more than a century before. This chart had been constructed as the *Coquille* stood well clear of the western side of the island on 26 April 1823.[14] As a result, the surveying officer had no opportunity to record anything more than its approximate outline; and the vessel's commander, Captain L. I. Duperrey, could sum up his impressions of the atoll in a couple of sentences. 'Its length from north-east to south-west,' he wrote, 'is about 15 miles, and it encloses an immense lagoon, into which it is no doubt possible to penetrate by two passes which we noticed on the western side. Its vegetation is magnificent, but all the eastern part seemed to be a necklace of rocks and islets, strung out on an uninterrupted, circular reef.'[15]

Hervé's ship, the *Mouette*, was better suited for surveying Amanu than a large sailing ship such as the *Coquille*. She was a 64-ton motor schooner, built specially for the Islands, and could thus venture closer to the reefs than any large sailing ship could dare to do.[16] Moreover, Hervé had the advantage of being accompanied by a man with much local knowledge—the island's chief.

Hervé had been busy with his survey for some time when he happened to remark to the chief that, unlike most other atolls in the Tuamotus, Amanu had no wrecks on its reef. The chief replied that there was, in fact, a wreck; that eight generations earlier, a white man's ship had run aground on the island, and all of its crew had been eaten by the local people. Asked where this wreck was, the chief conducted Hervé to the atoll's eastern side, where, on the reef, near the northern tip, four heavy cannon were lying in shallow water, partly embedded in coral. Nearby was a pile of stones, which, as Hervé later put it, 'never were native to the Tuamotu Islands'. With the aid of gear on board the *Mouette*, Hervé prised one of the cannon from the reef and took it, together with the alien stones, to Tahiti. There he presented his finds to the local museum, which, then as now, was run by the Société des Etudes Océaniennes, an association of local historians and ethnologists, established in 1917.[17]

Normally, in those unhurried, pre-war days, the society took pains to record all gifts to its museum in its quarterly journal, the *Bulletin de la Société des Etudes Océaniennes.* However, for some reason, it failed to do so on this occasion; and as Hervé, an occasional journalist, wrote nothing about his discoveries himself, and as there was no newspaper or radio station in Tahiti to make a fuss about them, the finding of the four strange cannon at Amanu went almost unnoticed. Indeed, had it not been for a chance encounter in Papeete between Hervé and a visiting American yachtsman, all knowledge of the cannon might now be forgotten, except, perhaps, at Amanu.

The yachtsman was Gifford Pinchot, a wealthy Pennsylvanian, who arrived in Papeete in October 1929 while Hervé was still in town. With his wife, young son and a couple of scientists, Pinchot had been making a cruise through the Galapagos, Marquesas and Tuamotu Islands, gathering specimens for American museums. Pinchot and his wife called on the governor, Louis Bouge, soon after their arrival in Papeete. The governor found them congenial company and invited them to lunch. It was a pleasant, leisurely meal that reminded the Pinchots of 'old days in France'. There were about twenty people at the table, among whom was François Hervé. Hervé and the Pinchots struck up a friendship, and Hervé told them of the cannon he had brought from Amanu. Later, he took them to the museum to show it to them, and he gave them some of the strange stones that had come with it.

In a book on his voyage published in 1930, Gifford Pinchot recorded that the cannon was in the courtyard of the museum; that it was 'a very short iron cannon (carronade)'; and that Hervé thought it had come from 'a Spanish exploring ship sent out from Peru'. As for the alien stones, it was Hervé's view that these were from the ship's ballast. Pinchot added that on his return to the United States, one of the scientists from his schooner—Dr Henry A. Pilsbry of the Philadelphia Academy of Natural Sciences—had tried to establish the origin of the stones, 'and so perhaps to reconstruct a little the history of the ship that carried them'. However, these efforts were of no avail.[18]

Only one other contemporary writer recorded details of Hervé's discoveries at first hand. This was Samuel Russell, British vice-consul in Tahiti for many years, who published a guidebook called *Tahiti and French Oceania* in 1935. In this, in a reference occupying barely three lines, he gave one or two minute details not mentioned by Pinchot. 'In 1929,' he wrote, 'an extremely old iron cannon was discovered on the Amanu barrier reef, on the eastern side, and taken to Papeete by the Government schooner *Mouette* to be placed in the local museum. The cannon is supposed to be of Spanish make, but there is no record to show how it came to be embedded in the coral of Amanu.'[19]

A shortened version of Russell's statement was included in the second edition of the *Pacific Islands Year Book* published in the same year as Russell's book and by the same publisher.[20] It has been repeated in all editions of the *Year Book* to appear since then.[21] However, despite all the publicity and the obvious mystery of the cannon's origin, no one seems to have expressed any further interest in the cannon until May 1963 when I speculated about it in the *Pacific Islands Monthly,* of which I was then a staff writer. The occasion was the announcement by the French Government of plans to use several atolls in the Tuamotus, including Hao and Mururoa, as bases for nuclear experiments. I did not then know of Pinchot's book, and wrote:

> Hao and Mururoa, two of the four little-known atolls in the Tuamotu Archipelago which will figure in the French Government's H-bomb plans, both have some sort of claim to fame in the history of the Pacific. . .
>
> Hao, which has guarded an intriguing secret for 350 years, was the first atoll in the Tuamotus on which Europeans are known to have made a landing; and Mururoa was the scene of the first wreck of a British merchant ship in the Pacific. Hao is about 500 miles east of Tahiti; and Mururoa is about 775 miles south-east.
>
> Hao was discovered on February 10, 1606, by the Spanish navigator Pedro Fernandez de Quiros while he was crossing the Pacific from Callao, Peru, to establish a settlement in the Solomons. Quiros named his discovery San Pablo.
>
> When the Spaniards landed on the atoll, they found the natives friendly and exchanged presents with them. They also noticed half of a cedar pole of Peruvian or Nicaraguan style, and saw an old woman wearing a gold ring with an emerald.
>
> As there is no record of any European ships having been among the Tuamotu Archipelago before Quiros' voyage, the presence of the ring, emerald and cedar pole on the atoll are puzzling, to put it mildly.
>
> Andrew Sharp said in his book, *The Discovery of the Pacific Islands,* that these articles were 'relics, perhaps, of a vessel from Peru, not necessarily European, and not necessarily on a two-way voyage.' However, it seems almost certain that the ring, emerald and pole *were* relics from a European ship because in 1929 an ancient cannon was found embedded in the reef on the eastern side of Amanu atoll, nine miles north-east of Hao. The cannon was taken to Papeete in the French Government schooner *Mouette* and placed in the local museum. At the time of its discovery, it was supposed to be of Spanish make, but no one could explain how it came to be at Amanu.
>
> As far as I know, no one has managed to explain its presence there

yet; but there seems to be little doubt that it was from the same ship that brought the relics that Quiros saw at Hao. . . .[22]

Like many another article that one writes as a journalist, my speculations about the Amanu cannon produced no apparent response from readers. However, some four and a half years later when I again wrote on the same subject, my article led to the recovery of two more cannon from the Amanu reef. My second article followed my discovery of Pinchot's book and his account of what Hervé had found. This set me speculating along a new line that had not occurred to me before. Supposing—I asked myself—that the four cannon seen by Hervé really had come from a European ship that had been wrecked on Amanu before Quiros' visit to Hao in 1606 . . . and supposing that the crew of that ship had not been eaten by the Amanu cannibals, as Hervé's chief had said, but had settled down and intermarried with the local women . . . and supposing that those sailors had included a sprinkling of red-haired, blue-eyed men . . . and supposing that some of the sailors and their descendants had emigrated or drifted in canoes from one island to another over the next couple of centuries . . . might not all that account for the blondeness, the light skins and marked European features that the explorers of Captain Cook's era had noted among the Tahitians and their neighbours when they first discovered them two hundred years ago?

From research I had done in the 1950s for a popular history of Tahiti and from subsequent reading, I knew that dozens of scientists had put forward theories on where the Polynesians had come from. South America (by means of Kon-Tiki style rafts), Indonesia, Southern India, Egypt, Arabia, Malaysia, Babylonia, Indo-China and the Philippines had all been suggested at various times.[23] On the other hand, most Pacific ethnologists were agreed that there was a Caucasian (i.e. European) strain among the Polynesians; but this was thought to have been acquired thousands of years ago, before the Polynesians had entered the Pacific.[24] No one, as far as I knew, had ever suggested that the explanation for that Caucasian strain might be that a party of Europeans had been shipwrecked in the Tuamotus in quite recent times.

To test the feasibility of my new theory, I began re-reading the accounts of Polynesia's early explorers with an eye for ethnographic details that had only mildly interested me before.[25] I also combed through Pacific literature for information about any ships, particularly Spanish ships, that had ventured into the eastern Pacific in early times and had not been heard of again. My researches into both these fields seemed to confirm my theory, rather than confound it. Indeed, I came up with the name of one Spanish ship that could well have left its bones on Amanu; and as this ship, the caravel *San Lesmes,* had disappeared early in the sixteenth century, it seemed to me that a mere handful of survivors could have had a profound influence on the genetic make-up of the Eastern Polynesians.

I was still engrossed in my researches into these matters when, in November 1967, the *Pacific Islands Monthly* sent me on a reporting assignment to Tahiti.

PLATE 1. A Tahitian taxi driver poses with one of the two cannon recovered from Amanu by Captain Hervé Le Goaziou. The second cannon is in the background. The photograph was taken outside the entrance to the Museum of the Discoverers at Point Venus, Tahiti, in August 1969. The cannon have since been placed on wooden mounts.

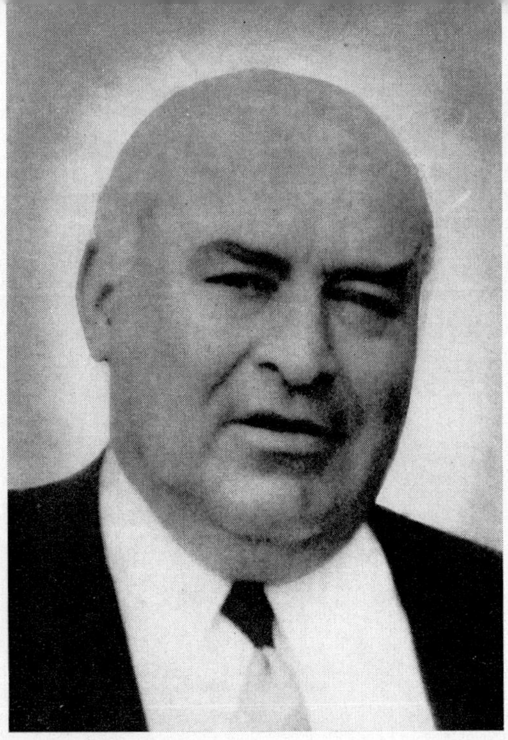

Captain Hervé Le Goaziou (left) recovered two cannon from Amanu in 1969 while serving with the French Navy at neighbouring Hao Atoll. At right is the late Captain François Hervé who recovered the first cannon in 1929 while serving as Administrator of the Tuamotu Archipelago.

Two built-up cannon which resemble those of Amanu have been recovered in England over the years. That at left, dating back to the fifteenth century, was found in a swamp in Cumberland and is now in the Metropolitan Museum of Art, New York. The other is an 8 ft iron gun from the 'Mary Rose', recovered in 1970 off Portsmouth with an iron cannonball still in position. Photographs: Metropolitan Museum of Art and Portsmouth Corporation.

The assignment could scarcely have come at a more opportune time, for if I was to pursue my castaways theory fruitfully, it was important for me to establish whether Hervé's cannon was a sixteenth century Spanish cannon, or, at least, whether it dated back to early times.

On arriving in Tahiti I took the first opportunity to visit the museum, but was disappointed to find that the cannon was no longer there. The museum secretary, Miss Aurora Natua, a mine of information on matters Tahitian, explained to me that since 1929 many things had happened. The museum had shifted its premises, first, from a building in the Avenue Bruat to an old, disused building on a park-like property at Mamao, and then, in 1956, to its present premises in the Rue Brea.[26] Moreover, the war had intervened, and all of the people associated with the museum in 1929 had either died or moved on. However, Aurora—everyone seemed to call her Aurora—had a vague idea that an old cannon from the museum had once been given to the Tahitian Battalion of the French Army for its arms museum at Taravao, some thirty miles from Papeete. She tried to confirm this during my stay in Tahiti, but as frequently happens on that island, no one could be found who knew anything about it. On the other hand, Aurora expressed keen interest in my castaways theory; and her big, brown Tahitian eyes lit up excitedly when I took down a copy of Pinchot's book from the museum's own shelves and showed her the passages describing Hervé's discovery of the cannon.

On my departure from Tahiti, Aurora promised to try to solve the vanished cannon mystery and let me know the result. However, when, after several weeks, no letter had arrived from her, I decided to publish an article on my castaways theory, using such information as I already had. As a busy journalist—I was then in my fourth year as assistant editor of the *Pacific Islands Monthly*—I was reluctant to waste the time and effort I had put into my researches.

My article, entitled 'Were Europeans Living in the Eastern Pacific in the 16th Century?' appeared in the *Pacific Islands Monthly* for January 1968.[27] This time, two or three readers were moved to write letters to me about my speculations and a newspaper in New Zealand sought permission to republish the article.[28] But the most interesting reaction was passed on to me by Aurora some time later.

Meanwhile, I had resigned from the *Pacific Islands Monthly* to take up a new post in the Research School of Pacific Studies at the Australian National University, Canberra. This kept me so busy for the next nine months or so that I had little time to devote to other matters. Then another event occurred that set me thinking again about 'my' castaways. In December 1968 I was invited to attend a World Conference on Records in Salt Lake City in the following July, and to deliver a paper on 'European Migrations to Australia and the Pacific.' When I suggested to the sponsors of the conference that I should like to pay particular attention to the question of 'European Castaways in the Pacific before Captain Cook,' they readily agreed, and so I set about preparing a paper with that emphasis. In doing this I wrote to Aurora to ask if she had located the missing cannon. She replied in the negative; but she did have some exciting news from Amanu itself.[29]

Some time previously, she said, a French naval officer (whose name she could not remember because it was 'a long Breton one') had come into the museum, having read my castaways article in the *Pacific Islands Monthly*. The officer was stationed at Hao, the forward base for the French nuclear tests at Mururoa. He was an amateur marine archaeologist, and was interested to try to recover the three cannon that Hervé had left on the Amanu reef. His purpose in visiting the museum, he said, was to find out if anything was known about the cannon beyond what I had stated in my article.

Aurora told me that she had shown the officer Pinchot's account of Hervé's discovery, and he had expressed particular interest in the strange stones that Hervé had found. Later, he had come to the museum again, having visited Amanu in the interval. At Amanu he had recovered two cannon, and these had been brought to Tahiti. 'They are also iron cannon,' Aurora wrote, 'and the officer said they seem to be of English make. I asked him how deep [deeply embedded] they were in the coral and he said ten centimetres [about four inches]. As soon as I know more, I will write to you. . . .'

Although I wrote to Aurora immediately urging her to find out everything she could about the cannon in case they, too, disappeared, I still had no precise information about them when I left for the conference in Salt Lake City. However, on my return flight to Australia I stopped off in Tahiti and—after a week of inquiry to establish where they were—I saw them for myself. They had been handed over to the newly-opened Museum of the Discoverers at Point Venus, owned and run by a French journalist, Bob Putigny.[30]

Armed with a camera, a tape measure and a notebook, I took a taxi to Point Venus. The cannon were lying on the ground outside the museum entrance. Each bore a small plaque inscribed in French: 'Gift of the French Navy to the Territory of French Polynesia.' But there was nothing to indicate who had found them, where they had come from, or when. Still, the cannon did seem quite different from any such weapons I had previously seen in that their barrels were corrugated. They were obviously made of iron, and this seemed to be extremely hard and virtually free from rust. Although only fifty-six inches long and forty-and-a-half inches in circumference at the widest part at the breech end, they were so heavy that I could not lift or even move them.

Using my taxi driver to add to the photogenic effect, I photographed the cannon from a variety of angles, took all the measurements I could think of, and then returned to Papeete to try to make certain that they were, indeed, the cannon from Amanu. As Putigny was away in Europe, I sought out a friend of his, Marc Darnois, Directeur des Affaires Culturelles in the local administration. Darnois, a former yachtsman and co-author of a book with Putigny, had seen the cannon at Amanu in 1947. He showed me on a rough sketch map where they then were, and this, as I later confirmed, was precisely where Aurora's naval officer with the long Breton name had found them.[31]

The naval officer, as Aurora had meanwhile discovered, was Capitaine de Vaisseau Hervé Le Goaziou. He was still stationed at Hao Atoll, as far as she knew, and she suggested that I write to him there seeking details of his discovery. I did this on my return to Australia. Several months later, I received a reply from him, not from Hao, but from the French naval base at Brest, to which he had been transferred. Writing on 5 May 1970 Captain Le Goaziou answered all the questions I had put to him about the cannon. He also sent me two sketches indicating their location on the Amanu reef when he had found them. Translated from French, his letter read in part as follows:[32]

> While I was in Papeete, Miss Aurora Natua spoke to me of your interest in the wreck at Amanu. . . . Here is an account of the events which resulted in my recovering the cannon:—
>
> Last year I was in service at Hao, which is the forward base for our nuclear testing area in the Tuamotus. I was the most senior naval officer, being in charge of all maritime matters. Amanu Atoll is 'next door' to Hao, and has always been closely linked with it. In earlier times, the people of Amanu exercised a sort of supremacy over all the atolls of the region and had conquered Hao. Family relations are very close, and at least once a week we made a trip to Amanu to deliver supplies and to enable the Amanu people, who were working at the base at Hao, to rejoin their families.
>
> In going to that atoll myself in November 1968 I made contact with some pearlshell divers; and in talking to them about one thing and another, I asked them for information about wrecks, since I have been interested in underwater archaeology for many years. My interlocutors understood French, but spoke it very badly and my Tahitian is rudimentary.
>
> [However, through a schoolmistress from Raiatea who speaks both French and Tahitian] one of the divers told me of a wreck and of cannon, and indicated to me roughly in which part of the island the wreck was. He proposed on the spur of the moment to take me there, but, this was not possible for me on that particular day as I had to go back to Hao.
>
> Fifteen days later I went back to try to obtain further information. Meanwhile, I had searched for details in Papeete, and Miss Aurora Natua had pointed out that around 1930 Monsieur Hervé had seen those cannon, and that one had been taken to Papeete, where it subsequently disappeared.
>
> On my return to Amanu, I was unable to obtain any further information except from the schoolmistress. She told me that the diver who had spoken to me had been criticised for doing so by his comrades as the cannon were 'tabu'. Even the schoolmistress was reluctant to speak. However, according to her, the wreck was a Spanish one, and there had been 35 survivors from it. She was unable to give me the reason for the 'tabu'. . . .
>
> Soon afterwards I learned where the cannon were, and as I had at my disposal at Hao a number of Navy helicopters, they were easily recovered by my friend Captain Maureau, commander of the aero-naval base at Hao.
>
> They were found some 15 metres from the edge of the reef. At low

VIEW OF COAST FROM POINT A

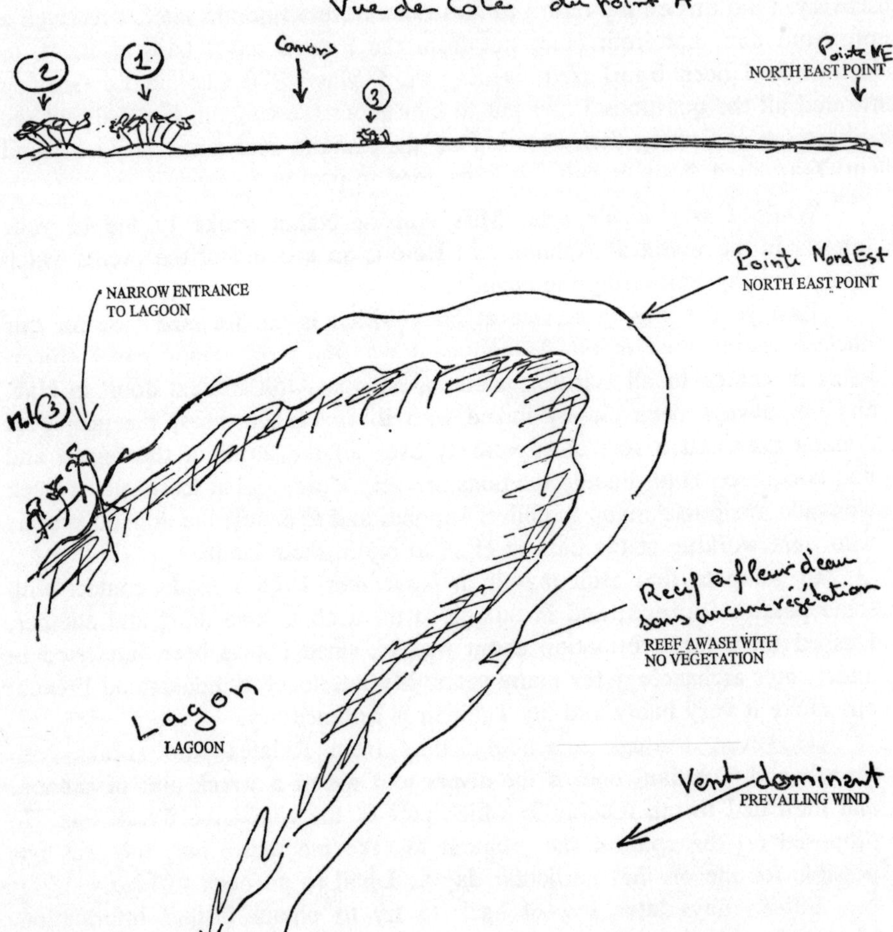

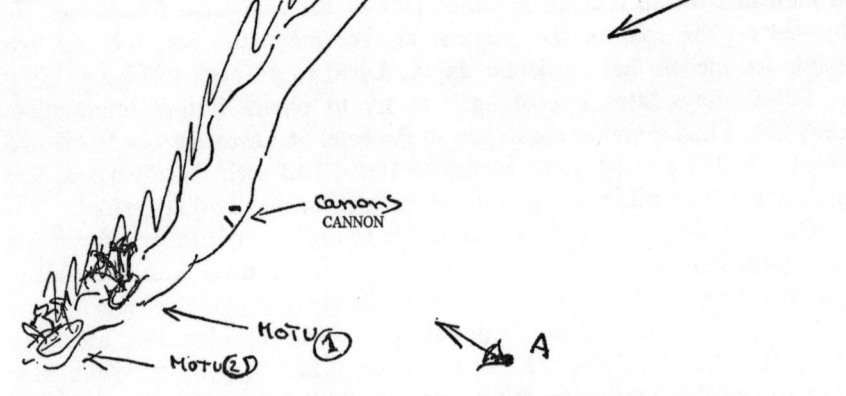

Captain Le Goaziou's sketches indicating the location on the Amanu reef of the two cannon recovered by him, and the view of the northern part of the atoll as seen from a ship approaching it from the east.

tide, the reef is exposed, and it is only covered by the waves in bad weather. At high tide, the cannon were awash, as there is little variation in the tides at Amanu—1.4 metres [4 ft 7 in.] at the most.

The nearest *motu* to the cannon was about 500 metres to the south. [On the other side] the reef is awash to the northernmost point of the island, and in poor visibility, or at night, a ship could expect to leave the atoll to the south in the belief that the last clump of trees marked the end of the island. The cannon were about 10 metres apart and partly covered with coral. On average they had a coral crust of 20 cm [8 in.], and it was necessary to use levers to get them out.

As we did not wish to upset the Amanu people, I had the cannon lifted from their site by helicopters and taken direct to Hao. The Amanu people did not learn about this until after the cannon were in Papeete and there was no reaction. The Admiral has given the cannon to the territory and they are now at Point Venus.

[After recovering the cannon], we searched for relics on the nearest *motu,* which is normally inhabited, but found nothing. We also took advantage of a spell of calm weather (because this is the island's windward side where the sea is always breaking) to dive to a depth of 20 metres along the edge of the reef in search of other relics . . . I searched particularly for an anchor, or some other metal object, but found nothing. However, I hope to return to that spot, because, several hundred metres from where the cannon were found, our divers discovered some wreckage which was sheathed in copper. This, though, seemed to be part of a much more recent shipwreck.[33]

Bad weather and my return to France prevented me from continuing my researches . . . [In any case], I was by no means preoccupied with them, as there were plenty of other things to be done at Hao . . .

Captain Le Goaziou added that he was curious to know why there had only been two cannon on the reef rather than three. 'Monsieur Hervé saw four cannon and recovered one', he said. 'I found only two. What has become of the fourth one?'[34]

Needless to say, it would be interesting and instructive to know more about both the fourth cannon—and, for that matter, the third. Were they similar in size and design to the two that lie at Point Venus? Were they, when found, nearer to the outer edge of the Amanu reef, or further away? However, at the time I received Captain Le Goaziou's letter such questions as these did not seem important. What was important was to try to establish the approximate age of the two cannon whose location was known, and so determine whether they could have come from the caravel *San Lesmes* or some other early ship.

Several of my scientific friends claimed that the only way to do this would be to get a metallurgist to examine a sample of the iron from the cannon. This was easier said than done, considering that I was in Canberra and the cannon were in Tahiti, four thousand miles away. However, eventually I located a specialist in old guns, who was able to deduce a great deal about the cannon merely by studying one of my photographs and a rough sketch giving their dimensions. The specialist, Mr A. N. Kennard, then assistant master of the Armouries in the Tower of London, wrote to me on 29 July 1970 as follows:

> The gun shown in your drawing and photograph is a strange looking affair. Its corrugated surface leads me to suspect that it is not cast [as I had suggested] but is 'built up', being composed of wrought iron rings shrunk on to an interior tube, this being the old method of constructing large iron guns before the art of casting them was perfected in the mid-sixteenth century. The trunnions seem very small, almost too small for their purpose and the gun has altogether an archaic look. It could well be of sixteenth century date. If, however, there is any possibility of the guns being Chinese or from anywhere in that part of the world, then they could be as late as 1800 since the Chinese were making cannon of incredibly primitive methods at a very late date indeed . . .

A day or two after Mr Kennard's letter reached me, I noticed a news item in *The Canberra Times* about the recovery, off Portsmouth, England, of an 8 ft iron gun from the wreck of the *Mary Rose,* one of the finest ships of King Henry VIII. This ship had sunk in 1545 while putting out to fight the French. The gun was said to be identical to one taken from the same wreck in 1842.[35] I immediately wrote to Mr Kennard to ask whether he had seen the newly-found gun and whether it resembled the two cannon from Amanu. Mr Kennard replied: 'I have just examined the newly-discovered *Mary Rose* gun and it is "built-up" just like the others from the same vessel. I suspect that these guns were old when installed on the ship and were probably made long before she sank in 1545. They are something like your guns from Amanu, but more slender and longer . . .'[36] Mr Kennard also gave me references to the scanty literature on 'built-up' guns.[37]

With this information, any lingering doubts about the antiquity of the Amanu cannon seemed to be removed. Either the cannon were of a type that was in use in Europe before 1550 (when the development of the blast furnace made the casting of iron guns possible),[38] or they were Chinese or Asian guns of no later than 1800. However, on the face of things, the possibility of the cannon being Chinese seemed rather remote; and on investigation even more so. For one thing, the Chinese have never been a Pacific-minded maritime people. As the Chinese scholar Dr Chiao-Min Hsieh wrote in a recent paper: 'Through most of their long history of cultural and scientific development, the Chinese people have been but passively interested in the Pacific Ocean. Believing that no land existed beyond the Pacific, most early Chinese explorers directed their expeditions westward. . . . Apparently there have been few, if any, planned deep penetrations of the Pacific Ocean by the Chinese. . . .[39]

Thus, for the four cannon of Amanu to be Chinese, it was necessary to conjure up a Chinese ship that was at least six thousand miles from her normal waters. Furthermore, the ship must have been heading towards China rather than away from it because the cannon were found on the eastern, or South American, side of the atoll—in such a position that only a ship coming from the east could reach. In short, to think in terms of a Chinese ship being wrecked on Amanu's reef was to toy with a highly improbable idea for which no evidence was known. The same, as far as I could discover, could be said for a ship from any other part of Asia. On the other hand, to postulate that the Amanu cannon were relics of a European ship of the pre-1550 era was in accordance both with probability and known facts, for, as I had already established, there was one such ship, the *San Lesmes,* that did disappear in the eastern South Pacific in the first half of the sixteenth century. The *San Lesmes* was last seen on 1 June 1526, six days after passing through the Strait of Magellan en route to the East Indies. At the time of her disappearance, she was one of a fleet of four ships—originally there had been seven—that had left Spain in 1525 under the command of Garcia Jofre de Loaisa. The fleet was the first from Europe to venture into the Pacific after the pioneering voyage of Magellan; it was also the last to attempt to cross that ocean from the southern tip of South America for almost a hundred years. The story of the expedition was one of almost unmitigated disaster and failure; and as the world soon forgets those who fail, the unfortunate exploits of Loaisa and his men have long since been consigned to oblivion. Thus, whereas details of Magellan's successful voyage are still widely known, most books on the history of Europeans in the Pacific have little or nothing to say about Loaisa's. J. C. Beaglehole's *The Exploration of the Pacific,* for example, dismisses the Loaisa expedition in two and a half sentences. The authoritative four-volume British Naval Intelligence Division handbook on the Pacific Islands does the same in a line and a half without mentioning Loaisa's name; while such books as Grattan's *The Southwest Pacific to 1900* ignore it altogether.[40] Perhaps, though, the historians of the past have dealt too summarily with the Loaisa expedition. For if the crew of the *San Lesmes* survived their shipwreck, intermarried with the local women, and spread their seed—to use a Biblical expression—throughout the surrounding islands, that would surely cast an entirely different light on much that has previously been written and assumed about the people and culture of Eastern Polynesia.

But one should not be hasty and jump to conclusions. The two cannon that Captain Le Goaziou recovered bear no markings that positively link them with the *San Lesmes.* So all one should say at this stage is that they may have come from that ship. However, as no other ship is known that is likely to have left her guns at Amanu, it will henceforth be assumed—to facilitate discussion—that the guns in question did come from her, although the possibility that they may have come from some other, unknown ship should be constantly borne in mind.

2

The lost caravel

FOR two thousand years before the start of the sixteenth century, the people of Europe obtained silks, spices, precious stones, aromatics, exotic woods and other Oriental luxuries by means of a long overland route from the Far East. Through a series of middlemen using camel and mule trains, the goods of the Orient were marched over half the world, via Lanchow, Lob Nor, Samarkand, Baghdad, Damascus, Aleppo and other caravan cities until they reached the eastern Mediterranean port of Antioch.[1] From there they were carried on in the trading vessels of many nations to their European markets. Other trade routes were developed over the centuries to take Chinese, Indian and other Asiatic merchandise to the eastern Mediterranean by way of the Red and Arabian Seas, the Persian Gulf and the Euphrates River valley.[2] The merchandise was much sought after, and the trade through the Levant, as the eastern Mediterranean was called, was a profitable one to those who controlled it. It was also an apparently immutable feature of European life. However, towards the end of the fifteenth century it suddenly appeared that two new routes to the riches of the East had been discovered. Bartholomeu Dias, sailing south from Portugal in 1487, succeeded in rounding the Cape of Good Hope, thereby opening the gateway to India. Five years later, Columbus, sailing west from Spain, discovered some islands in Central America that he thought were Japan.[3]

Columbus' discoveries inspired the Spanish monarch, Emperor Charles V, to try to steal a march on the Portuguese king. He persuaded Pope Alexander VI, himself a Spaniard, to issue a bull granting sovereignty to Spain over all lands more than 100 leagues west of the Spanish Azores. He also got the Pope to rescind all earlier papal grants ratifying Portuguese claims to Africa and the route to the Orient. Not surprisingly, these edicts did not please the Portuguese king. But by clever diplomacy, he succeeded in obtaining an agreement with the Spaniards that suited him. This agreement, the Treaty of Tordesillas of 1494, cancelled the effect of the Pope's rulings, and it divided the newly-discovered world between the Portuguese and Spanish kings. The line of demarcation was fixed at 370 leagues west of the Portuguese Cape Verde Islands. Everything east of that line was to be Portuguese; everything west, Spanish.[4]

For the next twenty years, as explorers of both countries added new lands to their globes and charts, the Tordesillas line served its purpose without dispute. For the Portuguese, Vasco da Gama found the way to India, and others pushed on to the East Indies and China. For the Spaniards, Columbus followed up his first voyage of discovery with three others to Central America; Balboa struck across the Isthmus of Panama to the Pacific; and others explored the Atlantic coasts of North and South America.[5]

Both Spain and Portugal were satisfied with their own discoveries and territorial conquests, and no problems arose over whose sphere they lay in until the Portuguese pushed their frontiers to the spice-rich Moluccas in 1512. It then occurred to a Portuguese officer, Fernão Magalhães (known in English as Ferdinand Magellan), that perhaps his countrymen had now gone so far round the world that they had actually got into the Spanish sphere. Magellan was then serving in the Portuguese Indies, where he took a keen interest in the problem of establishing longitude.

Returning to Portugal in about 1516, he told the Portuguese king of his suspicions and put forward a proposal to settle the matter one way or another. This was to sail to the Moluccas by way of the 'bottom' of South America and so find out whether that route was longer or shorter than via the Cape of Good Hope. The proposal was dear to its author's heart, and when the king rejected it, Magellan publicly renounced his citizenship, crossed into Spain, and entered the service of Emperor Charles V. He arrived in Seville in October 1517; saw the emperor in Valladolid in the following February; and almost immediately obtained support for his proposed expedition. His success was undoubtedly due to two claims: (1) that his expedition would prove the Moluccas to be in the Spanish sphere, and (2) that the South American route would prove to be the best way of reaching them.[6]

With a fleet of five small ships and a complement of 239 men, Magellan sailed from Seville in September 1519. After wintering at Port St Julian in what is now Argentine territory, and putting down a mutiny among the Portuguese members of his crew, Magellan entered the strait that now bears his name. In the strait, one of his ships was wrecked and another deserted. But the expedition pressed on and so entered the ocean that Magellan called the Pacific. Nearly two months later, on 24 January 1521, the expedition came upon a small island with trees on it, which was named San Pablo. This island, which modern scholars identify as Pukapuka, in the north-eastern corner of the Tuamotus, was thus the first Pacific island to be discovered by Europeans.[7] On approaching it, the Spaniards found it to be uninhabited, and as they could find no bottom with the lead, they sailed on, apparently without landing.

Eleven days later, another island was sighted. This, too, was small and uninhabited, and although it abounded in birds and trees, it provided the expedition with neither water nor fruit. 'We saw there many of the fish called Tiburoni', wrote Pigafetta, an Italian chronicler of the expedition. Accordingly, the island was named Isla de los Tiburones, or Shark Island; and the two islands that the Spaniards had seen were bracketed together as Las Desaventuradas—the Unfortunate Islands—clear evidence of what they thought of them.

From Tiburones, which was almost certainly Flint Island,[8] 410 miles

These five drawings representing the first voyage round the world and its aftermath appeared in a book published in Madrid in 1601-15. The book is a history by Antonio Herrera y Tordesillas concerning Spanish exploits in the Americas and South Seas. The picture above, with an inset of Magellan, depicts the discovery of Magellan Strait. Those at left show Magellan's ships passing through the strait into the Pacific; the death of Magellan at the hands of 'Indians' in the Philippines; and the return to Seville of the 'Victoria' after circumnavigating the world. An oared galley or galleass is at left in the last-named picture. Below is an artist's impression of the Badajoz-Elvas conference when representatives of Spain and Portugal tried unsuccessfully to determine whether the Moluccas were in the Spanish or Portuguese half of the world.

north of Tahiti, Magellan sailed for thirty days before seeing any more islands. These were some of the southern Marianas chain—Guam, Rota and possibly Saipan—which the Spaniards called both Islas de las Velas Latinas (Islands of Lateen Sails), and Islas de los Ladrones (Islands of Thieves). Despite the islanders' thievish propensities, the Spaniards were able to trade for fresh food and water, and they thus ended ninety-eight hungry days on the vast, empty Pacific.

From the Marianas, the expedition sailed to the Philippines. After six weeks in those islands, Magellan was killed in an affray with the natives. Later one of the expedition's three ships was burned. The remaining two, the *Trinidad* and *Victoria,* then wandered southward, finally reaching Tidore in the Moluccas on 8 November 1521. Here, both ships were soon loaded with rich cargoes of cloves, mace, cinnamon, nutmeg and sandalwood, and their crews prepared to return to Spain. However, when the *Trinidad* sprang a leak, the captains decided that the *Victoria* should not wait for her, but should sail at once to take advantage of the east monsoon. The *Victoria* set off on 27 December 1521. She had a complement of forty-seven Europeans and thirteen Malays under the command of a Basque seaman, Juan Sebastian Elcano. After touching at several Indonesian islands, including Timor, Elcano headed for home by way of the Cape of Good Hope.

For the next five months, the *Victoria's* crew subsisted on nothing but corn, rice and water. Being now in the Portuguese sphere, Elcano did not dare go near any land for fear of capture. But after twenty-two of his men had died of hunger, he was finally compelled to stop at the Cape Verde Islands. Claiming that he had come from the Antilles, on the Spanish side of the Tordesillas line, Elcano got a quantity of refreshments before the truth leaked out and the Portuguese arrested thirteen of his men who went ashore in a boat. Elcano then noticed that the Portuguese were preparing four caravels to come and overpower the *Victoria.* Determined to die rather than fall into Portuguese hands, he ordered his men to clap on all sail, and although, as he later claimed, they were 'more exhausted than men have ever been before', they jumped to it and made a narrow escape.

About eight weeks later, on 7 September 1522, the *Victoria* arrived at San Lucar on the Guadalquivir River in southern Spain; and on the 9th she moved upriver to Seville. The *Victoria* thus became the first ship to circumnavigate the world. Already from San Lucar, Elcano had written to Charles V informing him of the *Victoria's* arrival and giving him a brief account of the expedition's proceedings. His crew, he said, was now reduced to only eighteen, for he did not count four Malays who had also survived the voyage. He urged the emperor to use his influence to obtain the release of the thirteen men captured in the Cape Verde Islands. 'They will count it as their gain', he said, 'to know that we have given practical proof that the earth is a sphere; having sailed round it, going from the west, we have come back from the east . . . I ask Your Majesty, in recognition of the hard work, hunger and thirst, cold and heat which our men have borne in the service of Your Majesty to graciously ensure their release and to award them their share of spice which is due to them from the freight we have brought home'.[9]

Elcano's letter reached the emperor at his court in Valladolid with unusual speed for those days. Indeed, in less than a week the emperor had replied expressing his 'infinite thanks' to the Basque captain for bringing the *Victoria* safely back to Spain. He also commanded Elcano to appear at court to give an account of his voyage in person, and to bring with him two of his most reliable and best-informed men.

Elcano, with Francisco Albo, the pilot, and Hernando de Bustamente, the *Victoria's* barber and surgeon, presented themselves in Valladolid towards the end of September. For several weeks, they were closely and separately questioned about all aspects of the voyage. Their questioners were especially curious about the location of Magellan's Strait, the mutiny at Port St Julian and the route the *Victoria* had taken. They also asked whether the *Victoria's* crew had, perhaps, smuggled some spices ashore at San Lucar or elsewhere for their own use.

Elcano's answers and those of his companions were deemed satisfactory; and on 23 January of the following year, the emperor announced rewards for them and the rest of the *Victoria's* crew. Elcano himself was to be paid an annual pension of 500 gold ducats and was to receive 'a fourth part of the twentieth' of the Crown's share of the spice cargo. Later, Charles V also announced that Elcano had the right to use a coat-of-arms.

Meanwhile, the *Victoria's* cargo had been shipped to Antwerp and sold for a handsome sum, and the emperor, with the backing of the noted Spanish financier Cristobal de Haro, decided to send another, larger fleet to the Moluccas for more spices. However, when news of this reached Portugal, the Portuguese king, João III, insisted on an inquiry to decide whether the Spice Islands were, in fact, in Spanish territory. The emperor, apparently confident of his position, agreed.

The inquiry was held in the Spanish and Portuguese border towns of Badajoz and Elvas from 11 April to 1 June 1524. Pilots, cosmographers, and other experts were invited to give evidence and sixteen survivors of the Magellan expedition—five of whom had been released from the Cape Verde Islands—were interrogated. Among Spain's chief delegates were Elcano, Hernando Colon (son of Columbus), Sebastian Cabot and Juan Vespucci, all notable figures in the field of exploration and geography. Meetings of the delegates took place alternately in the two border towns. Elcano's evidence was of major importance; and because he feared that the Portuguese might kill him, he successfully petitioned the emperor for two armed bodyguards.

Elcano gave his evidence on the last day of the inquiry. It consisted of a summary of the Spanish case, illustrated by a chart showing his nation's claims. The chart was presumably based on the wildly inaccurate longitudes of the pilot Albo, whose position for the Philippines, for example, was more than fifty degrees in error.[10] As with all the rest of the Spanish evidence, the chart failed to convince the Portuguese, and the inquiry broke up without a conclusion being reached. The stalemate did not really worry the Portuguese king, for his forces had already vitiated the outcome by occupying the Moluccas. Charles V, on the other hand, was not perturbed, either, for he now felt free to proceed with his plan to send a second expedition to those islands.

The new expedition, it was decided, would consist of seven ships—four large ones, two caravels and a pinnace.[11] No Portuguese were to be allowed to serve in it, to avoid the discord that Magellan had experienced. The command of the expedition was given to a veteran soldier, Comendador Garcia Jofre de Loaisa (or Loaysa), who was to assume the governorship of the Moluccas on his arrival in those islands.[12] Elcano, the Basque, was offered the posts of chief pilot, second in command, and commander of one of the ships; and to make sure he acted loyally, the emperor ordered his annual pension of 500 gold ducats to be withheld until he returned from the new voyage.[13]

As the emperor foresaw a prosperous future for the spice trade, he decided that Loaisa's ships should be assembled in the Galician port of La Coruña, rather than in Seville, the port Magellan had used. He also ordered facilities for the handling of spice cargoes to be built there. La Coruña was preferred to Seville, the usual port for ships trading with Cuba, Mexico and Spain's other new colonies in the Americas for several reasons. One was that, being in the north of Spain, it was nearer to northern Europe, and therefore cheaper for ships from those countries to use. Costs at La Coruña were also lower; more and bigger ships could gather in its ample harbour than in the Guadalquivir River at Seville; and ships did not get worms in them as they did in Seville's river water. Finally, there was less risk of attack by Portuguese pirates; and fewer opportunities for captains to bring contraband ashore.[14]

The decision in favour of La Coruña, the ban on Portuguese seamen, and the appointment of Elcano as chief pilot had a significant effect on the nature of Loaisa's crew. Instead of the motley band of Spaniards, Portuguese, Basques, Genoese, Sicilians, Germans, Greeks, Neapolitans, Flemings, Corfiotes, Frenchmen, Ligurians, Negroes, Malays and the single Englishman that Magellan took with him[15]—the typically cosmopolitan crew that a Mediterranean port such as Seville provided—Loaisa's crew was much more of a piece. With a few exceptions, the crew seems to have been entirely drawn from Spain itself. The exceptions included three of the four Malays brought back by Elcano, several Flemish gunners and a Negro or two. Many of the men were recruited by Elcano himself in his own home territory, the Basque country. So a notable proportion of the crew were Basques.

No list of the 450 men who filled the berths in the seven ships seems to have survived. But the names of nearly 120 of them are scattered through

VOYAGES TO THE MOLUCCAS 1520–1537

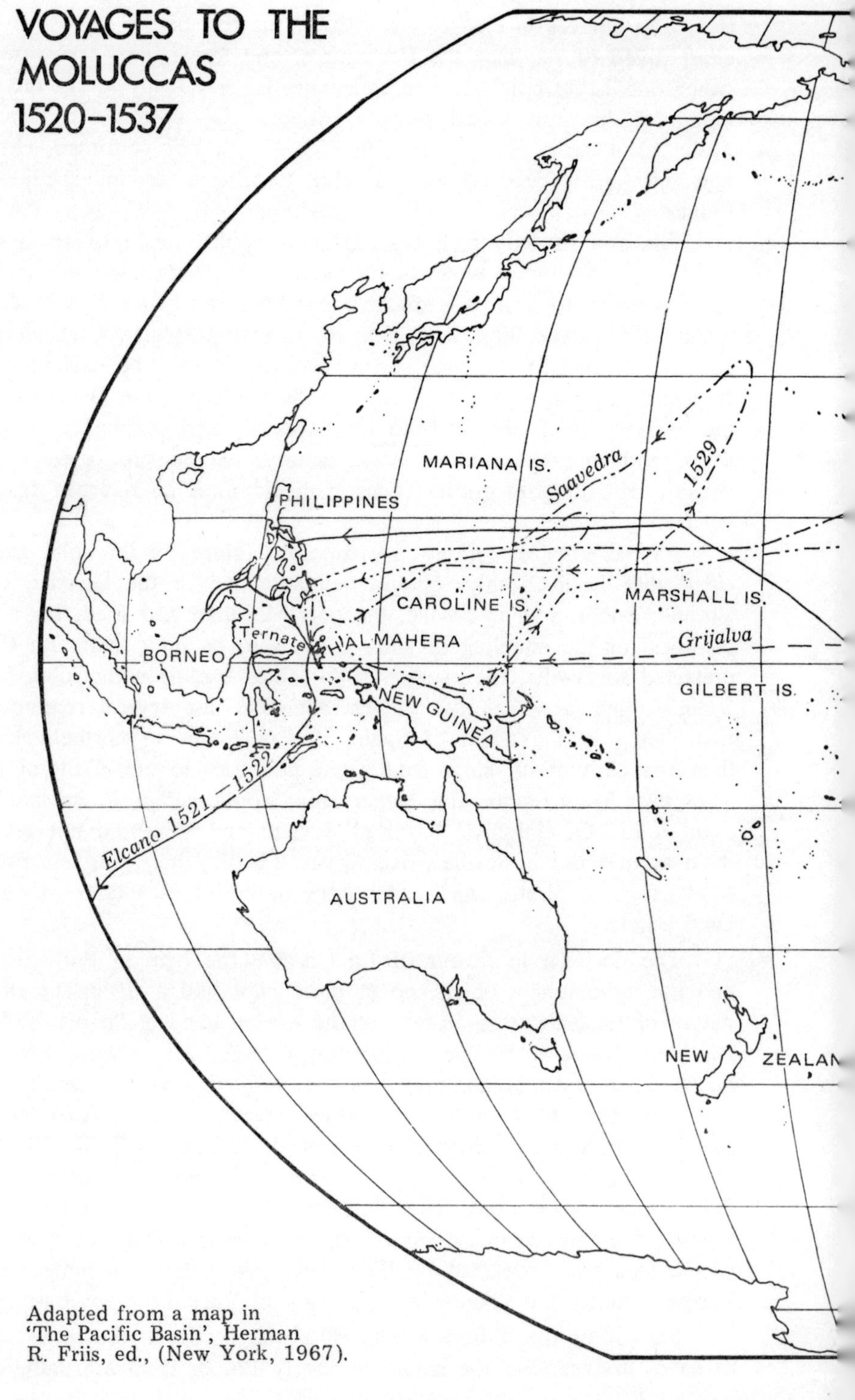

Adapted from a map in 'The Pacific Basin', Herman R. Friis, ed., (New York, 1967).

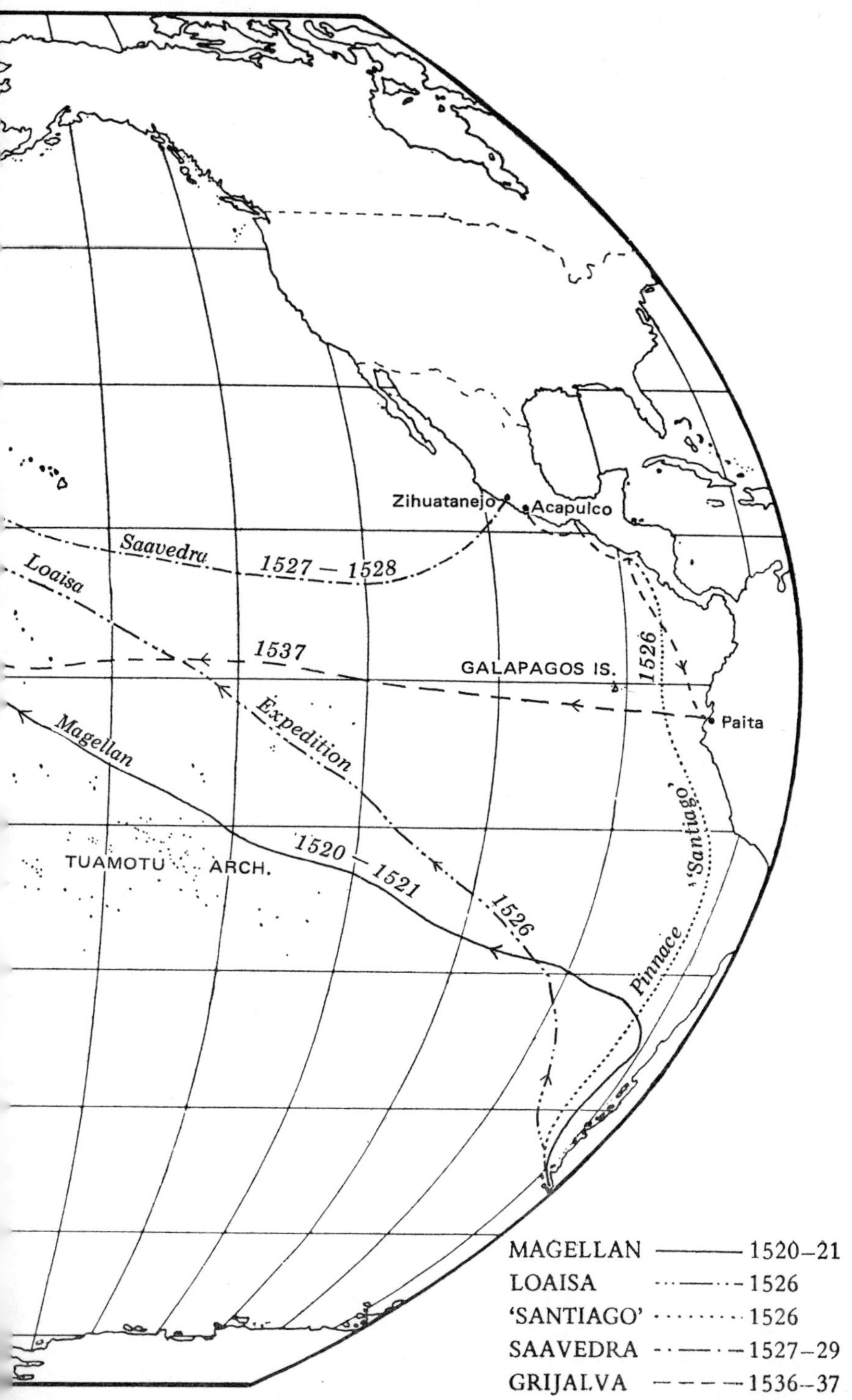
Zihuatanejo
Acapulco
Saavedra
1527 — 1528
Loaisa
1537
GALAPAGOS IS.
1526
Paita
Expedition
Magellan
'Santiago'
TUAMOTU
ARCH.
1520 — 1521
1526
Pinnace
MAGELLAN 1520–21
LOAISA 1526
'SANTIAGO' 1526
SAAVEDRA 1527–29
GRIJALVA 1536–37

the extant documents.* Of these, one third are either described as Basques, were domiciled in the Basque provinces, or have unmistakable Basque names such as Arreizaga, Elorriaga, Goiri, Galarraga, Gorostiaga, Leparazu, Lexundi, Sabugal, Urdaneta, Uriarte, Urtiaga, Zabal and Zeoraga. At least five members of the crew were relatives of Elcano—three brothers, a cousin and a brother-in-law.[16]

As the voyage was likely to be highly profitable to those who took part in it, it was natural that Elcano should favour his own relatives and countrymen. But the Basques, in any case, were renowned as the best seamen in Spain, with a long tradition of deep-sea voyages behind them. At least 120 years before Columbus discovered America, Basque whalers are reputed to have fished for whales off the coast of Newfoundland—a skill they had first developed in the stormy waters of their own Bay of Biscay.[17] Thus, for a long voyage requiring daring, courage, endurance and a high standard of seamanship, Elcano had good reason to seek a crew among his own people. Four of Loaisa's ships were, in fact, purchased, manned and fitted out under Elcano's supervision in the Basque port of Portugalete, eight miles north of Bilbao, on the River Nervion, in Viscaya province; and it is known that from there Elcano visited his own province of Guipúzcoa to recruit men at his birthplace, Guetaria, and in other fishing villages of the Bay of Biscay.[18]

* For details, see Appendix A

PLATE 3. An imaginative painting by the Basque artist Pablo de Uranga of the departure of the Loaisa expedition from La Coruña in 1525. Juan Sebastian Elcano, Loaisa's second-in-command, is addressing the principal captains. The painting was done in 1922 to commemorate the 400th anniversary of the return to Spain of Magellan's 'Victoria' under Elcano's command. It is housed in the palace of the Diputación Provincial de Guipúzcoa in San Sebastian and is reproduced by courtesy of the president of the Diputación.

PLATE 4. Portugalete (above) on the western, i.e. left, side of the River Nervion is the spot where four of Loaisa's ships were fitted out. These undoubtedly included the shallow-draught 'San Lesmes'. Portugalete is eight miles north of Bilbao and only a few hundred yards from the sea. At left is Guetaria, a Basque fishing village on the Bay of Biscay. It was the birthplace of Juan Sebastian Elcano. The Cantabrian mountains descend steeply to the sea along this coast. In this respect, the Basque country closely resembles many of the volcanic islands of the Pacific.

Some time after the middle of April 1525, Elcano's four ships left Portugalete to join the rest of Loaisa's fleet in La Coruña. There the preparation of the other three ships had been in the hands of Estevão Gomes, captain of the ship of the Magellan expedition that had deserted in South America and returned to Spain. Gomes seems to have recruited a number of local seaman for the voyage, as several Galicians are mentioned in the extant documents.[19]

Together, the seven ships had a total tonnage of 1,010. This was more than twice that of Magellan's five ships, and Loaisa's crew list of 450 men was correspondingly longer. However, whereas the tonnage of each of Loaisa's ships is known, no record appears to have survived of how many men sailed in each. Nevertheless, an estimate can be obtained by comparing the known details with the fuller records for Magellan's ships:

MAGELLAN EXPEDITION[20]			LOAISA EXPEDITION[21]		
Ship	*Known Tonnage*	*Known Crew*	*Ship*	*Known Tonnage*	*Estimated Crew*
Trinidad	110	62	Santa Maria de la Victoria	300	135
San Antonio	120	57	Sancti Spiritus	200	90
Concepcion	90	44	Anunciada	170	75
Victoria	85	45	San Gabriel	130	60
Santiago	75	31	Santa Maria del Parral (caravel)	80	35
			San Lesmes (caravel)	80	35
			Santiago (pinnace)	50	20
Known totals	480	239	Known totals	1,010	450

It will be seen from this table that the *San Lesmes*—the ship that this book is primarily concerned with—was slightly smaller than the celebrated *Victoria,* which Elcano sailed back to Spain. The *Victoria,* however, was probably a broad, bluff, heavily-built carrack,[22] while the *San Lesmes* was a caravel. This was a fast, versatile type of ship, much used in Spain and Portugal in those days because its shallow draught and ease of handling made it ideal for nosing in and out of estuaries. Maritime experts of the time considered the caravels the handiest and best-found vessels afloat. They could use either square or lateen sails, and it was because of their versatility that Columbus and Bartholomeu Dias took them on their voyages of exploration.[23]

Beyond knowing what type of ship the *San Lesmes* was, and her tonnage, the only specific details about the ship that have come down to us are that her captain's name was Francisco de Hozes and that he came from Cordoba, Andalusia.[24] However, the crew lists of the *San Lesmes* and *Victoria* were no doubt fairly similar, so the caravel's crew would have been something like this: captain, pilot, purser, master, boatswain, master-at-arms, steward, ship-

Although caravels are frequently mentioned in sixteenth century writings, there are remarkably few extant pictures of them. These five, based on contemporary drawings, demonstrate the variety of rigs employed. They have been redrawn from illustrations accompanying an article on caravels by R. Morton Nance in the 'Mariner's Mirror' 1913, vol. 3, p. 265-71.

CARAVELS

wright, carpenter, gunner, ten able seamen, nine ordinary seamen, one cabin boy, two captain's servants, two blacksmiths and one cooper (total, 35).[25]

Herrera, the chief historian of the Spanish Indies from 1596 to 1625, recorded that the Loaisa expedition was 'well-provisioned and well-equipped with artillery and other arms', and that it carried 'a good supply of cloth, haberdashery and other items of exchange'. But no inventory of the armament and stores seems to have survived, so one must again go to the detailed records of the Magellan expedition to get an idea of what items were shipped.[26]

As artillery, Magellan's five ships carried at least fifty-eight culverins, seven falcons, three large bombards and three *pasamuros,* together with shot and cannon balls of iron and stone, and a large quantity of powder.[27] All of the cannon were of iron and made in Bilbao. The culverins were long weapons in relation to their bore, and about 200 lb in weight.[28] The falcons were heavy cannon of 800 lb each, and possibly similar to those from Amanu.[29] The bombards were a type of mortar. So, too, no doubt, were the 'pasamuros' (wall-penetrators), which are not further described. Other armament carried by the Magellan expedition included 100 corselets, with their shoulder plates and helmets; 100 breast-plates with accompanying throat pieces; sixty cross bows; fifty arquebuses (portable guns used with tripods); 200 shields; ninety-five harpoons; ten dozen javelins; and 1,000 lances.

In the food line, the chief items were biscuit, beans, chick-pease, lentils, olive oil, anchovies, dried fish, dried pork, cheese, sugar, garlic, rice, flour, dried fruit, and enough wine to last each man for 1,134 days at the rate of 1-1/3 pints per day, or for 756 days at two pints per day. Several cows were carried to provide fresh milk, and there were three pigs. There may also have been some goats, as these animals, although not mentioned in the Magellan records, were much favoured by later voyagers. Other animals that do not figure in the records, but which almost certainly were carried, were cats and dogs.[30] The dogs would probably have included the type known in Spain as *perros de agua* and, in English, as spaniels. These shaggy animals, which swim admirably, were frequently carried in Spanish ships in the sixteenth century because of their ability to retrieve fallen game or anything else that fell into the sea.[31]

In the case of the Loaisa expedition, there is no doubt that dogs were carried as one such animal figures in an anecdote recorded by the Spanish historian Fernandez de Oviedo y Valdés. Oviedo, who obtained his information from a survivor of the expedition, also recorded that the expedition carried fowls.[32]

Loaisa's ships, with whatever equipment and animals they carried, slipped out of La Coruña in the early hours of 24 July 1525, and set sail for the Canary Islands.[33] All hands had confessed and had taken the sacrament before departure, for Loaisa had orders not to receive anyone on board who had not done so. Loaisa, of course, sailed in the flagship, the *Santa Maria de la Victoria,* but as he was a landsman, with no knowledge of navigation, the ship's master,

Juan de Huelva, was in effective command. Elcano had command of the second largest ship, the *Sancti Spiritus*. Each captain had a set of instructions, approved by the king, which laid down how the expedition should proceed and what was to be done in emergencies. Among the instructions were the following:

> On no pretext was the expedition to discover or touch at any land within the limits of the king of Portugal.
>
> The captains were to look out every night for the flagship, which would flash a lantern once to know if the other ships were in sight. A single flash in reply would be an affirmative answer.
>
> Two, three and four flashes from the flagship would mean go on another tack, shorten sail and strike sails respectively.
>
> Many flashes of the lantern would be the signal for disaster.
>
> The pilots, masters and mates were not to drop anchors without first sounding and ascertaining that the bottom was clean and safe.
>
> If, during the voyage, any inhabited islands were discovered within the Spanish line, speech was to be had with the inhabitants, and a sign left to show that they were discovered by order of the king. If any religious were willing to remain voluntarily, arrangements could be made for them to land.
>
> If a ship parted company from the fleet, she was to make the best of her way to the Moluccas and there wait for a month. If the fleet did not arrive, a signal was to be placed on the ground consisting of five stones arranged as a cross, a wooden cross was to be set up, and a document was to be left in a jar giving the date of arrival and other particulars. The same signals were to be left if other lands were met with.[34]

Seven or eight days after leaving La Coruña, Loaisa's fleet anchored at Gomera Island in the Canaries to take in supplies. The next landfall was a small island below the Equator where the sailors landed, killed some boobies and caught some excellent fish. Crossing to Brazil, the fleet crept southwards along the coast until a storm separated them below the River Plate. Although all but the flagship were reunited within a few days, one of the ships, the *San Gabriel*, again went astray. The remaining five then stuck together until reaching the Santa Cruz River, about 150 miles north of Magellan Strait, where the pinnace was sent to a small island near the mouth to erect a cross and leave a message for Loaisa. The message said that all five ships were going to the strait to refit and obtain wood and water, and that they would wait for Loaisa at the port of Sardinas. However, on reaching the strait another violent storm blew up, and all was again confusion. Elcano's ship was driven ashore with the loss of nine lives, and next day she broke up in a tremendous gale, which destroyed all her bread and much of her wine and merchandise. In these doleful circumstances, Elcano transferred to the *Anunciada* to resume his acting command of the squadron, leaving his crew to live on shore as best they could. Shortly afterwards the missing flagship and the *San Gabriel* turned up. This event was recorded with infinite pleasure by Elcano's young attendant, Andres de Urdaneta, the chief chronicler of the expedition. His joy, however, was short-lived. Yet another gale blew up, forcing the two caravels to put to sea to avoid being smashed up in the strait.

Over the next few days, the *San Lesmes'* crew gained the unsought honour of approaching nearer to the South Pole than any Europeans had done to that time, for their ship was driven 200 miles south to the fifty-fifth parallel before she could battle back to the strait. Meanwhile, the *Anunciada* had also put out to sea, never to be seen again; and Loaisa's flagship, like the *Sancti Spiritus,* was driven ashore in the strait. When the weather moderated, the flagship was refloated; but the whole fleet was now so battered that Loaisa decided to go north again to the Santa Cruz River for a complete overhaul. This decision apparently displeased the *San Gabriel's* captain, for he suddenly sailed off and eventually returned to Spain. En route, in southern Brazil, he found five Spaniards who had been cast away about ten years earlier when a galleon from the expedition of Juan Diaz de Solís was wrecked. The Spaniards were living with Indian women and had had several children by them.[35]

In the Santa Cruz River, Loaisa's men laboured for several weeks to repair the damage that all ships had suffered. The flagship presented the greatest difficulties as three fathoms of her keel were broken, and despite wintry weather, the men had to work in the water to fix it. The caravels and the pinnace, on the other hand, were reasonably easy to repair, there being 'very convenient tides, rising five fathoms', as Urdaneta put it. Meanwhile, some of the sailors took in wood and water, and caught fish, seals and seabirds to preserve for the voyage. Four members of the *Santiago* had an unforgettable adventure when, accompanied by a dog, they marched overland and encountered a party of giant Patagonians.

On 29 March 1526—more than two months after Elcano had first reached Magellan Strait—the depleted squadron of four ships was ready to tackle it again. All ships were now overcrowded with men, as each had had to accommodate some of the survivors of the wrecked *Sancti Spiritus.* However, there was more room in at least one respect, for only one rooster and one hen remained alive of all the poultry the Spaniards had brought from Spain. These birds belonged to the commander of the *Santa Maria del Parral,* who resisted a handsome offer for them from the *San Lesmes'* captain, Francisco de Hozes.[36]

At the second attempt to negotiate the strait, the squadron had a few early difficulties, and one near-disaster. Otherwise the passage was plain sailing, enabling the officers to observe the landmarks at leisure and to bestow on them such zealously Catholic names as San Juan de Portalatina, Puerto de la Ascension, Espiritu Santo and San Alifonso. One particularly striking landmark was called Santoña, the name of a spectacular rock in the Bay of Biscay, near Laredo.[37]

The four ships reached Cape Deseado at the western end of the strait on 26 May 1526, and so entered the Pacific. One of the pilots, Martin de Uriarte, noted in his journal for the day that the wind was from the south-east and that it was the day of St. Alifonso and eve of Trinity.[38] Juan de Arreizaga, one of the fleet's two chaplains, who was in the pinnace, recalled several years later that the weather was extremely cold.[39] For the next few days, the ships laboured under sunless skies, and on the first day of June they were 157 leagues from Cape Deseado.[40] 'At this point,' as Arreizaga related, 'they were dispersed by a gale and never succeeded in joining company again. When the gale went down the pinnace sought for the fleet, but only sighted the *San Lesmes*. Those in the pinnace supposed that the others had gone ahead. . . .'[41]

Thus, from being a squadron of four ships with strict instructions to keep closely together, the *Santa Maria de la Victoria,* the two caravels and the tiny pinnace *Santiago* were now lonely, isolated units in the vast emptiness of the Pacific. Their crews were further from home and more helpless than any Europeans had ever been in such a situation. It was like a modern astronaut being left to fend for himself on the dark side of the moon.

In accordance with their instructions, the captains knew that they must head for the Moluccas with all haste and there await their companions. This, however, was more than the captain of the 50-ton pinnace dared to do. Not only was the pinnace grossly overmanned with fifty people on board, but all of her stores, except 400 lb of biscuit and eight barrels of water, were in the flagship for want of room. As Arreizaga afterwards related: 'The crew were without any food whatever, while they reckoned they were 2,200 leagues from the nearest land, the Ladrones, where they could get anything to eat.' In the circumstances, the *Santiago's* captain decided to head for Mexico, which was reckoned to be only 800 to a thousand leagues distant.[42]

It was a terrible voyage lasting fifty days. The men's daily ration was only 2½ oz of biscuit and a few teaspoons of water, apart from a few fish they caught. Their situation was so desperate when they reached Mexico that Arreizaga volunteered to float ashore in a box to seek help, there being no boat on board. Commending himself to God and taking a sword, the chaplain started for the shore in his shirt and drawers. Although his box capsized halfway, he managed to swim the remaining distance and was pulled out exhausted by five Indians.

Indians from a nearby town later rescued the rest of the *Santiago's* crew. Arreizaga then set off for Mexico City, some 500 miles away, to give an account of what had happened to the celebrated conquistador, Hernan Cortes, governor of what was then called New Spain. Cortes received his unexpected visitor with interest, for Charles V had just ordered him to send an expedition to the Moluccas to search for Magellan's *Trinidad,* last heard of in Tidore in December 1521. Cortes was hopeful that the *Santiago* could be used for this purpose. However, the pinnace had been 'rendered unseaworthy by the barnacles,'[43] and some twelve months passed before other ships could be prepared for the voyage.[44]

Meanwhile, the storm that had separated Loaisa's fleet had caused severe

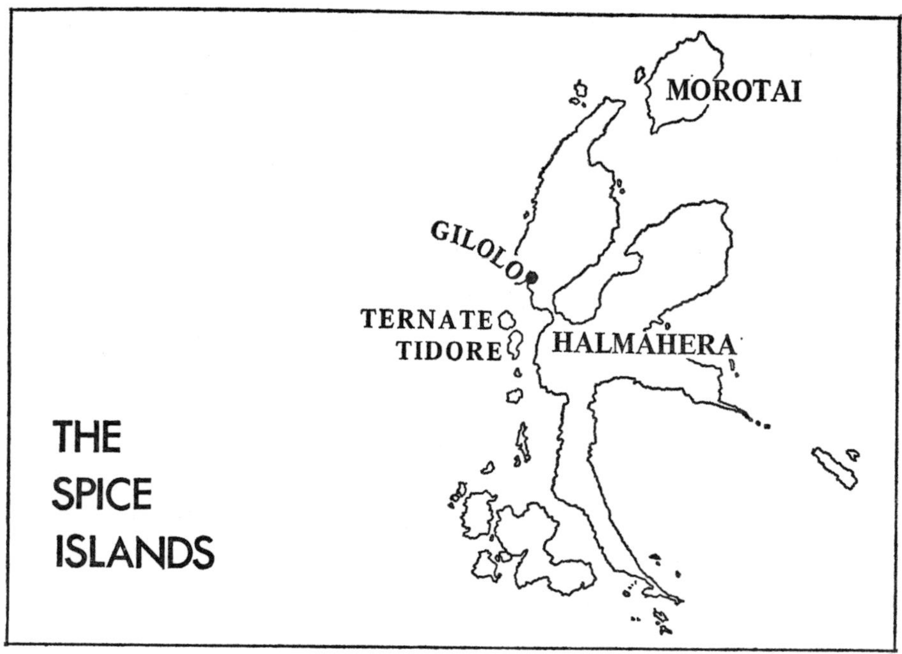

damage to the flagship. She became so leaky that the crew could not keep the water down even with two pumps constantly going. 'Each day we expected the end to come,' young Urdaneta wrote gloomily. 'On the other hand we had to reduce the rations by reason of the number of additional men who had come on board from the ship that was wrecked. Thus, while on the one side we worked hard, on the other we were insufficiently fed. We passed through much misery and some perished.'[45]

In climbing into the tropics from the Strait of Magellan, the *Santa Maria de la Victoria* sailed to the east of the Tuamotu Archipelago, and did not change course for the west until well clear of it.[46] She did not encounter a single Pacific island until 21 August 1526 when Taongi, the northernmost of the Marshall Islands, was reached.[47] By then, both Loaisa and Elcano were dead, and their immediate successor died soon after bringing the ship to the Marianas. The command of the expedition then passed to the master-at-arms, Martin Iñiguez de Carquisano, and the Spaniards sailed on to the Philippines and Gilolo (now called Halmahera). At Gilolo, Carquisano learned from a fugitive slave of the Portuguese that a Portuguese force had occupied the spice island of Ternate and had attacked its neighbour, Tidore, for supplying cloves to the ships of Magellan. Undeterred, the Spanish captain sent a message to Tidore stating hopefully and a little untruthfully that seven Spanish ships had been sent to the Moluccas, and that although only one had yet arrived, the rest were 'coming behind'. About two months later, the Spaniards (now numbering about a hundred) sailed south to Tidore, landed their valuables and some artillery, and built a fort with local help.

On the ground that the Moluccas were in their half of the world, the Portuguese, with growing threats, repeatedly asked the Spaniards to leave. After the Spaniards had just as often refused, the Portuguese attacked them with a well-armed fleet. The battle was indecisive. But it did put an end to the *Santa Maria de la Victoria* which began leaking uncontrollably when the firing of her own heavy guns opened her seams. The Spaniards later started to build another ship, but when work on it was well advanced, the Portuguese infiltrated a spy into their shipyard and blew it up. The Portuguese also disposed of the Spaniards' commander, Carquisano, by poisoning his wine, and they threatened to poison their water supply. Despite all this, the Spaniards kept their spirits up, confident that the other three ships in their fleet would eventually come to their aid.

It was March 1528 before they learned what had become of the *Santiago*. They learned at the same time that the *Santa Maria del Parral* had been wrecked in the southern Philippines with the subsequent loss of most of her men by death or enslavement. The news of the two ships was brought to Tidore by a Spanish captain, Alonso de Saavedra, who had touched at the Philippines on his way to Tidore in the caravel *Florida*. Fifteen months earlier, Cortes had sent him from Mexico to ascertain the fate of Magellan's *Trinidad* (which had long since been captured by the Portuguese) and also to see how Loaisa's fleet was faring. The *Florida* had originally been accompanied by two other small ships—the *Santiago,* of forty-five men, and the *Espiritu Santo,* of fifteen. However, these ships became separated from her near the Marshall Islands and were not seen again.*

The *Florida* remained at Tidore for three months. She then set out with a cargo of spices to return to Mexico by way of the north coast of New Guinea, but was eventually forced back by contrary winds. She made a second attempt in the following year, but was again defeated.[48] By this time, three years had passed since the Spaniards had arrived at Tidore. Many of them had died of disease; some had been killed in desultory fighting against the Portuguese; while others again, disheartened by the lack of reinforcements, had deserted to the enemy. The few loyal men no longer posed a threat to the Portuguese. It was all they could do to keep themselves alive.

Meanwhile, at home in Spain, Emperor Charles V was having his own troubles. A war with France had brought him to the brink of insolvency, and the lack of news from the Moluccas had dampened his hopes of obtaining relief from that quarter. In these circumstances he hit on the ingenious idea of selling or pawning his claim to the Spice Islands before its value could drop any lower. Put to the Portuguese king, the idea proved highly acceptable. And so the Treaty of Zaragoza of 1529 was drawn up whereby Charles V formally renounced his claim and ceded it to the Crown of Portugal for 350,000 ducats.[49]

News of their monarch's astonishing sell-out reached the Spaniards in the Moluccas in 1532. Another year or so passed before the Portuguese could

* Their apparent fate is discussed in chapter 21.

provide transport home for the last seventeen survivors. Their departure from the East Indies after nearly eight years of warfare and suffering in the emperor's cause closed a chapter in Spain's colonial history. Henceforth, Portugal's sovereignty in those islands was acknowledged unreservedly. The Spanish Crown therefore had no further reason to send furtive expeditions to that part of the world through the Strait of Magellan. Thus, if any seamen from the caravel *San Lesmes* were waiting hopefully for a Spanish sail to rescue them from some unknown island in the South Pacific, they were doomed to disappointment.

3

The laws of chance

WHEN the *San Lesmes* was last seen from the decks of the pinnace *Santiago* on 1 June 1526, the storm that had separated Loaisa's four ships had abated, and the caravel was apparently not in distress. If her captain had then done what he was instructed to do, he would have again set his course for the Moluccas. And if, in sailing north, he took a somewhat more westerly track than either Magellan or Loaisa did, he could scarcely have missed one or another of the unknown, low-lying Tuamotus. That this, indeed, is what must have happened seems evident from the four guns that were found on the Amanu reef four centuries later.* What is not evident, or, at least, not immediately evident, is what became of the caravel itself and the caravel's crew.

In basic terms, the number of things that could have happened is extremely limited. The ship could have been driven on the reef so hard that there was no moving her; or, lightened of her heavy gear, she could have been washed or hauled off again, either to sink or swim. As for the crew, some might have been lost, all might have been lost, or none. There were thus three possible outcomes for both the ship and her crew. But in each case, these can be reduced in even starker terms to two: either the ship came through the accident in a seaworthy state or she did not, and each man either lived or died.

On the face of things, it might seem that in any reef collision there is a 50-50 chance of survival for both ship and crew. In reality, the odds vary according to such factors as the state of the tide and weather, the nature of the reef, the draught of the ship, the captain's competence in handling the situation, the crew's obedience, quickness, knowledge of seamanship and ability to swim, the availability of boats and the proximity of dry land. Above all, there is the natural instinct of human beings to survive.[1] This last factor, particularly, tends to upset any purely theoretical conclusion, so that if one examines the records of reef mishaps in the South Pacific, one finds that the survival rate for crews, if not for ships, is considerably better than 50 per cent.

In the first fifteen recorded cases in which European ships on the high seas collided with uncharted South Seas reefs, four of the ships were safely refloated, three sank, and the rest, as far as is known, remained stuck fast where they came to grief. However, in no case was there complete loss of life. In eight there was none; in three the losses were minimal; and in the remaining four, the losses ranged from 26 per cent to an imprecise maximum

* This is bearing in mind the proviso in the last paragraph of chapter 1.

of about 70 per cent.* On these figures, therefore, it is safe to say that when the *San Lesmes* struck the reef at Amanu in 1526, some of her crew would have survived, regardless of what happened to the ship itself.

How many men were on board the *San Lesmes* at that time, we do not know. But the number was no doubt many more than her original complement of perhaps thirty-five, as each of Loaisa's ships had taken in some of the crew of the wrecked *Sancti Spiritus.* As that vessel had a crew estimated at ninety men at first, and as nine lost their lives in Magellan Strait, the remaining four ships probably had to find berths for an average of twenty men each. Arreizaga tells us that when the 50-ton pinnace *Santiago* set out for Mexico she had fifty men on board (compared with her original crew of perhaps twenty).[2] Urdaneta recorded that the crew of the flagship on leaving the strait was 145—possibly ten or twenty more than her original figure.[3] So the *San Lesmes'* complement from Magellan Strait onwards was probably between fifty and sixty, possibly seventy.

As it was then mid-year, the weather, as the *San Lesmes* sailed into the tropics, should generally have been fine, clear and pleasant. This was the case for Loaisa's flagship, whose voyage was logged by the pilot, Uriarte.[4] It was also the case when HMS *Dolphin,* under Captain Samuel Wallis, passed that way at about the same season of the year some two and a half centuries later.[5] The winds then were mainly from the southeast, with no hint of the hurricanes that sometimes sweep those waters from December to March.[6]

Like the *Dolphin,* the *San Lesmes* probably took about five weeks to reach the tropics; and like her she may have sighted or touched at one or another of the atolls in the Vahitahi area, or, perhaps, the high islands of Mangareva. At any rate, it was probably during the first half of July when she reached the vicinity of Amanu. Whether the nights were then dark or whether the moon was as full and clear as only a tropical moon can be, the caravel's moment of disaster no doubt came with horrifying suddenness.

Captain Cook has left a vividly simple account of how such things happen —of how one of his ships collided with a reef in the best possible conditions on the night of 11 June 1770. The disaster occurred as he was skirting Australia's Great Barrier Reef in HMS *Endeavour.* 'My intention was,' he wrote, 'to stretch off [the coast] all night as well to avoid the dangers we saw ahead as to see if any Islands lay in the offing . . . having the advantage of a fine breeze of wind and a clear moonlight night . . . Before 10 oClock we had 20 and 21 fathom and continued in that depth untill a few Minutes before a 11 when we had 17 and before the Man at the lead could heave another cast the Ship Struck and stuck fast.'

Cook's first reaction was to take in all the sails and hoist out the boats to make soundings round the ship. Then, several anchors were carried out and his men heaved strenuously on them to try to prise the ship from the reef. When this manoeuvre failed all heavy and useless articles—six iron

* For details, see Appendix B.

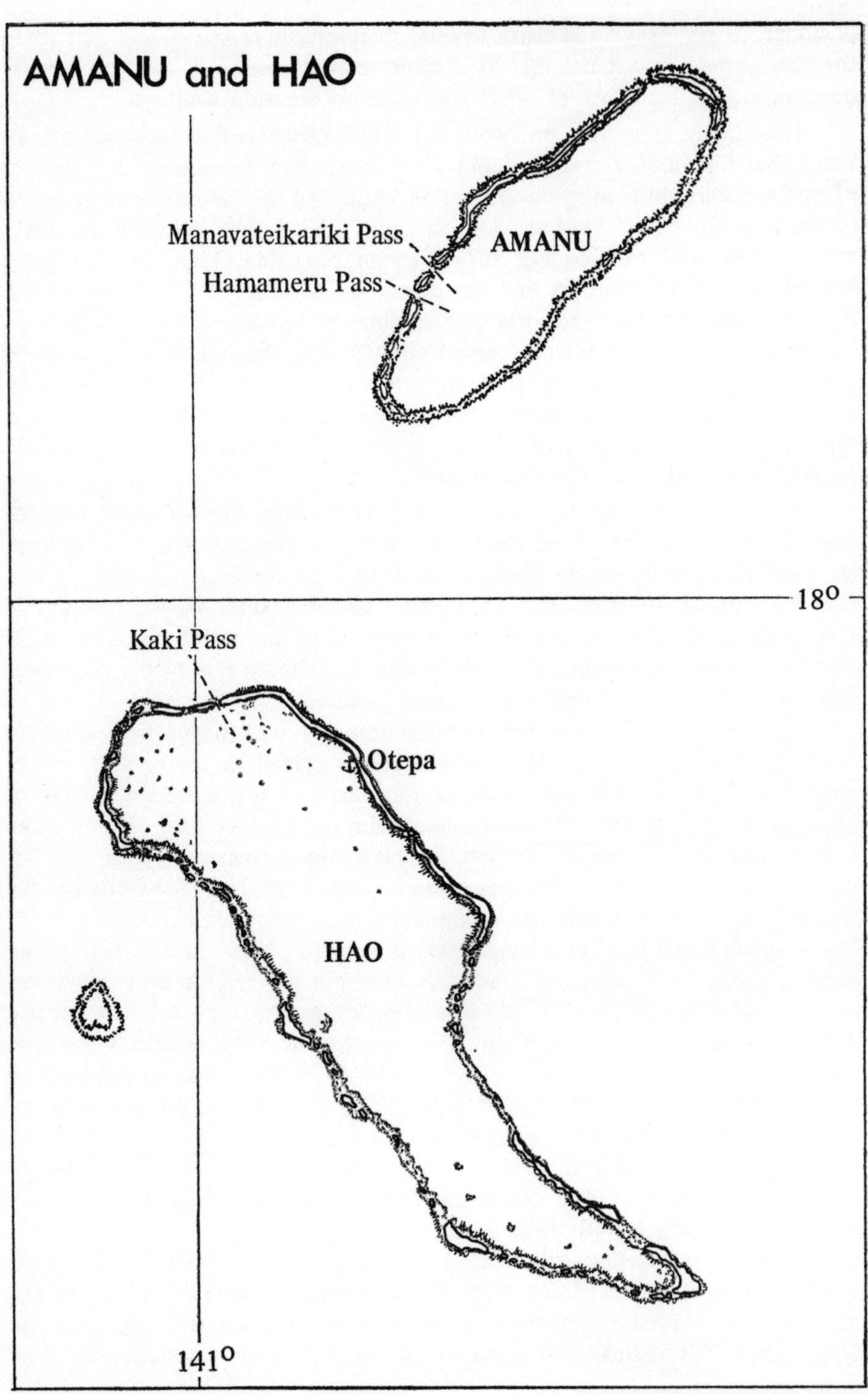
AMANU and HAO
Manavateikariki Pass
AMANU
Hamameru Pass
18°
Kaki Pass
Otepa
HAO
141°

cannon, the stone and iron ballast, casks, hoops, staves, oil jars and decayed stores—were thrown overboard. But even then the ship could not be moved. Meanwhile, water poured in through a hole in the ship's bottom and gained considerably on the men at the pumps. This, as Cook put it, was an 'alarming' and 'terrible circumstance' for it threatened immediate destruction when the ship was refloated by the high tide. However, Cook risked everything and finally heaved her off, losing an anchor and some cable in doing so. Subsequently, the ship was warped away from the reef, her sails were hoisted again, and Cook stood in for the land. At the same time, a sail was prepared to fother (or bandage) the leak, and this reduced the leak so much that soon it could easily be kept clear with only one pump. It was then merely a matter of finding a spot where the damage to the *Endeavour* could be repaired—the spot chosen being the Endeavour River near presentday Cooktown.[7]

There is good reason to suppose that something similar to this happened to the *San Lesmes*. Indeed, it would seem that the *San Lesmes* was refloated from the Amanu reef with even greater ease than the *Endeavour*. If it had been otherwise—if the caravel had stuck fast—then François Hervé or Captain Le Goaziou and his divers would undoubtedly have found evidence of this. This evidence would have been in the shape of anchors, chain cable and other heavy, immovable gear, as well as bits of crockery, earthenware, coins and other small items that would have fallen to the reef when the vessel broke up.[8] As it was, there were only four heavy cannon and a few alien stones—probably primitive cannonballs, like those carried by Magellan. The inference is therefore clear. By jettisoning those items, the *San Lesmes*' crew were able to haul or refloat their ship from the reef. Yet even a shallow-draught caravel could scarcely have escaped damage on a reef where there is little water even at high tide. So the captain's first task would have been to find a haven where he could beach his ship to inspect her hull and, if necessary, make repairs. From the spot where the disaster occurred, he could have plainly seen that there was no haven on the surf-battered eastern side of Amanu. But across the lagoon to the west, he would have seen the same tree-covered body of land that Captain Duperrey saw from the *Coquille* in 1823.

To reach this land, the *San Lesmes*' captain could have done two things. He could have sailed north, then west, then south to negotiate the 'top' side of the oval-shaped atoll. Or he could have gone south, then west, then north to reach his destination by the 'bottom' side. If he had taken the first course, a voyage of ten miles or so would have brought him to the first of the two entrances into Amanu's lagoon.[9] If he had taken the second, he would have seen, on reaching the southern end of Amanu, that there was more land further south—this being the northern side of Hao, which is separated from Amanu by a nine-mile channel. An investigation of the Hao coast would have revealed a second lagoon entrance that the caravel could have entered.[10] On the other hand, by continuing round the coast of Amanu, the *San Lesmes* would have come to yet a third opening—the second reef passage that Duperrey saw. Thus, within easy reach of the disaster scene, there were three escape routes from the open sea. And as the evidence suggests that the caravel sustained less damage than the *Endeavour,* it seems likely that she would have reached one of them without great difficulty.

As will later appear, there is evidence to suggest that the caravel reached Hao and that the crew got ashore there. If so, her crew would have found a convenient anchorage and careening place on the north-eastern side of the lagoon, about six miles from the entrance. This spot, now called Otepa, is known to have been a village site as far back as 1606.[11] So people may well have been living there in 1526. The caravel's crew, at any rate, appear to have found a native community at whatever place they did reach after their collision; and as it is not material whether this was on Amanu or Hao, Otepa will serve for the purpose of discussion.

Without the benefit of a time machine, there seems to be no way of knowing what sort of people were living at Otepa at the time of the shipwreck. But it is probably safe to say that they would have had blackish, brown or copper-coloured skins, black hair and dark brown eyes, as this was the usual description of people in the eastern Pacific in later times.[12] Where these people came from originally can only be surmised. However, various items of evidence suggest that they were probably of diverse origins—an amalgam of Polynesians who originated in the west and of South Americans who came from the east. Certainly, the language of Hao and of several other Tuamotuan atolls differed substantially in historical times from the Polynesian dialects of the western Pacific. So it seems reasonable to assume that the Tuamotu Archipelago was subject to influences that were never known in the west.[13]

Whatever the truth was on the ethnic origins of the Hao people, there can be no doubt that they must have lived simple, primitive lives. For clothing, they probably had no materials other than grasses and the leaves of the coconut and pandanus palms. For food, they would have had to subsist on fish, sharks, shell-fish, octopuses, coconuts, pandanus nuts, purslane, taro, the berries of the *Morinda citrifolia* shrub, sea birds, sea birds' eggs, and occasionally a turtle.[14] Only if they or their ancestors had been lucky enough to reach Hao with any of the three domestic creatures known to the Polynesians —pigs, fowls and dogs—would they have been able to vary their diets occasionally with a feast of pork, chicken or dogs' flesh. However, few Polynesian islands had all three domestic creatures when the European explorers discovered them. The Marquesas, for example, did not have the dog.[15] And most atolls were especially poor in them. So Hao probably had little, if anything, to boast of in that respect. If it had, the animals would probably have been of the same Asiatic species as were usually found in Polynesia in later times. The fowls would have been a domesticated variety of the jungle fowl; the pigs, small; and the dogs something like terriers, being descendants of the pariah dogs of Asia, with small eyes, sharp snouts, short legs, prick ears, short smooth hair usually, and sometimes a bushy tail.[16]

In building their canoes and houses, the Hao Islanders must have exercised both parsimony and ingenuity. As Hao, even today,* has few, if any, trees other than coconuts, pandanus palms, *Pisonia, Cordia, Erythrina* and *Hibiscus tiliaceus,* and as they do not grow freely, no tree could be recklessly appropriated for use.[17] In any case, getting timber from a tree, small as they usually were, would have been no easy task for a people with no metal tools and without even stone to make them from. The islanders must therefore have either used fire to do this or adzes made from the pearl oyster, clam or other shell. Their only other tools for carpentering would have been what could be fashioned from coral rock, turtle shell, sharks' teeth, wood, stingrays' tails, and perhaps human bone. To make a canoe would therefore have been a work of much labour. Without trees with large enough trunks to make dugouts, the islanders would have had to make their canoes from many small planks sewn together with sinnet. Canoes from the area seen in later times usually had narrow hulls, seldom much wider than a man's body; and as they could easily be upset, they had outriggers attached to balance them.

In any isolated community where life is harsh and only the fittest can survive, the arrival of strangers is always likely to produce a hostile or cautious reaction. Such reactions were seen repeatedly when Europeans began exploring the Tuamotus in the early part of the seventeenth century. So one may assume that when the *San Lesmes* reached Hao after her encounter with the Amanu reef, the people of Otepa would immediately have been on their guard. Possibly they would have been extremely frightened by the appearance of a ship whose like they had never seen before; and the strange, white-skinned sailors on board might have seemed to them like ghosts or gods. In the circumstances, a few shots from the caravel's culverins, arquebuses and cross-bows might have been sufficient to drive them off to some other *motu* of the atoll. On the other hand, the Spaniards might have had to fight a bloody battle before they could get ashore. Two things, at least, seem clear from the evidence that will be presented hereafter. The caravel's crew somehow reached land and established relations with the island's women.[18]

On getting ashore, the Spaniards would presumably have erected a cross (in accordance with instructions) as a signal to any of their companion vessels that might have come looking for them. They would then have turned their attention to the state of the vessel that had landed them in their unhappy predicament. An inspection of her hull would have revealed one of two things. Either her encounter with the reef had not seriously damaged her; or her timbers were so warped and holed—and perhaps damaged by barnacles, like the *Santiago's*—that simple repairs were impossible. Everything seems to suggest that the latter proved to be the case. So the Spaniards may have salvaged such good timbers as remained in the vessel, and then set to to build

* All references in this book to the 'present' situation in the atolls of the eastern Tuamotus must be interpreted as that existing before the French Government began using those atolls for nuclear experiments and closed them to outsiders. Hao, now, has an 11,000 ft airstrip on its eastern flank, so much of its former vegetation has been destroyed.

another, using whatever local materials they could get. This would undoubtedly have been a long and difficult job, and it could well be that more than a year elapsed before the caravel's crew was able to build a new ship or repair the old. Meanwhile, human nature being what it is, disputes over women, food, wine, the division of labour and so on would probably have broken out among them, and some of the seamen may have broken away from the main group to live with islanders in other parts of the atoll.

Two traditions gathered at Hao in the first three decades of this century certainly suggest that some noteworthy events occurred there at some time in the not-too-distant past. One of the traditions was gathered by a Catholic missionary, Father Hervé Audran, who died in 1918 after several years in the Tuamotus. It concerns a castaway (but, more probably, a group of castaways) who arrived at Hao in former times and caused such havoc that he was the 'terror of the country'.[19] The castaway belonged to a race of strangers called Hiva or Kura. When he was in a bad humour, he would uproot (chop down?) a coconut tree, and 'break it up' as if it were nothing, setting at defiance those who opposed him.* As this was in the days when coconut trees on Hao were rare and therefore precious, this was a serious thing. The castaway was also troublesome when he went out fishing. On such occasions he would amuse himself by hurling ashore enormous blocks of coral (cannonballs from a bombard?) as if they were little stones. 'At each instant', Audran wrote, 'some people were naturally wounded.'†

The other tradition, possibly complementary to that of Audran, was gathered by an American linguist, J. Frank Stimson, compiler of the first and only Tuamotuan dictionary. Stimson first heard it in 1929 when he visited the Tuamotus as a member of an expedition from the Bernice P. Bishop Museum of Honolulu. The islanders of Hao then told him that in former times 'a great sea-going canoe'—the largest ever built at Hao—had left there for unknown lands and had never returned. Its name was *Tainui—tai* meaning 'ocean' and *nui,* 'big.' It was said to be capable of carrying perhaps a hundred voyagers. Stimson also learned that the same tradition was known to the people of Vahitahi Atoll to the south-east of Hao and at Fangatau to the north. But their name for the great canoe was *Tainui-Atea*—Atea being the word for 'god.' The Vahitahi and Fangatau people added that the navigator of the canoe was one, Tahoro-Takarari; while on Napuka, an atoll some 200 miles north of Hao, tradition had it that the captain's name was Hotu-Roa, and the canoe itself, *Tainuia.*[20]

* People who cannot climb a coconut tree—and how many Europeans can?—are constrained to cut the tree down if they desperately want the fruit. F. D. Bennett, a naturalist who visited the Pacific in the 1830s, remarked on this practice in relation to uninhabited Caroline Island: 'That some ship had lately touched here was evident . . . from several of the cocoa-nut trees having been recently cut down to obtain their fruit—a practice . . . at all times selfish and mischievous, and more particularly so here, where cocoa-nut palms although increasing in number are as yet but few.' (Bennett 1840:I:369.)

† As coral is the only rock on Hao, Audran would naturally have assumed that the projectiles referred to could only have been of that material.

As will later be shown, there is a good deal of evidence to suggest that *Tainui, Tainuia* or *Tainui-Atea* was, in fact, a ship built or repaired by the *San Lesmes*' crew. It will also be shown that on leaving Hao (where a few of the crew seem to have stayed behind), the castaways apparently reached Anaa, another atoll, considerably more fertile than Hao, about 250 miles east of Tahiti. Here the castaways seem to have made a second sojourn—a few of them finding it so much to their liking that they decided to make their homes there. The rest, it seems, eventually sailed on until they reached the lush, volcanic island of Raiatea, about 120 miles north-west of Tahiti. This, for some of them, was apparently journey's end. But the rest seem to have resumed their voyage after a lapse of several years, there being evidence to suggest that they eventually reached New Zealand. Meanwhile, the castaways apparently took wives and had children, and thereby established exclusive Hispano-Polynesian dynasties that lasted down to Captain Cook's time two and a half centuries later. In addition, they seem to have introduced various elements of Iberian culture to the Pacific, not only to the islands already mentioned, but to many others (see p 56-7) to which their descendants later migrated, either by accident or design. All this, at first sight, might seem far-fetched. Yet a little consideration should make it clear that, in theory, at least, it is not so.

If it is assumed, for example, that only thirty members of the caravel's crew survived, that all took wives and had three children, that those children and all descendants thereafter had three children, and that each generation was of twenty-five years, the number of part-European descendants of the castaways at the end of 250 years would have ranged from 3,405 to 1,771,470. The minimum figure would apply if *all* descendants of the original mixed marriages were always equally divided by sex and if all intermarried only with each other. The maximum figure would hold good if all the descendants married only outside the Hispano-Polynesian circle.[21] Needless to say, the real figure would have been somewhere between the two, with more inbreeding occurring on small, isolated islands than in large, well-populated groups.

As the castaways (except perhaps for one or two Negroes or Malays) would have been white- or olive-skinned,[22] and as the people of Polynesia in the early sixteenth century were almost certainly darker, one would expect that wherever the castaways or their descendants settled, the skins of some of the islanders would have become considerably lighter than in other parts of Polynesia.[23] In the first generation, the skin colour of all children born to the castaways would have been halfway between that of the fathers and the mothers. This is because each child of a mixed marriage receives one set of dominant dark-skin genes and one set of recessive light-skin genes from its parents. These genes, being 'blended', produce a medium or 'mulatto' skin colour. However, when 'mulattos' marry each other, they may pass any one of nine combinations of skin-colour genes to *their* children.* One of their children, for example, may

* This assumes a four-gene model, each gene having an additive effect on pigmentation. Some geneticists believe that human skin colour is determined by five genes.

get two sets of dark-skin genes (i.e., four pairs of such genes) passed down from its two dark-skinned grandmothers, and so will have the same skin colour as they had. Another may inherit four pairs of white-skin genes and so be as fair as its two grandfathers. Others, again, may inherit, one, two or three pairs of dark-skin or light-skin genes and so turn out to be a gradation of colours between their four grandparents. Subsequent generations will vary in skin colour according to the way the genes of the parents 'blend'. But most of the descendants of mixed marriages will be fairer than their dark-skinned folk-mothers and darker than their fair folk-fathers—provided no other genetic factors intervene. The reason is that when hybrids marry, the chances of their children inheriting four pairs of dark-skin genes or four pairs of light-skin genes are always very low—only one in 256.[24]

The laws of heredity as they concern skin colour are basically the same in all other heritable features. However, the gradations observable in the case of skin colour are frequently absent elsewhere because many of the other features are passed on *in toto* rather than by halves. Some, again, appear to be passed on *in toto,* but gradations are observable on close examination. In eye-colour, for example, dark-eye genes are dominant over light-eye genes, and the former will always obscure the latter, so long as the dark-eyed partner has no light-eyed ancestors.[25] In other words, if a blue-eyed man marries a brown-eyed woman in a completely brown-eyed community, all of their children will have brown eyes—although the pigmentation in the eyes of some of the children may be slightly less than in those of the mother. Regardless of this, each child will inherit one set of blue-eye genes from the father and one set of brown-eye genes from the mother; and these may be passed down in many different combinations to the next generation.* The blue eyes of the father may therefore reappear in subsequent generations—but only if two people happen to mate, who, between them, are carrying fifty per cent or more blue-eye genes.[26] In an overwhelmingly brown-eyed community, this would be an infrequent event unless the descendants of the original mixed folk-parents kept inter-marrying, and even then it would be uncommon. If, therefore, any seamen from the *San Lesmes* had blue eyes and the eyes of the islanders were dark-brown, the lighter features would become swamped in a sea of brown after a few generations. However, the castaways' blue-eye genes, having once been released in the genetic pool, would always be waiting in the wings, so to speak, to make a reappearance; and they would inevitably do so from time to time. As all other eye colours are recessive to dark-brown, any light-brown, green or grey-eye genes released by the castaways would have tended to be obscured like the blue-eye genes. But like them, they would sometimes have lessened the pigmentation (or melanin content) of the eyes of the children who received them, thus making the eyes of some descendants of the castaways a lighter brown than those of the islanders generally. Needless to say, such people would have been less distinctive than

* The exact number of combinations depends on the number of genes involved. Geneticists say that eye colour is determined by at least four, and probably six, genes.

those with blue eyes. Indeed, they would scarcely have been noticed except by the keenest observers.

There is little doubt that the *San Lesmes* did carry some men whose light-eye genes could have left tell-tale signs in Polynesia several generations later. As has already been said, a third of the known members of the Loaisa expedition were Basques and a good number were Galicians—both types having significant numbers of light-eyed people among them.* In recent years, more than 19.5 per cent of the people of Guipúzcoa, Elcano's home province, were estimated to have blue, grey or green eyes—or what Spaniards call *ojos garzos*. The same was so throughout Galicia, the Celtic region from which the Loaisa expedition took its departure. Large numbers of light-eyed people are also found in other parts of Spain, contrary to popular belief; and because of the way the laws of heredity work in the case of eye colour, the proportions of such people may have been much greater in the sixteenth century.[27]

As light eyes and red or fair hair frequently go together, and seem to be related genetically, it is not surprising that the light-eyed Spanish provinces also have significant numbers of red or light-haired people. Guipúzcoa has more than 15.5 per cent. The same proportions are found in the Mediterranean provinces of Huelva and Cadiz; while the Galician province of La Coruña, the Basque province of Viscaya, and several others have between 10.4 and 15.5 per cent.[28] It may be assumed from this that some of the *San Lesmes'* seamen almost certainly had red or fair hair. So if such men intermarried with dark-haired islanders, they would inevitably have added their hair-colour genes to the genetic pool. However, as dark-hair genes dominate light-hair genes in the same way as brown eyes dominate blue, any blond-haired castaways could not have left many replicas of themselves among their Hispano-Polynesian descendants. On the other hand, traces of their blond locks might turn up in later times in piebald form, such as dark hair with yellowish roots. Or their blond-hair genes might produce an even more distinctive hair colour—red.

> It seems very probable [says anthropologist E. A. Hooton] that red-haired individuals often result from the crossing of a black-haired parent in whom there is a good deal of recessive red-gold pigment, with a blond mate in whose hair is little pigment of any kind, and some of that little the red-gold pigment. Thus, by a process of segregating out recessive red-gold pigment, pure red-haired individuals result. This supposition becomes more plausible when we consider the usual combination of red hair with a milky white skin that freckles. The freckles represent the tanning capabilities of the brunet stock irregularly distributed in the epithelial cells. The milky white background on which the freckles form represents the inheritance from the blond stock which is incapable of acquiring a protective pigmentation under the stimulus of solar rays.[29]

If blond-hair genes can produce red hair in a black-haired community, it may be expected that red-hair genes will also behave in a distinctive way. And

* For a summary of the provenances of the crew, see Appendix C.

this, indeed, appears to be the case. The red-hair gene, as the geneticist Amram Scheinfeld has noted, is a special one which shows its effect if not masked by very dark-hair genes. Only when the melanin gene is very active, making the hair black or dark brown, is the red-hair gene obscured. But where the melanin gene is not so strong, the red-hair gene manifests itself and the result is a reddish brown or chestnut shade. And if the brown-hair gene is an 'utter weakling', to use Scheinfeld's expression, or if it is absent, distinctive red hair will be produced.[30]

Skin colour, eye colour and hair colour are the three human features in which the processes of heredity can be most easily observed. In such features as the shapes and sizes of eyes, noses, ears, lips, etc., and the waviness or otherwise of head hair, the results of gene-mixing are much harder to study and classify. Even so, geneticists have discovered, among other things, that narrow and small eyes are recessive to wide and large eyes; that long eyelashes are dominant over short lashes; and that straight eyes dominate slant eyes. The geneticists know, also, that broad nostrils are dominant over narrow nostrils; that prominent and convex noses are dominant over those that are moderate and straight; and that kinky hair dominates curly hair, that curly dominates wavy, and that wavy dominates straight. They are less sure of themselves concerning the shapes of lips and the sizes of ears; and Scheinfeld says that so many environmental factors are involved in the skeletal and constitutional aspects of the body that 'the classification of peoples on this basis is a formidable, if not impossible, task'.[31]

It will be gathered from all this that if castaways from the *San Lesmes* did intermarry with islanders in the eastern Pacific, their genes, in succeeding generations, would have produced results in a regular pattern—even in those heritable features that are difficult to study and classify. It is safe to say, therefore, that a good proportion of the castaways' most direct descendants would have inherited enough of the features of their male forebears to look like Europeans. Yet few of those descendants would have looked quite as European as the castaways themselves. If the castaways' wives had had brown skins, the skins of their descendants would generally have been lighter than their wives' but darker than their own. If their wives' hair had been black and theirs otherwise, the hair of their descendants would still have been black—except where blond or red-hair genes occasionally produced crops of reddish-brown, chestnut or completely red hair. Large eyes in the castaways' wives would generally have reappeared as large eyes in subsequent generations. Brown eyes would almost invariably have reappeared as brown—except when a rare pair of blue eyes from the Bay of Biscay or elsewhere came 'smiling through'. Flat Polynesian noses with broad nostrils would have tended to stay flat; but straight Polynesian hair would have got such kinks, waves and curls in it as the castaways had in theirs. In short, any island where the castaways' genes had a chance to assert themselves would have developed a new ethnic type, unlike anything to be found in the 'pure' Polynesian islands. This new breed would, of course, have inherited many other features besides those mentioned, for example, blood types, fingerprint patterns, the ability or otherwise to sing, and probably intelligence.[32] In addition, it would probably have been taller and stronger than either of the original types, for the mating of people of diverse racial origins is apt to produce a hybrid vigour, which geneticists call heterosis. Heterosis is said to have occurred on Pitcairn Island among the Anglo-Polynesian descendants of the *Bounty* mutineers. It has also been noted among descendants of Maori-European marriages in New Zealand and those of European-Asian marriages in Hawaii.[33] In the case of the castaways, the effect of heterosis could have been especially marked in later times as the Basques are the tallest people in Spain.[34] Another factor that would undoubtedly have distinguished their descendants is a propensity to wear clothes where their darker compatriots in tropical Polynesia had no need of them.

Like the castaways themselves, any fowls, pigs or dogs that the castaways brought with them would have betrayed themselves genetically in subsequent generations if they had mated with Polynesian counterparts of different breeds. They would have been even more obvious if they remained apart. However, Oviedo's anecdote about the failure of the *San Lesmes*' captain in the Santa Cruz River to buy the last two fowls in Loaisa's ships leaves little doubt that no alien breed of fowl could have arrived in the caravel. But there is no such certainty about pigs and dogs. If European pigs were introduced, they would probably have been detectable in later times by their superior size.[35] As for European breeds of dog, they are likely to have stood out even more clearly because dogs come in a greater variety of shapes and sizes. If, for example, the caravel's crew had carried some spaniels with them, as was customary in sixteenth century Spanish ships,[36] the spaniels' long, silky hair and distinctive appearance would have clearly differentiated them from the short-haired, prick-eared dogs that the Polynesians bred for food. Naturally, the distinction would have become blurred if the two types were interbred. But, as with human beings, examples resembling the original types would occasionally have been seen—if Nature were allowed to take its course. However, where interbreeding did take place the long hair of the original spaniels would have tended to disappear in subsequent generations, as long hair in dogs is recessive to short.[37] Floppy ears would probably have disappeared also, as upright ears are known to be dominant in some breeds.[38]

It need scarcely be said that if some of the seamen of the *San Lesmes* (not to mention their livestock) survived the loss of their ship to leave their genetic imprint in Polynesia, one would also expect them to have made an impact in other ways. They could have done this in four main fields. They could have left their mark on the material culture of the region; they could have influenced its folk culture (including religion and language); they could have dominated or influenced political affairs and social mores; and they could have brought in diseases that were unknown in the area previously.

From the point of view of disease, the mere arrival of the castaways or their descendants at any island could have had the same devastating effect on the inhabitants as the arrival of Europeans in the Pacific in the eighteenth century. In the latter case, the islanders died in their thousands through having no resistance to the commonplace germs that the cosmopolitan Europeans brought with them.[39] So there is good reason to suppose that the castaways might have quickly lessened their numerical inferiority in the islands they reached in the same unwitting way. In such circumstances, it would naturally have been easier for them to leave their marks on the political, social and cultural life of the region than if they were always heavily outnumbered.

There is no knowing now, of course, what the social and political systems of Eastern Polynesia were in the early sixteenth century. Nor can we do more than guess at the range of capabilities of any survivors of the *San Lesmes* disaster. However, it is probably safe to say that a group of men who had battled halfway around the world would have been more aggressive than any community of insular sixteenth century Polynesians; and being in a desperate situation, they would have been more ruthless. The castaways might therefore have quickly attained positions of political power even in a large community. But they are more likely to have made a strong impression on the culture of an island with a small population.

On any island where the castaways did achieve important positions, one may readily imagine that, with the object of inspiring continuing fear and respect, they might have fostered the notion that their white skins were closely associated with their superior 'know-how' and technology. White men have frequently done this where they have won sway over people of a darker complexion. One of the consequences is that lightness of skin becomes politically and socially desirable. In such communities the duskier descendants of mixed marriages frequently go to considerable lengths to keep their skins as light as possible, both because white skins are looked on as more attractive and because it 'pays' to be white. On the other hand, the people with no white-skin genes are obliged to put up with their condition as best they can, and this—as in the United States or South Africa—frequently means standing on the bottom rungs of the political and social ladder.[40] Colour consciousness, therefore, is likely to have been an important fact of life in any place where the crew of the *San Lesmes,* or the lighter of their descendants, won positions of power; and one would expect the local language to have acquired an array of words to describe the various shades of skin colour.[41]

In the field of material culture, the castaways are likely to have made their greatest impact in those areas where Spanish forms and techniques were clearly superior to those of the local people or where local forms did not exist. In the main, the castaways would have known more about their own profession of the sea than anything else. So one would expect their influence to have been most marked in matters pertaining to boats, fishing and navigation. Yet the castaways' influence could scarcely have become paramount in some of those matters. Rather, features from both Spanish and Polynesian culture must have been blended out of sheer necessity. For example, once the castaways' supplies of iron, nails, sailcloth and the like were exhausted, any boats they built must have taken on a somewhat Polynesian appearance. Thus woven mats would have had to serve as sails, and the castaways would have had to learn the art of using sinnet to sew the planks of their hulls together. Likewise, the lack of large timber trees would have forced them into unaccustomed economies, so that the hulls of their boats are likely to have become narrower until, in the end, they had to adopt the Polynesian practice of using outriggers to balance them. This, in turn, could have led to the invention of, or, at least, the construction of, the double canoe, whereby two narrow hulls were lashed together with the aid of staves to create a vessel beamy enough and stable enough to carry bulky cargoes and to go on long voyages. Yet despite the modifications that their environment must have forced upon them, one may imagine that the castaways would have continued to build their boats much as they had always done. If, therefore, their techniques survived, their sailing vessels should have been just as distinctive in later times as a person with white skin, red hair and blue eyes. Similarly, one may imagine that once the castaways' metal tools were lost, stolen or worn out, they would have made replicas of them in shell, wood, bone or stone. One may further imagine that the castaways would have adapted their navigational lore to their new environment—that, despite the immediate or eventual loss of their navigational instruments, they would have divided the horizon into its accustomed cardinal points, and that they would have continued to steer by the stars on long night voyages.[42] Needless to say, the castaways would have discovered many stars in the southern sky that had previously been but little known to Europeans. So if, in accordance with centuries-old European practice, they had grouped them into constellations, that would not have been surprising. Nor would it have been surprising if the constellations they fixed on did not correspond with those of modern times, for it was not until 1603 that Johann Bayer, a German astronomer, added twelve constellations—all in the southern sky—to the forty-eight proclaimed by Ptolemy in the second century A.D.[43] The astronomy of Ptolemy would, in fact, have been the only astronomical system known to the castaways, as their departure from Europe preceded the heydays of both Copernicus and Galileo. So apart from understanding that the world was round, the castaways would have been inclined to picture the earth as the centre of the universe, enclosed within an elaborate series of cycles and epicycles in which the sun, moon, stars and planets had their courses.[44]

Because of the limited resources of their new environment and their limited metal tools, the castaways' impact on the material culture of the islanders could not have been extensive. In the Tuamotus, for example, any knowledge they may have had about building a stone house with a tiled roof, chimneys, glass windows, etc. would have been of little avail on an atoll where the only possible building materials were coral rock and what could be had from bushes and trees. Nor could they have usefully used any knowledge they may have had about

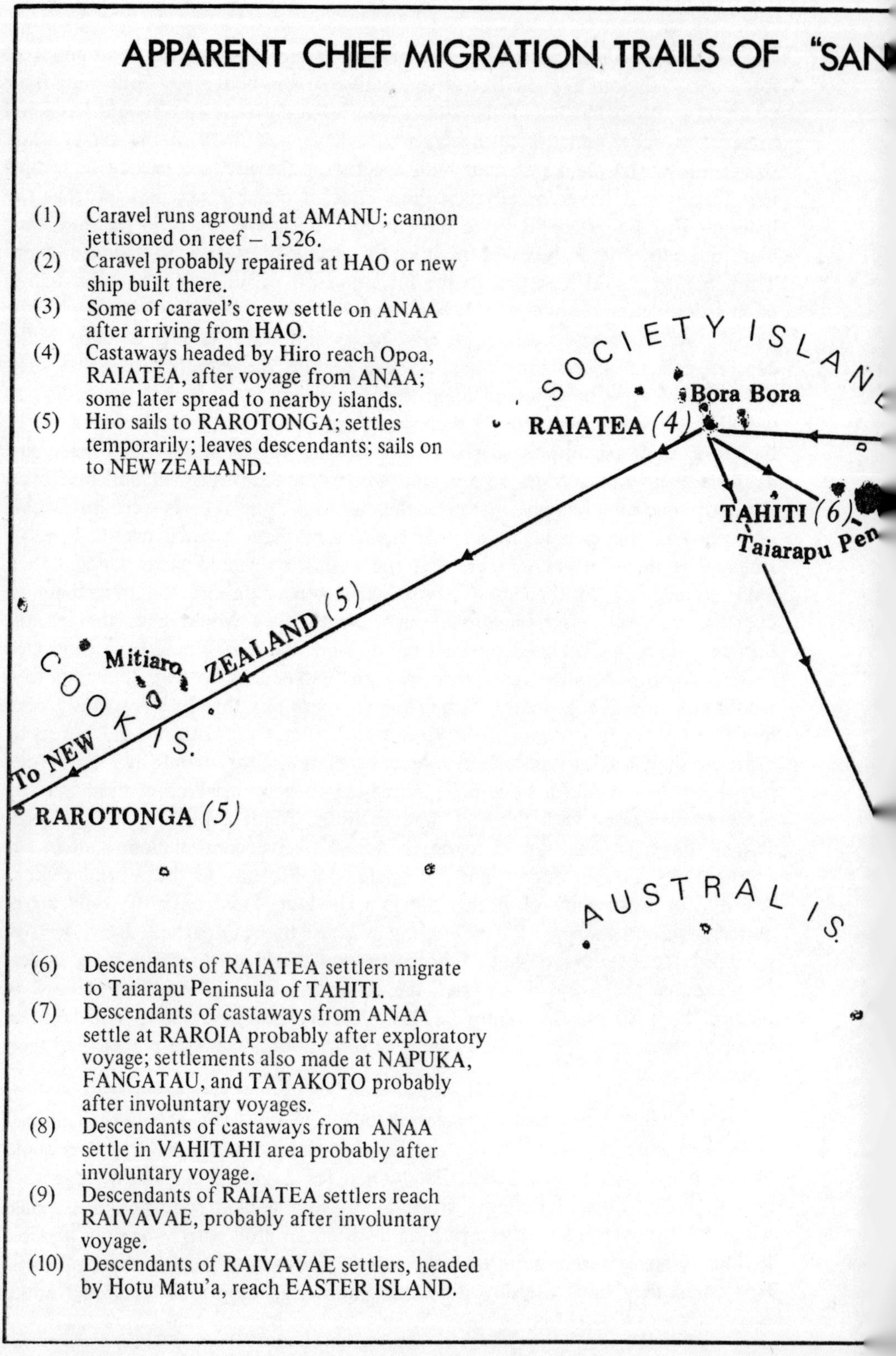

APPARENT CHIEF MIGRATION TRAILS OF "SAN

(1) Caravel runs aground at AMANU; cannon jettisoned on reef – 1526.
(2) Caravel probably repaired at HAO or new ship built there.
(3) Some of caravel's crew settle on ANAA after arriving from HAO.
(4) Castaways headed by Hiro reach Opoa, RAIATEA, after voyage from ANAA; some later spread to nearby islands.
(5) Hiro sails to RAROTONGA; settles temporarily; leaves descendants; sails on to NEW ZEALAND.

SOCIETY ISLAN
Bora Bora
RAIATEA (4)
TAHITI (6)
Taiarapu Pen
COOK IS.
Mitiaro
To NEW ZEALAND (5)
RAROTONGA (5)
AUSTRAL IS.

(6) Descendants of RAIATEA settlers migrate to Taiarapu Peninsula of TAHITI.
(7) Descendants of castaways from ANAA settle at RAROIA probably after exploratory voyage; settlements also made at NAPUKA, FANGATAU, and TATAKOTO probably after involuntary voyages.
(8) Descendants of castaways from ANAA settle in VAHITAHI area probably after involuntary voyage.
(9) Descendants of RAIATEA settlers reach RAIVAVAE, probably after involuntary voyage.
(10) Descendants of RAIVAVAE settlers, headed by Hotu Matu'a, reach EASTER ISLAND.

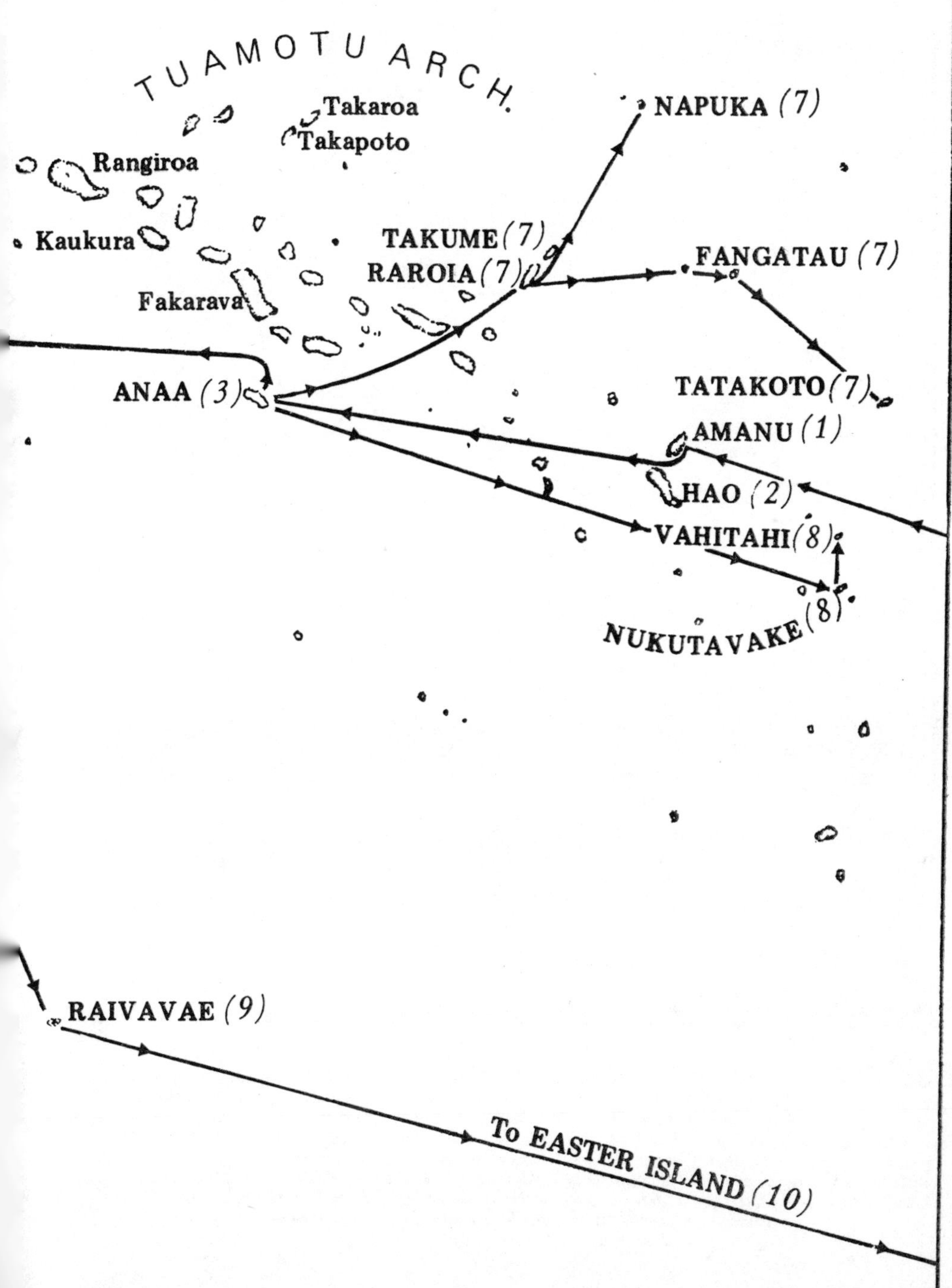
.ESMES" CASTAWAYS AND THEIR DESCENDANTS
TUAMOTU ARCH.
Takaroa
Takapoto
Rangiroa
Kaukura
Fakarava
NAPUKA (7)
TAKUME (7)
RAROIA (7)
FANGATAU (7)
ANAA (3)
TATAKOTO (7)
AMANU (1)
HAO (2)
VAHITAHI (8)
NUKUTAVAKE (8)
RAIVAVAE (9)
To EASTER ISLAND (10)

When the Loaisa expedition left Spain in 1525, Europeans still believed that the earth was the centre of the universe and that the sun, moon, stars and planets revolved around it in a series of spheres. The idea had first been propounded by the Egyptian astronomer Ptolemy, who flourished in the second century A.D. This illustration of the Ptolemaic conception, with the universe borne on the shoulders of Atlas, is from William Cunningham's 'The Cosmographical Glasse' (London, 1559). Part of Cunningham's book is devoted to a discussion on the number of celestial spheres, as this was a matter of considerable doubt to scholars of the time.

farming where there was no soil to speak of, no familiar fruits or vegetables, and a tropical climate. As for the wheelwright's craft, there would have been little point in practising this where there were no beasts of burden and everything could easily be transported by sea. Nor would they have been likely to introduce such crafts as weaving and pottery—even supposing they were skilled in them—when there was no thread and no clay to use.

Much of the practical knowledge of the castaways could, therefore, have been lost in a single generation. However, their knowledge, ideas and beliefs in matters of morals, religion and other things of the mind could have considerably altered much of the folk culture of the islands they settled. If, for example, the castaways had found cannibalism practised, it seems likely that their Christian morality would have been outraged and they would have done their best to overthrow it. No expertise in the local language would have been needed to protest about such matters. As the early explorers and missionaries found in Tahiti, effective communication is possible without being an accomplished linguist. However, the castaways could not have become effective immigrants in Polynesia without learning the local language; and the probability is that they would eventually have adopted this even among themselves. The reason is that the castaways, almost certainly, had a variety of languages as their native tongues. The Basques would have spoken Basque, a strange, ancient, immensely difficult language that is unrelated, so far as is known, to any other living tongue.[45] The Galicians would have spoken Galician, a descendant of the Vulgar Latin of Roman times, which has more in common with Portuguese than the Spanish of Castille.[46] The Flemish gunners (if any) would have spoken the Germanic language of Flanders; and the Malays and Negroes (if any) would have spoken their own languages. So only the castaways who came from parts of Spain other than Galicia and the Basque provinces would have been native speakers of a language approximating that of the Spanish court. Although the others would undoubtedly have known Spanish more or less, and used it as a lingua franca, they would certainly not have spoken it from preference. In any case, even if all the castaways had spoken the same native tongue, they are unlikely—as a small group of immigrants—to have had any more impact on the dialects of Polynesia than, say, the million-odd foreign migrants have had on English in Australia since World War II. As the American ethnologist Charles Pickering wrote more than a century ago, it is false to think that 'nations' go about in masses, the strong overcoming the weak, and imposing their customs, religion and languages on the vanquished. 'The adoption of a language,' he said, 'seems to be very much a matter of convenience, depending on the numerical majority. A stranger learns the language of the community in which he may happen to fix his abode; and his children often know no other.'[47]

If the castaways had had their own women with them there is, of course, a possibility that an enclave of Spanish, Basque or Galician speakers might have survived in some remote corner of the Pacific. But as they did not, it goes almost without saying that any children they had could only have learned the language of their mothers at their mothers' knees, and would have learned nothing of their fathers' languages unless the castaways made special efforts to teach them. Thus within a single generation all trace of the Spanish, Basque or Galician languages would probably have been effaced—except, perhaps, for a few Polynesianised words from the Iberian peninsula for hitherto unknown concepts. However, as Tuamotuan has only fifteen sounds and Tahitian only thirteen, the Iberian words could easily have become modified virtually beyond recognition within only a day or two. This is what happened to European words in Tahiti some two and a half centuries later. Names such as Bougainville, Cook and Banks became Putaveri, Tute and Opano overnight and words like governor, Chinese and July became tavana, Tinito and Tiurai respectively.[48]

As the castaways could not have taught their children anything of consequence until they were at least five years old—or at least five years and nine months after their shipwreck—it is reasonable to assume that some of them would have acquired a good knowledge of the local language by then. They would thus have been able to use the vernacular to instruct their children and perhaps other islanders in some of the mysteries of their Catholic religion, which, then as now, played an all-important part in Spanish life. Here, however, the castaways would have been limited in what they could pass on by a number of fortuitous factors. If, for example, a copy of the Old Testament survived with them, but the New Testament did not, their religious teachings would almost certainly have taken on a more Jewish cast than was customary in Spain at that time.[49] On the other hand, if no books survived at all, or if no one survived who could read, the castaways could only have passed on what they could recollect of the chants, prayers, Bible stories and so on that they had learned at home, and what they could invent. In this respect, it is worth noting that the cult of images which is popularly associated with the religion of Spain is not universal in that country. The Basques, in particular, do not make use of the crucifixes, Madonnas, sacred hearts, etc. that are so beloved of Latin Spaniards. So this aspect of Iberian culture would not necessarily survive a sixteenth century Spanish shipwreck.[50]

Another cultural item that could be expected to become an early casualty, at least in its original form, is the art of writing. With no means of replenishing their stocks of books and writing materials, and faced with the problem of adapting their knowledge to a foreign language, it may be readily imagined that the Roman script of the castaways would have tended to degenerate into more primitive forms—if it were passed down to their part-Polynesian descendants. Such degenerate scripts are known to have developed in several previously illiterate communities once the art of writing became known to them, and these thereafter served as a means of communication.[51] Thus, on any island where the castaways or their descendants settled, some form of script could well have been used to pass down knowledge from one generation to another. In the main, however, it might be expected that the chant, endlessly repeated, would have been the principal means of instruction and record.

Apart from introducing European notions of music and dancing, a diversion or two, and such everyday customs as handshaking (as opposed to the traditional Polynesian greeting of pressing noses),[52] a shipload of sixteenth century Spaniards could scarcely have influenced communities of Stone Age Polynesians in many other ways. Certainly, any castaways from the *San Lesmes* left no overwhelmingly obvious traces of themselves in the Pacific islands. If they had, the story of the lost caravel would have become common knowledge long before now. However, a careful reading of Pacific literature of the past four and a half centuries has convinced the writer that there are, or were, many anomalies about the people and culture of the region that can only be explained by assuming the survival of the caravel's crew.

These anomalies, set against the background of the European exploration and penetration of the Pacific islands, will be brought into focus in the following pages. Particular attention will be paid to what the various observers recorded about the skin, hair and eye colours of the islanders, about their general appearance, their clothing and ornaments, their dogs and pigs (if any), their boats and other maritime accoutrements, their houses, furniture, tools, religion, morals, customs, dances, music, ability to sing, diseases, and such other matters as seem relevant. Where possible, sufficient data will be given so that the reliability or bias of any subjective statement may be assessed. Thus, if the information is known, it will be indicated whether an observer had minutes, hours, months or years to study any particular subject. Likewise, each observer's competence will be recorded—whether he was a ship's captain, scientist, ordinary seaman, missionary, businessman and so forth, and whether he was Spanish, French, English, Belgian, Dutch, Russian, etc. All this information should, in the end, enable each reader to make up his own mind on four questions:

1. Can it be assumed that the four cannon of Amanu did come from the *San Lesmes?*
2. If so, did any of the caravel's crew survive the shipwreck and intermarry with the local women?
3. What was the extent (if any) of their genetic influence in the Pacific islands?
4. And what cultural and other impact (if any) did they have in the Pacific?

It need scarcely be said that, unless a time machine is one day invented, absolute truth will probably never be arrived at in these questions. But one verity can be stated concerning them. This is that of the numerous observers who will be called to give evidence in the following pages, only one—Philibert de Commerson—ever gave serious thought to the possibility of an early Spanish shipwreck in the eastern Pacific and what the consequences of such an event might be.

4

A gold ring, red hair and dogs of Castille

FOR eighty years after the Loaisa expedition passed through the eastern Pacific, no white men's ships are known to have sailed within several hundred miles of Hao or Amanu. Nor are they likely to have done so. The Spaniards, initially the only Europeans with a frontier on the Pacific's eastern margin, had, in the main, more rewarding things to do than to explore it. As for other nations, they had no reasons for wanting to enter the Pacific at all—until Spain in the east and Portugal in the west had built up colonies and trading monopolies that were worth attacking.

Spain's conquest of Mexico, the rich Aztec empire, took place in 1521. This was followed soon afterwards by the conquest of Guatemala, the Mayan empire. The Spaniards' thoughts then turned to a golden kingdom called Biru or Peru that was rumoured to lie somewhere to the south of Panama. In 1531, Francisco Pizarro, an illiterate adventurer, succeeded in reaching this land after two earlier attempts had failed. Having captured and murdered the Inca Atahualpa, Pizarro and his followers soon overcame the Inca's subjects. By January 1535 Pizarro had founded Lima as the city of his government, with nearby Callao its port. Meanwhile, expeditions pushed south into what are now Bolivia and Chile, and eventually those regions were conquered also. However, opposition to Pizarro's rule developed among some of the Spaniards, and this, indirectly, led to the first Spanish attempt to explore the eastern Pacific.[1]

When news of Pizarro's difficulties reached Mexico, Cortes sent him a party of reinforcements in a ship commanded by Hernando de Grijalva. In April 1537, Grijalva landed the troops in the Peruvian port of Paita. While there he learned of some reputedly wealthy islands that were said to lie somewhere in the Pacific to the south-west and he resolved to go in search of them. He pushed down to the 29th parallel without finding anything, then turned about to return to Mexico. His crew, however, opposed him in this, urging him to sail for the Moluccas. When he refused, they murdered him and steered for those islands themselves, on a course somewhere near the Equator. Four months later, wracked by hunger, exhaustion and disease, they reached some islands to the north of New Guinea. Soon afterwards, their rotting ship fell to pieces, and the crew were either killed by the natives or captured and enslaved. A few of the latter eventually reached the Moluccas, where the Portuguese governor took pity on them, despite a conviction that Cortes had sent them to try to regain the Moluccas for Spain.[2]

Meanwhile, Andres de Urdaneta, one of the few survivors of the Loaisa expedition, had returned home. In a report to the Council of the Indies, he spoke of the rich trade that Spain would enjoy if she again occupied the Moluccas. He also mentioned the possibility of trade with China and the 'Islas del Poniente', as the Philippines were then called. Although Emperor Charles V could not be tempted to reopen the Moluccas question with Portugal, he did grant a request from Pedro de Alvarado, the conqueror of Guatemala, to trade in spices elsewhere in the Far East. Alvarado, himself, never took advantage of this grant. But in November 1542, an expedition of six ships left Mexico under Ruy Lopez de Villalobos and crossed the Pacific to the 'Islas del Poniente'. Villalobos renamed the islands the Philippines after the emperor's son and established a base on Sangani Island, but was eventually driven south to Tidore through shortage of food. Meanwhile, his flagship *San Juan* made two attempts to return to Mexico, but as with Saavedra's *Florida,* she was defeated by contrary winds. After the second attempt, Villalobos accepted a Portuguese offer of transportation to Spain; and so, for the second time in two decades, Spanish dreams of rich commerce in the Far East came to nought. Moreover, the problem of how to cross the Pacific from west to east remained unsolved.[3]

For the rest of the reign of Emperor Charles V, the Spaniards did no more about the potential Far East trade. However, new plans were laid soon after his son, Philip II, came to the throne in 1556. Among the planners was Urdaneta, now a venerable Augustinian priest. After several years of preparation, a fleet of four ships left Mexico under Miguel Lopez de Legaspi. Urdaneta accompanied him as chief navigator and adviser. Legaspi's instructions were to explore, colonise and Christianise the Philippines, to look for gold and spices, and to investigate the possibility of trade with other countries. He was also to try to discover a return route to Mexico.

Soon after leaving Mexico, one of Legaspi's ships, the *San Lucas,* under Alonso de Arellano, became separated from the others. She reached the Philippines independently in January 1565, having narrowly escaped shipwreck in the low and dangerous Marshall Islands. Arellano remained in the Philippines for three months, then set out to return to Mexico. In doing this, he ran north to the 40th parallel and thus got into the zone of westerly winds and the east-flowing Japanese current. In this region, it proved quite easy to cross the Pacific to North America, from where the passage to Mexico was equally straightforward. The *San Lucas* thus became the first ship to complete a voyage from Mexico to the Philippines and back. Meanwhile, Legaspi's other ships had also become entangled in the Marshall Islands. But having got clear of them, they duly reached the Philippines where some of the Spaniards landed and formed a settlement. Legaspi's flagship, *San Pedro,* eventually set out to return to Mexico under Urdaneta's command; and by coincidence, she, too, was taken into the same high latitudes as the *San Lucas* and reached the North American coast without difficulty.[4]

With the practicability of return voyages between the Philippines and Mexico now demonstrated, the way was open for a rich trade to develop between those two countries. Indeed, from then until the end of the Napoleonic wars, a year seldom passed without the voyage of at least one ship from Acapulco to Manila or vice versa. These ships, the largest and richest merchant vessels of their age, were the celebrated Spanish galleons. They carried the luxuries of the Orient to Mexico for onward shipment to Spain, and returned to the Philippines with silver ingots. Outward from Mexico, they sailed with the north-east trade winds in or about 13 deg. North latitude, thereby avoiding the troublesome Marshall Islands. On the way back, they took the same course as the pioneering ships of Arellano and Urdaneta. A feature of the galleon trade was its remarkable safety record. Only three ships in 250 years are known to have been wrecked in the islands between Mexico and the Philippines; and only six set out from those places, never to be heard of again.[5] Whether any of the six lost galleons left European castaways on islands that were not 'officially' discovered until many years later will be discussed towards the end of this book. Meanwhile, suffice it to say that the development of the galleon trade was undoubtedly a factor behind the first official attempt by Spaniards to explore the South Pacific in 1567; that this, in turn, led to a colonising expedition from which two more ships disappeared; and that when a third voyage was made to the South Pacific in 1606, the Spaniards made the first and only contact with either Hao Atoll, or its neighbour Amanu, until the era of Captain Cook.

Almost from the time of Pizarro's conquest of Peru, rumours had persisted among the Spaniards that islands of great wealth existed somewhere in the South Pacific. Years earlier, it was said, the Inca Tupac Yupanqui had discovered two islands called Hagua Chumbi and Niña Chumbi, and had returned from them with gold and silver, a copper throne, black slaves and the skin of an animal like a horse. Other tales told of islands of great riches called Coatu, Qüen and Acabana.[6] Whatever the origin of these tales, they created the notion that the islands in question were the fabled Islands of Solomon, source of the wealth of the celebrated Biblical king. One of the ablest conquistadores, Pedro Sarmiento de Gamboa, became convinced that these islands were the outposts of a great continent, which stretched north-west from Tierra del Fuego to within fifteen degrees of the Equator, some 600 leagues from Peru. Sarmiento's theory and other considerations finally persuaded the viceroy of Peru to provide two ships to go in search of the supposed land. Under the command of the viceroy's nephew, Alvaro de Mendaña, the ships left Callao in November 1567 with instructions to find the continent and settle there. They sailed for fifty-eight days before making their first landfall—a small island in the Ellice Group. From there they turned south and after about three more weeks they came to a large, high island which Mendaña named Santa Isabel. Several other large islands—including Guadalcanal, San Cristobal and Malaita—were discovered over the next six months. All were inhabited by naked, woolly-headed black men who were often inhospitable or positively hostile to the Spaniards. Despite this, many of the Spaniards were excited by the islands they had found. The glitter of pyrites in the islanders' clubs convinced some that the rocks of the islands contained gold. Others thought they saw traces of gold when they panned the streams. Those who had visions of quick wealth wanted to settle in the islands and exploit their imagined riches. But Mendaña was still eager to discover the continent he had set out to find, and he was convinced that if the expedition sailed further south he would find it. In the end, the pilots were the ones who had their way. With provisions and ammunition running short, the two ships worn and leaky, and many of the men sick, the pilots declared that the expedition's only hope of survival was to return to Peru at once. After a last token search for the southern continent, they headed north to cross the Pacific in the track of the galleons.[7]

No hero's welcome awaited Mendaña in South America. He had not found the continent he had set out to find; nor had he returned with any valuable articles of trade. Nevertheless, rumours soon began to circulate that he had, in fact, discovered some islands of great wealth and that these were actually the Solomon Islands—the name his discoveries still bear today. Mendaña, himself, does not seem to have believed in this wishful propaganda. But he certainly thought his islands were the outposts of a continent; and with his uncle, the viceroy, he went to Spain to seek permission to go there again. The king granted his wish in 1574, but on his way back to Peru to prepare his fleet, he called at Mexico, fell foul of enemies of his uncle, and was imprisoned. When, finally, he reached Peru, a series of other events occurred to delay his voyage. In 1578-9, Francis Drake, the first foreign interloper to enter the Pacific, sailed up the west coast of South America from Magellan Strait, looting towns, capturing treasure ships, and causing fear and confusion from Chile to Mexico. This unprecedented piracy caused the Peruvian government to veto Mendaña's new expedition on the ground that a new, inadequately defended colony would only tempt other English privateers to make more raids. Besides this, the government sent an expedition to Magellan Strait to establish a garrison.[8]

However, Thomas Cavendish, the next English privateer to come along, slipped past the Spanish defences, went on to capture a Manila galleon, and like Drake, completed a triumphant and highly profitable voyage round the world. This second blow to Spanish morale further delayed the Mendaña expedition. But when, in 1594, yet another British privateer, Richard Hawkins, was captured off the Peruvian coast in trying to emulate his countrymen's exploits, a new feeling of confidence spread among them. Furthermore, Hawkins' capture coincided with the arrival in Peru of a new viceroy sympathetic to foreign exploration and settlement, and Mendaña was thus able to renew preparations for his long-deferred voyage.[9]

In June 1595, Mendaña sailed for the Solomon Islands with a fleet of four ships carrying a large number of prospective colonists. A thirty-year-old Portuguese, Pedro Fernandez de Quiros,* acted as pilot. Five weeks out from

* This is the Spanish spelling of his name.

Paita, the expedition came upon four islands on the eastern edge of the Polynesian triangle which Mendaña named after the viceroy, the Marqués de Mendoza— a name since shortened in English to Marquesas Islands. The Spaniards spent a fortnight among those islands repairing their ships and taking in wood and water. Although there were some bloody affrays with the islanders, Quiros was much impressed by some 'beautiful youths', who, in his opinion, had 'much cause to praise their Creator'. These youths were later to inspire Quiros with a desire to perform heroic deeds. Meanwhile, Mendaña's ships pressed on to the west, passing only two small islands before approaching the outliers of the Solomons. Here the expedition ran into a heavy fog near the volcano island of Tinakula, and when this cleared up, one of the four ships had disappeared, never to be seen again. Mendaña subsequently tried to establish a settlement on the island of Ndeni, which he called Santa Cruz. However, disagreement soon broke out among the colonists; the islanders were frequently hostile; and sickness and death struck many of the Spaniards down. After ten weeks, and following the death of Mendaña himself, the settlement was abandoned and the remaining three ships set sail for the Philippines. Only two, however, reached their destination. The third disappeared near the little-known Caroline Islands, and was never afterwards heard of.*[10]

About four years later, Quiros, one of the few survivors of the expedition, went to Rome for the jubilee Holy Year celebrations of 1600. While there he had an audience with the Pope and told him of the new lands he had seen and how the natives of the Marquesas Islands were among the most comely in the world. He said he was prepared to devote his life to their conversion to Christianity. Impressed, the Pope promised to support such an enterprise and to grant spiritual favours to all who engaged in it. Quiros also won the ear of the Spanish ambassador; and when he left Rome for Spain in 1602, he had valuable letters of recommendation to the Spanish court. The letters helped Quiros to gain royal approval for a new South Seas expedition, for which the viceroy of Peru was ordered to provide the necessary ships and equipment.[11]

Quiros returned to Peru in March 1605. Nine months later, he sailed from Callao with two ships and a launch having a total complement of ninety-two men.[12] His first objective was to try to discover some islands or a great body of land that he thought must exist near the four Marquesas Islands.[13] To do this, he shaped his course well to the south of that previously taken by Mendaña, and after four weeks he reached the southeastern fringe of the Tuamotu Archipelago.[14] Having passed the atolls of South Marutea, the Actaeon Group and Vairaatea, his three ships swung northward and so came upon Hao Atoll, which Quiros, with his customary Catholic fervour, called La Conversion de San Pablo (St Paul's Conversion).[15]

The three ships approached the atoll at its north-eastern corner, where many palm trees were growing. As no anchorage could be found in that

* Mendaña's two lost ships are further discussed in chapter 21.

vicinity, the launch was sent southwards to search for one along the eastern coast. Here and there, smoke could be seen rising and presently those in the launch cried out: 'People, people on the beach'. To Quiros, anxious for fresh water, 'the sight was hailed as if they had been angels'. The launch and two other boats were sent in to land a party of well-armed men. As they pulled towards the shore, about thirty islanders, armed with clubs and lances, stood in a row, awaiting them.[16] They were quite friendly, however, and beckoned and called on the Spaniards to land. Two soldiers jumped overboard and began to swim ashore, whereupon the islanders threw down their weapons and bowed three times from the head and shoulder. When one of the Spaniards was knocked over by a wave, some of the islanders plunged in and grabbed him, embracing him and kissing him on the cheeks. This, Quiros noted, was 'a way of showing friendship used also in France'.[17]

The friendly reception accorded to the two Spaniards encouraged a couple of their companions to swim ashore too. One of these had an especially white skin. This apparently fascinated the islanders, for Quiros noted that they 'came and felt his back, breast and arms, showing much astonishment'.[18] The islanders themselves were like the half-caste offspring of whites and Negroes. 'They are the colour of mulattos but with well-made limbs and good features', wrote Fray Juan de Torquemada, a historian of the expedition.[19] To the accountant, Juan de Iturbe, the islanders had a 'tawny complexion like mulattos' and were 'well disposed'.[20]

The islanders and the Spaniards talked by means of 'well-understood signs'. The islanders pointed to the thatched houses of their village and invited the Spaniards to go there for a meal. The Spaniards, for their part, offered to take the islanders to their ships. As neither party could prevail, and as it was getting late, the Spaniards swam back through the surf to their boats. Eight or nine islanders followed them; but although the Spaniards gave them such things as cheese, knives, biscuits, cloth and garters, which greatly pleased them, they still could not persuade them to go out to their ships. Finally, after inviting the Spaniards to come back next day, the islanders swam ashore, and the boats returned to the ships just as the sun was setting.

That night the three ships beat to windward, as it was Quiros' intention to return to the atoll next morning to try to get water. Meanwhile, from the masthead, the chief pilot had sighted a bay to southward which, in his view, was much better than the bay of Cadiz. Everyone was 'rather joyful at finding this port', Quiros wrote. However, when dawn broke, the Spaniards were about three leagues to leeward of where they had met the islanders the previous day, and instead of finding a bay there was merely a long, narrow reef almost covered with water. Only at one spot, a slightly elevated island, were there some palm trees. To this island, Quiros sent two boat parties to search for water. The surf broke on the reef with great fury. But the

Spaniards jumped into the surf with their arquebuses, spades, crowbars and jars, and except for one accident, they got ashore without difficulty.

Marching in order, they went for about half a league until they entered a grove of palms, which surrounded a small square. In the middle of the square was a stone structure, some twenty feet long and three feet broad, bordered with white coral stones up to three feet high. Palm leaves plaited together and fixed to the trunk of a tree fell over the higher stones, which seemed to be 'in the form of an altar'. The Spaniards thought that this was a place where 'the devil spoke to and deceived those miserable Indians without anyone to stop him'. For this reason they cut down a tree and erected a cross to sanctify the spot. Then, they fell to their knees to thank God for 'having been the first to raise his royal standard in the unknown lands'.[21]

The Spaniards dug for water in several places but found it brackish. However, they did get a good supply of coconuts, with which they marched back to the beach. On the way they saw a figure coming towards them. It seemed at first to be a man but proved to be a woman. She was so old that some thought it a miracle she could stand on her feet. Others estimated her age at from sixty to 100. She was tall and large, with a brown, wrinkled face. Her teeth were few and decayed; while her fine, black hair, interspersed with grey, was 'dressed in the Spanish fashion'—to use the words of Fray Martin de Munilla, one of the priests. In a basket she carried some dried cuttlefish, a knife made from mother of pearl shell, and a skein of thread. A small white dog with patches of a darker colour ran at her heels. Gonzalez de Leza, the second pilot, recorded that it was 'a dog like ours'.[22] Leza also noted that the landing party found half of a cedar pole on shore which he thought had been 'worked on the coast of Nicaragua or Peru'.[23]

The old woman agreed to accompany the Spaniards to the flagship. Quiros was delighted to see her. He seated her on a box and gave her meat and soup from a pot, which she ate without scruple. However, she could not manage the hard ship's biscuit except when it was softened in wine, and this 'she indicated she knew well', as Quiros himself put it. The old woman expressed much pleasure when Quiros gave her a looking glass, and everyone agreed that she was well-mannered and would not have been bad-looking when young. She looked at the men with attention, but displayed the greatest interest in the boys. And when she was shown the ship's goats, she looked at them 'as if she had seen others'. Although she wore only a loin cloth, the woman had a gold ring with an emerald set in it on one of her fingers. Quiros asked her to give him this, but she replied by signs that she could not do so without cutting her finger off, and for this she seemed sorry. When a brass ring was offered to her, she did not care for it; but she was glad to accept a length of Rouen cloth and other things to dress in.[24]

At this point, Quiros noticed that several canoes had come from the village on the other side of the lagoon, bringing seventy-two islanders in them. He sent his boats ashore to meet them, and the old woman went too. Each of the canoes contained fourteen or fifteen men, except the largest which had twenty-five. 'This little fleet consisted of vessels like well-made galeots,' Leza recorded. 'They were not of one tree trunk, but very subtle, with curious mat sails. Better ones could not have been made in Castille'.[25]

Leaving their canoes well secured, the islanders jumped ashore to meet the Spaniards. As soon as they saw the old woman, they ran to embrace her, surprised at seeing her clothed. Meanwhile, a robust, broad-shouldered man of about fifty with a 'good-complexioned face' was pointed out as the islanders' chief. He wore on his head a crown of small black feathers, which were so fine and soft that they looked like silk.[26] 'From the back of his head', Fray Torquemada recorded, 'there fell a mass of red and rather curly hair, reaching half way down his back. This caused great astonishment among our people, to find that, among a race which is not white, there should be such red hair, though they believed it to be his wife's, knowing that he was married'.[27]

By signs, the Spaniards invited the chief to visit their ships. He and several companions got into the boats, but they had scarcely done so when, apparently fearing treachery, all but the chief jumped out again and swam ashore. The chief wanted to do likewise, but some of the boat party grabbed and held him, and finally tied him down, while the rest rowed rapidly to the flagship. He struggled violently all the way, but became calmer when Quiros climbed down to the boat with a palm frond as an emblem of peace and personally untied his bonds. The chief looked at the ship with much attention, 'wondering at its build and talking a good deal'. But as he made it clear that he did not want to stay, Quiros gave him some presents, and the boat took him ashore again. Quiros' presents included a pair of breeches, a yellow silk shirt, a hat, a tin medal to go round his neck, a case of knives, a fowl, and some quince jam and other things to eat. Back on shore, the chief gave a Spanish sergeant his crown of feathers and red tresses as a present for Quiros, plus some fish and water that his people carried in coconut shells. The islanders then took to their canoes to return to their village. The Spaniards fired their arquebuses in farewell and returned on board.

Quiros wanted to make yet another attempt to contact the islanders next day. But the chief pilot advised against this because, he said, their village was well to windward and water would be wasted in trying to reach it. The three ships therefore lay to for the night, ready to resume their voyage in the morning. During the night, the crews never ceased talking of what they had seen and 'giving thanks to God for the way the islands had been explored, and for the good conduct of the natives.'[28] No doubt the Spaniards discussed such things as the carved cedar pole, the old woman's gold ring, her white spotted dog like those at home, her apparent familiarity with goats and wine, and the red hair in the chiefs' head-dress. However, they still knew too little about the great ocean around them to suspect anything odd about such things.

Summing up his impressions of the island, Quiros merely wrote: 'It is in latitude 18 deg., distant from Lima 1,180 leagues. Its circumference is 40 leagues, and in the centre there is a large shallow lake. The people are corpulent, and of a very good shape and colour. Their hair is fine and loose, and they have their parts covered. Their arms are thick and heavy lances of palm-wood, about 30 palmos long, and clubs of the same wood . . .'[29]

Leza, for his part, wrote: 'These Indians do not have knives nor any sort of iron to cut things. They make their knives from shells, as was seen when the old woman came on board.' Referring to the head-dress given to Quiros, Leza said: 'Among many feathers, there were tresses of a woman's hair arranged like a diadem. . . . The hairs were long and very golden, like gold threads, and there could not be better in our Spain even if they were dyed.'[30]

Munilla, the priest, made some pertinent remarks about the Hao canoes. 'The canoes of the natives were made in pieces, sewn together with hemp,' he wrote. 'The sails consisted of mats, and there was a counterpoise to prevent the canoes capsizing with the force of the waves.' He added: 'A pole made of cedar wood and some dogs like those of Castille were found there.'[31]

On leaving Hao, the Spaniards first coasted the southern part of the atoll and then ran up the western side on a nor'westerly course. Their next landfalls seem to have been Tauere, Rekareka and Raroia, three atolls that they did not approach.[32] Having passed the last of these, the expedition got clear of the Tuamotus, and did not see land again until isolated, palm-clad Caroline Island appeared on the horizon a week later. After another week, the three ships came upon Rakahanga Atoll, one of the northernmost atolls of the present-day Cook Group. The Spaniards landed in search of water. Then they sailed westwards for five more weeks before seeing land again—Taumako Island in the Duff Group of the Solomons. From there, they worked southwards, and as the double chain of islands now known as the New Hebrides came in sight, each overlapping the other as far as the eye could see, Quiros became convinced that he had found the great south land he sought. He named the new land La Austrialia del Espiritu Santo, and made grandiose plans for building a city on the shores of St Philip and St James Bay in the island now known as Santo. When these plans came to nothing at the end of a month, the expedition set out to return to Peru. Quiros, in the flagship, eventually reached Mexico; while his second-in-command, Louis Vaez de Torres, took the other two ships to the Philippines after passing through the strait between Australia and New Guinea.[33]

Although the expedition was an utter fiasco commercially, Quiros was still enthusiastic about the potential of the Pacific Islands, and he pestered officialdom for the rest of his life to send him on another expedition.[34] However, officialdom could see no profit in the islands he had discovered and always fobbed him off. After Quiros' death in about 1615, no new visionary arose to take up the torch of his enthusiasm for South Seas voyages. Indeed, more than 160 years passed before any of his countrymen were again sent to traverse the lonely expanses of that ocean; and it was not until that period that Europeans again set eyes on Hao or its sister island, Amanu.

5

'Three Spanish dogs, very lean'

IN 1580, some twenty-six years before Quiros made his last, inconclusive voyage to the Pacific, King Philip II of Spain, who was already king of the Netherlands, succeeded also to the crown of Portugal. But having gained Portugal, he soon lost the Netherlands. From 1572, the Dutch had been in revolt against him, and they finally gained their independence about the time that England defeated the Spanish Armada. These events made conditions ripe for the Dutch to challenge the trading monopolies that both the Portuguese and Spaniards had established over the previous century. Among other things, they sought to break Portugal's stranglehold on the East Indies spice trade; and from 1595 onwards scores of their ships sailed to the Moluccas to trade for spices directly. Most of these went out by way of the Cape of Good Hope. But a few tried the Strait of Magellan route, sometimes with the dual aim of attacking Spanish shipping on the Chilean and Peruvian coasts.

The first Dutch ships to enter the Pacific from the South American side were the *Liefde* and *Trouw,* which left Rotterdam in June 1598 under Jacob Mahu. The *Liefde* eventually reached Japan; the *Trouw* disappeared in a storm in about 27° or 28° N. Although little is known of the routes they took across the Pacific, they seem unlikely to have touched at any islands below the Equator. Other Dutch expeditions that passed through the eastern Pacific were commanded by Oliver Van Noort (1599-1600), Joris Van Spilbergen (1614-17), Willem Cornelisz Schouten and Jacob Le Maire (1615-16) and Jacob l'Hermite (1624-25). Of these, only Schouten and Le Maire touched at any islands south of the Line.[1]

Schouten and Le Maire, with two ships, *Eendracht* and *Hoorn,* left Holland in June 1615.[2] Their aim was to try to find the great south land that Quiros had sought, and, failing that, to reach the East Indies and trade there. As the newly-formed Dutch East India Company had been granted exclusive use of the Strait of Magellan, Schouten and Le Maire sought a more southerly passage, and in so doing they rounded Cape Horn (or Hoorn, as they spelled it). As their ship of that name had been burned a few days earlier, the *Eendracht* was alone when she entered the Pacific and headed north for the Juan Fernandez Islands to refresh. The Dutchmen then steered to the north-west, and later west, 'looking out eagerly for the southern land,' as Schouten wrote, 'but almost despairing and fearing there was no such land.' On 10 April 1616, about five weeks after leaving Juan Fernandez, the expedition sighted a small island, which was reckoned to be situated in 15° 12' to 15° 15' S. lat. and 61° 40' from the coast of Peru. This was Pukapuka Atoll

SPANISH, DUTCH VOYAGES IN THE PACIFIC 1542–1722

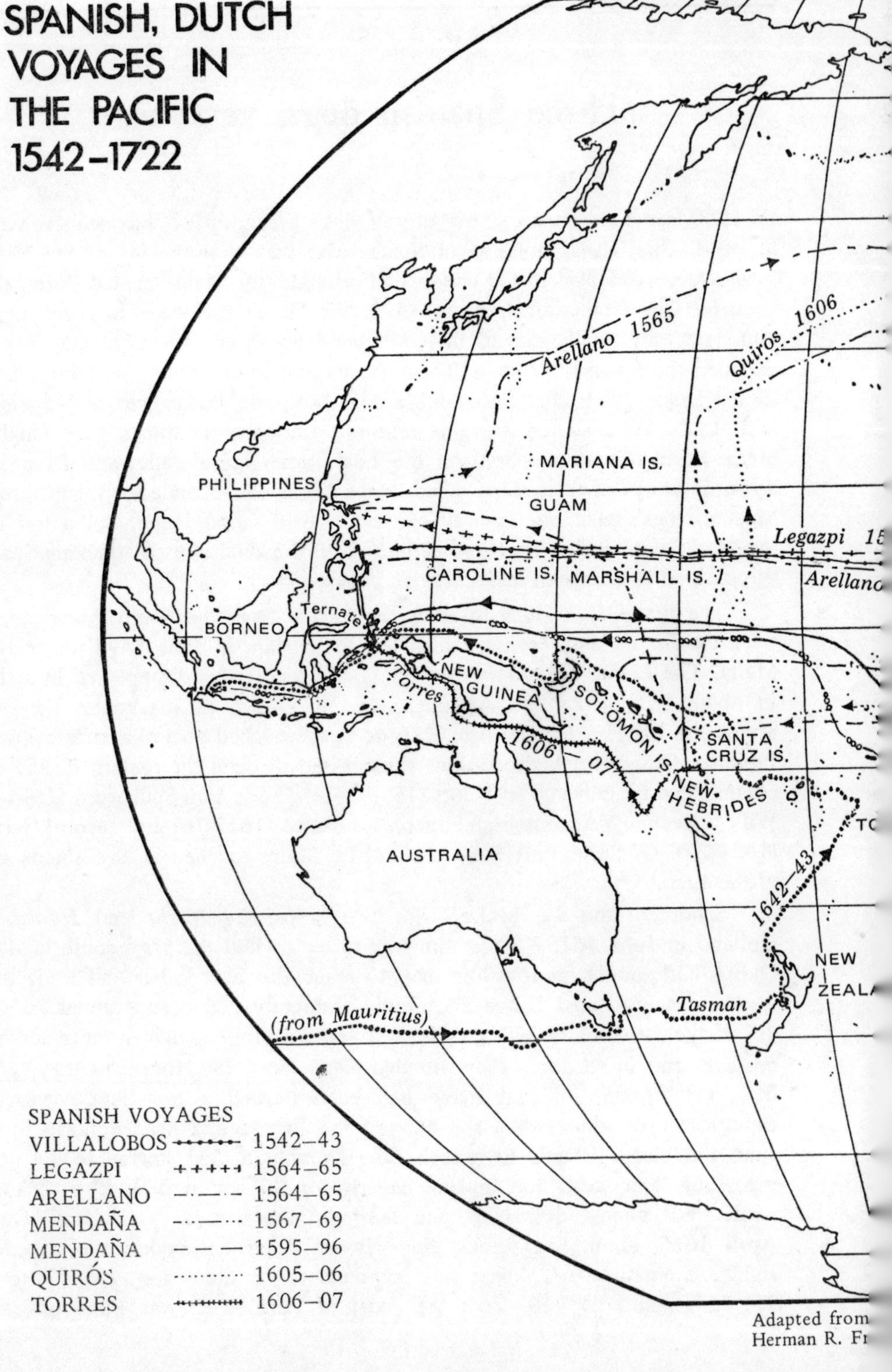

Adapted from
Herman R. Fr

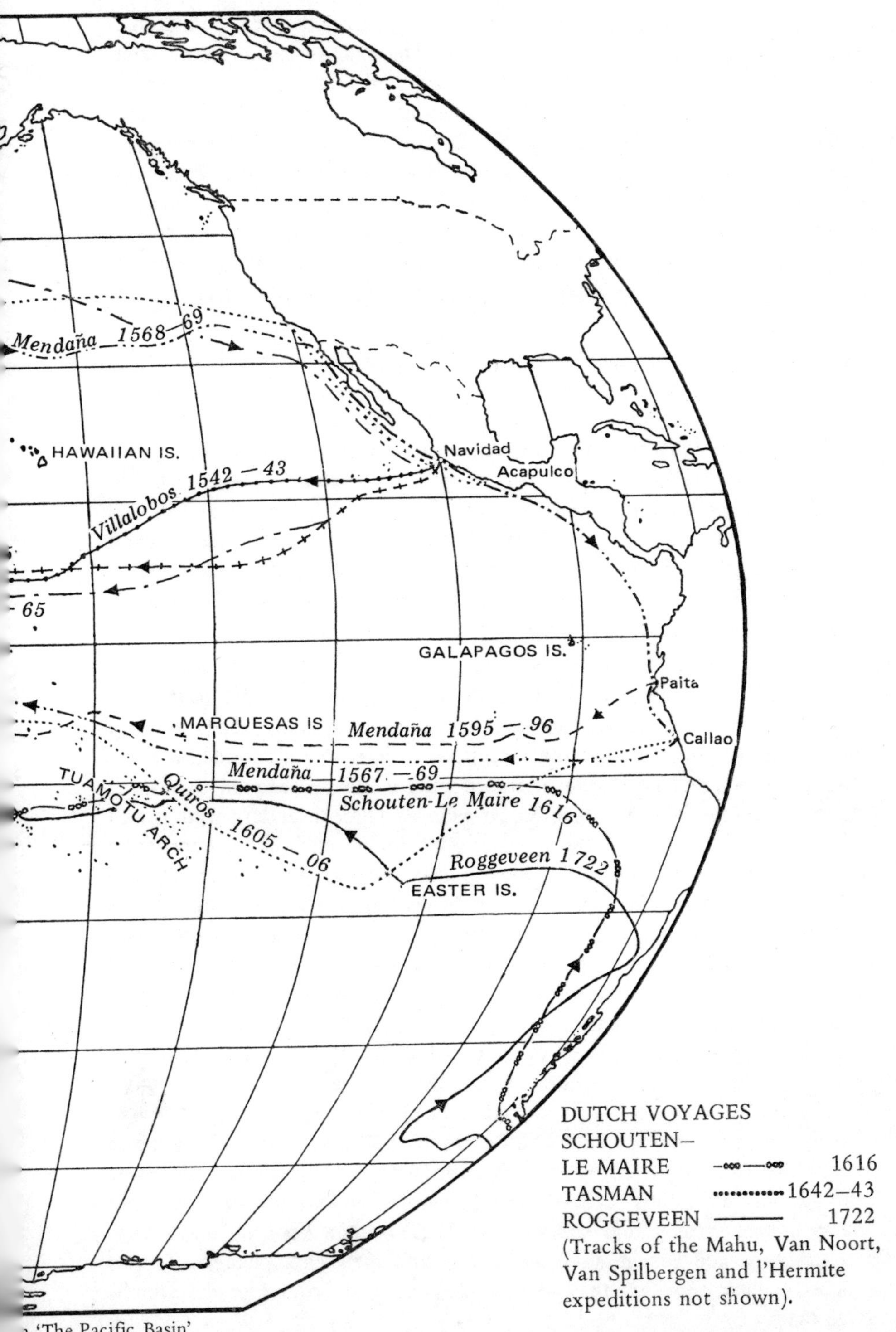

ı 'The Pacific Basin'
York, 1967)

(or Magellan's San Pablo) in the north-eastern corner of the Tuamotus.[3] Being badly in need of fresh food and water, the Dutchmen tried to land a boat, but were foiled by a heavy surf. Finally, they anchored their boat some distance off the island and either swam ashore or hauled each other ashore with ropes. The island had no human inhabitants, but the Dutchmen did find three dogs which apparently could not bark or make a noise. Le Maire described them as 'three Spanish dogs, very lean'.[4] They were the easternmost dogs ever recorded in the 'aboriginal' Pacific by the early European explorers. So it was appropriate that the Dutchmen should call their outpost Honden Eylandt (Dog Island), a name it bore on European charts for the next two and a half centuries.[5]

Having collected some plants that tasted like cress, Schouten and Le Maire continued westwards and soon reached another, larger atoll—Takaroa. Hopeful of getting food and water, the Dutchmen sailed towards it. As they closed in, they met a canoe containing four naked red men with long, black hair, who kept their distance but made signs for them to go ashore. The *Eendracht* approached the land within a musket shot. But as the crew could find no bottom, she stood out to sea again. During these manoeuvres, many naked islanders were seen on shore. Their complexion was 'very yellow, inclining to red', and they had 'long hair extremely black, tucked up behind'. The Dutchmen spoke Spanish, Malay, Javanese and Dutch to some who came off in a canoe, but the islanders did not understand them.[6]

That night the *Eendracht* sailed south and south-east to get round the island, but they were still abreast of land when morning came. They had, in fact, got beyond Takaroa without realising it, and were now alongside its sister atoll, Takapoto. A great multitude of naked men could be seen on the beach shouting and making signs for them to go ashore. Three islanders who rowed out to the *Eendracht's* sloop as she was sounding for an anchorage, were given presents of beads and knives. They then pulled over to the *Eendracht,* and ventured near enough for the Dutchmen to throw them a rope. Eventually one of them screwed up his courage to climb into the ship's balcony. In doing so, he pulled out nails from the window shutters of a couple of cabins and hid them in his hair. His companions acted in similar fashion when they ventured on board. 'Being very desirous of having iron,' Schouten wrote, 'they pulled out the nails everywhere, and even thought to pull out the bars and great iron bolts about the ship.' The islanders were entirely naked except for a small mat over their genitals. Schouten recorded that their skin was marked with various figures—'serpents, dragons and such like figures of strange kinds'—and it seemed to him that these had been burnt on with gunpowder.[7] Le Maire, on the other hand, noted only that their skin—particularly of their fingers—was marked with 'many figures, long, round and square.' The islanders were 'fat and bulky, of large structure and robust, their noses flat and their ears pierced'. It was in the holes in their ears that they hung some nails and beads that the Dutchmen gave them.[8]

An armed boat's crew was sent ashore to try to trade for pigs and fowls, which the islanders indicated they had in plenty. However, about thirty natives attacked them with clubs, staves and slings; stole some nails and pieces of iron; and provoked the Dutchmen to fire on them. Several of their number were killed and wounded, which put an end to any hope of trade.

Having bestowed the name, Zonder Grondt Eylandt (Bottomless Island), on this unfriendly place and its seemingly connected neighbour, Takaroa, the Dutchmen again set sail for the west. 'It appears clearly that hitherto this island was unknown and unfrequented, for it is in want of everything,' Le Maire wrote. 'The women wear some little coverings from the belly to below the knees and scolded their husbands, as appeared to us, for having behaved so treacherously and barbarously to us.'

A day after leaving Takapoto, the Dutchmen discovered another atoll, Manihi. It was uninhabited and provided them with food and water. Their next landfall was Rangiroa, the largest of the Tuamotus. Here another boat party was sent off for water. But on reaching the shore, the men saw an islander who seemed to be carrying a bow, and this was sufficient to send them scurrying for their boat. Five or six other islanders who were later seen from the boat deterred them from trying to land again. Because the hands and faces of the boat's crew were covered with flies when they returned to the *Eendracht,* the atoll was dubbed Vliegen Eylandt (Island of Flies).

To the west of this pestiferous place, the Dutchmen noticed a great swell from the south which convinced them that no land lay in that direction, or that if it did, it was a long way off. The *Eendracht* was, in fact, now clear of the Tuamotus, and more than three weeks passed before they saw land again—two of the northern outliers of the Tonga group, Tafahi and Niuatoputapu. After a brief stop at these islands and at neighbouring Niuafo'ou, the Dutchmen reached Futuna and Alofi, two high, contiguous islands to the north-west, where they spent ten days wooding and watering. They then continued on a westerly course, passing to the north of New Guinea, and finally reaching Java. In Java, which the Dutch had occupied several years earlier, Schouten and Le Maire were arrested for infringing the monopoly of the Dutch East India Company and their ship and goods were confiscated. Schouten was sent home in a Dutch ship. Le Maire died on the way. Two years passed before Le Maire's father, by means of petitions and litigation, had the *Eendracht* and her cargo handed over to him.

Meanwhile, an account of the *Eendracht's* voyage, attributed to Schouten, was published in Amsterdam. It went through thirty-eight Dutch editions during the next few years. An account by Le Maire, based on a journal retrieved by his father from the East India Company, was published in 1622. This, too, was republished many times.[9] However, public interest in the *Eendracht's* voyage did not inspire anyone to imitate it. There was, in fact, only one other European voyage into the heart of the South Pacific during the remainder of the seventeenth century. This was the voyage of Abel Janszoon Tasman, who set out from Java in August 1642 at the behest of the Dutch East India Company to search for the great south land. Tasman's voyage took him via Mauritius to New Zealand and Tonga. But it revealed nothing to excite his employers, and for the next eighty years no further attempts were made to discover the land that Sarmiento had postulated.[10]

Except for the Spanish galleons, the only European vessels to cross the Pacific during this period were a few French merchantmen and British privateers. None of these ventured far into the eastern South Pacific. The French ships, mainly from St Malo, traded in Chile and Peru from 1695 to 1726, and occasionally crossed the Pacific to Guam and China in the track of the galleons.[11] The privateers preyed on Spanish shipping off the South American coast and sometimes crossed the Pacific on a similar course. They were manned by such celebrated buccaneers as William Dampier, Lionel Wafer, John Clipperton, George Shelvocke, Woodes Rogers and Edward Davis.[12] Davis was the only seaman of the period to add anything new to South Pacific geography. In 1687, according to both Wafer and Dampier, he discovered some land about 600 leagues west of the Chilean port of Copiapo, which was placed on the charts as Davis' Land.[13] Although no land was subsequently found in the position assigned to it, many years elapsed before geographers and seamen ceased to believe in its existence.

Meanwhile, imaginative fiction writers took up the theme of the unknown south land, or Terra Australis Incognita as it was frequently called. One such writer, Bishop Joseph Hall, who described an imaginary voyage to Terra Australis in the early part of the seventeenth century,[14] is said to have inspired Jonathan Swift's *Gulliver's Travels.* Another, Gabriel de Foigny, made his 'Terres Australes' the scene of a shipwreck where a Frenchman, Jacques Sadeur, lived for thirty-five years before returning to civilisation with many curious details about the manners, customs, religions, laws, studies and wars of the inhabitants. In 1693, an English translator of de Foigny's book used the word 'Australia' in place of 'Terres Australes' and described its inhabitants as 'Australians', thereby anticipating the birth of present-day usage by well over 100 years.[15] A third writer, Henry Neville, in a short novel published in 1668, was perhaps the most imaginative of all. His novel, entitled *The Isle of Pines, or A late Discovery of a fourth Island in Terra Australis, Incognita,* claimed to be 'A True Relation of certain English persons, Who in the days of Queen Elizabeth, making a Voyage to the East India, were cast away, and wracked upon the Island near to the Coast of Terra Australis, Incognita, and all drowned, except one Man and four Women, whereof one was a Negro. And now lately Anno Dom. 1667, a Dutch Ship driven by foul weather there, by chance have found their Posterity (speaking good English) to amount to ten or twelve thousand persons, as they suppose.'[16]

The stories of such people as Hall, de Foigny and Neville helped to keep the notion of the great south land alive, and new proposals were occasionally put forward to go in search of it. In 1675, Arend Roggeveen, a Dutch mathematician, obtained permission from the Dutch authorities to make an exploratory voyage. Although the project fell through for lack of money, Roggeveen's son Jacob successfully revived it about forty-five years later.[17] He persuaded the Dutch West India Company to provide him with three ships for a voyage into the Pacific from the South American side. The ships were the *Arend, Tienhoven* and *Afrikaansche Galei* (*African Galley*) which sailed from Holland on 1 August 1721. Roggeveen's instructions were to search for Davis' Land and also for some land further west in 15° S., that Schouten had surmised to exist. After rounding the Horn Roggeveen's expedition touched at Juan Fernandez, then headed WNW and later west in search of Davis' Land. No land answering Davis' description was found, but on Easter Day (5 April) 1722, the expedition came upon a small, inhabited island which Roggeveen named Paasch Eylandt (Easter Island). The Dutch ships stayed there for five days; made a last attempt to find Davis' Land in its vicinity; then proceeded north-west. Roggeveen's aim was to reach the Honden Eylandt of Schouten and Le Maire, and from there to search for the land mentioned in the second part of his instructions. It turned out, however, that all three ships missed Honden and their next landfall was Tikei, an island of similar size and almost in the same latitude, but some 400 miles further west. Roggeveen viewed his landfall uneasily, but decided that it was Honden, despite a big difference between his estimated position for it and Schouten's estimate for the real Honden. This error led to disaster in the early hours of the following morning. The *African Galley,* a small, flat-bottomed ship, was running ahead of the *Arend* and *Tienhoven,* as was her custom, when those on board suddenly saw reefs ahead. The reefs were those of Takapoto Atoll (part of the Zonder Grondt of Schouten and Le Maire), which was not expected to be seen for several days. Although the *African Galley's* crew had time to fire distress signals to warn the other ships of impending danger, they could do nothing to save their own ship. In a trice, she was on the reef and stuck fast.

All that day and the following day, the crew strove to refloat the ship, but to no avail. The *African Galley* had split open and filled with water. Meanwhile, the *Arend* and *Tienhoven* sailed round to the lee side of the island to escape the wind; and for five days their boats toiled to get the stranded crew and their effects off the reef. During the rescue operations, five sailors from the two ships got drunk and decided to stay on the island. As the last boat left the disaster scene, they shouted out: 'We wish you a successful voyage. Say goodnight to our friends in Amsterdam. We shall stay here.' Roggeveen predicted an early death for these men, the first known European deserters in the South Pacific. 'Being driven by drunkenness or wanton lust to have bodily intercourse with the women of the Indians,' he wrote, 'they will surely be killed.'[18] However, Roggeveen and his companions do not seem to have seen much of the Takapoto people, for they apparently fled to the opposite end of their island when the *African Galley* fired her distress signals. Roggeveen, himself, gave no account of them in his daily journal, nor did the *Tienhoven's* captain, Cornelis Bouman.[19] On the other hand, Carl Friederich Behrens, a sergeant in the *Arend,* who published a book on the Dutch expedition, was so addicted to falsehood and exaggeration that what he did say must be regarded with caution.[20] He averred, for example, on the testimony of his shipmates, that the islanders' footprints were twenty inches long and that they painted their bodies all over and in all colours. He said also that their hair was 'black and brown, inclining a little to red,' and that they were all very cruel and wicked.[21]

For a day or two after leaving Takapoto, Roggeveen sailed west, then south, past four more atolls—Manihi, Apataki, Arutua and Rangiroa. Then, having got clear of these dangerous places, he came upon an upraised island, Makatea. Here, he got some badly needed refreshments after his men had driven some hostile islanders from the landing place, and had fired at others who ambushed them and pelted them with stones. In the circumstances, the Dutchmen's visit to Makatea was not conducive to detailed ethnological observations. However, Behrens recorded that the islanders had long, black shining hair, anointed with coconut oil; that their bodies were painted, i.e. tattooed; that the men wore only a net, which passed through their thighs to cover their 'middle'; and that the women were entirely covered with a stuff 'as soft to the touch as silk.'[22] An anonymous chronicler of Roggeveen's voyage remarked that the Makateans were 'of an excellent shape, well proportioned and comely in person, and what is surprising, their skin is as clear and white as that of a native of Holland.'[23]

On leaving Makatea, Roggeveen and his officers agreed that as they had failed to find Schouten's supposed land along the 15th parallel, they should sail with all haste for the East Indies to join the annual fleet for Holland—and this they did. As a result, the expedition did not trouble to investigate two high islands, probably Bora Bora and Maupiti, that they saw two days after leaving Makatea. Nor did they spend more than a few hours among the Samoan islands, which they discovered in mid-June 1722.

The positive results of Roggeveen's voyage were so negligible that the Dutch henceforth lost all interest in the Pacific and their exploratory voyages to that ocean came to an end. It will therefore be seen that, during the Dutch period of exploration, there were few opportunities for anyone to gather clues to the fate of the *San Lesmes* and her crew. However, two observations made on Roggeveen's voyage and two on that of Schouten and Le Maire were, perhaps, clues of that kind. Those of Roggeveen's voyage were Behrens' remark about the hair of the islanders of Takapoto being 'black and brown, inclining a little to red,' and the anonymous chronicler's statement about the light skin colour of the Makateans. The possible clues gathered on the voyage of Schouten and Le Maire were the observations about the Takaroans' familiarity with iron and eagerness for it; and Le Maire's remark about the three silent 'Spanish' dogs of Pukapuka. Of all these, Le Maire's canine 'clue' is probably the most positive.

Considering that Le Maire was a Dutchman and that he might also have compared the dogs to, say, French poodles, Scottish terriers, Great Danes or German shepherd dogs, his use of the word 'Spanish' seems to suggest that he must have had a breed especially associated with Spain in mind. Such dogs, of course, can usually bark. But as a modern writer on the Polynesian dog has said: 'European dogs which become feral may lose their ability to bark and resort only to howling. They recover their bark if they return to a domesticated life.'[24]

Where could Pukapuka's barkless 'Spanish' dogs have come from? As the Marquesas Islands to the north of Pukapuka did not have dogs in historical times,[25] there seem to be only two possibilities. One is that they were descended from dogs that got ashore from Magellan's ships when they touched at Pukapuka in 1521. However, as Magellan's men apparently did not land and are likely to have eaten their dogs by then, this seems unlikely. The other possibility is that they came from some island to the west or south. Pukapuka's nearest neighbours are Fakahina and Fangatau, two small atolls about 100 and 130 miles to the south-west respectively. About 100 miles or so further south are Amanu and Hao. Hao, as has already been noted, was inhabited by dogs 'like those of Castille' when Quiros called there in 1606, ten years before Schouten and Le Maire entered the Pacific. Nothing is known about Fakahina and Fangatau at that period, as European explorers did not discover them until the first quarter of the nineteenth century. However, as will later be seen, the Tahitians of the 1770s already knew of Fangatau's existence, and in their eyes one of its chief claims to fame was that it was an island of dogs. . . .

6

'A thing most difficult to account for'

APART from the Spanish galleons which plied annually between Mexico and the Philippines, only one European ship crossed the Pacific in the first forty years after Roggeveen's return to Holland. This was HMS *Centurion,* the flagship of Commodore George Anson, who was sent from England in 1741 with a fleet of six ships to attack Spanish shipping in the Pacific. Two of Anson's ships failed to round Cape Horn and another, HMS *Wager,* was wrecked on the bleak south coast of Chile. The remainder did great damage to Spanish commerce on the American coast; but because the crews were much reduced by sickness and death, Anson destroyed two of the ships and set out to return to England with only the *Centurion.* After crossing the Pacific north of the Line, Anson captured a Spanish treasure galleon off the Philippines and returned to England with booty worth £400,000.

An account of Anson's exploits published in 1745 aroused great interest in England and helped to set men thinking once more about the unknown South Seas. It was Anson's view that the South Seas would offer great commercial possibilities if settlements were established on strategic islands in the Atlantic and Pacific for the refreshment of British ships. The islands he suggested were the Falklands, nearby Pepys Island, and Juan Fernandez, 400 miles west of Chile.[1]

Although nothing came immediately of Anson's proposals, other influences kept them alive. One of these was the publication in 1744-8 of a new edition of John Harris' *A Collection of Voyages and Travels,* edited by one John Campbell. In this, Campbell argued that the long-sought-for southern continent lay somewhere between New Zealand and South America, and that the islands sighted in the South Seas from Quiros to Roggeveen were, in fact, 'promontories' of this great land. Campbell claimed that the Terra Australis Incognita would be a promising field for British trade, and he, too, urged that the Falklands and Juan Fernandez should be settled so that British merchants could exploit it.

Campbell's cry was taken up in France. In 1756, Charles de Brosses, president of the Parlement of Dijon, published his *Histoire des Navigations aux Terres Australes* in which he proclaimed that the unknown southern continent probably covered from eight to ten million square miles, and was fabulously rich in minerals, fruits, fish, etc. In his view, the continent lay somewhere in an area which he called Polynesia (a word that he was the first to use); and it was because previous navigators had sailed too far north of Polynesia that the continent remained undiscovered. The discovery of this great land, he said, was 'the grandest, noblest, most useful enterprise a sovereign could undertake', and he urged his countrymen to act quickly so that it would not fall into British hands.[2]

Nevertheless, the English were the first to attempt to find it. On 21 June 1764 Commodore John Byron, a survivor of the *Wager* wreck of 1741, left England with two ships, HMS *Dolphin* and *Tamar*. Byron had orders to search for unknown lands in the South Atlantic, to take possession of the Falkland Islands and to search for a north-west passage to Europe from the North Pacific. Nothing was said in his instructions about the southern continent or lands in the South Pacific. However, after carrying out the first part of his orders, Byron simply ignored the rest and went off to look for Davis' Land—the land that Roggeveen had sought in vain. Having failed in this, he continued on a westerly course, apparently in the hope of finding the southern continent.[3]

On 7 June 1765, Byron came upon two previously undiscovered islands in the northern part of the Tuamotu Archipelago, Tepoto and Napuka. As he urgently needed fresh vegetables for many of his crew who were down with scurvy, he steered towards Tepoto, the smaller and more westerly of the two. A number of islanders soon appeared on the beach, carrying spears fifteen or sixteen feet long. They lit several fires which were immediately answered by people on the other island. Byron thought the islanders were 'a deep copper colour', although one of his officers described them as 'of a very black complexion'. Apart from coverings to hide 'what nature taught them to conceal', they were naked.

As a boat party could not get soundings less than a cable's length from the beach, Byron worked over to Napuka. Numerous islanders appeared on the beach armed with spears, clubs and other weapons. But they had no occasion to use them for the Englishmen could find no bottom even close to the surf; and Byron had finally to bear away, 'greatly grieved' that he could get no refreshments for his sick men.[4]

Having named his landfalls the Islands of Disappointment, Byron resumed a westerly course. In two days he came upon another atoll, Takaroa. As soon as the inhabitants saw the two ships they lit fires and followed them along the beach. Others came down inside the lagoon in large canoes. When Byron sent his boats in to make soundings, hundreds of armed islanders waded into the water, making 'a terrible noise'. Some swam out to the *Tamar's* boat, and one man got in and stole a seaman's jacket. Further along, towards the atoll's south-west point, about sixty armed men came out in two large canoes, apparently intent on chasing the boats away. However, they quickly paddled off when the boats chased them, ran their canoes through the surf and hauled them up on the beach. Later, after they had attacked the Englishmen with clubs and stones, the Englishmen opened fire on them, killing several and putting the others to flight. The Englishmen were thus able to capture one of their double canoes, which was taken out to the *Dolphin*. One hull was thirty-two feet long, the other somewhat shorter. They were joined together about six or eight feet apart by stout spars. Each had a mast, but a single sail, neatly made of matting, served them both. 'There must be an infinite deal of labour in making one of these Canoes,' Byron wrote, 'the Plank is extremely well worked & carved in many places. It is sewed together, & over every Seam is a strip of Tortoise Shell to keep the water out. Their Cordage is as good & well laid as any I ever saw tho' made of the rind of Coco Nutt.'

Having discovered that his ships could not anchor at the western end of the island, Byron worked back to a reef entrance he had previously seen. After a shot fired over their heads had driven the islanders away, a boat party landed and gathered a few coconuts. Byron himself went ashore next morning. He found the islanders' village delightfully situated in a grove of stately trees. Except for some dogs which kept up 'a dreadful howling' all day, it was deserted. Byron did not say what the dogs looked like, but he recorded that the islanders' houses were 'mean and low'. However, there were many fine, large, newly-built canoes nearby and the islanders had left 'a thousand marks of their Ingenuity behind them'. In looking through the huts, Byron and his men found the carved head of a Dutch long boat's rudder, which was very old and worm-eaten. A piece of hammered iron, a piece of brass, and some iron tools were also seen. Byron had obviously never heard of the wreck of Roggeveen's *African Galley* on neighbouring Takapoto, for he thought the islanders' ancestors must have got these items 'by cutting off one of those Dutch ships who attempted to make discoveries this way many years ago & who were never afterwards heard of'. He added: 'they make use of a Tool exactly like a Carpenters Adze made out of a Pearl Oyster Shell, which is I suppose in imitation of those they saw on board that Ship, & which in all probability are now worn out . . .' [5]

The Englishmen got several boatloads of coconuts and scurvy grass on Takaroa. Then they sailed over to Takapoto where the islanders were friendly and gave them coconuts and water. As no anchorage could be found, Byron decided to sail on. 'I honor'd these Two last Islands by the name of King George's Islands', he wrote. He noted also that he had seen two or three large boats in Takapoto's lagoon, one of which had two masts, and some rigging overhead to support them.

A day or so after leaving Takapoto, the *Dolphin* and *Tamar* reached Rangiroa, which Byron named Prince of Wales Island. As a 'prodigious surf' was running and many dangerous reefs were seen, no attempt was made to land on it, and the two ships continued on a westerly course. Soon afterwards they encountered a mountainous swell from the southward, which had not been felt since a day or two before the discovery of Tepoto and Napuka. This, combined with the fact that flocks of birds had been seen flying southward in the evenings, convinced Byron that land must lie in that direction. 'Had not the winds failed me in the higher latitudes . . .' he wrote, 'I make no doubt that I should have fell in with it, & in all probability made the discovery of the S° Continent'.[6] As it was there were so many sick men in his ships that he had to hurry on, intent on reaching Tinian in the Marianas, where he knew from his voyage with Anson that fresh food could be obtained.

In the 4,000 or so miles from Rangiroa to Tinian, Byron passed only three small islands—Puka Puka in the Northern Cook Group, Atafu in the Tokelaus, and Nukunau in the Gilbert Islands. His voyage across the Pacific was therefore scarcely of a kind to place him in the front rank of the world's explorers. However, his opinion about the location of the long-sought-for southern continent carried great weight at the British Admiralty;[7] and within three months of his return to England, the *Dolphin* under a new commander, Captain Samuel Wallis, was fitted out for a second Pacific voyage. A sloop, HMS *Swallow* (Captain Philip Carteret), was assigned as her consort; and a merchant vessel, the *Prince Frederick,* was commissioned as a store ship.[8]

When the *Dolphin* left Deptford on 26 July 1766 to sail to Long Reach on the River Thames to take in her guns and gunners' stores, exactly 241 years had passed since the Loaisa expedition's departure from La Coruña. In all those years only eight European expeditions had ventured into the eastern South Pacific, and only thirty or so islands, mostly atolls, had been discovered. Of the inhabited atolls—about half—landings had been made on only seven—once because of shipwreck. No landing party had ever stayed ashore more than a few hours, so little had been learned of the islands' inhabitants. The great difficulty in exploring the region had been the lack of safe harbours where ships could refit, refresh their crews and take in food, water and firewood after the long, exhausting haul from the Strait of Magellan. However, the new voyage of the *Dolphin* was to change all that.

The *Dolphin, Swallow* and *Prince Frederick* sailed from England a month after the *Dolphin's* departure from Deptford. Captain Wallis' instructions were to round Cape Horn or pass through the Strait of Magellan, and then to search for the 'Land or Islands of Great extent' that were believed to exist between Cape Horn and New Zealand. In mid-January 1767 the expedition reached the eastern entrance to the strait, where the *Dolphin* and *Swallow* took in stores from the *Prince Frederick*. The store ship then sailed for the Falkland Islands, and the *Dolphin* and *Swallow* began a tedious passage of the strait. They entered the Pacific on 11 April. That same day, the *Swallow* became separated from her consort and the two ships did not meet again.[9] The *Swallow,* as it turned out, took a more southerly course than the *Dolphin* and passed through the eastern Pacific in lower latitudes than any previous ship had done. She came upon several previously unknown islands, but all were uninhabited and no landings were made. The first was Pitcairn Island, then Mururoa, Nukutupipi and Anuanu Raro, three small atolls on the southern fringe of the Tuamotus. Four weeks later the *Swallow* reached Ndeni Island (Mendaña's Santa Cruz) on the other side of the Pacific without sighting any more land.[10]

Meanwhile, Wallis in the *Dolphin* had made a new, but unsuccessful search for Davis' Land, and had then steered northward and westward into the tropics. Nearly seven weeks after leaving Magellan Strait, the *Dolphin's* crew sighted birds, dolphins and other indications of land, which set everyone wishing that the *Swallow* was still in company in case of night-time shipwreck. George Robertson, the *Dolphin's* master, reflected grimly that after such a disaster the crew would have no means of getting home. 'The loss of our Ship', he wrote in his journal, 'is the loss of our Lives to our King and Country—besides the Loss of any Descovery that we may make'.[11] Robertson, at this time, was one of the few fit men on board. Both the captain and first lieutenant were ill with a bilious disorder; eighteen to twenty seamen had scurvy and other ailments; and many of the others were weak and unwell. However, the sight of two small islands on 6 June 1767 revived their drooping spirits and raised hopes of fresh food.

The first island—which Wallis called Whitsunday—was Pinaki, a tiny, almost perfectly circular atoll, 100 miles or so south-east of Hao and Amanu. The other was Nukutavake, eight miles north-west of Pinaki. Pinaki, at first, seemed to have little to offer. But when two canoes were seen paddling off towards Nukutavake, Tobias Furneaux, the second lieutenant, was sent ashore to bring off all the fresh food he could. As no anchorage could be found near the atoll, Furneaux' party had to don cork jackets and swim through the surf to reach the beach. They returned to the *Dolphin* well-laden with coconuts, scurvy grass and purslane, plus several pearlshell fish hooks and pieces of tortoiseshell. The island, they said, was uninhabited, but it had on it three neatly-thatched shelters and several canoes in the course of construction.[12]

Another boat tried to land on the island next morning. But as the surf was too high, Wallis decided to bear away for Nukutavake. Furneaux was sent ahead with two armed boats. About fifty men, women and children, armed with long, bone-tipped spears gathered on the beach to oppose Furneaux' approach. Other, older men and women lit fires at every possible landing place. The Englishmen made all the friendly signs they could think of, and held up beads, ribbons, nails and shears. But the islanders still shook their spears threateningly. Only when the *Dolphin* stood close in and fired a nine-pound shot over their heads did they act more peaceably and respond to the Englishmen's sign-language requests for water and coconuts. Indeed, when three of Furneaux' party jumped ashore, the islanders 'Shaked hands and seemed very friendly', as Robertson put it. Before long they had brought some 200 coconuts and several large coconut shells of water to the beach. They put their offerings in the *Dolphin's* boats and were paid for them in nails, beads and small hatchets—the nails being the most popular. When all business was concluded, everyone parted seemingly good friends. But when the Englishmen indicated that they would return next morning, the islanders stared and did not seem pleased.[13]

The *Dolphin* lay to for the night. At sunrise, Furneaux went off with two boats to take possession of the island, to honour it with the name of Queen Charlotte, and to get all the fresh food he could. The island's men, armed with spears, were drawn up on the beach as he approached their village. The women and children were embarked in four large double-canoes, apparently ready to make off somewhere. The men's display of resistance was brief. When Furneaux ordered a musketoon to be fired to frighten them, they, too, took to the canoes and made sail to the westward. A fifth canoe joined them off the western end of the island. Robertson noted that the canoes were about thirty feet long, four feet broad and three to three and a half feet deep. They were built of small planks sewn together, and fixed to several small timbers 'not unlyke the frame of our Boats'. They were made double by lashing two hulls together about three feet apart. Three beams fixed to the gunwales were used to do this. One was for'ard, one aft, and one amidships. A mast was stepped in the middle beam, and was supported by a pair of shrouds belayed aft—or supported by a set of ropes, coiled round a cleat, to use a less seamanlike expression. In Robertson's view, the sails looked like topmast steering sails with the tack part uppermost, which was a shellback's way of saying that the sails were triangular in shape. Wallis, himself, who was no mean artist, made a sketch of the canoes as they sailed off. As for the islanders, Robertson described them as middle-sized and of a dark copper colour with long black hair hanging loose round their shoulders. They had some sort of cloth or mat round their middles, but no other clothing, except for one man who had a head-dress of feathers.[14]

Other than rats, Furneaux and his men found no living creatures ashore; and although the palm trees had been stripped of their nuts, there were still enough to fill the *Dolphin's* boats. The discovery of three small ponds of fresh water prompted Wallis to stay near the island overnight and send watering parties ashore in the morning. The captain and several officers landed with the waterers. Robertson, who was among them, took the opportunity to stroll round the island. He found the village to consist of about twenty houses. They were 'built after the Indian manner' and thatched with palm leaves 'as net [neatly] as any Farmers office house in England'. Three large sailing craft were being built on stocks. Two were of about eight to ten tons; the third, of about twelve tons, was only in frame and had no planks on her. 'What Trade they Carie on with this large Craft I know not', Robertson wrote, 'but am certain they are not for fishing round this Island, but built in purpos for careing on a trade to some distant shoar thats of greater Extent nor this Island'.[15]

William Hambly, a midshipman, who also saw the partly-built boats, recorded that they were 'made with planks about ½ an inch Thick Sowd together.' Each had a keel. They were built 'very regularly, tapering at each end and Broad in the Middle.' Hambly also noticed several hatchets and fishing nets that the islanders had left behind. 'The hatchets,' he wrote, 'are made of shell about four inches long and three broad, which is fixed to a piece of wood 13 or 14 inches long & resembles a Coopers Adze.' The fishing nets were stout, strong and well made, and 'in ye same form as our English Netts.'[16] Hambly's opinion about the fishing nets was shared by Robertson, who wrote: 'We likeways saw several pices [*sic*] of Small Nets here made after the same manner that they are in England with Great Balls of ready-made line . . .'[17] Wallis, for his part, recorded nothing about the nets, but he seemed to find European affinities in the islanders' tools. 'The tools they make use of for building their canoes,' he wrote, 'are shells sharpened and fixed on sticks and made like Adzes, Chizles and Awls . . .'[18] Both Wallis and Robertson recorded that the islanders did not bury their dead, but left the bodies to putrefy above ground, under canopies.[19]

Besides getting a good supply of water from the island, the Englishmen took possession of several of the islanders' artifacts, including a small canoe, and left a Union Jack, some hatchets, billhooks, knives, nails and beads in exchange for them. The *Dolphin* then made sail to westward, steering the same course that the islanders had been seen to take. By doing so, the Englishmen hoped to reach 'a mutch finer country' than either Pinaki or Nukutavake had proved to be. However, the next island, which was seen within a few hours, was only a crumb of land like the others. It was, in fact, Vairaatea Atoll, the same island that Quiros had seen in 1606, the day before reaching Hao. Wallis called it Lord Egmont's Island. No bottom could be found even close to the shore and no attempt was made to land on it. As the *Dolphin* sailed by, the crew saw seven double canoes hauled up on the beach, and about fifty men waving their pikes. Robertson thought they included the same people who had set out from Nukutavake.[20]

In the seventy-two hours after passing Vairaatea, the *Dolphin* passed three more atolls—Paraoa, Manuhangi and Nengonengo. Only Paraoa was seen to be inhabited and there the islanders ran along the beach with long spears and lit fires, apparently to make it clear that they wanted no visitors. Three and a half days beyond Nengonengo, the *Dolphin* reached a lofty island covered with coconut and other trees. This was Mehetia, or Osnaburg Island, as Wallis called it. Boats were sent off to it in the hope of getting refreshments. However, as the only possible landing place was occupied by more than 100 armed men and women, the Englishmen decided not to attempt to get ashore. As a result, two fowls, a pig and some fruit were all the provisions they obtained. Furneaux, who was in charge of the boats, reported that the inhabitants seemed to be more numerous than the island could support; but as he saw several large double canoes on the beach, he surmised that there must be other larger islands not far distant. As this seemed a reasonable conjecture, Wallis ordered the boats to be hoisted in, and the *Dolphin* resumed a westerly course.[21] Next day, the Englishmen reached a much larger, much more fruitful island—Tahiti. It appeared at first as a lofty mountain covered at the top by clouds. 'This made us all rejoice and fild us with the greatest hopes Imaginable,' Robertson wrote, 'we now lookt upon our selves as relived from all our distresses as we was almost Certain of finding all sorts of refreshments on this great Body of Land. . . . We now suposed we saw the long wishd for Southern

Continent, which has been often talkd of, but neaver before seen by any Europeans.'[22]

As the *Dolphin* approached her new landfall, a thick fog came down and obscured everything from sight. When it cleared up, the easternmost point of the land was only two leagues away, and a hundred canoes could be seen paddling out to the ship. On coming within pistol shot, the paddlers lay to, looked at the ship in apparent astonishment, and held 'a sort of council of war.' The *Dolphin's* men made all the friendly signs they could think of, held up trinkets, and tried to entice the islanders on board. The islanders replied by holding up plantain branches, paddling round the ship, and laughing and talking a great deal. After one of them had made a speech lasting fifteen minutes, the canoes came closer and some of the islanders ventured aboard. The first to do so accepted a few trinkets and, as Robertson recorded, 'shaked hands with us', thereby demonstrating that—like the Nukutavake people—he was familiar with the Englishmen's mode of greeting.[23]

With perhaps as many as 800 islanders milling about the ship in about 150 canoes, the English sailors made signs to them to bring off food in exchange for cloth, knives, beads and other trinkets which they showed them. Some sailors grunted like pigs to suggest the notion of pork; others crowed like roosters to indicate that poultry was wanted. The Tahitians quickly understood, and some went off in their canoes to bring the desired goods. Others began to pull at the iron stanchions and other iron work; and when the sailors showed them some nails 'which they appeared very fond of,' those on board became most unwilling to leave the ship without something made of iron. Finally a nine-pound shot was fired over their heads to frighten them, and this cleared the ship at once. The *Dolphin* then bore away to westward to seek a place to anchor in. Robertson thought the island had 'the most Beautiful appearance its posable to Imagin'. It was densely populated all along the coast, the houses being 'lyke long Farmers Barns'. Robertson and his companions were now fully convinced that they had found the southern continent.[24]

Early next morning the barge and cutter were hoisted out to sound for an anchorage. However, hundreds of Tahitian canoes crowded round, sometimes trying to ram the English boats, and sometimes trying to board them. The Englishmen fired their muskets in the air in the hope of frightening the Tahitians away, and when this failed they fired *at* the Tahitians, killing and wounding one or two. For the next day or two, the *Dolphin* lay precariously off a low sandy spit, which Captain Cook later called Point Venus. Some Tahitians came out in their canoes to trade, but they did not always barter fairly and several of their number were shot for their dishonesty. Meanwhile, the *Dolphin's* gunner, John Gore, was sent off with a boat's crew to get water, which was now desperately needed. He was still diffident about landing and tried to get the Tahitians to fill his casks for him. The Tahitians filled four, but kept two, and then tried to inveigle the English sailors ashore by getting some handsome women to play 'a great many droll, want[on] tricks'. Robertson noted that some of the women were a light copper colour, some a mulatto, and others 'almost if not altogeather White.'[25] The sailors were agreeably stirred by their antics, but deferred going ashore until they became better acquainted with the Tahitian temper.

The day after this incident, the *Dolphin's* barge and cutter were again sent to sound for an anchorage; and this time they found one in Matavai Bay, to the west of Point Venus. The *Dolphin* followed the two boats in; got stuck briefly on a reef that is still known as the Dolphin Bank; and finally anchored, unscathed, in seventeen fathoms. Next morning some 4,000 men in about 500 canoes crowded round the ship. After acting peaceably for a time, and using some young women to play the same 'droll and wanton tricks' of the previous day, the men suddenly bombarded the *Dolphin* with stones. A lively engagement ensued, but the Englishmen's artillery soon drove the Tahitians off, and by noon that day not a single canoe was to be seen in the water and not ten people along the beach. A day or two later, Wallis sent Lieutenant Furneaux ashore to run up the British flag and take possession of the island in the name of King George III. The significance of this ceremony was lost on the Tahitians, for they again gathered in large hostile numbers to make yet another attack on the *Dolphin*. However, their warlike spirit soon evaporated in the face of further artillery fire and Wallis completed a rout of them by sending his men ashore with axes and saws to disable their canoes. From then on, the Tahitians did everything they could to make friends with the Englishmen and by the time the *Dolphin* sailed from Tahiti after a stay of six weeks, Anglo-Tahitian relations were most cordial.

Wallis' purpose in staying in Tahiti was to obtain wood, water and food and to allow his sickly crew to recover their health. Boat parties were therefore sent ashore each day to barter nails, hatchets, ear-rings and toys for the desired commodities, and to allow the sick to stretch their legs and breathe the land air. The first boat party met with a pleasant reception, for the Tahitians brought a number of handsome young girls to the riverside for their delectation. Robertson noted that as on the previous occasion some of the girls were a light copper colour, others a mulatto and some almost white.[26] Several old men who were with them made them stand in line and made signs to the English sailors 'to take which they lyked best and as many as they lyked,' and they even showed them 'how to use the poor young Girls.' This agreeable encounter soon led to a brisk commerce in what Robertson called 'the old trade,' the medium of exchange on the English side being a nail. All went well for ten days or so—until the *Dolphin's* carpenter reported that every cleat in the ship had been drawn and all the nails carried off. At the same time, the boatswain stated that most of the hammock nails had been pulled out and that two-thirds of the men were sleeping on the deck for want of nails to hang their hammocks on. This was alarming news, for not only was the 'old trade' causing considerable damage to the ship, but the prices for provisions were rising steeply. Instead of a small nail purchasing a medium-size pig, large spikes were now demanded. An inquiry to try to discover the nail thieves proved of little avail because all the sailors were apparently involved. Moreover, as warnings did not deter them from continuing to pull the ship apart, most shore excursions were finally forbidden except by the wooding, watering and trading parties. Because of this and because Wallis also forbade exploratory work, Robertson, who seems to have had the most inquiring mind in the ship, did not see as much of Tahiti as he would have liked. Nevertheless, he made the most of his opportunities and was always diligent in noting down what he saw.

Among the many things that he briefly described were the islanders' double canoes, fishing gear, and bows and arrows. Two double canoes that he saw drawn up on the reef as he was taking bearings from a boat in Matavai Bay were about fifty feet long. They seemed capable of carrying about eight tons. The two vessels were raised about two feet off the reef with several large logs of wood—'after the same manner that we would rais a ship to put on a new keel.'[27] Subsequently, through a spy glass from the *Dolphin's* deck, Robertson saw several such canoes under sail. At first sight they seemed like large schooners or sloops, and because of the way the Tahitians greeted their arrival he thought they might be 'Strangers come from some other Country' or 'trading Vessels that hade been some distant voyage.' Although eager to see them at close hand, Robertson never had an opportunity to do so.[28] On the other hand, he did examine some Tahitian fishing lines. They were made of 'silk grass', and were as neat as any fishing lines in England and 'made in the same manner.'[29] As for the bows and arrows, he 'scarce saw any that was fit for War' and neither he nor his shipmates ever saw a Tahitian use them to kill anything.[30] Robertson noted also that the Tahitians had three domestic animals—pigs, fowls and dogs. He thought the pigs were of a Chinese breed, and that the fowls were 'the same as ours in England.' But beyond saying that two dogs he saw were 'fine' and 'fatt' he did not further describe them.[31]

The Tahitians' clothing, Robertson recorded, was made from a 'sort of willow.' A woman called 'Oberea', whom the Englishman took to be Tahiti's queen, wore white under-garments of this cloth, while those on top were yellow and red. Robertson and the queen became quite friendly, and on one of his shore excursions, she dressed him in the Tahitian manner. Having cut off a ten foot length of Tahitian cloth, she made a hole in the middle of it for his head, put it on him, then tied the garment round his waist with a sash of even finer cloth.[32] Later, the queen took Robertson into some of the Tahitian houses and introduced him to the residents. The appearance of some of the people seems to have surprised him.

> At the last House where we Calld, [he wrote] their was two of the handsomest Young Ladys that I ever saw upon the Island. One in particular was fully as fair and hade as Good features as the Generality of Women in England. Hade she been drest after the English manner, [I] am certain no man would [have] thought her of Another Country. I first shaked

> hands with two fine Jolly old people, which I supose was the Young Ladys parents; but they were both of a Mullato colour. I then shaked hands with the Young Ladys who was both fine, brisk, spirited women. The fairest seeing that I took more notice of her than the oyther began to be very Merry and we compaird skinns and hers was rather fairer and Whiter nor mine.[33]

The fairness of some of the Tahitians and the variety of skin colours among them were a constant source of interest and puzzlement to Robertson. A few days after the *Dolphin's* arrival in Tahiti he had written:

> There is three distink colours of people here, which is a thing most difficult to account for of anything which we have yet seen. The Red people are ten times more numerous nor the Mustees,* which is a Medium between the Whitest sort and the red or Indian Colour, and the Mustees are near ten times as numerous as the Whitest sort.[34]

Although the white and 'mustee' people were heavily outnumbered, Robertson noted that they were of the chiefly class and that the red or copper-coloured people were invariably their servants. When, for example, three of the fairest men that Robertson saw arrived at Matavai Bay from some other part of Tahiti to visit the *Dolphin* towards the end of her stay, their canoe was paddled by 'Eight of the Red sort of people.'[35] Similarly, the red people did the paddling for the white-skinned people when several large double canoes went out to the *Dolphin* on the day of her departure. These canoes had apparently just arrived from some other island. They each had a canopy under which ten or a dozen people could sit, 'not unlyke the place where the Gentlemen Sits in the City Barges.' In Robertson's view the occupants were 'Jolly, fatt, well made people.' They were 'mutch fairer nor any that we ever saw before, the two Young Ladys which the Queen introduced me to only Excepted.' The new arrivals were also dressed much more neatly than Robertson's previous acquaintances, and seemed to have great power over the copper-coloured people who paddled for them. 'I enquired at all our trading party if any of them hade ever seen any of this people before,' he wrote, 'but they all said they neaver saw any of them before—neather did any Onb[d] ever see so many fair people at one time.' To establish whether an old man among them understood the use of firearms, Robertson pointed a musket at him, but the man 'took no notice and only smild . . .' Robertson thought these white people were 'fully as fair as the Generality of Spainiards or Portugees,' and that they bore 'a great resemblance to the Jews.' Indeed, he speculated whether they might not be 'a part of the ten tribes of Israel.' On the other hand, he concluded that the red or copper-coloured people were 'Exactly lyke the Malayos in Batavea or Princes Island [in the Straits of Sunda]'—two places that the *Dolphin* visited on her way home.[36] Robertson

* 'Mustee', now virtually obsolete, is a corruption of the Spanish word *mestizo*, meaning 'mixed blood'. It is one of several such words, describing the offspring of mixed marriages, that found their way into English from Spain's American colonies. For others, see p. 132.

added that the Tahitians had 'a very particular Custom,' which was to paint (i.e. tattoo)* their thighs black and to paint 'cureous figures' on their legs and arms.[37]

Because Wallis and his first and second lieutenants were on the sick list during much of their stay in Tahiti, they did not take the same interest in ethnographic matters as the always-robust Robertson did. Nevertheless, Wallis (who went ashore only twice) did record a few details that Robertson did not. He noted, for example, that three types of canoe were in use. One variety, hollowed from a single tree, carried from two to six men and was used mainly for fishing. The second kind was built of planks 'very dexterously sewed together' and was generally made double by lashing two hulls side by side. Such canoes were of different sizes, could carry from ten to forty men, and were sailed far out of sight of land. If they were double, they had two masts stepped between them; if single, they had only one mast, but an outrigger on one side. The third kind of canoe, which only went out in fine weather, seemed mainly intended for processions and show, being without sails and shaped like a Venetian gondola. These vessels had large awnings amidships on which and under which the passengers could sit. 'Three or four times a week,' Wallis wrote, 'we saw a Procession of eight or Ten with Streamers Flying and thousands of people running along the shore, and Numbers of small canoes attending them.' Their passengers were always dressed in red and white, while the rowers and steerers wore white only. The plank for the canoes was obtained by splitting a tree with the grain into as many thin pieces as possible. Then, with tools 'made like shipwright's adzes,' it was dubbed level. Six or eight men sometimes worked on the same plank together, and as their adzes quickly lost their edges, each man had by him a stone and a coconut shell filled with water with which to sharpen them. The planks were generally made about an inch thick and were fitted in place with the 'exactness of an expert joiner.' To fasten the planks together, holes were bored with a piece of bone fixed to a stick, and through these holes 'a kind of plaited cordage' was passed to hold the planks firmly together. The seams were then caulked with dried rushes, and the whole outside of the vessel was paid with the gum from a certain tree which served as a substitute for pitch.[38]

Describing the Tahitians themselves, Wallis said that the men were generally from five feet seven to five feet ten inches tall, but some were taller. The women were from five feet to five feet six. The men's complexion was tawny, but those who were sailors were much redder than those who lived on shore. They had strong black hair which they tied on their heads in various ways. However, there were a few men who did not tie their hair up, and in their case it was usually curly and of different colours—black, brown,

* Europeans had no word for 'tattoo' until they adopted the Tahitian word 'tatau' in various forms.

red, whitish or flaxen.* The hair of the children, especially, was of a light colour.[39]

Wallis made no specific statement in support of Robertson's view that there were distinct racial types in Tahiti. But such a view was held by at least one other member of the *Dolphin's* crew, Midshipman Henry Ibbot. Writing in his journal on 4 July 1767, he said:

> There are two different sorts of People among y^{m} [them] one having long Black Hair and of a dark copper colour, in gen'ral Stout, well made & handsome featur'd, & by what I saw of y^{m} are the poorer sort such as Fisher Men & (which appears to be their chief employment) Canoe Builders . . . The most part of them go naked except a Bag where they put their Privities. The other sort have short curly Black Hair, are not so yellow as a Mulatto . . . and are in gen'ral I dare to say as tall & Stout as the Patagonians. Of the women I saw some that were quite white and had a red colour in their Faces: they are in gen'ral very small, but quite handsomely Featur'd.[40]

Besides being handsome and of different skin colours, the Tahitians proved to be most friendly and affectionate as the Englishmen got to know them better. When Wallis announced on 27 July that he intended to sail on the following day, the queen entreated him to stay longer and burst into a flood of tears when he would not. 'This Great freindly Woman,' as Robertson called her, came out to the *Dolphin* as the ship was getting under way, shook hands with everyone she could, and wept 'with as mutch tenderness and Affection as any Wife or Mother could do at the parting with their Husbands or children.'[41]

It was on this note that the *Dolphin* bore away from Tahiti and steered towards the lofty island of Moorea, ten miles to westward. Robertson was disappointed that Wallis would not stop to explore Moorea; but Wallis had few of the qualities of a good explorer, and his one aim on leaving Tahiti was to cross the Pacific as quickly as possible. Having passed Moorea and three other islands—Maiao, Mopihaa and Fenua Ura—a couple of days' sail further west, the *Dolphin's* crew did not see land again until the twin Tongan islands, Tafahi and Niuatoputapu, were reached about a fortnight later. Wallis subsequently discovered a small hummocky island, Uea, which he named after himself. From there he went on to Tinian, Batavia and Cape Town, and anchored in the Downs on 20 May 1768 after a voyage of twenty-one months.[42] The London newspapers were quick to publish details of the most exciting event of his journey—the discovery of Tahiti. Almost simultaneously with his arrival home, the *St James Chronicle, Lloyd's Evening Post,* the *London Chronicle* and the *Gazeteer and New Daily Advertiser* all reproduced a letter from someone in the *Dolphin* setting out the principal facts. Among other things, the letter said: 'The Natives of Tahiti are pretty much civilized

* The OED defines 'flaxen' as pale yellow-brown.

considering that the Arts have made but little Progress among them. They are in general taller and stouter than our People, and are mostly of a Copper Colour, with black Hair; others are fairer, especially the Women, some of whom were observed to be red-haired.'[43]

Wallis' discovery of Tahiti with its safe anchorage at Matavai Bay, its ample food supplies, and its friendly, even amorous people completely altered the nature of Pacific exploration. Instead of being faced with a vast, empty, havenless ocean, the explorers could now confidently head for an attractive, centrally-situated island that could supply them with all their needs before they ventured elsewhere. Tahiti thus became a focal point for Pacific explorers, as it did for the whalers, traders and missionaries who followed them. In consequence, mariners from Wallis' time onwards rarely sought food and water in the low and dangerous Tuamotus, and decades sometimes passed between the European discovery of an atoll and the next visit by a European ship. This was particularly so in the small, remote and isolated atolls in the eastern part of the archipelago. Pinaki and Nukutavake, for example, which provided the *Dolphin's* crew with their first fresh food and water beyond the Strait of Magellan, were not visited again until Captain F. W. Beechey of HMS *Blossom* passed that way in 1826—fifty-nine years later. Two more decades then passed before a far-ranging pearler from Tahiti learned the native names for the islands, and three more decades went by before the first European missionary paid the islands a fleeting visit. If, therefore, there were any clues to the fate of the *San Lesmes* and her crew in those islands—if, indeed, George Robertson and his companions had already gathered some there—Europeans had few opportunities in the century after the *Dolphin's* voyage to discover or confirm them.

7

Philibert de Commerson's forgotten theory

WHEN Louis-Antoine de Bougainville, a French nobleman-turned-navigator, arrived in Tahiti in April 1768, he was unaware that Wallis had been there eight months earlier. His visit was the fortuitous outcome of a series of events that began in 1764 when he undertook to colonise the Falkland Islands at his own expense for the benefit of French commerce. However, Spain soon complained that the Falklands were part of the South American continent; and France promised to surrender them to Spain provided Bougainville was indemnified. When the Spanish government agreed to this, Bougainville was given command of an expedition to hand the Falklands to a Spanish force and then to cross the Pacific to the East Indies.[1]

Leaving France in the frigate *Boudeuse* in November 1766, Bougainville carried out the first part of his instructions within six months. He then sailed to Rio de Janeiro where the storeship *Etoile* joined his expedition. In January 1768, the two ships entered the Pacific by the Strait of Magellan. After making yet another vain search for Davis' Land, Bougainville steered west. On 22 March he discovered two of the easternmost islands of the Tuamotu Archipelago, Vahitahi and Akiaki.[2]

Vahitahi, which was seen only from a distance, was named Les Quatre Facardins because it reminded Bougainville of a well-known novel of the day. Akiaki, a much smaller island, with many coconut and other trees, was called Ile de Lanciers because some men armed with lances were seen on it. Several square houses were also seen among the trees. To Pierre Caro, an officer of the *Etoile,* the islanders seemed to be dressed in mats with square hats of some kind on their heads. 'We never would have imagined,' he wrote in his journal, 'that such a small island could have been inhabited.' And apparently thinking that the islanders might be descendants of European castaways, he added: 'Few ships must surely have passed this way. Indeed, since Quiros in 1603 [*sic*], we are the first in 165 years.'[3] Bougainville, himself, thought at first that the islanders *were* castaways, and he ordered his ships to lay to, as he was determined to do all he could to save them. However, he changed his mind about them when fifteen or twenty naked men came out of the woods brandishing long pikes in a threatening manner. 'These men seemed very tall, and of a bronze colour,' Bougainville wrote. 'Who can give an account of the manner in which they were conveyed hither, what communications they have with other beings, and what becomes of them when they multiply on an isle, which has no more than a league in diameter?'[4]

On the morning after leaving Akiaki, Bougainville came upon yet another low, but much larger island with a lagoon in its centre. Because of its shape, as seen from the masthead, he called it La Harpe (the Harp). It was covered with low wood and occasional coconut trees, but in one place the coconuts seemed to be arranged in a man-made plantation. The *Boudeuse* and *Etoile* ran along the southern side of the atoll. Caro recorded seeing several canoes in the lagoon with six to eight black men in each. Their sails seemed to be brown and square. Some small boats of two kinds were moored near a *motu* on the reef; and a number of islanders were seen on foot. Bougainville and his officers were not sure if La Harpe was the same as the Conversion de San Pablo of Quiros. Its appearance seemed to fit his description of that island, but its position did not. However, it is now clear that the two islands were the same—that Bougainville's landfall was Hao Atoll, where the Spaniards saw the old woman with the gold ring and Castilian dog, and other curious things. Bougainville recorded that the islanders he saw were tall and well-proportioned, while François Vives, the *Etoile's* surgeon, noted that six men who began following the two ships in a sailing canoe were a reddish mulatto (*rouge mulâtre*) colour. Bougainville was anxious to communicate with these men to learn something of their island, but nightfall prevented this.[5]

The French ships subsequently passed five more atolls—Marokau, Ravahere, Hikueru, Reitoru and Haraiki—before they got clear of what Bougainville named the Dangerous Archipelago.[6] No more land was then seen until the high sugar loaf peak of Mehetia came into view nearly a week later. That same day, the Frenchmen sighted the peaks of Tahiti, and as fresh food and water were desperately needed, Bougainville steered towards them. The Frenchmen were charmed by Tahiti's beautiful appearance as they approached its eastern side. They could see many attractive, well-built houses, but no likely anchorage. Presently a canoe came out with a man and two children in it. Vives noted that they were a mulatto colour with curly black hair and very white teeth. The children were almost white.[7] Before long more than 100 canoes of different sizes, all with outriggers, had surrounded the *Boudeuse* and a smaller number were hovering round the *Etoile*. All carried banana leaves as emblems of peace. 'All these savages seemed very affable and unembarrassed,' Charles Fesche, a young seaman, wrote in his journal. 'They are well-formed, robust and of ordinary size. Some are mulattos, some are whitish, others are reddish and others black. All have curly hair and usually big beards like the Capuchins.'[8]

It was too late for Bougainville to find an anchorage that day, so the two ships lay off the island for the night. Next morning, 6 April 1768, the canoes again came out, bringing fish, fruit, fishing tackle, stone chisels, cloth and other things to sell. All the islanders seemed familiar with the art of commerce, for no one would give anything without receiving something in exchange. A canoe that approached the *Etoile* had a man and a white-skinned girl of sixteen to eighteen years in it. The girl had a piece of cloth around her head and another around her waist. Otherwise, she was naked. To Caro, she looked more attractive, or at least the equal, of any girl in Europe of similar age, and he was puzzled how such white and charming people could be found so far from Europe when all the others previously seen on the voyage were black and without *rapport*. 'We were not slow to express the wish that we would soon put into port,' he wrote in his journal.[9]

After a good deal of trouble, the *Boudeuse* and *Etoile* found an anchorage off the north-eastern coast of the island, in the district of Hitiaa. Bougainville was fascinated by what he saw as his ships manoeuvred to their haven.

> As we came nearer the shore [he wrote], the number of islanders surrounding our ships increased. The canoes were so numerous . . . that we had much to do to warp in amidst the crowd of boats and the noise. All these people came crying out *tayo,* which means friend, and gave a thousand signs of friendship; they all asked nails and ear-rings of us. The canoes were full of females; who, for agreeable features, are not inferior to most European women; and who, in point of beauty of the body, might, with much reason, vie with them all. Most of these fair females were naked; for the men and the old women that accompanied them had stripped them of the garments which they generally dress themselves in. The glances which they gave us from their canoes seemed to discover some degree of uneasiness, notwithstanding the innocent manner in which they were given; perhaps because nature has everywhere embellished their sex with a natural timidity; or because even in those countries where the ease of the golden age is still in use, women seem least to desire what they most wish for. The men, who were more plain, or rather, more free, soon explained their meaning very clearly. They pressed us to choose a woman, and to come on shore with her; and their gestures, which were nothing less than equivocal, denoted in what manner we should form an acquaintance with her. It was very difficult, amidst such a sight, to keep at their work four hundred young French sailors, who had seen no women for six months. In spite of all our precautions, a young girl came on board, and placed herself upon the quarter deck, near one of the hatchways, which was open to give air to those heaving at the capstan below it. The girl carelessly dropped the cloth which covered her and appeared to the eyes of all beholders much as Venus showed herself to the Phrygian shepherd—having, indeed, the celestial form of that goddess. Both sailors and soldiers endeavoured to come to the hatchway, and the capstan was never hove with more alacrity than on this occasion. . . .[10]

As soon as the ships were safely moored, Bougainville went ashore to see where water could be had. Among his companions was the Prince of Nassau-Siegen, a rich young passenger in the *Boudeuse*. The prince thought the landscape was as beautiful as could be and the people 'superb'. The men were all handsome, well made, and from 5 ft 6 in. to 6 ft tall. The women were 'of a becoming size, with beautiful big eyes, attractive teeth, European features and soft skin.' 'The colour of these Indians,' he went on, 'is that of copper,

A Raiatean priest wearing a gorget or 'taumi' fringed with dog's hair. The artist was Sydney Parkinson who visited Tahiti in 1769.

the women being whiter. It seems that there is also another browner race among them.'[11]

Bougainville and his companions were met by the chief of the district whose name, as they presently learned, was Ereti. They were conducted to his house, where domestics brought them fruit, water and dried fish. Meanwhile, Ereti sent for several pieces of cloth and two large gorgets to be given to them. The gorgets were made of wickerwork covered with black feathers and sharks' teeth. One was placed round Bougainville's neck; the other round that of one of his officers. 'Their form,' Bougainville wrote, 'closely resembled the enormous ruffs that were worn in the time of Francis I.'*[12]

On the day after Bougainville's reconnaissance ashore, Ereti visited him on board the *Boudeuse,* bringing gifts of fowls and pigs. Relations being so good, the Frenchmen landed their sick and water casks and prepared to build an armed camp near a small stream. Ereti and his councillors objected to this

* Francis I (1494-1547) was king of France when the Loaisa expedition sailed for the Moluccas. Bougainville recorded in a vocabulary of Tahitian words that a 'gorget of ceremony' was called *taoumi* [properly, *taumi*]—Bougainville 1772:474. Later visitors stated that the *taumi* were usually fringed with long dogs' hair obtained from the Tuamotus.

at first, but finally acquiesced when Bougainville pointed out that he intended to stay only eighteen days. A friendly trade soon began in nails, tools and other items. The Tahitian men helped the French sailors to get wood and water, while the women and children collected shells and scurvy grass for them. Apart from the Tahitians' propensity to filch things, the Frenchmen were delighted by almost everything about them.

The French sailors were constantly invited into the Tahitians' houses and offered food and even young girls; and if they accepted the girls, the houses were immediately filled with curious onlookers. 'Here Venus is the goddess of hospitality,' Bougainville wrote, 'her worship does not admit of any mysteries, and every tribute paid to her is a feast to the whole nation.'[13] The French commander noted that the Tahitian girls were enchanted by his men's white skin, and that they showed their admiration for it in 'the most expressive manner.'[14] He recorded also that he took all possible measures to prevent his men from communicating venereal disease to them, especially as he 'could not suppose that they were already infected with it.'[15] Although the Frenchmen eventually learned that the native name for the island was Tahiti, Bougainville dubbed it La Nouvelle Cythère because the amorous practices of the Tahitians called to mind Cytherea, birthplace of the Greek goddess of love.[16]

Tahiti's lofty mountains, pleasant streams and lush vegetation made Bougainville feel that he had been 'transported into the Garden of Eden' or the Elysian fields. He noted approvingly that the houses were built 'without order and without forming any villages,' although there were 'public paths, very judiciously laid out and carefully kept in good condition.'[17] Writing of the Tahitians themselves, he said:

> The inhabitants . . . consist of two races of men, very different from each other, but speaking the same language, having the same customs, and seemingly mixing without distinction. The first, which is the most numerous, produces men of the greatest size; it is very common to see them measure six (Paris) feet and upwards in height. I never saw men better made, and whose limbs were more proportionate: in order to paint a Hercules or Mars, one could no where find more beautiful models. Nothing distinguishes their features from those of Europeans: and if they were clothed, if they lived less in the open air, and were less exposed to the sun at noon, they would be as white as ourselves: their hair in general is black. The second race are of middle size, have frizzled hair as hard as bristles, and both in colour and features they differ little from the mulattoes. . . .[18]

Bougainville noted that polygamy seemed to be established among the chiefly class; indeed, a greater number of women was 'the only luxury of the opulent.'[19] However, the lower order of men frequently wore no other clothing but the breech-cloth, while the chiefs generally wrapped themselves in a large piece of cloth hanging down to the knees. This, likewise, was the only dress of the women, who knew 'how to place it so artfully as to make it susceptible of coquetry.' Bougainville added: 'As the women of Tahiti never go out into the sun without being covered, and always have a little hat made of canes and adorned with flowers to defend their faces against its rays, their complexions are, of course, much fairer than those of the men.'[20]

Bougainville could not immediately discover whether the Tahitians had any religion, although he noticed that in all the principal houses there were two human figures, one of each sex, carved in wood. 'The only religious ceremony which we have been witnesses to concerns the dead,' he wrote. 'They preserve their corpses a long while, extended on a kind of scaffold, covered by a shed. . . . When nothing but the skeletons remain, they carry them into their houses, and I do not know how long they keep them there.'[21]

As far as Bougainville could ascertain, the island produced no minerals, but the Tahitians used the word *aouri* to describe all the metals that were shown or given to them. There were only three quadrupeds—hogs, rats and 'a pretty sort of dogs'; and only one rich article of commerce—pearls. However, pearls were not the only things the Tahitians got from the pearl oyster. 'They make a kind of castanets of the shells,' Bougainville said.[22]

Bougainville was particularly interested in a red dye that the Tahitians used, and which seemed to him to be superior to that used in the celebrated 15th century tapestries of the Gobelins.[23] The Tahitians' fishing gear also impressed him. 'It is amazing with how much art their fishing tackle is contrived,' he wrote. 'Their hooks are made of mother-of-pearl, as neatly wrought as if they were made by the help of our tools; their nets are exactly like ours. . . .'[24] Bougainville did not see any European affinities in the Tahitians' canoes;[25] and one of his companions asserted that they corresponded to 'no known model'.[26] However, Bougainville thought the black stone chisels used to make them were 'exactly of the same form as that of our carpenters.'[27]

Among other things that the French commander noted was the practice of wearing mourning for the dead. The mourning garb consisted of a head-dress of black feathers and a veil over the face. 'When the people in mourning go out of their houses,' he wrote, 'they are preceded by several slaves, who beat the castanets in a certain cadence; their doleful sound gives everybody notice to clear the way. . . .'[28] Bougainville also noticed that the Tahitians had the custom of letting blood to cure the sick. This was performed by a *tahua,* or priest, who struck a sharp piece of wood on the cranium of the patient, thereby opening the sagittal vein. When sufficient blood was let out, the wound was bandaged, and next day it was washed with water.[29]

Although the Frenchmen had intended to stay at Tahiti for eighteen days, their sojourn was reduced to ten because of the poorness of their Hitiaa anchorage. On their departure, they took with them a young Tahitian called Ahutoru, who had expressed the wish to visit Europe.[30] He was a member of what Bougainville described as Tahiti's second race, being a son of Ereti and a woman from Opoa, Raiatea, who had been captured in war. 'To this [kind of] mixture I attribute the difference of the races we have observed among [the Tahitians],' he wrote.[31]

Ahutoru and Bougainville had many conversations as the *Boudeuse* and *Etoile* continued their voyage across the Pacific. It was thus that Bougainville learned of Wallis' visit to Tahiti eight months earlier. 'From hence,' he wrote, 'doubtless proceeds the knowledge of iron and the name *aouri* by which [the Tahitians] call it. I am yet ignorant whether . . . they . . . may not likewise be indebted to the English for the venereal disease which we found had been naturalised among them.'[32]

Bougainville also learned that the Tahitians were not of 'almost equal rank' as he and his companions had supposed. On the contrary, the 'distinction of ranks' was very great. The 'kings and grandees' had the power of life and death over their servants and slaves; and, as far as Bougainville could make out, they had the 'same barbarous prerogative' over the common people, whom they called *tata-einou* (properly, *taata ino*). It was from these people that victims were chosen for human sacrifice.[33]

Another matter that Ahutoru revealed was that the Tahitians worshipped a superior god, whom they did not represent by any material image, and that they had several others, some beneficent, some evil, called *eatoua,* i.e. *atua.* Bougainville was surprised to learn that these gods were invoked when a Tahitian sneezed—that his companions would say: '*Evaroua-t-eatoua*' (that the good *atua* may awaken thee, or that the evil *atua* may not lull thee asleep). 'These are marks which prove that [the Tahitians] have the same origin as the people of the old continent,' Bougainville wrote.[34]

Two and a half weeks after leaving Tahiti, the French ships came upon the Samoan islands of Manua, Tutuila and Upolu. They later touched at several in the New Hebrides and Solomons, skirted the northern coast of New Guinea and passed into the Indian Ocean by way of Batavia. Mauritius, then a French colony called Ile de France, was reached in November 1768, and Cape Town two months later. In mid-March 1768, Bougainville was back in France.

Meanwhile, Philibert de Commerson, who had been the expedition's surgeon-botanist as far as Mauritius, had written a long letter to a fellow scientist in France giving a detailed account of Tahiti. The letter was published in the *Mercure de France* for November 1769.[35] It differed from all other writings published on Tahiti for almost two centuries in that it propounded the theory that the Tahitians were a mixed race, descended from some aboriginal islanders whom Commerson called Protoplasts and castaways from a Spanish ship of the early days of Pacific exploration.

> It will undoubtedly be asked [Commerson wrote], from which continent and from which people have these islanders come? . . . I have formed only a conjecture, but I willingly submit it to those who delight in discussing this kind of subject.
>
> I found in the Tahitian language four or five words derived from Spanish.

Among them are *haouri,* which evidently comes from *hierro,* iron, and *mattar, mate,* which means *to kill* or *killed.* Could it be that some Spaniards, shipwrecked during the first crossings of the Pacific, could have furnished these words in giving the Tahitians their first knowledge of the things described? . . . If one admits this supposition, which I do not wish to make in prejudice of a nation I respect, I will soon explain several customs and the origin of several animals, that seem to me to have been borrowed from Europeans. It may have been thus that a pregnant dog and a pregnant sow brought to that island a race of pigs and small European dogs. It may have been thus that the Tahitians learned the art of knotting and mounting their fishing nets like ours; that they learned the practice of bleeding [the sick] with splinters of pearl shell sharpened in the form of lancets. It may be due to the castaways that their seats resembled the low, four-legged stools that our carpenters make for children; that their ropes and lines of vegetable fibre look like ours; that they have plaited hair, baskets, adze-shaped hatchets, and clothing for men like dalmatics;* that they have a passion for earrings and bracelets, and several other customs, which, taken singly, establish nothing, but which, collectively, indicate a series of imitations of European fashions. Finally, the small amount of iron that escaped the shipwreck would long since have rusted away, so it is not surprising that we did not find the least vestiges of it. But the tradition and the name, though somewhat corrupted, may have been preserved among them. Indeed, the Tahitians could have obtained these notions without having had any direct communication with Europeans. The wreck may have occurred on an island about a hundred or two hundred leagues from Tahiti, as [Ahutoru] has assured us that his countrymen are in contact with such places.†

Commerson's theory did not provoke any contemporary discussion in print. If it was read by any officers or sailors from the *Dolphin, Boudeuse* or *Etoile,* they kept their views to themselves. No one else at that time, of course, could possibly have had an informed opinion about it, so it is not surprising that the theory was soon forgotten. It was not brought to light again until a French writer published a biography of Commerson in serial form in 1885-8;[36] and it did not appear in any English publication until after the turn of the century.[37] By that time Pacific scholars were generally agreed that the Tahitians and other Polynesians were a homogeneous people who had originated in Asia; that their dogs, pigs and fowls were all Asiatic species; and that their language was of the Malay family. In the circumstances, not even the writers who re-published Commerson's letter seem to have taken his theory on the Tahitians very seriously.‡

* A dalmatic is a long, loose, wide-sleeved vestment with slit sides worn by Catholic deacons and bishops.

† This is a free translation of Commerson's theory, which is written in rather long-winded French. The last sentence in the original runs to 214 words!

‡ The present writer did not discover Commerson's theory until several months after beginning serious research for this book.

8

Traders in fine, white dogs' hair

News of Bougainville's voyage round the world had not reached England when Lieutenant James Cook left London in HMS *Endeavour* on 7 August 1768 on the first of his three great voyages to the Pacific. The purpose of the voyage was twofold: to observe the transit of Venus across the sun and to make yet another search for the southern continent. Observations of the transit—a once-in-a-century event—were expected to yield accurate measurements of the earth's distance from the sun, thereby simplifying the determination of longitude at sea. Astronomical expeditions organised by Britain's Royal Society were sent to several places in the northern hemisphere, but Cook's was the only one to the southern half of the world and was therefore of special importance. The Royal Society had originally suggested that Cook should go to either the Marquesas Islands or Tonga for the observations. However, when Wallis arrived home with news of the discovery of Tahiti, the venue was soon changed to that island. Cook's expedition consisted of eighty-four officers and seamen, and eight civilians. Among the civilians were Joseph Banks, a wealthy, well-connected botanist of twenty-five; and Sydney Parkinson, a botanical draftsman.[1]

The *Endeavour* entered the Pacific via Cape Horn on 27 January 1769. After the South American coast disappeared from sight, no land was again seen until Vahitahi Atoll—Bougainville's Les Quatre Facardins—appeared on the skyline on the morning of 4 April. The *Endeavour* came within a mile of it and Banks counted twenty-four inhabitants through his glasses. They were tall, black-haired people of a 'brown copper colour,' who seemed to have very large heads 'or possibly much hair upon them.' Eleven of the men walked along the beach abreast of the ship, each with a six-foot pole or pike in his hand. They were naked except for coverings over their genitals. However, as soon as the ship had passed the island, they seemed to put on some clothing that made them look lighter in colour. Some people dressed in white were also seen under the trees, and these were thought to be women.[2]

During the next twenty-four hours or so, the *Endeavour* sailed past Akiaki and Hao, which Cook called Thrum Cap and Bow Island respectively. No inhabitants were seen. The next landfalls were the twin atolls of Marokau and Ravahere. These were dubbed the Two Groups. The *Endeavour* hauled into a bay on the south-western side of Ravahere, but soon sailed out again when no bottom could be found near the shore. Meanwhile, a number of islanders assembled on the beach with their canoes, some of which could carry three men, others six or seven. One of the canoes followed the *Endeavour* out to sea, hoisting a sail which Banks described as 'not unlike an English lugsail and near as lofty as an English boat of the same size would have carried.' Banks, however, did not make it clear how big the canoe was. On the other hand, he described the islanders in some detail, although he admitted that none was seen at closer range than about half a mile. 'As well as we could judge,' he said, the people seemed to be 'about our size and well made, of a dark brown complexion, stark naked, wearing their hair tied back with a fillet which passed round their hair and kept it sticking out behind like a bush.' Most of the islanders carried poles from ten to fourteen feet long, each having a small knob or point 'not unlike the point of a spear.' They also had 'weapons' about four feet long, although Banks thought that these might have been paddles.[3]

Beyond Ravahere, the *Endeavour* sighted two more atolls—Reitoru and Anaa—before reaching Tahiti. Cook hauled up for Anaa and found it to be an oval-shaped 'double range of low woody Islands join'd together by reefs.' The islets and reefs seemed to surround its lagoon like a chain, for which reason Cook called it Chain Island, a name it bore for many years thereafter. It had plenty of large trees on it and smoke could be seen rising among them.[4]

On the morning of 13 April, the *Endeavour* anchored in Tahiti's Matavai Bay. Some of the crew were soon ashore. Those who had been to Tahiti before noticed at once that many houses had been razed and far fewer people were living in the area than on their previous visit. However, those who remained gave 'evident signs' that the Englishmen were 'not unwelcome.' With the permission of the chiefs, Cook began erecting a fort and an observatory on a tongue of land that he called Point Venus. Except that the Tahitians constantly pilfered things, including a quadrant required in the astronomical observations, the Englishmen and Tahitians got along well. Banks, who superintended most of the trading, took special pains to investigate the local customs and culture, and he frequently rambled through the surrounding countryside.

Among the many visitors who came to the fort was the chiefess Purea—the 'Queen Oberea' of Captain Wallis' visit—who seemed to have lost some of her authority. Cook thought she was 'very Masculine' in appearance;[5] but others were a little more kindly. Parkinson saw her as a 'fat, bouncing, good-looking dame,'[6] while Banks described her as 'tall and very lusty,' with white skin and eyes full of meaning.[7] Purea was frequently accompanied by Tupaia, a chief and priest of the island of Raiatea, who had fled to Tahiti after being driven from his possessions by invaders from neighbouring Bora Bora. He and Banks became close friends, and it was from him that Banks, Cook and others obtained much of their knowledge of Tahiti and the surrounding islands. Robert Molyneux, the master's mate, and a veteran of the *Dolphin's* voyage, described Tupaia as 'infinitely superior in every respect' to all the other islanders he knew;[8] while Cook said he was 'a very intelligent person' who knew 'more of the Geography of the Islands situated in these seas, their produce and the religion laws and customs of the inhabitants than any one we had met with.'[9]

On one of Purea's visits to the Englishmen with Tupaia, she brought them a large quantity of food and a very fat dog. This led to the discovery that the

Tahitians bred their dogs to eat, whereupon Cook, Banks and others expressed interest in a dog's-flesh dinner. Purea's offering was accordingly given to Tupaia, who killed it by suffocation and dressed it, Banks wrote, 'as we would a pig.' The dog was subsequently baked in an earth oven, or *umu,* and all who tried it declared that they had never tasted sweeter meat. 'I cannot however promise,' Banks said, 'that an European dog would eat as well, as these scarce in their lives touch animal food, Cocoa nut kernel, Bread fruit, yams, &c, being what their masters can best afford to give them and what indeed from custom I suppose they preferr to any kind of food.'[10]

Continuous contact with the Tahitians enabled the more diligent of the *Endeavour's* crew to make good progress in learning their language; and after four weeks on the island, Banks recorded: 'We have now got the Indian name of the Island, Otahite, so therefore for the future I shall call it.' About the same time the Englishmen learned that a foreign ship, which they took to be Spanish, had recently visited the island and had carried away an islander by his own consent. They also learned that the crew of the *Dolphin* had not been the first white men to be seen in the area, although their ship was the first to anchor at Tahiti. Molyneux recorded—in an apparent reference to Roggeveen's *African Galley* and the five deserters from his ships—that some years previously a ship had been stranded on a reef 'belonging to a small Island adjacent,' and that the crew had bravely defended themselves for some time. However, either because they were wearied or starved out, or because their ammunition was exhausted, they were finally overpowered and killed. Soon afterwards, some islanders had come to Tahiti from the scene of the wreck, bringing two of the dead men and some iron bolts. 'They were so well receiv'd,' Molyneux added, 'that they never since have return'd Home & I saw two of them some days agoe.'[11]

A few days later, Molyneux recorded that 'many of the Principal Natives' had come to the fort for divine service, and that they had behaved very quietly throughout—kneeling, standing or sitting as the Englishmen did. 'They understood perfectly that we were Parowing the Etuah, that is talking to God,' Molyneux wrote, 'this they easily comprehended as they themselves worship an Invisible & Omnipotent Being.'[12] Banks, however, was not so certain. He wrote in *his* journal that although a couple of chiefs imitated all they saw him do, they did not ask any questions about the service once it was over, nor would they attend to any explanations concerning it. 'We have not yet seen any traces of religion among these people, may be they are entirely without it,' he added.[13]

As the day for the observation of the transit of Venus approached, the *Endeavour's* carpenters made repairs to the ship's longboat so that an astronomical party could be sent to Moorea, Tahiti's sister island, as a safeguard against bad weather marring the observations at Point Venus. Banks, who accompanied the party to Moorea, took advantage of the opportunity to examine the people and produce of that island—or, at least, its north-western corner.

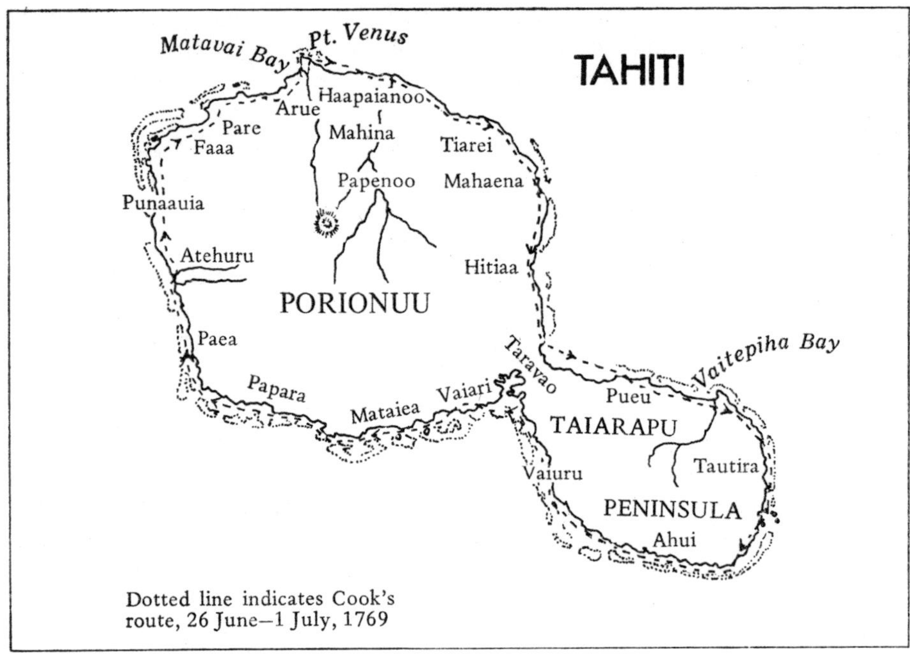

Dotted line indicates Cook's route, 26 June–1 July, 1769

However, he found very little that was new. Indeed, as far as he could see, the people were 'exactly the same'—some of them being 'the Identical same people' that he had seen at Tahiti.[14]

The transit of Venus took place some seven weeks after the *Endeavour's* arrival in Tahiti. The day turned out to be as favourable as Cook could wish and the observations, both on Tahiti and Moorea, were made without difficulty. With this important task over, Cook had leisure to investigate his surroundings more thoroughly. On 26 June, he and Banks, with a Tahitian as guide, set out in the *Endeavour's* pinnace to make a circuit of the island. Sometimes they travelled by sea, and sometimes overland. The excursion took six days. It revealed, among other things, that some parts of Tahiti were at war with others; and that the material culture and customs of the islanders were not everywhere exactly the same. For example, Taiarapu, the smaller peninsula of the island, which was ruled by an old white-bearded chief called Vehiatua, was at war with the Porionuu people of the larger part. Taiarapu also had an 'almost innumerable' number of double canoes that varied considerably from those of other parts, being larger and of a different build, with very high sterns ornamented with carvings and with awnings supported on carved pillars.[15] Some of the information that Cook and Banks gathered on their round-the-island tour was incorporated into detailed ethnographical accounts that both appended to the journals of their Tahitian sojourn. These accounts are basically the same, Cook having copied much of his from Banks, although he added many minor points of his own.[16]

Both men agreed that the Tahitians were of various skin colours; that their hair was almost universally black; and that the 'superior' people were much lighter-skinned and generally taller than the 'inferior' people. The inferior people, who were much exposed to the elements in fishing and other outdoor tasks, were 'of a very dark brown.' On the other hand, the superior people, who spent most of their time in their houses or under shelter, were 'not browner,' in Cook's view, 'than people who are born or reside long in the West Indias.' Some of the women, in fact, were 'almost as fair as Europeans.' To Banks, the superior people, especially the women, were 'seldom browner . . . than that kind of Brunette which many in Europe preferr to the finest red and white.' And he said he had seen some of them 'shew a Blush very manifestly.' Cook, but not Banks, remarked that the people generally had fine white teeth, short, flat noses, thick lips, and generally agreeable features. But both men said much the same thing in describing some islanders who were undoubtedly albinos. Cook said their skin was 'whiter than any Europeans, being of a dead colour like the nose of a white horse.'* Their eyes, eyebrows, hair and beards were also white; their bodies were more or less covered with a kind of white down; and their skins were spotted—some parts being much whiter than others. They were short-sighted and their eyes were often full of rheum. They always looked 'unwholesome' and had neither the spirit nor activity of the other islanders. 'I did not see above three or four upon the whole Island,' Cook added, 'and these were old men so that I concluded that this difference of Colour &c[a] was accidental and did not run in families, for if it did they must have been more numerous.'[17]

Both Cook and Banks gave detailed descriptions of the Tahitian custom of tattooing their bodies—usually their buttocks, arms and legs, but not their faces. Banks said that despite numerous inquiries he could not discover the reason for 'so apparently absurd a custom.' However, he thought that the smaller marks tattooed on the fingers and arms of the women were 'intended only for beauty,' although whiteness of complexion was considered 'the first essential in beauty.'[18]

Banks' description of the dress of the Tahitians was more detailed than Cook's, although, again, the two men obviously compared notes. Banks said that the richer people had clothing of two kinds—woven mats and that made from the bark of the paper mulberry tree. They wore their clothing in a thousand different ways. The 'dress of form' for women was a *pareu,* or kind of petticoat, wrapped round the hips, and one, two or three *tiputa* slipped over the head. The *tiputa* was a thick piece of cloth about two and a half yards long and one wide, with a hole in the middle. It hung down before and behind, giving full liberty to the arms, but was tied round the waist with two or three large pieces of thin cloth. Sometimes one or two additional pieces of cloth were

* In comparing the skin of these islanders to that of a white horse, Cook used exactly the same simile as the buccaneer Lionel Wafer in describing some white Indians of a Panamanian tribe in 1681.—Wafer 1934: 80-2. These Indians are now known to have been of the San Blas tribe, among whom there is a higher percentage of albinism than anywhere in the world.—Gates 1952: 272-3. For photographs of the San Blas albinos, see Harlan 1932: 319-22.

thrown loosely over the shoulders, as the rich seemed to take great pride in wearing 'a large quantity of cloth.' The dress of the men was similar to that of the women, except that their bodies were rather more bare, and, instead of the *pareu,* they wore a *maro* which passed between their legs and round their waists. 'Both sexes,' Banks added, 'shade their faces from the sun with little bonnets of cocoa nut leaves which they make occasionally in a very few minutes.' Some had them of fine matting, but that was less common. Cook noted that the turban was also used as a head-dress, and that the women sometimes wore long lengths of plaited human hair wound tastefully round their heads.[19]

Cook and Banks were agreed that the Tahitians had few diversions. The one they saw most frequently was archery, which was confined almost entirely to the chiefs. Another was wrestling. In the archery contests, targets were not used, nor were fledged arrows. The contestants shot their arrows solely for distance, kneeling on one knee and dropping the bow as soon as the arrow parted from it. One chief had been seen to fire an arrow 274 yards, yet he complained that as the bow and arrows were bad, he could have done much better.[20]

Although the Tahitians were fond of music, it seemed to both Cook and Banks that this art was little known among them. Both men stated that the Tahitians had only two instruments, the drum and the nose-flute—a hollow bamboo with three holes into which the player blew with one nostril.[21] However, there was also a third instrument—the castanet, which Bougainville had mentioned. Parkinson described this as 'a clapper made of two mother of pearl shell' which was used by the Tahitian girls in dancing the *'taowree whaow'*.[22]

In writing of the Tahitians' canoes or *vaa**, both Cook and Banks made it clear that these were of primitive design, being flat-bottomed and wall-sided. The bottoms were made from one or more tree-trunks hollowed out to a thickness of about three inches. Planks of similar thickness were sewn to them to form the sides. The *vaa* ranged in length from 10 to 72 ft, depending on whether they were intended for fishing, travelling or fighting. They were never more than one to two feet wide and two and a half to three feet deep. The single *vaa* had outriggers attached to give stability; otherwise, two hulls were fastened together to make double canoes. In either type, the sails were made of matting in the shape of a leg of mutton.[23]

Both Cook and Banks wrote glowingly of the Tahitians' ingenuity as carpenters, joiners and stone cutters.[24] And Banks said they were 'vastly ingenious' in every expedient to catch fish—their seines and nets being 'exactly like ours.'[25] Banks went on to assert that the language, manners and customs of Tahiti 'agreed almost exactly' with those of the other, neighbouring islands

* The word *vaa* should properly be written *va'a* to indicate that the 'k' sound, which once existed in Tahitian, is now heard only as a glottal catch. Likewise, *arii* (chief) should be written *ari'i* to show that it was once *ariki;* and Raiatea should be Ra'iatea to indicate a missing 'ng'. However, as the use of the glottal stop (') has only recently been adopted by scholars, great inconsistency can arise in quoting from the works of earlier writers. In this book, glottal stops are *not* used except in personal names and where it seems necessary to emphasise a linguistic peculiarity.

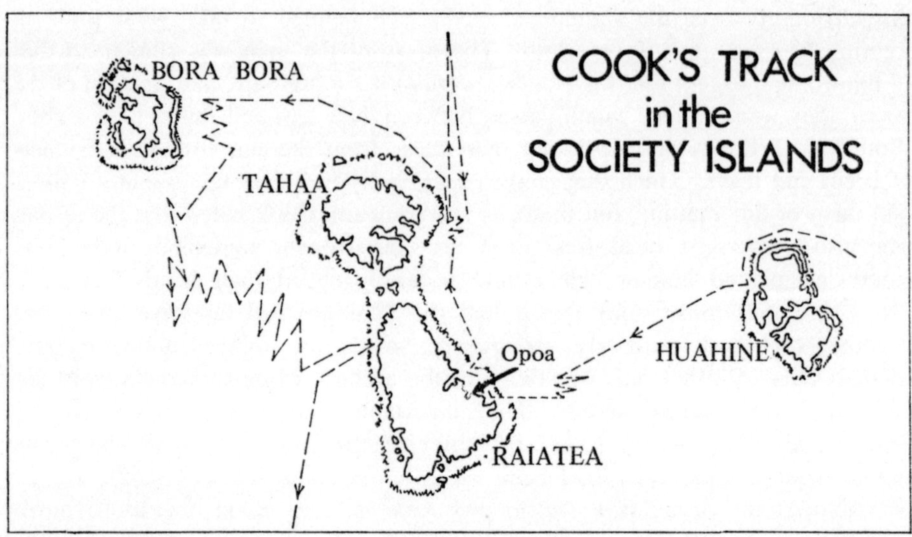

to westward that the *Endeavour* visited subsequently.[26] Cook expressed a similar view.[27] However, it is plain from the narratives of both Banks and Cook, as well as of Parkinson, that there were, in fact, some notable differences.

After staying three months in Tahiti, the *Endeavour's* first landfall was Huahine, some eighty miles northwest. There, Banks soon noticed, among other things, that the islanders had large shelters for their boats, a type of structure unrecorded in Tahiti.[28] Banks was also struck by a difference in the god houses (*fare no atua)* in which the islanders kept their 'oblations to the Gods.'[29] But even more remarkable was the difference in the people. Cook wrote that, unlike the Tahitians, the Huahineans were not addicted to stealing. They were also 'rather fairer' and 'more uniformly of one Colour.'[30] Banks, for his part, thought the Huahineans were 'less timid as well as less curious' than the Tahitians; that the men were all 'large made and stout;' and that the women were 'very Fair'—'more so than at Otahite,' although there was 'none so hansome.'[31] Parkinson, who sketched a couple of Huahinean women with distinctly Caucasian features (see plate 8), did not entirely share Banks' view. 'The natives of this island,' he wrote, 'are not of such a dark complexion as those of Otahite, and the other neighbouring islands; and the women are, in general, as handsome, and nearly of the same colour as Europeans; from which we may draw a reason for the name of this pretty island,* which I left regretting that I did not see more of it.'[32]

The *Endeavour* stayed only four days at Huahine. She then crossed the 20-mile channel to its nearest neighbour, Raiatea, or Uliatea as it was then more frequently called. For four days she lay at Opoa, at the south-east corner of that island, which, unbeknown to the Englishmen, was the site of the most

* In a footnote, Parkinson explained that *Huahine* meant 'wife'. It seems to be a variant of *vahine,* meaning both 'wife' and 'woman'.

sacred *marae* in Eastern Polynesia.[33] On 25 July 1769 Cook sailed north to 'take a view' of Tahaa and Bora Bora, two islands that he had heard of from Tupaia, Banks' knowledgeable Raiatean friend of Tahiti, who was being taken to England at Banks' expense. Off the eastern coast of Tahaa, Banks was given the opportunity to go ashore for a few hours in a boat. Then the *Endeavour* rounded the northern shore of that island, sailed past Bora Bora, and finally anchored for a week at Haamene, on Raiatea's north-west coast. During the *Endeavour's* peregrinations the Englishmen sighted two other small islands, Tupai and Maupiti, which, with Huahine, Raiatea, Tahaa and Bora Bora, Cook named the Society Islands 'because they lay contiguous to one another.'[34]

While the *Endeavour* lay at Haamene, Cook made a couple of trips to Tahaa. He also saw a number of Bora Borans, including their chief, Puni, who had invaded Raiatea. On the strength of what he saw, Cook later affirmed that the Society Islanders in general were 'rather of a fairer Colour than the generality of natives of [Tahiti], but more especially the woman who are much fairer and handsomer.'[35] Banks did not specifically describe the Society Islanders, other than the Huahineans;[36] but he observed that the Raiatean language differed from that of Tahiti in that the Raiateans used a 'k' where the Tahitians used 't', so making it much less soft.[37] Both Cook and Banks also noted that the Raiateans had the same god houses and boat houses as those seen at Huahine,[38] and both men as well as Parkinson observed that the Society Islanders in general had a type of canoe that was quite different from, and much superior to, the generality seen in Tahiti.

The canoes of the Society Islands were called *pahi*. Parkinson described them as 'very long, bellying out on the sides' and with a very high peaked stern. They were housed in what he called a Catanarian arch, thatched all over, and were only used at 'particular seasons.'[39] Cook spoke of them as 'full bellied' and of the same model as six he had seen in Tahiti, but which he was told were not built there. They were constructed with far more ingenuity 'than one could expect,' and the islanders, by building shelters for them, seemed to take great care of them.

> In this Proes or Pahee's . . . [Cook added] these people sail . . . from Island to Island for several hundred Leagues, the Sun serving them for a compass by day and the Moon and Stars by night . . . Tupia tells us that during the Months of Novr Decemb^r & January, Westerly winds with rain prevail & as the inhabitants of the Islands know very well how to make the proper use of the winds, there will no difficulty arise in Trading or sailing from Island to Island even tho' they lay in an East & West direction.[40]

Banks noted that the islanders at Opoa were particularly busy in building and repairing their *pahi* during the *Endeavour's* sojourn there. He thought the *pahi* were 'much better embarkations' than the *vaa* and were built in 'a more ingenious manner.' Unlike the flat-bottomed, square-sided *vaa* of Tahiti, the *pahi* had round, bilging sides and a sharp bottom like a keel. The keel-like bottom was 'hollowed out like a trough' from a long tree. This was surmounted on each side by a section made of planks sewn together; then came another section hollowed like the keel; and finally more planks. The planks were about four feet long, 15 inches wide and two inches thick. 'When they have prepared their planks &c,' Banks wrote, 'the keel is layd on blocks and the whole Canoe put together much in the same manner as we do a ship, the sides being supported by [stanchions] and all the seams wedg'd together before the last sewing is put on.'[41] Cook added several construction details that Banks overlooked. The *pahi,* he said, had timbers (i.e. ribs) in the inside which the *vaa* did not. They also had high curved sterns and slightly curving heads, both of which were ornamented 'with the image of a Man carved in wood, very little inferior [to] work of the like kind done by common ship carvers in England.'[42]

Banks said the *pahi* varied considerably in length, being from thirty to sixty feet long. Their round sides made them capable of carrying much greater burdens than the *vaa* and made them much safer at sea. For these reasons they were used for fighting and long voyages. In the sailing *pahi,* two hulls were generally fastened together. The vessels of middling size were said to be the best and least liable to accidents in stormy weather. 'With these boats,' Banks went on, 'they venture themselves out of sight of land; we saw several of them at Otahite which had come from Ulhietea [i.e. Raiatea] . . .'[43] He added:

> . . . in these if we may credit the reports of the inhabitants, they make very long voyages, often remaining out from home several months, visiting in that time many different Islands of which they repeated to us the names of near a hundred. They cannot however remain at sea above a fortnight or 20 days tho they live as sparingly as possible, for want of proper provisions and places to put them in safe, as well as water of which however they carry a tolerable stock in hollow Bamboes.[44]

Neither Banks nor his companions recorded the names of the islands that the Society Islanders visited in their *pahi.* But there is little doubt that they had contact with the Tuamotus, for on one occasion, while walking on shore at Raiatea, Banks noticed a girl with an earring of three large pearls which must almost certainly have come from that archipelago. The girl was a member of a team of strolling players who were much in evidence on Raiatea. Banks saw them perform twice. On the second occasion, he was accompanied by Parkinson, who made a sketch of the women's full, pleated dresses, which fell from their armpits to the ground. In Banks' view, the women handled their

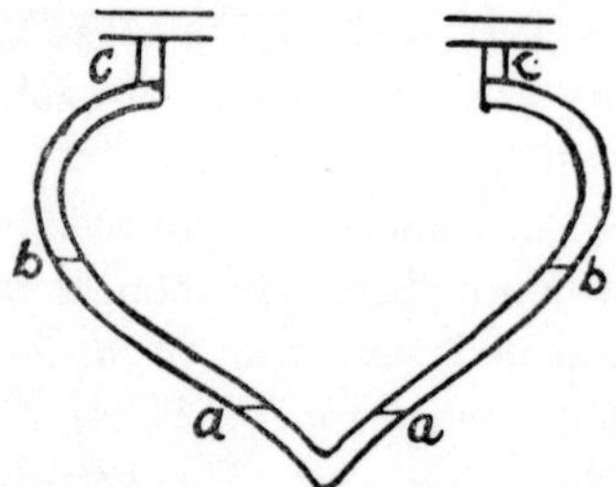

Cross section of the hull of a Raiatean 'pahi', as drawn by Joseph Banks.

skirts 'with as much dexterity as our opera dancers could have done;' while Cook wrote that their dress was of a kind he had not seen before, being 'neat decent and well chose and in many respects not much unlike a European dress.' The women performed dances to music in which they moved their arms, hands and fingers with great agility but made very little use of their legs and feet. Neither the music nor the dancing, in Cook's opinion, was 'att all calculated to please a European.' But he took a kindlier view of a kind of farce performed by the men, which 'shew'd that this people have a notion of Dramatick performances.' Banks went even further. To him, some of the performances of the men 'resembled much the Drama of an English stage dance.'[45]

The *Endeavour* took in a good supply of fruit, vegetables and livestock at Raiatea. Cook then sailed south in search of some new islands that Tupaia had described to him. After four days, the expedition came upon the island of Rurutu, which Tupaia said was called Hiti-roa.[46] Banks, Tupaia and others attempted to make a landing from the ship's pinnance, but the islanders opposed them. However, the party did manage to barter with the islanders from their boat, and so to observe them at close hand. Considering that Rurutu is more than 300 miles south of Raiatea, the skin colour of the islanders was not, perhaps, what the Englishmen would have expected. 'The people,' Banks wrote, 'seemed strong lusty and well made, but were rather browner than those we have left behind.' Banks also noted that the islanders tattooed themselves differently; that their clothing, although made from *tapa* like that of the northern islands, was coloured differently; and that their arms consisted of long lances and clubs of hard *toa* wood. 'Of the few things we saw among these people,' Banks added, 'every one was ornamented infinitely superior to any thing we had before seen: their cloth was better coulourd as well as nicely painted, their clubs were better cut and polished, [and] the [only] Canoe which we saw, tho a very small and very narrow one, was nevertheless carvd and ornamented very highly.'[47]

After leaving Rurutu, the *Endeavour's* next landfall was New Zealand, which was reached on 6 October 1769, halfway down the eastern side of the North Island. As no European had visited this country since Tasman's brief passage in 1643, Cook immediately set about surveying it to determine whether it was part of the supposed southern continent. The survey occupied almost six months, during which both the North and South Islands were circumnavigated. Tupaia proved useful as an interpreter, for it was found that his language and that of the New Zealanders closely resembled each other. However, Tupaia and the New Zealanders did not always see eye to eye, especially after it became known that the New Zealanders practised cannibalism, a custom unknown in Tupaia's part of the Pacific. 'Tupia who holds this custom in very great aversion', Cook wrote, 'hath very often argued with them against it but they always strenuously supported it and never would own that it was wrong . . .'[48]

From New Zealand, the *Endeavour* sailed westward and on 19 April

1770 reached the east coast of Australia at a spot that was named Point Hicks. For the next four months, Cook followed the coast northward until he reached Torres Strait. From there he made his way to the Dutch settlement of Batavia, and then home via the Cape of Good Hope.

Within two months of the expedition's return, an anonymous chronicler —probably James Magra—rushed out the first account to be published of the *Endeavour's* voyage.[49] In general, it is a poor, slipshod production. But occasionally it contains observations on subjects that the other chroniclers failed to mention. Two such observations which can be checked against other sources are significant in the context of this book. Describing the Tahitians, the anonymous writer said: 'Their complexion is brown, but much lighter than that of the natives of America; some few among them appeared almost as white as Europeans, and several had red hair, though commonly it is black and straight.'[50] Elsewhere, the anonymous writer referred to voyages that were made from Tahiti to the Tuamotus for a prized commodity—dogs' hair:

> The natives of Otahitee visit the islands lying to the eastward, which we had discovered in our passage hither, for the sake of traffic, in their canoes, waiting the opportunity of winds, which blow favourably about three months of the year. With the inhabitants of those islands they barter their cloth and provisions for pearls and a fine white hair, which grows on a species of dog peculiar to themselves, and with this they ornament their breast plates.[51]

Parkinson, who sketched a Raiatean priest wearing a breast plate, or *taumi,* confirmed the anonymous writer's statement that the hair in them was fine and white.[52] But like him, Parkinson failed to mention that the hair in the breast plates was remarkably long—far longer than could be obtained from any but a long-haired species of dog. Many examples of the *taumi* of old Tahiti and the Society Islands are still preserved in museums around the world.[53] One in the Peabody Museum of Salem, Massachusetts, contains grey, white and yellow dogs' hair up to almost eight inches in length; and another has hair more than six inches long.[54] In the British Museum there are five *taumi* with creamy hair, usually silky in texture, ranging from five to six inches long;[55] and others with hair of similar length are to be found in the Australian Museum, Sydney;[56] the National Museum of Ireland, Dublin;[57] the Musée d'Histoire de Berne;[58] and the Dominion Museum, Wellington.[59]

The length of the hair in the extant *taumi,* the fact that the Tahitians had to go to the Tuamotus to get such hair, and the anonymous writer's statement that the Tuamotuans had dogs 'peculiar to themselves,' all suggest that the dogs of the Tuamotus were introduced from the east rather than the west, and at no very distant date. If it were otherwise, one would expect that the Tahitians, who prized long dog's hair so highly, would have had numerous long-haired dogs themselves, and that such dogs would also have been found in the Society Islands and the other islands to the west, whence the Polynesians are supposed to have originated.

Dancing girls at Raiatea, sketched by Sydney Parkinson during Cook's first visit to the Pacific in 1769. The clothing is made of tapa and the girls are wearing headdresses of plaited hair. Original drawing, British Museum.

The dogs encountered among the Polynesians by the early explorers are now extinct. They are thought to have been descended from the pariah dogs of Asia—like this one photographed in South China. Reproduced from H. Epstein's 'Domestic Animals of China' (Farnham Royal, 1969).

This 'taumi' or breastplate fringed with dogs' hair was photographed many years ago in the British Museum. Obviously, the dogs' hair could not have come from a short-haired dog such as the pariah.

PLATE 6. Islanders of Eastern Polynesia drawn by Sydney Parkinson and published in his 'A Journal of a Voyage to the South Seas . . .' (London, 1773). The two at left are Tahitians; the two at top right are Huahinean women; and the two below, Rurutuans. Parkinson described the people of Huahine as fairer than the Tahitians, the women being 'as handsome, and nearly of the same colour as Europeans'.

9

Blue eyes at Taiarapu

For nearly 200 years from Drake's time onwards, English and Dutch pirates had made occasional raids on Spanish ships and settlements along the western coast of South America. They operated without bases and appeared without warning, and it was therefore difficult for the Spaniards to take preventative measures against them. Now, it seemed, a new, more organised era of harassment was about to begin. News of Byron's voyage to the Falkland Islands and of his and Wallis' incursions into the Pacific suggested to the Spaniards that the British were about to establish bases adjacent to South America, or had already done so; and that henceforth their ships and ports would be liable to more frequent attack. Accordingly, in October 1769, the Spanish king ordered the viceroy of Peru to send an expedition to the South Seas to see what the British were up to. In particular, the expedition was to search for Davis' Land and to examine other islands, including those off the coast of southern Chile, 'whereat the English may have established themselves.'

Two well-armed frigates, the *San Lorenzo* and *Santa Rosalia* were fitted out. They sailed from Callao in October 1770 under a veteran naval officer, Felipe Gonzalez.[1] With French and Dutch charts to guide him, Gonzalez sailed south-west until reaching the 27th parallel, and then west. After a voyage of five weeks, he sighted a treeless island, which he first thought was a new discovery. He named it San Carlos. However, he soon realised that it was the Easter Island of Roggeveen. The island had a population estimated at 900 to 1,000. The Spaniards stayed at the island for six days, took formal possession of it, and satisfied themselves that no Englishmen had settled on it. They then set sail to search for another island, which, according to a Dutch chart, lay nearby. After sailing sixty leagues west without seeing any sign of land, they turned about to look for a third island said to lie in 38° 30' S. Unsuccessful in this search, they carried on to the coast of Chile; investigated the island of Chiloé without finding or learning of any foreign settlements; and then returned to Peru.

Having received a report from Gonzalez, the viceroy, Manuel de Amat, suggested to the Spanish government that some action should be taken to ensure that foreign pirates could not make use of Easter Island and its inhabitants. Either it should be occupied and fortified, he said, or its inhabitants should be removed to Peru so that the pirates could not employ them as troops in raids on South America.[2] The viceroy's suggestions struck a sympathetic chord in Spain, and the king authorised him to send a second expedition to Easter Island to cultivate the islanders' friendship, pending a decision on whether the island should be occupied or not. However, just as the king's message was about to be dispatched, news reached Spain of Cook's visit to Tahiti. Coming so soon after the voyages of Byron and Wallis, this seemed so ominous to the Spaniards that the viceroy was hastily ordered to send an expedition to seek out that island as well.[3]

On 26 September 1772, a frigate, the *Aguila,* sailed from Callao under a Basque naval officer, Domingo Boenechea.[4] On board were two priests who had been engaged to settle on Easter Island as missionaries. Boenechea's instructions gave him discretion as to whether he should visit Tahiti or Easter Island first. However, the viceroy ordered that his visit to Tahiti should not be 'so cursory and brief as to leave us with the same confused ideas about it as did that made by the two vessels sent to explore [Davis' Land].' He was also told to ensure that no foreigners had settled on Tahiti; to investigate any other islands he saw; and to bring back four or five smart young Tahitians to be instructed in the Spanish language and the rudiments of the Catholic faith.[5]

Boenechea decided to head for Tahiti first, and to go to Easter Island after refreshing at Valparaiso. As a result, he approached the Tuamotu Archipelago from a different angle from his predecessors, and so came upon two small atolls not previously recorded on European charts. The first was Tauere, some fifty miles north-west of Amanu. The other was Haraiki, about a day's sail further west. About twenty brown-skinned islanders were seen on the beach at Tauere. They had bristly hair cut short at the neck, and were naked apart from a whitish-grey *maro,* or breech-cloth. They carried spears and clubs, yelled vociferously, and made various signs, which the Spaniards interpreted both as acts of defiance and invitations to go ashore. Although two canoes were seen, there seemed to be no huts and no women.[6] At Haraiki, from twelve to sixteen people were seen. They were dressed like those of Tauere and were similarly armed.[7]

A couple of days later, the *Aguila* came upon another, larger atoll. This was Anaa, which Cook had seen from a distance some eighteen months earlier and had named Chain Island. A sub-lieutenant, Raimundo Bonacorsi, was sent inshore in a boat to seek an anchorage. This attracted a number of islanders to the beach, who signalled to the Spaniards with green boughs to come closer in, and followed their boat along the coast with a great show of merriment. Bonacorsi noted that their build, clothing and weapons were the same as at the other atolls, but they varied considerably in appearance. Some were 'pretty blonde in hue,' others were of a 'tawny colour with frizzly hair,' and others again had 'purely Indian features and the hair lank.' Their shoulders, buttocks, trunks, arms and legs were tattooed blue in various patterns and stripes. But the women were draped from the waist to the knees in the same material as the men used for breech-cloths.[8] As no anchorage could be found, Boenechea resumed his voyage, having named the atoll Todos los Santos.[9]

The *Aguila* reached Mehetia two days later. This was the small, lofty island to the eastward of Tahiti that Wallis had named Osnaburg. A boat's crew was sent off to make a circuit of it. Meanwhile, two islanders of medium build paddled out to the ship. 'They were of a mulatto colour,' Boenechea wrote, 'with features of a pleasant cast.' Their hair was cut short; their thighs and hands were tattooed; and like the men at the atolls, their only clothing was a breech-cloth.[10] Bonacorsi described them as 'fairly light in hue, being merely browned by the sun.' They were 'somewhat tawny about their features and hair', which was crinkly and stuck up in an even mass all over. Bonacorsi added that they asked for *uri,* which the Spaniards later understood was their name for nails and other bits of iron.[11] Having exchanged some coconuts for a few trifles, they paddled ashore seemingly contented.

As the *Aguila's* boat party met similarly well-disposed islanders on their circuit of the island, Boenechea stood off and on for the night so that a further reconnaissance could be made in the morning. This time, a party headed by a sub-lieutenant, Diego Machado, made a landing. The islanders were in a 'lightsome mood' and helped them to get ashore. Then they led them to a cluster of five thatched huts. A human jaw bone was hanging up in one hut, and a neatly-carved concave stool was seen in another. The only other household chattels were baskets and mats made of palm leaves and what seemed to be rushes. On noticing an *umu,* or earth-oven, Machado asked by signs how the islanders kindled fire, and was told that they rubbed two sticks together. Beyond the cluster of huts, Machado saw a black and tan puppy following some women. It was 'of ordinary size' and had pointed ears. Further on, there was a cultivated area containing coconuts, plantains and other plants; and beyond that a pen with several fat, fine-looking pigs in it, 'as large as the biggest ones at Lima.' Machado also saw a *marae,* or place of worship, of stepped stone platforms. It was adorned with carved posts, on which the 'figure of a small dog was pre-eminent in every case.'[12]

When the boat party returned to the *Aguila,* Bonacorsi obtained some information from them that Machado did not put in his journal. He recorded that, in addition to the breech-cloth, the men had *ponchos* of fine matting, and that the women had a 'certain white drapery that they get from the bark of a tree after much beating out and working up.' They used this to clothe themselves from the waist downwards, and sometimes the whole body. Bonacorsi added that the islanders used stone hatchets and adzes in their woodwork 'after the manner of our iron ones'.[13] Father Joseph Amich, one of the missionaries intended for Easter Island, noted that the island's men were well-built and of a light hue, with scanty beards. Some had somewhat frizzly hair; in others it was lank.[14]

On leaving Mehetia the Spaniards took an islander with them who indicated that he wanted to go to Tahiti. They reached that island next day; but eleven days elapsed before the *Aguila* was safely anchored at Vaiurua, on the eastern side of the Taiarapu Peninsula. In the meantime, the ship was briefly aground on a coral bank—an accident that smashed her tiller and tore away three chunks of protective planking under her stern. This damage, at the time, seemed of no great consequence; and Boenechea proceeded to carry out the viceroy's orders by sending a boat under Lieutenant Tomas Gayangos to make a circuit of the island. Gayangos kept a journal of the voyage, as did Father Amich who accompanied him. The launch cast off from the frigate on the morning of 5 December 1772, and proceeded northwards round the island's windward side. In some districts, the Spaniards stopped and went ashore; in others the islanders came out to meet them in their canoes. The voyage took six days. One of its highlights was a formal meeting at Matavai between Gayangos and the high chief Tu, whom Gayangos described as a man of twenty or twenty-two, taller than most of his countrymen, well-proportioned, swarthy in hue, with black eyes and an aquiline nose.[15] Tu received Gayangos at his residence, sitting on the floor with three women and in the presence of 400 or 500 Tahitians. Four men armed with pikes acted as bodyguards.

> As soon as I came into his presence [Gayangos wrote] he welcomed me with the word *taio* of which they customarily make use to express friendly intent: I replied with the same, whereupon he immediately embraced me and kissed me on the temples, and divesting himself of a shawl or wrap of native cloth with which he was draped . . . he placed it around my shoulders. The ladies he had by his side then greeted me in the same affectionate fashion, to which I made similar response.[16]

Gayangos' journey round Tahiti proved that no foreigners had settled on the island. It also helped Boenechea to compile a reasonably comprehensive report on the island and its people for the viceroy. He said in this that the number of inhabitants at 'the lowest computation' was 10,000.* The people were of four distinct types or castes. There were pure-bred Indians, hybrids, others of a light-brownish tint, and three or four albinos. In general, the people were taller than Spaniards, many being 'of huge stature and well-proportioned.' They wore long, but not very bushy beards, and their hair was short—not reaching below their shoulders. However, it was so tangled that it gave them 'a very wild look.'[17]

Much of Boenechea's report naturally duplicated what Tahiti's earlier European visitors had written. But among its novelties was the statement that the Tahitians practised circumcision.[18] Other novelties were recorded by the other diarists of the *Aguila's* voyage. Father Amich, who described the Tahitians generally as 'stout and well set up', and mostly of a mulatto colour, wrote of three islanders who differed markedly from the norm. 'On two occasions,' he said, 'a couple of men quite white came on board the Frigate, with blonde hair, reddish beards and eyebrows, and blue eyes.' He added that the chief of Taiarapu, Ti'i-torea, was 'very fair and ruddy, notwithstanding sunburn.' As for the women, they were 'remarkably fair', despite going about exposed to the weather.[19] Amich noted that the Tahitians glued several lengths of tapa together to make bed coverlets, and he highly praised the Tahitians' skill as joiners. The

* This figure differs so markedly from other early estimates that there is reason to suppose that a nought was omitted and that the real estimate was 100,000.

tools used to build their canoes were a sort of adze made of small fillets of a black stone, which, although very hard, were easy to whet with other stones. 'They fit them so perfectly to their hafts of stick,' Amich wrote, 'that they look just like the tools of a skilled wright.'[20] Bonacorsi, for his part, recorded a novelty that escaped the notice of all other early visitors to Tahiti. This was that the Tahitians had several breeds of dog—some quite small, and others 'very large and hairy.'[21]

The Spaniards stayed at Taiarapu for four weeks, then sailed for Valparaiso to take in stores for the second part of their voyage. In accordance with the viceroy's instructions, they took with them four Tahitians to be indoctrinated into the Spanish way of life in Lima. By the time they reached Valparaiso, the Tahitians could communicate reasonably well with the Spaniards, and the *Aguila's* master, Juan de Hervé, gathered a good deal of new information from them about Tahiti and the surrounding islands. One item confirmed the observations of Cook and Banks that the Society Islanders were lighter-skinned than the Tahitians; another, that the canoes of that island were both larger and different from the generality of those of Tahiti.

> They say [Hervé wrote] that a youth of very pleasing features who came on board the Frigate while we were at Tahiti and whom, at first, we took for a woman, belonged to Raiatea. He came again with four others equally well favoured, and they tell us that they were all from thence, and that the people there are much fairer than those of Tahiti, especially the women.
>
> They also tell us that there is in that island a very great abundance of good timber trees, some very large, and that the canoes built there are much larger than those of the other Islands.
>
> Each *arii* owns a large vessel that they call *paxia* [i.e. *pahi*], according to the signs they make to us as much as 44 ft in length, and carrying fifty men of a crew. They say there is one of the same kind at the island of Mehetia, which they keep hauled up on the hillside in order that she may not be stolen from them: no doubt she is taken to pieces in sections. They say that the largest vessel in these islands belongs to Raiatea and that each hull is 55 ft in length, and two in breadth; both being of even size and placed at a distance of 8 ft apart, with spars fixed athwartships from the one to the other, by means of which they are well lashed together. Each canoe-body is fitted on the inside with knees, which project upwards above the gunwales; and to these they fix wash-boards. So that, besides having a length of 55 ft, each hull has a breadth of 5½ ft, which, together with the 8 ft of intervening space, gives each vessel a total beam of 19 feet. They raise on them with the wash-boards as much as they wish. . . .
>
> They rig some of these with two masts and their sails. The heel of the mast fits or rests on a stout plank fixed across the two canoe-bodies, with the mast at the middle part. When they have to carry women on board they build a small deck-house on the canoes, and when they reach port it is put ashore with the women, and then they only step one mast in the vessel.

> On remarking to our natives that although we made the entire tour of the Island we never saw a single example of this class of vessel, they replied that they were all away at that time at the Island of Raiatea, and that there is one season of the year when they go over there, and there are other times when those of that Island come to the Isle of Tahiti. And they give us to understand that they choose their time to avoid the bad weather, for . . . there are occasions when Tahiti is swept by gales of wind from the N. or from the E., both of them of such force that they snap off the trunks of coconut-palms.[22]

Hervé's report was sent to the viceroy from Valparaiso on 31 May 1773 and shortly afterwards the *Aguila* sailed for Easter Island. However she had not gone far when the damage she had suffered in Tahiti caused her to leak badly, and Boenechea deemed it prudent to return immediately to Peru. Three Tahitians whom he had brought from Taiarapu—the fourth had died in Valparaiso—were presented to the viceroy and installed in the vice-regal palace in Lima. There they were placed in the charge of various instructors, whose task it was to teach them Spanish and something of the Catholic faith, it being the viceroy's view that this knowledge might later be useful in converting their compatriots to Christianity.

Two of the Tahitians, named Pautu and Tetuanui, lived to return home about a year later, having gained 'a moderate insight into Spanish' and 'other kindred matters', as the viceroy himself put it.[23] The Tahitians also enabled the Spaniards, particularly a young marine called Maximo Rodriguez, to gain a good knowledge of their language, for during their stay Rodriguez and others drew up a Tahitian vocabulary of some 1,500 words. This vocabulary, easily the most extensive Polynesian word list compiled up to that time, contains one word of especial interest in the quest for clues to the fate of the *San Lesmes*' crew. This word is *purepure,* which is defined in the list as 'blue-eyed'.[24] It is virtually the same word that the Tahitians used as a nickname for the English poet Rupert Brooke, whose blue eyes, fair hair and light skin made him a conspicuous figure when he visited Tahiti in 1913.[25] Brooke was called 'Pupure', meaning 'fair'—the word *purepure* in Tahitian having come to mean 'spotted', 'chequered' or 'of diverse colours.'[26] However, in Tuamotuan, *purepure* still means much the same as it did in the Tahitian of 200 years ago. In that dialect, it is an adjective meaning 'blond' while *pupure* is 'a blond person.'[27]

10

A problem for the learned

After Cook returned to England in July 1771 from his first voyage round the world, he put forward a plan to settle the long-discussed question of the southern continent. This was to approach the Pacific by way of the Cape of Good Hope; to pass through the strait between New Zealand's North and South Islands; and then to run in a high latitude towards Cape Horn. If no continent was found, Cook suggested that the exploration of the Pacific could be completed by hauling to the north to search for islands that Tupaia had said existed there.[1]

The Admiralty soon approved Cook's plan, and, having promoted him to the rank of captain, appointed him to command a new expedition. This time there were two ships, HMS *Resolution* and HMS *Adventure,* with a total complement of nearly 200 men. Cook's second-in-command was Captain Tobias Furneaux, the second officer on Wallis' voyage. Other officers included Lieutenant Richard Pickersgill, a veteran of the voyages of both the *Endeavour* and *Dolphin;* and Lieutenant Charles Clerke, who had been in the *Endeavour*. In addition, there were several civilians—two astronomers, William Wales and William Bayley; an artist William Hodges; and two naturalists, Johann Reinhold Forster and his gifted 18-year-old son George. J. R. Forster was a difficult, but erudite man of Scottish-Prussian descent, who had translated Bougainville's voyage into English.[2] This work had given him an opportunity to familiarise himself with the Tahitian language, as Bougainville had obtained a list of several hundred Tahitian words from Ahutoru, the islander whom he took to Paris.

The *Resolution* and *Adventure* sailed from Plymouth on 13 July 1772 and reached Cape Town three and a half months later. After making a deep sweep into the hitherto unexplored Antarctic, they headed for New Zealand. In June 1773, they set off to explore 'the unknown parts of the sea to the East and North.' For about five weeks they sailed east between latitudes 41° and 46° S. Then they turned north and crossed Captain Carteret's track in the vicinity of Pitcairn Island. Having seen no signs of land in two months of sailing Cook was virtually convinced that the southern continent did not exist. But as this was 'too important a point to be left to conjector,' he turned west to investigate 'some of the remaining parts of this Sea.' Within a week, the expedition was among the atolls of the Tuamotu Archipelago, where Tauere, Tekokoto, Marutea, Motutunga and Anaa were sighted one after another. Normally, Cook would undoubtedly have made a close examination of these atolls. But because several of the *Adventure's* crew were down with scurvy, he pushed on to Tahiti with all speed. On 17 August, the expedition anchored at Vaitepiha Bay on the eastern side of the Taiarapu Peninsula.[3] They stayed there for seven days trading with the islanders. However, none of the islanders would sell any pigs, claiming that all belonged to Vehiatua, the chief of the district, who was then absent.*[4]

No doubt because Cook had been to Tahiti previously, he did not show the same interest in the island's ethnology as he did on his first visit. However, to the two Forsters, everything was excitingly new, and it is to their writings that one must turn for the most detailed ethnographical accounts of Cook's second sojourn in Tahiti. The elder Forster was quick to notice that the Tahitians were a 'well-limbed people.' But there was a marked difference between the chiefs who were 'very tall and athletic' and the common people who were 'seldom tall.' The women, Forster wrote, 'are all small & slender limbed.'[5]

George Forster noted that the first islanders to come out to the *Resolution* 'expressed several marks of affection and admired the whiteness of the Englishmen's bodies.'[6] He was particularly struck by a man called O-Tai, who came on board with his wife and two sisters. He was about six feet tall and was 'remarkabl[y] fairer' than any of the islanders young Forster had previously seen, being like a West Indian mestizo in colour. 'His features were really handsome and regular,' Forster wrote, 'he had a high forehead, arched eyebrows, large black eyes, sparkling with expression, and a well-proportioned nose; there was something remarkably sweet and engaging about his mouth; the lips were prominent, but not disagreeably large; and his beard was black and finely frizzled; his hair was of a jetty colour, and fell in strong curls down his neck.' O-Tai's sisters were 'still fairer' than he was, but nine or ten inches shorter; and one, in particular, was a 'graceful figure, with the most delicate and beautiful contours.'[7]

During the week that Cook spent at Vaitepiha Bay, the Forsters went ashore almost every day in search of natural history specimens, which gave them a chance to see a good number of Tahitians. Meanwhile, Cook became impatient at the absence of Vehiatua and his inability to buy pigs, and after five days he decided to move round to his old anchorage at Matavai Bay. However, at this juncture, Vehiatua arrived in the district, and when some of Cook's crew happened to meet him on shore, he assured them he would like to see Cook and that he had plenty of pigs for him. The same men also reported seeing a man who resembled a European both in colour and features, but on speaking to him he disappeared into a crowd, and he was not seen again.[8]

News of Vehiatua's arrival caused Cook to postpone his departure, and he went ashore to meet him accompanied by the Forsters and several officers. They found him sitting on a large stool cut out of solid wood. This was big enough for two people to sit on, for as soon as Vehiatua saw Cook and recollected him from his previous visit, he moved over to make room for him. The younger Forster described him as a sturdy youth of between seventeen and eighteen years of age, about five feet six inches tall, and likely to grow

* Since Boenechea's visit, Vehiatua had taken over as chief from his 'fair and ruddy' step-father, Ti'i-torea, who had acted for him during his minority.

taller. 'His colour was of the fairest of his people,' he wrote, 'and his lank hair [was] light brown, turning into reddish at the tips or being what is commonly called sandy.' On both sides of Vehiatua were several chiefs, who were 'distinguishable by their superior stature.' One of these, Ti'i-torea, was tattooed in a 'surprising manner', having 'large black blotches of various shapes, almost covering his arms, legs and sides.'[9] Ti'i-torea asked the Forsters whether they had a god in their country and whether they prayed to him.

> When we told him [George wrote] that we acknowledged a Divinity, who made everything and was invisible, and that we also were accustomed to address our petitions to him, he seemed to be highly pleased, and repeated our words with notes of his own to several persons who sat around him. To us he seemed to signify that the ideas of his countrymen corresponded with ours in this respect. . . .[10]

Although Vehiatua was eager for Cook to stay in his district, Cook had made up his mind to go, and his two ships put to sea next morning. However, Lieutenant Pickersgill was left behind with the *Resolution's* cutter to buy pigs, and after a certain amount of trouble he obtained eight. In so doing, he, too, had an opportunity to see Vehiatua, whom he described in his journal in similar terms to the younger Forster. He was, he wrote 'a tall likely young man about 18 years of age, with fine flaxen hair, his features regular and his complexion a Dark Olive.'[11]

The *Resolution* and *Adventure* anchored in Matavai Bay on 26 August. Cook immediately paid a call on Tu, and Tu later presented Cook with a pig. However, as pigs seemed to be just as scarce at Matavai as they were at Taiarapu, Cook sent Pickersgill down the coast to Punaauia to see if he could get some from Potatau, a friendly chief on his previous voyage. In recording details of this embassy in his journal, Pickersgill said he had seen a man who was 'the colour of a Flemmen' (i.e. a Fleming, or native of Flanders). He had red hair, bad teeth and grey eyes, all of which were 'differant from the Natives of these countries.' Pickersgill and his companions at first took him for a European, but on closer examination they found him to be a native. 'How or by what means a white man comes to be born amongst a set of copper colour'd Indians,' Pickersgill added, 'I leave the learned to account for.'[12]

Although Potatau eventually produced a couple of pigs and several more were obtained elsewhere, the total taken on board the two ships after seventeen days of trading was so meagre that Cook decided to try his luck at Huahine. There the Englishmen soon found that livestock was plentiful, and in three days they obtained about 300 pigs, and numerous fowls and (edible) dogs. The dogs prompted the younger Forster to write the only detailed description of the dogs of the Society Islands that has come down to us; and, curiously, considering all the other breeds he could have mentioned, he compared some of them to spaniels.

> The dogs of all these islands [he wrote] were short, and their sizes vary from that of a lap-dog to the largest spaniel. Their head is broad, the snout

pointed, the eyes very small, the ears upright, and their hair rather long, lank, hard, and of different colours, but most commonly white and brown. They seldom if ever barked, but howled sometimes, and were shy to strangers to a degree of aversion.[13]

In George Forster's eyes, the people of Huahine seemed exactly like the Tahitians, and he could not agree with the 'assertions of former navigators' that the Huahinean women were 'in general fairer and more handsome,' although he admitted that one's view of this could 'vary according to circumstances.' On the other hand, he did find the Huahineans less troublesome in begging for beads and other presents, and less forward in bestowing their favours on new-comers.[14] Forster's father, for his part, took especial interest in a Huahinean war canoe that was then in the course of construction. It consisted of two hulls, each built 'sharp towards the keel,' with 'a belly upperwards & a Gunnel set upon that.' The hulls measured $87\frac{1}{2}$ feet from stem to stern, the stern being $15\frac{1}{2}$ feet above the keel. 'The parts of the Canoes,' the elder Forster wrote, 'are joined together by ropes of Coco-Nut Strings, & some of them Strings looking like Oakum, were laid between the planks & in the holes, which were not filled by the lashing. . . .'[15]

After three days at Huahine, Cook sailed for neighbouring Raiatea 'to procure an addition of Fruit to our present stock.' As the *Resolution* warped into Haamanino Harbour on the north-western side of that island, two chiefs from Bora Bora came on board. One, 'Oruwherra', was extensively tattooed, having large square blotches on his arms; black bands on his chest, belly and back; and blackened buttocks. The other, Herea, was described by J. R. Forster as 'the stoutest and most corpulent man I have ever seen,' his waist measuring 54 inches and his thighs, $31\frac{3}{4}$. 'All these people who are Chiefs,' Forster went on, 'are tall, well made, commonly fatt & lusty & less coloured than the common people. All have very smooth & soft skin, which would hardly be expected in people that constantly go exposed to the Sun.'[16]

Soon after the *Resolution* and *Adventure* were safely anchored, Cook, Furneaux and the Forsters went ashore to visit the local chief, Oreo. Cook, who seldom concerned himself with personal appearances, did not describe him; nor did the elder Forster. But George Forster noted that he was 'a middle-sized lusty man, with a very lively intelligent countenance, and a thin red[d]ish brown beard.'[17] He had a fourteen-year-old daughter, Poetua, who was an especially striking figure. To George Forster, her skin was 'of a very white colour,' while her other features had 'not much of the general character of the nation.' Her nose and eyes were 'remarkably well shaped', her body elegantly proportioned, and her hands 'graceful beyond description.' Forster thought her eyes gave her 'some resemblance to a Chinese,'[18] but this view was not universally held. Pickersgill, who saw her later and called her Miss Poedoua, thought she had 'good teeth and Eyes and a regular set of features.' Her hair was black, but her complexion extremely fair. 'I have seen many Ladies in England much more of a Brunett,' Pickersgill wrote.[19]

On the day after Cook's first meeting with Oreo and his family, the chief invited his visitors to what Cook called 'a Comedy or Dramatick Heava.' The actors were seven men and two young women—Poetua and another 'tall well shaped lady, of very agreeable features, and likewise a very fair complexion.'[20] The women's dress, George Forster recorded, was very different from the usual fashion in the islands. It consisted of a piece of cloth 'closely wrapped round the breast so as to resemble the close dresses which our ladies wear,' and a kind of ruff of four rows of cloth, alternately red and white, which was tied on to their hips with a great quantity of white cloth and descended to their feet, forming ample petticoats.'[21] Music was provided by three drums; and several boys sang. The performance consisted of dancing and dramatic interludes. Cook thought the only entertaining part of the performance was a theft committed in one of the interludes by a man and his accomplice, 'which sufficiently desplayed the Genius of the people in this art.'[22] Wales, the astronomer, was considerably more impressed. To him, the performance demonstrated that drama in the islands had advanced 'very far beyond the Age of Thespis,' and he was not certain that he 'ever saw Mr. Garrick perform with more propriety than one Man did most of his parts.'[23] The younger Forster was particularly impressed by the graceful arm movements and continual gesticulation of the fingers in the women's dancing. But like Wales, he was offended by their 'frightful custom of writhing their mouths into the strangest distortions.' He added that after the dancing, the women sat 'in a most profuse perspiration'—Poetua's companion having a 'suffusion of red in her cheeks, which was the strongest proof of her fair complexion.'[24]

A day or two after the *heiva,* Cook sent a trading party to Raiatea's sister island, Tahaa, which is enclosed by the same barrier reef. The elder Forster accompanied them. Besides obtaining a good supply of plantains, Forster noticed a couple of strikingly anomalous people like the one who had so puzzled Pickersgill in Tahiti. One was a man with 'perfectly red hair' and a 'fairer complexion than the rest,' who was 'sprinkled all over with freckles.' The other was 'a very fine woman both in face & shape,' whose hair was 'all of a yellowish-brown & in ringlets, quite in the Van Dycks taste.'[25] Meanwhile, those who had stayed at Raiatea were entertained at further dramatic performances, at one of which, in George Forster's view, were several of the prettiest women in the country. 'One of them,' George wrote, 'was remarkable for the whitest complexion we had ever seen in all these islands. Her colour resembled that of white wax a little sullied, without having the least appearance of sickness, which that hue commonly conveys; and her fine black eyes and hair contrasted so well with it that she was admired by us all.'[26]

On the morning after the trading party returned from Tahaa, Cook resumed his voyage westwards. He took with him a seventeen-year-old Raiatean called Hitihiti—'a very handsome youth', George Forster thought—'who appeared to be of the better sort of people by his complexion and good garments.'[27] In the next few weeks Cook discovered two small, uninhabited islands, which he called the Hervey Islands; and he spent a week or so at the Tongan islands of Eua and Tongatapu. On 22 October 1773, his two ships reached New Zealand, only to be separated in a few days by a storm. Furneaux, in the *Adventure,* subsequently decided to return home by way of Cape Horn. But Cook prepared for further exploratory work, and on 26 November, he again set sail for the Antarctic. During the next five months he penetrated to a record southern latitude of 71° I0'; made a fruitless search in 38° S. latitude for land reputed to have been discovered by Juan Fernandez; spent five days at Easter Island; and paid the first visit to the Marquesas Group since Mendaña was there in 1595. On 13 April 1774, Cook again steered for Tahiti, and five days later, he reached Takaroa, an atoll in the north-western corner of the Tuamotu Archipelago, which Byron had briefly visited in 1765.[28]

As Cook had not previously tarried at an atoll, he sent two boats ashore 'with a view of having some intercourse with [the islanders], to get some refreshments and to give Mr. Forster an oppertunity to collect some Plants.'[29] The elder Forster was accompanied by Hitihiti and his son George. The boat parties landed without opposition among fifty or sixty well-built islanders. George Forster described them as 'of a dark brown,' and his father as 'very tawny.'[30] Their chests, abdomens and hands were tattooed—in 'imitation of fishes,' George said—and their features were 'not disagreeable.' Indeed, they were 'more mild than those of all the high islands about them.' Apart from a very small piece of cloth about their loins, they were naked; and the few of their women who were seen at a distance wore only a slightly larger piece of cloth. 'The hair and beards [of the men],' George added, 'were generally black and curling, but sometimes cut; however I took notice of a single man, whose hair was quite yellowish at the points.'

The islanders greeted their visitors by touching noses 'after the custom of New Zealand,' and brought coconuts and dogs for sale to the boats. Hitihiti bought five dogs in exchange for nails and some ripe bananas he had brought from the Marquesas. The dogs, according to the younger Forster, were 'not unlike those at the Society Islands, but had fine long hair of a white colour.' Hitihiti was therefore eager to purchase them, because that very sort of hair was 'made use of in his country to adorn the breast-plates of the warriors.' The Forsters walked along the island for some distance, picking plants. The islanders explained their names. Hitihiti was able to act as interpreter because their language was similar to Tahitian except that the pronunciation was 'more coarse and gutteral.' In passing through the village, the younger Forster noted that the islanders' huts were small and low, and that their only occupants at the time were dogs. Nearby were some boat houses containing some short, stout canoes, pointed at both ends and with a sharp keel. However, the Forsters had no time to make a minute examination of anything, for presently some islanders appeared with long spears and clubs in their hands, and it was thought prudent to return to the boats.

Although the Forsters spent only half an hour on Takaroa, the younger man subsequently filled several pages of his *A Voyage Round the World* with information on the Tuamotus and their inhabitants. Some of this was apparently obtained from Hitihiti, as Forster could not have learned of all he wrote from his own observation. He said, among other things, that the Tuamotuan dogs [unlike their vegetarian counterparts in the Society Islands] lived on fish, and they were reckoned 'excellent meat' by the people of the Society Islands to whom they were known.[31]

On leaving Takaroa, Cook steered south-west by south. In the next twenty-four hours, he discovered four atolls—Apataki, Toau, Kaukura and Arutua—which he called Palliser's Isles after the Comptroller of the Navy. No attempt was made to land on them. A day or so later, the *Resolution* again reached Tahiti and anchored in Matavai Bay.

At first, Cook intended to stay in Tahiti only a few days to enable Wales to check his astronomical instruments. But finding that hogs and other supplies were again plentiful, he extended his sojourn to three weeks. During this time, long white dogs' hair from the Tuamotus must have been much in evidence, for drawn up at Pare, near the *Resolution's* anchorage, was a magnificent fleet of more than 300 war canoes, whose chiefs were dressed in 'a vast quantity of Cloth Turbands, breast Plates and Helmmets.' The canoes themselves were decorated with flags, streamers, etc. so that the whole fleet, in Cook's view, 'made a grand and Noble appearance such as was never seen before in this Sea.'[32] Both the *vaa* and *pahi* were represented in the fleet, for George Forster observed that some canoes had 'flat bottoms and sides nearly perpendicular upon them,' while others were 'bow-sided with a sharp keel.'[33] This statement suggests that many of the canoes had come from Raiatea and were manned by Raiateans, for both Cook and Banks in 1769 and Hervé in 1772 had all stated that the *pahi* were peculiar to that island. This fact, however, now escaped Cook's recollection and he proceeded to estimate Tahiti's population on the basis of what he saw before him. By adding up the men needed to man each canoe, as well as about 170 smaller ones that seemed designed as transports or victuallers, Cook arrived at a figure of not less than 204,000.[34] George Forster, for his part, thought 120,000 was a reasonable figure—'at a most moderate computation.'[35] The fleet had been assembled to attack a usurping chief on Moorea, Tahiti's sister island, and Cook was eager to see it in action. However, the chiefs made it clear that the fighting would not begin until after the *Resolution* had gone, so he and his companions were deprived of a sight that seemed 'well worth seeing.'

On the other hand, the Tahitians had a chance to see a gruesomely fascinating sight in the *Resolution*. This was the head of a murdered Maori youth that Pickersgill had bought in New Zealand and had preserved in spirits. News of the grisly relic was spread among the Tahitians by Hitihiti, whose stories of New Zealand, the Antarctic and elsewhere always attracted eager listeners, although his account of cannibalism among the New Zealand Maoris 'filled them with horror.' George Forster, who was present when several Tahitians came on board to see the Maori head, noted that they unanimously called it *'te Tae-ai'*, which seemed to be the equivalent of 'man eater.' He later asked about 'this extraordinary circumstance' among the chiefs and others and found that, according to tradition, Tahiti had also had cannibals at some 'indefinite but very remote period of time.' The cannibals were said to have been 'a very strong robust people' who had 'made great havock among the inhabitants,' but had 'long since been entirely extinct.' Forster added:

> The influence of this fact upon the ancient history of Taheitee is very striking; but shall we conclude that a set of canibals [*sic*] have by some accident made a descent upon the island, and committed depredations upon the indigenous people, or is it not rather evident, that the original state of the whole nation is concealed in this tradition, and that all the Taheitians were anthropophagai, before they arrived at that state of civilization, which the excellence of the country and climate, and the profusion of vegetables and animal food, has introduced?[36]

Among other observations that George Forster made at this time was one in which he contradicted Bougainville's assertion that the people of Tahiti were of two distinct races. However, he immediately tempered this view by stating that the chiefs were 'so much superior in stature and elegance of form' to the common people that they looked like people of a different race.[37] Forster also revealed—albeit unconsciously—that the 'mixing' of unlike genes had produced a striking contrast in the skin colour of the seven children of Hapai'i, father of the high chief Tu.[38] 'A healthy, but not corpulent habit of body, and a large bushy head of hair, were extremely characteristic of the whole family,' he wrote. 'Their features in general were pleasing, but their complexions rather brown, except that of Neehourai [the eldest daughter] and O-too [i.e. Tu].'*

When Cook left Tahiti on 14 May 1774, he sailed first to Huahine, where he spent six days, and then to Raiatea to return Hitihiti to his home island. At Raiatea, the Englishmen's sojourn lasted a fortnight. It was notable for further dramatic entertainments like those seen on the previous visit. Everyone was highly amused by a farce called 'The Child is Coming,' one detail of which led Cook to suppose that many of the islanders' noses were not naturally flat, but were artificially flattened soon after birth. The chief actor in the farce was a large, brawny man with a big, black, bushy beard, who sat on the ground with his legs straight out to play the part of a woman in labour. Another man sat behind him to act as midwife; and the bodies of both were partly covered by a white cloth that was held over them by several other actors who kneeled around them. After numerous wrigglings and twistings of the body on the part of the he-mother, 'a great lubberly fellow' crawled out from under the cloth and ran across an open place between the audience and the actors. The he-mother straddled after him, squeezing his breasts between his fingers and dabbing them across the 'baby's' lips, and occasionally, to heighten

* It is now known that Hapai'i was of Tahitian and Tuamotuan descent, and that his wife was the daughter of a Raiatean high chief—Davies 1961: Appendix I.

the relish of the entertainment, stroking them up his backside.[39] Cook, who saw this farcical interlude twice, noticed on the second occasion that as soon as they got hold of the fellow who played the part of the child, they 'f[l]atened his nose or press'd it to his face.' From this he concluded that the islanders did the same with all their children, and that this was possibly the reason why all in general had flat, 'or what we call pug noses.'[40]

The sojourn at Raiatea was a profitable one for J. R. Forster, for he discovered among other things that the chief of the district where the *Resolution* lay was a '*tata-orrero*' or divinity teacher. From this man Forster learned that the islanders counted by scores; that they had fourteen months of twenty-nine days; and that each day had a name. He learned also that each island had its own supreme god, the creator of the earth and sky; that the sea had thirteen gods; and that the sun, moon, stars, winds and earthquakes each had their separate gods. The islanders believed that man had a soul which could think, speak, smell, taste, feel, see and hear and that this retired after death to the wooden images set over their burial grounds. 'I likewise learned the Names of the 4 Cardinal & the 4 intermediate points of the Compass,' Forster added.[41]

On the *Resolution's* departure from Raiatea, Cook steered west with the object of visiting the islands in the New Hebrides that Quiros had discovered 168 years earlier. This project resulted in the discovery en route of three islands—Palmerston, Niue and Vatoa—and subsequently of New Caledonia and Norfolk Island. Cook then returned to New Zealand for refreshments and headed home via Cape Horn and Cape Town. He anchored at Spithead on 29 July 1775 after an absence from England of three years and eighteen days.[42]

Among the numerous trophies that the expedition brought home was a large collection of paintings and drawings done on the voyage by the artist William Hodges. Hodges was primarily a landscape artist, but he tried his hand at other types of work, including portraiture, and it is from his efforts that we can now get a visual idea of what the Pacific Islands and their people looked like in his day. A comparison of Hodges' portraits of Tahitians and Society Islanders with written descriptions of the same subjects where they exist makes it clear that Hodges was a realist who drew what he saw. His portrait of Tu, for example, confirms Gayangos' statement of 1772 that his nose was aquiline, as well as George Forster's that he had a bushy head of hair. His portrait of Hitihiti, on the other hand, leaves no doubt that that youth's nose was very flat; while those he did of the Melanesian New Hebrideans and New Caledonians closely resemble the people of those territories of today. If, therefore, some of his portraits of Eastern Polynesians seem to have more of the Caucasian in them than anything else, the explanation surely is that his subjects must have looked Caucasian, and not that Hodges wanted them that way.[43]

11

The cross of Anaa and other oddities

FOUR months after Cook's second departure from Tahiti in the *Resolution* and *Adventure,* the Spanish government sent a second expedition to that island. It had a threefold purpose: to foster friendly relations with the Tahitians, to explore the island more thoroughly, and to set up some mark or inscription in token of its discovery and possession by emissaries of Spain. This time there were two ships—the *Aguila,* which had undergone extensive repairs, and a small storeship, the *Jupiter.* Many officers and men from the previous expedition embarked again. The *Aguila* was again commanded by Boenechea. Tomas Gayangos sailed as his first lieutenant, and Raimundo Bonacorsi was again a junior officer. The commander of the *Jupiter,* on the other hand, was a newcomer—José de Andía y Varela, a merchant skipper. Other members of the expedition included two Franciscan friars, who were to be left on Tahiti as missionaries; the Tahitians, Pautu and Tetuanui; and Maximo Rodríguez, the marine, who had helped to compile the Tahitian vocabulary in the viceroy's palace.[1]

The *Aguila* and *Jupiter* left Callao in company on 20 September 1774. But fifteen days out they became separated, the *Jupiter* being unable to keep up with her swifter, larger consort. This, however, was not a serious matter as the captains had agreed to meet at Anaa—Boenechea's Todos los Santos—in the event of such an occurrence. Meanwhile, the two ships kept on approximately the same course, their first landfall being Tatakoto, an isolated, hitherto-unknown atoll about 150 miles NE by E of Amanu. The crew of the *Aguila* saw that it was well covered with trees, including coconuts and plantains. Its inhabitants were naked and seemed to be very swarthy and above medium height.[2]

Beyond Tatakoto, the *Aguila* sailed almost due west, sighting Tauere and Haraiki before reaching Anaa forty-four days out from Callao. At Anaa, Gayangos was sent ashore to seek an anchorage. This resulted in a curious discovery which has been described as 'one of the many mysteries of the Pacific'.[3] After getting within a boat's length of the reef, Gayangos was confronted by 100 to 150 islanders, 'droning a sort of chant as if a prayer.' Although they were armed with slings and stones, they made signs to the Spaniards to land. The surf was too high for the Spaniards to do this; but Pautu, the Tahitian, jumped into the water to tell the Anaans who their visitors were. However, he had scarcely done so when the islanders let fly with a volley of stones. This caused the Spaniards to retreat out of range and to continue their search for an anchorage further along the coast. Nevertheless,

PLATE 7. William Hodges, the artist on Cook's second voyage, did these portraits of islanders during visits to Tahiti and Raiatea in 1773 and 1774. Above are two Tahitians, Tu, later Pomare I (left), high chief of Te Porionuu, and Potatau, chief of Atehuru. Below are Tainamai (left), daughter of the Raiatean chief Oreo and sister of Poetua; and Hitihiti, a Raiatean, who accompanied Cook on an extensive cruise of the Pacific. The portrait of Potatau is a steel engraving from an account of Cook's second voyage; all the others are original crayon sketches in the National Library of Australia, Canberra.

PLATE 8. William Hodges' painting (as engraved above) of war canoes at Pare, Tahiti, in 1774 gives no hint of European influences. However, as George Forster recorded that some of the vessels were 'bow-sided with a sharp keel', it may be that Hodges concentrated on the more fantastic features of the fleet. Certainly, John Webber's sketch of a Raiatean 'pahi' (below) suggests that some of the war canoes may have been more European-looking than Hodges represented them. Yet there is no doubt that some Tahitian canoes had a very strange appearance. Bougainville's companion, Philibert de Commerson, was probably referring to the single-hull outrigger (at left) when he wrote that the Tahitian canoes corresponded to 'no known model'. The top two pictures are reproduced from the narratives of Cook and Bougainville; the other is in the British Museum.

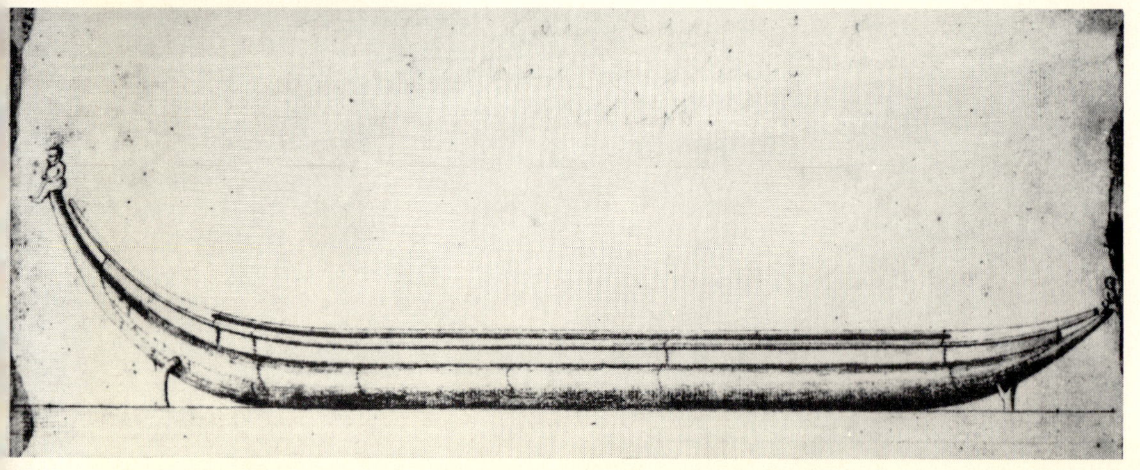

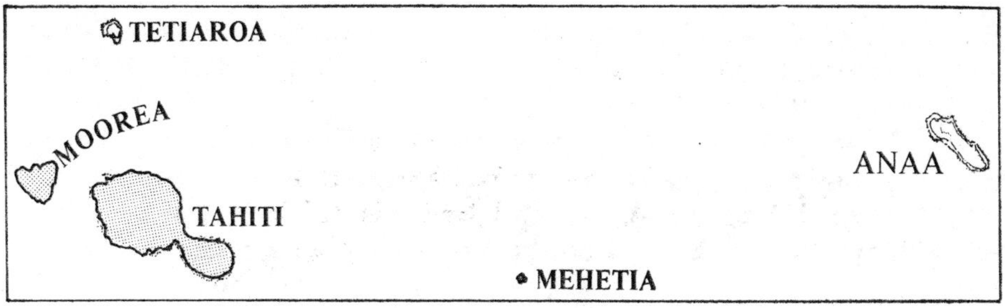

the islanders still followed them—until a gap in the reef prevented their further progress and they turned back. 'Just then,' Gayangos wrote afterwards, 'we caught sight of a wooden cross, standing on a sandy beach on the inner side of the reef near the skirt of a wood. It was of moderate size, regular in all its proportions, and showed signs of having been erected a long time ago.'[4]

Seeing that the islanders were now too far off to do any harm with their slings, Gayangos put back a little and ordered a seaman to jump ashore and leave a couple of knives on the beach. When the islanders saw this, they emerged from the wood near the cross and ran towards him, gesturing angrily. However, when they found what his offerings were, they dropped their slings and gathered near the boat, making signs of peace. The Spaniards threw them more knives and some biscuits, and the islanders offered them coconuts, a pearl-shell necklace, a bow and some strips of matting in exchange. Several of them sprang into the water and swam out to the boat. They tried to talk to the Spaniards through their Tahitian interpreter. But Pautu could not understand them very well, although he said they knew he was a Tahitian by the tattooing on his arms and legs.[5]

Eventually, Gayangos returned to the *Aguila* without having found an anchorage, and for the next six days the frigate stood off and on the island in expectation of the *Jupiter*. The Spaniards had no further contact with the islanders and no further opportunities to examine their cross. On the sixth day, a heavy storm drove the frigate many miles NNE to within sight of Tahanea and Motutunga Atolls. After the crew worked her back to Anaa, she remained for another day or two before Boenechea decided to press on to Tahiti. En route the Spaniards stopped briefly at Mehetia. Several canoe loads of islanders came out to the ship, and on recognising Pautu, they clambered on board. The Spaniards understood from them that they knew of Anaa and that their name for it was Tapuhoe. They said it was inhabited by 'a very fierce people' who did not maintain intercourse with any neighbouring islands.[6]

A day after leaving Mehetia, the *Aguila* reached Tahiti. The *Jupiter* was seen off Taiarapu shortly afterwards. That ship, it turned out, had taken a slightly more southerly course than the *Aguila* after passing Tatakoto, and had come in sight of Amanu more or less opposite the spot where François Hervé found the four iron cannon in 1929. Captain Andía y Varela felt sure that the island had not previously been seen by Europeans, and named it Isla de las Animas (Island of Souls) because it was 'the eve of the day sacred to the memory of the departed.' He reconnoitred the island's north-western coast, where the coconut palms reared up to a great height and the beaches were dazzlingly white. Columns of smoke indicated the presence of inhabitants, but no people were seen. Andía was eager to make a landing and explore the island thoroughly. But as he had 'no instructions to prosecute discoveries,' he reluctantly proceeded on his way. All the land was strikingly low—so nearly flush with the sea that it could not be seen more than a league and a half away.[7]

A day after leaving Amanu, the *Jupiter* sighted Tauere, where the islanders lit bonfires and appeared on the beach with long, stout spears. They seemed deep tawny in colour, well-proportioned and lithe, with a tuft of some kind on their heads. Except for one man who wore a white wrap, they were all naked.[8] The *Jupiter* subsequently passed Tekokoto and Haraiki, and reached Anaa the day after the *Aguila* had first arrived there. Although the *Aguila* was somewhere in the offing, the *Jupiter's* crew failed to see her, and her commander decided to sail on to Tahiti. He had been at Taiarapu for almost a week when the *Aguila* finally put in an appearance.

Reunited, Boenechea and Andía spent twelve days investigating various harbours before deciding to anchor at Tautira, otherwise known as Vaitepiha Bay, a few miles from the *Aguila's* former anchorage. As soon as the anchors were down, two important chiefs went out to the *Aguila*. One was Tu, whose home was at Matavai at the opposite end of the island. The other was Vehiatua, chief of Taiarapu. Boenechea and the two chiefs exchanged gifts, and the Spanish commander obtained their approval to leave the two Franciscan friars on shore as missionaries, with Rodriguez as their interpreter. The chiefs also agreed to grant them a plot of land for the erection of a house.

For the next month, the *Aguila's* carpenters were busy putting the house up, while other members of the crew felled timber to fence a garden for the missionaries. Among the events recorded by the expedition's diarists during that time was one recounted by the priests under date of 15 December 1774. On that day, a canoe went out to the *Aguila* containing two men, a boy of ten, and a woman nursing a baby of about fifteen months. The baby's appearance immediately attracted attention. Indeed, Gayangos was so interested that he climbed down to the canoe and took the child in his arms, subsequently passing it from person to person. The priests described it as 'very pretty.' Its skin was 'very fair in hue' and its hair red. As soon as the Spanish seamen saw it, they exclaimed: '*Hey aqui un inglesito*' ('Here is a little Englishman'), being under the impression that the child was the offspring of some English sailor who had previously visited the island. The priests, themselves, were also inclined to that opinion.[9] However, had they known the dates of Captain Cook's various visits, they would have realised that they were in error in this, for any Anglo-Polynesian children conceived during his sojourns must then have been nearly five years old, no more than seven months, or still unborn.[10]

Around the time of the red-headed baby incident, some cattle, pigs, sheep and goats were landed from the *Jupiter* for the priests' use. A couple of weeks later, their dwelling was ready for occupation; and as soon as they were installed in it, the *Aguila* and *Jupiter* sailed to Raiatea for a brief visit. On their return, Boenechea died from a sudden illness and was buried on shore. Next day, 28 January 1775, the expedition set out for Peru, leaving the two priests on Tahiti, with Rodriguez and a seaman to act as cook. Two islanders—a pilot called Puhoro from Makatea and a Raiatean chief, Mabarua—were embarked in the *Aguila,* and two others were taken in the *Jupiter*.

To pick up a favourable wind, the expedition (now under the command of Gayangos) sailed SE, then SSW. After a week, the two ships discovered an island of 'more than middling height' which Gayangos named Santa Rosa. It was, in fact, Raivavae, one of the four well-separated Austral Islands that lie some 300 miles to the southward of Tahiti. A boat under Sub-lieutenant Bonacorsi, with Puhoro and Mabarua on board, was sent off to investigate. They found an anchorage in a small bay where 400 or 500 islanders were 'shouting and hullaballooing.' An islander presently swam out, clambered on board, and began capering and shouting wildly. Other islanders followed him, so that the Spaniards were hard pressed to prevent their stealing the many strange objects that met their eyes. Through all this, Puhoro and Mabarua managed to talk to an old man of somewhat quieter demeanour than the rest, and to learn from him that the island's name was 'Oraibabae'; that the islanders had never seen a ship before; and that they knew of no other lands nearby. However, the Polynesian interpreters could understand only a few words of the old man's language, and as the islanders became increasingly troublesome, Bonacorsi decided to return to the *Aguila*.

Writing of the Raivavaeans in his journal,[11] Bonacorsi said: 'The people are like those of Otahiti: some white, many mulatto-coloured, and the rest somewhat more swarthy. They are not pigmented [i.e. tattooed] in any part of their bodies, which are tall and well made. They have holes [pierced] in their ears, and wear the hair fastened in a tuft on the head. Their clothing consists of wraps like those of the Otahitians. . . .' Bonacorsi added that the islanders' canoes were twin-hulled, with bows and sterns that sheered up high. They were made of a wood that looked somewhat like mahogany and were painted along the gunwales. For weapons they had 'nicely made' pikes and cudgels.*

After Bonacorsi's boat returned from its reconnaissance, the *Aguila* and *Jupiter* resumed their voyage to Peru. Some eighteen days later, the two ships became separated in a thick mist and they did not meet again until reaching

* Bonacorsi's description of the Raivavaeans is quoted from the journal of Andía y Varela, who said he made a word for word copy of it from Bonacorsi's own journal. However, a report from Bonacorsi, which Gayangos said he received from that officer, and which he incorporated in *his* journal, contains several slight differences and some additional material. In that report, the Raivavaeans are described as 'somewhat fairer skinned' than the Tahitians, some being 'like Europeans in hue.' They had long beards and 'large perforations' in their ears. A spear bartered from them looked as if it had been turned in a lathe. Their canoes were 'better-constructed' than those in Tahiti, and they were ornamented with parti-coloured fringes which hung from the gunwales.—Corney II:176-9.

Callao about ten weeks out from Tahiti. During their long voyages, both Gayangos and Andía had leisure to interrogate the islanders on board their ships and to prepare their journals for submission to the viceroy.

Gayangos included in his journal a list of forty-three islands known to the 'most trustworthy Indians of eminence in Tahiti' and 'checked by others of similar degree'. Fifteen of the islands were described as lying to the eastward of Tahiti, and Puhoro was said to have cruised among them several times for pearls.[12] All fifteen islands are identifiable as atolls of the Tuamotu Archipelago, although one of them, Anaa, was included twice—as Oanà and Tapuhoe.[13] According to the list, the most distant atoll known to the Tahitians was Fangatau, which lies 500 miles NE by E of Tahiti and about 120 miles due north of Amanu. Gayangos listed it under its old name, Maropua.[14] To the Tahitians, Maropua was a small, low island inhabited by 'bad' people, and with coconuts, yams, dogs and fish in plenty. Two days were needed to reach it from Maemo (i.e. Makemo), an island that also had plenty of dogs. Five of the other eastern islands in Gayangos' list were also noted for their dogs, these being Kaukura, Anaa, Rangiroa, Tikehau and Matahiva. The dogs of Kaukura were specifically stated to have had 'good coats', while those of Anaa and Rangiroa were plentiful. On the other hand, none of the Tuamotuan islands was said to have pigs or fowls, although these were usually described as being products of the islands to the immediate west of Tahiti.[15]

Except for its information about the islands known to the Tahitians, Gayangos' journal contains little other information of ethnological value. That of Andía, on the other hand, is a mine of ethnographic detail, which shows its author to have been an unusually curious and observant member of his profession. Beginning with an account of Tahiti's physical features, Andía went on to describe the physical and personal characteristics of the islanders, their traditions about their own origin, their religion, funeral ceremonies, marriage customs, system of government, warfare, archery competitions, clothing, dwellings, furniture, diet, cookery, fishing methods, canoes, seamanship, methods of navigation, dances and many other such things. Much of what he wrote had already been described by earlier European visitors; but much of it was new. Some of it is of special value in that Andía was the only important chronicler of early Tahiti whose observations were confined to Taiarapu.

Writing of the Tahitians' physical appearance, Andía reiterated what various predecessors had said, but was somewhat more explicit:

> There is much variety in their hue [he said] and in their hair. Some have the appearance of zambos, others of [full-blooded] Indians, others mulattos, others quadroons, and others still are even fairer.* The same

* 'Zambo', 'quadroon' and 'mulatto' are all words of Spanish origin that found their way into English from Spain's American colonies. Another such word is 'mestizo' (mixed blood). A zambo (sometimes spelled 'sambo') is a person of mixed Negro and Indian, or European blood. A quadroon (*cuateron* in Spanish) is the offspring of a European and a mestizo. A mulatto is the offspring of a European and Negro. See the OED for variant meanings.

[variety] obtains in regard to their hair; for in some it is quite curly, in others less so, and in most it is smooth. There are a few very fair-skinned ones with blue eyes. They possess good features, for the most part, and would look still better were it not general amongst them all to be snub-nosed. . . .

The women are few in number, as compared with the men; but they are for the most part tall, with handsome figures, and as regards beauty need not envy those of other countries. They are very endearing, and possess great charm; and although there are some dissolute hussies amongst them, as in every place, those who do not belong to that class evince modesty in their habiliments, their mien, and their behaviour.[16]

Andía said that the Tahitians varied in their statements about the original inhabitants of their island. But all agreed that the first settlers were castaways who had been travelling in a canoe from Raiatea to one of its neighbours when a strong westerly wind arose, forcing them to scud before it until they sighted Tahiti and gained one of its harbours. In one story the castaways were said to have found the island very fruitful and abounding in all things necessary for human life. They therefore decided to stay 'since it afforded a wider domain and greater wealth than they possessed in their own country.' In another story, the castaways' canoe was said to have been wrecked on reaching Tahiti, leaving the survivors without means of returning home. Subsequently, two Raiatean men were miraculously flown from Raiatea on the backs of two great birds to marry the daughters of a castaway couple. 'From their nuptials,' Andía added, 'and from alliances between certain other families, who, gaining intelligence of Otahiti in course of time, went to it from Oriayatea and other islands, the teeming numbers of inhabitants who now people the place are descended.'

Andía inferred from what he learned of the Tahitians' origins that they and the other islanders to the southward and eastward were of Asiatic stock rather than from South America. He had two reasons for this opinion. One was that, at the time of the Spanish Conquest, the American Indians had 'no knowledge of vessels capable of making long voyages.' The other was that, as a rule, the American Indians were beardless, whereas 'those of Otahiti and the other islands we saw are a hirsute people, and wear their beards long, after the style of Asiatics.'[17]

In describing the Tahitians' fishing methods, Andía observed, as several of his predecessors had done, that nets made of fibre were commonly used, some of them being thirty to forty fathoms in length. The nets were fine or coarse according to the class of fish the Tahitians expected to catch in them, and the mesh or knots were 'the same as that of our fishing nets.'[18]

Andía did not name the various types of canoes in use in Tahiti during his sojourn. But it is plain from his remarks that he saw both the Tahitian *vaa* and the Raiatean *pahi,* and that he admired them both. He was obviously referring to the *pahi* when he wrote:

For long voyages they [the islanders] employ two canoes coupled together by means of cross scantling securely lashed, and leaving space enough between them for the crew of both canoe-bodies to scull in. These canoes have no outrigger, because they need none, each hull sustaining the other; and they generally set two sails, one in each canoe-body. I have seen some of these [double canoes] more than 54 ft in length, built up of several sections admirably fitted together; for, though they have no tools but those they fashion out of sundry stones, they fit, smoothen, and complete a piece of work with as workmanlike a finish as the best of our carpenters could turn out. They do not use either nails, treenails, dowels, or ties, for they secure one plank to the next by lacing them edgewise together with plait made of the fibres of the outer husk of the coco-nut. They pass this through holes bored along the margins of each plank, supplemented by some caulking of the same fibre, which they pay outside with a kind of pitch or blackish resin—not very lasting but sufficiently so to prevent water from getting in through the seams. Their canoes have nevertheless to be constantly baled, on account of the water they ship over the side.[19]

According to Andía, there were many sailing masters among the islanders who were competent to make long voyages, such as from Tahiti to Raiatea and further afield. Although they had no mariner's compass, they divided the horizon into sixteen parts, taking for the cardinal points those at which the sun rose and set. Andía described the method of using these points and other guides when sailing by day, but said it was easiest for the islanders to navigate on clear nights, for then they could steer by the stars. They noted by them the bearings of the various islands and harbours they visited, and they could make straight for a harbour entrance by following the rhumb of the particular star that rose or set over it. The planets were distinguished from the fixed stars by their movements, and were given separate names; while the stars used in sailing from one island to another were given the names of the islands in question. '. . . the same occurs with those that serve them for making the harbours in those islands,' Andía added.[20]

Soon after the *Aguila* and *Jupiter* returned to Callao, the viceroy ordered the larger ship to be fitted out for yet another voyage to Tahiti, to take stores to the Franciscan missionaries and their interpreter. This time the *Aguila* was placed under the command of Captain Cayetano de Langara, who sailed from Callao on 27 September 1775. The pilot Puhoro was among the passengers, but not his three compatriots, as they had elected to remain in Peru. The *Aguila* reached Tahiti after an uneventful voyage of five weeks.[21]

Meanwhile, the Franciscan mission to that island had proved a virtual fiasco. The two priests, Géronimo Clota and Narciso Gonzalez, were a peevish, narrow-minded, pusillanimous pair, who made no effort to learn Tahitian and seldom ventured from the mission house. The Spanish seaman who had been assigned to cook for them made things worse by being unruly and causing trouble with the Tahitians. Only the interpreter, Maximo Rodríguez, got along well. Rodríguez, or Marteemo, as the Tahitians called him affectionately, roamed freely through the island, enjoying the confidence of both chiefs and commoners, and noting in a diary details of what he did, heard and saw. The diary, being the first continuous record of Tahitian life when no foreign ships were present to disrupt normalcy, is of great value to historians and ethnologists.[22] Two remarks in it are of especial interest in the context of this book. They confirm the impression given by other writers that there was a blond element among the Taiarapu people that was more evident there than elsewhere in Tahiti.

Describing Vehiatua, the young chief of Taiarapu who died in August 1775, Rodríguez said he was 'very fair skinned though not of the blondest.'[23] He wrote similarly of a woman called Oviriau, a first cousin of Vehiatua and a person of 'extreme beauty' in his eyes. 'Her complexion was very blonde, her hair ruddy and curling, and she had blue eyes,' he said. 'She was much admired by the people of Atehuru, her district.'[24]

Rodríguez' impressions of Oviriau are among the last of their kind in his diary. A few weeks after recording them, the *Aguila* returned to Tautira and the Franciscans demanded to be taken back to Lima. 'We are left unprotected and are in imminent danger of losing our lives,' they said in a letter to Captain Langara. The frigate's commander vainly tried to persuade them to stay. Then, much of the livestock that had been left for them on the previous voyage was rounded up, and the *Aguila* set sail for Lima after a stay at Tautira of only nine days. Spain's association with Tahiti thereby came to an end, for despite several royal commands over the next few years that the Catholic mission should be resumed, these orders were never carried out.[25]

One of the last of the Spanish accounts of Tahiti of this era was a letter written by Lieutenant Don Blas de Barreda, an officer of the *Aguila* on her last voyage. Writing to a friend from Lima on 24 April 1776, Barreda described various Tahitian customs that he had noticed, including a dance in honour of the late Vehiatua. He also described the Tahitians themselves. 'There are several castes of people,' he said, 'the greater part, by their physiognomy, resemble Asiatics; but there are others like Europeans. They are tall and well-built; the chiefs, as a rule, are men of finer presence, and are much respected by the commoners.' Of the dance for Vehiatua, Barreda wrote: 'They [the mourners] wore garments interwoven with feathers of very gloomy shades, with head-dresses to match and masks of mother of pearl shell; and they held castanets of the same with which they clacked a mournful measure to the accompaniment of a drum, executing, as they danced, many gestures and weird grimaces.'[26]

An important point to be noted about the three Spanish voyages to Tahiti is that, except for the diary of Father Amich, virtually nothing was published about them in any language until an English scholar, B. G. Corney, brought out English translations of almost all known documents in 1913-19. In the main, therefore, the observations of the Spaniards were unknown to, and had no influence on, the views of any other visitors to Tahiti until after World War I.

12

The enigmatic 'Miss Poedoua'

When Captain Cook left London in June 1776 to make his last, fatal voyage to the Pacific, he had two main objectives in view. First and foremost, he was to try to discover whether a North-West Passage existed between the Pacific and Atlantic Oceans. Secondly, he was to return Omai, a Polynesian in his early twenties, to his home island of Huahine.[1]

On the previous voyage, Captain Furneaux had taken Omai aboard the *Adventure* while she and the *Resolution* lay at Huahine in September 1773; and later, after the two ships had become separated in New Zealand waters, he had carried him on to England. At the time, Cook was of the opinion that Omai was a poor specimen of his countrymen to be exhibited abroad, being 'dark, ugly and a downright blackguard.' However, during the two years he spent in England, Omai impressed everyone with his assurance and easy manner, and, as a result, he became one of the social lions of the times. He went to the opera, visited country houses, dined at banquets, had his portrait painted, attended the House of Lords, walked through the streets, and conversed with the king as if he had been used to such things all his life. Everyone made a fuss of Omai and much was written about him.[2] Daniel Solander, a companion of Cook on his first voyage, who met Omai soon after his arrival in England, shared Cook's opinion about his appearance. He also reiterated previously expressed notions that a light skin colour was a matter of considerable importance in Omai's country. In a letter to a friend, Solander said that Omai was 'not at all hansome' and 'allmost a[s] brown as a Mulatto.' He added: 'I believe we have to thank his wide Nostrills for the Visit he has paid us—for he says that the people of his own country laughed at him upon the account of his flatish Nose and dark hue, but he hopes when he returns and has so many fine things to talk of, that he shall be much respected.'[3] Omai, indeed, had more than fine things to talk of when he left England. The king and 'other gentlemen and Ladies of his acquaintance' loaded him with gifts of everything they thought would be useful or ornamental in his country. Or, as Cook, himself, put it, everything was done 'to make him convey to his Countrymen the highest opinion of the greatness and generosity of the British Nation.'[4]

Cook's expedition on this occasion consisted of two ships, *Resolution* and *Discovery,* the latter being under the command of Captain Charles Clerke. The ships entered the Pacific via the Cape of Good Hope, Van Diemen's Land (Tasmania) and New Zealand. On 30 March 1777, they made their first tropical landfall at Mangaia in what are now known as the Cook Islands, the group immediately SW of the Society Islands. Cook hove to off Mangaia for a few hours and noted that its inhabitants were 'both numerous and well fed.' In their language and actions, they seemed to come nearer to the New Zealanders than the Tahitians, their skin colour being somewhere 'between both.'[6]

At the next island, Atiu, two degrees north of Mangaia, Omai found four of his countrymen. They had drifted there about ten years earlier in a canoe that had missed its way in sailing from Tahiti to Raiatea. All but one of sixteen others who had been in the canoe had died of privation, having had neither food nor water for many days before being washed up at Atiu. Omai offered thc survivors a passage home in Cook's ships, but they were so well satisfied with their new situation that they declined. 'This circumstance,' Cook wrote, 'very well accounts for the manner the inhabited islands in this Sea have been at first peopled, especially those which lay remote from any Continent and from each other.' He added that the Atiuans were equally understood both by Omai and two New Zealanders who had joined his ships in Queen Charlotte Sound.[6] One of his officers further noted that they were like the Tahitians 'in allmost Every respect.'[7] But William Anderson, the *Resolution's* surgeon, who went ashore for several hours, was of the opinion that there were two distinct types among them. One, apparently small and dark-skinned, was the 'lower class.' The other, the chiefly class, was made up of people of a 'much whiter cast' who had 'a superior dignity in their air' and were 'commonly distinguish'd by their size & corpulency unless very young.' Some were extensively tattooed on the sides, back and legs.[8]

Two days' sail to the north-west of Atiu, the expedition came upon the two small Hervey Islands which Cook had discovered on his previous voyage. On that occasion they were apparently uninhabited. But this time a number of islanders came out to the ships who 'spoke the Otaheite language more perfect than those of either of the other two islands.' These people were very dark, and not tattooed, although they gave the Englishmen to understand that they were subject to the king of Atiu.[9]

From the Hervey Islands, Cook sailed west to the Tonga group where he spent the period from 2 May to 17 July 1777 visiting the islands of Nomuka, Lifuka, Tongatapu and Eua. He then turned eastwards again and set sail for Tahiti. En route, he discovered an island some 300 miles south of Tahiti and learned from some islanders who came out to his ships that it was called Tubuai. According to Anderson, the islanders were strong, copper-coloured people with straight black hair and roundish faces, but 'rather flat' features. They wore only the *maro,* although some were seen on shore who were 'clothed in white.' Their canoes, which were single with outriggers, were broader than usual and something like those of New Zealand, but 'incomparably better,' in the eyes of one of Cook's officers. Both their heads and sterns were raised, the sterns being ornamented with carved work.[10]

The *Resolution* and *Discovery* reached Tahiti on 12 August and anchored at Vaitepiha Bay. They stayed there for twelve days before going on to

Matavai. Cook's chief concern at both places was to get all the fresh provisions he could before sailing north in search of the North-West Passage. He was as diligent as usual in writing up his daily journal. But as he had been to Tahiti three times before, and as he thought that 'so much, or rather too much' had already been published about it, he had less to say about ethnographical matters than on previous occasions.[11] Of his officers, only John Williamson and James King, third and second lieutenants respectively in the *Resolution,* had anything to say about the Tahitians' physical appearance. Williamson described Tu, high chief of Matavai Bay and its surroundings, as 'a tall stout man, of a very dark complection,' with short 'rather frizled hair.'[12] King, for his part, made it clear that Tu was not a typical representative of the chiefly class. 'We certainly saw some Chiefs,' he wrote, 'whose fine smooth and fair skins made them much more beautiful than those at Tonga-taboo.' As for the Tahitians in general, it was King's view that they fell far short of the Tongans in shape, air, sweetness and manliness; and he thought that the beards worn particularly among the 'lower cast' gave their faces a ferocious appearance. On the other hand, the Tahitian women had more regular and beautiful features than the Tongan women, and were 'superior in womanly perfections.' Their figures had 'all the softness and effeminacy' which was 'so much want'd in Tonga.'[13]

Cook's stay in Matavai Bay lasted five weeks. He then sailed over to neighbouring Moorea, which no Europeans had previously visited apart from the boat party sent in 1769 to observe the transit of Venus. Having moored in fiord-like Papetoai Bay on the north-western side of the island, Cook remained somewhat longer than he intended because the islanders stole a ship's goat. Determined that the culprits should not go unpunished, he marched several miles inland in search of them and thus saw a good deal of the countryside at first hand. When he left Moorea for Huahine after nearly a fortnight, he wrote in his journal with some authority: 'I do not know that there is any difference between the produce of this island and Otaheite, but there is a striking difference in the Women which I can by no means accou[n]t for.' The Moorean women, he said, were short, dark and generally of forbidding features. 'If one sees a fine Woman among them, one is sure, on enquiry, to find she is of some other Island,' he added.[14] David Samwell, the *Discovery's* surgeon, was of much the same opinion. 'The girls we met with here are not half so beautiful as those we have left behind [in Tahiti],' he wrote in his journal.[15]

The *Resolution* and *Discovery* reached Huahine on 12 October and stayed there for nearly a fortnight while the ships' carpenters built a house for Omai. This gave Samwell ample opportunity to take stock of the local girls, and he did so with the same approving eye as Parkinson had done on Cook's first voyage. 'Great numbers of fine girls for which this island is famous came daily on board the ships,' he wrote.[16]

As soon as Cook had satisfied himself that Omai was comfortably settled in his new house, he sailed over to neighbouring Raiatea for a final visit. He had not yet come to an anchor at Haamanino when his old friend Oreo, the chief of the district, paid him a visit. Oreo's two daughters, Poetua and Tainamai—'so much famed for their Beauty,' as Samwell put it—went on board at the same time. Poetua, the young woman whom Pickersgill had previously called 'Miss Poedoua,' must then have been about nineteen. Her sister was somewhat older. The ship's officers studied them with interest. 'We all allowed they were as fine Women as we had ever seen,' Samwell wrote, although he added that, as at the other islands, 'great Numbers of fine Girls' also visited the ships.[17]

Because of contrary winds and the desertion of two of his men, Cook stayed at Raiatea for more than a month. His crew were treated to the same entertainments as on his previous visits. But these were now so commonplace to Cook that he did not even mention them in his journal and on some days his journal remained a complete blank. His officers, however, still found a good deal to interest them. John Webber, the expedition's 24-year-old artist, made sketches of Raiatea's dancing girls, while some of the officers poked about and made inquiries about various matters, thereby adding a few small details to the stock of knowledge on Raiatea and the neighbouring islands. King, for example, confirmed Banks' discovery of 1769 that there were linguistic differences between Tahiti and the more westerly Society Islands. 'Otaheite,' he wrote, 'has many words & phrases, as I am told, quite unknown among the Islands to the Wtward which all agree [i.e. have identical vocabularies].' King also concluded that the islanders did not travel as extensively as some of his predecessors had supposed. He ascertained that they visited all the high islands from Mehetia to Maupiti, as well as a low island to the westward called 'Mopeehe' (i.e. Mopelia). In addition, they maintained contact with 'a small low island' to the eastward of Mehetia—presumably Anaa. 'But,' he added, 'they say that their farthest visits are only two days sail, with a fair wind; their knowledge however of Islands is more extensive, but only traditional, & most likely [derived] from people driven from them in bad weather.'[18]

Undoubtedly the most notable memento of Cook's last sojourn at Raiatea is a portrait by Webber of Oreo's daughter, Poetua. The portrait, which is in oils, was possibly done after Captain Clerke had seized Poetua and two of her relatives as hostages following the desertion of a midshipman and a seaman from the *Discovery*. A copy of the painting—probably the 'master' copy—is now in the National Maritime Museum, Greenwich, England, on loan from the British Admiralty.[19] Another is in the National Library of Australia, Canberra.[20] And a third is in the possession of Princess Takau Pomare, of Tahiti, at her home in Nice, France.[21] All three were apparently done by Webber, himself. One was exhibited at the Royal Academy, London, in 1785—the year in which Webber was elected ARA.[22] The paintings depict Poetua as a handsome, light-skinned, almost statuesque woman, with dark, wavy hair and decidedly European features. Cook's editor and biographer, J. C. Beaglehole, has described the subject as of 'lavish charm' and 'a little enigmatic.'[23] Bernard Smith, in his *European Vision and the South Pacific, 1768-1850,* has called the painting a 'highly romantic image of a firm-breasted Raiatean girl' with 'a Gioconda look upon her face.'[24]

Smith's remarks seem to imply that, in his view, Webber did not paint Poetua as she was, but as he or others would have liked her to be. Yet if he did, one may well wonder in what way his portrait differed from the original. Was she not one of the finest women that Samwell and his fellow-officers had ever seen? Did not George Forster, on the previous voyage, praise her eyes and nose as 'remarkably well shaped,' her body as 'elegantly proportioned,' and her hands as 'graceful beyond description'? And was it not Pickersgill's view that there were 'many Ladies in England much more of a Brunett'?

When viewed in conjunction with the various literary descriptions, there seems, in fact, to be little doubt that the portrait is *not* a highly romantic image of a South Seas beauty. Rather, it is a faithful likeness of a chiefly Raiatean woman—albeit an exceptionally handsome one—at the beginning of the era of modern European contact. Certainly, Webber does seem to have depicted Poetua with an enigmatic, Gioconda smile. But this perhaps was inevitable, for in what better way could a sensitive artist have expressed his puzzlement at finding such a woman—not among the fashionable ladies of a London art salon—but deep in the heart of the South Pacific 'amongst a set of copper colour'd Indians'?

13

Traditions like 'our books of the Old Testament'

Eleven years passed after the departure from Raiatea of the *Resolution* and *Discovery* before any other European ships visited the eastern Pacific. The first was the British transport vessel *Lady Penrhyn* which anchored in Matavai Bay on 10 July 1788. She had been one of the First Fleet to take convicts to New South Wales. On sailing from there for China, contrary winds had forced her far out of her way until, finally, the captain decided to run for Tahiti to seek rest and refreshments for his scurvy-ridden crew. The *Lady Penrhyn* spent two weeks at Matavai Bay, and then a few days at Huahine. Because the situation was 'not very eligible' for her few fit men to go ashore in Tahiti, little of ethnographic value was recorded there apart from the fact that 'great numbers' of the islanders had been 'carried off' by venereal disease. This observation was made by Lieutenant John Watts, who had visited the island in 1777 in the *Resolution.* According to him, the disease had been contracted from the crews of Cook's ships. He noted also that the women of the 'lowest class' were not as free from the complaint as formerly, but that the 'better sort' of women apparently did not wish to 'hazard the catching of so terrible a disorder.'[1]

Three months after the *Lady Penrhyn* sailed, another British ship dropped anchor in Tahiti. This was HMS *Bounty,* of mutiny fame. Under the command of Lieutenant William Bligh, she had come from England in quest of breadfruit for transplanting to the West Indies. Bligh, who had been sailing master in the *Resolution* on Cook's last voyage, soon obtained permission of the chiefs to collect a cargo of breadfruit. But because it was then the wrong time of year to gather young plants, he had to stay in Tahiti for five months to achieve his objective. During this period, he seldom wandered far from his anchorage—first at Matavai Bay and later at nearby 'Toahroah' harbour*—except when he chased some deserters to Tetiaroa, a small atoll some twenty-six miles north of Tahiti. Nevertheless, he made good use of his time. By persistent enquiry, he learned much more about some aspects of Tahitian life than any of his predecessors, and he wrote up his discoveries in his log book.[2]

Like Watts, Bligh soon discovered that venereal disease had caused great havoc among the Tahitians since the *Resolution's* departure, being told that 'many fine girls' had died of it. However, after making many inquiries he was not so sure that the disease was of European origin. Indeed, he thought some of his predecessors had 'assuredly been mistaken' on this point and that it had probably existed 'before the Natives had any intercourse with Europeans.'[3]

* Part of what is now called Taaone.

From Cook's former travelling companion Hitihiti, who apparently arrived in Tahiti from Raiatea just after the *Bounty,* Bligh learned that Poetua, 'the lady who Mr. Webber made a painting of,' was dead. Dead, too, was Omai. The news of Omai's death prompted Bligh to inquire whether he had attained a higher rank after Cook had left him at Huahine. The answer was that he had remained 'just the same,' which was 'only one class above a *teuteu.*'* Bligh then asked what the ranks among the islanders were, and was told: *arii rahi* (king or greatest chief); *arii* (chief or lord of a district); *'taatatoo-ow'* (barons); *raatira* or *manahune* (citizens) and *teuteu* (servants). This led to the discovery that the chiefs of all the districts were independent of each other; that the 'king' had no power over them; and that they would either fight for, or against him, as they felt inclined, and this they did with impunity. As Bligh understood the situation, the *arii rahi* of the island was a boy of six, who had been born since Cook's last visit. His home was in the Pare district, near Matavai Bay. The boy (who was later known as Pomare II) had inherited the title of Tu from his father (later called Pomare I). However, in accordance with Tahitian custom, the father was acting as regent during his son's minority and was then called Teina. There were two other personages on the island of considerable importance. These were Vehiatua, chief of Taiarapu, and Potatau, chief of the western district of Atehuru. Both sent messages to Bligh inviting him to visit them. But neither would 'venture to come themselves,' nor could Bligh get Teina to accompany him to see them—such was the 'Mutual jealousy of these People.'[4]

The friction among the chiefs and apparent restriction on movements between districts no doubt prevented Bligh from learning all he would have liked about Vehiatua and Potatau. In fact, one of the few things he did learn was that the 'first and only connection' between Tu's family and Vehiatua's was that Tu's great-great-grandfather, Taaroa Manahune, had married a sister of the reigning Vehiatua† of that time. On the other hand, Bligh discovered that Tu's family had formed several marriage alliances with the chiefs of Raiatea. One such chief, Tutaha, was then in Tahiti, as was Tutaha's uncle, Moaroa. Tutaha, a priest and a man 'of much consequence,' was considered to have great knowledge, and it was either to him or to his uncle that the Tahitian chiefs frequently referred Bligh when he sought information on various subjects.[5]

It was from them, for example, that Bligh learned that both the Tahitian and Raiatean months consisted of thirty days, and that both the days and the months had names. But whereas the Tahitian year consisted of twelve months, that of Raiatea had an extra one—apparently brief—to 'make up some deficiency . . . in the 12 Lunar Months.' The extra month came between February and March when no breadfruit was to be had. From these and other details, Bligh concluded that the islanders kept a regular account of time. But they

* Where known, the modern Tahitian spellings are given in this chapter rather than the phonetic renderings of Bligh and others.

† Vehiatua was a title rather than a name.

seemed to have no record of past time, as no one could tell him how many months had elapsed since Wallis and Cook had visited Tahiti. Nor could he learn if there was a fixed day when the year began.[6]

Bligh noted among other things that the practice of circumcision among the Tahitians was 'not the same as among the Jews'; that the needle and thread were unknown to them; and that when the *Bounty's* barber made a model of a European woman as a joke, some of the Tahitians 'joined noses' with it while others kissed it.[7] Like several of his predecessors, he was of the opinion that the Tahitians were of several racial types, although he found less variety in some of their physical features than other visitors had recorded. On 30 December 1788, two months after his arrival in Tahiti, he wrote:

> It is difficult to judge from the complexion of these people if there has been any difference among them, because as they are more or less exposed to the Sun the Skin shows it considerably. Neither have I yet seen anything in the features to discover it by, but here are three Classes of People, if I was to judge by the Hair of the head. One has it very short and frizled, something like a Negroes, the others becomingly curled, and the last long and lank like an Indian, but the frizled is not so jet black as the others.[8]

Less than two weeks later, Bligh recorded his first impressions of the islanders' religion, a matter on which earlier visitors had gleaned little information. The Tahitians' *atua,* or god, seemed to him to be a being capable of all power, but subject to violent passions that might either be turned to their advantage or destruction. Their success in an enterprise or the mitigation of some offence could be secured by addressing the deity and making an offering suitable to the occasion. 'It therefore happens,' Bligh went on, 'that they apply to their *atua* as a Roman Catholic would to a confessor, and having Idealy discharged their duties to him in this Manner, they have no others moral or divine on their minds, but what they easily get rid of in the same way.'[9]

After further conversations with the principal islanders, Bligh wrote that he had accepted their assertions that they believed in virgin births. Whoever the queen of the island was, he said, it was the islanders' belief that she had her first-born son, or the one who became 'Heir to the Crown,' through the inspiration of the *atua.* The islanders claimed that while the queen slept, with her husband by her, the *atua* would hover over her and have connection with her, and that she would thereby conceive. All her other children, however, were 'begot by the Husband.' 'Yet [the islanders] imply nothing more,' Bligh thought, 'than that it was their God that gave them a King, without whose assistance they would have been without one.'[10]

Bligh went on to say that to speak loosely of the islanders' tenets was probably to do them a great injustice. They believed in the omnipresence of a divine being who was both all-powerful and 'the great ruler of all things.' This god, who was called Oro, had been begotten by Taaroa and Heuamaiterai, before whom no gods existed. Although Taaroa was as great as Oro, it was to

Oro that the islanders made their offerings and addressed their prayers. There were also many inferior deities to whom 'certain Evils or good' were attributed. But as far as Bligh could learn, the islanders had no idea of a future state. 'They worship no Idol,' he added, 'for wherever their devotions are paid, they suppose the real God present hovering about them. On being asked where their God resides or where he is, their constant answer is *"Arre te po,"* which properly interpreted is—'He is invisible.'[11]

Although much that Bligh recorded in his log book was published in his *A Voyage to the South Sea . . .* (London, 1792), his remarks on the Tahitians' religious beliefs were not deemed of general interest and were edited out. They did not appear in print until the 1930s when a revival of interest in the *Bounty* mutiny produced a spate of literature on that subject, including a verbatim edition of the logbook. Also published at that time was the so-called journal of James Morrison, the *Bounty's* boatswain's mate.[12]

Morrison's work is undoubtedly the best-informed and fullest ethnographic account of pre-Christian Tahiti that has come down to us. It also contains the only detailed account of eighteenth-century Tubuai, an island some 300 miles south of Tahiti. Its author, a well-educated man—although a somewhat erratic speller and punctuater—spent more than two years on Tahiti and three months on Tubuai. Morrison was not a mutineer, but was one of twenty-five men who remained in the *Bounty* in April 1789 after some of the crew had mutinied in Tongan waters. These men subsequently tried to form a settlement on Tubuai. When this failed, the *Bounty* returned to Tahiti where Morrison and fifteen companions went ashore, leaving Fletcher Christian and eight others to take the ship where they chose. Morrison and his associates remained on Tahiti for the next eighteen months, mainly in the vicinity of Matavai Bay. Some of them helped him to build a schooner in which to sail to the East Indies. However, before they could set off, Captain Edward Edwards arrived at the island in HMS *Pandora* and arrested them. This was in April 1791. Meanwhile, Morrison had acquired a good knowledge of the Tahitian language, and this had enabled him to make many inquiries into the islanders' beliefs and institutions. In 1793, after he had returned to England and had survived a gruelling courtmartial, he wrote up his observations in a bulky manuscript. The manuscript was intended for immediate publication. But because it contained some bitter criticism of Bligh, its publication was withheld, although some of Morrison's ethnographic information did appear in print at the turn of the nineteenth century.[13]

On the subject of Tubuai, Morrison said that the chief of the district where the mutineers tried to form their settlement was called Tamatoa. He was a great-great-grandson of a chief of Raiatea who had drifted to the island in a fishing canoe and, not knowing his way home, had settled there. The island was then 'but thinly inhabited'. Some of the people had been driven to it from an island far to the westward which they had called 'Paroodtoo,' and

PLATE 9. Portrait of Poetua, daughter of the Raiatean chief Oreo, by John Webber. The original oil painting, measuring 144.8 cm (57 in.) x 93.9 cm (37 in.), is in the Nan Kivell Collection, National Library of Australia, Canberra. Other virtually identical copies are in the National Maritime Museum, Greenwich, England, and in the possession of Princess Takau Pomare, of Nice, France. In the Greenwich portrait, Poetua's right cheek is a fraction less fleshy and this gives her an even more European appearance than here.

PLATE 10. Most early writers on Tahiti and the leeward Society Islands did not differentiate between the cultures of the two places. As a result some aspects of culture which were found only on Raiatea and its near neighbours were erroneously ascribed to Tahiti also. This representation of a dance at Raiatea is a case in point. When published in John Webber's 'Views in the South Seas . . .' (London, 1808), it was captioned 'A Dance in Otaheite'. Compare this picture with the drawing by Sydney Parkinson, plate 5.

others had come from another island to the eastward called 'O'Gweeva.'* These people had accepted the Raiatean castaway as their chief, and he (with evident homesickness) had named three of the districts of his new home Raiatea, Tahaa, and Huahine.

Morrison said the Tubuaians of his time numbered about 3,000, and were nearly of the same colour as the Society Islanders, but were more robust and savage in appearance. They were not tattooed and the men were not circumcised. The women were generally handsomer than those of the Society Islands. At fourteen or fifteen, their long hair, which flowed in soft ringlets, set them off to much advantage. In their dances, which seemed to resemble those of Tonga, they did not make the 'Lewd Motions or gestures' that were so much in use in the other islands.

The language of Tubuai was a cross between that of Tonga and the Society Islands, but not so different from either as to prevent its being understood by people of both places. On the other hand, the canoes of the island were different from those of the other islands Morrison had seen. They were from thirty to forty feet long, sixteen to eighteen inches at the gunwale, about two feet deep, and sharp towards the head and stern. The head resembled the head of some animal with a large mouth, while the stern rose into a scroll, neatly finished and carved. Several pieces of breadfruit and tamanu wood, neatly trimmed and joined together by seizings of coconut fibre, were used in their construction. The Tubuaians, however, had no sailing vessels and never left their island, except when they were blown off it, as all the islands they knew of were 'at too great a distance for them to hold intercourse.' Other matters that Morrison mentioned in respect of Tubuai were that the houses were oval in shape and at a distance resembled haystacks; that the islanders used *kava* or 'Intoxicating peper' in the same manner as the Society Islanders, preferring the method of chewing it to any other; that they had no slings or bows for use in war; and that their *marae* differed from those of the Society Islands.[14]

In writing of Tahiti, Morrison, like Bligh, had a good deal to say about the islanders' religion. Much of what he recorded corresponded closely with Bligh's findings, but on some points he diverged markedly or even contradicted him. In Morrison's opinion, the islanders' religion was 'without form or Regularity' and in many respects peculiar to themselves. In many other ways it was comparable to that of some of the ancient Jewish tribes, while numerous traditions of the islanders corresponded with 'our books of the Old Testament.' There were three deities, called by the general name of *atua,* but worshipped as three distinct 'persons' and spoken of separately. Tane, the first or father of the gods, was called *atua nui* (great god) and sometimes *atua mana* (tremendous or awful god). He was the maker of the world and of all things—the

* Neither 'Paroodtoo' (Parutu) nor 'O'Gweeva' can now be positively identified. 'Paroodtoo' may be a rendering of Pulotu, a place name in Tonga, where the word is also used to mean 'the land of the departed' and is considered the home of certain gods.—Gifford 1923: 197. 'O'Gweeva' is probably a rendering of Hiva, which simply means 'foreign parts', 'faraway', 'over there', etc. See chapter 19, note 51.

cause of light, darkness, thunder, lightning, rain, etc. His son was Oromatautua (presumably Bligh's Oro) who presided over war and peace, and punished the chiefs with sickness and death for any neglect of their duty. The third god, Tipahoamanu was the friend of both Tane and Oromatautua and their messenger on earth. The three gods were said to have been born of, or brought forth from, darkness or eternal night. Only in time of war or when a chief became sick did the people apply to them for help, as they were looked on as too great to interest themselves in trivial affairs.[15]

According to Morrison, the Tahitians did believe in a future state. They also had notions of guardian angels and an evil demon. 'Their traditions respecting the Creation,' he went on, 'are in many respects the same as we find in the Bible; they do not limit the time but say that God produced all things from nothing and set evry [*sic*] thing in Motion by his Command.' As for the Tahitians' accounts of the stars, these seemed to Morrison to be similar to the Greek fables. For example, a girl called Taurua, who was both a great beauty and a great whore, was banished to the planet Venus for cursing the god Tane. Similarly, Castor and Pollux (whom the Greeks called The Twins) were said to be two brothers who had begged Tane to be taken away from their parents because the parents had refused them some fine fish.

> As they are superstitious in all their Customs [Morrison continued] and think that evry transgression against God or Man is attended with punnishment, so they have but few that may be calld real Crimes among a People who have no other law but that of Nature. They firmly beleive what they are taught by their priests and Forefathers and which they suppose to be the command of God—they know that from him all their blessings proceed, and when they approach their places of worship it is with a Reverential Awe that would be an honor to Christianity, and when in the Act [of] praying always behave with due Decorum.[16]

Morrison said that the islanders' *marae* or places of worship were oblong areas thickly planted with trees and enclosed by walls of stone, four, five and six feet high. In the centre of each was a table or altar on which offerings were made. At a great *marae* in the Pare district there was a moveable *marae* —'something similar to the Ark of the Jews.' This was a box about three feet long by two wide and one deep containing images representing the three deities, which were kept for remembrance rather than for worship. The ark, in turn, was part of a moveable house called *fare atua* (house of god) where a girdle of red and yellow feathers, or *maro ura,* was kept. This girdle, the symbol of royalty, had been in the possession of the chiefs of Atehuru for about twenty years. But at the end of September 1789, the *Bounty* people, with their superior arms, had helped to retrieve it, together with the *fare atua,* and had carried it back to Pare.[17] According to Morrison, there were two classes of priest—*tahua marae* and *tahua atua*. They were the only people who had any knowledge, and it was their business to keep the lower classes in ignorance, although some were from the lowest class themselves. The *tahua marae,* who were in charge of *marae* ceremonies, chanted their hymns and prayers in an 'unknown tongue'. Those who were not of their profession, including many chiefs, could not understand it.[18]

In describing the Tahitians' physical characteristics, Morrison said much the same as some of his predecessors. The chiefs, in his view, were generally taller and stouter than the common people, were more serious and thoughtful, and were of a different appearance. Their women were also larger and fairer. Few of the chiefs were shorter than six feet. Indeed, the people could not conceive that a short man could be a chief. Moreover, no chief could ever lose his rank, and no one could become a chief who was not born one. On the birth of a child, however, the titles and honours of the father passed to it.[19]

In general, the women were finely shaped and brunette. Some who were constantly exposed to the sun were very dark. The others were a 'fine bright Collour' and had a 'Glow of Blood' in their faces, and as their skin was as tender as a European's, they burned as readily in the sun. The islanders' eyes were black 'almost without exception', their noses of different descriptions, their mouths small, and lips thin and red. The hair of both sexes was mostly black or dark brown, sometimes coarse and sometimes fine. The limbs of the women were generally 'neat and delicate,' and although they went barefooted, their feet did not spread like those of the inhabitants of Africa and other hot climates. Many with the help of a fashionable dress 'would pass for handsom weomen even in England.'[20]

Morrison said that any commoner who spoke disrespectfully of a chief was 'sure to suffer death,' while the chiefs would 'instantly bring on a War' if they spoke ill of each other. It was because Vehiatua, the chief of Taiarapu, had refused to acknowledge the boy chief Tu as the 'son of the Deity' that several bloody battles had occurred between his people and those of Tahiti-Nui. In fact, Morrison said, Vehiatua claimed that Tu was not even the son of his reputed father, but of a favourite minion of his mother, who had invented the story of his virgin birth so that he would not be disinherited if he 'did not attain his proper size.'[21]

Morrison estimated Tahiti's population at nearly 30,000, of whom about one-third were warriors. However, whereas the chief strength of Tu's family had formerly been their naval force, this had dwindled to no more than '20 sail of War Canoes,' of which most had been brought from Raiatea by Tu's aunt, Ariipaea Vahine. In writing of the canoes, Morrison indicated that they were similar to the double-hulled *pahi* of Raiatea that Cook, Banks and Hervé had described. He said they often went from island to island in fleets of ten or twelve. By this means, the iron left at Tahiti by European visitors was distributed among all the islands the Tahitians knew, in return for which they got pearls, pearlshell, etc. Some of the islands the islanders sailed to were more than a hundred leagues away. In making such voyages they used their judgement and their knowledge of the 'Motion of the Heavenly bodys' which was more expert than a European astronomer would be willing to believe. Moreover,

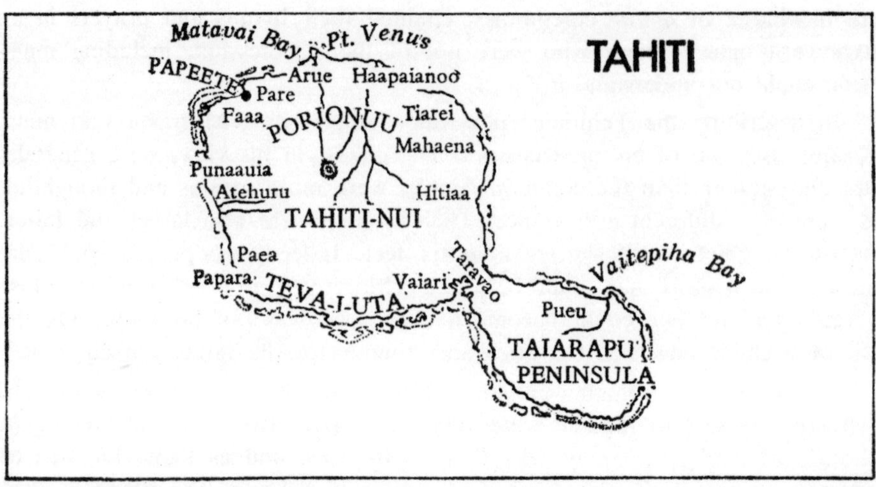

they could foretell a change in the weather with great precision from the appearance of the heavens, and could prepare for it accordingly. When they went to sea they steered by the sun, moon and stars and shaped their course with 'some degree of exactness.'[22]

Morrison described Tahiti's system of government in some detail, stating among other things that the chiefs were of two 'houses'—the Porionuu and the Teva-i-uta. The Porionuu included the chiefs of Pare and all the districts on the northern side of Tahiti-Nui, while the Teva-i-uta took in those of Vaiare, Vaiuriri and Papara on the western side.[23] Although, in reality, the situation seems to have been somewhat more complex, Morrison was certainly correct—by Bligh's definition—in stating that only one chief could be *arii rahi.*[24] On this point, Morrison concurred with Bligh that the *arii rahi* of his time was the boy chief Tu. However, he said the rightful sovereign was Tu's aunt, Ariipaea Vahine, the first-born of her family, who had returned to Tahiti from Raiatea in September 1790 after an absence of some years. Having no children of her own, she had transferred her sovereignty during her absence to her brother, Teina, and he in turn had transferred it to his son Tu. Ariipaea Vahine and a large party of Raiateans were present when Tu was invested with the *maro ura* in an elaborate *marae* ceremony at Pare on 13 February 1790. Morrison was also in attendance, but no Taiarapu chiefs were present because they did not recognise Tu's paramountcy.[25]

Because Morrison was arrested by the *Pandora* only a few weeks after Tu's investiture, he did not learn the details of one of the extraordinary consequences of it. This was that, in accordance with a custom called *pi,* any Tahitian word containing the syllable *tu* or the key syllable in Tu's title, Vaira'atoa, became outlawed and was either modified or replaced. Thus, for example, the island then known as Te*tu*roa became Te*tia*roa, as it is today; fe*tu* (star) became fe*tia*; *vai* (water) became *pape*; and numerous place names such as *Vai*ete and *Vai*uriri became *Pape*ete, *Pape*uriri, etc. The names of many of the principal chiefs were also changed, and these changes, in turn, affected abourt forty or fifty of the commonest words in the language. Tu's father, for example, took the name Pomare—from *po* (night) and *mare* (cough) —and these two words were replaced by *ru'i* and *hota* respectively.[26]

The first outsider to notice these word and syllable changes was Captain George Vancouver, who dropped anchor in Matavai Bay in late December 1791 in HMS *Discovery* and *Chatham.* Vancouver, who was on a surveying voyage to the north-west coast of America, knew something of the Tahitian language through having visited Tahiti twice before with Cook. He noted that the words in the newly-adopted vocabulary bore no affinity to the former expressions, and that anyone who did not use them was severely punished. 'Were such a pernicious innovation to take place, generally, at the arbitrary will of the sovereigns throughout the South-Sea Islands,' he wrote, 'it would be attended with insurmountable difficulties to strangers; but it appears to be a new regulation, and, as yet, confined to these islands. . . .' Vancouver thought it would be interesting to try to learn the reasons for the change. However, this required a better knowledge of the language than he possessed, and, in any case, he was too busy with shipboard matters to devote his attention to it.[27]

Vancouver, in fact, recorded very little information of ethnographic interest during a sojourn of nearly four weeks. But he did note a number of significant political developments. One was that following the death of the last Vehiatua, Tu's father had ousted the legitimate claimant to that title and had installed one of his own brothers as chief of the Taiarapu district. This meant that the whole of Tahiti now acknowledged Tu's authority. Indeed, his paramountcy was also recognised in the neighbouring islands of Moorea, Makatea, Tetiaroa, Maiao and Huahine, and, in consequence, the young chief was paid much more respect than either his father or grandfather had been.[28] Vancouver noted also that a disease introduced by the Spaniards, causing a large swelling in the throat, had brought about many deaths at Taiarapu, and that Tahiti's women were not as handsome as when he first knew them. On this second point, he wrote: 'The natives themselves freely admit the alteration which in a few years has taken place and seem to attribute much of the cause to the lamentable diseases introduced by Europeans visitors, to which many of their finest women, at an early period of life, have fallen sacrifices.'[29]

Vancouver's remarks, first published in an account of his voyage in 1798, were among the last on Tahiti to be recorded before a band of Protestant missionaries settled on the island in 1797. The arrival of the missionaries was the beginning of a new era in the history of the Society Islands for it led to the adoption of Christianity among the islanders and the abandonment of many old customs and beliefs. Meanwhile, several other ships put into Tahiti, but as their crews recorded nothing of importance in the context of this book, they may be quickly passed over.

The first ships to appear after Vancouver's departure were the British whalers *Matilda* and *Mary Ann,* which spent three days at Tautira in mid-

February 1792 on their way to the whaling grounds off Peru.[30] A month later, the British schooner *Jenny* was at Matavai Bay for six days en route to North America.[31] And in less than another month, two more British naval vessels put in an appearance. These ships, HMS *Providence* and *Assistant,* were under the captaincy of the *Bounty's* ill-fated commander, William Bligh. They stayed in Tahiti for three months gathering a second cargo of breadfruit which, on this occasion, Bligh succeeded in taking to the West Indies.[32] The next visitor was HMS *Daedalus,* a storeship sent from North America by Captain Vancouver, which spent a fortnight at Matavai Bay in February 1793.[33] Finally, on 28 November 1795, Bligh's old ship, the *Providence,* hauled into her old anchorage again en route to Asia on a surveying voyage under Captain W. R. Broughton.[34] Each visitor from the *Jenny* to the *Daedalus* took off several seamen belonging to the *Matilda,* who, having lost their ship on Mururoa Atoll in the Tuamotu Archipelago, had sailed back to Tahiti in the ship's boats. However, six of the *Matilda's* men were still beachcombing on Tahiti or its neighbours when the *Providence* sailed after a fortnight's sojourn, and there was also a Swedish deserter from the *Daedalus*. Some of these men remained in the Society Islands* until they died, being the pioneers of the European community in those islands that has persisted to this day.

In the twenty-five years that preceded the arrival of these settlers, more than a score of ships from Britain, France and Spain had visited the Society Islands, and dozens of diligent scientists and seamen had filled their diaries with accounts of what they did, learned and saw. No islands in the Pacific, in the early years of European contact, were described more fully and so often. Yet for all the tens of thousands of words that were put on paper, Europeans still knew remarkably little about some aspects of Society Islands life at this stage. One important fact that they had failed to learn was that, as in Christendom with its Vatican, or Islam with its Mecca, there was one place in those islands that was especially venerated. This place, Opoa, on the south-eastern side of Raiatea, was the site of the islanders' most sacred *marae,* the spiritual home of the most powerful chiefs, and the centre of worship to the great god Oro. Bougainville, it is true, had recorded in 1768 that Opoa was the birthplace of Ahutoru's mother, who, he inferred, was racially distinct from the generality of Tahitians. And both Cook and Banks in 1769 had actually set foot there and had written at length of Opoa's ingeniously constructed *pahi,* which, in their eyes, were vastly superior to the primitive sailing craft of Tahiti. However, it was left to some of the Protestant missionaries of the next era of Society Islands history to discover something of the real significance of Opoa in the local scheme of things.

* Cook, it will be recalled, applied the term Society Islands only to the islands of Raiatea, Tahaa, Huahine, Borabora, Tupai and Maupiti. However, from the end of the period of exploration it gradually came to include Tahiti, Moorea, Maiao and Mehetia as well: and this is the meaning it has today. In this book, the term will henceforth be used in its modern sense; and such expressions as 'leeward islands of the Society Group' will be adopted to differentiate Raiatea, Tahaa, etc., from Tahiti and its neighbours.

14

The great white chiefs of Opoa

On 5 March 1797, a new era began in the South Pacific with the arrival of the ship *Duff* at Matavai Bay. On board were thirty Protestant missionaries. They had been sent to the Pacific by a newly-formed London body, the Missionary Society (later called the London Missionary Society), to evangelise the heathen. Eighteen of the missionaries had decided to work in Tahiti; ten in Tonga; and two in the Marquesas. Those destined for Tahiti were kindly received by the *arii rahi* Tu, now a youth of fourteen or fifteen. Tu (who was soon to adopt his father's name Pomare, and will hereafter be described as such or as Pomare II) placed a large house at Point Venus at the missionaries' disposal and offered them his protection. Within three weeks, the missionaries had made themselves comfortable, and the *Duff* sailed for Tonga and the Marquesas to land the other brethren at their chosen stations. She returned to Tahiti about three months later to ensure that those left at Point Venus were being properly treated, and stayed three more weeks before heading for China.[1] During the interval her captain and chief officer made a circuit of the island to estimate the population. This confirmed the statements of Watts, Bligh, Morrison and Vancouver that the Tahitians had greatly declined in numbers since Cook's time. Whereas Cook had probably grossly exaggerated the population at 204,000 and George Forster had put it at 120,000, the *Duff's* officers found only about 16,000 people. This compared with an estimate by Morrison only seven years earlier of 30,000.[2]

The estimate of the *Duff's* officers, being based on a house count, was possibly accurate to within two or three thousand. Whatever the exact figure was, it proved to be more than a sufficiency for the missionaries, for the Tahitians were far less amenable to the teachings of Christianity than they had hoped or imagined. Many of the Tahitians told the missionaries flatly that they did not want to hear their teachings. Others took delight in ridiculing them or in setting dogs and roosters fighting near them when they tried to preach. The missionaries, moreover, found the Tahitian language much harder to master than they had expected; and the tropical climate and sensuous Tahitians lulled some of them into moral lapses with resultant loss of faith. Thereafter, only a small incident was needed to discourage the weaker-willed brethren from going on with their work. Such an incident occurred in March 1798 when a group of Tahitians waylaid several missionaries and stripped them of their clothes. The result was that eleven of their number left the island soon afterwards in a visiting sealing vessel bound for Sydney.[3]

Although eight new missionaries reinforced the mission in July 1801, the evangelists made little headway against the islanders' beliefs during their first decade or so on the island. Meanwhile, occasional whalers put into Tahiti for refreshments and repairs in sailing to and from the whaling grounds off the coast of Peru; and from August 1801 a trade in salted pork developed with the infant colony of New South Wales.[4] A total of forty-five ships called at the island between the departure of the *Duff* and October 1808.[5] Many of these increased the missionaries' difficulties by bartering muskets and gunpowder with the islanders, thereby increasing the deadliness of the frequent affrays between Pomare's people and those of other districts. Although Pomare's people got most of the firearms through being on hand near Matavai Bay, their opponents eventually gained the upper hand. By November 1808, Tahiti was in a state of anarchy, and as Pomare could no longer guarantee the missionaries his protection, most of them suddenly evacuated their station and sailed for the safety of Huahine in a visiting trading vessel. Four who stayed behind soon took refuge on Moorea, and three later went on to Huahine. Those at Huahine hoped that they would eventually return to Tahiti. But in late October 1809 they received such melancholy news from that island that all but two—both single men—took passages in a ship bound for Sydney.[6]

The refugees reached Sydney in mid-January 1810 and remained there for the next eighteen months or so—until reports of improving conditions in Tahiti encouraged them to return. They drifted back in small groups on various trading vessels. By mid-1812 ten adults and several children had made the voyage. As Tahiti was still in turmoil, they established new headquarters at Papetoai on neighbouring Moorea. Pomare, who was living at that place on their return, went back soon afterwards to Tahiti and the missionaries saw little of him for the next two years. Meanwhile, his ageing mother, Itia, who lived nearby, proved a good friend and protector. But as she was 'one of the strongest advocates in the nation for the old religion and customs,' they had little hope of making wholesale conversions. Nevertheless, they gradually gained ground. Having greatly improved their knowledge of the Tahitian language, they opened a school and began to teach their servants to read and write. Later, a few chiefly Tahitians, Raiateans and Huahineans also became their pupils, and every now and then one of them would profess a desire to become a Christian. With every passing month, the times became more propitious for the missionaries. Because of war, disease and depopulation, the islanders had begun to lose faith in their old gods.[7]

Itia's death in January 1814 seems to have been the signal for the start of a new order. Within weeks, Tahitians who had previously scorned the missionaries began to flock to them, eager to learn the mysteries of reading and writing, to receive religious instruction, and to join the previously thin ranks of *Pure Atua,* or praying people. Pomare, himself, having returned from Tahiti, regularly attended the missionaries' prayer meetings, and by the end of 1814 some 2,300 of his people were doing so. However, it was not until mid-November 1815 that the old religion was completely overthrown and Christianity triumphed. The event occurred on Tahiti and was brought about by force of arms. Pomare and his followers were attending a prayer meeting in the district of Punaauia when they were suddenly attacked by members of a rival clan, who were still resolute heathens. The attack threw the Christian party into temporary disarray. But they quickly regrouped and routed their assailants with firearms they had with them. After the battle, Pomare gave orders that the vanquished should not be ill-treated—a command so contrary to normal usage that the heathen were moved to abandon their old gods forthwith and to accept the new religion. Pomare was subsequently acknowledged as the supreme chief of both Tahiti and Moorea; and within a few days he invited the missionaries to send two of their number to visit Tahiti.[8]

The spell of Christianity soon spread to Huahine, Raiatea and other islands. It brought hundreds of eager islanders to Moorea in search of spelling books, catechisms and religious instruction. The small band of missionaries, then numbering only seven, could not cope with the sudden and heavy demands on them, and after long years of lamenting their lack of progress, they now yearned for more evangelists and more books. Nine new missionaries, mostly with wives, arrived at Papetoai in 1816-17, having been on their way from England and Australia when the mass conversions began. They brought with them a small printing press to produce whatever literature was needed. Until February 1818, all the missionaries remained on Moorea. They then began to split up and go to other islands. By September, six had moved to Tahiti, two to Huahine and two to Raiatea.[9] The first two missionaries to Huahine, the Revs J. M. Orsmond and William Ellis, were somewhat kindred spirits. Both quickly learned the Tahitian language and took pains to discover all they could of the islanders' own former beliefs and customs. Orsmond, who lived on one or another of the Society Islands until 1856, was a tireless recorder of ethnographical information. Unfortunately, several manuscripts in which he wrote up his material were subsequently lost. But thanks to his Tahiti-born granddaughter Teuira Henry, many of his original notes were re-edited after his death, and published with much additional material as *Ancient Tahiti* in 1928.[10] Ellis, for his part, lived in the Society Islands, mainly on Huahine, only until 1822. But with the help of Orsmond and other missionaries who corresponded with him after he returned to England, he amassed sufficient data to fill three volumes of his celebrated book, *Polynesian Researches*. This was first published in 1829.[11]

Both *Ancient Tahiti* and *Polynesian Researches* seem to contain further evidence that there were European settlers in the eastern Pacific at a much earlier period than has generally been supposed, and that they and their descendants left their mark on the political, social and cultural life of the region. Indeed, the two works, combined with material from other sources, seemingly provide enough clues to reconstruct some of the history of those aliens in considerable detail. In brief, it seems clear that a dozen or so

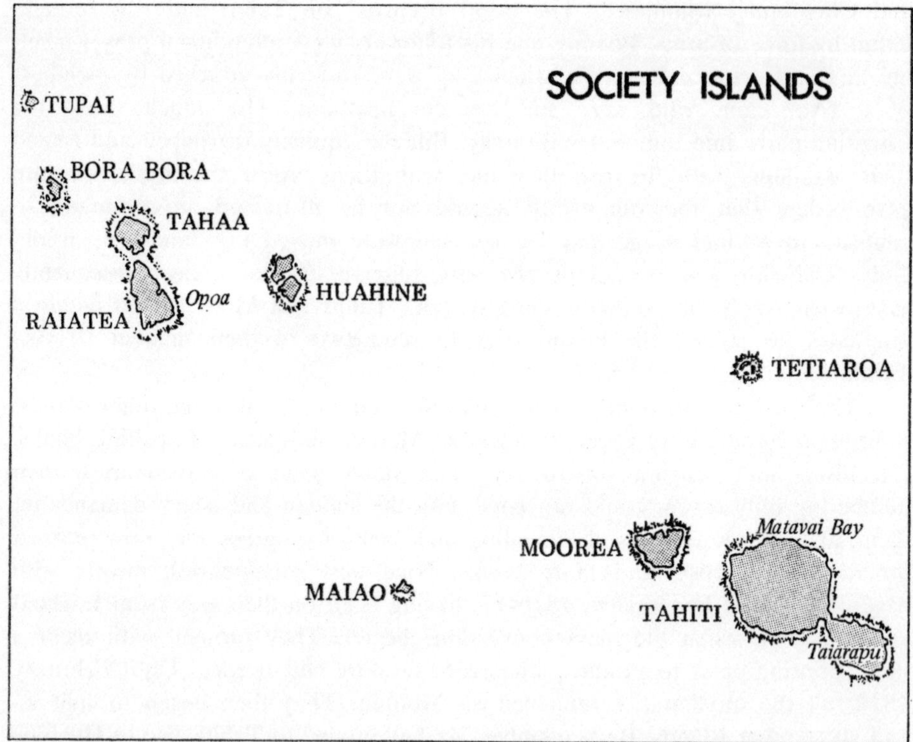

generations before the arrival of Wallis, Bougainville and Cook, a party of light-skinned immigrants settled at Opoa on the south-eastern side of Raiatea. There, under the leadership of a man called Hiro, whose name was that of a night of the moon in the Tahitian calendar, they established a chiefly dynasty; introduced new and superior canoe-building techniques and other maritime expertise; and inaugurated a new religion which combined some of their own beliefs with those of the local inhabitants. Wars occurred with a local chief called Puna. But the Opoa colonists triumphed and multiplied, and gradually spread throughout Raiatea and also to the neighbouring islands of Tahaa, Huahine, Borabora and others. Hiro himself and some of his followers eventually left Raiatea and sailed to Rarotonga in the Cook Islands, some 450 miles south-westward. There another new dynasty was established; and then Hiro apparently went on to New Zealand. A generation or two later, some of the Opoa colonists established a foothold on the Taiarapu Peninsula of Tahiti. This resulted in a constant migration of those people to that island over the next century or so; and when the European explorers burst on the scene in the late eighteenth century, descendants of the Opoa people had spread through the whole of Taiarapu and the entire southern portion of Tahiti-Nui.

Although both Ellis and Orsmond recorded that Opoa was the cultural centre of the eastern Pacific and that it had been settled by the chiefly dynasty within the memory of man, neither missionary gathered any traditions as to where those people came from. Nor did they suspect anything strange about their origins, although Ellis, in particular, must occasionally have been on the verge of doing so.

Writing of the Society Islanders' physical appearance, Ellis said their profile often bore 'a most striking resemblance to that of the European.' The nose was generally rectilinear or aquiline, often with a fullness about the nostrils. It was seldom flat, even though it was formerly the custom of the mothers and nurses to press the nostrils of the female children. The facial angle was 'frequently as perpendicular as in the European structure, excepting where the frontal and the occipital bones of the skull were pressed together in infancy.' The only eye colour that Ellis mentioned was 'jet black'; but he described the islanders' hair as either 'a shining black or dark brown.' The hair was frequently soft and curly, but seldom as fine as in 'civilised nations of the temperate zones.' On the other hand, where it was straight, it was never lank and wiry like an American Indian's. The prevailing skin colour was olive, bronze or reddish brown. But there was a considerable variety in the islanders' complexions, and most of the reigning family of Raiatea were 'no darker than the inhabitants of some parts of Europe.' 'At the time of their birth,' Ellis went on, 'the complexion of Tahitian [i.e. Society Islands] infants is but little if any darker than that of European children, and the skin only assumes the bronze or brown hue as they grow up under repeated or constant exposure to the sun . . .'[12] Darkness of skin colour, Ellis said, was 'generally considered an indication of strength.'[13] But lightness was preferred among the chiefly class.[14] Tetiaroa, an atoll some twenty-six miles north of Tahiti, had long been frequented by the 'females of the higher class' for the purpose of *haapori,* or 'increasing the corpulency of their persons, and removing . . . the dark tinge which the vertical sun of Tahiti might have burnt upon their complexions.'[15]

Referring to the traditional history of the Society Islanders, Ellis remarked that this was 'necessarily involved in obscurity' because of the lack of written records. Much of it was contradictory and perplexing.[16] Nevertheless, some of the islanders' traditions inclined him to think that 'the nation, whence they emigrated, was acquainted with some of the leading facts recorded in the Mosaic history of the primitive ages of mankind.'[17] Taaroa, their principal god, was invisible, uncreated and existing since the beginning of time.[18] He was said to have made the sun, moon, stars, heaven and hell, and, according to a very generally received tradition, he also made the first human pair.[19]

> On more than one occasion [Ellis wrote], I have listened to the details of the people respecting his work of creation. They say that after Taaroa had formed the world, he created man out of *araea,* red earth, which was also the food of man until bread-fruit was produced.* In connexion with this, some relate that Taaroa one day called for the man by name. When he came, he caused him to fall asleep, and that, while he slept, he took out one

* In another creation myth recorded by Ellis, Taaroa is said to have used sand to make the first man.—Ellis 1831:I:115.

of his *ivi,* or bones, and with it made a woman, whom he gave to the man as his wife, and that they became the progenitors of mankind. This always appeared to be a mere recital of the Mosaic account of creation, which they had heard from some European, and I never placed any reliance on it, although they have repeatedly told me it was a tradition among them before any foreigner arrived.[20]

In Ellis' opinion, there was a 'striking analogy' between the islanders' account of the deluge and the Mosaic version. This seemed to indicate 'a high degree of antiquity belonging to this isolated people.' The principal facts in the story were the same in the various groups, although there were minor differences. In one group, it was said that Taaroa, being angry with men because of their disobedience to his will, overturned the world into the sea, whereupon the earth sank, except for a few projecting points which became 'the present cluster of islands.' In the Tahitian version of the story, only one man and his wife remained alive, and these took up their young chickens, pigs and dogs and climbed to a high mountain, Pito-hiti. There they remained for ten nights until the sea subsided, after which they climbed down again. The couple subsequently had several children, and although there was no food, they thrived and grew up. Then breadfruit trees and coconut palms appeared again as well as other food plants. And the land again became 'covered with men' who were all descended from the Polynesian Noah and his wife.[21]

Ellis stated that, according to an 'extensive and popular tradition,' the islanders originated at Opoa, on Raiatea, where only *tii* or spirits had formerly dwelt. Opoa was the hereditary land of the reigning family and the 'usual residence of the king and his household;' and it was from there that the islanders had 'subsequently spread themselves over the whole cluster'. Opoa had the distinction of being the birthplace of Oro, the son of Taaroa and his wife Hina, and a great *marae* was built there called Taputapuatea. It had formerly been the centre of Oro worship; and it was there that the practice of offering human sacrifices, which had been adopted in the Society Islands only a few generations before Europeans discovered them, had originated. Opoa was also a shrine for members of the Arioi Society, a body of 'strolling players and privileged libertines,' whose ceremonies and practices (including the murder of their own offspring due to vows of celibacy) were closely linked with Oro worship.

The priests of the national temples (i.e. *marae*) were a distinct class, Ellis said, and their offices were hereditary. The king was generally the chief priest, and the high-priesthood of the principal idols was usually held by a member of his family or a near relative. On many occasions the king also personified the god, and received the prayers and offerings of his people. There was therefore 'an intimate connexion' between the islanders' religion and political despotism. Indeed, the chiefs and the gods seemed always to have exercised a combined influence over the people. The 'power of the gods' was often exercised only to establish the authority of the king, whom the people considered to be descended from them. Likewise, the measures of the government were apparently often carried out only to inspire fear, and secure acknowledgment for the gods. Hence, when a human sacrifice was required, a priest would apply to the king, and the king would give orders to provide the victim.[23]

Ellis described the government of the Society Islands in former times as an arbitrary monarchy. The supreme authority was vested in the king and was hereditary in his family. 'In many respects . . .,' he said, 'their institutions indicate great attention to the principles of government, an acquaintance with the means of controlling the conduct of man, and an advancement in the organisation of their civil polity, which, under corresponding circumstances, is but rarely attained, and could scarcely have been expected.' Their society was divided into three distinct ranks. The highest, the *hui arii,* included the king or 'reigning chieftain' in each island, the members of his family, and all who were related to them. Next came the *pue raatira,* the landed proprietors, or gentry and farmers. Finally, there were the *manahune,* or common people, who included *titi* (prisoners of war) and *teuteu* (slaves).[24]

The *hui arii,* though not numerous, were the most influential in the state. They were 'exceedingly pertinacious of their distinction, and jealous of the least degradation by the admission of inferiors to their dignity.' If a marriage took place between one of the *hui arii* and someone from a lower order, all children of the union were destroyed unless certain *marae* ceremonies were held which removed the inferiority and made both parties 'equal in dignity.' The sovereignty descended from the father to the eldest son, although sometimes daughters inherited the 'throne.' The 'most singular usage' concerning this was a father's abdication of the throne on the birth of his son. The same custom prevailed for the inheritance of other *hui arii* titles, as well as those of the *raatira.* Ellis could not trace the origin of this custom, and he thought its advantages were 'not very apparent,' unless it was to ensure a son's undisputed succession to his father's dignity and power. 'If this was the design,' he added, 'the plan was admirably adapted to its accomplishment; for the son was usually firmly fixed in the government before his father's decease. . . .'[25]

Ellis wrote at length of the homage that was paid to the kings and queens, of the elaborate ceremonies that accompanied their inauguration, and of the adulatory language used towards them. As the islanders, in his view, were 'but slightly removed from barbarism,' he was 'almost surprised' that they paid their rulers the homage and respect they did. He noted, moreover, that the difference between the rulers and the ruled was far greater than in most civilised countries. However, although the authority of the king was supreme and his power undisputed, he was apparently never considered the absolute proprietor of any land but the royal domains. The other districts were regarded as belonging to their 'respective occupants or proprietors,' who were generally *raatira.* The *raatira* inherited these lands from their ancestors, and bequeathed them to their children or anyone else they chose. These people formed the most important body in times of peace and the strength of the armies in times of war, and without their co-operation, the king could carry out 'but few of his measures.'[26]

Other matters on which Ellis commented included the islanders' division of the horizon, their use of numbers and their computation of time. He said that although the islanders were unacquainted with the compass, they had names for the cardinal points.[27] 'Considering their uncivilised state, and want of letters,' he went on, 'their method for computing time is a matter of astonishment, and shews that they must have existed as a nation for many generations, to have rendered it so perfect. . . . Their acquaintance with, and extensive use of numbers, under these circumstances, is still more surprising. . . . They did not reckon by forties, after the manner of the Mexicans and the Sandwich Islanders [i.e. Hawaiians], but had a decimal method of calculation.'[28] Ellis added:

> The precision, regularity, and extent of their numbers has often astonished me; and how a people, having, comparatively speaking, but little necessity to use calculation, and being destitute of knowledge of figures, should have originated and matured such a system, is still wonderful, and appears, more than any other fact, to favour the opinion that these islands were peopled from a country whose inhabitants were highly civilised.[29]

In writing of nautical matters, Ellis stated that the Society Islands chiefs usually kept canoe-builders 'attached to their establishments.' However, his account of the types of canoe that these artisans made is somewhat confused, for he jumbled his facts about single and double canoes, and referred to the *pahi* as if it were a purely Tuamotuan type of vessel. He said, for example, that several of the principal chiefs owned a *pahi Paumotu,* or Tuamotuan canoe, because this was 'a more safe and convenient mode of conveyance than their own canoes.'* He went on to say, correctly, that although the *pahi* were built of much smaller pieces of wood than those employed in the various Tahitian canoes, they were 'much superior both for strength, convenience and sustaining a tempest at sea.' They were always double, one hull having permanent covered quarters for the crew. Their two masts were stationary, and there was 'a kind of ladder, or wooden shroud' extending from the sides to the head of the masts. When equipped for deep-sea voyaging, they were fitted with wash-boards—'planks, twelve to fifteen inches wide . . . after the manner of wash-boards in a European boat.' The sails were large and made of fine matting, and were 'commonly used in the same manner as sprit or lugger sails . . . in European boats.'[30]

Ellis noted also that the servants of the Society Islands chiefs had to provide the chiefs with fishing nets, and that the needles used to make these were 'not unlike [those] used by European workmen.'[31] On this small but curious point, Ellis was a pioneer, for although several of the early explorers

* The explanation for Ellis' error probably is that, by his time, the Society Islands chiefs were employing Tuamotuans to build their canoes for them. Indeed, J. A. Moerenhout, who settled in Tahiti about five years after Ellis' departure, has left it on record that this was the case.—Moerenhout 1837:I:159.

had noticed the similarity between the knots used in Society Islands nets and those of Europe, he was the first to record that the netting needles were also similar. His statement was later reiterated by a German writer, Friedrich Gerstaecker, who visited the Society Islands, including rarely touched at Maiao Island, in 1851 and wrote:

> It is a singular fact . . . that the inhabitants of the South Seas, when the first white men stepped upon their shores, knew the art of making nets, with exactly the same knots, and employed the same tools in their manufacture as the Europeans. They had at that time, and have now, the same wooden netting-needle sailors and fishermen use in our country.*[32]

Ellis said the islanders had numerous gods of the ocean. These were 'probably men who had excelled their contemporaries in nautical adventure or exploit, and were deified by their descendants.' The most conspicuous was Hiro, although he was not exclusively a god of the sea. The period of his adventures was 'probably the most recent of any thus preserved,' as there were more places associated with his name in the leeward islands of the Society Group than any other. A pile of rocks in Tahaa was called the Dogs of Hiro; a mountain ridge (in Maupiti) was known as the Pahi, or Ship of Hiro; and a large basaltic rock, near the summit of a mountain in Huahine, was called the Hoe or Paddle of Hiro.[33] Ellis added that in a chant that the islanders sang before going to war, Hiro was described as:

> The king of the black purple deep,
> The king of the depths unknown,
> The king who fills with consternation.

He was also said to have a broad back, and dark, deep-fixed eyes, while his body hair—an unusual attribute among the Polynesians—was 'like the pike-fish.'[34]

Teuira Henry's *Ancient Tahiti* reiterates many of Ellis' remarks about Hiro, but has a good deal more to say about him. It contains a series of legends that Orsmond recorded in 1818 in which Hiro is credited with building the first *pahi* in the Society Islands as well as introducing a new method of making fire. The legends also tell how, in building one *pahi,* Hiro murdered his wife† after snaring her fingers in the lashings of its hull, and how he buried

* The similarity was also noted by an English cleric, Charles Bathurst, who published the first English-language treatise on netmaking in 1837. Bathurst examined Society Islands netting needles that had been brought back to England and deposited in the Ashmolean Museum, Oxford. With the aid of illustrations, he explained that there were two types of European netting needle: one with an eye and tongue and one with an open fork at each end.—Bathurst [1837]:15, 129. Illustrations of two eye and tongue netting needles from the Society Islands, like those depicted by Bathurst, appear in W. C. Handy 1927: 110. Buck 1944:223 depicts a Tahitian netting needle of the open fork type which was collected in Tahiti by G. Bennet 'before 1829'. It is now in the British Museum (No. 7052). See also Blandford 1961:11-13.

† Society Islands genealogies give the name of Hiro's wife as Vai-tu-*maria.* This is the only instance of a European-seeming name in the genealogies before the nineteenth century.

her body under a heap of wood chips.* Finally, Hiro built a great *pahi* called *Hohoio* (Interloper) in which he left the Society Islands and never returned.[35]

The legend about *Hohoio* is so explicit that it must surely be a folk recollection of an actual event. It says that Hiro stole the timber for the vessel from the land of King Puna on Raiatea, and that he built a shed for it thirty fathoms long, six wide and five high on rising ground, facing the sea endwise. He was assisted by his own chief artisan, Hotu, and by the chief artisan of Opoa, Memeru. Having marked out the keel, beams and planks, Hiro and his assistants cut their material to the required shape. Next, they set the keel of *avai, toi* and *mara* wood on rollers in the shed, these being polished and firmly spliced together. Knees were then fastened to the keel with spikes and sennit, and the parts were painted with red clay mixed with charcoal to preserve them from wood borers. Holes were bored into the keel and planks at even distances, and the planks were laced in place with sennit. Every seam and all the holes were well caulked with fine coconut-husk fibre and pitched with gum, which Hiro drew from sacred breadfruit trees. When all the strakes were on, the canoe was washed clean, dried well, and painted inside and out with red clay and charcoal. As the hull then reached almost to the roof, the builders broke the shed away from it. Then they fixed the boards of the deck on cross beams with spikes and sennit.

The tradition says the *pahi* had two deck houses and three masts that were fitted into the keel through holes in the deck. After the props were removed from the sides of the vessel, the *pahi* was launched on its rollers in the presence of a large crowd. Soon afterwards Hiro embarked as captain and pilot of the vessel. Other seamen, who, like him, were 'acquainted with the heavenly bodies and their rising and setting.' went on board as his crew. Women and children also embarked, and one day the great *pahi* sailed out to sea 'never to return to Tahitian waters. . . .'

Orsmond did not attempt to assign a date to the period of Hiro's exploits. However, in a genealogy of the royal family of the Society Islands which he obtained in 1846, Hiro is shown as having lived twenty generations (or reigns) earlier. The genealogy indicates that Hiro left two sons in those islands, and that one of them became the father of the first chief to be called Tamatoa—a name or title still in use in Orsmond's day.[36]

Edmond de Bovis, a French naval officer, who published a valuable study in 1855 entitled *Etat de la Société Tahitienne a l'Arrivée des Européens,* confirmed some of Orsmond's information about Hiro and added other details. He stated specifically that Hiro had lived twenty generations earlier, and that everything before then was in the realm of the fabulous. He claimed that Hiro was the first king of the Society Islands; that he introduced the *maro-ura,* or

* The name of the canoe associated with the murder of Hiro's wife is not given in Orsmond's legend. However, in a series of Hiro legends recorded by the American linguist J. Frank Stimson and published posthumously, the name is given as *Hotu-tahi-nui.*—Stimson 1957:154. It is not stated in Stimson's work where, when or from whom Stimson obtained his information on this point.

PLATE 11. 'A Royal group of Society Islanders' was the caption for the above photograph when it appeared in Edward Reeves' 'Brown Men and Women . . .' (London, 1898). The first three women in the back row were identified as (from left) the queen of Raiatea, the queen of Borabora, and a princess of Huahine. The others were not identified. Below (left) is a portrait of Tati, chief of the Tahitian district of Papara early last century. It was done by the Belgian merchant J. A. Moerenhout and appeared in his 'Voyage aux Iles du Grand Ocean', (Paris, 1837). Fourteen years earlier, R. P. Lesson, assistant-surgeon of the 'Coquille', had described Tati as 'remarkable for the whiteness of his skin as well as for his plumpness and the regularity of his facial features'. The portrait at right is of an early nineteenth century Raiatean pastor, Papeiha. It is reproduced from Richard Lovett's 'The History of the London Missionary Society' (London, 1899).

LA FAMILLE ROYALE
PAPEETE, TAHITI

PLATE 12. Opposite is a composite photograph of Tahiti's royal family prepared by Mrs S. Hoare, a Papeete photographer, about 1886-7. Most of the people depicted are descendants of Pomare I and the consorts of those descendants. Except for two part-Europeans, Isabella Shaw (4th row) and Norman Brander (5th row) all are directly descended from the Hiro lineage of Raiatea or the Mai lineage of Borabora. Prince Hinoi Pomare (4th row) and John Brander (5th row), are the only others not known to be 'pure Polynesian'. The portraits are in rows of five.

First row: *1. Teriimaevarua I (1841-1873), queen of Borabora, daughter of Pomare IV; 2. Pomare II (c.1774-1821), king of Tahiti; 3. Pomare III (1820-27), king of Tahiti; 4. Teremoemoe, daughter of Tamatoa III of Raiatea, wife of Pomare II and mother of Pomares, III and IV; 5. Haamanahia (1849-1911), grandchild of Mai, king of Borabora and great-grandchild of Tati, high chief of Papara, as were Nos. 14 and 15 below.*

Second row: *6. Princess Teriinavahoroa of Raiatea (1877-1918), daughter of Tamatoa V, granddaughter of Pomare IV; 7. Pomare IV (1813-77), queen of Tahiti; 8. Pomare V (1839-91), king of Tahiti; 9. Ariifaaite a Hiro (1820-73), grandson of Tamatoa III of Raiatea, husband of Pomare IV; 10. Princess Aimatarii of Raiatea (1878-94), daughter of Tamatoa V, granddaughter of Pomare IV.*

Third row: *11. Prince Teriitapunui of Tahiti (1846-88), son of Pomare IV; 12. Tamatoa V (1842-81), king of Raiatea, son of Pomare IV; 13. Pomare I (d. 1803), ancestor of Pomare dynasty; 14. Moeterauri a Mai (1850-90); 15. Teriinavahoroa of Tautira.*

Fourth row: *16. Prince Hinoi Pomare (1869-1916), part-European grandson of Pomare IV; 17. Prince de Joinville (1847-75), son of Pomare IV; 18. Teriitaria, queen of Huahine, daughter of Tamatoa III of Raiatea and titular wife of Pomare II; 19. Isabella Shaw (d. 1918), part-European, wife of Prince de Joinville; 20. Teriimaevarua II (1871-1932), queen of Borabora, daughter of Tamatoa V, granddaughter of Pomare IV.*

Fifth row: *21. Tapiria, (adopted) daughter of Ariipeu a Hiro; 22. Princess Teriivaetua (1869-1918) of Raiatea, daughter of Tamatoa V, granddaughter of Pomare IV; 23. John Teriinuiotahiti (Jock) Brander (1885-1918), part-European, son of Princess Teriivaetua; 24. Norman Teriitua Brander (1864-1930), part-European husband of Princess Teriivaetua; 25. Ariipeu a Hiro, grandson of Tamatoa III.*

(Caption prepared by Dr Niel Gunson, Australian National University, Canberra.)

PLATE 13. This photograph was captioned 'Tahitian women (old style)' when published in 1898 in Edward Reeves' book 'Brown Men and Women . . .' Two of the women have a strong Oriental cast of feature and appear to confirm a statement by one of the early Spanish visitors to Tahiti that 'the greater part (of the people), by their physiognomy, resemble Asiatics.'

Charles Bathurst, author of the pioneer treatise 'Notes on Nets; or the Quincunx Practically Considered' (London, 1837) was among those who noted that the netting needles brought back from the South Pacific by the early explorers were like those of Europe. This illustration depicting the open-fork and tongue-and-eye types of needle is from his book. The other implements are gauges.

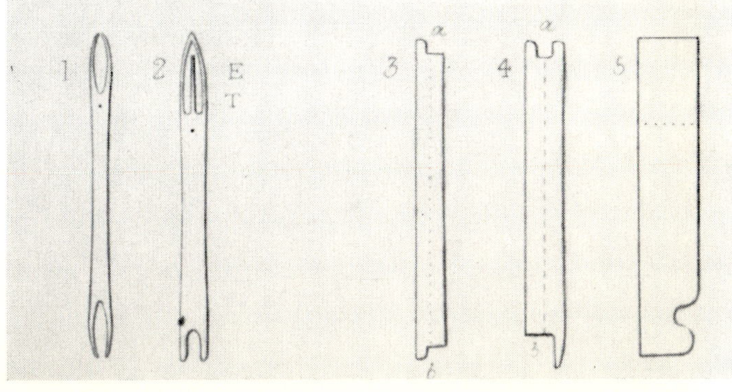

PLATE 14. Among the pictorial evidence suggesting that New Zealand was reached in pre-Cook times by previously unsuspected Europeans is this painting from George French Angas' book 'The New Zealanders Illustrated' (London, 1847). It depicts a chief's family in the middle of New Zealand's North Island. The second child is an 'urukehu'—a blond or red-head. According to the New Zealand scholar Elsdon Best, the 'urukehu' strain reached New Zealand from Eastern Polynesia and was quite distinct from albinism. For further details, see chapter 19.

red-feather girdle, as a symbol of royalty; and that it was he who founded the great Taputapuatea *marae* at Opoa and dedicated it to the god Oro.[37] Other writers attributed other achievements to Hiro. For example, a French ethnologist, J. L. A. de Quatrefages, who obtained his information from French sources in Tahiti, stated in a book in 1866 that Hiro was supposed to have thrown a spear through a mountain on Moorea—the spot where the weapon passed through being still pointed out.* He was also famous for having conquered the great god Tane. Quatrefages went on to say that when a Tahitian genealogist reached Hiro's name in reciting the genealogy of the Raiatean kings, he interrupted his recital to repeat some of the legends associated with him. The genealogist also emphasised that Hiro was not superhuman, but a man—a wise man. In Quatrefages' opinion, the genealogy attested 'very positively' that Hiro had been a king of Raiatea, and he estimated that he must have lived 'about the middle of the sixteenth century, at the very latest.'[38]

None of the writers who gathered traditions about Hiro's career in the Society Islands recorded anything about him after his departure from Raiatea. It therefore seems certain that nothing was known about this in the Society Islands in their time. Likewise, because the Society Islands traditions either remained unpublished for many years or were not widely disseminated, there is little likelihood that they inspired or influenced what was recorded of Hiro in the Cook Islands and New Zealand.

The Cook Islands traditions state that after leaving a place called Avaiki, Hiro (or Iro, as the h-less Cook Islanders call him) reached Rarotonga. After living for a time at Tui-tui-k'a-moana on that island's north coast, he visited the island of Mauke. There he met Tangiia, a chiefly friend from Avaiki, whose children had been killed. Tangiia begged Hiro to allow him to adopt his son Tai-te-ariki, who was with him, and Hiro agreed. Subsequently, Tai-te-ariki settled at Rarotonga, married, and became a progenitor of the Pa Ariki family of Rarotonga's Takitumu tribe. Meanwhile, Hiro visited Aitutaki, Atiu and Mangaia, where he is also said to have left descendants.[39]

No tradition apparently exists recording Hiro's departure from the Cook Islands. However, several Maori traditions claim that he eventually reached New Zealand. One such tradition is that Hiro (or Whiro, as he is known in New Zealand), landed in the Taranaki district, eight miles south of New Plymouth on the western side of the North Island in a canoe called *Tawhiti*. He later marched inland to Karioi† o Whiro (the loitering place of Hiro) and married a Taranaki woman, whose name was the same as that of his son in Rarotonga. Another tradition states that Hiro reached New Zealand in the canoe *Nukutere,* which made the land near Opape in the Bay of Plenty. What-

* The mountain, Mouaputa (2,592 ft), has a hole through its summit just below the top. For a picture, see *Pacific Islands Monthly,* July 1964, p. 82. Another legend about Mouaputa is that the hole was made by a Tahitian warrior called Pai, who hurled a spear at Moorea in an attempt to prevent 'Hiro and his band of thieves' from removing Mount Rotui from that island to Raiatea.—Henry 1928:589.

† Note the similarity between this name and *arioi* (properly *'arioi*), the name of the society of 'strolling players and privileged libertines' in the Society Islands.

ever the truth was, Hiro apparently had further children or was looked upon as a folk father, as several North Island tribes—the Ngatihau, Ngatiporou, Ngapuhi and Whanganui—all trace their descent from him.[40]

Both the Cook Islands and New Zealand traditions describe Hiro as a great navigator. They also recount versions of the murder he is said to have committed in the Society Islands—the detail about the disposal of the body under a heap of wood chips being the same in all cases. Likewise, the genealogies of the two places contain details about Hiro's antecedents that coincide with the genealogy collected by Orsmond. Most of them also place his lifetime in approximately the same period—20, 23, 24 and 25 generations before 1900. The New Zealand traditions agree with those of the Cooks that Hiro's homeland was Avaiki, or Hawaiki as it is written in New Zealand. They also link him with places called Vavau (or Wawau) and Kuporu (or Kupolu). Some scholars have been mystified by these names or have wrongly identified them.[41] But Society Islands sources leave no doubt that they are the old names of Raiatea, Borabora and Tahaa respectively, which in the now k-less Society Islands are written Havaii, Vavau and Uporu.[42]

A feature of the Cook Islands traditions is that they give many details about Hiro's wars on Raiatea with the *ngati* Puna (Puna tribe) that were never recorded in the Society Islands themselves. They also suggest that Hiro was a stranger in those parts, but one who quickly learned to use local customs to ingratiate himself in the local society. One tradition tells how Hiro arrived in a canoe at the entrance to the harbour of Vavau (i.e. Borabora), and how the local chief, Moe-tara-uri, tried to prevent him from landing. When Hiro succeeded, Moe-tara-uri called out:

'Stay where you are, we will each give our descent and our ancestors: Who are you that you are able to reach my land?'

Hiro replied: 'You are of the land, the land is yours, you commence first, I am a visitor and may err.'

Moe-tara-uri then gave his genealogy: 'My ancestor Te Ariki-tapu-kura begat Moe-itiiti, who begat Moe-rekareka, who begat Moe-metua, who begat me Moe-tara-uri.'

Hiro in his turn repeated Moe-tara-uri's genealogy and added a few details that he had apparently learned previously: 'My ancestor Te-Ariki-tapu-kura begat Moe-itiiti, who begat Moe-rekareka, who begat Moe-metua,* who begat Moe-tara-uri, who took to wife Akimano, the daughter of Ngana-te-tupua the descendant of Kaukura-ariki, and they begat me, Iro-ma-oata; my name is the name of the night when Moe-tara-uri visited my mother.'

The Cook Islands tradition goes on: 'When Moe-tara-uri heard this he was overjoyed, and sprang into the sea and rubbed noses with his son Iro,

* Moe-metua does not figure in the genealogy of Hiro that Orsmond collected, nor in those of the New Zealand tribes. Moe-tara-uri (or Moe-te-ra-uri) is also missing from the New Zealand genealogies, but it immediately precedes Hiro's name in that of Orsmond. Moe-te-rekareka (or Moe-te-re'a-re'a) is common to all the genealogies.—Smith 1893:29.

and conveyed him to the land. . . . The father then called all the people together and caused a great feast to be made in Iro's honour. . . . He appointed Iro *ariki* [chief] over the land in his stead, the name of his *koutu-ariki* (court of royalty) was named Nuiapu.'[43]

Because of the numerous legends concerning Hiro's career in the Society Islands and the many landmarks associated with him there, it is evident that he lived in those islands for several years and was looked up to as an extraordinary man. His influence, it seems, lived on long after his departure. Not only did the keeled, plank-sided *pahi* become the usual means of conveyance for the Raiatean chiefs, but the Oro cult and all its trappings became a matter of contention throughout those islands. Battles over Oro were still going on when the *Duff* missionaries arrived.[44]

Traditions recorded by Orsmond and published in *Ancient Tahiti* give details of the Oro cult's spread both to the islands in the immediate vicinity of Raiatea as well as to Tahiti and Moorea. The traditions state that the cult was first taken to Tahiti in the reign of the first Tamatoa, Hiro's grandson. Its first emissary was a priest called Tupua-nui-te-faaonoono, who was accompanied by his two brothers and a sister. They took with them a stone from the Taputapuatea *marae* which they intended to present, with other gifts, to the Tahitians of what is now Papeete. However, while their canoe was moored on the reef near the entrance to Papeete harbour, the warriors of that district came out and tried to seize it. In this predicament, the priest's sister invoked the aid of Oro, whereupon the canoe and its occupants were 'caught up into the clouds and borne speedily by a strong wind to Opoa.' After presenting offerings to Oro in gratitude for their deliverance, these 'zealots of Oro' set out for Tahiti again. This time they landed at Taiarapu where they were 'received with due ceremonies and allowed to set up their cornerstone.' Subsequently, 'a great national *marae*' was built there which was named Taputapuatea, like the parent temple at Opoa. Later the priests of Oro went to Paea, where they were 'allowed to take possession and were also aided in the building of their *marae*.' Gradually, as the priests of the new order increased, new *marae* to Oro were erected all around Tahiti. And eventually a *marae* called Taputapuatea was also built at Papetoai, Moorea, following a marriage between a high chief of the Manea family of Papetoai and 'a princess of Opoa.' 'Meanwhile,' Orsmond's account adds, 'many princes and princesses of the royal house of Opoa intermarried with the families of the high chiefs of Tahiti, in consequence of which more royal *marae* were erected to Oro and some to other gods. . . .'[45]

It will be seen from the foregoing that Orsmond's account of the spread of the Oro cult to and within Tahiti corresponds closely with Andía y Varela's story of the settlement of that island, recorded at Taiarapu in 1774. It will likewise be noted that the places in Tahiti that were especially associated with the cult were also the places where the early explorers most frequently saw islanders with light skins, red hair and sometimes blue eyes. This, of course, is not surprising. As the Raiateans were invariably said to be fairer than the generality of Tahitians, enclaves of blondism must have been created wherever they established new Oro colonies. It was therefore in the nature of things that the early European visitors to Taiarapu—but not those to Matavai Bay—should have repeatedly remarked on the light features of the people of that area, for it was there that the Oro cult had been longest established. Light-featured people were also conspicuous in the vicinity of Paea, where the priests of Oro were 'allowed to take possession.' However, as Europeans rarely visited that district in the first half-century of contact, only a few such people were specifically described. These included Captain Wallis' light-skinned 'Queen Oberea', a high chiefess of Papara, which adjoins Paea; Maximo Rodriguez's red-haired, blue-eyed beauty, Oviriau, whose district, Atehuru, included Paea; and the white man at Potatau's headquarters in Atehuru who so puzzled Lieutenant Pickersgill.

Further genetic evidence of the truth of the tradition recorded by Orsmond is provided by the variegated skin colours of the offspring of Tahitian-Raiatean marriages. One example, already recorded, is that of the Tahitian-Raiatean family of Hapai'i or Teu, Pomare II's grandfather, among whom George Forster noted that two children were much fairer than the others. Another example is that of the family of Pomare II himself. Pomare II, as Ellis stated, was 'not dark, but rather tawny,' while his Raiatean wife was of a comparatively fair complexion.[46] They had two children, both of whom were evidently much fairer than the father, although one was darker than the other. The younger one, a boy, reigned briefly as Pomare III following his father's death in 1821. The other, a girl, Aimata, assumed the title of Queen Pomare IV when her brother died in 1827. The two children were described by R. P. Lesson, assistant-surgeon of the French exploring vessel *Coquille,* which visited Tahiti in May 1823. Pomare III, then three years old, was seen as 'an interesting figure, of delicate features' who would have passed as 'a beautiful child even in England, the country *par excellence* for chubby, fresh-faced, ruddy-cheeked children.'[47] His sister Aimata, then ten, was of a somewhat darker complexion. 'Her features are slender and delicate, and her colouration is a very light yellow, verging on white,' Lesson wrote.[48] The light colour of other Tahitian chiefs also attracted Lesson's attention. Tati, the head of the Teva clan of Papara, was described as 'remarkable for the whiteness of his skin as well as for his plumpness and the regularity of his facial features.'[49] Likewise, the wives of the chiefs who did not work in the sun were said to have skins that were 'rather less dark than that of the people of Provence' and to be 'remarkable for a very great whiteness.'[50] Other visitors to Tahiti wrote similarly; and at least two confirmed Lesson's statements about the complexions of Pomare II's children.[51]

Tahiti by that time also had its share of half-caste European children—the offspring of sailors from the numerous European ships that had put into the island since the turn of the nineteenth century.[52] On the other hand, the massive depopulation that followed the European discovery of that island seems to have wiped out some ethnic types; or, perhaps, intermarriage among those who remained blurred the distinctions. Whatever the reason was, writers from the 1830s onwards were less conscious of the different types that had so struck the early explorers, and some even maintained that they had never existed. Thus, J. A. Moerenhout, a Belgian trader who settled in Tahiti in 1829, wrote emphatically after several years' residence that he had never seen a single Tahitian with crisp hair—*cheveux crépu*—a term much used by the early explorers. He claimed also that any differences in skin colour were entirely due to different modes of life and different habitats, and that these disappeared when the people lived under similar conditions.[53] Moerenhout's views were later held by no less a person than Marau Taaroa, consort of Pomare V, Tahiti's last king, and a noted authority on her people. In 1930, a few years before her death, she was reported as saying that in former times the *manahune* were 'not distinguishable from any other Tahitians in stature or color.'[54]

Yet if time, disease or miscegenation did, in fact, ring such genetic changes in Tahiti that former ethnic differences became obscured and forgotten, they were still observable in the less-frequented leeward islands of the Society group well into the nineteenth century. Frederick Debell Bennett, a Fellow of the Royal College of Surgeons, London, was one who noticed them. In 1834, on a visit to Raiatea in a whaler, he recorded that the royal chief of that island, Tamatoa IV, was 'much lighter' in complexion than most of his countrymen. He also found a variety of skin colours among the Raiateans generally, as well as 'a somewhat paradoxical taste' for a fair complexion or 'the nearest approach to one.' '*Taata ere ere,* or black man,' he said, 'they regard as a term of reproach; each, probably, thinking himself less dark than his neighbour.' Yet the 'clear brown complexion' of some Raiateans was sometimes many shades darker than in others. In a few cases, it almost amounted to blackness, without any apparent cause, such as extraordinary exposure to the sun, to account for it. Bennett also noted, particularly among the 'higher ranks', that there was a regularity in the features, a thinness of the lips, and a prominence of the nose (approaching the aquiline) that brought them 'nearer to the European cast.' He added that although the Raiateans' hair was generally black and glossy, that of the adults was occasionally of a light reddish colour, while a 'flaxen hue' was sometimes seen among the children.[55]

Another of Bennett's observations was that the Raiateans had a musical instrument called a *hoe,* which was made of bamboo and played with the mouth and fingers like a flageolet.* The *hoe* was not recorded by any other early visitor to Raiatea, nor to any other part of Polynesia. If it was indigenous, as it seems to have been, it was an unusually sophisticated instrument for the Pacific Islands. Bennett said it produced a tone 'similar to the drone of a bagpipe.' He went on:

The upper extremity, or embouchure, of this instrument is split on one

* An instrument like a flute, but blown at the end instead of the side.

side, and encircled by a ring of tow or other soft material, by raising or depressing which the aperture is enlarged or diminished, with the effect of producing a graver or more acute tone at the option of the performer. The *hoe* is usually played in concert, or as an accompaniment to the native dances; the reeds being tuned with extreme accuracy previous to each performance. The musicians sit in a circle, huddled close together, with their heads depressed to their knees, and thus play native tunes with much precision and great regard to time. A few of the more exquisite musicians embellish their performance with a flourish of the fingers, rivalling in grace that of Paganini's bow.[56]

Although the *hoe* was not seen or, at least, described again, Bennett's remarks on the blond features of some Raiateans were echoed some seventy years later by Paul Huguenin, a Swiss, who spent four years in the leeward islands as director of Protestant mission schools. In his book *Raiatea La Sacrée,* Huguenin wrote:

. . . the families of the *arii* or great chiefs are of a type apart. The members of these families are always distinguished by an above-average stature, a marked propensity to obesity, and a lighter skin than that of the Tahitians in general. Their eyes are not black. I have observed that those of the Tamatoas, the royal family of Raiatea, are pale, with bluish lights, as are those of the royal family of Huahine. Their beards and hair are very light also, verging, in fact, on the reddish.

In Huguenin's opinion, there were two main reasons why the *arii* were genetically different from other Society Islanders. One was that they were the last invaders of the group—people who, by their greater strength and superior intelligence, had conquered the *raatira* and *manahune* who preceded them. Secondly, they kept their blood lines pure by avoiding misalliances and by holding in contempt any children who were born of such marriages. According to Huguenin, the Pomares were not of the same racial type as the other *arii,* their skins being darker, their chins receding, and their lips thick like those of the Tahitians in general.[57]

Huguenin noted that the Tahitian language contained many synonymous words for the same objects, and he deduced from this that there had been two distinct waves of immigrants in the Society Islands. However, he believed that the islanders had all come from the same place—that they had originated in India and had entered the Pacific after sojourns of various lengths in Indonesia. The first migration, dating back to about the first and second centuries of the Christian era, had probably come via the north of New Guinea, the Solomons, New Hebrides, Fiji and Samoa. It was reasonable to believe, he said, that it had brought the *manahune* to Tahiti and Hawaii as well as the first inhabitants to New Zealand and the Marquesas. Huguenin believed that a second wave of immigrants—more warlike and much more subject to Malayan influence—had reached Samoa by the same route as the first between the tenth and twelfth centuries, and that these people had later spread to the other Polynesian groups. 'This migration gave the islands kings and chiefs (*hui arii, hui raatira*),' he said, 'while the primitive inhabitants were reduced to an inferior condition, that of *manahune*.'[58]

In broad terms, an American ethnologist, E. S. Craighill Handy, came to the same conclusions as Huguenin a generation or so later after studying the Society Islanders' traditions, archaeology, material culture, social organisation, religion and mythology for several years. Handy, however, went considerably further than Huguenin in that he attempted to separate the cultural traits of the two waves of immigrants. On the other hand, he saw nothing noteworthy in the physical appearance of such *arii* as he himself met; and, with one exception, nothing in the descriptions of the explorers whose works he consulted.

In his monograph *History and Culture in the Society Islands,* Handy contended that the civilisation of those islands when eighteenth century Europeans discovered them was a product of the blending of the cultures of the *manahune* and the later-arriving *arii*. The 'intermediate class' of *raatira,* he thought, had come about through intermarriage between the 'followers of the conquering *arii*' and the 'superior element of the old population.'[59]

Like Huguenin, Handy believed the *manahune* were 'old Polynesians'—'like the Maoris of New Zealand.'[60] They were cultivators who wore the *maro,* lived in communal, democratic clans and tribes, and practised sexual freedom. They were skilled stoneworkers and carvers who used terraced hilltop forts in time of war. Their *marae* were inland rather than on the coast. They were head-hunters and ancestor-worshippers who venerated skulls and other relics. Their gods were Tane, Roo (Rongo) and Tu, but Atea, Maui, Tii and others played important roles in their mythology.[61] Their seacraft was the *vaa*—a vessel with a dugout hull, elevated sides, bow and stern. The *vaa,* Handy said, was unquestionably the ancient Polynesian type of canoe, being preserved in the structure of the Hawaiian *waa* and Marquesan *vaka*.[62] In the heyday of the *manahune* the names applied to Tahiti and its neighbours were 'undoubtedly those now spoken of as the ancient names of the islands.' Thus, Raiatea was called Havaii, Tahaa was Uporu, Borabora was Vavau, Tahiti was Hiti, Moorea was Eimeo, and so on.[63] Handy did not speculate on where the *manahune* had originated. But he thought there was 'little reason to suppose' that they spoke the same language as the *arii,* although that of the *arii* 'may have been, in fact probably was, of the same family.'[64]

In Handy's view, the *arii* had much in common with the people of Tonga and Samoa. Their houses were 'characteristic of the region of central western Polynesia' which was 'dominated by descendants of Taaroa (Tangaloa),' and there were similarities in such matters as kava drinking, oratory, and certain titles and ceremonies.[65] Handy attributed to the *arii* such items of household furniture as stools, headrests and bowls. He claimed they were specialists in plaiting and weaving fibre, and in printing *tapa* in geometric and naturalistic patterns; that they had elaborate political institutions, court etiquette, dynastic traditions and insignia; that they were lovers of costume and the drama; and that they had a high respect for chastity, purity of blood and a light skin.[66] In addition, he said, they had a remarkable body of laws, precepts and maxims called *ture* that was transmitted orally from one generation to another. One group of *ture* impressed on the *arii* his duty towards himself and his family; another concerned the rules of government. Handy obtained his information about the *ture* from Queen Marau, whose family seat was Papara. Among those he recorded were the following:

- Let not your eyes be blind to the errors of your family. Sin will be like an oven in your home.
- Let not your ears, but your eyes, be open to the reports of evil persons. You will be the first wounded if you believe them or are blind to them.
- Allow not your head to be touched by the hands of the woman of low birth. Your head does not belong to them.
- Take care in choosing the polisher of your spear case.
- Guard yourself against courtesans, who anoint themselves with sweet-scented oils in your household; they will be the cause of the drowning of your soul with the false pride that is the mark of the low-born.
- Let not folded legs and the love of soft couches be known in your household. They will be the cause of your ruin.
- Keep a ready ear for the agitated cries of the night bird, *torea*. It is the herald of the warrior of death.
- Let not the decrees of death be too frequent, for your own bones will follow the road to death. It will be like the tearing down of your own home by the warrior when the night of darkness is enveloping you, the night that hides sin.
- The people are like a crying child, easily coaxed with gentle words, easily enraged by ill treatment.
- The heart of the *arii* must be as great as his power; he must be ever ready to do good, never weary of listening to the cry of his people, with ears and eyes open to the demands of the law.
- Beware of the soft-voiced flatterer. Flattery is the commencement of deception.

Commenting on the *ture,* Handy said they gave the essence of the principles which underlay the Tahitian social order under the *hui arii*. Whether they were edicts of a benevolent ruler, or crystallisations of mores evolved through the centuries, they assuredly pointed to a 'high order of civilization.' They also revealed the *hui arii* as a dynasty with traditions and institutions 'belonging to a phase of cultural evolution wholly different and entirely removed from that exemplified in the tribal life of the Marquesans and Maoris.'[68]

Handy thought there was every reason to believe that the original *arii* were 'a distinctly maritime people.' In both Samoa and Tahiti the *arii* had clung to the littoral and, in cooperation with an ideal environment, had developed a highly perfected art of fishing. Tradition revealed that certain of their stock were skilled navigators and fearless adventurers by land and sea. There was no doubt that the *arii* had introduced the *pahi,* or 'built-up composite vessel with keel,' to the Society Islands. 'Tradition definitely attributes this form of vessel to Hiro, an early *arii* of the Leeward Islands,' Handy said. 'In principles of construction and fundamental form, as well as in the word employed by the natives to describe it, this style of craft stands in marked contrast to the old Polynesian *vaa* style. . . .'[69] In a later study, *Houses, Boats and Fishing in the Society Islands,* Handy wrote further about the *pahi.* He was convinced, he said, that it was introduced to the Society Islands by 'an experienced boat-building and seafaring group of immigrants.' And he added:

> My impression is that the chiefs of the Leeward Islands were much more active traders, voyagers and explorers than those of Tahiti. Tradition bears this out . . . and history points to Raiatea as the center of the dynasty of seafaring chiefs who spread their domain throughout the Society Islands and beyond, to the Cook and Austral Islands, and the Tuamotus.[70]

Using genealogical information supplied by Queen Marau, Handy tentatively fixed the founding of the *hui arii* settlement at Opoa in the late sixth or seventh century. This was sixty-seven generations before 1930, taking twenty years for each generation. However, Handy believed the Taputapuatea *marae* at Opoa was founded long after the era of *arii* domination began. Its very size, he said, precluded its being built except by an *arii* capable of calling on a large force of laborers, and such a force would not have been available in the early period of settlement.[71] Handy also believed that the foundation of the *arioi* society at Opoa dated only to the time of the first Tamatoa, which he estimated to be in the early sixteenth century.[72]

Some ethnologists subsequently challenged Handy's view that the *arii* and *manahune* arrived in the Society Islands separately and with distinct cultures.[73] But they did not dispute his main thesis that the culture of those islands when modern Europeans discovered them was derived from Tonga and Samoa. This thesis was first expounded in the 1840s by Horatio Hale, a brilliant young ethnologist with the United States Exploring Expedition.[74] It is still generally held.[75] And on most issues it seems unlikely that it will ever be seriously disputed. Yet it is clear from the evidence already brought forward in this book and from other data in the literature of Tonga and Samoa (see Appendix D), that the Tonga-Samoa theory, particularly as Handy expounded it, does not explain several striking anomalies in the ethnography of the Society Islands. These anomalies pose such questions as:

1. Why invaders from Tonga and Samoa, in the *western* Pacific, would have chosen Opoa, on the *eastern* side of Raiatea, as the site of their first settlement—particularly as a barrier reef (see map) makes access to Opoa virtually impossible except from the east.
2. Why such invaders would have abandoned the names Havaii, Uporu and Vavau in favour of Raiatea, Tahaa and Borabora when the first group—with slight sound differences in two cases—were, and still are, the names of three of the principal islands in Tonga and Samoa.

3. Why the *hui arii,* whom Handy identified as 'active traders, voyagers and explorers', took so long to establish themselves in Tahiti if they did, indeed, arrive in the leeward Society Islands sixty-seven generations before 1930.
4. How the *raatira* could have become a numerous body through intermarriage between the *manahune* and 'followers of the conquering *arii*' when the *arii* had strict rules to keep their blood lines pure and the children of mis-alliances were destroyed except in exceptional circumstances.
5. Why the *raatira* owned more land than their superiors, the *arii,* and why the *arii* apparently had no control over their land rights.
6. Why no vessel resembling the *pahi* was known in Tonga or Samoa in historical times and why the word *pahi* (or something similar) was also unknown, although both the primitive *vaa* and the word for it were known in both places.
7. Why the building of the *pahi* was still confined to the leeward Society Islands in Cook's time.
8. Why the navigational lore of the Society Islands included features that were never recorded in Tonga and Samoa. (One such feature was the practice of dividing the horizon into eight or sixteen equal parts, a practice which a specialist in early European navigational techniques has claimed could not have been conceived without prior knowledge of the magnetic compass.)[76]
9. Why the Society Islanders used netting needles like those of Europe—including the distinctive eye and tongue type—to make their fishing nets.
10. Why the most knowledgeable Society Islanders, such as Tupaia and Tutaha, were almost invariably Raiateans, and why much of their abstract knowledge was unknown in Tonga and Samoa.
11. Why the Raiateans had dramatic entertainments and a wind instrument, the *hoe,* that were unknown in Tonga and Samoa, and even in Tahiti.
12. Why the Raiatean women wore a seemingly European-style dress for their entertainments unlike anything ever seen in the other islands.
13. Why the Oro cult or something resembling it was unknown in Tonga and Samoa.
14. Why the coincidences between Society Islands religious beliefs and Biblical teachings, which Morrison and Ellis noted independently, were not found in Tonga and Samoa.
15. Why the Tahitians frequently shook hands as a form of greeting while the Tongans and Samoans rubbed noses.
16. Why the Raiatean *arii* and their relatives elsewhere were generally light-skinned and sometimes red-haired, blue-eyed and of Caucasian features while the Samoans and Tongans were almost invariably dark-complexioned and with non-Caucasian features.

A consideration of the foregoing questions and the evidence concerning them must inevitably lead to several broad conclusions. These are that the Raiatean *arii* were ethnically and culturally distinct from the Tongans and

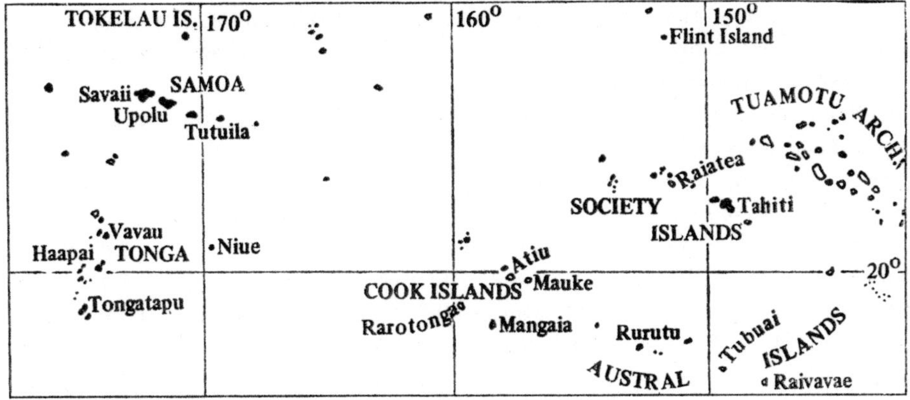

Samoans, and that they must therefore have come from some other place; that they reached the Society Islands in quite recent times; that they conquered the *manahune* and *raatira* but did not dispossess them or interfere with most of their customs; that they grafted their own culture on the existing culture, but kept some of their skills and knowledge to themselves; and that their infiltration and cultural conquest of Tahiti were incomplete when Europeans discovered it in 1767.

If Tonga and Samoa are ruled out as the immediate places of origin of the Raiatean *arii,* only a few alternatives remain. To the north, the only land mass of any size is Hawaii, almost 2,000 miles away. To the south, there are only the five insignificant Austral Islands. To the west, apart from Tonga and Samoa, there are only a few small islands such as the Cook group, Niue and Tokelaus before the islands of Melanesia are reached. And to the east are the seventy-six islands of the Tuamotu Archipelago, the Marquesas, Pitcairn and Easter Island.

Without considering whether any of those places had inhabitants with the physical characteristics, the seacraft and other attributes of the Raiatean *arii,* a study of geographical factors reveals that the east is the most logical homeland for those chiefly people. Not only are the nearest of the eastern islands closer to the Society Islands than any others, they are also to windward of them. This means that the prevailing south-east trade wind and east-to-west currents would have favoured a voyage towards those islands, whether by drift or design.[77] Moreover, Opoa would have been a natural landfall for vessels involved in such a voyage, particularly if they originated in the western or central Tuamotus and could not make the land at Tetiaroa, Tahiti or Huahine.[78]

Of course, if these *arii* did reach the Society Islands from the east and were not of Tongan or Samoan origin, the names Havaii, Uporu and Vavau would have meant nothing to them. So if they succeeded in conquering their predecessors, it would have been natural for them to change those names, as conquerors have done throughout history. A typical example is that of New York where English forces defeated a community of Dutch colonists in 1664 and immediately substituted the English name New York for the Dutch name

New Amsterdam. However, as a modern encyclopedia puts it, 'the terms of the surrender were highly favorable to the Dutch colonists, whose institutions and customs persisted in the Hudson Valley for many years.'[79]

That the names of the leeward Society Islands had not long been changed when Captain Cook discovered them is evident from the fact that the old names were still remembered in Orsmond's time. Yet they must have been changed at least five generations before 1789 because James Morrison of the *Bounty* found that the great-great-grandson of a blown-away Raiatean chief was using the names Raiatea, Tahaa and Huahine for his lands on Tubuai.[80] On the other hand, the old names must still have been known in Hiro's time, otherwise Hawaiki, Vavau and Kuporu could not have been associated with him in Cook Islands and New Zealand tradition.[81]

As has already been seen, Ellis considered Hiro to be 'the most recent' of the Society Islanders' deified ancestors. A genealogy obtained by Orsmond in 1846 indicated that Hiro had lived twenty generations (or reigns) earlier—a period with which Bovis agreed. Quatrefages fixed Hiro's lifetime at 'about the middle of the sixteenth century, at the very latest.' Handy considered that Hiro's grandson had lived in the early sixteenth century. And most of the genealogies of the Cook Islands and New Zealand indicate that Hiro flourished from twenty to twenty-five generations before 1900. There is therefore broad agreement among a wide variety of authorities on the period of Hiro's career. In fact, provided only fifteen years are allowed for a generation—as Queen Marau suggested for the Society Islands[82]—even the longest genealogy fixes Hiro's lifetime within the sixteenth century. In other words, it is compatible with the genealogies to suppose that Hiro may have been either a survivor, or a descendant of a survivor, of the ill-fated *San Lesmes*, or whatever ship left her guns on the reef at Amanu. It therefore follows that people of European origin could have settled in the Society Islands, Cook Islands and New Zealand some two and a half centuries earlier than has hitherto been supposed.

Several coincidences in the ancient lore of Eastern Polynesia and that of New Zealand lend weight to this notion, and these will later be examined. Meanwhile, the question is: is there any evidence that Hiro and his band of followers did reach the Society Islands from the Tuamotus, and that they were, in fact, linked with the *San Lesmes?* One piece of information that immediately suggests an affirmative answer is to be found in the writings of the Pacific canoe specialist James Hornell. According to him, probably the best sailing craft ever built in Polynesia were constructed in the Tuamotus[83]—and this despite the fact that those islands are among the worst-endowed in the Pacific with good timber trees . . .

15

Anaa: land of 'immense vessels like our ships'

When the first LMS missionaries arrived in Tahiti in the ship *Duff* in 1797, at least a third of the seventy-six atolls and islands of the Tuamotu Archipelago had never been seen by Europeans, as far as anyone then knew. Of those that had been sighted, some had not been revisited since the pioneering voyages of Quiros, Schouten and Le Maire in the early seventeenth century. No Europeans were known to have spent more than a few hours on any atoll, except for the five deserters from Roggeveen's expedition of 1722. And no Europeans had voluntarily landed on one since Cook's brief stop at Takaroa in 1774. Apart from the whaler *Matilda,* which was wrecked without loss of life on uninhabited Mururoa in 1792, only six ships had sighted islands in the archipelago between Cook's second voyage and the *Duff's* arrival in Tahiti. These six were the *Aguila* and *Jupiter* (1774), *Aguila* (1775), *Pandora* (1791), and *Providence* and *Assistant* (1792).[1] Their voyages had added five new atolls to European charts, but only at one of these, Tatakoto, were any people seen.

The *Duff* herself found some new islands in or near the archipelago on her voyage from Tahiti to the Marquesas. The first were the high islands of Mangareva and the neighbouring atoll, Temoe, which were named Gambier Islands and Crescent Island respectively. Then, nine days later to the northward, another atoll, Pukarua, was discovered and named Serle's Island. Of these, both Mangareva and Temoe, were inhabited, but the *Duff's* crew did not communicate with them.[2]

Following the *Duff's* voyage, no other European ship is known to have been among the Tuamotus until 1802 when the British ship *Margaret* (Captain John Buyers) touched at several atolls en route from Hawaii to Tahiti. The atolls included previously undiscovered Makemo, where one of several naked islanders was seen to have a few pearl oyster shells hanging around his neck. This observation led the *Margaret's* people to suspect that pearls were to be found thereabouts, and the *Margaret's* captain decided to head for Tahiti with all speed to equip his ship for a pearling voyage. Within a few weeks, the *Margaret* was back in Tuamotuan waters. But on the night of 17 April 1803, she was wrecked on Arutua Atoll, one of Cook's Palliser Islands, and her crew was lucky to get back to Tahiti on a rudely-made punt.[3]

Four years then passed before another British ship, the *General Wellesley,* made a second voyage to the Tuamotus in quest of pearls. However, because of bad weather, the hostility of the islanders, poor interpreters and lack of divers, this venture was also a failure.[4] The third attempt to exploit the archipelago's resources was not made until 1809 when Captain William Campbell, master and owner of the Sydney brig *Hibernia,* succeeded in obtaining a small cargo of bêche-de-mer and pearlshell in the north-western atolls.[5] This prompted him to make a second voyage to the archipelago in 1811. Although on that occasion his ship, the *Venus,* was wrecked on Manihi Atoll, he did obtain enough pearls and pearlshell to make the voyage worthwhile.[6]

News of Campbell's successes soon brought other would-be pearlers to the Tuamotus.[7] But there was never anything like a gold rush—only a thin trickle of ships that took nearly forty years to investigate the archipelago from end to end. The pearlers soon discovered that one atoll stood out from all the rest. This was Anaa, some 250 miles east of Tahiti and about seventy miles from its nearest neighbours, Faaite and Tahanea. Besides being the most fertile and densely populated atoll in the archipelago, Anaa was remarkable for its fierce, tattooed warriors, its expert shipwrights and daring navigators who wandered over much of the archipelago in huge, double-hulled *pahi,* being the terror of the other inhabitants. The Anaans, indeed, seem to have been masters at that time of the entire double chain of atolls stretching from Arutua in the west to Taenga and Nihiru in the east; and they tried to ensure that no hostile foreigners could settle on them by destroying any coconut trees that chanced to grow there.[8]

In the early years of the pearlshell trade, the pearlers sometimes engaged wandering bands of Anaans to dive for them, although they usually depended on Society Islanders. However, in the early 1820s, it was the common practice for several years for the pearlers to hire their divers at Anaa itself. Anaa, by that time, had adopted Christianity, for the teachings of the LMS missionaries in Tahiti had been carried there by Anaan converts. Meanwhile, the atoll itself had remained virtually unknown to Europeans. The only European who can be said with some certainty to have landed there before 1820 was Captain R. S. Walker of the sandalwooder *King George*. Walker called there in 1817 after the first Anaan convert had begun missionary work.[9]

Anaa is undoubtedly one of the few islands in the eastern Pacific where Christianity is known to have been taught before the first recorded white man set foot on shore, and where that religion was adopted without any European being present. However, there seem to be substantial reasons for believing that, long before the period of recorded history, the white man and his religion had already reached that atoll; that the white man had brought a long-haired species of dog with him, besides other things that were then unknown in the islands further west; and that the Anaans' huge double-hulled *pahi* of the pearling era were, in fact, modelled on vessels of European origin, but adapted to suit the local, timber-scarce conditions.

Evidence to support these notions began accumulating in 1769, soon after Captain Cook discovered Anaa and named it Chain Island because of the chain-like formation of islets on its oval-shaped reef. He himself recorded nothing more about the atoll beyond the fact that smoke could be seen rising from it and that the trees were too far off to be identified.[10] However, later

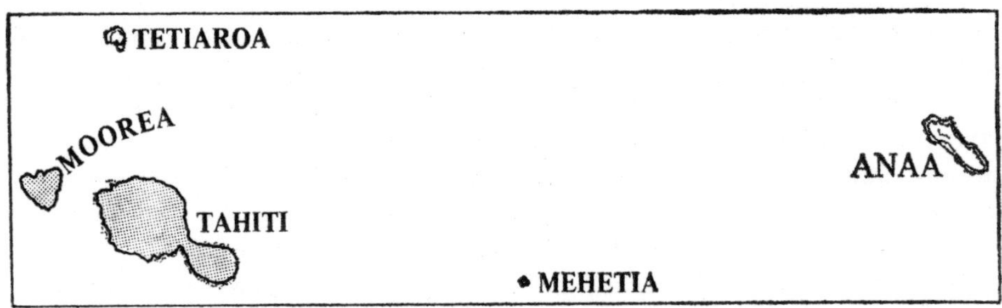

in Tahiti, an anonymous chronicler of his expedition was told that the Tahitians visited Anaa to barter for a fine white dogs' hair that 'grew on a species of dog peculiar to themselves.'[11] Three years later, when the Spanish explorer Boenechea touched at Anaa, he sent a boat in close to seek an anchorage under a young officer, Raimundo Bonacorsi. This exercise revealed that although the Anaans were heavily tattooed on the shoulders, buttocks, trunks, arms and legs, some of them were 'pretty blonde in hue,' while others were 'of a tawny colour with frizzly hair' or of 'purely Indian features and the hair lank.'[12] After an interval of two more years, when Boenechea called at the atoll again, his first officer, Tomas Gayangos, discovered another curious anomaly while reconoitring the atoll's northern coast. This was the wooden cross, referred to in chapter 11, which Gayangos described as 'regular in all its proportions' and showing signs of having been erected a long time previously.[13] Gayangos later learned that Anaa was known both as Tapuhoe and Oana, while his companion Andía y Varela wrote of it as Topufue.*[14] Gayangos also recorded—on the authority of the Tahitians—that the atoll abounded with coconuts, yams, fish and dogs; that it also produced pearls; and that its inhabitants were 'a bad lot of people.'[15]

Although some Tahitians undoubtedly held the Anaans in mortal dread, several references in the early literature of Tahiti make it clear that they carried on a trade with them by way of lofty Mehetia Island. Mehetia was then under the control of the chief of Taiarapu. The first reference to the Tahiti-Mehetia-Anaa trade is an entry in the diary of the Spanish interpreter Maximo Rodríguez. On 26 September 1775, Rodríguez recorded that a *pahi* had reached Tahiti from Mehetia; that it had been smashed on the reef at Taiarapu; and that the Tahitians had 'made havoc' of the goods it brought.[16] Thirteen years later, Bligh learned of a canoe—presumably a *pahi*—that had arrived at Mehetia from Anaa, and whose crew, except for a woman and a young boy, had been killed.[17] Finally, there is a detailed account by James Morrison of how the chief of Taiarapu kept a canoe plying regularly between Taiarapu and Mehetia, which linked Mehetia with the more easterly islands. On its outward voyage the canoe carried iron and other commodities obtained from Europeans. On its return, it brought pearls, pearlshell, matting, cloth, oil, hogs, etc. and stools, headrests and dishes made of tamanu wood. To reach Mehetia, the canoe's crew took advantage of a northerly wind. They then

* The 'f' and 'h' were almost interchangeable in eighteenth century Tahitian—perhaps for the reason advanced later in this chapter.

waited at that island until the wind changed so they could 'stretch to the Northward' to reach a group of small islands whose capital was 'Tapoohoe.'[18]

There is evidence in LMS sources that the trade through Mehetia was still going on in 1803.[19] But it broke down about 1806 when a party of Anaans invaded that island and drove its inhabitants out.[20] The trade was never resumed. One of the consequences seems to have been that the term Tapuhoe quickly fell into disuse among the Tahitians and was forgotten,[21] while another word, *papaa,* lost its old meaning. Originally, the Tahitians had used *papaa* (which literally means 'sunburnt shoulderblades') as an epithet for the Anaans. But after the advent of Captain Wallis and the *Dolphin's* crew, they also used it to mean white men or Europeans—as they still do today.*[22] The Tahitians thus seem to have seen some resemblance between the Anaans and Europeans. In addition, there is no doubt that the *pahi,* in their eyes, had more in common with European ships than their own canoes, or *vaa,* for it was *pahi* rather than *vaa* that they adopted as the generic term for ship.

The word *pahi* was first recorded as the Tahitian equivalent of ship in 1769, and the word *papaa* as their equivalent of European about 1790.[23] But it was not until September 1807, when four large Anaan sailing craft were driven to Tahiti in a storm, that any European seized the opportunity to describe what the Tahitians had originally called a *pahi papaa.* The four vessels had been caught in a strong easterly wind while sailing from Anaa to Kaukura, one of the north-western Tuamotus. They landed at Point Venus, where Pomare II kindly received them. One of the *pahi* had seven men and one woman on board; the rest had about twenty people each, including six or seven women. To the LMS missionary John Davies, who saw them arrive, the Anaans seemed a 'wild daring people,' although they were much afraid at first both of Europeans and of Pomare's red-coated guards.

> These islanders [Davies wrote] appear in many things to be very far short of the Taheiteans in civilization, but notwithstanding this, these savages display no small degree of ingenuity in the construction of their *Pahe's,* or Canoes, for tho' their islands scarcely afford a single timber tree of any kind, yet they find means of building large and strong vessels, far superior in respect of convenience, strength and safety in operation, to any of those built by the Taheite or Society Islanders. Their vessels are made of small pieces of wood† . . . well fitted and strongly sewn together with sinnet made of the fibres of cocoa nut husks. To those that have not seen or known the state of manners of these islands previous to their intercourse with Europeans it would hardly appear credible that such work could be accomplished by means so inadequate, for it ought to be remembered that these eastern islanders have not only a scarcity of materials but that all their work is accomplished by means of such tools as they can make of stones, bones or shells. But surely their work must cost them an immense labour and much time. On an inquiry

* However, the word is now spelled and pronounced *popaa.*

† Several words describing the type of wood are illegible in the original manuscript.

PLATE 15. Model of an Anaan 'pahi' or double canoe, made under the supervision of Admiral F. E. Paris, for the Musée de la Marine, Louvre, Paris. Admiral Paris saw such craft in Tahiti in 1839 and made minute measurements of them. But he did not see them rigged or under sail and was only told that their sails were triangular. The only known contemporary representation of such craft under sail is that of Captain Wallis, plate 20. Photograph: Musée de la Marine.

The only practicable pass into the lagoon at Anaa is at the north-western end of the atoll. It was at the point at left that the Spaniard Tomas Gayangos reported seeing a cross in 1774 that was 'regular in all its proportions, and showed signs of having been erected a long time ago.' The photograph was taken by a member of the 'Albatross' expedition to the Pacific at the turn of the present century.

PLATE 16. The atolls of the Tuamotu Archipelago are all much alike—rings of coral surrounding fairly shallow lagoons, with some vegetation at those places where deposits of coral sand and other detritus provide footholds for it. The reef islets are called 'motu'. This photograph is of the north-eastern part of Raroia Atoll. In that area the conditions are much the same as in the same part of Amanu. The photograph is reproduced by courtesy of Dr Bengt Danielsson from his book 'Work and Life on Raroia' (London, 1956). Below is a sketch of a sailing ship emerging from the lagoon at Hao Atoll, through Kaki Pass—reproduced from an Admiralty chart.

being made whether they had any of their stone adzes on board, they answered in the negative, saying that they had left them at home, but [they] produced three *Toges* [axes] as they call them that they had with them. One of these was made of iron, and the other two of Copper; they had also a small English Tomahawk. These things they said were taken from the Au ura [i.e. Kaukura] people, who in all probability got them from the wreck of Capt. Byer's [*sic*] vessel lost at Arutua in 1803.

Davies, who was an accomplished linguist, noted that the islanders called their island Anaa or Ngana, 'sometimes prefixing the article O according to the manner of the Taheiteans.' However, their dialect differed considerably from Tahitian, particularly in the frequent use of the consonant *k*, the hard *g*, and the nasal *ng*. On the other hand, most nouns and verbs were the same, except that certain consonants were retained that the Tahitians dropped. Yet their numerals, with one or two exceptions, were quite different from Tahitian as well as Hawaiian, Marquesan, Maori, Tongan and even Fijian. Moreover, they frequently had five or six different names for the same thing—one like the Tahitian word, one like the Maori, Marquesan &c. 'This makes it very probable,' Davies wrote, 'that their islands have been peopled by accidental colonies from different places, and that these in the course of time mixed together and formed one common jumble out of their several dialects, retaining at the same time those different names of object[s] that had been peculiar to each.'

Davies noted also that the Anaans called themselves Parata and sometimes Tapuhoe. These were not the names of an island, but of a 'party' (i.e. clan or tribe) such as the Porionuu, Teva and Oropaa in Tahiti. Auura was also the name of a party—one that had conquered the Palliser Islands. However, those islands were then almost if not entirely uninhabited because the Parata had either extirpated their inhabitants or forced them to flee to other islands.[24]

The islanders of whom Davies wrote eventually sailed down to the Taiarapu Peninsula to await a favourable wind to return home. During the next few years, although it remained rare for European ships to touch at Anaa, the Anaans became increasingly familiar to Europeans because of their contact with pearling vessels in the north-western Tuamotus. Captain Campbell, the pioneer of trade in the archipelago, told the *Sydney Gazette* in January 1814 that the Anaans were 'universal travellers' and were generally to be found in 'detached parties' in all the other islands. Although not such expert divers as the Tahitians, they served to keep those islanders in check by their ready example and the awe which their 'peculiarity of character and manners' seemed to inspire. They were usually dreaded for their 'determined courage and superiority in warlike exercises.' 'Between two and three years ago,' Campbell added, 'they made a descent on some of the leeward islands [of the archipelago] . . . and after putting all the inhabitants to death who could not by flight avoid their vengeance, they destroyed the cocoa nut trees that had been their chief support.'[25]

Although the pearlshell trade was temporarily abandoned in 1814 following the discovery of sandalwood in the Marquesas Islands, its brief flowering seems to have prompted the Anaans to begin making frequent and regular visits to Tahiti.[26] Davies, who claimed they had never much done this in the past, recorded that a large party of them arrived in Tahiti in several *pahi* early in 1813. From then on many were to be found on both Tahiti and Moorea. Pomare II, particularly, was always surrounded by them and employed them as bodyguards.[27] In fact, one contemporary writer claimed that it was chiefly due to their military prowess and to the generalship of an Anaan chief, Ariipaea, that Christianity triumphed on Tahiti in 1815.[28] Some Anaans were later among the pupils in the LMS schools in Tahiti; and in 1817, a small group of them sailed home in the hope of introducing their new faith to their countrymen. Although rebuffed after a promising start and compelled to return to Tahiti, they renewed their efforts a couple of years later and were successful. Several months before Pomare II died in December 1821, the whole of Anaa and most of the neighbouring atolls were said to have renounced idolatry and to have accepted the mission-inspired Tahitian code of laws. In addition, the Anaans, headed by Ariipaea, acknowledged Pomare as their supreme chief.[29]

When adventurers from Sydney resumed the pearlshell trade in 1822, they continued to limit their activities to the northwestern Tuamotus like Campbell and his contemporaries.[30] However, after an English pearler, Captain Richard Charlton, discovered in 1823 that Hao Atoll was rich in shell and had a practicable entrance into its lagoon, the operations of the pearlers moved further eastward. Charlton's discovery seems to have been made with the help of Anaans he met in Tahiti. It also seems that it was Charlton who initiated the practice of calling at Anaa to engage divers, and that it was he who inspired adventurers in Valparaiso to try their luck in the pearling trade.[31] At any rate, when the first Chilean pearling ship made a voyage to the Tuamotus in 1825, she first went to Anaa for divers, as did those who immediately followed her.[32] Meanwhile, the Sydney-based pearlers had begun to lose interest in the trade, and from 1827 onwards Valparaiso was the pearling capital for the eastern Pacific. It remained so for the rest of the century.[33] The practice of engaging Anaan divers, however, did not remain constant. After several affrays in which the Anaans attacked their European employers and pillaged their ships, many of the pearlers took to engaging the more tractable Rapa Islanders to dive for them.[34] The consequence was that European contact with Anaa at this period was short-lived, and little was learned of the Anaans at Anaa itself. On the other hand, because of the Anaans' penchant for long sea voyages, they and their *pahi* were occasionally encountered many miles from home and more was added to the Europeans' stock of knowledge of them through such meetings.

The Russian explorer Captain Thaddeus von Bellingshausen, who made the first extensive survey of the Tuamotus in 1820, found no permanent inhabitants at most of the twenty atolls he visited in the central and western part of the archipelago. But he met small parties of Anaans at both Nihiru

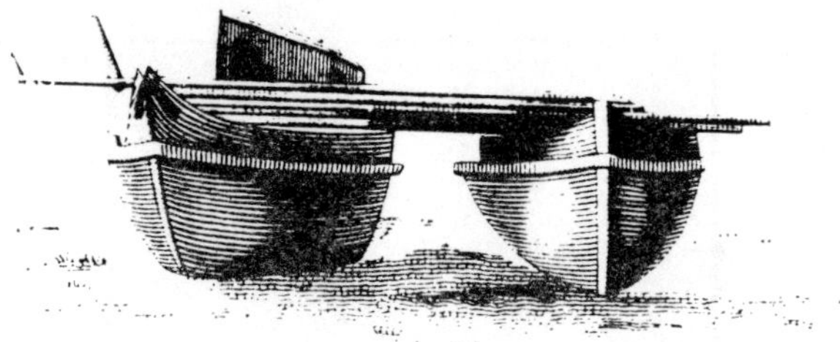

The hulls of an Anaan double canoe—from the Atlas accompanying L. I. Duperrey's 'Voyage autour du Monde dans . . . la 'Coquille' (Paris, 1827).

and Makemo Atolls, north-east of Anaa, as well as at the upraised island of Makatea to the north-west. Other islanders who were almost certainly Anaans were seen at Fakarava as Bellingshausen sailed past that atoll late one afternoon. In that case the islanders were standing by several canoes, the largest of which had two masts, and they gave the impression of being on a fishing or food-gathering expedition. Several of them had 'woven cloaks or mats' over their shoulders—possibly to protect them from sunburn. Later at Kaukura, which the Anaans had conquered, Bellingshausen was struck by the appearance of two men who paddled out to his ship. Although they were 'very dark of face and body, probably on account of constant exposure to the sun whilst fishing,' their features 'did not differ from [those of] Europeans.' Bellingshausen later met other Anaans in Tahiti, and finally expressed the view that they were 'indistinguishable from the Tahitians' except for long loose hair and tattoo marks on their thighs. 'They are all daring navigators and undertake long and difficult sea voyages,' he added.[35]

About three years after Bellingshausen's voyage, R. P. Lesson, naturalist and assistant surgeon of the French exploring ship *Coquille,* also met a party of Anaans in Tahiti. He took the opportunity to examine several of their *pahi* which were drawn up at Papaoa, near Point Venus. They were 'solidly built for distant navigation' and about the size of fishing sloops in Europe. Their hulls were surmounted by a gunwale, were pointed at each end, and strongly linked by beams about two feet apart. The beams supported a solid platform, the planks being firmly fixed in place with wooden pins. Over the whole length of the port side hull was a cabin of 'pliant branches' woven together like basketwork. The steering oars consisted of long pieces of wood widening at the end like the tail of a fish. They were remarkable for the simple way they were fixed in place, each turning only on a pin. The masts of the *pahi* were made of long bamboos supported by ropes of hibiscus bark. 'A big square mat serves as a sail,' Lesson added, 'and what is of particular interest to a sailor is that the tack does not differ from that in our boats in Europe, and the sheet is fixed on one side or the other with a small wooden pin.'*

* The tack of a sail in a sailing ship (such as the *Coquille*) is a rope, wire, or chain and hook, used to secure the windward clews or corners of the courses (lower square sails) to the ship's side when close-hauled on a wind. It is also a rope, wire, or lashing used to secure amidships the windward lower end of a fore-and-aft sail. The sheet is a rope or chain from a lower corner of a sail to extend it or move it.

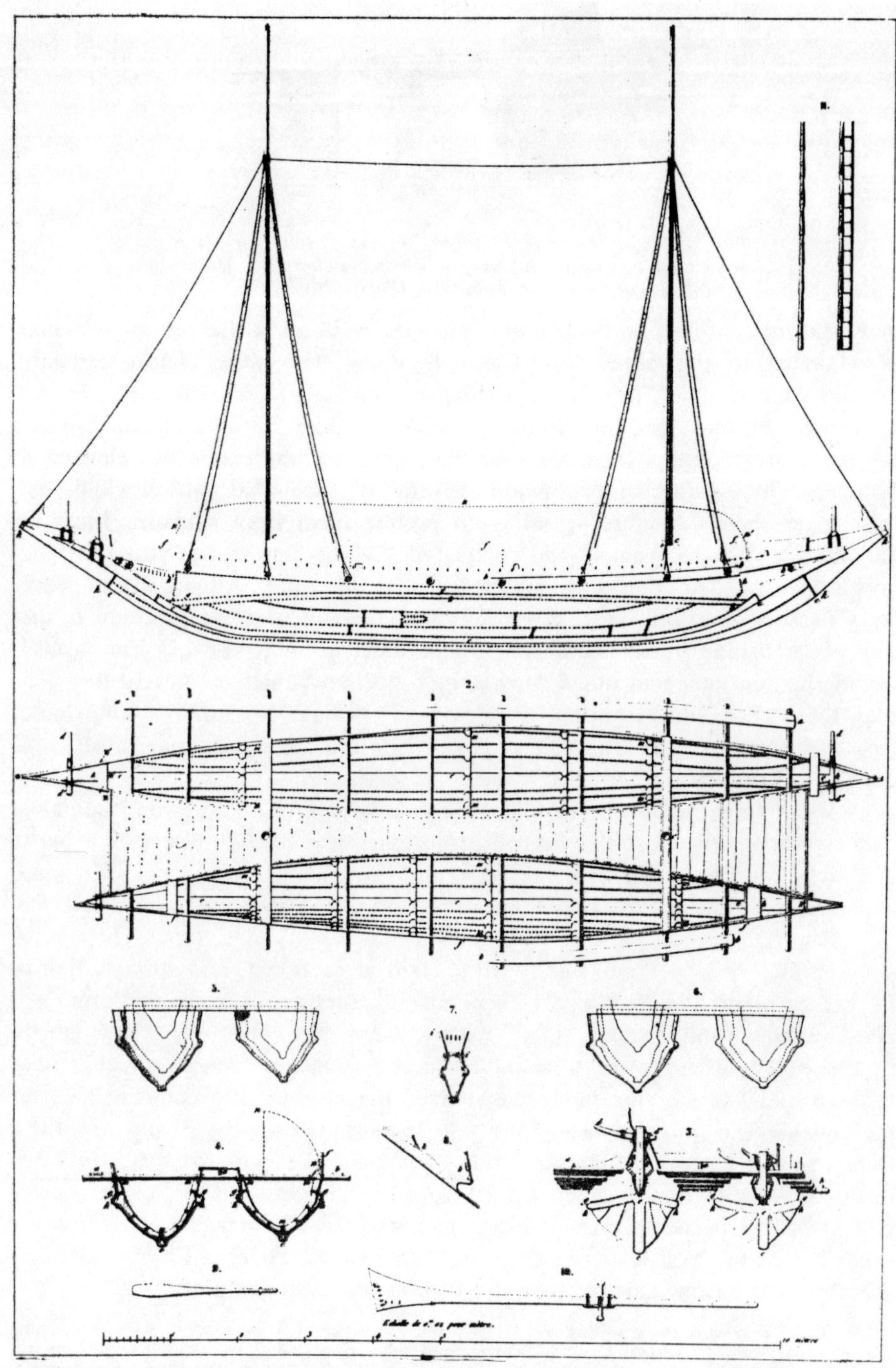

Construction details of an Anaan pahi, or double canoe—from F. E. Paris' 'Essai sur la construction navale des peuples extra-Europeens' (Paris, [1841]).

Lesson reiterated Bellingshausen's assessment that the Anaans resembled the Tahitians.* But in his opinion, they were more vigorous and did not have the same kindly character and affectionate manners. Their features were rough and wild, and their whole character bore the 'stamp of ferocity.' These characteristics were accentuated by heavy tattooing on the body, forehead, and cheeks, which made them more closely resemble the Maoris and Marquesans than the Tahitians, who were only lightly tattooed and in simple designs. The islanders used a very hard wood, which was rare in their islands, to make their spears. These were often fifteen feet long, widened at the end like the head of a halberd,† and covered with delicate carvings. Their clubs were also ornamented with graceful designs, as were their axes.[36]

The next European to learn anything substantial about the Anaans was Captain F. W. Beechey of HMS *Blossom,* who surveyed a large part of the Tuamotu Archipelago in 1826. Beechey found parties of Anaans on three atolls, excluding Anaa itself. At Ahunui, a small, previously undiscovered atoll about 325 miles south-east of Anaa, three islanders who proved to be Anaans paddled fearlessly out to the *Blossom* in a canoe. Instead of being 'deep-coloured uncivilized Indians' like those of 'the coral islands in general,' Beechey thought they were 'comparatively fair.' Inquiry revealed that nearly two years earlier they and about twenty other men, women and children on shore had been drifted to Vanavana, about five hundred miles south-east of Anaa, after leaving home to go to Tahiti in a double canoe. Nine men, eight women and three children died during the voyage. The survivors remained on Vanavana for thirteen months before setting out to try to return home. However, on reaching Ahunui, about one hundred miles to the north-west, their canoe was stove in on the reef; and when the *Blossom* arrived, they had been there for eight months preparing to resume their voyage.[37]

Beechey visited the castaway community on shore and examined their canoe. It was about thirty feet long, and, from his description of it, obviously a *pahi*. Beechey offered to take the castaways to the 'next' island, but the Anaans declined on the ground that 'the greater part of the inhabitants of the eastern islands of Polynesia were cannibals.' Beechey then offered to take several of them to Anaa itself, and this he did about a month later. In the interval he called at Hao where he found a party of Anaans working as divers for an English pearler.[38] Twenty-three others were later seen at Marokau, about sixty-five miles west of Hao—the atoll where Banks, in 1769, reported

* The physiognomy of the Tahitians,' Lesson wrote, 'is generally stamped with a great softness and an appearance of good humour. Their heads would be European if it were not for the flatness of the nostrils and the thickness [*grosseur trop forte*] of the lips. Their hair is black and coarse. The colour of the skin is of a slightly darkish yellow-red, or what is commonly known as a light copper colour. This coloration varies, however, in intensity, and many of the natives of the two sexes are 'no browner than the people of southern Europe'. Lesson thought that the 'singular enlargement' of the features of the face was possibly due to the Tahitian mothers' practice of 'compressing the heads of their children, in a manner which results in an enlargement of the mouth, the flattening of the nostrils and the projection of the cheekbones'.

† A combined spear and battle-axe used in Europe in the fifteenth and sixteenth centuries.

seeing a canoe with a sail 'not unlike an English lugsail.' At Marokau, Beechey's crew also saw 'a great many dogs' on shore—the largest number reported in a single place in the early literature of the eastern Pacific.[39]

On reaching Anaa, Beechey sent his passengers ashore in the ship's barge, but made no attempt to land himself. He thus missed an opportunity to see and write of the Anaans on their home soil, and it was not until 1837, when the Belgian merchant J. A. Moerenhout published his *Voyages aux Iles du Grand Ocean,* that the first such account appeared in print. In 1829, Moerenhout had spent about twenty-four hours on Anaa when he went there to recruit a team of divers. He thought the Anaans were a dangerous and unsociable people, and most of his account of them is a tale of how, in his own view, he narrowly escaped from them with his life. On first landing, however, Moerenhout had had leisure to examine their canoes, which he saw everywhere 'of different shapes and sizes.' The largest of them, their *pahi,* were 'immense vessels,' one being seventy-five feet long by twenty-five feet wide. Like Cook, Banks, Ellis and Lesson before him, Moerenhout thought the *pahi* were similar in some respects to European ships. 'They are built on the same plan as our ships, with a keel, but rarely of a single piece,' he wrote, 'and they are provided with ribs which are attached to the keel in a manner similar to that used by our boatbuilders. . . .' Elsewhere in his book, Moerenhout claimed that many *pahi* were over one hundred feet long. 'In Tahiti,' he added, 'these same vessels used to be employed for travelling; but to build them, they [the Tahitians] needed the help of men from the low islands. They called them *pahi,* the name used nowadays to describe our ships.'[40]

The Anaans were still using the *pahi* on long voyages when the French frigate *Artémise* called at Tahiti in 1839. Several *pahi* were then visiting that island. An officer of the frigate, Lieutenant F. E. Paris, whose hobby was the study of non-European sailing craft, took the opportunity to make a plan of one, which he later published in his monumental *Essai sur la Construction Navale des Peuples Extra-Européens. . . .* He also made a model of a *pahi* for the

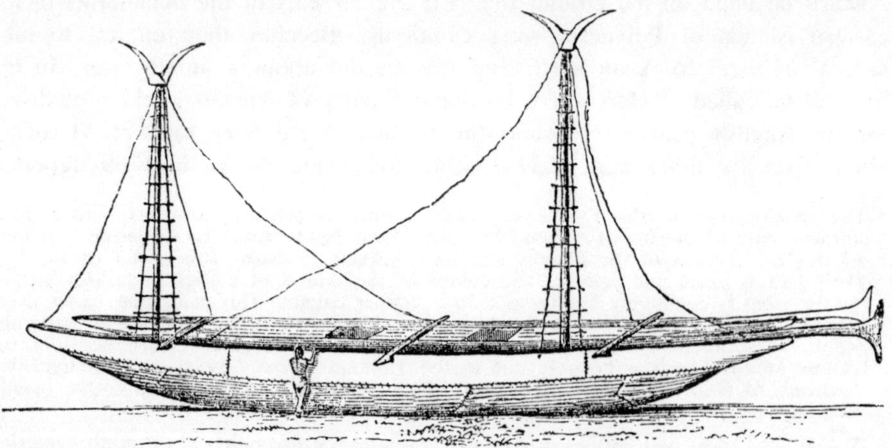

'A trading double canoe' of the Tuamotus—sketched in 1839. Both this and the sketch on the previous page are from Charles Wilkes' 'Narrative of the United States Exploring Expedition' (Philadelphia, 1845).

Musée de la Marine in Paris, of which, as an admiral, he became the first director.[41] Both the model and the plan readily explain why Europeans saw similarities between the *pahi* and their own ships, and why the Tahitians immediately adopted the word *pahi* as the generic term for them.

Commodore Charles Wilkes of the United States Exploring Expedition, who visited Tahiti a few months after the *Artémise,* published sketches of two *pahi* that also illustrate their European appearance. One sketch was done in Tahiti and the other at Raraka Atoll which Wilkes also touched at. At Raraka Wilkes encountered a party of Anaans who had sailed there on a pearling expedition. Their *pahi* was 'neatly put together' and well-secured with twine and sennit, no iron or other metal being used. Although the Anaans were beginning to learn the use of the compass, they still preferred to sail by the sun and stars, and, according to Wilkes, 'seldom made any material error.'[42]

Writing of the Anaans themselves, Wilkes spoke highly of their advance in civilisation. 'They showed a modest disposition and gave us a hearty welcome,' he said. 'Here all shipwrecked mariners would be sure of kind treatment and a share of the few comforts these people possess. No savage mistrust and fear were seen. . . .' Wilkes noted that all the men were tall and well-made. The children were handsome, well-formed and 'as cheerful as could be.' But the women were 'anything but good looking.' Extensive tattooing was common. The islanders' chief, an old man, was so marked on the chest and arms that he had the appearance of a blue and brown checkerboard. Others had large rosettes on their legs, and horizontal bands on their backs extending outwards from the spine.[43]

Wilkes found the chief's brother-in-law—whom one of his officers described as a 'tall, good-humoured Yankee-looking individual'—to be 'quite an intelligent native.'[44] The man had a 'surprising knowledge' of the western Tuamotus, and drew a map of all the islands he knew on the deck of Wilkes' flagship. It was done with 'considerable accuracy' and included several small atolls that were not then shown on European charts, but were later found by one of Wilkes' ships.

Another member of the Wilkes expedition who found much to interest him at Raraka was Horatio Hale, the expedition's thirty-two-year-old linguist and ethnologist. Hale made a study of the Anaans' language which he found to be quite different from Tahitian—the difference being much greater than between Tahitian and Hawaiian. According to Captain William Hudson, Wilkes' second-in-command, the islanders told Hale that their language prevailed throughout the Tuamotus, but that they also understood Tahitian. 'When Mr. Hale asked the name of any article,' Hudson said, 'they would first tell him what it was called in the "parau Paumotu" (Tuamotuan language) and then in the "parau Tahiti" (Tahitian language).' Hale thus learned, for example, that the Anaan word for coconut was *hakari* but that in Tahitian it was *niu*.[45]

Hale continued his study of Anaan when the expedition reached Tahiti. This convinced him that the Anaan dialect was made up of two distinct elements —one similar to Tahitian and another quite unlike it. The words in the second element were 'not only numerous' but were such as were 'usually original in a language, and very rarely introduced from abroad.' They included those for man, woman, fire, water, good and bad. Some Anaan words such as *ruki* (dark), *hene* (six) and *kavake* (moon) had recently been introduced into Tahitian as replacements for those outlawed under the custom of *pi,* but their pronunciation had been modified in the process. Hale believed that the strange Anaan elements had once formed part of some primitive tongue that had been 'corrupted and partially destroyed by an infusion of Tahitian.' But the intermixture with Tahitian had apparently occurred a long time previously, as the existing form of the Tahitian words in the Anaan language was that which prevailed before the *k* and *ng* had fallen into disuse in Tahiti itself. Moreover, the Tahitian words had been 'perverted and disfigured' as they would have been in the pronunciation of foreigners.

Hale compared the 'peculiar' Anaan words with their counterparts in other Pacific tongues without finding a clue to their origin. 'Perhaps, when the idioms of Melanesia are better known,' he wrote, 'the attempt may be resumed with more success.' Yet in looking to the west for an answer to his linguistic problem, Hale realised that he was only creating problems of another kind. For if the Anaans had originated in the west, Hale reasoned that they must have reached the Tuamotus without sighting the more desirable Society or Marquesas Islands, otherwise they would surely have chosen to settle on them, rather than on their own more or less barren atolls. Moreover, as they were the best warriors in that part of the ocean, they must have remained confined to the Tuamotus until after the high islands were settled. Otherwise, having once established themselves in the high islands, the 'half-starved crews of a few wandering Samoan canoes' could never have pushed them out.

Hale could visualise that the early Anaans may well have come from a great distance without stopping at 'intermediate points', as they were the most skilful navigators and best canoe-builders in the eastern Pacific. However, he could not imagine why such skilful navigators and canoe-builders—whose techniques, he said, were 'not borrowed from the Tahitians'—would have remained in the atolls if they had, indeed, reached them from the west in the manner he suggested. Nor could he suggest how the Tahitians could have conquered such accomplished warriors, thereafter corrupting and partially destroying their language; nor yet why the Tahitian element in their language had been 'perverted and disfigured' as if by foreigners. In short, although Hale came to a similar conclusion as the missionary Davies about the complexity of the Anaan tongue, he could not solve the mystery of it.[46] Scholars since Hale's time have been equally unsuccessful, even though many more words peculiar to Anaan have been recorded.[47] Edward Tregear, compiler of the monumental *The Maori-Polynesian Comparative Dictionary* of 1891, could only remark that, although the Anaan language was 'in bulk Polynesian,' it had been 'crossed with some foreign tongue in a remarkable manner.' An American linguist, Isidore Dyen wrote in 1966 that there was clearly 'something . . . queer about the lexicostatistics' of Anaan in relation to other Polynesian languages. But he had no explantation for the anomalies.*[48]

Although a French pearler Eugene Ricardi wrote at some length about Anaa and the Anaans around the time that Hale's speculations were published,[49] nothing else of importance in the context of this book was recorded on those subjects until the 1850s. This was after an American Mormon had become the first Western missionary to reside on Anaa, and after several French Roman Catholic priests had established a mission station there. The Mormon missionary was Benjamin Grouard, one of several members of his faith who arrived in the eastern Pacific in the early 1840s. He landed on Anaa in May 1845. Apparently because he was prepared to live as the Anaans did and because other Western missionaries had previously kept well clear of the atoll, he was immediately successful.

Within five months of his arrival, six hundred islanders had joined his church, branches of it had been set up in each of the atoll's five villages, and seventeen islanders had been ordained. After this 'glorious and successful' beginning, Grouard went to Tubuai and persuaded a fellow Mormon, Addison Pratt, to return to Anaa to help him. Then, while Pratt remained on Anaa, Grouard began a proselytising tour of the western Tuamotus. As some of

* It should be noted that Hale, Tregear and Dyen did not speak of the Anaan language, but of Paumotuan or Tuamotuan. There is little doubt that they were referring only to the language of Anaa. Except for a few hours at Napuka, Hale had no opportunity to meet any Tuamotuans other than Anaans. Tregear used information supplied to him by Bishop Jaussen of Tahiti, which must have come from the Catholic missionaries who had been based on Anaa for the previous forty years. And Dyen used Tregear's material.

Grouard's Anaan converts had preceded him, he was sympathetically received, and in three months he baptised 116 people on the islands of Faaite, Fakarava, Toau, Kaukura, Makatea, Tikehau, Rangiroa, Arutua and Apataki. He and Pratt left Anaa soon afterwards; but another Mormon, John Hawkins, who had married a Tuamotuan, continued missionary work from Arutua.[50]

News of the Mormons' success reached the ears of Tepano Jaussen, the first Catholic bishop of Tahiti, soon after he arrived there in February 1849. He wasted no time in trying to combat it. Within three months, two priests from the mission at Mangareva, which had been established in 1835, were sent to open the first Catholic mission in the central Tuamotus. The priests were taken to their destination in a French gunboat. As Anaa seemed too dangerous a place for them to begin their work, they built their first station on neighbouring Fakarava. They found a pretext to move to Anaa in 1851. But they soon ran into difficulties with another Mormon missionary, James S. Brown, who arrived there within a few weeks of them. Brown, a tactless man of little education, found the Anaans hostile to the protectorate that the French had established over Tahiti and Moorea in 1842, and which they had later claimed included the Tuamotus. Brown counselled the Anaans to resist the French; and when the priests, who now numbered three, complained that he was preaching sedition, the French sent a gunboat from Tahiti to remove him. This event further inflamed the Anaans and provoked them to attack the priests and also a French gendarme who had been stationed on the atoll. The gendarme was killed. The upshot was that another gunboat was sent to Anaa; several Anaans were publicly hanged on the spot; and others were sentenced to hard labour in Tahiti. All but two of the Mormon missionaries then in the protectorate returned to the United States soon afterwards.[51] This left the Tuamotus virtually free to the Catholics for nearly forty years. However, it did not immediately help their cause on Anaa. For the next ten years, most Anaans shunned them, and they made few converts.[52] The priests naturally had little incentive to record their observations on the Anaans in print during this period. In fact, only one letter from them was published before the end of the 1860s. This was written in April 1854 by Father Albert Montiton who had arrived on the atoll seven months earlier. He was still optimistic about the future and said among other things:

> It must not be imagined that our islanders are behind their neighbours in point of civilisation, handicrafts, and even beaux arts. Their cosmopolitan instincts have long put them in continual contact with the Europeans and Americans who rove these seas, and, through mixing with them, they have become refined and now dress in an easy, almost elegant, manner. Their power of understanding has also broadened; but above all, their innate taste for harmony has been admirably developed and perfected.
>
> They are mad about music. Squatting in a circle or negligently stretched out in their houses . . . they pass whole days singing in chorus. This and the reading of the Bible are the only occupations in a good many of the small

islands, and everywhere it is the principal thing they love and look for in religion.[53]

Montiton's letter was written about six months after the French authorities in Tahiti had formally extended their administration to the Tuamotus.[54] They did this by vesting authority in Paiore, an Anaan high chief, who was regent in the archipelago for Queen Pomare IV of Tahiti. Paiore, a staunch Protestant, was the principal representative of the French government in the Tuamotus until 1861.[55] However, in 1858, a French naval officer, Lieutenant Xavier Caillet, was sent to Anaa for nearly two years as special commissioner, apparently to work alongside him.[56] The two men evidently got along well, for Paiore told Caillet a great deal about the Anaans' ancient religious beliefs and notions of creation. Some of this information was published anonymously in the *Annuaire des Etablissements français de l'Océanie* . . . for 1863. Other details appeared in later publications. In total, Paiore's material reveals that the Anaans formerly believed in a heaven, a hell, and the immortality of the soul; that they pictured the universe in a somewhat similar fashion to sixteenth century Europeans; and that they had Pythagorean notions about the transmigration of the soul.* The account published in 1863 stated among other things that:

> According to the ancient [Anaan] traditions, the earth was composed of three layers superposed. Each of these layers had its own sky. The upper layer was designed for happy souls; the living inhabited the middle layer; and in the third layer wandered the souls in distress. However, many of these unfortunate souls escaped their sad fate by hiding in the bodies of birds. . . .[57]

A more detailed account of Paiore's version of the Anaans' religious and cosmogonic beliefs—as recorded by Caillet—was published in 1928 in Teuira Henry's *Ancient Tahiti.* That account tells how the universe was originally like an egg which contained Te Tumu (The Foundation) and Te Papa (The Stratum Rock). Eventually it burst and produced three layers superposed, the lowest one propping up the two above. Te Tumu and Te Papa remained on the lowest layer and created man, animals and plants. These included Hoatu and Hoatea who were the progenitors of the human race. When the people had greatly multiplied, Hoatea proposed to expand their dominion by raising the layer above them. This strong men did with their arms, mounting on each others' shoulders, until the highest trees could stand upright. The people got from one layer to another by making an opening through the middle of the one above until they had three abodes. The skies were raised in a similar manner. Then the

* The belief in metempsychosis or the transmigration of the soul, now chiefly confined to Buddhists and Hindus, was once widespread. In Ancient Greece, the followers of Pythagoras adopted it as a doctrine, while Plato incorporated it into his teachings. Several heretical Christian sects from the second to the thirteenth century held it; it was popular among the Jews of the Middle Ages; and it was revived during the Renaissance. A playful reference to it appears in Act IV, Scene II, of Shakespeare's *Twelfth Night* (written in 1601-2) where the Clown asks Malvolio: 'What is the opinion of Pythagoras concerning wild fowl?' and Malvolio replies: 'That the soul of our grandam [i.e. grandmother] might haply inhabit a bird.' Shakespeare also referred to metempsychosis in *As You Like It* and *The Merchant of Venice.*

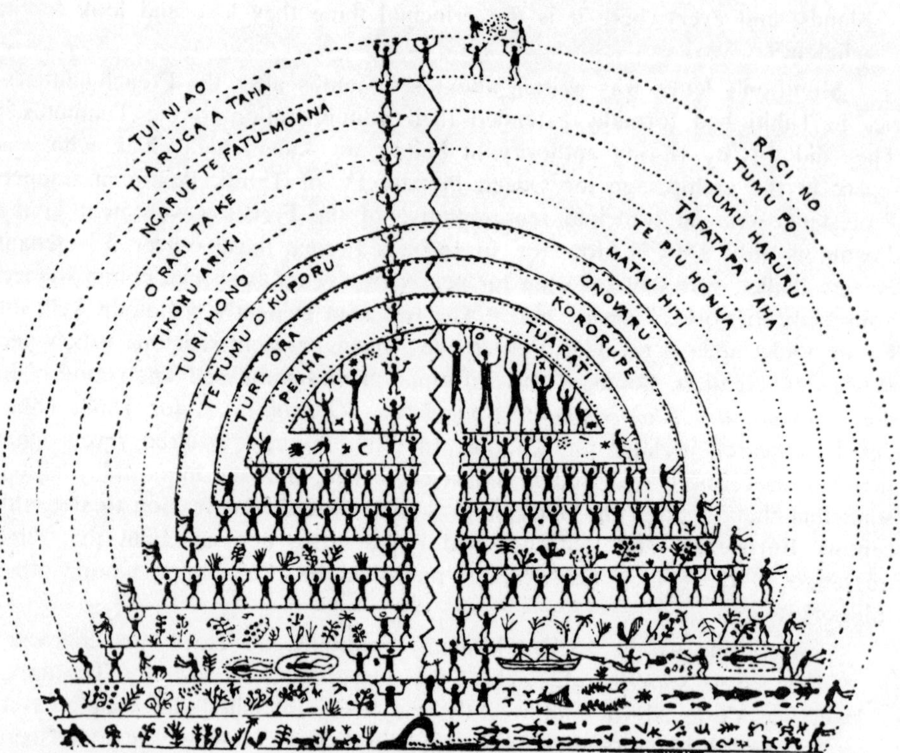

Paiore's conception of the universe, as reproduced in Teuira Henry's 'Ancient Tahiti'. Compare this with the Ptolemaic conception reproduced on p. 58.

stars were created to illumine the highest heavens, the sun to shine lower down, and the moon to shine nearest to the earth. The celestial bodies rose up through shafts in their horizons to the east, and set through others in corresponding horizons in the west, all in regular succession except the sun, which caused the days and nights to be irregular. However, the hero Maui regulated the sun by seizing it by its rays as it was rising one morning from its hiding place. The creation of the universe was scarcely terminated when Tangaroa, an evil spirit, set fire to the highest heaven, seeking thus to destroy everything. Fortunately the fire was seen spreading by three men on earth who quickly ascended to it, extinguished the flames, and bore Tangaroa to the lowest layer of earth. Tangaroa was banished to that region, which was in utter darkness, and he became its ruler and the powerful god of death. Thereafter human beings became mortal. Te Tumu, the god of life, rewarded spirits according to their deserts: the spirits of the good soared up to the higher regions, while those of the wicked went down to dwell with Tangaroa.[58]

Several sketches illustrating the Anaan cosmogony, apparently drawn by Paiore, were among Caillet's papers when he died in 1901. One, bearing Paiore's signature, was dated 1869—the year in which Caillet was posted to the Tuamotus for a brief second term, this time as resident administrator.[59]

Similar sketches also found their way into other hands. All have two things in common. They bear no resemblance to the work of artists in other parts of Polynesia, but are somewhat similar to illustrations in European books of the sixteenth century depicting the then-current Ptolemaic notion of the universe. In the latter the earth is surrounded by a series of spheres in which the sun, moon and planets have their courses—the whole being sometimes supported on the shoulders of the Greek figure Atlas.*[60]

The Paiore drawings, which reiterate a kind of Atlas concept and depict a notion approximating that of the spheres, have been copied or reproduced in several publications. The first to appear was a copy done by Father Montiton, who was based on Anaa until 1873. It was published in the French Catholic mission journal *Les Missions Catholiques* in 1874 with a series of articles by Montiton on the Tuamotus, and it bore the caption 'sketch imagined by the natives to represent their cosmogony.'[61] Another drawing, that signed by Paiore in 1869, was reproduced in F. W. Christian's *Eastern Pacific Lands* in 1910; with an article by J. L. Young in the *Journal of the Polynesian Society* in 1919; and in *Ancient Tahiti* in 1928.[62] Finally, copies of all known Paiore drawings were published in the *Journal of the Polynesian Society* between 1939 and 1943, when Kenneth P. Emory, an ethnologist with the Bernice P. Bishop Museum of Honolulu, examined the drawings in conjunction with Tuamotuan cosmogonic chants.[63] Three of the writers, Montiton, Christian and Henry, accepted the drawings that they copied or reproduced as genuine Polynesian productions. But Young and Emory were of the opinion that Paiore's notions of cosmogony had been influenced by missionary teachings or based on ideas derived from books.[64] However, Young, for his part, did not suggest which missionary or missionaries (excluding Montiton, of course) could have influenced Paiore.[65] And Emory did not mention what illustrated books—depicting a Ptolemaic, rather than Copernican, conception of the universe—are likely to have found their way to Anaa in Paiore's time.[66] Indeed, if these two matters had been

* The theory of the universe of the Egyptian astronomer Ptolemy, who lived in the second century A.D., was accepted in Europe until well into the eighteenth century. Its fundamental doctrine was that the earth was the fixed centre of the solar system and that the stars revolved about it in a complicated system of cycles and epicycles. The Ptolemaic system was not challenged until the Polish astronomer Nicolaus Copernicus (1473-1543) published his *De revolutionibus orbium coelestium* in the year of his death. In this he maintained that the sun was the central fixed body around which the planets revolved in concentric circles, and that the earth rotated on its axis once a day, thereby accounting for the apparent diurnal rotation of the heavenly bodies. Copernicus' theories were hotly debated for the next sixty-six years until the Italian astronomer Galileo Galilei (1564-1642) built a telescope which enabled him to find evidence in support of them. He expounded this evidence in *A Dialogue on the Two Principal Systems of the World*, published in 1632; but because the Copernican system deposed man from his previously self-assumed station at the centre of the universe, Galileo was forced to recant. Subsequently, the new ideas were gradually accepted, although, as Sir James Jeans pointed out in *The Universe Around Us* (Cambridge 1929), 'Human vanity, reinforced by the authority of the Church, contrived to make a rough road for those who dared draw attention to the earth's insignificant position in the universe'. Jeans added that even in the eighteenth century the University of Paris still taught that the motion of the earth round the sun was 'a convenient but false hypothesis', while the new American universities of Harvard and Yale taught the Ptolemaic and Copernican systems of astronomy as if they were equally tenable.

seriously investigated, it seems unlikely that the sceptics would have found any evidence to support their views. For one thing, Paiore himself lamented in 1864 that 'the church of our Lord' was dormant in the Tuamotus because of the lack of Protestant missionaries.[67] Secondly, a French Protestant missionary who visited Anaa that same year found that the only books in the Anaans' houses were Bibles, hymn books and a few breviaries.[68] Finally, as no religious books were ever translated into the Anaan dialect, it is almost certain that the books that the Protestant missionary did see were in Tahitian, in which case it can readily be demonstrated that they were not illustrated.[69]

Except for a few remarks by the pearler Ricardi,[70] the information and drawings that Caillet obtained from Paiore comprise the only data on the Anaans' ancient religious beliefs and practices to be recorded in the nineteenth century. In fact, little other ethnographic material of any kind was recorded on or about Anaa for sixty years or so after Caillet's second sojourn on that island. There were several reasons for this. First, in 1878, a devastating hurricane struck the atoll, sweeping 150 houses away and crippling the trade in copra and coconut oil that had developed over the previous two decades. This prompted the French to transfer the seat of their administration in the Tuamotus to Fakarava, which meant that few outsiders had occasion to call at Anaa until its coconut plantations were replanted and bearing again. However, the atoll had scarcely recovered from the 1878 disaster when another hurricane, in 1906, caused further havoc. Nearly 100 people were drowned, three villages were utterly destroyed, and almost every tree for twenty kilometres was uprooted and carried off. Anaa was thus reduced to little more than bare rocks, with virtually nothing to support the few hundred people who had stayed on after the previous disaster. By 1911, the atoll's population had dropped to a miserable 199 compared with a flourishing two thousand or so in the early 1840s.[71]

That any of Anaa's ancient lore survived the two hurricanes to be recorded in modern times was largely due to two Anaan men, Tiapu-a-Parepare and his nephew, Paea-a-Avehe. About the time of the 1906 hurricane, they were living together on another atoll, Taiaro, which happened to escape the death and destruction of their home island. To while away the long evenings, Tiapu, one of the most learned Anaans of his time, taught his nephew numerous ancient chants and traditions, insisting that he commit them to memory and never forget them. Paea, then a teenager, thus acquired an unusual body of learning for an islander of his generation; and twenty years later, when most such knowledge had been forgotten in the western atolls, his fellow islanders looked on him as the most learned Tuamotuan then living. Paea was still barely forty years old when a party of scientists from the Bishop Museum arrived in the Tuamotus in 1929 bent on recording whatever ancient lore they could. He was soon enlisted as one of their principal informants. One of the scientists, the linguist J. Frank Stimson, obtained from Paea a great deal of information about the distinctive Anaan language, besides recording much of the traditional knowledge that his uncle had passed on to him. The latter included details of an esoteric religious cult, whose principal god was called Kiho, Kio or Io. Another scientist, the ethnologist Emory, questioned Paea on other aspects of Anaan culture.[72]

Some of the knowledge that Paea passed on to Stimson and Emory seems to throw further light on the subject of this book. He said, for example, that in former times Anaa was divided among three *ngati* or tribes. The most important of these was the Tangihia, whose genealogies went back seventeen generations before 1900 to a chief of the same name. This chief was the son of a mythical female forbear called Te Kura who reputedly came from 'a non-human superior world called Paparangi.'[73] An ancestor of one of the other *ngati* was an Amanu man, Maehanga-tua-ira, who settled on Anaa in the time of Tangihia after arriving there in a ship called Te-kainga-o-Hiro (literally, the homeland of Hiro).[74] In addition, Paea gave Emory details of several string figures that were said to depict Hiro's house, his swing, his canoe cabin, his net for catching spirits, his mountain or grove of trees, his *marae* stone, and his reclining seat.[75] All this information seems relevant here because:

1. Tangi(h)ia was the name of the chief at Mauke, Cook Islands, to whom Hiro gave his son Tai-te-ariki who became the ancestor of Rarotonga's Pa-Ariki family (see p. 161).

2. Kura was the name of the troublesome castaway(s) belonging to a race of strangers who once invaded Hao, uprooting coconut trees and hurling missiles ashore as if they were little stones (see p. 48).

3. Paparangi (or, at least, Papalangy) is given in the first Tahitian-English dictionary of 1851 as a term for Europeans.[76]

4. Whereas *kura* or its equivalent in the languages of Polynesia usually means 'red', on Anaa it also means 'the blond skin of the white races.'[77]

5. The fact that an Amanu man arrived at Anaa in Tangihia's time in a a ship called—or, more likely, from—the homeland of Hiro suggests that Hiro himself arrived in that ship, that he was a contemporary of Tangihia, and that the ship must previously have visited Amanu or some atoll in its vicinity.

6. The string figures collected by Emory suggest that Hiro lived on Anaa for some time, while the one depicting his reclining seat indicates that he was a foreigner, as such items of furniture were unknown among the Polynesians.

In total, Paea's information leaves little doubt that when Hiro arrived in the Society Islands, he came from Anaa; and as his homeland was obviously not familiar to the Anaans, there is further reason to suspect that he may have been a European. This suspicion is strengthened by the fact that Tangihia's mother was of fabulous origin and that her name was synonymous with a white skin. In short, everything seems to point to the fact that Bonacorsi's light-skinned Anaans of 1772 were descended from survivors of the *San Lesmes* or whatever ship left her guns on the Amanu reef; that Gayangos' cross was a symbol of Christianity introduced by them; and that the constructional similarities between the Anaans' *pahi* and European ships were not due to mere coincidence.

But what of the strange element in the Anaan language that has baffled linguists from Davies to the present day? Was it a relic of Spanish, Basque, Galician or some other European tongue spoken aboard the *San Lesmes?* The answer, undoubtedly, is 'no.' Nor, it seems, was it a relic of any of the Melanesian languages of the western Pacific, for if it were, it could scarcely have been carried across several thousand miles of island-studded seas without leaving some trace of its passage.[78] This leaves only one other likely provenance for it: the west coast of South America.

South America, at present, does not find much favour among Pacific specialists as a Polynesian homeland or source of Polynesian culture. Despite Thor Heyerdahl's successful drift voyage in the raft *Kon-Tiki* from Peru to the Tuamotus in 1947; despite several similar drift voyages since then; and despite the mass of argument in Heyerdahl's *American Indians in the Pacific* and subsequent writings on Easter Island, most Pacific specialists have remained convinced that virtually all things Polynesian originated in the west. Yet several factors still strongly support Heyerdahl's basic contention. Some of the most striking are:

1. The ease with which a voyage may be made from the west coast of South America to Eastern Polynesia once a sailing craft breaks free of the coast-hugging Humboldt Current.[79]

2. The fact that botanists are agreed that the *kumara* or Polynesian sweet potato (*Ipomoea batatas*) was carried by man from the Americas to the Pacific, although some now doubt whether the word *kumara* is related to *cumar* of the Quechua dialects of Ecuador or Peru.[80]

3. The probable South American origin of two other Polynesian plants, the *totora* reed of Easter Island and the bottle gourd *(laganaria siceraria)*.[81]

4. The precisely-fitted stone work of Vinapu, Easter Island, which has striking parallels in the prehistoric masonry of Peru.[82]

5. The fact that the huge stone statues of Peru and its neighbours are highly reminiscent of those of Eastern Polynesia, despite many divergencies of style.[83]

6. The fact that the further one goes west in the South Pacific, the rarer does prehistoric stonework become.[84] (For example, Reao, the most easterly of the inhabited atolls in the Tuamotus, has more stone *marae* than any other in that archipelago).[85]

7. The custom of dilating the ear lobe, which was common to the ancient Peruvians, to the Easter Islanders, Marquesans, Raivavaeans and people of Takapoto Atoll, but not to the islanders of Western Polynesia.[86]

8. The close blood genetic relationship between American Indians and Polynesians, and the fact that no similar relationship is evident when Polynesians are compared with Melanesians, Micronesians and Indonesians, except, in the main, in adjacent areas of direct contact.[87]

9. The fact that the people of Reao and some Napukans are of a physical type quite unlike the generality of Polynesians—the Reao people having been described as resembling American Indians.

10. The existence of synonyms in the language of Easter Island and the fact that an early European explorer recorded a series of numerals there that was quite different from that of other Polynesian tongues.

11. The fact that twice between 1947 and 1954 small parties of Easter Islanders drifted in boats to the Tuamotus—once to Reao and once to Kauehi Atoll.

12. The existence in the language of Reao, and also in those of Anaa and Napuka, of many basic words that have no parallels in other Polynesian languages.

13. The fact that the Tahitian language has a number of synonyms for the same objects or concepts, some of which are common to the Tuamotuan dialects, but not to those of Western Polynesia.

Points 9 to 13 above are elaborated in Appendix F. Most of them have not been used by Heyerdahl to support his arguments for American Indian influences among the Polynesians. So there are more reasons for believing that the first human inhabitants of Anaa may have been of South American origin than even he suggests.[88] If Anaa's first settlers were, indeed, American Indians, they could have drifted all the way from Ecuador or Peru in the manner of *Kon-Tiki*. Or they could have been descendants of a party of American Indians who had formed a settlement on Easter Island or one of the more easterly atolls of the Tuamotus. In either case, it is highly probable that any such settlers of Anaa would have been the occupants of a single sailing craft and that they would not have numbered more than a dozen or so people. Such people would inevitably have been 'of purely Indian features and the hair lank', to repeat Bonacorsi's description of 1772; and several generations would undoubtedly have passed before their numbers could have reached a hundred. Meanwhile, if immigrants from Tonga, Samoa or thereabouts had already moved eastwards to the Marquesas or Society Islands, then people of a different ethnic type would have been on hand to provide Anaa with a second wave of settlers. These people, no doubt, would have resembled many Tongans or Samoans of historical times, and so would have been 'of a tawny colour with frizzly hair'—like the second type of Anaan whom Bonacorsi described.[89] And if some or all of them had intermarried with descendants of the first arrivals when the numbers of both groups were not too uneven, then it would have been in the nature of things for their children to make a 'common jumble' of Anaa's two tongues. However, so long as the Indian settlers remained in the majority, their language would have predominated, and words that are 'very rarely introduced from abroad'—to use Hale's expression—would have been lost. Later, however, if other Polynesians drifted to Anaa from Tahiti, the Indian language would have been further 'corrupted and partially destroyed by an infusion of

Tahitian.' In addition, the new arrivals could have strengthened the influence of other Polynesian practices, such as extensive tattooing. Then, if, in the year 1526 or thereabouts yet another disparate group of foreign immigrants arrived, the remaining anomalous elements in Anaa's pre-history could be accounted for. Thus, if the new immigrants were 'pretty blond in hue' and therefore prone to sunburnt shoulder blades, words such as *papaa* and *kura* would have been needed to describe them. If they arrived from the east rather than the west and were expert shipwrights, that would explain why the Anaan method of canoe-building of later times was 'not borrowed from the Tahitians.' If, in addition, the blond immigrants were accomplished warriors and had never been near Tahiti or the Marquesas, the reason for their non-seizure of those islands would be obvious. And if they brought a non-Polynesian type of dog with them, that would explain why the dogs of the Tuamotus differed from those of the islands further west. Finally, if the new arrivals were too small in numbers to impose their language on the Anaans, but sufficiently numerous and ingenious to conquer them and influence their culture, that could explain why Hale found many Tahitian words in Anaan to be 'perverted and disfigured' as they would be in the pronunciation of foreigners.

It is unfortunate that Hale did not specify how, in his opinion, the pronunciation of Anaa's Tahitian words had been perverted and disfigured. However, a comparison of Anaan words with similar words in Tahitian and other Polynesian languages suggests that he may have had two sounds—*ng* and *f*—especially in mind. The first of these obviously caused difficulty to some Anaan speakers even in historical times, for Davies recorded in 1807 that they pronounced the name of their island both Anaa and Ngana. Similarly, the *f* was frequently converted to *h* so that the Anaan form of such basic Polynesian words as *fenua* (land), *faka* (to do), etc. was *henua, haka,* etc.[90] Interestingly, the *ng* sound is the only one in any Polynesian language that does not exist in Spanish, while *f* is one that Spaniards have increasingly converted to *h* in recent centuries. Moreover, the *f* sound does not exist in the Basque language at all.

William J. Entwistle, in his book *The Spanish Language together with Portuguese, Catalan and Basque,* makes the point that the substitution of *f* by *h* in Spanish apparently owes its origin to the influence of the *f*-less Basque language on the Castilian dialect of northern and central Spain. He describes the substitution as the most outstanding phenomenon of modern Spanish. It was a development that began about the fourteenth century in the areas bordering the Basque provinces where the *h* gradually became a substitute for *f*. But as time passed and the use of *h* spread southwards, it became increasingly weak, and from about 1580, it ceased to be heard at all. From then on, in written Spanish, the *h* merely represented zero, as is the case today.[91]

It will be gathered from this that when the *San Lesme*s left Spain in

1525, the *h* in Spanish was still an aspirated sound. So castaways from that ship may well have influenced the *f* to *h* sound shift in Anaan, not to mention the partial elision of the *ng*. Similar changes also occurred in the Society Islands. But in those islands, where, because of the larger population, any castaways from the *San Lesmes* must have exercised a smaller influence on the language, the conversion of *f* to *h* was less complete, although the *ng* was dropped entirely.

As the reasons for sound changes in a language are complex, it would be rash to draw any positive conclusions from those noted in the Anaan tongue. Nevertheless, enough has probably been said on other matters to demonstrate that the prehistory of Anaa may well have been subject to hitherto unsuspected European influences. Additional evidence could, in fact, be presented on this subject, in the shape of information on the cult of Kiho, Kio or Io, which Stimson obtained from his informant Paea. However, as several scholars have claimed that much of what Paea told Stimson on that topic was influenced by the teachings of modern Christian missionaries, it seems best to present this additional material in the course of the next two chapters which deal with the remote atoll of Fangatau and the equally remote islands of the Vahitahi area. Fangatau and the Vahitahi islands were among the last islands in the eastern Pacific to be evangelised. Yet the Kiho cult, according to Stimson, existed in both areas, and with much the same features as Paea claimed for the cult of Anaa.

16

The 'remarkably European' people of Fangatau

The Tuamotuan atoll for which the most varied evidence can be presented for the survival of castaways from an early European shipwreck is Fangatau. This is an isolated crumb of land about 120 miles due north of Amanu, and 500 miles north-east by east of Tahiti. The atoll is also known as Angatau,* and was originally called Marupua.[1] It is roughly triangular in shape, only twenty-five miles around, and with no entrance into its lagoon. Its nearest neighbour is Fakahina, some forty miles almost due east, with which it seems to have been closely linked in pre-European times. The only other atolls within 100 miles or so are Takume and Raroia, about seventy and eighty miles to the west; tiny Rekareka, about ninety miles south-west; Napuka and Tepoto, 100 miles or so nor-nor-west; and isolated Pukapuka, some 130 miles north-east.

In early times, Fangatau was noted among other things for dogs. No European ever described these in print. But there is reason to suspect that they may have been of the same ilk as the 'three Spanish dogs, very lean' that the Schouten and Le Maire expedition saw at Pukapuka in 1616, as Fangatau is the nearest island to Pukapuka known to have had dogs in early times. Certainly the Fangatauans had seacraft capable of reaching Pukapuka and much more distant islands before the period of modern European contact. Not only do local legends describe voyages to faraway places; but when the European discoverer of Fangatau came upon the island in 1820, he found the islanders' canoes superior to any he had previously seen in the Pacific. Moreover, they were occupied by men who, although swarthy, were otherwise not much different from Europeans.

Over the next fifty years, Fangatau had only sporadic and fleeting contacts with Europeans and other outsiders. Yet the first European missionary to reside on the island found that some of the islanders' religious beliefs were seemingly Biblical in character; that, among other things, they worshipped a saviour god and knew of a figure who appeared to correspond with the Virgin Mary. Half a century later when Stimson recorded and translated some of the ancient Fangatauan religious chants, he was astonished by the 'lofty' philosophical ideas embodied in them and he found it 'difficult to imagine how they could have arisen among barbaric peoples.' At the same time a physical anthropologist found that the Fangatauans were 'remarkably European' in appearance and he thought that this fact might lead to the solution of 'some of the disturbing questions with regard to the racial position of the Polynesians.' However,

* The spellings Agatau and Fagatau are also used. The 'g' or 'ng' represents the soft 'ng' in 'hanger'. The 'ng' spelling in this and other words is used in this book, except in quotations.

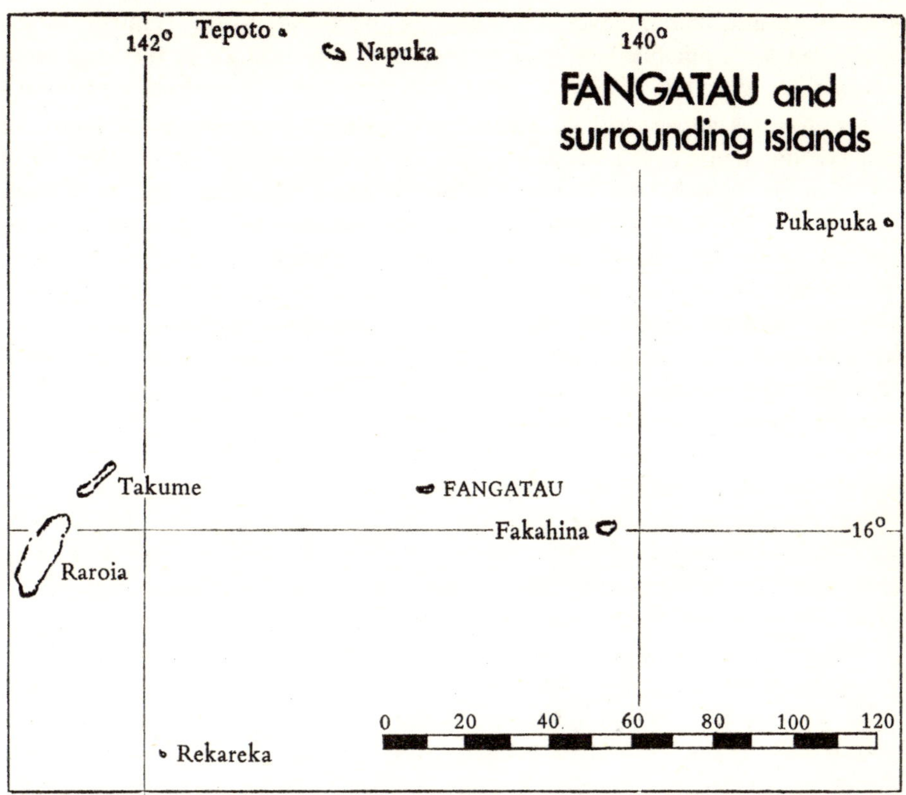

neither Stimson nor the anthropologist did more than speculate and neither imagined that the oddities confronting them might have been explicable in terms of an early European shipwreck.

One of the earliest traditions relating to Fangatau is that it was the birthplace of a celebrated voyager, Mapu the Great, or Mapu the Traveller.[2] He was the son of Varoa Nui, a high chief of Takume, whose dominions also included Amanu, Hao, Raroia, Fakahina and Fangatau. Mapu's mother was a Fangatauan. Mapu is said to have travelled constantly. On one occasion, having set out from Fangatau to visit his father at Takume, he went on to Raroia, Takaroa[3] and Niau, and then determined to make for Tahiti. Instead, he was carried to Mopelia, at the far western end of the Society Islands, where he caught a red bird and changed the name of his canoe to commemorate the event. His next stopping place was Anaa, where he was involved in a battle and killed a good number of people. Finally, he sailed on to Raroia and Takume, where he settled down, had children, and left descendants.

Although Mapu's name does not appear to figure in Tahitian traditions, the name of his home island was known to the Tahitians long before Europeans discovered it. Information about the atoll was first recorded in 1774-5 when the Boenechea expedition made its second visit to Tahiti. On that occasion, the Tahitians gave the Spaniards the names of fifteen islands that lay to the eastward, among which was Marupua. According to the Tahitians it was 'small and low', inhabited by 'bad people,' and at a distance of two days from 'Maemo', or Makemo. Coconuts, yams, dogs and fish were said to be plentiful.[4]

Europeans appear to have gleaned no further information about Fangatau until Bellingshausen, the Russian explorer, discovered it on 10 July 1820 in his ships *Vostok* and *Mirnyi*. Bellingshausen approached the atoll from the south, a day and two nights after leaving Amanu. At noon when his ships were about twelve miles from it, some of the Fangatauans surprised him with their great daring. First one canoe, then a second, then a third, and finally as many as six pushed off from the shore and made their way out to the Russian ships. They came quite close and stopped abreast of them, but seemed doubtful about coming alongside. Finally one did approach the *Vostok,* Bellingshausen's flagship. The men in her caught hold of a rope that was let down from the stern. Bellingshausen noted that all the islanders were of medium height, and thin rather than stout. They had small beards; their hair was tied at the tops of their heads in a knot; and their only clothing was a belt of grass around their waists and a strip to cover their genitals. 'Face and body were swarthy,' Bellingshausen added, 'and therein chiefly differed from Europeans.'

The Russian commander described the islanders' canoes as better suited to the open sea than any such vessels previously known to him. They were about 20 feet long, and (unlike those described by previous navigators in the eastern Pacific) they were wide enough for two men to sit abreast. Several planks 'very skilfully put together' were used in building them, and they had outriggers on one side to steady them. In cross-section, they looked like low milk pans. There were three or four 'active, lithe islanders' to a canoe, each with a spear, a small club, and a lasso made of plaited grasses.* 'It seemed to us . . . ,' Bellingshausen wrote, 'that they had come out to attack us from different sides and if possible get possession of the ship.'

The islanders stayed in the vicinity of the Russian ships for about four hours. They resisted all offers of friendship, and one of them tried to wound one of the officers with a spear when he leant out of a porthole. Finally, the islanders returned to the shore, and, with the help of others, carried their canoes to the interior lagoon. They then set fire to trees and underbrush and made a huge blaze. Meanwhile, Bellingshausen began a quick reconnaissance of the atoll, during which he noted that coconut trees were especially evident on its northern side. As no European navigator had previously reported it, he claimed the atoll as his discovery and named it Arakcheev Island.[5]

The next European to sight Fangatau was another Russian, Otto von Kotzebue, who came upon it on 2 March 1824 in his ship *Predpriatie*. Earlier the same day, Kotzebue had discovered Fangatau's easterly neighbour, Fakahina. On this occasion, no islanders were to be seen on Fangatau and Kotzebue would have concluded that it was uninhabited 'had not Captain Bellingshausen

* Bellingshausen was the only European explorer to record seeing lassos among the Eastern Polynesians.

ascertained the contrary.' The truth probably was that the Fangatauans had migrated temporarily to Fakahina, for on passing that island Kotzebue had seen numerous large, well-built canoes that were seemingly 'intended for other and even distant lands.'[6]

Following Kotzebue's brief encounter, no other European seems to have touched at Fangatau for more than a dozen years. However, when Captain Robert Fitz-Roy of HMS *Beagle* was in Tahiti in November 1835, he learned the name 'Maropua' from John Middleton, a young Englishman who had lived on Anaa for the preceding ten years and had accompanied the Anaans in many of their wanderings. Middleton sold Fitz-Roy a chart on which all the Tuamotuan islands were supposed to be marked;[7] but when Fitz-Roy published a chart of the area in 1839, he showed Fangatau as Araktcheef, and 'Maropua' was merely included in a list of islands whose locality, he said, was unknown to him.[8] These facts clearly show that neither Middleton, the far-ranging Anaans, nor any other knowledgeable people whom Fitz-Roy consulted knew where Fantagau (or Marupua) was, and that no one of that period connected it with Bellingshausen's Arakcheev.

The first European to have contact with the Fangatauans and to learn the two names for their island was a French pearler, Captain Arnaud Mauruc. In 1838, while searching for new sources of pearlshell, Mauruc touched at Fangatau on a west-bound voyage.[9] About twenty canoes, each carrying three or four men, put off boldly to his ship. Each man was armed with an ironwood spear, a club of turtle bone and numerous ironwood missiles. The islanders surrounded the ship, and Mauruc learned from them that their island was called Aatao (or Nanatao) and also Maroupo.* After acting amicably for a time, they began hurling their missiles on board. Although no one was hit by these, one of Mauruc's men was wounded by a spear. The visitors retaliated by opening fire with a hunting rifle loaded with buckshot, wounding one and killing two. The remainder fled. Writing later of this visit, Mauruc's first officer, Eugene Ricardi, said:

> All the people . . . are in general of medium height, but well-made; their features are regular and their physiognomy agreeable. The hair is long in both sexes; sometimes it is allowed to hang down; sometimes they wear it drawn up and tied to the tops of their heads like the women of Europe. Of those that we saw, none was tattooed. The men are generally not as copper-coloured as the women, which we attribute to the fact that they [the women] are more exposed to the sun in gathering food for their families.[10]

About four years after Mauruc's visit, an English pearler, Edward Lucett, was prompted to call at Fangatau by a party of divers whom he had engaged at Anaa. The Anaans told him that 'many years' earlier, a few 'half-starved beings' had been blown from 'Angatau' to Anaa in a canoe; that their island was northward of Hao and Amanu; that no white men had ever visited it;

* In Mauruc's published account—Mauruc 1848—there are several misprints, including his own Christian name, which is given as Armand. 'Maroupo' may therefore have been a misprint for Maropuo or, at least, something nearer to Marupua.

and that many large canoes from Anaa had tried unsuccessfully to reach it. The Fangatauans were said to be still in their primitive condition, and to wear pearls round their necks and in their ears.

Lucett reached Fangatau via Hao in mid-May 1842. When he and his divers went ashore, the islanders greeted them cautiously at first. But after Tiemu, one of the Anaans, had made it clear that their intentions were peaceful, their chief made an 'energetically wild and savage' oration and offered Lucett a coconut to drink. All the islanders then dropped on one knee and celebrated the event with a 'chant to the gods.' Thereafter Lucett was the object of boundless curiosity. 'I was the first white man they had ever touched,' he wrote, 'and they examined my naked breast and arms, forcing up the sleeves of my coat and opening my shirt bosom. The light colour and softness of my hair was another object of admiration. . . .' The Anaans and Fangatauans hit things off like old friends, with much singing, dancing, laughing, rubbing of noses and embracing. Tiemu told Lucett that the Fangatauan language was similar to that of Anaa 'before they had seen white men, or intercourse was so common with Tahiti.'

Lucett described the Fangatauans as 'a harmless, inoffensive race.' They were all but naked, wild and savage-looking, with matted, dishevelled hair, thick mustachios on the upper lip and long beards. They were not tattooed, were thinner than the other islanders, but, generally speaking, taller. Several were nearly seven feet. Only four or five women were seen—'tall, reedy-looking beings, but with rather a soft and pleasing expression of countenance.'

Lucett did not see any pearls among the islanders, nor did they comprehend when his divers asked if they had any. There was therefore nothing to detain Lucett on the island, and after a few hours, he and his divers returned to their ship. A large double canoe was seen on the beach.

Later at Takume Atoll, Lucett found two double canoes from Anaa that had been to Fangatau shortly before his own visit, and had been involved in an affray of some sort. One had left Anaa before he called there to engage his divers; the other had done so soon afterwards. 'It is rather singular,' he wrote, 'after so many years of bootless trial, that both should succeed in reaching Angatau at this time.' Lucett could not get a clear picture of what precisely had happened. But there was a 'whispered rumour' that those in the first canoe had 'wantonly fired' on the Fangatauans and that four of the 'unoffending islanders' had been killed. One man from the second canoe was said to have been killed, and another was said to have been speared in the back and right arm. Whatever the circumstances were, Lucett thought they probably accounted for the Fangatauans' timidity when he had first landed and for the fact that all the islanders had appeared armed.[11]

Following Lucett's visit, Fangatau had little to do with the outside world for a generation or so. The French administration in Tahiti did not trouble about it; and it was therefore not in the list of atolls that were reported in 1858 to have 'received and freely accepted' the protectorate flag.[12] However, in 1861, after the regent Paiore had attempted to bring neighbouring Fakahina under French control, the gunboat *Cassini* apparently called there with Lieutenant Xavier Caillet on board. Caillet later wrote that 'among the savages of Angatau and Fakahina one still recognises the intelligent type of Tahitian and Nukuhivan, but among the children only, since the men especially deviate from this type at a certain age.'[13]

A further eight years passed before Fangatau had its first visit from a European missionary. This was Father Montiton, who called there briefly in 1869 on the first of two evangelical voyages he made from Anaa to the eastern atolls. Montiton sowed a few vague seeds of Christianity, baptised the islanders *en masse* and left two catechists, a man and his wife, to try to consolidate his work.[14] Nine months later, Montiton's colleague, Father Germain Fierens, also called briefly at Fangatau. He baptised the children born since Montiton's visit and replaced the catechist couple with a single catechist. Fierens later reported that Fangatau—'where the people until recently were still savages and cannibals'—had become entirely Catholic. Nevertheless, the islanders were 'still in a state of almost complete nudity', having no clothes other than girdles of pandanus leaves. 'Their island is very poor,' Fierens said. 'The fruit of the pandanus and fish are basically their only food.'[15]

In April 1870, Montiton returned to Fangatau in the mission schooner *Vatikana*. His intention was to stay there for three months, but six months passed before the schooner returned for him.[16] He busied himself in the interval with many tasks. First, he persuaded the islanders to build their principal settlement on the atoll's mainland, for they were then living on a small lagoon islet, whence they had fled about thirty years earlier 'to protect themselves from sudden invasions by Tuamotuan pirates.'* Montiton then set about building a schoolhouse, church and cemetery. He also did his best to instil in the Fangatauans some serious notions of the Catholic faith, for he found that the native catechists had done little more than teach a few prayers and the 'letter of the catechism.' The islanders, however, 'preferred to keep their own company or to sleep rather than take part in these different exercises.' Moreover, as the island had few coconut trees, they were frequently busy gathering shellfish or extracting the edible fruit from pandanus nuts—a long, tedious task. Montiton's efforts to indoctrinate the islanders were therefore 'without great success,' as he himself put it. On the other hand, he did learn a good deal about their own religious beliefs, some of which struck him as remarkably Biblical. He found similar beliefs at Tatakoto,† an isolated atoll about 160 miles south-east of Fangatau, where he lived from November 1870 to July 1871.

About two years later, while Montiton was in Europe for the treatment of a skin disease,[17] he published a series of five articles on Tuamotuan traditions and customs in the missionary journal *Les Missions Catholiques*.[18] He drew

* These invasions must have been the Anaan incursions described by Lucett.

† The name of this atoll appears as Tatakoto on official charts and in other official documents. However, its true name is apparently Takoto, as this is the spelling used by Montiton and others who have visited it. In this book, the official spelling is used, except in quotations.

attention in these to the Biblical nature of some of his discoveries. 'For many years,' he wrote in an introduction, 'I had tried to make this study, but, unable to find sufficient information at Anaa and the other islands to the west, I was forced to give it up. It was not until I was among the savages of Fangatau and Takoto that, with time, patience and labour, I was able to gather a few worthwhile details and positive facts.'[19]

In his first article,[20] on the cosmogony of the Tuamotuans, Montiton told a story about two giants, Tahitiofenua, and his brother Ronamakaitua, who killed another man called Maraukura. 'These are the first murderers known among the Tuamotuans,' he wrote, 'and their history, with the circumstances of brother and sacrifice, is evidently a much altered but recognisable copy of the history of Cain, murderer of his brother Abel.' Further on, Montiton told of a battle in the heavens between Tane and Oatea, Maraukura's brother. The battle ended in victory for Tane, who 'threw [Oatea] out of the sky and into the great fire.' Commenting on this, Montiton said: 'No one, in their different ways, will fail to recognise in this the history of the revolt, the fall and punishment of the bad angels. In both Tuamotuan mythology and the account of Moses, the story comes before the story of creation, so that it conforms closely with the order revealed by the Holy Scriptures.'

Montiton next recounted the Tuamotuan story of how Tane, 'now sole master of Heaven and Earth,' gathered the angels together and ordered them to carry the firmament into the sky, where he established his throne and reigned as sovereign master of all things. Meanwhile, the land remained submerged until one, Tefaafanua, 'untied it from the waters.' A single point then appeared above the surface, which gradually grew larger and soon became the earth as it now is. Imperceptibly, the land became covered with vegetation, bushes and great trees. 'This detail of the Polynesian cosmogony,' Montiton went on, 'carries us back quite naturally to the Biblical story where the Spirit of God is represented to us as incubating and fertilizing the inert and unformed mass of the earth, which then comes out from the bosom of the waters on the third day of creation, and soon becomes covered with luxuriant vegetation.'

Continuing, Montiton told the Tuamotuan story of how the Earth (Fakahotufenua), the source and mother of all things, gave birth to the day, the night, the moon, the sunrise, sunset, and, in short, all animate and inanimate things, including man, who, according to some, was called Magamaga. 'However,' he said, 'the first man known in all these islands seems to have been Tiki, the veritable Polynesian Adam, who, like the one in the Bible, was the first great sinner, the murderer of all his posterity, even before he had become its father.' Montiton said there were two versions of Tiki's birth. Some claimed he was born spontaneously of the sand and sea; others that he emerged alive from a shell. Whatever his origin was, it was he who formed Vahuone, the first woman, from a heap of sand and made her his wife and companion. Of their union, a daughter, Hina, was born. Tiki later fell in love with her and she, being discovered by Vahuone, fled in shame to the moon 'where one still sees her figure.'

Before this, Hina gave birth to Maikuku 'who begat Finiafu, who begat Pagahuruhuru, who begat Hiro, who begat Rii, who successively begat men and dogs, since he himself was changed into a dog by Maui who shared Rii's wife and was jealous of the preference she showed for him.'

After recounting some stories about Maui, 'a powerful and evil genius,' whom he called the Polynesian Joshua, Montiton described some further similarities between the Bible and Tuamotuan mythology. 'The Holy Bible tells us,' he said, 'that the posterity of Adam, having become carnal, was swallowed up in the waters of the deluge which God used to punish and purefy the contamination of Earth. Tuamotuan mythology tells us equally that the depraved race of Tiki, having been transformed into dogs, was partially submerged in a more or less general deluge.' After giving a brief outline of the Tuamotuan 'cataclysm,' Montiton affirmed that there were yet other stories among the 'pagan traditions' of the Tuamotus 'whose themes and manifest types are found in the Bible.' He added, 'I shall here mention only those that relate to Jonah and Goliath,' which he described as follows:

> Kae, a giant eight feet high, a glutton and a sacrilegious person, had returned furtively to the *marae* after a sacrifice to eat part of the idol. Afterwards, as he went at high tide to rejoin some native fishermen, his canoe was attacked by an enormous shark in which the soul of the idol had entered. The sacrilegious Kae was swallowed by the monster in one gulp, and he remained alive in its entrails for several days. Meanwhile, the shark swam about as usual, going from one island to another. Finally, it went so close to an island that its passenger, from the depths of his dark dwelling, could distinctly hear the surf breaking on the reef. Kae then armed himself with a shark's tooth that he had in the hole of his ear and resolutely tore at the entrails of his powerful courser, which, in rage and pain, suddenly jumped on the reef. There Kae managed to disembowel the monster and escape to the land.
>
> The Tuamotuan Goliath, Patira, was another giant. He could walk from one island to another. Being arrived at Makemo, he set about seducing the wife of Moeava. However, the latter was warned by his demon, who arrived in time, tied the giant's foot with lianas, and, having thus made him fall to the ground, he jumped on him and cut off his head.

Montiton's second article was subtitled 'Biblical and Messianic Traditions —Immortality of the Soul.'[21] Among other things, it recounted the stories of two legendary figures, who, in Montiton's eyes, seem to have corresponded closely to the Virgin Mary and Jesus.

> It is consoling to find [he wrote], even among those islands scattered like grains of sand in the immensity of the ocean, a striking, although incomplete form of the virginal motherhood of the august Mother of God. Tekurotoga supplies this.
>
> This woman, eminently holy and privileged, conceived and gave birth, in all virginity and by the miraculous work of Tane, to a son named Tuku-

hakia. She was the daughter of Keha. Tane found her in her father's house, in the sky, when he went there, pursued by Oatea. This Virgin Mother was especially venerated at Fangatau, where some said she was invoked for the cure of headaches. When one recalls the *conteret caput* of the original and Biblical type, this makes the copy resemble it even more closely.*

But the most faithfully and uniformly preserved character, and the most strongly accented in all the islands, is that of the Messiah, Tama, the son *par excellence,* or Atua Fakaora, Saviour god. He was the sole and unique refuge of the sinful and unfortunate race of Tiki.

Montiton said that under the double name that the islanders gave to 'this mysterious personage,' they seemed to have preserved—perhaps more religiously than any other pagan people—the true notion and proper character of the Messiah. Tama, the son *par excellence,* was the god's true name, describing his nature, his personality; Atua Fakaora, the saviour god, was his role, his mission before men. It was he, who, during their lives, cured the islanders of their injuries when they fell from pandanus and coconut palms, and who cured them of shark bites, and other maladies and infirmities. It was also Tama who, after their deaths, conducted their souls to Heaven or *kororupo.* Souls that Tama did not save were thrown pitilessly into a miry swamp from which they could never escape. According to the Fangatauans, Tama descended upon their island one day to find and instruct Tangata, the man. Tangata in turn taught his compatriots the 'word that saves', and all the islanders subsequently practised this word and prayed to Tama.

Describing the Tuamotuan idea of the underworld, Montiton said that the guardian and king of this was called Tukuhiti. He apparently had the double character and functions of Cerberus and Pluto. He had four eyes, two in front and two behind, so that no one could escape him. Under his orders was a body of evil spirits who, mounted like him on great canoes, chased souls day and night. 'As one sees,' Montiton went on, 'our Oceanic savages believed in the survival and immortality of the soul. After its separation from the body, they assigned three distinct dwelling places to it in keeping with the social or moral state that each had occupied on earth.' The three dwelling places were *paparagi, kororupo* and the 'redoubtable swamp' already mentioned. The swamp was reserved for the souls of the impious and for those of thieves, drunkards, murderers and cannibals which Tama could not or did not wish to save. *Paparagi* or Paradise was the 'Olympus of the gods and demi-gods, the dwelling place exclusively reserved for the bravest warriors and people of noble and powerful race here below.' *Kororupo* was the dwelling place for the souls of the good common people who had learned and followed the word

* The phrase *conteret caput* (it will crush the head) is from Genesis III:15 of the Vulgate (Latin) version of the Bible. The verse refers to the crushing of the serpent's head, and has been assumed traditionally to be a prophesy concerning the Virgin Mary and her offspring, Christ, who would crush the Devil. In connecting all this with the curing of headaches, Montiton seems to have been indulging in oblique symbolic argument. To nineteenth century readers of *Les Missions Catholiques,* this symbolism may have been more obvious than it probably is to most Europeans of the present day.

of Tama, the saviour god. There, exempt from all care, all work and all sickness, and abundantly provided for with all kinds of food, they passed a life solely employed in feasting, voluptuousness, dancing, the game of *baton kitoa,* and many thousands of other amusements. But *Paparagi* and *kororupo* were not so far apart that the souls in each could not easily pass from one to another, and this they did when a feast or some other circumstance made the reunion of all the souls in the same place useful or necessary.

Montiton recorded much else about the traditions and customs of the Fangatau and Tatakoto people. But only in one other instance did he remark on a similarity between customs and traditions among the atoll-dwellers and his own religion. This was in respect of the prayers spoken by the Tuamotuan priests after a person's death. The prayers were addressed not to Tama, nor to Tane, but to Tiki, the father of mankind and the first great prevaricator, who, by his sin, had introduced death to the world. 'This body,' the priests would say, 'that thou hast transmitted to us, thou hast thyself received from the earth, and if we must render it inanimate to thee, it is because thou hast killed it through the sin that thou hast fatally transmitted with life.' Commenting on this, Montiton said: 'Who will not recognise here the doctrine of St Paul and the teachings of the Church. . . .?'[22]

Although medical treatment in France enabled Montiton to return to the Pacific, he was not sent to the Tuamotus again,[23] and for the next eighteen years, the work of evangelisation in the eastern atolls was the responsibility of Fathers Fierens and Vincent de Paul Terlyn.[24] Such visits as they made to Fangatau were brief and apparently infrequent. Only two were specifically recorded in print. The first, by Fierens, was in the early part of 1873 to deliver many thousands of planting coconuts to the islanders to relieve them of their poverty and to make them less dependent on pandanus nuts and shellfish for food.[25] Terlyn paid the second visit in 1887 when the population stood at 152.[26] Meanwhile, passing trading schooners apparently touched at the atoll occasionally and the islanders acquired some slight knowledge of money. Thus, when the French gunboat *La Voie* called at Fangatau in April 1883, a passenger, J. C. Bell, found that the islanders charged a dollar for all their trade goods—shark hooks, fish hooks and cord made from coconut fibre. They also accepted old European clothes. Their canoes were still being made of many thin slabs of wood sewn together. Bell thought they were 'very graceful' and similar to Canadian canoes, except for their outriggers.[27]

Fangatau's sewn canoes were still much in evidence some twenty years later when a French scientist, L. G. Seurat, visited Fangatau. By then many coconut trees were bearing, but the production of copra was 'absolutely nil' because the islanders ate all the nuts themselves. 'These natives, having no needs, live in the most complete idleness,' Seurat wrote. 'Even the making of mats and hats from pandanus leaves, which enabled them to exchange a few things with passing schooners, is on the point of disappearing.'[28] Yet despite their idleness, the Fangatauans had somehow managed to acquire European tools, so that their own Stone Age implements were becoming rare. Seurat described those that were still to be found in meticulous detail. The axes or hatchets, he said, were made from big tridacna shells, fixed in wooden, L-shaped handles. These tools were used to cut down trees, the cutting edges of their blades being parallel to the plane of the two branches of the handle, 'the same as in our European axes.' Another type, used to hollow out trees for canoes, had an almost V-shaped handle, which reminded Seurat of the European adze. Holes in the planks for the canoes were pierced with a kind of brace and bit which 'showed great ingenuity among these Indians.' The bit drove rapidly through the wood and bored even holes. Through the holes, a cord made of sennit was passed, and other ingenious devices were used to ensure that, when drawn taut, it was inflexible.

Writing of the canoes themselves, Seurat said the small ones were propelled by paddles and the big ones used sails. The rigging of the *pahi* in which the ancient Polynesians made their long voyages comprised a big mast (*tira*) and a yard-arm (*tahatu*) attached to the top of the mast. A square sail, made of pandanus matting, was attached to the yard-arm and held in position at its lower extremities by two cords which enabled it to be moved about according to the wind. Seurat added:

> They [the islanders] used the stars to find their way. The oldest among them still know the names of these, which they group in different constellations from us. The new generation is ignorant of almost all these astronomical notions as well as of the fishing devices of their ancestors. In a few years it will be impossible to obtain any information on this subject.[29]

Although nothing appears to have been recorded concerning the eventual demise of the sewn canoes of Fangatau, an event occurred soon after Seurat's visit that undoubtedly hastened their disappearance. This was the arrival on the atoll in September 1905 of a European settler named Marechal, who opened a store and encouraged the islanders to develop a copra industry.[30] He was so successful that by 1916 two Chinese traders had also opened stores there; another was in the hands of an islander; and yet another was being opened by a French company. The quickening of commerce naturally brought more trading vessels to the island and there was some intermarriage with outsiders.[31] Nevertheless, the Fangatauans were still a predominantly homogeneous community and much of their ancient culture was still intact, or at least remembered, when three scientists from the Bishop Museum visited the island in October 1929. The scientists were the linguist Stimson, the ethnologist Emory, and a physical anthropologist, Harry L. Shapiro. They spent about three weeks on the island. While Shapiro investigated the islanders' physical characteristics, Stimson studied their language and recorded their chants and traditions, and Emory surveyed the atoll's well-preserved *marae*.

In reports on their work to the director of the Bishop Museum, all three scientists remarked on the European, or Caucasian, appearance of the Fangatauans. Shapiro, who had previously spent a total of ten months surveying the physical characteristics of the Marquesans, Tuamotuans and Society Islanders,[32] said in his report:

> In studies of this kind the intricate relationships between various groups are determined only after considerable study. . . . However, from preliminary surveys of the data and from observation, several interesting facts stand out. In the first place, the people of the northwestern Tuamotus appear to be very closely related to the Society Islanders. This, one might expect from the juxtaposition of these islands to Tahiti, but, as one goes eastward towards the more remote islands, one becomes impressed with the population of the Tuamotus as a kind of geographical cul-de-sac which has received various elements from central Polynesia* no longer existent in the Tuamotus. Furthermore, in Fagatau and Napuka† I was especially struck by a marked Caucasian strain which I have never found so clearly indicated anywhere else in Polynesia. Some of these islanders, of undoubtedly pure descent, are remarkably European and to my mind solve some of the disturbing questions with regard to the racial position of the Polynesian and the elements that go to make up the Polynesian physical complex.[33]

Stimson, for his part, quoted Shapiro as saying that the Fangatauans were distinctive among Polynesian tribes for 'an extraordinarily Caucasian cast of features'; and he added that their island was unique for the number of ancient words preserved in its pagan chants or *fangu*. The words were what he called 'old Tahitian.' They were unknown in common speech except where they had been reintroduced in very modern times. 'It would seem possible,' Stimson wrote, 'at least as a working hypothesis, that these words were brought in by conquerors who imposed their own religious ceremonies upon the earlier peoples, maintaining unchanged the actual wording of the *fagu* (chants) through the *mana* (power) of a sort of tapu, although they themselves eventually adopted the corresponding words in common speech.'[34]

Emory reported that Shapiro had measured thirty-seven Fangatauans who were all of a 'uniform, very Caucasoid type.' This, coupled with the fact that their language was old Tahitian rather than the Tuamotuan of the central Tuamotus, made them 'a most interesting group.' Emory added that he and his party had recorded a chant commemorating the rediscovery on Fangatau twelve generations before 1900 of the sacred learning or *vananga*. This learning had become almost lost in other parts of the Tuamotus, so the chiefs joined together in a desperate search for some family who still knew it. On Fangatau, so the tradition went, the search party found that Mahinui, the atoll's chief, had received and preserved the *vananga* and he was thus able to pass it on to them.

Emory said that two great sages, both descendants of Mahinui, were still living on Fangatau. They were cousins, Temiro a Pahoa and Kamake a Ituragi. Temiro, born in 1841, had 'witnessed with adult eyes the full flourishing of

* Shapiro presented no evidence to support this statement, and was presumably hypothesising on the only lines that then seemed feasible.

† At the time of writing, Shapiro had visited only nine Tuamotuan atolls—Takaroa, Takapoto, Katiu, Napuka, Fangatau, Fakahina, Amanu and Hao.—Gregory 1932:50.

pure native culture.' Kamake, born in 1858, was the most learned islander the expedition encountered. In addition, the expedition was 'immensely helped' by Fariua a Makitua, a young and brilliant sage of Hikueru, who had married Temiro's daughter.[35]

When the expedition left Fangatau, it was Emory's hope that he and Stimson could return to the atoll in the following year for further investigations. This, however, proved impossible, so Emory arranged for Fariua a Makitua to travel to Tahiti to help them there. He arrived in April 1931 accompanied by his wife Reva. 'They proved of such invaluable assistance,' Emory later wrote, 'that Stimson kept them in Papeete until November 1931. Through them we were able to record the Fagatau songs on the dictaphone . . . Stimson has obtained from Fariua his most complete data concerning the Tuamotuan belief in the creator, Kiho-tumu.'[36]

Two years after his recording sessions with Fariua, Stimson published a monograph entitled *The Cult of Kiho-Tumu* in which he suggested that the 'lofty ideas' embodied in the cult were derived from 'some highly developed ancient civilisation.'[37] The monograph supplemented Stimson's *Tuamotuan Religion* which had appeared earlier in the same year, based mainly on data obtained from informants from Vahitahi and Anaa.[38] In an introduction to the second work, Stimson wrote:

> The present record seems to confirm in many essentials the main conclusions of my previous study and brings new and welcome support to the thesis already elaborated. In brief, this thesis maintains that an early ethnic wave of Polynesians—termed, for convenience, palae-Polynesians—brought with it a conception of cosmogenesis and of a supreme god which formed an esoteric religion taught only to the priests and nobles. The philosophical ideas involved are so lofty that it is difficult to imagine how they could have arisen among barbaric peoples. It would appear more logical to infer that they were derived from some highly developed ancient civilization somewhere in southeastern Asia in prehistoric times. Whatever the explanation may be, the fact remains that this brief and imperfect fragment of a nobler past bears living witness to the genius of the palae-Polynesian race, whose capacity for philosophic reflection and introspection has, perhaps, never been surpassed and rarely equalled by any people of a similar cultural level.[39]

Stimson explained that the Tuamotuan texts of the chants given in his monograph had been written down from memory by Fariua a Makitua in the Fangatau dialect as it was taught to him by his grandfather, Temiro-Tehina-a-Makitua. The account of cosmogenesis was derived from Temiro, but had been 'corroborated in full' by Kamake-a-Ituragi, 'the celebrated Fagatau sage.' There was internal and external evidence to establish the authenticity of the Kiho-tumu chants. Among other things, François Hervé, the administrator of the Tuamotu Archipelago*, had volunteered in a letter of 30 July 1931 that he had heard of the Kiho cult as far back as 1915. Stimson mentioned also that the

* And discoverer of the four Amanu cannon in 1929.

PLATE 17. This model of a Fangatauan double canoe in the Bishop Museum, Honolulu, is reputed to have been made in 1854. The date is questionable because Fangatau had little contact with the outside world until the first Catholic missionaries visited it in 1869. Whether the sail has been correctly modelled is also a moot point. Nevertheless, the model is of interest because it has the same open-ended bows as the 'pahi' of Anaa, Vahitahi and Raiatea pictured elsewhere, a feature that demonstrates a common ancestry.—Bishop Museum photograph.

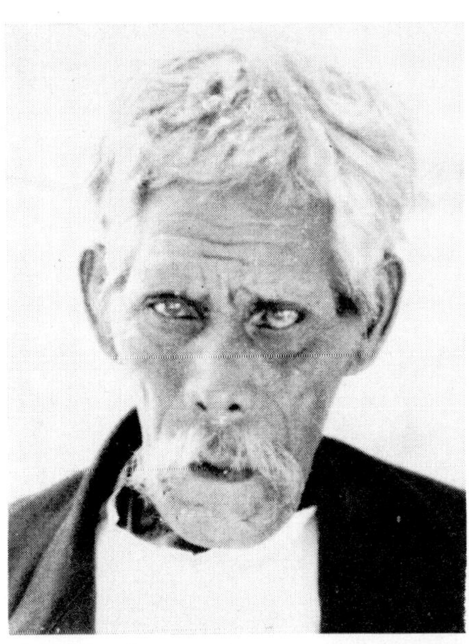

Three Fangatauans who greatly assisted the Bishop Museum's Tuamotus expedition in 1929. They are Kamake-a-Ituragi (left) and Stimson's informants, Fariua-a-Makitua and his wife Reva.—Bishop Museum photographs.

PLATE 18. Although somewhat swarthy, some of the Vahitahi people of the 1930s were distinctly Caucasian in features. The man at right seems, from his appearance, to have been related to those above—a man called Tagi and his daughter Kohenigo.—Bishop Museum photographs.

It would be hard for anyone to guess the racial origins of these girls from their appearance. They are, in fact, 'native girls of Nukutavake' of the 1930s.—Bishop Museum photograph.

'Takaoa, his family and friends' is the caption of this Bishop Museum photograph taken at Vahitahi in the 1930s. It clearly demonstrates that the people of that island were of diverse physical types and various skin colours.

chants had been shown to leading sages from many sections of the Tuamotus, all of whom had expressed the unqualified opinion that they were 'genuine archaic compositions.' They had agreed that such compositions were impossible of imitation at a time when the 'ancient modes of expression and often the meanings of the words themselves' had become widely forgotten and often corrupted by the invading and almost universal Tahitian language. 'It is unlikely,' Stimson added, 'that there is a Tuamotuan native alive today capable of composing these, or similar, cosmogonic chants.'[40]

It is not clear from published sources why Stimson was so insistent about the authenticity of the Kiho chants. It may have been that he merely wanted to show what he had done to try to ensure their genuineness. Or he may have been prompted by misgivings on the part of his associate, Emory. Whatever the reason was, Emory claimed several years later that he had developed doubts about the genuineness of the god Kiho at the very time that Stimson was recording the chants and that he had urged Stimson not to publish them. After Stimson insisted, he began to gather information, which, in his view, 'proved that [Stimson's] informants were unreliable in what they gave in support of the Kio, or Kiho, cult.' [41] In 1939 and 1940, Emory published three papers in which he set down the information he had collected; and in 1947 he broached the subject again in a monograph entitled *Tuamotuan Religious Structures and Ceremonies*.[42] The burden of Emory's misgivings was that Stimson had been misled into believing in the Kiho cult through attempting to find a 'Tuamotuan equivalent of [the supreme god] Io of the Maoris.' He did not challenge the authenticity of the chants that Stimson had recorded. But he claimed that Stimson's informants had deliberately interpolated or substituted the names of Kio or Kiho in them, or that Stimson had read the names into the text when those three or four letters happened to come together. The names Kio or Kiho, Emory said, were not recorded in the manuscript books of any of Stimson's informants before he and Stimson knew them. Moreover, Fariua, Stimson's informant, had been embarrassed and unable to repeat the Kiho chants when he (Emory) unexpectedly paid Fangatau a two-day visit in July 1934.[43]

A friend of Emory, the anthropologist Bengt Danielsson, has since averred that Emory was 'completely right' over Kiho and that Stimson was 'altogether wrong.'[44] On the other hand, a friend of Stimson, the linguist D. S. Marshall, has announced that he intends to publish a monograph, using unpublished material recorded by Stimson, which will be a detailed analysis of the term Kiho and the implications of the difference of opinion between the two men.[45] Until Marshall's monograph appears, there is little point in discussing the merits of the Kiho dispute at length. In any case, the authenticity or otherwise of Kiho is not necessarily relevant to this book.* However, several points that

* The existence of Kiho in ancient Tuamotuan lore could be relevant in that the name could be derived from the Spanish word 'Dios', meaning God. As there is no 'd' and no 's' in Tuamotuan, the word 'Dios' would become either Tio or Kio in that language if normal sound changes were followed. Both Kio (or Kiho) and Dios are accented on the second syllable. See chapter 15, note 70, for a reference to a god called Varoua-Kiro, recorded in 1844.

emerged in the dispute are worth mentioning here because they show that if some of Emory's initial assumptions about the Tuamotus were erroneous, much of his thinking thereafter, no matter how logical, is likely to have been erroneous. These points are:

1. Like Shapiro and Stimson, Emory took it for granted that the Tuamotuans originated in the west. It therefore followed that the transmission of cultural influences between the Society Islands and Tuamotu Archipelago was in a west-east direction. 'For centuries,' Emory wrote (without citing any evidence), 'the Tuamotus have served as a refuge area for those who have been refractory to the constant changes taking place in Polynesia's great cultural center, the Society Islands.'[46] (By contrast, the pioneer LMS missionary John Davies wrote: 'It seems that in old times, there was very little designed intercourse between the Paumotu people and the Tahitians and Leeward islanders. Now and then Paumotu canoes drifted to the islands [i.e. from east to west] and returned when they had favourable wind . . .')[47]

2. Emory stated that when he and Stimson began collecting material in the Tuamotus, they were 'surprised and puzzled' that the islanders did not describe Tangaroa as a supreme god and creator 'in view of the close relationship between Tuamotuan and Tahitian culture.' 'Everywhere we repeatedly met with statements and vague accounts in which the supreme god was Tane or Atea,' Emory said. '. . . we naturally assumed that the elevation of Tane and Atea . . . was due to the century and more of vigorous Christian teaching of a supreme god and creator, and our assumption was borne out by the unmistakably Biblicized accounts of creation recorded in manuscripts of the natives, accounts which had been in existence for more than seventy-five years.'[48]

3. As with Stimson, it never occurred to Emory that the ancient Fangatauans and other Tuamotuans could have been subject to Biblical influences. Therefore, any Biblical ideas encountered in questioning the islanders about their ancient beliefs were assumed to be due to the ancient lore being 'overlaid and obscured' by modern influences. 'Any present-day recording of Tuamotuan beliefs is sure to meet with Biblicized accounts,' Emory said. 'To inform the Tuamotuans that these accounts are not ancient, and to inquire as to what their ancestors actually were taught concerning creation, is to invite reconstructions based upon whatever the informants may have learned but turned in whatever direction he [*sic*] believes may please the investigator.'[49]

4. In Emory's view, the most reliable information on ancient Tuamotuan religious beliefs was that derived from chants which informants recited before they were questioned and from chants, recitations, songs and genealogies which they wrote down for their own benefit in their own manuscript books.[50] However, by inference, Emory excluded the 'Biblicized accounts of creation recorded in manuscripts,' mentioned in paragraph 2 above; and, as stated in paragraph 5, he specifically excluded the Biblicized accounts that Montiton obtained from the 'savages' of Fangatau and Tatakoto before the 'century and more of vigorous Christian teaching' began.

5. By citing without question much of what Montiton learned about the islanders' ancient religion at Fangatau and Tatakoto, Emory acknowledged that Montiton was a reliable reporter. Indeed, he stated that Montiton was 'anxious to obtain genuine native beliefs.' However, he explained away the Biblical side of Montiton's material by asserting that Montiton was 'eager to find Biblical parallels,' and he thereafter refrained from discussing any of the parallels he did find.[51]

It will be seen from the foregoing that, whatever the truth may have been about Kiho, Emory's thinking on the origins, culture and Biblical notions of the Tuamotuans was firm-fixed and unimaginative. It is therefore hardly surprising that he failed to see any possible link between the 'very Caucasoid' people of Fangatau and the 'Biblical and Messianic traditions' that Montiton described, or, indeed, between them and the lofty philosophical ideas that Stimson found embodied in their chants. On the other hand, it is little short of astonishing that Shapiro, who confidently proclaimed to the director of the Bishop Museum that his discovery of the 'remarkably European' Fangatauans had solved some of the 'disturbing questions' about Polynesian origins, should never have published another word about them—not even his measurements. In brief, it can fairly be said that the remote, rarely-visited Fangatauans—'a most interesting group' as Emory described them—received disappointingly short shrift from two of the few scholars ever to study them.

Apart from Emory, Stimson and Shapiro, only two people have published anything of consequence on Fangatau since 1930.[52] One was an American journalist, Clifford Gessler, who paid a two-day visit to the atoll with Emory in July 1934 after a ten-week stay on Napuka. Gessler's contribution to the literature of Fangatau was an article, which first appeared in the American journal *Asia* in September 1935, and was later incorporated in his book *The Dangerous Islands,* published in 1937. In this, he described Stimson's informant Fariua as 'a fine, jolly Tuamotuan, with a face like an American Indian.' His father-in-law, the sage Temiro, was seen as 'a wild bearded figure like some Old Testament prophet.'[53] Gessler also told how Fariua and his wife Reva had regaled both him and Emory with a series of ancient chants, including one concerning 'the Root or Source'—a supreme god whose name, it was said, was 'not to be spoken in ancient times save by the priests of the highest rank.' It was a 'majestic, somber creation chant,' Gessler added, which described how the Source 'slept from time without beginning,' how he eventually awoke, created the universe, and placed subordinate gods 'in command of its several spheres.'[54] Gessler did not say whether Fariua had mentioned the name that had previously been applied on Fangatau to the Root or Source. But it is interesting to note that only four months earlier, in an *Asia* article on Napuka, Gessler had spoken of 'Kiho the Root.'*[55]

* Gessler's reference to Kiho in his *Asia* article on Napuka was expunged when the article was incorporated in *The Dangerous Islands*. This and the namelessness of the Root or Source in his Fangatau article suggest that it was not until after he and Emory returned to 'civilisation' that Emory told him of his misgivings about Fariua and Kiho. In fact, a contemporary report by Emory suggests that—contrary to what Emory later wrote—he

(continued overleaf)

The only other person to write at length about Fangatau in recent years was a Bishop Museum ethnologist, Edwin G. Burrows. In 1933, he published a monograph, *Native Music of the Tuamotus,* in which he analysed 350 songs and chants that Stimson and Emory recorded at Fangatau, Vahitahi and Reao in 1929-31.[56] The monograph reveals that there were many similarities between European music and that of the ancient Tuamotus. But as Burrows shared the same preconceptions as Emory, Stimson and Shapiro about the origins and culture of the Tuamotuans, he naturally did not look any further back than the nineteenth century to account for the similarities he found.

Burrows was particularly struck by the parallels between European music and a type of Tuamotuan love song called a *mereu.* The *mereu,* he said, was characterised by a 'distinct introductory section' before the main theme was sung, and by a 'prolonged final note.' Moreover, the melody of the main theme was 'more varied' than in the simpler *teki,* or ditties, of the atolls. Two *mereu* recorded at Fangatau had a range of an octave in their two parts, and one had a range of a seventh in the lower part alone. 'European influence appears particularly strong in the *mereu,'* Burrows said. And he added: 'Despite the thesis of Margaret Mead's *Coming of Age in Samoa* that Polynesian mores eliminate many of the conflicts common among adolescent girls in European cultures, [one *mereu* recorded at Fangatau] seems to indicate that Freudian wish-fulfilment dreams are not unknown to Polynesian women.'[57]

In discussing the possible sources of European influence on the music of the Tuamotus, Burrows named only two—hymns introduced by the missionaries and 'the chanteys and forecastle songs of sailors, especially those of the whaling ships that cruised the South Seas in the first half of the nineteenth century.' Burrows stated that 'in all probability' whaling ships never put in at the Tuamotus. But he thought it likely that some Tuamotuans reached Tahiti in canoes, shipped from there on whalers, and 'returned and sang the songs of the square-riggers to their countrymen.'[58]

In the case of the western Tuamotus, Burrows was probably right. But in the remote eastern atolls such as Fangatau, all evidence indicates that there was virtually no contact with the outside world until Fathers Montiton and Fierens began visiting them in 1869-70. That means that the responsibility for the European influence in the love songs of Fangatau must either be laid at the doors of a couple of celibate priests, or some other explanation for its existence must be found. In the circumstances, it seems that a new study of Fangatau's music in conjunction with that of sixteenth century Spain could well reveal the correct answer.

(Emory) had had no misgivings on those subjects *before* visiting Fangatau with Gessler in 1934, and that even while there no such misgivings occurred to him. Emory's report, published in 1935 in the annual report of the director of the Bishop Museum for 1934, described his and Gessler's arrival at Fangatau. It went on: 'Our informant, Fariua, came out to meet us and during our stay we lodged with him. Aside from Fariua and his wife Reva . . . there are no reliable informants left on Fagatau. I recorded 31 Fagatau chants and songs . . . Fariua and Reva assisted me in every way possible, cooking our meals, bringing informants and answering the questions I had prepared for them.'—Gregory 1935:62-3.

17

Vahitahi: land of the Holy Trinity

Lying at a distance of eighty to one hundred miles south-eastward of Hao is a cluster of five small islands, which seem to offer decisive evidence for the survival of castaways from the caravel *San Lesmes*. The five islands are Akiaki, Nukutavake, Pinaki, Vahitahi and Vairaatea. For convenience, they may be described as the Vahitahi group. Two of them, Akiaki and Nukutavake, are unusual for the Tuamotus in that they have no lagoons and are therefore not atolls. Nukutavake, which is low and flat, otherwise conforms in most respects to the characteristics of an atoll. But Akiaki, which is only about a mile in circumference, is somewhat upraised, extremely fertile, and supports an exceptionally heavy growth of timber trees. The greatest distance in the group from one island to another is twenty-nine miles, and the smallest, eight. In ancient times, the islanders moved freely from one island to another, as they still do today. However, Akiaki and Pinaki are so small that they seem never to have had any permanent inhabitants, being used only as sources of food and timber. The other islands were inhabited only semi-permanently—the islanders moving on when the supply of food became exhausted.[1]

The timber trees of Akiaki enabled the islanders of former times to build large and solid sailing craft, which struck several early European visitors to the group as having much in common with European vessels. The islanders, moreover, were light-skinned, and, as in other parts of the Tuamotus, were sometimes compared to Europeans. But the most remarkable feature about the Vahitahi group was the wealth of poetic chants that were part of the islanders' lore until well into the present century. Some of these chants, when recorded and translated in the 1930s, were found to be remarkably Biblical in character. Indeed, one was virtually a verse-for-verse rendering of the first chapter of Genesis, while others were reminiscent of the Psalms and other parts of the Bible. Several recent scholars have assumed that the chants and boats of the Vahitahi islanders owed their character to modern European influences. However, a survey of the known history of the area does not seem to support their view . . .

The first island in the group to be recorded by Europeans was Vairaatea. This was sighted on 9 February 1606 as Quiros was sailing northwards to Hao.[2] More than a century and a half then passed before the next European navigator, Captain Wallis, passed that way in HMS *Dolphin*. Wallis discovered Pinaki on 6 June 1767 and later sailed on to Nukutavake. When a boat party from the *Dolphin* approached Nukutavake, about fifty islanders gathered on the beach to oppose their landing; but next day the entire population fled to

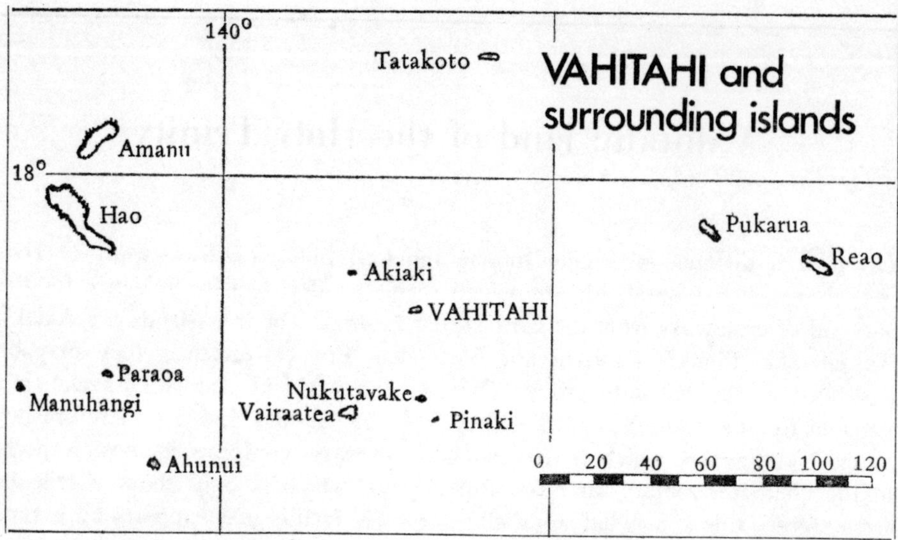

Vairaatea in five double canoes. George Robertson, the *Dolphin's* master, noted that the canoes' hulls were about thirty feet long, built of small planks sewn together, and fixed to small timbers 'not unlyke the frame of our Boats.' Their masts were supported by ropes coiled round cleats at the stern and their sails were triangular. On going ashore, Robertson found three large sailing craft being built on stocks. Two were of eight to ten tons and one of about twelve tons. A midshipman, William Hambly, noted that they were built 'very regularly, tapering at each end and Broad in the Middle.' He also saw some hatchets with blades of shell that reminded him of coopers' adzes, and some fishing nets that were 'in ye same form as our English Netts.' Robertson wrote similarly of the nets, saying that they were 'made after the same manner that they are in England.'[3]

On leaving Nukutavake, the *Dolphin* sailed westward past Vairaatea where the refugees from Nukutavake were seen on shore. In the following year, the French expedition under Bougainville discovered Vahitahi and Akiaki, but did not see much of their inhabitants.[4] Captain Cook passed the same two islands in 1769.[5] Sixty-six years then passed before the next known visitor appeared. This was Captain Peter Dillon of the brig *Calder,* who sighted Pinaki and Vairaatea on 9 November 1825 on his way from Valparaiso to Sydney. No people were seen at either island.[6]

About two and a half months later, Captain F. W. Beechey of HMS *Blossom* began a survey of the area. His first landfall was Pinaki where a landing party found several well-trodden paths, many low huts, and other traces of human inhabitants, but none of recent date. That same evening the *Blossom* bore away for Nukutavake. This, too, was uninhabited, although several huts and sheds were also seen there.[7]

From Nukutavake, the *Blossom* sailed north to Vahitahi. Two boats were sent ashore to a small inhabited village. The islanders assembled on the beach with long, bone-tipped poles and short clubs like billhooks. But they laid them down before the boats reached the surf and beckoned the Englishmen to land. As the breakers were too high for the visitors to do this, the islanders 'suffered themselves to be bribed by a few pieces of iron,' as Captain Beechey put it, and swam off to the boats. A brisk trade soon began, the Englishmen exchanging nails, beads and pieces of iron for coconuts, mats, lines made of human hair, finely-plaited coconut fibre and sinnet made from hibiscus bark. The islanders used the word *toki* to describe the nails and iron the Englishmen offered them.

> The strictest integrity was observed by these people in all their dealings [Beechey wrote]. If one person had not the number of cocoa-nuts demanded for a piece of iron, he borrowed from his neighbour; and when any of the fruit fell overboard in putting it into the boat, they swam after it, and restored it to the owner. Such honesty is rare among the natives of Polynesia, and the [Vahitahians] consequently ingratiated themselves much with us.[8]

Lieutenant Edward Belcher, the ship's surveying officer, who was in one of the trading boats, thought the Vahitahians' honesty 'would have done credit to many civilised nations.' He also noted 'a sort of well-bred politeness' in the smile of one or two of them. As for their appearance, they were well-made, with 'open and pleasing countenances,' the men having bushy hair and 'much hair on the lips and chin.'[9] Beechey described the islanders as a fine athletic race, with thick frizzled hair. They were not tattooed. Their complexion was much lighter than the islanders of Reao, 135 miles eastward, which the *Blossom* had visited a few days earlier. 'One man, in particular, and the only one who had whiskers, was so fair, and so like an European,' Beechey said, 'that the boat's crew claimed him as a countryman.'[10]

Beechey noted the dress of the men was simply a *maro* 'of straw' and 'sometimes a straw sack hung over their shoulders to prevent the sun from scorching their backs.' That of the women was a mat wrapped round the loins. Two of the men wore crowns of white feathers. The women were inferior to the men in appearance and were generally bow-legged. However, they 'exercised an authority not very common among uncivilized people, by taking from the men whatever articles they received in exchange for their fruit, as soon as they returned to the shore.' Beechey compared the Vahitahians favourably with the people of the Mangareva or Gambier Islands among whom he had spent a fortnight a short time earlier. 'The good-natured countenances of these people, the honesty observed in all their dealings, and the great respect they paid their women, bespeak them a more amiable race than the avaricious Gambier Islanders,' he wrote.[11]

On leaving Vahitahi, the *Blossom* sailed northward to Akiaki where a hut and some slabs placed erect indicated it was occasionally inhabited. Her next landfall was Vairaatea, where Beechey thought the islanders were so similar to those of Vahitahi as to need no description. 'We noticed only one canoe,' he wrote. Then, apparently recalling how the people of Nukutavake had fled to Vairaatea in Wallis' time, he added, 'but no doubt they have others, as a constant communication is kept up with the islands to the windward.'[12]

Some seventeen years after the *Blossom's* survey, the English pearler Edward Lucett sighted both Vahitahi and Akiaki on a voyage from Valparaiso to Hao. He did not stop to investigate them, but on reaching Hao he met an islander who had drifted there from Vahitahi about two years earlier. According to the Hao Islanders, he did not speak their dialect, and several months had passed before they could understand him. The man had then told them that he had fled from his own island (which Lucett recorded as 'Faeatae') after several canoe loads of armed men had made a 'murderous descent' on it and had butchered many of his countrymen. The castaway had no idea in which direction his island lay, but he named seven others as being in the same group. Their names, as Lucett understood them, were Pinaki, Uoapuni, Uairatea, Moru, Nukutivaki, Uoakiaki and Reau.* All were then unknown as such to Europeans.[13]

About a year later, while on another voyage from Valparaiso to Hao, Lucett was again in the vicinity of Vahitahi. Eager, on this occasion, to examine the atoll for pearlshell, he lowered a boat and pulled ashore with two Rapan divers and one from Tubuai. About a hundred islanders, many armed with spears, soon showed themselves. From their 'peculiar, crouching, stealthy gait,' Lucett was convinced that they had seen 'little, if anything, of those who held intercourse with civilised man.' And on closer acquaintance he found that their dialect differed from that of his divers. The islanders, however, resembled those of Hao, except that they had a 'wilder and more savage air.' Although Lucett's divers claimed that the lagoon was full of pearlshell, Lucett made no attempt to prove the point and sailed on.[14]

Only six weeks later, another pearler visited Vahitahi and the other islands thereabouts. This was Captain d'Hondt, of the Belgian schooner *Industriel,* out from Tahiti. On 9 August 1844, he reached Vairaatea, and thinking it an unknown island, he named it Ile Industriel. Several parties of Anaan divers were sent ashore to examine the lagoon for pearlshell. They returned instead with various items they had stolen from the inhabitants and five captive islanders who were remarkable for their European appearance. Three were men aged 40 to 45, 25 to 26, and eighteen, and two were children of ten and five.

When the *Industriel* returned to Tahiti several weeks later after an eminently unsuccessful pearling voyage, the Papeete newspaper *l'Océanie Française* reported that the five prisoners were strong, well-made people, of the same skin colouring as the Tahitians, and without any tattoo marks. Their

* The identification of the first, third, fifth, sixth and seventh islands in this list presents no difficulty. They were obviously Pinaki, Vairaatea, Nukutavake, Akiaki and Reao. Uoapuni also seems to have been a name for Reao, as, according to Stimson and Marshall 1964:51, that island was formerly known as Ao-puni-pehu. Moru cannot be identified. It was possibly Pukarua, Reao's nearest neighbour, or a misprint for Motu, meaning 'island'. Stimson and Marshall 1964:314 record Motu-Nui as yet another name for Reao.

only clothing was a narrow girdle of bark strips artistically plaited. The Anaans could not understand their language.

> The natives of this island had never seen a ship before and had never before seen Europeans [the newspaper went on]. They were therefore among the most primitive people of the human race. However, far from being repulsive, these men have an agreeable appearance. Their physiognomy is intelligent and they are not of the same type as in Tahiti where the lips are thick and the nose flat. Their profile is that of Europe.

The same newspaper also reported that on Nukutavake, the Anaan divers had 'devastated the temple of the gods' and had carried off the 'holy ark' containing the 'fetiches of the people.' These consisted of a bundle of red feathers of the tropic bird arranged around a hank of coconut fibre containing wisps of black and white hair, teeth, fingernails, etc. The ark itself was two and a half feet high, six to eight inches wide, and nearly three feet long, with two stakes fixed to its sides to enable it to be carried on men's shoulders in religious processions. The Vairaatea people had shown it great reverence on first seeing it, *l'Océanie Française* added, and had 'disposed themselves' to pray before it.[15]

Following d'Hondt's voyage to the Vahitahi islands, no other European ships apparently visited that area until the French naval vessel *Lamothe-Piquet* made a survey of Vairaatea in 1869.[16] That same year, Father Germain Fierens paid Vahitahi a brief visit, being the first missionary to land in the group. His visit, however, was unfruitful, as almost everyone fled or hid themselves on his approach. Only a few men and three or four old women, all trembling with fear, remained on the beach; and when Fierens asked if he could baptise their children, they replied that their chief had gone turtle-fishing, and they could do nothing until he came back.[17]

As it happened, the Vahitahi chief and several of his fellow-islanders were blown to Hao in a canoe. They were found there some eighteen months later by Father Montiton, following his six-month stay on Fangatau. Montiton immediately seized the opportunity to try to convert the castaways to Catholicism. He also offered to take them home—on the way to his next destination, Tatakoto. However, during their sojourn on Hao, the Vahitahians had learned something of the Mormon faith from native converts, and only the chief had become a Catholic by the time they reached Vahitahi in October 1870. In the hope of winning other converts, Montiton decided to hold a public baptism for the chief, his family, and a Christian Mangarevan woman who had accompanied him from Hao. But despite the 'novelty and strangeness of the spectacle,' only a few islanders 'dared' to attend, as the 'Mormon ministers'—as Montiton described the chief's mentors—had given the order not to attend. Nevertheless, Montiton was grateful for the small progress he had made, and before embarking for Tatakoto, he arranged for his few followers to build a temporary chapel. A young islander skilled in masonry was left to help them.[18]

Montiton returned to Vahitahi about nine months later and stayed a month while his schooner, the *Vatikana,* went to Hao for provisions. The chapel, such as it was, had been completed. 'I found my little Christian group fervent and assiduous at prayers,' Montiton recorded. 'If a few scandals had taken place, I happily did not have to deplore either defections or apostasy.' Montiton's return emboldened his neophytes to build 'a sort of sanctuary' within their chapel with stones taken from a neighbouring *marae*. This act of sacrilege, combined with several other events, soon led thirty-six other Vahitahians—nineteen of them children—to adopt the Catholic faith. At the time, this number represented almost the entire population of the atoll, as some of the people were away at another island.[19]

Montiton paid a call at Vahitahi for provisions in September 1871.[20] Thereafter it remained unvisited until mid-March 1873 when his colleague Fierens called there during an eight-month voyage to the eastern atolls. Fierens also visited Nukutavake where the islanders greeted him with 'the greatest demonstrations of joy.' At Vahitahi, he conducted further baptisms, blessed all the marriages, and sent a boat to a 'neighbouring island'—presumably Akiaki—to seek out the rest of the population who were then living there. 'No one failed to respond,' he wrote, 'and all demanded to be baptised. I then laid the foundations for a church and blessed the first stone, and after a distribution of clothing, I departed, leaving Louis Matii and Gabriel Tehoutika [two converts from Anaa] to direct the work.'[21]

On another tour of the eastern atolls a year or so later, either Fierens or his colleague, Father Terlyn, apparently called at Vahitahi and left the islanders a supply of coconuts for planting.[22] However, the next evangelistic visit to be recorded in the mission journals was not until 1883. Meanwhile, in January 1874, the French hydrographic vessel *Mesange* called at Vahitahi on a mission of mercy, having on board forty-six Vahitahians who had been lost in a storm. Several months earlier, the Vahitahians had learned from their Anaan teachers that the French administration at Anaa had issued a code of laws for the people of the Tuamotus and that there was also a protectorate flag. Eager to possess these symbols of civilisation, a large party of them had sailed for Anaa in several canoes, apparently guided by Gabriel Tehoutika. They covered the 350 miles of the outward journey without mishap. But on their way home, possessed of their booty, a storm drove them to Anuanuraro Atoll, about 200 miles south-east of Anaa. Here their canoes were wrecked on the reef and two of their number died.

Half-starved and almost naked, the survivors were found early in January 1874 when the *Mesange* happened to put into their landfall. Lieutenant A. Mariot, the French Resident Agent at Anaa, who was then on board, recorded that the Vahitahians were a very gentle people and also ingenious. To sail on the atoll's lagoon, they had built several small canoes, their only tools being an axe and some iron obtained at Anaa, plus nails taken from wreckage found on the beach. To sew the planks of the canoes together, they had used fibres from the roots of pandanus palms. On being returned to their home island, Mariot noted that the castaways were received by their relatives with the 'habitual demonstrations of these people on rediscovering dear and long-lost friends.' He added:

> This island has previously been visited by Rev. Father Germain [Fierens]. The mission schooner is almost the only ship they know. A native of Anaa devotes himself to civilising them. He built their school and teaches them what the government of the protectorate is, and how it is better to settle their quarrels by regular laws than by violent means . . .
>
> The island has very little pearlshell and the coconut trees have been planted very unintelligently, as everyone wanted to plant in the same place . . . Happily, they are still young enough to be transplanted . . .
>
> I took advantage of my visit to make this island [an administrative] district. One Tamahere, to whom I gave the provisional title of chief, has been given an annual salary of 120 francs. The situation of the inhabitants is in the process of being improved, thanks to the intelligent action of Mohi* the voluntary teacher, from whom the chief docilely receives advice.[23]

Mariot was almost certainly the only French official to visit Vahitahi before the turn of the twentieth century. Brief as his visit was, he suggested to the islanders various improvements; and when Fierens called there in November 1883, he recorded that much had changed for the better. The islanders' houses were more comfortable, roads had been built, and the bush had been cleared away. On the other hand, Fierens found that the islanders still knew little of Christian teachings. Moreover, he was disappointed to find that many of them were absent on a turtle-fishing expedition, which prompted him to lament that his long and arduous evangelistic voyages often accomplished very little.

> What can a single missionary do in some forty islands situated at distances of seven to eight days one from another? [he wrote]. Half the time is spent in travelling. Often the missionary arrives in the evening, gathers the Christians together, does some teaching and passes the night hearing confessions. At dawn, he says Holy Mass, distributes the bread of life to these hungry, abandoned people—who sometimes have not seen a priest for two years and who may never see one again—and he departs.
>
> . . .
>
> Another difficulty of our ministry is the wandering life of the people. After a troublesome and costly voyage, we land on the beach somewhere—and not a person is to be found. They have all gone fishing to other islands and will not be back for several weeks.

The islanders who were absent when Fierens arrived at Vahitahi seemed unlikely to return during his sojourn there. So 'putting a good face on bad fortune,' he began preparing the others for a special communion service on Christmas Day. Each evening for a month, he taught them the catechism for two or three hours until, in the end, they could comprehend what he called 'our holy mysteries.' He also gave them clothes to wear so the occasion would be as

* This presumably was a misprint for Matii, the surname of one of the two Anaans whom Fierens left at Vahitahi in 1873; or Matii may have been a misprint for Mohi in Fierens' account.

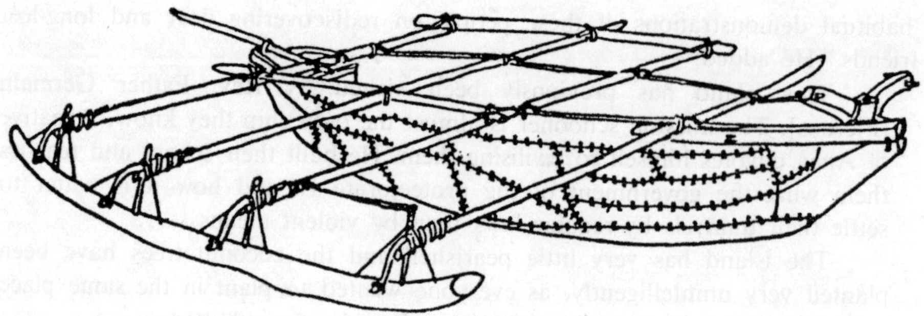

solemn as possible; and when the great day came the islanders were agog with enthusiasm. 'If St Paul had been present at Vahitahi [on this occasion],' he wrote, 'he would have felt that he was still witnessing the earliest days of the Church.'[24]

Whether St Paul would have noticed any further progress in the affairs of the Church at Vahitahi over the next few years is doubtful. No further news about that island or its neighbours was published in the Catholic mission journals during the rest of the century. So it seems that the Catholic missionaries either did not visit them again, or that if they did, they had nothing noteworthy to report. Certainly, the Vahitahi islands remained untouched by most outside influences. When a United States fisheries expedition visited Nukutavake in the steamer *Albatross* in 1899, the islanders' village was 'the most primitive' of any that the expedition encountered during an extensive tour of the Tuamotu Archipelago. The fisheries men spent about an hour on the island. Two of them, Charles H. Townshend and H. F. Moore, later compiled a joint report in which they said:

> Generally speaking, the Paumotuans have given up their own style of house construction, and have adopted European ideas and 'tin roofs' whenever they can afford it [sic]. Here [at Nukutavake] in an entirely native population of about 100 people . . . (only one half-caste* and no whites at all) primitive ideas and methods prevail. Household furniture and utensils are few and rude, the products of the cocoa-palms and pandanus entering chiefly into their domestic economy. The lava-lava or pareu is the usual work-a-day dress, both for male and female, the men donning a shirt and the women a Mother Hubbard gown for state occasions; the children are without clothing until 10 or 11 years old. The houses are of palm-leaf with woven and plaited walls, and thatched roof, with a number of pandanus sleeping mats on the gravel floors . . .

Despite the backwardness of the Nukutavakeans in many ways, Townshend and Moore thought their canoes were 'very ingeniously constructed'. Moreover, they were 'of an entirely different model' from any others they saw

* This, presumably, was an assumption, based on the physical appearance of the person concerned.

in the archipelago, being 'quite deep and sharp' and with keels that were 'decidedly rounding, or rocking.' They were made of small wooden slabs lashed together with sennit. The 'usual out-rigger float' was fixed to them for stability.[25]

Other members of the *Albatross* expedition were equally impressed by the canoes. One, A. G. Mayer, made a sketch of one of them, together with a section of it, to show the essential parts.[26] Another, A. B. Alexander, described the canoes in detail. In Alexander's opinion, the canoes—as well as everything else in the Nukutavakean village—'had the appearance of having undergone little change through the introduction of modern things.' Yet they were 'put together in somewhat the same manner as a boat or vessel' and were 'altogether different from the ordinary dugout.' No metal was used. All canoes examined at other atolls were 'crude' by comparison—those of Nukutavake being of 'original design and workmanship' and of 'very superior quality.' The largest Nukutavakean canoe to be measured was seventeen feet long, 3¾ feet wide and 2½ feet deep. Two others were fourteen feet long and thirteen and a half feet long. The seams of the planking were covered with bamboo strips, and between them was a coating of gum and narrow strips of pandanus leaves. Each canoe had two sets of floor timbers, one three feet from the bow and the other six feet from the stern; also a mast step. However, no masts, sails, or paddles were seen.

Alexander noted that the bow and stern were alike in each canoe; that a head rail extended out 2½ feet from the main body of the vessel; and that a cutwater running up from the keel connected with this, 'giving strength and adding considerably to the general appearance.' There was a cleat at the stern for 'making fast the sheet.' The steering paddle was also placed against the cleat when going through the surf and narrow passages. Two braces, one for-

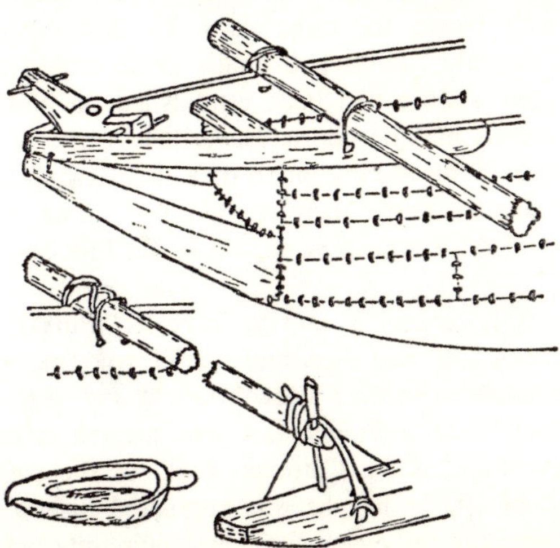

Construction details of the outrigger canoe of Nukutavake (opposite) drawn by A. G. Mayer of the 'Albatross' expedition. Note the steering cleat in the stern with two belaying pins athwart the distinctive head rails.

ward and one aft, answered as thwarts. 'Getting out the planks, head rails, cutwater and outrigger float from the rough log, made smooth and fitted together so perfectly must indeed be a long and laborious task,' Alexander went on. And he added: 'We saw no tools of any kind lying about, and the time being short we had no opportunity of investigating among the houses for such implements as are used in building either house or canoe.'[27]

In the thirty years after the *Albatross* expedition's brief call, the Vahitahi islands again figured only rarely in published literature. But such references as there are strongly suggest that there was little change in their 'primitive' condition. Indeed, in the first decade of the twentieth century the islands regressed rather than advanced, for they suffered severe damage in the famous hurricane that devastated much of the Tuamotus in 1906. For several years thereafter the Catholic missionaries could apparently pay little attention to them for when, in 1911, Bishop Athanase Hermel of Tahiti visited them, he wrote: 'On 11 June, I was at Nukutavake. There, also, the church was destroyed by hurricane in 1906, and having been rebuilt, I blessed it solemnly.' Three days earlier, the bishop had paid a call at Vahitahi and next day he set foot on tiny Pinaki. 'Never since the beginning of the world,' he recorded, 'had a priest landed on that last-named island . . . the church and the episcopal palace were very primitive, being simply the shed where the village coaster [*côtre*] was kept . . .'[28]

There is no evidence that any European ever settled in the Vahitahi islands to encourage a copra industry, as was the case at Fangatau. However, in February 1913, an Englishman, Charles Edward Howe, landed on Pinaki to search for a treasure that was supposedly stolen from Peru and buried there in 1859. The American writer Charles Nordhoff, who met Howe at Pinaki in 1920, found he had dug extensive trenches in his quest for the treasure. Nordhoff stayed with Howe for three days. In describing this sojourn, he indicated that the Vahitahi islands had finally come within the orbit of a few Tahiti merchants; that a store had been established on Nukutavake; and that the islanders had started making copra. Nevertheless, the islands were still far from the beaten track. 'With the exception of a small group of Papeete traders,' Nordhoff wrote, 'I don't suppose there are a dozen white men who have ever heard of [Pinaki]; and those who have seen it or set foot upon it must be fewer still.'[29]

Howe, the treasure-seeker, is said to have left Pinaki in 1926.[30] In the interval between that event and Nordhoff's brief sojourn with him, probably only one European spent more than a few hours at any of the Vahitahi islands. This was Father Paul Mazé, a Frenchman, who arrived in the Pacific in 1911 and was placed in charge of the Catholic 'flock' of the eastern Tuamotus in 1920. From then until 1937 when he was appointed bishop of Tahiti, he was something of a legend for his evangelistic and humanitarian work among the atoll-dwellers. Mazé had no headquarters, but travelled constantly in trading schooners or in his own small sailing vessel, the *Saint Pierre*. He spent a month here, a week there, and a few days somewhere else. He knew the Tuamotuan dialects intimately; lived only for the Tuamotuans; and moulded his life according to the traditions of his hardy predecessors, Fathers Montiton, Fierens and Terlyn.[31] But despite his great energy and apostolic zeal, Mazé's charges were not always the tractable Catholics he might have wished. In September 1932, for example, he wrote from Reao that he had recently spent four months on Vahitahi—much longer than he had originally intended—because of the 'work of perversion' that the heretics (i.e. Mormons) were carrying on on that island.[32]

This remark of Mazé's, written after twelve years' experience in the eastern Tuamotus, is of particular interest, for less than two years earlier, the linguist Stimson had recorded a number of supposedly ancient chants on that island that were unmistakably Biblical, but which scholars of the time ascribed to the teachings of modern missionaries. Stimson, accompanied by his colleague Emory, arrived at Vahitahi on 29 June 1930 and remained there for the next four months. Emory, meanwhile, made brief visits to the surrounding islands, besides a quick trip to Tahiti for supplies and equipment. In a report on his and his associate's work to the director of the Bishop Museum, Emory wrote:

> The Vahitahi area has been occupied for an unknown number of generations by a people speaking a language very closely allied to the Maori. Favoured by isolation, such aspects of native culture as songs, dances, ceremonies, and navigation have clung to them with greater tenacity than to any other peoples of eastern Polynesia. From our entry into the Tuamotus, we had heard of the Vahitahi people. Failing to reach the island on our first cruise [i.e. when Fangatau was visited], we shaped our course directly for it on our second. From the first of July to the end of October, 1930, Stimson worked steadily recording the great *tipara* festival which the people performed for our benefit. The festival was anciently held only in times of famine to secure an even distribution of existing food and to hearten the people.
>
> Every chant and formal speech employed was taken down by Stimson and translated with the help of the ablest natives. The chants were recorded on the dictaphone, and the dances, spear exhibitions, and some of the ceremonies on cinematographic film. This furnishes a record of many phases of Polynesian life, for which, heretofore, we have had no adequate or reliable data . . .[33]

Emory did not mention in his report—possibly because he was not present and did not know—that Stimson had also been busy recording what he could of Vahitahi's ancient religion. This material, with English translations, was published in 1933 in Stimson's monograph, *Tuamotuan Religion.* In an introduction, Stimson explained that the monograph was 'essentially a record of Tuamotuan religion of pre-Christian times in the islands of Anaa and Vahitahi, as partially revealed through the lost cult of a supreme god called Kiho, Kio, or Io at Anaa, and Kio at Vahitahi.' The study was based on the memories of three living witnesses—one from Anaa and two from Vahitahi.

Stimson said he had first heard of Kiho from his Anaan informant, Paea-a-Avehe, before his association with the Bishop Museum began in 1929. Paea had told him that Kiho had flourished at Anaa before the Tuamotus were evangelised. But about the middle of the nineteenth century, at a meeting at Fakarava of *tahunga* (high priests), 'those who upheld the cult of Kiho were ruled out of court.' From then on the cult was 'utterly discredited.' The protagonists of Christianity maintained that Kiho was Satan, the Lord of Hades, and his sacred name became altered to Kino, meaning 'evil.' As such it had remained in the popular estimation. Nevertheless, the cult of Kiho was still treasured in the hearts of some of its former adherents and was secretly handed down to a few members of the succeeding generation.

Stimson explained that Paea had learned about Kiho from his uncle, Tiapu-a-Parepare, while living at Taiaro (see p. 190). He added that on going to Vahitahi he (Stimson) had asked if Kiho was also known there. At first, he was 'put off the track' by the local chief who denied any knowledge of the god. Subsequently, however, the chief had told him a legend about a female ogre of that name. Also, a woman called Ruea-a-Reka, who was possibly Vahitahi's oldest inhabitant, had confessed to him that, as a girl and the first-born of her family, she had been taught the lore of a primal and supreme god called Kio, but that for fifty years or more she had 'banished him utterly' from her thoughts.

> Ruea finally consented to disclose to me all she could remember of the cult [Stimson said], imposing a condition of strict secrecy, for she was fearful of public resentment. Ruea went on to say that she could not bear to hear Kio described as the Devil by the younger ignorant generations, and to see prayers pertaining to the Supreme God wrongfully ascribed to Tane and Oatea. At first she would never mention Kio in the presence of another, but later on, when she found that Tuhiragi-a-Miti was recounting to me his recollection of the Kio cult and lore, she would speak before him without reserve. It was interesting to listen to their discussions, for Ruea and Tuhiragi by no means always agreed as to the details of the cult.

Tuhiragi, as Stimson explained, was a man of pure Vahitahian ancestry on both sides. Like Ruea, he was one of the island's oldest inhabitants. He was 'not in good standing with the Church' and could not be given the sacrament because his granddaughter was not married to her 'accepted lover.' Stimson implied that it was because of this that Tuhiragi had no scruples about disclosing what he knew of the Kiho lore. When it became known that he was doing this, and other islanders took him to task for it, he would reply sententiously: 'Let not children instruct their elders.' 'There is no doubt,' Stimson added, 'that it was largely owing to Tuhiragi's unflinching attitude in the face of universal condemnation and resentment that Ruea plucked up sufficient

PLATE 19. In 1930, this 'outriggerless canoe', built of small pieces of timber sewn together with sinnet, was still in a seaworthy state at Nukutavake. The shape of its hull suggested at the time that it had been modelled on a modern European whaleboat. Yet it still retained the open-ended bows common to Anaan and Fangatauan 'pahi' of ancient times and its steering oar (above) was fitted in place in much the same way as those of the ancient 'pahi'. The vessel is now in the Papeete Museum.—Bishop Museum photographs.

PLATE 20. HMS 'Dolphin' standing off Nukutavake in June 1767 while the islanders make off in four double canoes. The drawing, by Captain Samuel Wallis, is the earliest known representation of Tuamotuan canoes and the only one showing them under sail. The triangular sails were described by the master of the 'Dolphin' as 'lyke topmast steering sails with the tack part uppermost.' Original drawing, National Library of Australia, Canberra.

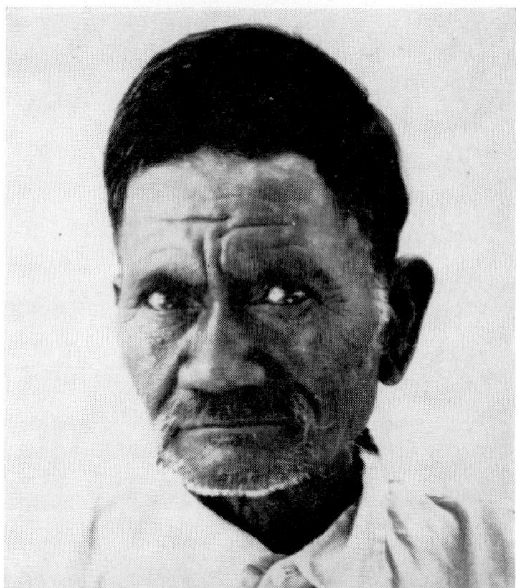

Three outstanding Tuamotuans of recent times were Tuhiragi (top right), Paea-a-Avehe (lower right) and Te Iho (above). Tuhiragi was the Vahitahi sage who gave Stimson an elaborate creation chant in 1930. Paea was Stimson's Anaan informant who first told him about the esoteric god Kiho. And Te Iho was Bengt Danielsson's principal informant on Raroia—a man whose features were 'not too foreign', Danielsson said, 'for him to have played Father Christmas in any English home.' The photographs are reproduced by courtesy of the Bishop Museum and Bengt Danielsson.

courage to defy her relatives and to see the matter [of revealing what she knew about Kiho] through to the end.'[34]

In discussing the Kiho chants that he recorded, Stimson said the 'complete Christianization of the natives' had 'tended to obliterate the last vestiges of ancient religious systems.'[35] He said in another context that there was a danger in accepting evidence from islanders who had been brought up as Christians, because, no matter how learned they were, their views could not be considered as 'entirely unaffected by Biblical theology.'[36] In yet another context, he said the various names applied to Kiho in the chants did not appear to reveal 'any evidences of contact with Christian theology.'[37]

In the light of these remarks, it is clear that Stimson closely scrutinised everything the islanders told him for possible missionary influence before accepting it as authentic ancient lore. There is no doubt, therefore, that he failed to realise that one of the chants he took down from Tuhiragi was, in fact, virtually a verse-for-verse rendering of the first chapter of Genesis, and that others were reminiscent of the Psalms and other parts of the Bible. Here is Stimson's translation of the Genesis-like chant with corresponding verses of the Authorised Version of the Bible placed alongside:

(Asterisks indicate omissions from the Tuamotuan text.)

TUAMOTUAN	GENESIS
Kio was the first original god; it was he who created and brought to completion the whole universe by means of the magical powers and god-like attributes of his divine assistants.	1. In the beginning God created the heaven and the earth.
Kio-the-sleeper slumbered immemorially in the Void— in the Night-of-utter-blackness, in the Night of profound darkness, * * * *	2. And the earth was without form, and void; and darkness was upon the face of the deep. And the Spirit of God moved upon the face of the waters.
Kio-the-sleeper spoke to his merely divine assistants, saying, 'Who will cause the Night-realm to be infused with soft light that it be illuminated with the shaded glow of twilight?' Then Shades-of-night replied to Kio, 'I will cause the Night-realm to be infused with soft light that it be illumined with the shaded glow of twilight!' And Shades-of-night caused the Night-realm to be infused with soft light so that it be illumined with the shaded glow of twilight, and the Night-realm was indeed infused with soft light; it was illumined with the shaded glow of twilight,—and this was finished.	3. And God said, Let there be light: and there was light.
Then Kio looked; it was sightly. Now, Kio spoke again to his divine assistants, saying, 'Who will cleave apart the bedrock of the Night-realm that it be sundered?' Then Cleaver-below replied to Kio, 'I will cleave apart the bedrock of the Night-realm that it be sundered!' And Cleaver-below clave apart the	4. And God saw the light, that it was good: and God divided the light from the darkness.

bedrock of the Night-realm so that it be sundered, and it was indeed cloven apart; it was sundered,

—and this was finished.

5. And the evening and the morning were the first day.

* * * *

Now, Kio spoke again to his divine assistants, saying, 'Who will divide the oceans that wave be separated from wave?'

6. And God said, Let there be a firmament in the midst of the waters, and let it divide the waters from the waters.

Then again Cleaver-below replied to Kio, saying, 'I will divide the oceans that wave be separated from wave!'

And Cleaver-below divided the oceans so that wave be separated from wave, and the oceans were indeed divided; wave was separated from wave,

—and this was finished.

7. And God made the firmament and divided the waters which were under the firmament from the waters which were above the firmament: and it was so.

Then Kio looked; it was sightly.

Now, Kio spoke again to his divine assistants, saying, 'Who will hold up the land above that it rise, riding clear?'

9. And God said, Let the waters under the heaven be gathered together unto one place, and let the dry land appear: and it was so.

Then Tane-up-thruster-of-the-land replied to Kio, 'I will support the land above that it rise, riding clear!'

And Tane-up-thruster-of-the-land held up the land above so that it rise, riding clear, and the land was indeed supported above; it rose, riding clear,

—and this was finished.

Then Kio looked; it was sightly.

10. . . . and God saw that it was good.

* * * *

Now, Kio spoke again to his divine assistants, saying, 'Who will cause the verdure of the land to appear that it grow?'

11. And God said, Let the earth bring forth grass, the herb yielding seed, and the fruit tree yielding fruit after its kind . . .

Then Forest-grove replied to Kio, 'I will cause the verdure of the land to appear that it grow!'

Then Kio again spoke to Forest-grove, saying, 'Who will assist you to cause the verdure of the land to appear that it grow?'

Then Forest-grove again replied to Kio, 'My two bands of demon-creatures shall aid me to cause the verdure of the land to appear that it grow!'

* * * *

And Forest-grove and his two bands of demon-creatures caused the verdure of the land to appear so that it grow, and indeed the verdure of the land was made to appear; it grew,

12. And the earth brought forth grass, and herb yielding seed after his kind, and the tree yielding fruit . . .

—and this was finished.

13. And the evening and the morning were the third day.

Then Kio looked; it was sightly.

12. (continued) . . . and God saw that it was good.

* * * *

Now indeed the land had been given over by Kio to Oatea,—and the oceans, and the atmosphere;

26. And God said, Let . . . man . . . have dominion over the fish of the sea, and over the fowl of the air, . . . and over all the earth . . .

and Kio gave his crimson-girdle to Oatea.	27. So God created man in his own image . . .
* * * *	
Now indeed were the deeds of Kio concluded; and he returned to his abode in Havaiki-the-source, there to sleep.	Chapter ii, 2. And on the seventh day God ended his work which he had made; and he rested on the seventh day.

The extraordinary resemblances between the two foregoing accounts of creation were first noticed by an Australian scholar, Dr (later Professor) Ralph Piddington. In 1939, he wrote:

> Whatever the cult of Kiho may have been, it appears, upon analysis, that the chants presented by Stimson primarily embody Polynesian versions of Christian teaching. The versions are attenuated in parts and elaborated in others, but they show such striking affinities to their originals that their source cannot be doubted.

Piddington took it for granted that the ancient Vahitahians had never been subject to Biblical influences, and he therefore reproached Stimson for accepting at face value what he called 'a *pot-pourri* of Biblical allusion and Polynesian elaboration.' He also criticised him for not approaching his field-work free from preconceptions. 'In view of the Biblical source of the Tuamotuan material,' he went on, 'the whole of Stimson's hypothesis of an "archaic" "esoteric" cult of Kiho as a "Primal Cause" falls to the ground.' And he added: '. . . it is not surprising that [Stimson's] informants, driven into a situation of conflict, with the sanctions of Christian teaching on the one hand and an insistent ethnographer on the other, should have magnified the worship of Kiho . . . and produced from the mists of their failing memories a jumble of Biblical theology and Polynesian metaphor, expression and poetic elaboration.'[38]

Piddington's strictures must have seemed completely justified at the time, for no one took up the cudgels on Stimson's behalf. Yet if Piddington had troubled to investigate the history of Vahitahi and to pursue his inquiries further, he must surely have realised that his explanations were not as pat as he imagined, and that he, himself, was apparently a victim of preconceptions. Further inquiries would have revealed that:

1. As the Bible has never been translated into any Tuamotuan dialect, the only Bible that modern Vahitahians could conceivably have read was the Tahitian Bible, translated by the LMS missionaries and first published in 1838.[39]

2. As the Tahitian language is *not* 'closely allied to the Maori' (as Emory said was the case with Vahitahian),[40] the Vahitahians would have needed considerable linguistic skill to read the Bible in Tahitian.

3. As it was the practice of Catholic missionaries until recently not to use the vernacular material of Protestant missionaries in public,[41] the possibility that a Tahitian Bible got into the Vahitahians' hands before 1930 is remote.

4. The account of cosmogenesis in the first chapter of Genesis in the

Tahitian Bible bears no verbal relationship to the account that Tuhiragi gave Stimson. (See Appendix E).

5. Although the first Vahitahians were baptised in 1870, the islanders that Fierens encountered at Vahitahi in 1883 were still so ignortant of Biblical theology that they had to be catechised for a month before they could comprehend what Fierens called 'our holy mysteries.'

6. As Tuhiragi was old enough to have a marriageable granddaughter when Stimson met him in 1930, he was probably no less than sixty years of age (i.e. born about 1870), and this notion is borne out by a photograph of him (see pl. 20) taken at the time.[42] If, therefore, he had learned the Biblical account of cosmogenesis from Fierens or some other Catholic missionary in or after 1883, he would have been mature enough to remember its origin in after years.

7. To have 'elaborated' and 'attenuated' the Biblical version into the form that Stimson recorded, Tuhiragi would have needed an extraordinarily vivid and poetic imagination.

8. For him to have foisted his version on Stimson as a genuine archaic chant, knowing it had emanated from the Bible, Tuhiragi would have needed the gall of a hardened criminal, the dexterity of an art forger, and—considering he was a member of the Church, though not in good standing—the duplicity of an arch-hypocrite.

9. As Stimson, an erudite linguist, was constantly on the watch for Biblical interpolations in the islanders' chants, he must have been exceptionally careless in this case to have been hoodwinked by an unsophisticated and possibly illiterate islander.

10. As Mazé, in 1932, complained of the 'work of perversion' of Vahitahi's heretics, there is reason to believe that the teachings of the Catholic missionaries had made no great impact on the islanders.

In short, it is not Stimson's hypothesis of an 'archaic' Kiho cult that falls to the ground. It is Piddington's view that 'whatever the cult of Kiho may have been,' it was basically of recent, missionary-inspired origin. This being so, some other source for Tuhiragi's cosmogonic chant must obviously be found—one sufficiently old for the elaborations and attenuations that Piddington noted to have taken place, yet not so old that the order and general tenor of the original had been lost. All the evidence suggests that Biblical teachings brought into the Pacific by survivors of the ship that left its cannon on Amanu's reef provide the only explanation that fits the case.

In the circumstances, it is hardly surprising that the early visitors to the Vahitahi area found the islanders light-skinned, thin-lipped and with European profiles; that some had to wear 'straw' sacks on their shoulders to prevent the sun from scorching their backs; and that one man, in 1826, was so fair and so like a European that a party of English sailors mistook him for a countryman. It is not surprising, either, that the islanders had 'holy arks' containing 'fetiches' in their religious processions;* that at Nukutavake in 1767 the officers of the *Dolphin* found hatchets shaped like coopers' adzes, fishing nets 'in ye same form as our English Netts,' and broad-bellied, plank-built canoes, complete with keels, stern cleats, and an interior frame-work 'not unlyke the frame of our Boats.' Nor is it surprising that the canoes' sails were not of some strange Oceanic shape, but triangular—'lyke a topmast Steeringsail with the Tack part Uppermost.'

Considering how informative the *Dolphin's* officers were about much of what they saw at Nukutavake, it is a pity that they did not say more about the three large sailing craft that were then being built on stocks. Neither Hambly nor Robertson gave the length, depth or breadth of the three vessels; neither said anything about the attachment of outriggers; and neither indicated whether any of the three hulls seemed intended to be a component for a double canoe. The only general description of the canoes was Robertson's speculative statement: 'What Trade they Carie on with this [i.e. these] large Craft I know not, but am certain they are not for fishing round this Island, but built on purpos for careing on a trade to some distant shoar thats of greater Extent nor this Island.'

The question of the precise nature of the Nukutavake canoes of 1767 is of especial interest. This is because, when Emory and Stimson were at the Vahitahi islands in 1930, Emory found four large, outriggerless craft that were keeled, plank-sided, broad in the middle and tapering at each end, and otherwise apparently similar to those described by the *Dolphin's* officers. Emory, who did not know of the accounts of Robertson and Hambly, which were then unpublished, assumed that the four vessels were adaptations of modern European whaleboats. That view has generally been accepted ever since. But were they, in fact, what Emory thought they were? Or were they, perhaps, lineal descendants of the whaleboats that were in use in the Bay of Biscay and beyond when the Loaisa expedition left Spain in 1525?

Two of the four craft that Emory discovered were in perfect condition at Vahitahi. One, rotting away, was at Nukutavake. And the other, beginning to decay, was at Akiaki. Emory purchased the Akiaki hull and presented it to the Papeete Museum, where it is still preserved. Parts of the Nukutavake vessel were given to the Bishop Museum. The Akiaki hull was 29 feet long, with a beam of eight feet three inches and a depth of three feet. The better of the two Vahitahi craft was 28 feet long, seven feet in beam and three feet five inches deep. According to Emory, the four vessels were built about 1880, the bow,

* The veneration of relics—i.e. the bodies of saints or parts of them, and of objects associated with them—has long been a Christian tradition. In the Middle Ages, gigantic pilgrimages were made to shrines containing relics, such as Santiago de Compostella, near La Coruña, Spain, where the body of St. James the Apostle is reputedly buried. The cult of relics also gave rise to street processions and fairs in which relics were carried in special receptacles, correctly called reliquaries, but also known as arks, pyxes, etc. Such was the demand for reliquaries in sixteenth century Spain that there was 'an illustrious legion' of artistic goldsmiths and silversmiths producing them. The veneration of relics was defined as 'good and useful' by the Council of Trent in 1563—thirty-eight years after the *San Lesmes* left Spain.

stern, keel and many of the side pieces being taken from 'famous double canoes of the past.' 'Although since 1880,' he said, 'the double sailing canoe has given way to the single canoe with a wide beam so as to sail without outrigger, the technique of constructing and manner of handling are very much the same.'[43]

James Hornell, who obtained numerous details from Emory about Vahitahi's outriggerless 'canoes' for volume 1 of the monograph *Canoes of Oceania,* stated that the wide beam of the Akiaki vessel had been obtained through raising its sides by the addition of one or two strakes. Thus widened, the vessel was able to sail 'without the adventitious aid of an outrigger.' Hornell went on: 'Although this vessel is an adaptation of material from old hulls to a modified whale-boat design, the steering method is of great value as elucidating that formerly in use in the twin hulls of the *pahi.*' After describing the steering oar of the Akiaki craft and outlining how it was fixed to a heavy cleat at the stern, Hornell added: 'This undoubtedly is the same method as that recorded by both Paris and Wilkes in their drawings of the double canoes existing in the first half of the last century.' Hornell also noted that the Akiaki craft had the 'characteristic head fittings peculiar to the Tuamotus.' These fittings comprised a headrail on each bow extending outwards to meet the 'free extremity of the end piece' which projected upwards from the stern and formed a cutwater.[44]

The head fittings in question are similar to those in the outrigger canoes of Nukutavake which Alexander described and Mayer sketched in 1899. They also resemble those in an Anaan *pahi* that Wilkes sketched in 1839 and those in a model of a Fangatau *pahi* reputedly made about 1854 and now in the Bishop Museum.[45] There is no doubt, therefore, that the head fittings were of ancient origin—that they were evolved before the ancestors of the modern Anaans, Fangatauans and Vahitahians became separated. What is not certain is what purpose they were intended to serve.

Such fittings bear no resemblance to anything to be found in the known sailing craft of other parts of the Pacific.[46] On the other hand, it cannot be said that they were common to Basque whaleboats of the early sixteenth century, as little is now known about the appearance of such vessels.[47] However, it *is* on record that some Spanish caravels of the sixteenth century had what is known as a beaked bow;[48] and it is likewise recorded that the Spanish and other galleys that took part in the Battle of Lepanto in 1571 also had beaks.[49] Moreover, early Spanish dictionaries contain the word *espolon,* which is defined as 'the iron point in which the bow of the galley or other ships terminate.'[50] On balance, therefore, the head fittings of the Vahitahi canoes seem more likely to have had their origin in Europe than to have been invented in the Tuamotus.

Certainly, no documentary evidence exists for the statements of Emory, Hornell and others that the outriggerless craft of Vahitahi were adaptations of modern European whaleboats, built after 1880. As the previous pages have shown, only one visitor to the Vahitahi area mentioned seeing any kind of sailing craft in the area between 1767 and 1880. That was Captain Beechey who reported a solitary vessel at Vairaatea in 1826, but did not describe it, although he implied that it was a *pahi*. On the other hand, only one man mentioned the existence of outriggerless craft between 1880 and 1930, and that was Bishop Hermel who referred vaguely to a Pinaki 'coaster'* in 1911. There is no certainty therefore that the *pahi* gave way to the outriggerless canoe in 1880; nor that the outriggerless canoe did not exist side by side with the *pahi* before 1880. Thus, Robertson's large sailing craft, which he thought were built for trading with 'some distant shoar', might well have been of the same kind that Emory discovered in 1930. And it might have been in such vessels that the intrepid Vahitahians made their voyage to Anaa in 1873 to obtain their copy of the code of laws and the French protectorate flag. In fact, one modern writer has positively stated that the Vahitahians *did* have outriggerless canoes in 'pre-discovery times.' This was Emory's friend Gessler, who accompanied him to Vahitahi in 1934. Gessler said in his book *The Dangerous Islands* that the pre-discovery canoes were much larger than those of his time, and that 'great grooves' had been worn in the reef where they had been dragged up out of reach of the waves. 'Vahitahi is an ancient land of voyagers,' he went on, 'there the old Tuamotuan sea-going vessels linger still in use; it is the land of sewn ships.' After describing the two outriggerless craft that still remained on Vahitahi, Gessler quoted remarks that two Vahitahians made to him about them:

> 'We go in them,' said Mokio, 'to Akiaki and to Nukutavake to get copra.'
>
> 'In old times,' added Tupuhoe, the stout young chief, 'they were two and three times as long, and men sailed in them to all the islands of the sea.'†[51]

If Gessler was right and Emory wrong about the outriggerless canoes of the Vahitahi area, and if Piddington was wrong about the origin of Tuhiragi's cosmogonic chant, then there is good reason to believe that Emory was also wrong in his interpretation of the contents of a remarkable manuscript book, a copy of which is now in the Bishop Museum. The book describes some aspects of the ancient religion of the Vahitahi area. It was written by a Nukutavakean called Te Poa, who died in 1927. Mazé first saw the book in 1923-4 when he was superintending the building of a church on Nukutavake. He told Emory about it in 1934. But he did not locate it again until 1938, when one of Te Poa's heirs allowed him to copy it for the Bishop Museum.

In his monograph *Tuamotuan Religious Structures and Ceremonies*, published in 1947, Emory summarised the contents of Te Poa's book and commented on its value. 'As Te Poa wrote his information for his own family, without having been questioned by a European,' Emory said, 'his manuscript

* *'Côtre paumotu'*—Tuamotuan coaster—seems to have been the term usually used by the French priests. See Maze 1933:229; also personal communication, 13 July 1972.

† Another writer, Earl Schenck, who accompanied Stimson to Vahitahi in 1934, said of the outriggerless canoes: 'Evidently, the Vahitahians had been inspired by their first sight of a ship, almost one hundred years before to attempt a reproduction.'—Schenck 1940:329.

is a valuable document for the new information which it supplies, for what it reveals of the break-down of native knowledge, and for a check on what we were told six and ten years later [i.e. in 1930 and 1934].' Emory said the book began with a brief account of the ancient worship and a list of the ancient equivalents for present-day features of the church and church ceremonies. Thus, the church (*fare pure*) was formerly called *fare heiau;* the altar was called *fata,* as in present-day speech; the ark of the covenant* (*aruna*) was called a *tapena* (literally, offering); the cross (*tatauro*) was called an *unu* (a decorated slab of wood or stone); the *komunio* (communion feast) was called the *uahau;* and *tumaimia* (incense) was called *kaunati* (magic fire). Te Poa's list of equivalents ended with the statement that the *uahau* (communion feast) was held after the offering to the god in heaven. In ancient times, he added, the god was called Te Atua-rere-pehu, Te Atua-noho-rangi, Te Atua-hangi-i-rangi —'three gods and those three were one.' The people prayed to him and offered feasts.

Emory did not offer any comment on the fact that, according to Te Poa, the ancient Vahitahians had had such obviously Christian, and particularly Catholic, paraphernalia as the cross, incense, and the ark of the covenant. Nor did he say anything about their communion feasts. But he did remark on Te Poa's statement that there had formerly been three gods and 'those three were one.' 'It is obvious,' he said, 'that in Te Poa's manuscript three names which bring Vahitahi concepts into closest line with the Biblical conception of a Trinity have been selected.'[52]

It is obvious, indeed, that Vahitahi's religion had much in common with the faith professed by Fathers Montiton, Fierens, Terlyn and Mazé. But, all things considered, it scarcely seems that it was for the simple reason that Emory supposed.

* The ark of the covenant of the Bible was a receptacle for the tablets of the law. The correct translation for the receptacle referred to here was probably 'reliquary'—see note, p. 229.

18

Of far-flung islands and 'hauntingly Caucasian faces'

In attempting to reconstruct the story of the lost caravel *San Lesmes,* there is one point that cannot be over-emphasised. This is that the period between the disappearance of the *San Lesmes* and Captain Cook's first voyage to the Pacific was almost half a century longer than the period between Cook's time and the present day. When this fact is borne in mind, it is easy to imagine that the genetic and cultural impact of a small group of European castaways of the early sixteenth century could have spread to almost every corner of the eastern Pacific before any other Europeans were on hand to record it. There is ample evidence to suggest that this did, indeed, happen—that besides the islands already dealt with, there are yet others where the mariners of the *San Lesmes* apparently left their marks. Most of these islands are on or near the outer perimeter of the Tuamotu Archipelago. In general, they are far-flung islands, remote from their neighbours. In ancient times, they probably had little contact with the outside world, except when a few hapless voyagers were drifted to them, perhaps over many hundreds of miles, from some other part of the Pacific. If visitors such as these were allowed to settle down, they no doubt contributed in some way to the culture of their new environment. But unless they were men of exceptional personality and ability, their cultural contribution must have been small. Thus, there are some islands where a few people of strikingly Caucasian appearance were reported in the early years of European contact; but no evidence was recorded suggesting that their ancestors made any contribution to the local culture that was particularly reminiscent of Europe. On other islands, on the other hand, genetic and cultural influences appear to have gone hand in hand.

An example of an island in the first category is Rapa, an isolated, volcanic outpost some 700 miles SSE of Tahiti. On two occasions in its first sixty years of contact, anomalous people of European appearance were seen there. But no one noticed any cultural items to match. The first such islander was seen in June 1820, when Bellingshausen, the Russian explorer, spent two days at Rapa on his way from New Zealand to the Tuamotus. From fifteen to twenty canoes went out to his ships each day. In general, their occupants were strongly-built men of medium height, bearded, curly-haired and with bright black eyes. Their faces and bodies were 'dark red'; their features pleasant and not 'disfigured' by tattooing. Yet one youth, of about seventeen or eighteen years of age, was so different from the rest that Paul Mikhailov, the expedition's artist, was moved to make a sketch of him.[1] The youth was very slimly built, Bellingshausen recorded, with 'light reddish hair, blue eyes, a rather aquiline nose and

the fair skin of northern Europe.' 'There is little room for doubt that he was the offspring of an Oparo [i.e. Rapan] woman and some European traveller,' the Russian commander added.[2]

Bellingshausen's conjecture, however, was almost certainly wrong. Before his own visit, only two 'European travellers' are known to have been at Rapa. Neither went ashore nor allowed his crew to do so. Moreover, neither was there at a time appropriate for a Rapan woman to have conceived a child who would have been seventeen or eighteen years old in 1820. And, in any case, unless the youth's mother had already been carrying blue-eye genes, it is genetically improbable that she could have given birth to a blue-eyed child even if the father's eyes had been a blue of the deepest dye.[3]

Bellingshausen's only known European predecessors at Rapa were the British explorer Vancouver, who discovered the island in HMS *Discovery* in 1791, and Captain John Powell of the brig *Queen Charlotte,* who made brief calls in 1816 and 1817 en route from Sydney to Tahiti.[4] Vancouver reported that the islanders bore a greater resemblance to the Tongans than to any other people he knew;[5] while William Ellis, who was on the *Queen Charlotte* in 1817, stated categorically in his *Polynesian Researches* that 'the English missionary from Tahiti was the first foreigner that ever landed [on Rapa].'[6] The missionary in question was the Rev. John Davies, who went ashore there in 1826. He himself later wrote: 'For many years little was known of this island or its inhabitants, [but] the name of Rapa was known both at Tahiti and the islands of Tupuai and Raivavae, and the general opinion was that the inhabitants of Rapa were exceedingly savage and that it was dangerous to go near them.'[7]

Rapa's population in Davies' time was possibly 2,000. Thereafter it declined rapidly as increasing contact with the outside world brought ravaging diseases. By 1867, there were only about 120 inhabitants.[8] As no European spent more than a few weeks on Rapa between 1826 and 1867, little was recorded of the island's ancient culture, and it is now impossible to say whether any cultural influences from Europe might have reached it in 'pre-discovery' times. On the other hand, the Mormon missionary James S. Brown, who visited the island in 1852, has left a record of a blond Rapan woman, reminiscent of Bellingshausen's light-featured youth. This woman, Brown said, was 'quite fair, with rather light brown or auburn hair.'[9] His description contrasts sharply with that of an English conchologist, Hugh Cuming, who said of the Rapans in 1828 that, in general, they had 'rather coarse features, face roundish, very dark complexions.'[10]

A few islanders answering the descriptions by Brown and Bellingshausen were also reported at Mangareva in the early days of European contact. Mangareva, the generic name for a cluster of volcanic islands surrounding an ample lagoon in the south-eastern corner of the Tuamotus, was first reported in 1797 by Captain Wilson of the *Duff*.[11] But no Europeans are known to have landed there until the mid-1820s. Captain Beechey, of HMS *Blossom,* who spent a fortnight there in December 1825, thought there was 'a great mixture of feature and colour' among the islanders; that several tribes from remote parts of the Pacific had met there and 'mingled their peculiarities;' and that in complexion and feature he could trace resemblances 'even to the widely separated tribes of New Zealand, New Caledonia, and Malacca.' In general, however, they had 'fine Asiatic countenances.'[12] Beechey's companion, Lieutenant Edward Belcher, was of much the same opinion. In his view, the Mangarevan countenance was 'of the Malay cast,' being of various tints approaching to white. The islanders were variously tattooed, the most prevalent form being the outline of a cross on the shoulder, hip or pectoral muscle. 'Some of their hands and feet,' Belcher said, 'were as neatly formed as any Europeans which is to be wondered at, considering they do not wear shoes.' In some instances, their hands were lighter than his own, which were much sunburnt. The Mangarevans' hair, he added, varied from black to 'a sort of umber or brownish auburn,' or even yellowish-brown among the women.[13]

These observations on the physical characteristics of the Mangarevans were reiterated and amplified in 1834 when the first European missionaries, a party of French Catholics, reached the island. One of them, Father Honoré Laval, who spent more than thirty years at Mangareva, wrote a description of the islanders on the day after his arrival. He mentioned among other things that their hair was generally black, but that in a very few it was 'sandy tending towards blond.' The light-haired islanders obviously struck him as European-looking, for he added: 'I learned afterwards that those people were not descended from white men, since [the Mangarevan] women were never given to strangers.'[14]

During his long sojourn on Mangareva, Laval compiled a detailed ethnography of its inhabitants. In this he wrote further about the Mangarevans' physical characteristics, and also mentioned two cultural items that could have been derived from Europe. On the first question, he said:

> The Mangarevans have brown skin, but among some of them it is almost white. Their body is hairless and covered more or less by extensive tattooing . . . Their hair is straight and glossy, usually black. But sometimes it is chestnut, tending towards red.[15]

Writing of the Mangarevans' cultural heritage, Laval remarked that the mesh of their fishing nets was 'exactly the same as in France' and that they had a wind compass that recognised sixteen wind directions.[16] A diagram by Laval indicating the eight principal winds of the Mangarevan compass reveals that this was almost exactly the same as that of Raiatea.[17] The two compasses may therefore be assumed to have been derived from the same source—very likely the great seafaring chiefs of Opoa.

Another island where blond people of European features were apparently to be found in 'pre-discovery' times is Reao, some 300 miles NNW of Mangareva. Reao is the easternmost inhabited atoll in the Tuamotus. Because of its remoteness from European shipping lanes, it was not discovered until June 1822.[18] When Captain Beechey touched there on 14 January 1826 following his sojourn at Mangareva, some of the islanders came out to his ship through a heavy surf. Their canoes were made of small pieces of wood 'well put together and sewed with the bark of a tree.' Beechey thought their occupants were 'a very inferior race' compared with the Mangarevans. Yet there was 'a great diversity of complexion' among them. 'In one of the canoes,' he wrote, 'there was a man nearly as dark as an African negro, with woolly hair tied in a knot like a Radackers;* and another with a light complexion, sandy hair and European features.'[19]

Beechey's sandy-haired man was the only one of his kind ever mentioned in the scanty published literature on Reao. But in 1900, the atoll's chief bore the name Henerike Kehu (literally, Henry Redhead),[20] so it may be that other sandy-haired people were to be seen there from time to time. Yet it is clear from the accounts of most visitors (see Appendix F) that darkness of feature was the most striking characteristic both of the Reao people and of those on

* A native of the Radack Chain of the Marshall Islands.

nearby Pukarua. This was in sharp contrast to that of the Tatakoto people, only 100 miles to leeward.

Tatakoto (also written Takoto) is a bean-shaped ring of land about nine miles long. It was first sighted by Europeans in 1774 when the Spaniards, headed by Boenechea, were on their second voyage to Tahiti. Other sightings were made in 1775, 1821, 1822 and 1824.[21] But it was not until the French pearler Arnaud Mauruc called there in 1840 that anything of consequence was learned of its inhabitants. Mauruc, himself, reported only that the islanders were 'too warlike' to deal with;[22] but his first officer, Eugène Ricardi, was somewhat more explicit. All the islanders were armed with lances and clubs of turtle bone, Ricardi said, and their war cry, although savage, 'did not lack a certain harmony'. In appearance, they were like the people of Fangatau and Taenga which Mauruc and Ricardi afterwards visited. They were generally of medium height, well made, and with 'regular and agreeable features.' The hair of both sexes was long and sometimes tied to the tops of their heads 'like the women of Europe.' No tattooed people were seen, and the men were generally less copper-coloured than the women. [23]

No other Europeans seem to have called at Tatakoto until 1867 when a brig from the Catholic mission at Mangareva paid a brief visit to tell the islanders that missionaries from Europe would soon come among them. [24] The first missionary, Father Montiton, put in an appearance in March 1869. Although the islanders 'refused to receive him,' he did succeed in leaving a native catechist and his wife on the island. These people were badly treated at first, and the woman fell ill and died. But some of the islanders eventually began to heed their teachings, and soon almost all the islanders were under instruction for baptism, and had built a small chapel.[25]

Father Fierens paid the atoll a fleeting visit towards the end of 1869. Finding many of the islanders well-instructed, he baptised them and married the couples who were living together.[26] About a year later, Montiton returned following his six-month sojourn at Fangatau (see chapter 17). His intention was merely to replace the native catechist with another convert, but a combination of circumstances resulted in his remaining on the atoll for eight months.

As Tatakoto was more productive than Fangatau, the islanders spent less time gathering food and were therefore 'more assiduous in the exercises of the chapel' than the Fangatauans. Soon they were attending morning mass, taking lessons in dogma and morality, reciting the rosary, the catechism and litanies for the Virgin Mary, singing the canticles, and so on.[27] Montiton was almost astonished at the change he wrought. 'These almost naked savages,' he recalled a year or so later, 'these same people, who, only yesterday, with flaming eyes and spears in hand, sped like eagles to the beach whenever a boat or ship dared to approach it—these people with the fury of a lion, the howl of a wolf and the blood-lust of a tiger have today become as gentle as lambs, humbly submitting to the voice of a simple priest.'[28] In subsequent writings, Montiton left no doubt that the Tatakotoans, when he first knew them, were much more cruel and savage than the people of Fangatau, and less religious.[29] Yet, they had the same creation myths as the Fangatauans and the same beliefs in a 'Virgin Mary', a saviour god, and other seemingly Biblical figures. In addition, they had one religious practice peculiar to themselves that further reminded Montiton of the Bible. It concerned the capture of a certain kind of eel and its use in funeral ceremonies for a dead woman. Commenting on this, Montiton wrote: 'In this strange symbolism, for which the islanders can apparently give no explanation, can one not see a degenerate image of the prophetic serpent of brass which Moses raised in the sky, as if woman, cursed at the time of the serpent, could only be rehabilitated through . . . the divine Redemptor, extended and immolated on the branches of the Cross?'[30]

Since Montiton's eight-month stay on Tatakoto, no other Catholic missionaries seem ever to have spent so much time on that atoll. But from that time onwards, they visited it sporadically, sometimes for a few days, sometimes a few weeks. Meanwhile, a Frenchman, Albert Javelot, made his home there, and in 1900 he was made the atoll's chief.[31] Like his compatriot Marechal at Fangatau, Javelot helped to develop a copra industry, which, in turn, brought a few trading schooners to Tatakoto from the outside world. An occasional traveller in these was Father Paul Mazé, the Catholic pastor to the eastern atolls from 1920 until he became bishop of Tahiti in 1937. In mid-1972, at the age of eighty-six, Mazé, then an archbishop, wrote to the present author in reply to a query about possible links between some Tuamotuans and castaways from the *San Lesmes*. Mazé's letter provided some unsolicited information about the people of Tatakoto.

> I have made many sojourns at Amanu [he wrote], but I never suspected that the people there were of European descent, from castaways from the *San Lesmes*. However at Takoto I had the impression that there were mixtures [*melanges*] with European blood. Why?
>
> 1. Because of the islanders' beauty, the fineness of their features, and their colour, which, in 1920, contrasted violently with the colour and features of the Reao and Pukarua people. It prompted me to ask the old missionary, who, for 13 years, had made an Easter tour of those islands, if there had not been a European (*popaa*) who had lived on that island. He replied that the whalers had probably sown some seeds there.
>
> 2. Because of their voices which were fresher than those of the surrounding islands, and, above all, because of the fall of a fifth at the end of each phrase in their recitation of prayers and responses to the catechism, in the manner of Spaniards.
>
> 3. Their physique, hair in corkscrew curls at the tops of their heads, and pointed chins.
>
> 4. Finally, they were generally more open, and more intelligent than those of other islands.[32]

These remarks seem to establish that the people of Tatakoto had (and have) the same Caucasian features as the islanders of Fangatau, whom Shapiro found so remarkably European in 1929. Tatakoto thus seems to provide further evidence of a correlation between islanders of that description and seemingly Biblical traditions; and this notion is further strengthened by Stimson's remarks on what he found at Tatakoto in 1934. During a stay of several weeks, he recorded more than seventy ancient chants, which, he thought, represented 'welcome support for the Fagatau lore of Kiho-tumu.'* 'Here, as everywhere,' he said in a report to the Bishop Museum, 'the cult of Kiho or Kio was esoteric, sacred and could not be divulged except to initiates; in this it parallels the Maori cult of Io.'[33]

Tests carried out before World War II show that the blood types of the Tatakoto people are remarkably similar to those of Spain's Basque provinces where most of the *San Lesmes*' crew were almost certainly recruited. On the other hand, they differ markedly from the Samoans, a Polynesian people who are not suspected of intermarriage with Europeans in 'pre-discovery' times. The blood tests at Tatakoto were made by Dr. George P. Lyman, surgeon of the yacht *Zaca*, in 1934. They reveal that group B is absent on Tatakoto, which is far from the case in Samoa, and that the figures for group A have little in common between the two places. Figures (in round numbers) for Tatakoto, Spanish Basques and Samoans are:[34]

Area and date	*No. tested*	*Percentage of group*			
		O	*A*	*B*	*AB*
Tatakoto (1934)	52	56	44	—	—
Spanish Basques:					
San Sebastian (1937)	91	57	42	1	—
San Sebastian (1937)	138	57	38	1	—
Guipúzcoa (1949)	444	55	40	4	1
San Sebastian (1949)	236	61	34	4	—
Samoa (1924)	51	41	37	14	8
Samoa (1930)	38	39	29	26	5
Samoa (1931)	500	59	17	19	5

Tatakoto is the only seemingly 'Caucasian' atoll in the Tuamotus where blood tests were carried out before World War II. So no comparable figures are available for such places as Anaa, Fangatau or Vahitahi where other evidence suggests that early European genetic influence was at work. Nor are figures available for Napuka, yet another atoll where such influence may be suspected. Napuka is one of the two Disappointment Islands in the north-eastern corner of the Tuamotus which Byron discovered in 1765. The United States Exploring Expedition visited it briefly in 1839 and a Peruvian slave raider was there in the 1860s.[35] Otherwise, it had virtually no contact with the outside world until 1870 when Father Fierens called there for the first time.[36] However, even as late as 1934 when Emory spent eleven weeks there with his friend Gessler, the Napukans claimed that no Europeans, other than the

* The chants were recorded in the year after Stimson's *Tuamotuan Religion* and *Cult of Kiho-Tumu* appeared. They are still unpublished.

Catholic missionary, had ever lived on the atoll.[37] Despite this, Shapiro, who touched at Napuka in 1929, remarked that, as at Fangatau, he was 'especially struck by a marked Caucasian strain' that he had never found so clearly indicated anywhere else in Polynesia. [38] Gessler said in his book *The Dangerous Islands* that the Caucasian strain was observable in about ten per cent of the people.[39] One of the first Napukans to greet him was 'a small, wiry Polynesian of the Caucasian type of features, with formidable black moustaches.' Another such person was 'an unusually blonde little girl' called Maruia, who seemed, from her appearance, to be the daughter of a white man. However, a Napukan chief assured Gessler that this was not so—that her parents were known to everyone, and that her family's genealogies went back thirty-five generations. 'You will see many blondes among our people,' the chief said. 'It has been so from the beginning.'[40]

Writing of the Napukans generally, Gessler said he could distinguish 'traces of the Caucasian features and reddish-brown hair that Wallis observed at his discovery of Tahiti, as did the sixteenth-century Spaniards in the Marquesas* . . .' And he said in another context: '. . . here, on one of the most remote atolls of the Tuamotu, were these hauntingly Caucasian faces, this red-gold hair, mingled with the high cheek bones that spoke of Asia, the dark curls of Melanesia, and the lineaments of who knows what vanished races that may have occupied these far islets before the conquerors came.'[41]

Elsewhere, Gessler spoke of Napuka's 'mysterious ancient chants.' These included chants about Hiro-of-the-Crimson-Girdle and Kiho the Root, creator of the lesser gods and 'the secret monotheistic god of the inner priesthood.' The Kiho chants, Gessler said, revealed a 'spirit of philosophical inquiry and a spiritual capacity not inferior to that of any race in its primitive state.' Indeed, for 'poetic imagery, cosmic vastness of conception and sublimity of expression,' the chants ranked with 'some of the noblest sacred writings of other lands.'[42]

Gessler's findings at Napuka have had their parallels in recent years at Raroia. This atoll, with its much smaller neighbour Takume, lies 100 miles or so SSW of Napuka. Following Bellingshausen's discovery of the two atolls in 1820, and visits by pearlers from Tahiti in the 'thirties and 'forties, Raroia had little contact with Europeans until Father Montiton called there for the first

* Although the Marquesans whom Gessler referred to had light skins and sometimes red or sandy hair, there seems to be no evidence that they were otherwise Caucasian in appearance. Nor, apparently, is there any cultural evidence to suggest that they were descendants of castaways from the *San Lesmes*. Such a possibility is feasible, however, as the Marquesas would have been directly in the route of any castaways who tried to reach Mexico from the Tuamotus. The Spaniards mentioned by Gessler were members of the Mendaña expedition who spent sixteen days in the Marquesas in 1595—sixty-nine years after the *San Lesmes* was last seen. Quiros, the pilot, wrote the only extant account of that sojourn.—Markham 1904:15-30. Captain Cook, the next European visitor, was there 180 years later. An American social anthropologist, Ralph Linton, who studied the material culture of the Marquesas in the early 1920s, claimed there was evidence of two distinct racial elements at the beginning of the historical period. One showed affinities with the Maori of New Zealand; the other with Western Polynesia. No important invasion of the Marquesas seemed to have occurred after the two racial elements had settled there.—Linton 1923:265. A physical anthropologist, Louis R. Sullivan, also concluded that there were two distinct racial types. He described these as Indonesian and Polynesian.—Sullivan 1923:233.

time in 1869.[43] About three-quarters of the islanders were then Mormons, having been converted by native missionaries from Anaa. Others had been baptised as Catholics during visits to that atoll. Montiton did not stay long on his first visit; and subsequent calls by him or his colleagues were also short. However, as an Anaan catechist was usually left on one of the two atolls between visits, the Catholic fold gradually increased. By 1888, 163 of the 274 inhabitants of Raroia were said to have been converted.[44]

An English traveller, J. C. Bell, who visited Raroia in 1883, thought the missionaries deserved every credit for trying to civilise the islanders. Their cottages and church were extremely neat; the people were well dressed; and the children could write and do sums. In fact, Bell concluded that although the islanders might be termed savages, their method of living, their dress, their primary knowledge and their intelligence would 'put in the shade many a village in Europe.'[45]

In the fifty years from 1870 to 1920, trading schooners are thought to have called at Raroia about five or six times a year.[46] However, no one seems to have written any further impressions of the Raroians until 1926 when the French yachtsman Alain Gerbault spent about a week at their island. One thing he emphasised was the European appearance of many islanders. 'The girls of Raroia,' he wrote, 'all seemed to me very pretty; strong and well-shaped. They had very slightly darkened skin and their features were nearly European in cast. Two little girls, in particular, were of a type almost exactly the same as that of the street beauties of Seville.'[47]

A generation later, another visitor, the anthropologist Bengt Danielsson, said much the same thing. Danielsson was aboard the *Kon-Tiki* raft when it was washed up at Raroia in 1947. He later spent eighteen months on the atoll doing research for a Ph.D. thesis and gathering material for a travel book, *The Happy Island*. In his book, Danielsson published several photographs of Raroians with distinctly Caucasian features, and he said of one, the island's chief, that he was 'the most European-looking of all the islanders.'[48] Elsewhere, Danielsson described his first encounter with an old man called Te Iho, whose unexpected European appearance so startled him that he almost cried out, 'But it's a white man!' Te Iho had been born on Raroia before Montiton's first visit. Nevertheless, his complexion was 'no darker than that of a southern European,' and with his greyish-white beard and hair, his features were 'not too foreign for him to have played Father Christmas in any English home.'[49]

Te Iho had been brought up to be a *tahunga* (historian), as the ancient culture, according to Danielsson, had persisted on Raroia until the end of the nineteenth century. He was a member of the atoll's most distinguished family and knew by heart numerous traditions, genealogies and sacred chants. Among them was a chant about the creation of the universe which began thus: 'In the beginning there was only void. Neither darkness nor light, neither sun nor sky yet existed. All was one great, silent, motionless void.' The chant went on to describe the formation of the sea and earth, and how the sky mother, Fakahotu, revealed herself, then the sky father, Atea. This pair had two sons, Tane and Tangaroa, and later two others, the Ru brothers, who formed a living pyramid by standing on each others' shoulders. In this way, three spheres were formed —the region below the sea and earth, the world we live in, and the sky above. After plants, animals and fish had begun to appear, Tangaroa created a man called Tiki. After a time, Tiki tired of being alone, so Tangaroa made a woman for him from a heap of sand. Her name was Hina-*ahu-one*—'Hina-made-of-sand'. She and Tiki were the progenitors of all mankind. When Danielsson asked Te Iho where the act of creation took place, Te Iho said it was in Paradise. And he added: 'All things considered, might not Tiki and Hina be only other names for Adam and Eve?'[50]

Te Iho and other Raroians also told Danielsson that their first Raroian ancestors came from a place called Hiva Nui. Te Iho put the date of his ancestors' arrival at thirty generations earlier (i.e. about 1500, if fifteen years are allowed for a generation). Danielsson thought that Hiva Nui was one of the Marquesas Islands because of its resemblance to the island names of Hiva-oa, Nukuhiva and Fatuhiva. But this identification is questionable. It may merely mean 'big, far-off land.'[51]

Hiva, at any rate (as chapter 3 has already revealed), was also the name of the troublesome castaway or castaways who invaded Hao in ancient times, tearing down coconut trees and hurling missiles ashore, as if they were little stones. Hao, in turn, was the large atoll next to Amanu where Quiros and his men, in 1606, saw the old woman whose hair was dressed in the Spanish fashion, whose finger carried an emerald-studded gold ring, and who had at her heels a small, spotted dog 'like the dogs of Castille.' Hao lies about 140 miles south-east of Raroia. One might think it would be a fruitful source of clues to the fate of the *San Lesmes*. And it does, indeed, offer further evidence on the subject of seemingly Biblical beliefs in 'pre-discovery' times.[52] But the most significant item in the present context appears to be another statement by Stimson, who spent seven weeks on that atoll in 1929 waiting for a schooner.

> At Hao [he wrote] there is a tradition of the departure of a great *pahi* (seagoing canoe) for lands unknown; it never returned, but was remembered as the greatest canoe ever constructed on the island, capable of transporting perhaps a hundred voyagers—its name was 'Tainui', the name of the great canoe that sailed to New Zealand with the great fleet of 1350. There are many words in the *fagu* which are identical with Maori, but unknown in the same signification elsewhere; one of these is *tupotu* (to be brought down to the sea).[53]

19

New Zealand: last loitering place of Hiro

In the National Museum in Wellington, New Zealand, are two metal objects of sixteenth century manufacture or thereabouts that have mystified New Zealanders for many years. Both were found in New Zealand, whose first known contact with visitors from the world of metals dates back only to Tasman's brief call in the mid-seventeenth century. One of the mysterious objects is the upper part of a bronze bell with an embossed inscription in the Tamil language of southern India; the other is part of a steel helmet, generally described as Spanish. Both the bell and the helmet, though seemingly unrelated, may be links in a long chain of evidence proving that New Zealand's first European settlers arrived almost three centuries earlier than has usually been supposed.

The bell was found in the Whangarei district of the North Island in 1836 or 1837. Its discoverer was the Rev. William Colenso, a missionary of the Church Missionary Society. He recovered it from a party of Maoris who were using it as a cooking pot. They themselves had found it when a large tree had been blown down, exposing it. But they are said to have told Colenso that it had belonged to their tribe for many generations. Colenso thought the inscription on the bell was in Javanese. However, when photographs were sent to India, the bell was recognised as a ship's bell such as was then commonly used among the Tamils. The inscription was translated as 'Mohoyideen Buks—ship's bell', although this was in an obsolete style, containing two characters no longer in use. Other Tamil-speakers have since translated the inscription as 'the bell of Mukaiyathan's own ship' and 'the bell of Moha Din Buksh's ship.' The last-cited is said to indicate that the ship's master belonged to a seafaring people called Marakkaiyar. These people were at one time Hindu, but were later converted to Islam. In the 1940s, a Tamil scholar, Professor Visvanathan, estimated the age of the bell at 400 to 500 years, and expressed the view that it might not have come from India, but from Java 'or adjacent lands,' where the Marakkaiyar had settled.[1]

Professor Visvanathan's information, if correct, provides two clues that could explain how the bell happened to reach New Zealand. One is that the bell is of approximately the right age to have been carried on a European ship of the sixteenth century. The other is that Marakkaiyar seafarers in Java or the nearby islands could have sold the bell to Elcano or a companion before he returned to Spain in Magellan's *Victoria* in 1522. The bell could therefore have been put on board the *San Lesmes* before she left Spain with Loaisa's fleet in 1525. Alternatively, it could have been transferred to that ship after

Elcano's vessel *Sancti Spiritus* was wrecked in the Strait of Magellan several months later. In either case, it could have been carried into the South Pacific in 1526.

As for the so-called Spanish helmet in the National Museum, that, too, it seems, could have come from the *San Lesmes*. The helmet—or, at least, the surviving part of it—is of a kind known as a morion (*morrión* in Spanish). In 1906, it was reported to have been dredged up from Wellington harbour and to have lain in the museum—then called the Colonial Museum—for about thirty years. However, no contemporary account has been found of its discovery, and the present museum authorities have no record of how, or from whom, the object was originally acquired. Moreover, the only attempts to establish its approximate age have been made from photographs. *Connoisseur,* a London magazine for antique collectors, has dated it to 1560-70, while an authority at London's Victoria and Albert Museum has fixed its period at 'about 1580.'[2] Both of these datings, of course, are far too recent for the helmet to have been carried in the *San Lesmes*. But as both are from British rather than Spanish authorities, they may be quite wrong. The morion, at any rate, is known to have been used in Spain in the first decades of the sixteenth century.[3] Moreover, several officers in Pablo de Uranga's painting of the departure of the Loaisa expedition (see pl. 3) are shown wearing such helmets.

New Zealand historian J. C. Beaglehole once said of the Wellington helmet that 'one piece of headgear does not make a discovery.'[4] He might equally have said that one Tamil bell does not make a Maori of a Marakkaiyar. Yet the two objects should scarcely be dismissed as clues to New Zealand's unwritten past—especially now that there are strong reasons for believing that Spanish seamen arrived in that country in the sixteenth century. Some of these reasons have already been mentioned in chapter 14. Briefly recapitulated, they are:

1. Ancient traditions and genealogies concerning Hiro, Iro or Whiro, are similar or identical in the Society Islands, Cook Islands and New Zealand. They therefore prove that either a person of that name, or knowledge of him, reached New Zealand in pre-Cook times.

2. In the Society Islands, Hiro is reputed to have founded the chiefly dynasty of Raiatea, whose members, in historical times, were remarkable for their light complexions and Caucasian features.

3. Provided only fifteen years are taken as a generation (or reign), Hiro's lifetime, even according to the longest genealogies, does not date back before the beginning of the sixteenth century. Hiro could thus have been the captain or a seaman of the *San Lesmes* and so could have reached New Zealand from the Society Islands some time after the first quarter of that century.

A great deal of other evidence can be brought forward to support the suggestion that New Zealand had its sixteenth century Spanish settlers. One item concerns the canoe *Tainui* (or *Tahi-nui*). On the one hand, there was a vessel of that name in the so-called fleet that brought the Maoris to New Zealand. On the other, *Tainui* was both the name of a canoe traditionally associated with Hiro (see footnote p. 159) and that of the great sea-going canoe that left Hao for unknown lands in ancient times and never returned. Moreover, the captain of the Hao canoe is said to have been Hoturoa, as is the one of New Zealand. And New Zealand's Hoturoa is said to have begun his voyage in Hawaiki, i.e. Raiatea; which means that he, too, can be traced back to the same island as Hiro. In addition, Hoturoa, like Hiro, is renowned as a Maori ancestor; and like him he also seems to figure in Society Islands tradition, but only under the name of Hotu, Hiro's chief artisan in the building of *Hohoio*.[5]

Numerous details about Hoturoa and his New Zealand descendants are recorded in a 484-page book called *Tainui,* published in 1949 by a part-Maori scholar, Leslie G. Kelly. Like most New Zealanders, Kelly assumed that the voyage of *Tainui* and the other canoes of the Maori fleet took place about 1350—a date based very insecurely on Maori genealogies.* He went on to say that little was now known about the construction of the New Zealand *Tainui*—that Maori elders were apt to picture their ancestral canoe as a single-hulled vessel, with a spiral carved sternpost and elaborate bow-piece, whereas everything suggested that this type of canoe was evolved in New Zealand. However, Kelly said that one or two seemingly accurate descriptions had been handed down from bygone times. According to these, *Tainui's* hull was 'built up by the addition of side boards,' she was fitted on one side with a smaller canoe, and had three masts and three sails supplemented by the usual supply of paddles.[6] If these details are approximately correct, then New Zealand's *Tainui* must have been similar in design to Hiro's *Hohoio.*

Maori traditions about the arrival of *Tainui* in New Zealand differ on some points, but agree on essential details. The canoe is said to have made the land near Cape Runaway in the Bay of Plenty, where the crew quarrelled with the occupants of another canoe, *Te Arawa,* over the ownership of a stranded whale. Later, the *Tainui* people coasted northward and (according to most versions) hauled their canoe across the isthmus where Auckland now stands. Having come out into the Tasman Sea through Manakau Heads, they sailed south to Kawhia Harbour where *Tainui* was drawn ashore. Two upright limestone slabs, 76 ft apart, are still said to mark her resting place. After they had settled on the shores of Kawhia Harbour, the *Tainui* people gradually spread inland until, after several centuries, they occupied much of the western and northern parts of the North Island. Their inland boundary lay in the mountainous country stretching from Coromandel south to Taupo. This divided them from the *Arawa* people, who are said to have spread inland from the Bay of Plenty. Nowadays, the Maoris of Hauraki, Waikato and the

* The date of 1350 has been repeated so often in New Zealand literature that most New Zealanders probably believe it has some sound scientific basis. In fact, it was arrived at by S. Percy Smith, one of the founders of the Polynesian Society, by taking the average length of fifty Maori genealogies that were supposed to date back to the 'fleet'. This produced the figure of twenty-two generations back from 1900, which was multiplied by twenty-five as representing the average number of years in a generation. The result was 550 years back from 1900, or 1350.—Smith 1921:19-20.

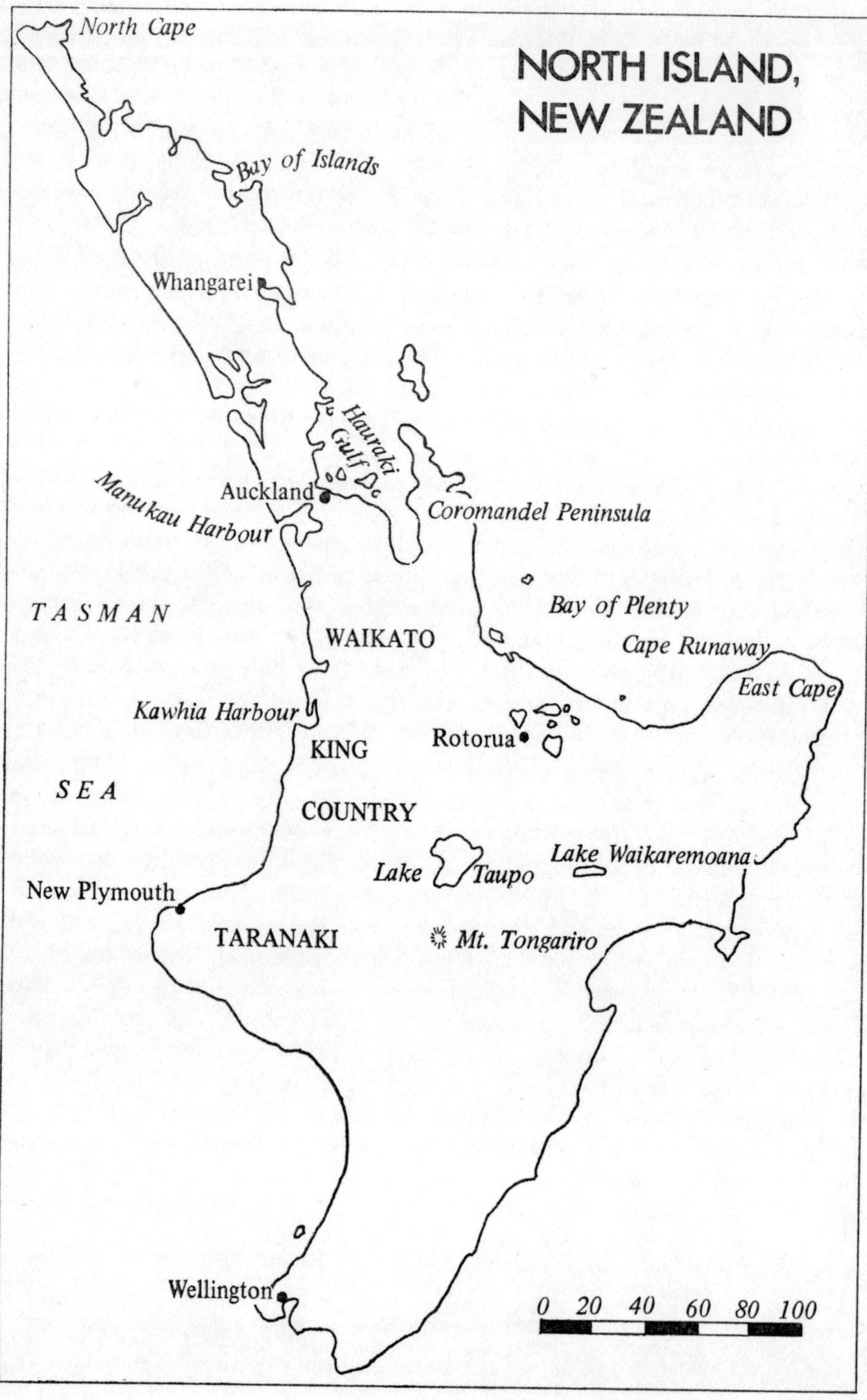
NORTH ISLAND, NEW ZEALAND
North Cape
Bay of Islands
Whangarei
Hauraki Gulf
Auckland
Manukau Harbour
Coromandel Peninsula
Bay of Plenty
Cape Runaway
East Cape
TASMAN
WAIKATO
Kawhia Harbour
Rotorua
KING
COUNTRY
SEA
Lake Waikaremoana
Lake Taupo
New Plymouth
TARANAKI
Mt. Tongariro
Wellington
0 20 40 60 80 100

King Country all claim to be descended from the *Tainui* immigrants, while those of Roturua and Taupo claim descent from the *Arawa* immigrants.[7] Other Maoris say their ancestors arrived from Hawaiki in canoes called *Aotea, Takitimu, Matatua, Tokomaru, Horouta,* etc. But none of those people place as much emphasis on their canoe origins as the *Tainui* and *Arawa* people, and this has raised doubts on whether the immigrant canoes from Hawaiki were as numerous as was once supposed.[8]

Tradition says that *Tainui's* commander, Hoturoa, was a middle-aged man when he made his voyage, and that he had two wives, Whakaoterangi and Marama. Whakaoterangi (who reputedly arrived in *Te Arawa*) is credited with being the first to cultivate the *kumara* or sweet potato in New Zealand.[9] But traditions recorded in the first half of the nineteenth century do not name her as the person who introduced the sweet potato to the new country. Instead, they describe that benefactor as a person called Pani, which is possibly a Maori corruption of the poetic name, Hispani, meaning Spaniards.[10] One of the chroniclers of the Pani tradition was Horatio Hale, of the United States Exploring Expedition. He was told at the Bay of Islands in 1841 that Pani had arrived from Hawaiki with his sister Hinakakirirangi; that their canoe was made of 'a number of pieces lashed together'; and this was one of four vessels—*Tainui, Arawa, Horouta* and *Takitimu*—that had arrived together. Hale also gathered the impression that the four canoes had reached New Zealand 'at a very late date', which suggests a more recent period than the usually-accepted date of 1350.[11]

Another chronicler of the Pani tradition was Ernest Dieffenbach, naturalist and surgeon to the New Zealand Company from 1839 to 1841. Dieffenbach also noted that the Maoris had two words for dog—*kuri* and *pero,* and that they had a seemingly non-Polynesian word for ship—*kaipuke.* Writing of the Maori dog in his book *Travels in New Zealand,* Dieffenbach said: 'The native name is *kuri,* the general name for dog amongst the Polynesians generally; but it is very curious that the Spanish word "pero" is also known to them'.* As for the word *kaipuke* Dieffenbach remarked that this was similar to the Spanish word *buque,* meaning ship, and he added: 'No other Polynesian nation has this word to designate a ship.'[12]

On the question of the sweet potato, Dieffenbach said that this item was 'gratefully remembered' by the Maoris and was recorded in many of their songs. These did not indicate when this vegetable had reached New Zealand, but the person who brought it was said to be E Pani or Ko Pani, the wife of E Tiki. She and her husband were reputed to have arrived from an island to the eastward called Taiwai. Finding that the New Zealanders did not have the sweet potato, E Pani offered to return to Taiwai to get it, which she did. Dieffenbach thought that this tradition might well conceal some 'remarkable tale of heroism.' 'Is it a tale connected with the Polynesian race itself,' he wondered, 'or does it not rather refer to the arrival in New Zealand of the

* The Spanish word is actually *perro* with a well-rolled double 'r'—*pero* being Spanish for 'but'. The double 'r', however, is not used in any Polynesian language.

early Spanish navigators, who may have brought this valuable product from the island of Taiwai . . ?' Then, recollecting the similarities between the Spanish and Maori words for dog and ship, Dieffenbach added: 'There can scarcely be any doubt but that New Zealand was visited by some [Spanish] people antecedent to Tasman [in 1642].'[13]

Despite his conviction about pre-Tasman Spaniards, Dieffenbach does not seem to have considered the possibility that such people might actually have settled in New Zealand and left descendants. Nevertheless, he did note that many Maoris looked like Europeans. He estimated the total Maori population at 115,000 and said he was convinced that originally it was composed of two races. Over the years, these had become mixed and 'a number of intermediate varieties' had resulted. However, some features of the two original types had been retained. One race, by far the more numerous, was tall, muscular and well-proportioned, very rarely inclined to *embonpoint,* and varying in size as much as Europeans. Many of their skulls in no way differed from those of Europeans, and often approached 'the best and most intellectual European heads.' In general, their skin colour was light brown, but it varied greatly in shade, and was sometimes 'even lighter than that of a native of the south of France.' The nose was straight, well-shaped and often aquiline; the eyes dark; the lips generally more developed than those of Europeans; and the hair generally black and lank, or slightly curled. However, the hair of some Maoris was a reddish or auburn colour, and they had a very light-coloured skin. Dieffenbach said that the people of the second race were characterised by a skull that was 'somewhat compressed from the sides,' as well as full and large features, prominent cheek bones, full lips, small ears, and coarse, curly (but not woolly) hair. This race had a much deeper skin colour than the other and a short, rather ill-proportioned figure.[14]

Dieffenbach was by no means the only writer who saw European likenesses in many Maoris. Another was Julien Crozet, a companion of the French explorer Marion du Fresne, who was in New Zealand waters in 1772. Crozet said the complexion of many Bay of Islands Maoris resembled that of the people of southern Europe and that some had red hair. 'There were some who were as white as our sailors,' he added, 'and we often saw on our ships a tall, young man, 5 ft 11 in. high, who by his colour and features might easily have passed for a European.'[15] The French explorer J. S. C. Dumont d'Urville mentioned seeing a similar youth in the Bay of Islands in 1826. Except for slight tattoo marks on his lips, he might 'easily have passed for a dark-skinned Provençal or Sicilian.'[16] Other Maoris with features resembling those of 'Brutus, Socrates, etc.' were reported by one of d'Urville's officers, M. Quoy.[17]

Yet another writer to remark on similarities between the Maoris and Europeans was J. S. Polack. He was an English Jew, who ran a trading store in the Bay of Islands for about six years from 1831 and wrote one of the earliest books on New Zealand. Like Dieffenbach, Polack believed the Maoris were of two distinct races, and he described their complexions as varying from the 'olive tinge of the Spanish peninsula' to a brown black. The olive, or copper-coloured race were 'a noble people,' often above six feet in stature, active and muscular. 'The highest classes,' Polack went on, 'are amply-chested, remarkably well formed and of dignified appearance. The countances of this class are often very pleasing; the hair glossy, black and curling, and the features approaching to the European.'[18]

Dr. Karl Scherzer, a scientist on the Austrian frigate *Novara,* which spent two and a half weeks in Auckland in the late 1850s, believed that even the extensive facial tattooing among some Maoris did not obscure their European features. He described the Maoris as a handsome race who closely resembled Europeans in features, in complexion and in the hair. The Maoris' complexion, he said, gave the impression of being 'embrowned' rather than naturally brown, while their hair, which was sometimes black and sometimes chestnut brown, was like that of Europeans because it was 'thin and weak.' 'Indeed,' Scherzer added, 'full-blooded Maories [*sic*] sometimes have such a European aspect, that even the numberless tattoo marks upon their faces do not destroy the impression, but have rather the appearance of those "painted faces" we are accustomed to see in actors, when they wish to give their countenances a more effective cast upon the boards.'[19]

Many other writers could be cited who shared the views of Dieffenbach, Crozet, d'Urville, Quoy, Polack and Scherzer on the physical appearance of the Maoris. Three others are worth mentioning for the additional light they throw on that subject. One, Elsdon Best, said in his book *The Maori* (Wellington, 1924) that among the black-haired natives of New Zealand, a fair-skinned type with wavy reddish hair was extremely persistent. 'Such folk are not, however, numerous,' Best added, 'though the strain is said to have come from Eastern Polynesia many generations ago.'[20] Elsewhere, Best said the light-haired, fair-skinned people were called *urukehu,* and that besides the two racial types frequently described as existing among the Maoris, they made up a third type. They were quite distinct from albinos, who were not uncommon.[21]

The *urukehu* were also described by Professor J. Macmillan Brown in his book *Maori and Polynesian* (London, 1907). Such people, he said, were 'not infrequent' among the Urewera tribe of the North Island. This tribe was only then coming into contact with Europeans, and was notable for a 'blond Caucasian strain.' The Urewera were reputed to have reached New Zealand in the *Matatua* canoe. Soon after their arrival, they passed into the highlands round Lake Waikaremoana, where they 'struggled with the inhabitants of the mountain and forest land' and ultimately amalgamated with them. Numerous other 'rufous people' were to be found in another district that had long been isolated from Europeans. This was the King Country, near Kawhia Harbour. '. . . the tribes there,' Brown added, 'speak of their ancestors, the immigrants of the *Tainui* canoe, [as] amalgamating with the aboriginals, the Ngatimokotorea.'[22]

The third writer, a novelist, Frank O. V. Acheson, stated in a foreword to his *Plume of the Arawas* that many *urukehu* were blue-eyed. He described the *urukehu* as 'an ancient and almost pure Caucasian strain' whose origin was shrouded in mystery. He added that he had seen 'many fair-haired but full-blooded Maoris, including many children, with fair skin and light blue eyes' in the Lake Taupo and Mt Tongariro region. Because of this, he was tempted to write a novel offering his own opinion on their origin.[23]

The links proclaimed in the literature between light-skinned redheads and the Bay of Islands (where the Ngapuhi people claim descent from Hiro),[24] between the *urukehu* and Eastern Polynesia, and between the 'rufous' King Country people and *Tainui* all tie in with the notion that the Caucasian strain among New Zealand's Maoris owed its origin to castaways from the *San Lesmes*. This notion is further strengthened by the fact that only among people of European origin are light skins, red hair and blue eyes found together. This being so, one should naturally expect to find traces of European culture among the Maoris. And as in the Tuamotus and Society Islands, such traces are apparently to be found in the ancient religion—to look no further. Pre-eminently, they comprise beliefs in a supreme god called Io, who had much in common with the seemingly Biblical Io, Kio or Kiho described by Stimson in the Tuamotus. The first European to learn about Io was one, C. O. Davis, a government interpreter and Maori linguist, who chanced on a few details in the 1850s which he published in 1876.[25] However, the only detailed account of Io is that contained in a manuscript dictated by a Maori named Te Matorohanga and taken down by another, Te Whatahoro. The manuscript, with English translations, appeared in print in 1913 as *The Lore of the Whare-wanaga or Teachings of the Maori College on Religion, Cosmogony and History*. Its editor, S. Percy Smith, president of the Polynesian Society, stated in an introduction that Te Matorohanga had died in 1884, but that Te Whatahoro—'the most learned man on these subjects it has ever been my lot to meet'—was still hale and hearty at the age of seventy-two. Smith said that the manuscript had been dictated in the 'fities of last century. He went on:

> It will possibly be thought that the idea of Io as the one supreme god, creator of all things, is derived from Christian teachers of the Maori people, and that it has been engrafted on to Maori beliefs in modern times since Christianity was introduced. But I am assured not only by the positive statement of the Scribe [i.e. Te Whatahoro], but by internal evidence—more particularly perhaps by prayers to Io, which contain so many obsolete words, and differ a good deal in form of composition from ordinary *karakias* [incantations]—that there is no foundation for such an idea. The doctrine of Io is evidently a bona-fide relic of very ancient times, handed down with scrupulous care generation after generation, as the centre and core of the esoteric teaching of the Whare-wananga. Had this grand old legend been derived from European sources, there can be no reasonable doubt that the life and doings of Jesus Christ would also have been incorporated. But there is nothing like it; not the slightest hint of it.[26]

The doctrine of Io was quite different from that of Rangi and Papa (the Sky-father and Sky-mother) who were known to the Maoris in general. One authority says that the Io cult was confined to the highest order of priests, termed *tohunga ahurewa.* Moreover, the name of Io was so sacred and secret that it was never mentioned under a roof, but only in the open between the initiated. People of the 'highest class' heard the ritual relating to Io only at the birth, sickness, death or exhumation of an important person.[27]

The exclusivity and other features of the Io cult prompted Smith to wonder whether two separate beliefs had not been amalgamated in ancient times—whether the doctrine of Io had not been superimposed on the doctrine of Rangi and Papa, or vice versa. 'The extreme sacredness of all connected with the name of Io, the much higher plane of thought which is embodied in all his attributes, the fact that his name was practically known to none but the few initiates, seems to point to a much higher degree of culture than the doctrines of Rangi and Papa . . . ,' he wrote. Smith also noted that many ideas permeating the lore of the Whare-wananga seemed to be based largely and originally on astronomy. The concept of twelve heavens was one such idea. 'It is certain,' Smith said, 'that the Polynesians were accurate observers of celestial phenomena. . . . They gave a name to the celestial equator, and every prominent star, and were fully aware of the rotundity of the earth as proved by the fact of finding new stars as they went further north or south. . . . Had someone with a knowledge of Astronomy been enabled to question these old Sages, I feel persuaded a great deal of information on that subject might have been obtained, but now, alas! it is too late.'[28]

Smith pointed out several parallels between the Io cult and the Bible, and went on to refer to two famous *toki,* or axes, that were associated with the Maoris' migration to New Zealand. The axes were called Te Whiro-nui and Te Awhio-rangi. The first was said to have been left in Tahiti when the *Takitimu* canoe began her voyage. The other had been brought with the Maori immigrants, having been used to 'fell' the storms encountered en route. 'This celebrated axe,' Smith said, 'was given as a marriage dower by its then owners to Tane-roroa, daughter of Turi, captain of the *Aotea* canoe, some time after the great migration to New Zealand . . . and still remains a venerated and sacred property of the Nga-Rauru tribe of the West Coast. No white man has been allowed to see it—it is far too sacred—but it is known by description to differ much in shape and material from the ordinary axe.'* Smith added that

* An account in the Maori language of the finding of the Awhio-rangi axe appeared in the Maori newspaper *Te Korimako* in 1888 and was republished in English in the *Journal of the Polynesian Society* in 1900. The account was written by Wiremu Kauika of the Nga-Rauru tribe of Wai-totara, near Wellington. It stated that all people in the North Island of New Zealand had heard of Awhio-rangi, but none had seen it since a certain ancestor had hidden it seven generations earlier. A girl called Tomai-rangi, who had married into the Nga-Rauru tribe, but who was unfamiliar with its sacred places, had chanced to find it on 10 December 1887 when she 'saw something gleaming' while searching for edible fungus in a *pukatea* tree. Later, the people of the tribe went to look at it, recognising it as Te Awhio-rangi from descriptions that had been handed down to them. Next day, at 5 a.m., 300 people of the Nga-Rauru, Whanganui and Ngati-Api

(Continued overleaf)

the reputed 'heavenly origin' of the two axes possibly meant that they were brought from the fatherland of the Polynesians' ancestors.[29]

Smith's volume on Io and the other lore of the Whare-wananga was enthusiastically received and accepted by Best and other Maori scholars of the time. But most scholars of recent years have tended to dismiss it as an unreliable compendium of ancient Maori knowledge and beliefs.[30] The noted part-Maori scholar Sir Peter Buck (Te Rangi Hiroa) was among those who found the Io cult impossible to accept in its entirety. In his book *The Coming of the Maori,* he said that the Io version of the separation of light from darkness, the division of the waters, and the creation of the earth were 'too reminiscent of similar episodes in the first chapter of Genesis.' Moreover, he and other scholars were suspicious of the fact that both Te Matorohanga and his scribe Te Whatahoro had become Christians before details of the Io cult were written down. Buck himself concluded that no authentic proof existed for the concept of a supreme creator named Io, Kio or Kiho in Eastern Polynesia before 'dispersal to the various island groups took place.' He was also convinced that the concept of Io in New Zealand was a purely local development. As for the notions reminiscent of Genesis, these were simply 'post-European additions to the Io cult, made after knowledge was acquired of the Biblical story of creation.' As a final comment on the Io cult, Buck said:

> The separation of the spirits at Hawaikinui so that the righteous went through the east door to ascend to supernatural realms and the sinners through the south door to the Underworld, is contrary to the Maori and Polynesian concepts of the future world. It is too closely allied to the Christian teaching of heaven and hell to have originated in a house of learning before European contact.[31]

It is perhaps ironical that Buck, with his great learning, should have overlooked the fact that few, if any, Maoris ever learned to read and write without becoming Christians. So there was really no good reason to suspect Te Matorohanga and Te Whatahoro of tampering with the ancient Io lore on the ground that they had been converted before recording what they knew of it. It is even more ironical that Buck's conclusions about Io should have comprised the last words in *The Coming of the Maori,* for it now seems probable that there would have been no coming of the 'fleet' Maoris to New Zealand had it not been for a small party of Europeans who settled in Polynesia nearly three centuries earlier than Buck could have supposed. Indeed, there now seems to be an obvious reason why the canoes seen among the Maoris from Captain

---

tribes assembled to see it. 'In appearance this axe is ruddy (kura) like a china cup,' Kauika's article went on, 'but it is also like the breast of the Pipiwharauroa (the little cuckoo, i.e. striped), at the same time it is like nothing else. One's likeness can be seen in it. It is eighteen inches long and one inch thick, the edge is six inches broad, and the slope of the sharp edge is two and a half inches thick, and it is shaped like a European adze.' An editorial comment on Kauika's article in the *JPS* stated that the Rev. T. G. Hammond of Patea had obtained a sketch of the axe from a Maori who had seen it, and it was obvious from this that it was unlike the ordinary Maori axe in shape and size.—Smith 1900:229-33.

Cook's time onward did *not* resemble the plank-built vessels in which the Maori ancestors reputedly reached New Zealand.[32] The reason is that the ancestral Maori canoes were *not* built by Stone Age Polynesian sea-rovers, who, over the centuries, acquired skills that fitted them for daring voyages of exploration. Rather, they were the handiwork of expert Spanish seamen and shipwrights who were possibly trying to reach the Cape of Good Hope and so return to Spain when they chanced upon New Zealand. Finding their new discovery green and temperate, like the Cantabrian coast and mountains of their own Bay of Biscay, they decided, instead, to settle there. Being a big island, there was land for everyone. There was a Karioi o Whiro, or Loitering Place for Hiro; a place in the sun for everyone else. Plank-built sailing craft were therefore no longer necessary for long sea-voyages, so there was no need to pass on the knowledge of how to build them to their part-Polynesian sons. For sea-weary, middle-aged men such as Hoturoa, New Zealand was journey's end—the westernmost terminal point of the *San Lesmes* castaways. Yet it was not, apparently, the farthest point to which the influence of those castaways spread. That honour seems to belong to Easter Island, at the opposite, far eastern extremity of the Polynesian triangle. . . .

20

A new key to an old Easter Island mystery

Easter Island, the remote, mysterious, isolated land at the far eastern extremity of the Polynesian triangle, has long captured the imagination of scholars and the public generally. Its unique stone statues with their long, scornful faces, its gigantic altars, its strange bird-man cult, its curiously-carved, hungry-looking wooden figurines, and its inscribed wooden tablets or 'talking boards' are all so different from anything found in other parts of Polynesia that controversies over their origin have inevitably occupied much attention. Some scholars such as Heyerdahl have looked to the ancient civilisations of Bolivia, Peru, Ecuador and Colombia, more than 2,000 miles eastward, for the source of Easter Island's remarkable culture. Others with less scholarship, but more vivid imaginations, have talked in terms of vanished archipelagoes and submerged continents. And others again have insisted that everything can be explained by invoking the genius of far-ranging Polynesians from the west.[1]

Heyerdahl's view, to do him full justice, is that Easter Island's ancient culture was actually an amalgam of influences from both South America *and* Polynesia. This was also the opinion of Father Sebastian Englert, a Catholic priest who lived on Easter Island from 1935 until just before his death in 1969.[2] There are several strong reasons for accepting such views (see chapter 15). Yet even the notion that both American Indians and Polynesians came together on Easter Island does not seem sufficient to explain all of the island's mysteries. What the island also seems to need, historically, are immigrants of European origin, including some of Basque origin, to account for two extraordinary facts. One is that many Easter Islanders, when the early explorers encountered them, were markedly European in appearance. The other is that the present-day Easter Islanders and Basques appear to be closely related genetically, being unlike any other people in the world in one curious respect. Castaways from the *San Lesmes* again seem to be the key to this situation; and it is to them also that Easter Island's unique system of writing can apparently be traced. However, no one from the *San Lesmes* herself may ever have set foot on Easter Island. What probably happened is that descendants of castaways who had settled in the Society Islands were caught in a storm that carried them 300 miles southwards to Raivavae, and that from there some of *their* descendants were subsequently drifted to Easter Island.

Raivavae is one of four widely-scattered islands in a group known as the Australs. The others are Rimatara, Rurutu and Tubuai. Several instances are on record of canoes and boats having drifted involuntarily to those islands from Tahiti and its neighbours.[3] No voyages of the same kind have been recorded from the Australs to Easter Island. But such a voyage could have been made, as all those islands lie in a region where the winds blow from west to east for at least half the year.[4] Of the four islands, Raivavae, the easternmost, lying in 23 deg. 51'S., is the best situated to be the starting point. It is just over 2,000 miles north-west of Easter Island, which means that a canoe travelling at four miles an hour could reach that island in approximately three weeks.

Raivavae first became known to Europeans in February 1775 when the Spanish ships *Aguila* and *Jupiter* were sailing southwards from Tahiti to pick up a favourable wind for Peru. Sub-Lieutenant Bonacorsi, who tried to land in a boat, reported that the Raivavaeans were like the Tahitians—'some white, many mulatto-coloured, and the rest somewhat more swarthy.' He also said they were 'somewhat fairer-skinned' than the Tahitians, and that 'some looked like Europeans in hue.' The islanders had twin-hulled canoes with bows and sterns that sheered up high, and these were better-constructed and of better wood than those of Tahiti. Bonacorsi added that the name of the island was Oraibabae—a close approximation to the true name for a Spanish speaker who is apt to confuse his *b*'s and *v*'s.[5] The name suggests, moreover, that the people responsible for it had emanated from the Society Islands, for only in that group was the Polynesian word *rangi,* meaning sky or heaven, abbreviated to *ra'i.*[6]

Following the *Aguila's* visit, Europeans had little contact with Raivavae until 1813 when Captain Michael Folger of the brig *Daphne* obtained the first of several cargoes of sandalwood there.[7] A few years later, a native convert from Huahine settled on the island and introduced Christianity.[8] The Raivavaeans were then estimated to number not less than two thousand. They adopted the new religion *en masse,* and were looked on approvingly by two inspectors of the London Missionary Society who visited them in 1821. The inspectors noted that they had formerly worshipped a god called Oronuitipapa, a personification, they thought, of the (Raiatean) god Oro.[9]

During the next few years, Raivavae's population was stricken by an epidemic which soon reduced it to a few hundred and caused its ancient culture to disintegrate.[10] Meanwhile, its sandalwood was exhausted, and, as it had little else to offer that Europeans wanted, few Europeans subsequently had occasion to go there, apart from an occasional missionary or French government official. Virtually nothing was done to record Raivavae's ancient lore until J. Frank Stimson spent several months on the island in 1937. He made a second visit in 1940. His principal informants were two Raivavaean men, Tauira'i and Hapai, the latter being a resident of Tahiti. Stimson eventually completed a 2,000-page typescript on the ethnology of Raivavae, which was still unpublished when he died in 1958. However, in 1957, the American anthropologist D. S. Marshall had access to Stimson's work and used it as the basis for a new, on-the-spot investigation of some aspects of Raivavae's culture.[11]

In 1961 Marshall published the first book entirely devoted to Raivavae.

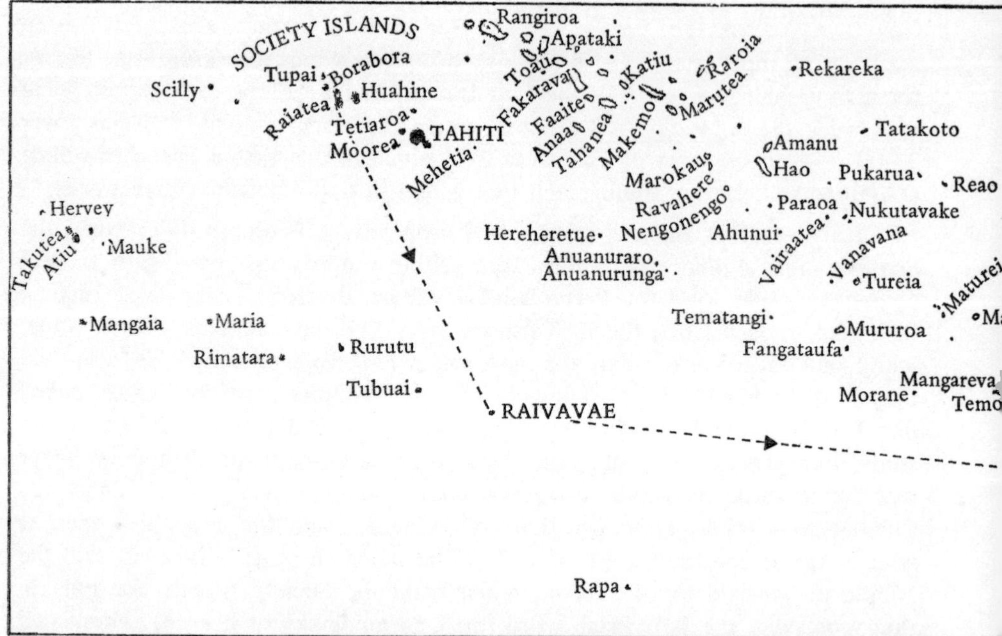

This contains several items which, in the light of the evidence in the foregoing chapters, strongly suggest European influences on Raivavae in pre-discovery times. One item is a statement that Raivavae's highest mountain, a peak of 1,434 ft, is called Mt Hiro.[12] Another is a statement that the Raivavaeans of the 1950s were still skilful builders of sewn, well-shaped, plank-built canoes with outriggers, although they were no longer using the double-hulled vessels—presumably *pahi*—that Bonacorsi described.[13] In addition, there are several photographs in Marshall's book that depict Raivavaeans who are so European in appearance that anyone who did not know them would almost certainly identify them as Europeans.[14] Two of these Caucasian-looking islanders were Stimson's informants, Hapai and Tauira'i—men of similar physical appearance to some of the sages of Anaa, Fangatau and Vahitahi who revealed to Stimson the lore of the esoteric god Kiho. On this account, it is interesting to note that one of Stimson's few published statements about the culture of Raivavae is that its language has 'marked resemblances' to that of Fangatau.[15] So it may well be that an examination of his Raivavae manuscript—which is now in the Peabody Museum at Salem, Massachusetts—would reveal other similarities in the cultures of the two islands.

One of the few scholars, other than Marshall, to have examined Stimson's manuscript is a German anthropologist, Thomas S. Barthel. Since the early 1950s, Barthel has been trying to decipher Easter Island's inscribed 'talking boards', which the islanders call *rongo-rongo*.*[16] Several items in Stimson's

* Barthel has found that the script consists of a vocabulary of about 120 basic elements which are combined to make 1,500 to 2,000 composite forms. Some of the signs represent flora that does not grow on Easter Island, such as the breadfruit tree, coconut palm and kava bush. Barthel believes the texts deal mainly with traditions and rituals, but that there is also a remnant of a kind of catalogue of tablets and their contents.

EASTER ISLAND in relation to RAIVAVAE and the SOCIETY ISLANDS

Broken line indicates apparent migration route of Hotu Matu'a

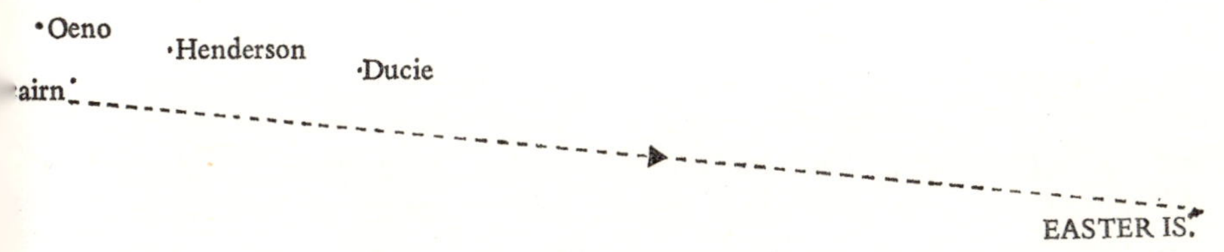

manuscripts have led him to suspect that Raivavae also had a system of writing in pre-contact times. These are legends that Stimson learned from Hapai, which claim that Raivavae once had 'carved wooden tablets of aligned glyphs called *taparakau*'. The tablets were six feet long and two wide, and were fastened over the doors of the priests' houses. They were incised with five rows of black guiding lines for carved signs to be engraved between them. The patterns of the symbols served the artists as models for tattooing or for the decoration of blankets and the clothes of people of high rank. The tablets were greatly venerated because they accurately transmitted ancestral knowledge as well as historical events. The priests knew the meaning of the signs and could recite the contents of the tablets by reading them.[17]

Barthel wrote in 1971 that Hapai's description of the Raivavae tablets was 'strikingly reminiscent' of *rongo-rongo* principles on Easter Island. In fact, some of Hapai's Raivavae terms were so similar to those of Easter Island that contact between the two islands could be assumed to have occurred at some time in the past. Moreover, as the Easter Island tablets revealed 'repeated and interlinking' references to Huahine and Raiatea, Barthel thought that those islands must have been the homeland of the 'literate immigrants' of Easter Island, whose leader, according to tradition, was Hotu Matu'a. Barthel therefore concluded that the Hotu Matu'a people must have reached Easter Island by taking a 'southern route' from the Society Islands to the Austral Islands, and proceeding eastward from there. This route, he believed, contrasted with that taken by earlier settlers of Easter Island who apparently originated in the Marquesas. Barthel added that the Hotu Matu'a immigration was thought to have occurred in 1400 A.D. 'plus or minus a century', and that the script carried to Easter

Island was 'an extract from that intellectual flowering of Polynesian culture which developed in the Leeward Islands [of the Society Group] . . .'[18]

Barthel expressed the view that proto-*rongo-rongo* must still have existed in the Society Islands about 500 years ago. He did not think the reason for its disappearance there could be reconstructed. But as the knowledge of writing 'must certainly have been limited to a small group of experts' it could easily have been lost by 'historical accidents'. Barthel went on to say that the system of writing might have been the discovery of 'a Polynesian school of priests in the Society Islands.' Alternatively, it could have been derived from a culture outside Polynesia that possessed a system of writing. However, Barthel claimed that 'neither of the two systems [of writing] recognisable in Ancient Peru' had any connection with *rongo-rongo*. And he cited another scholar, Fritz Kramer, as stating that attempts to find affinities with the writing of the Cuna Indians of Panama had proved abortive.[19] Barthel also made the point that the *rongo-rongo* signs followed a 'conventional canon of shapes' which clearly differentiated them from pictographs and brought them 'close to a genuine writing system.' Moreover, the signs seemed to reduce their messages to note form, so that their apparent purpose was to serve as 'memory joggers' or catchwords for the initiated.[20]

If *rongo-rongo* is, indeed, non-American in origin and close to a genuine writing system, and if Barthel has correctly deduced that it reached Raivavae and Easter Island from the Society Group, then it could well prove to have originated with the *San Lesmes* castaways. There seem to be only three objections to this proposition. First, Barthel's date for Hotu Matu'a's arrival on Easter Island—1400 A.D. 'plus or minus a century'—places the use of the script too far back in time. Second, the script bears no apparent resemblance to the Roman alphabet in use in Spain in the sixteenth century. Third, Barthel and other scholars agree that the script is written in reversed boustrophedon, i.e. the lines run horizontally from left to right, but every second line is inverted. These objections at first sight seem to rule out the possibility of a European origin. Yet none is really quite as formidable as it seems.

The first objection can be easily disposed of, as the date of Hotu Matu'a's arrival has been based only on genealogical evidence, or, to be more specific, lists of *ariki* or chiefs. Such evidence provides no means of knowing how many years should be allowed for a generation or reign; nor is there any certainty that each name in the lists represents a full generation or reign.[21] Moreover, there are six quite discrepant *ariki* lists.[22] One permits Hotu Matu'a's period to be calculated at approximately 475 A.D.[23] Others can be made to yield the uncertain figure mentioned by Barthel.[24] And then, again, it is possible to conclude, as Father Englert did, that Hotu Matu'a 'probably arrived in the sixteenth century.'[25] The genealogical evidence is therefore so imprecise that only two things can be said about it with certainty. One is that it substantiates local traditions that a person called Hotu Matu'a reached Easter Island in prehistoric times and left descendants.[26] The other is that among the Easter

Islanders whom Europeans have questioned, the island's history is reckoned to begin with him. The latter, of course, does not exclude the possibility that Easter Island was inhabited when Hotu Matu'a arrived there;* nor that he and some of his followers may have been of European origin.

This, therefore, reduces the number of objections to a European origin for *rongo-rongo* to only two: that it bears no resemblance to the Roman alphabet and is written in reversed boustrophedon. These objections can be countered in their turn by considering the only apparent alternatives, which are:

1. *Rongo-rongo* was invented on Easter Island or elsewhere in eastern Polynesia by a people with no previous knowledge of writing.

2. The script had its origin in Asia, and was carried to Easter Island by far-ranging Polynesians from the west, but all knowledge of it was lost in all the intervening islands, except Raivavae, before the era of European exploration.

3. The script was derived from a system of writing that once existed in South or Central America, of which all knowledge has now been lost.

If it is agreed that any one of the foregoing alternatives is a less likely explanation for the origin of *rongo-rongo* than its derivation from the script of sixteenth century Spain, then only the development of the *rongo-rongo* signs themselves and the manner of writing them remain to be explained. One possible explanation is that the signs were invented by the *San Lesmes*' castaways themselves as a sort of mnemonic shorthand when faced with a shortage of suitable writing material. Another, more likely explanation, is that *rongo-rongo* was developed by the castaways' Hispano-Polynesian children as a mnemonic system, after they had learned the rudiments of alphabetic writing from their fathers. Yet another possible explanation is that *rongo-rongo* is merely a series of meaningless symbols, developed by the castaways' children and their descendants in imitation of the castaways' writing system, which they themselves never learned.[27] As for the reversed boustrophedon—or perhaps, *apparent* reversed boustrophedon—manner of writing, this could have developed from European writing in two ways. One is through a writer turning his writing material upside down after completing a 'page' and then writing between the lines from bottom to top to conserve his material. The other is through a writer copying the *rongo-rongo* signs from each previous line upside down—in the manner of pre-school children and illiterate adults.

Of the foregoing suggestions, possibly the second of the first three and the first of the other two come nearest to the truth. It should be noted, in any case, that the *rongo-rongo* characters always proceed from left to right whether the tablets are held right side up or upside down. So it may be further stated that the script is not like those of China and Japan which are written perpendicularly. Nor is it like most Semitic scripts that run from right to left.[28]

* Most people when asked about their nation's past will take an event in the history of their own race as a starting point—not an event in someone else's history. Thus, most white Australians will hark back to Captain Cook's discovery of the east coast of Australia or the convict settlement at Botany Bay. They will ignore the fact that Aborigines had occupied their continent for thousands of years.

In short, a better case can be established for a European origin for *rongo-rongo* than any other. It should therefore follow that some of the inhabitants of Easter Island, when the first European explorers encountered them, should have been light-skinned and should otherwise have looked like Europeans. This, indeed, was certainly the case.

When Roggeveen, the Dutch explorer, discovered the island in 1722, his companion Carl Friedrich Behrens recorded that the islanders, in general, were 'brown, like the Spaniards', but that some were 'pretty black', others 'quite white', and others again of a reddish complexion as if burnt by the sun.[29] Roggeveen himself wrote that the natural colour of the people he saw was 'not black, but pale yellow or sallow.' He also mentioned that they had sewn, plank-built canoes with 'high and sharply tapering prows'—reminiscent of those seen by Bonacorsi at Raivavae.[30] Forty-eight years later, when Captain Felipe Gonzalez visited Easter Island from Peru, two of his officers stated specifically that some of the islanders resembled Europeans. The chief pilot, Francisco Antonio de Agüera y Infanzon, recorded that those he saw did not look like the Indians of Chile, Peru or Mexico in any way—that their appearance was 'thoroughly pleasing, and tallying with Europeans more than with Indians'. They were tall, well-built and well-proportioned, he said. Their skin colour was 'between white, swarthy and reddish'. They were not thick-lipped or flat-nosed; and their hair colour varied from black and chestnut to red and a cinnamon tint.[31] The other officer, Juan de Hervé, also a pilot, described the islanders as having complexions like quadroons. They had smooth hair and short beards, and bore no resemblance to the South American Indians. 'If they wore clothing like ourselves they might very well pass for Europeans,' he added.[32] Hervé, who made a circuit of the island in a launch, also reported that no trees were seen capable of furnishing planks as much as six inches wide. As a result, the island had few canoes and those few were poorly made. Two that were seen were made of five extremely narrow boards 'fitted together with wooden pegs in place of nails.' They had outriggers to prevent them from capsizing. The same chronicler added that the islanders had fishing nets made of fibre 'after the fashion of our small nets.'[33]

After Gonzalez had been at Easter Island for six days, he sent 250 officers and men ashore to take formal possession of it for the Spanish Crown. This act was carried out under the command of a senior lieutenant and a document was drawn up to record the proceedings. For the 'greater confirmation of so serious an act,' some of the islanders were persuaded to attest the document 'by marking upon it certain characters in their own form of script.'[34] The islanders thereby demonstrated that they already knew how to write—the only recorded instance of such skill in Polynesia when European contact began.[35]

Four years after the Spaniards' visit, Captain Cook spent five days at Easter Island during his second voyage to the Pacific. He himself was sick at the time, made only one brief excursion ashore, and relied chiefly on others for his account of the island. One of his collaborators was the astronomer William

Wales who noted that the first islander to board Cook's ships was a man of about fifty years of age whose features 'did not seem to differ materially from those of Europeans'. The man's complexion was a dark copper colour, his eyes a dark brown, his hair black, and his beard black and bushy.[36] Another of Cook's collaborators, Lieutenant Pickergill, recorded seeing a man 'seemingly of some note' whose skin colour was 'some thing whiter than the rest'. He was a 'stout made man', with a fine open countenance. His face was painted, his body tattooed, and his cloak was somewhat better than those of the other islanders.[37] Cook himself described the Easter Islanders as 'well-featured' and with 'agreeable countenances'. They were generally slim and black-haired, and seemed to him to be of the same race as other Pacific islanders he had seen because of the affinity of language, skin colour and some of their customs. However, he thought they resembled the Tongans and New Zealanders more than the Tahitians and Society Islanders.[38]

The French explorer J. F. G. de La Pérouse, who called at Easter Island in 1785, did not describe the inhabitants.[39] But nineteen years later, the Russian explorer Urey Lisiansky remarked that the islanders seen by his men were all stoutly built and tall, and of a colour resembling 'a sun-burnt European.' One man had a bushy brown beard.[40] Lisiansky's countryman, Otto von Kotzebue, wrote in 1816 that a few of the islanders were 'rather white', but generally they were copper-coloured.[41] In 1825, Captain Beechey described the islanders' skin colour as 'lighter than that of the Malays.' He added that their hair was generally black, but that of one man he saw was a reddish-ash grey. Beechey thought the islanders were a handsome race, particularly the women. They had 'fine oval countenances,' smooth, high-rounded foreheads, and well-proportioned aquiline noses. The men were notable for their 'regular features.'[42]

Several of the early explorers remarked on the Easter Island customs of perforating and distending the ear lobe, and of tattooing the body extensively. The accounts of lobe distension by such visitors as Roggeveen, Cook and J. R. Forster have given some scientists the impression that this practice was universal.[43] This, however, was certainly not the case. Some chroniclers, including those of the Gonzalez expedition, did not even mention the practice and presumably saw no examples of it. Lisiansky stated emphatically that the ears of all the islanders his officers saw were 'no longer than ours,' and he concluded that 'the fashion of expanding the ears' had probably come to an end.[44] Beechey, for his part, found that while the 'hideous practice' of lobe distension was still in use, it was 'not so general as formerly.'[45] On the other hand, Beechey said that tattooing was practised 'to a greater extent than formerly'—in contrast to Roggeveen who said that many youths he saw were not tattooed.[46]

As Beechey had not previously visited Easter Island, and as his stay was brief, his statements were largely guesswork. Yet his impressions appear to be borne out by two modern traditions. One is that in pre-contact times, the inhabitants were divided into two main tribes—one that distended the ear lobe and one that did not. The other is that those with long ear lobes were eventually

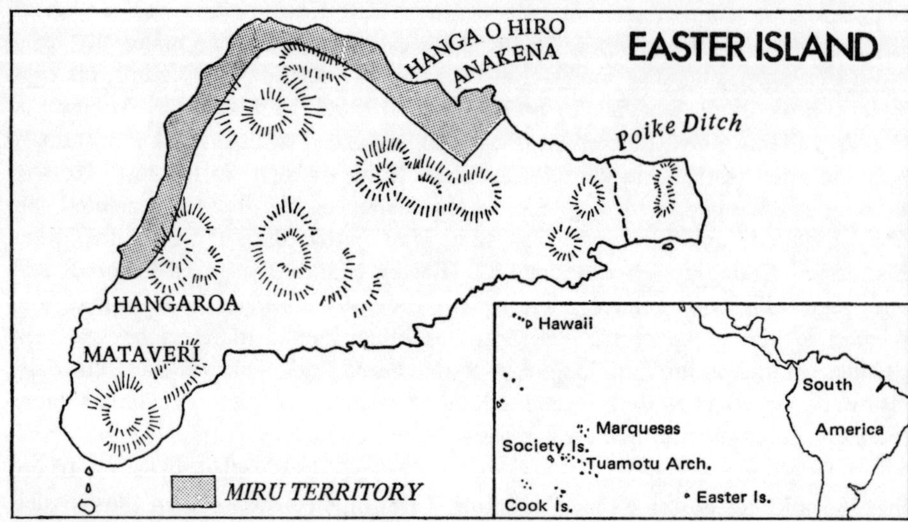

defeated in war and almost annihilated. Thus, the result may well have been that lobe distension had fallen into disuse by Beechey's time, and that the survivors among the vanquished had adopted the customs of the victors, including extensive tattooing.

According to tradition, the names of the two tribes of pre-contact times were Hanau Eepe and Hanau Momoko. These names are usually translated as Long Ears and Short Ears respectively, although the first, according to Father Englert, really means 'stocky or heavy-set people' and the other, 'slender people.'*[47] The Long Ears were evidently the builders of the great stone statues, as the statues themselves have long ears.[48] The great number of them—well over six hundred—makes it clear that their sculptors reached Easter Island many centuries ago.[49] Carbon-dated material from a recently-excavated temple site suggests 400 A.D. or thereabouts as a 'reasonable' date for the initial settlement of the island.[50] In view of this, it is not surprising that there are no reliable traditions as to where the Long Ears came from. However, several items of evidence (see p. 192-3 and Appendix F) strongly suggest that they originated in South America. If they did, they may have reached Easter Island directly or by way of the Marquesas, or they may have come from both places.[51] Whatever the truth was, the Long Ears are said to have spoken a different language from the Short Ears, and it was Father Englert's belief that relics of this might still exist in the present-day Easter Island language.[52] On the other hand, there is no evidence that the Long Ears knew *rongo-rongo,* as no examples of that script have been found on any statues or other stone work.[53]

That the Short Ears were much later arrivals than the Long Ears is suggested by the fact that traditions about the coming of the Short Ears are still

* Father Englert's statements on these points, as well as his interpretation of some traditions concerning the Long Ears and Short Ears, are open to dispute. *Epe* (one initial 'e') is the Easter Island word for earlobe, and *moko* or *momoko* is the Maori word for 'tattoo'.

well-known. The Short Ears were the people of Hotu Matu'a. Except in one discredited tradition, they are invariably said to have come from the west. They arrived in two double canoes, landing at Anakena on the north-east coast. Two spots near their landing place were named in honour of Hiro, these being Hanga o Hiro and Hiro Moko.[54] Hiro was subsequently invoked as the god of rain, as is shown in a fragment of an ancient hymn:

> O rain, long tears of Hiro,
> Fall,
> Strike the ground
> O rain, long tears of Hiro.[55]

Although the Short Ears and Long Ears lived apart, intermarriage is said to have occurred, so there was probably some cross-culturation. The war that eventually broke out between them was reputedly fought at the eastern end of the island, near a gully now known as the Poike Ditch. The Long Ears had hoped to drive the Short Ears into the gully and burn them alive. But through the treachery of a Long-Eared woman who was married to a Short Ear, the Short Ears turned the tables on them.[56] The war apparently occurred either just before or just after Roggeveen's visit. Several pieces of evidence support this supposition. One is that archaeologists have recently carbon-dated charcoal from the Poike Ditch to 1676 A.D. plus or minus a century.[57] Second, the genealogical researches of Father Englert have revealed that one Long Ear who survived the war and left descendants must have been born in the latter half of the seventeenth century.[58] Third, the islanders' attitude towards the stone statues underwent a drastic change around the time of Roggeveen's visit.

As far as may be gathered from Roggeveen's account, all the stone statues were intact in his time and apparently venerated—at least by the Long Ears. However, during the next century or so, the statues were deliberately toppled from their platforms, apparently in acts of contempt by the Short Ears. Cook wrote in 1774 that the statues, in his opinion, were 'not looked upon as Idols,' while Pickersgill and Wales remarked on the large number of images lying on the ground. La Perouse found even more thrown down in 1785. A French captain, Du Petit-Thouars, was hard put to find any still upright in 1838. And by 1864, when a French missionary, Brother Eugene Eyraud, became the first European to take up residence on the island, every statue had been desecrated or overthrown.[59]

Eyraud's arrival closely followed a tragic series of events that brought an end to Easter Island's ancient culture and obliterated much of the knowledge of the past. In 1862, a flotilla of Peruvian ships had abducted between 800 and 1,000 of the islanders to work on the guano islands off the Peruvian coast. Diplomatic protests soon forced the Peruvian government to agree to repatriate the islanders. But many died of disease, ill-treatment and homesickness before this could be done. The few survivors who did reach home carried smallpox with them that quickly decimated their remaining compatriots. Some of those who escaped the scourge later went to Mangareva and Tahiti. The result was that by 1877 the island's population had dropped to a record minimum of 110, compared with possibly three or four thousand in Roggeveen's time.[60] All modern Easter Islanders are descended from about fifteen couples among those 110 people, plus some who returned from Tahiti and Mangareva. However, there has been some intermarriage with outsiders, particularly since Chile annexed the island in 1888.[61]

When Eyraud arrived in 1864, the population stood at about 1,200. It was scarcely a time for detailed ethnographic observations, as smallpox was raging and many of the people were dying. Nevertheless Eyraud noted that, in build, the islanders were more like Europeans than other islanders in Oceania. Moreover, their complexion, although somewhat coppery, was 'not far removed from that of the European.' Eyraud also noted—and he was the first to do so—that all the islanders had *rongo-rongo* tablets in their houses, although they did not seem to understand their meanings or show much respect for them.[62] Several years later, another missionary collected several *rongo-rongo* tablets and tried unsuccessfully to learn their meanings.[63] Meanwhile, the islanders had adopted Christianity, and, apparently because they associated the tablets with their old religion, they either destroyed them or hid them in subterranean caves. As a result, only a few ever found their way into European hands.[64]

The first European to make a serious effort to learn the secrets of *rongo-rongo* was Bishop Jaussen of Tahiti. In the 1870s, he located an Easter Islander called Metoro Tauara, then living in Tahiti, who claimed to have been taught to chant from the tablets. However, when Metoro chanted from tablets in the bishop's possession, the bishop could not make much sense of his performance.[65] Others later obtained similarly disappointing results from other islanders; and several scholars have since expressed the view that Metoro and his compatriots could not really 'read' *rongo-rongo*—they either recited memorised texts that were unrelated to the tablets, or merely described the characters on them.[66]

Mrs Scoresby Routledge, an English archaeologist, who visited Easter Island in 1914, wrote in her book, *The Mystery of Easter Island,* that the knowledge of *rongo-rongo* was confined to only a few people, all of whom were members of the Miru clan. This clan lived on the central north coast, and was said to be descended from Hotu Matu'a. The Miru were unique in other ways. They were the only group on the island who had a headman, or chief. He was known as the *ariki,* or sometimes *ariki-mau* (great chief), to distinguish him from the *ariki-paka,* a term apparently applied to other members of his clan. The office of *ariki-mau* was hereditary, and he was the only man who was obliged to marry into his own clan. When he was old and feeble, it was customary for him to resign in favour of his son.

> The last man to fill the post of *ariki* with its original dignity [Mrs Routledge wrote] was Ngaara; he died shortly before the Peruvian raid, and becomes a very real personage to anyone inquiring into the history of the island. He was short and very stout, with white skin, as had all his family, but so heavily tattooed as to look black. . . . It was not permitted to see

PLATE 21. Sydney Parkinson's well-known sketches, such as that above, have helped to create an impression among Europeans that the Maoris of Captain Cook's day were a straight-haired, alien-looking people. Other early artists depicted some Maoris quite differently. An example is the watercolour portrait at right, attributed to the Rev. Samuel Leigh in 1823, of a chief called Te Puhi, otherwise 'King Tabooha', who appears to live up to Dr. Karl Scherzer's statement in the 1850s that some full-blooded Maoris had such a European aspect that even the 'numberless tattoo marks upon their faces' did not destroy that impression. The portrait is reproduced by courtesy of the trustees of the Methodist Missionary Society, London.

Two mysterious objects in the National Museum, Wellington—the Tamil bell found by the Rev. William Colenso in the Whangarei district of the North Island in the 1830s and the so-called Spanish helmet, reputedly dredged up from Wellington Harbour late last century.

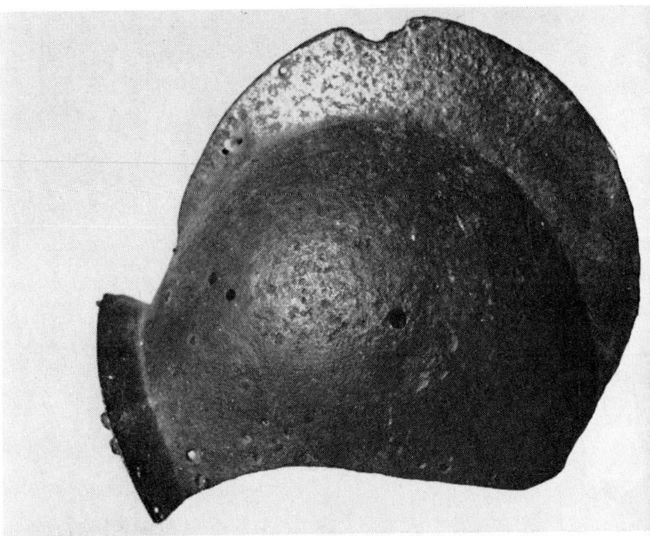

PLATE 22. The Trukese men pictured on this page were all photographed by members of the German South Seas Expedition which visited Micronesia before World War I. The Caucasian appearance of the four men at left and above is strikingly emphasised when compared with those in the lower photograph, despite their ponchos and elongated ear-lobes.

PLATE 23. *'A canoe of the Sandwich Islands, the rowers masked' was the caption of this painting by Captain Cook's artist, John Webber, when it was originally published. The picture at left below is by the same artist. The possibility that the 'masks' of the Hawaiians were modelled on European helmets is evident when compared with the Spanish helmet at right below, which was engraved and dated 1557.*

PLATE 24. A rongo-rongo tablet from Easter Island photographed in Tahiti in the 1880s. Only about two dozen of these tablets now exist, scattered in museums around the world. Every second line of the rongo-rongo script is inverted. At left is Kaituoe, 'the nearest descendant of the last king' of Easter Island, as photographed by H. W. Whitaker of the USS 'Mohican' in 1886.

That Easter Island's rongo-rongo might have been developed by islanders who were familiar with, but had not mastered, a European script is suggested by these examples of a modern New Guinean 'script.' The 'script' was the work of an East Sepik man who had attended Bible school and an adult literacy class but had not actually learned to write. The man filled two exercise books with the 'script' about 1959-61 and claimed that it told the story of his ancestors. These examples were obtained for reproduction from Mr. Bryant Allen of the University of Papua New Guinea.

[him and his family] eat, and no one but the servants was allowed to enter the house. His headquarters were at Anakena, the cove on the island where, according to tradition, the first canoe landed. . . .[67]

Mrs. Routledge also noted the same variety of skin colours that Behrens described in 1722, and said that when collecting genealogies the islanders were 'quite ready to give the colour of even remote relations.'[68] Mrs. Routledge's genealogies, now in the library of the Royal Geographical Society, London, contain a number of notations that this or that person was light-skinned, fair-haired and blue-eyed.[69] Her information about the Miru clan and Easter Island's blond strain is therefore in keeping with the notion that Hotu Matu'a's most direct descendants were of the same ilk as, and similar in appearance to, the exclusive *hui arii* of Raiatea. Her information is also compatible with what is revealed in a photograph taken in 1886 by an American surgeon, H. W. Whitaker, who visited Easter Island in the USS *Mohican*. The photograph depicts an islander called Kaituoe, 'the nearest descendant of the last king.'[70] He is a man of about fifty years of age and so European in appearance that no one, not in the secret, would be likely to identify him as a Pacific Islander. Kaituoe, moreover, was apparently fairly typical of the Easter Islanders who survived the disasters of the 1860s and 1870s, for when Professor Macmillan Brown visited Easter Island in 1920, the European features of many islanders strongly impressed him. 'Even the small remnant of natives that now lives in Hangaroa, the one village of the island, show strong Caucasoid traces in their features and their hair,' he wrote. He added that their faces were 'as European-like as one would find in an equal number of the south of Europe;' that their complexions varied, but were often nearly white; and that in the sunlight their hair showed brown and frequently red.[71]

Such observations as the preceding are now backed by the discovery that the Easter Islanders and Basques are remarkably similar genetically. This discovery was made in 1970-72 when teams of geneticists around the world carried out experiments in forty-six isolated communities to try to determine the genetic relationships of the human race.[72] The geneticists analysed blood samples for the presence or otherwise of any one of a series of about two dozen proteins. For technical reasons, certain combinations of these proteins are so peculiar that they are unlikely to occur in two different populations by chance. Because of this, the series of proteins has been dubbed 'the marvellous new marker for anthropological study.'[73]

In the 1970-72 experiments—called histocompatibility tests—geneticists found that a combination of proteins called HLA-12 and W19.1 was frequent in Easter Islanders and Basques, but rare in other peoples. One team of geneticists analysed blood samples from forty-nine Easter Islanders of reputedly pure descent. Meanwhile, another team examined samples from 144 people with no known non-Basque antecedents in the Basque village of Macaye on the French side of the Pyrenees. Eighty-eight of the Basques were unrelated. The experiments revealed that 39 per cent of the eighty-eight Basques and 37 per cent of the Easter Islanders had blood containing the protein HLA-12—the highest and second highest proportions in the world. The figures for W19.1 were similar. The Easter Islanders, with 37 per cent, had the highest proportion in the world, while the Basques were second with 24 per cent. Much more significantly, the two proteins were found together in 11 per cent of the Easter Islanders and 7.9 per cent of the Basques. No other peoples in the world had figures remotely resembling these. In fact, the combination was not found at all in Asia or the Americas, nor in Fiji and New Guinea, the only Pacific territories apart from Easter Island where tests were carried out.[74]

The geneticists who did the Easter Island experiments reported that in seeking out islanders of pure descent, they used genealogical data compiled by Father Englert. They also interviewed several of the oldest inhabitants about their knowledge of foreign admixtures. 'We aimed,' they said, 'at selection of individuals where no known foreign admixture had taken place, even from other Polynesian islands . . .'[75]

The team who blood-tested the Basques of Macaye said in their report:

> Fifty years ago it was suggested that the Basques were the last representatives of the primitive races . . . who lived in Europe during the late paleolithic period. Two waves of invaders, one coming from the East (the Alpine race) and the other from the South East (the Mediterranean race), forced the withdrawal of the Basques in the area west of the Pyrenees mountains. Under the shelter of the mountains, the Basques escaped the Eastern European invasions, preserving the biological and cultural inheritance of their ancestors . . . Inspired by such data, and incited by the peculiarities of their blood group distribution . . . , we invested our efforts in the study of this people. We chose a small village, Macaye, situated in a basin surrounded by mountains in the heart of the French 'Pays Basque.' [Our investigations] confirmed a very small radius of marriage beyond the limits of the village and no marriage with non-Basques.[76]

As the foregoing indicates, but does not entirely make clear, the people of Macaye are closely related to the Basques on the Spanish side of the Pyrenees, not only of today, but of many centuries past. This means that some of the Basque seamen whom Elcano recruited to sail in the *San Lesmes* and other ships of Loaisa's fleet must have carried the protein pair HLA-12, W19.1. The results of the histocompatibility tests of 1970-2 therefore seem to offer irrefutable answers to two of the four questions posed in chapter 3. One is that the four cannon of Amanu did come from the *San Lesmes;* the other that at least some of the caravel's crew survived to marry the local women and pass their distinctive genes down the centuries to the Easter Islanders of today. No precise answers can be given on the extent of the castaways' genetic, cultural and social influence in other parts of the Pacific. But the example of Easter Island leaves no doubt that it was remarkably widespread.

21

The legion of lost ships

In the two and a half centuries between the disappearance of the *San Lesmes* and Cook's first voyage to the Pacific, no less than a dozen European ships are known to have vanished in the 'trackless immensity' of the central Pacific, to use a Carlylean phrase.[1] As with the *San Lesmes,* historians, anthropologists, archaeologists and others have paid scant attention in the past to these lost ships. On coming upon such tragic words in the records as '. . . and so the frigate was lost to sight, never to be seen again. . . ,' they seem invariably to have assumed that the people on board were forthwith swallowed up by the sea, leaving no trace. Some such fate does, indeed, seem to have overtaken the crews of some of the lost ships. But not all of them. At least half apparently reached the safety of dry land, where, deprived of the means of returning home or of continuing their voyages, they settled down to make the best of things—intermarrying with the local women and adding their mite to the local culture. There is evidence that this happened in three widely separated parts of the Pacific—the Caroline Archipelago, the Solomons-Gilberts area, and the Hawaiian Islands. And in two of those areas, it seems to have happened more than once. In short, the loss of the *San Lesmes* was not an isolated incident: it was re-enacted several times over.

At least three ships were probably lost in the Carolines before the end of the sixteenth century. The first two were the caravel *Santiago,* of forty-five men, and the brigantine *Espiritu Santo,* of fifteen. They were units of a fleet of three ships that Cortes despatched from Mexico in 1527 on a twofold mission. One objective was to try to discover what had become of Magellan's ship *Trinidad,* whose fate was unknown after Elcano left her in Tidore with a cargo of spices in 1521. Secondly, they were to seek news of the Loaisa expedition, whose ships (including the *San Lesmes)* had not been heard of since they became separated near the Strait of Magellan in mid-1526. The *Santiago* and *Espiritu Santo* left Mexico in company with a third ship, the caravel *Florida.* They remained together in about 11° N. latitude until reaching the northernmost of the Marshall Islands. Then a squall blew up which drove the *Santiago* and *Espiritu Santo* quickly ahead of the *Florida,* never to be heard of again.[2]

Sixteen years later, the Spanish explorer Villalobos came upon an island in the Caroline Archipelago, immediately west of the Marshalls, where some islanders came out to his ships, hailed his men in perfect Spanish, and made the sign of the cross. *'Buenos dias, matelotes,'*—'good day, sailors,' they said. Villalobos accordingly named their island Isla de Matelotes, but as he could find

A Trukese woman using a Peruvian-style loom—a device used only in the central Carolines. This sketch and the one opposite are both from a book by Augustin Kramer, who visited the Carolines with the German South Seas Expedition of 1908-10.

no anchorage, he sailed on. Three days later, he came to another, bigger island in the same latitude where other islanders rowed out to his ships and gave the same salutation as before. Again no anchorage could be found, and Villalobos continued on his way, having named his second landfall 'Arrecifes' (Reefs).[3]

The two islands in question were Fais and Ulithi. Although they were among the first in the Carolines to be 'officially' discovered by Europeans, they were little known to the Western world until the United States navy used Ulithi as a base during World War II. Shortly afterwards, an American scholar, Professor William A. Lessa, began an anthropological study of the people of the two islands. Many of them, he found, had a 'strong European cast of features' and there was 'a fair amount of blondism.' In fact, some Ulithians seemed merely 'tanned Caucasoids.' However, as Lessa did not link the lost ships *Santiago* and *Espiritu Santo* with the Spanish-speaking islanders whom Villalobos encountered, he could not adequately explain his curious discovery. On the one hand, he suggested that some unidentified Spaniards might have 'stopped by' in the early days of Pacific discovery, leaving behind some 'gravid women.' Alternatively, he thought that some 'ancient white strain'—again unidentified—might have intermingled with the Carolinians before they left the Asian continent.[4]

Descendants of the castaways of Ulithi and Fais evidently spread to many islands of the central Carolines. One man who recorded information indicating this was Father Juan Antonio Cantova. In 1721, when some islanders from Faraulep Atoll were drifted to Guam, he was much struck by their light skins and European appearance. 'The colour of some is like that of pure Indians,' he wrote, 'there can be no doubt that others are mestizos, born of Spaniards and of Indians.'[5] Other writers later wrote to similar effect about the people of other atolls. And from their comments it may be inferred that castaways from the *Santiago* and/or *Espiritu Santo* became chiefs and made some impact on the culture of the region. In particular, they seem to have influenced both the navigational techniques and religious beliefs of some islands. In addition, they apparently introduced their system of writing, which, in subsequent years, degenerated into a non-alphabetic script, like Easter Island's *rongo-rongo*.[6]

The third European ship that apparently ended her days in the Carolines was the frigate *Santa Catalina*. She was one of the ships of the Mendaña expedition that tried to form a settlement on Ndeni Island, some 200 miles east of the Solomon Islands, in 1595. The frigate was lost in December of that year after the Ndeni settlement had been abandoned and Mendaña's fleet was heading northward for the Philippines. As the fleet approached the Caroline Islands, the *Santa Catalina,* which was leaking badly, fell behind her companions and was never afterwards heard of. At the time, she probably had thirty to forty people on board—Spaniards, Peruvian Indians (including women), and Negroes.[7]

More than three centuries later, ethnologists working on the seldom-visited island of Truk found that some of the islanders were strikingly European in appearance, while some aspects of their culture were both unique in the Carolines and oddly reminiscent of ancient Peru. Specifically, the islanders wore long ponchos woven on American-style looms, they distended their ear lobes, and mummified the dead.[8] However, as the disappearance of Mendaña's *Santa Catalina* had long been forgotten, no one could suggest how these curious practices could have been brought to Truk, together with people of apparently Caucasian origin. . . .

But the *Santa Catalina* was not the only ship of the Mendaña expedition to end her days in the great South Sea. Some ten weeks before she limped into oblivion, the *almiranta Santa Isabel,* one of the largest ships in the fleet, was lost in a fog as the fleet was nearing Ndeni. Although Mendaña caused an extensive search to be made for her, she had vanished as completely as if she had never been.[9]

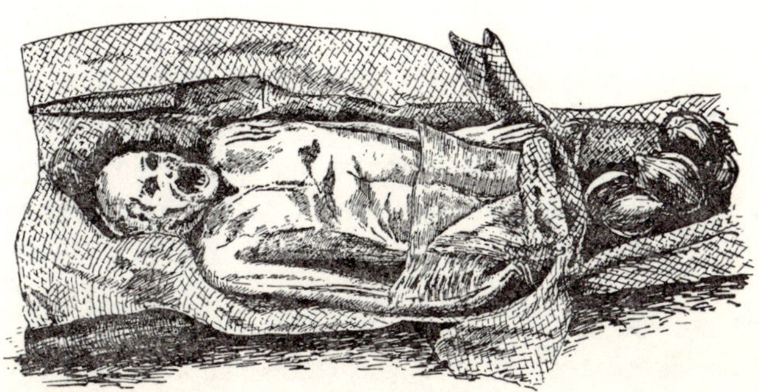

Like the loom, the mummification of the dead on Truk was typically Peruvian. The practice was not found elsewhere in the Carolines.

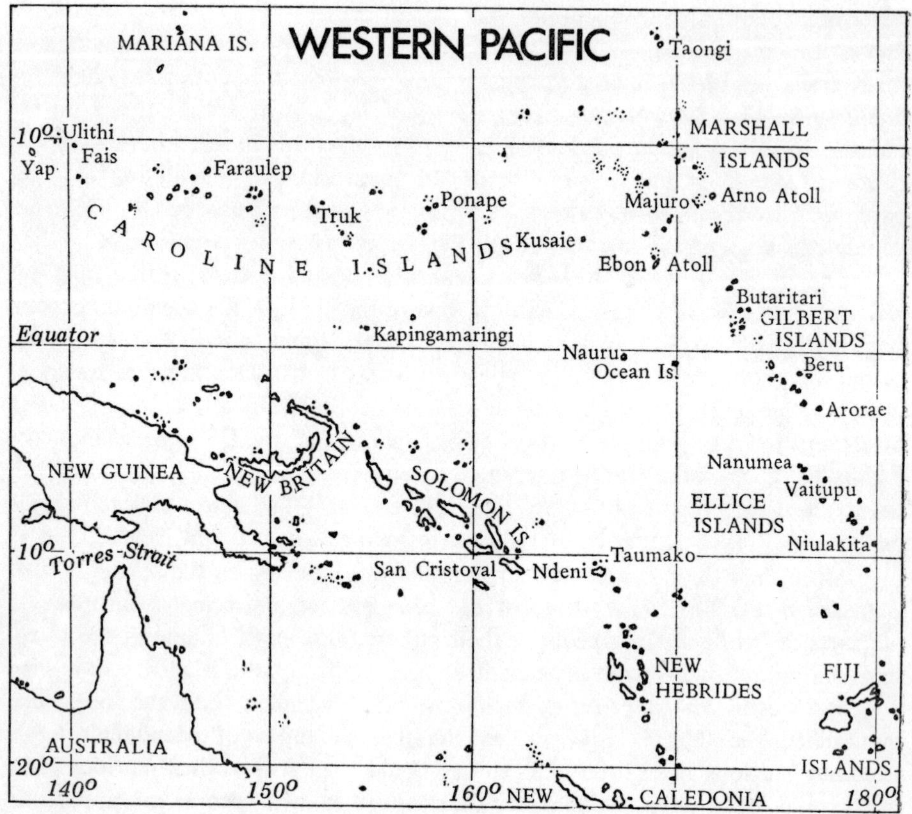

It was not until 1971, 376 years later, that two archaeologists, Jim Allen and Roger Green, made some discoveries that enabled the veil of mystery to be positively lifted for the first time. At a place called Pamua, on San Cristobal, one of the largest of the Solomon Islands, they found some broken pottery and other items that clearly established that the *almiranta's* passengers and crew had camped there for a short time.[10] But what became of them after that is still a mystery, although various possible clues have come to light over the past three and a half centuries or so. In brief, it seems that after the *almiranta's* captain had waited in vain for the other ships of Mendaña's fleet to appear, he set out from Pamua either to reach the Philippines or return to Peru. Whatever his intention was, the *almiranta* apparently did not get beyond the Gilbert Islands, from which point she turned southward until she finally reached Taumako, to the south-west of the Ellice Islands. Many of the passengers and crew died en route from hunger and thirst.

Among the evidence that suggests the foregoing reconstruction is a Gilbert Islands tradition about a white man who landed on Beru Atoll fifteen generations before the 1920s. He came ashore from a 'canoe without an outrigger, shaped like a box.' He had the bones of a giant, a white skin like a garfish's belly, and a narrow face 'like the blade of an adze.' In addition, he had red hair and a flaming beard. Although he was almost dead when he got ashore, he eventually recovered, took eight sisters of a local chief to wife, and became the father of twenty-three children. By the 1920s, his descendants were said to have become scattered over fourteen of the sixteen islands of the Gilbert Group.[11]

Other evidence about the ultimate fate of the *Santa Isabel* seems to have been gathered by members of the Quiros expedition when they touched at Taumako in 1606. In fact, one survivor of the lost ship was apparently then living there. This was a young man whose skin was so white and who was 'so brown as regards beard and hair' that the Spaniards dubbed him 'the Fleming,' although they learned that his name was Olan. The Spaniards also reported seeing the islanders eating meat which they were given to understand came from an animal with horns—something unknown in the Pacific in pre-European times. Moreover, Quiros learned from an islander whom he took to Mexico that some time earlier a large ship had arrived at Taumako. On board were seven men who were 'very white' and one who was brown, plus three women who were 'white and beautiful as Spanish.' The women had very long red hair, and were covered from head to foot in a kind of veil, either blue or black. Their ship was said to have come from an island called 'Guaytopo'—possibly Vaitupu in the Ellice Group—and to have had fifty people on board originally. However, forty had died of hunger and thirst before reaching Taumako; and the rest, except Olan, had died afterwards.[12]

Archaeological discoveries made at Taumako in 1801 and 1971 support the notion that it was at that island that the *Santa Isabel* ended her days.[13] However, there seems to be no evidence that either Olan or any of his companions left their genetic imprint at Taumako, nor that they significantly influenced its culture. The story of the *Santa Isabel* as it concerns Taumako is therefore quite different from those of the two or three ships that apparently left their bones in the Caroline Islands. Nor is it like those of some of the lost galleons of the Manila-Acapulco run, which, despite various opinions to the contrary, *do* seem to have deposited influential European castaways in the Hawaiian Islands long before Captain Cook discovered them in 1778.

The trade between Acapulco and Manila, it will be recalled, was inaugurated in the 1560s after the Spaniards proved the practicability of making return voyages between those points. For two and a half centuries thereafterwards, a year rarely passed without the passage of at least one galleon. Sometimes there were sailings in both directions; sometimes a sailing in only one direction, but with two or more ships. The voyages from Mexico were made about thirteen degrees north of the Equator; those back kept to the zone of the westerlies, well to the north of the Hawaiian Islands. The galleon captains were strictly enjoined to keep to their appointed tracks to avoid the low and dangerous Marshall and Caroline Islands. And so zealously did they follow their instructions that fewer than a dozen ships were lost in 250 years of

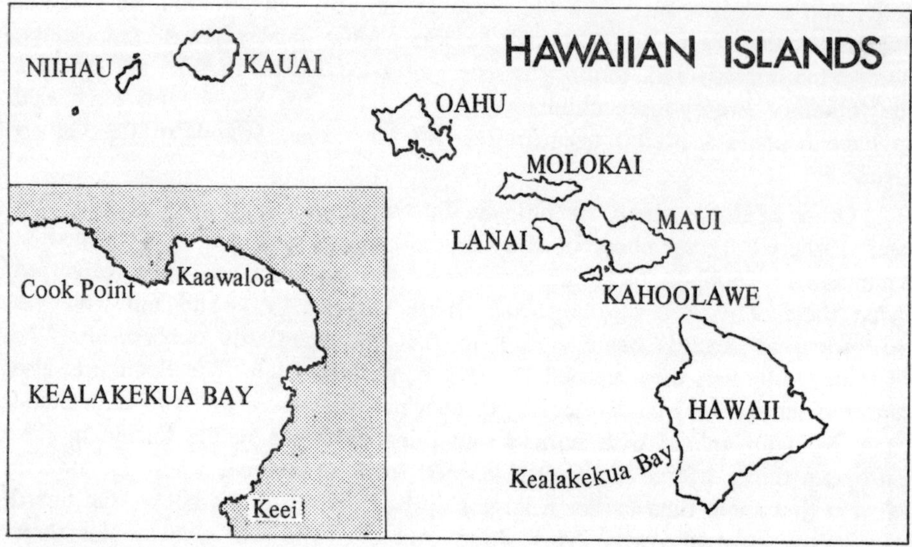

voyaging.[14] Of these, four were wrecked in the Mariana Islands;[15] one, whose name is unknown, disappeared after leaving Mexico for Manila in 1574;[16] and five never returned from voyages in the opposite direction. The five lost on the Manila-Acapulco run were: *San Felipe* (1576), *San Juanillo* (1578), *San Juan* (1586), *Santo Cristo de Burgos* (1693) and *San Francisco Xavier* (1705).[17]

It need scarcely be said that if any of the lost galleons were forced by storms to stray from their appointed course, they might well have been wrecked in the then-unknown Hawaiian Islands. Alternatively, if any of them had capsized in the early part of their voyages, some of their crews might have fetched up in Hawaii in boats. Such events in the case of four of the galleons would have occurred some two centuries before Cook's time. In the case of the other two, the events would have preceded his advent by less than a century. On the one hand, therefore, traditions relating to the arrival of European castaways could have been relatively fresh when Cook reached Hawaii; on the other, they could well have faded into the mist of semi-forgotten things.

Cook's discovery of Hawaii was made on his third voyage, as he was sailing northwards from the Society Islands in the *Resolution* and *Discovery* to search for the North-West Passage. He then touched at only two islands, Kauai and Niihau.[18] But in the following year, after almost twelve months in Arctic waters, he also called at the large islands of Maui and Hawaii.[19] He himself was killed at Kealakekua Bay, on the western side of Hawaii, on 14 February 1779—possibly by a type of weapon that castaway Spaniards had introduced to that island many years earlier. Certain it is, at any rate, that among the islanders at that time were some who wore remarkable helmets and feather cloaks, and who carried daggers called *pahoa*. Most of the daggers were of hardwood. But in a few instances, they were made of iron.

John Webber's sketch (left) of a Hawaiian man in his cape and helmet has often been reproduced. The picture of a similarly-attired Spaniard is from a history by Antonio Herrera y Tórdesillas published in Madrid in 1601-15.

The helmets, cloaks and daggers were in use from Kauai to Hawaii, which are almost three hundred miles apart. They caused some of Cook's officers to think that other Europeans had anticipated them in their Hawaiian discoveries. James King, the second lieutenant of the *Resolution,* wrote that the cloaks and helmets were 'a singular deviation' from the clothing worn in other parts of Polynesia and that they bore 'an exact resemblance' to those of Spaniards of former times. These factors prompted him to inquire whether there were 'any probable grounds' for supposing that the Hawaiian dress was, in fact, derived from Spain. Although his inquiries yielded no positive information, he concluded that the 'uncommon form of this habit' was 'sufficient proof of its European origin'. He added: 'We were driven, indeed, by this conclusion to a supposition of a shipwreck of some Buccaneer, or Spanish ship, in the neighbourhood of these islands. But when it is recollected that the course of the Spanish trade from Acapulco to the Manillas is but a few degrees to the Southward of the Sandwich Islands, in their passage out, and to the Northward, on their return, this supposition will not appear in the least improbable'.[20]

The *Discovery's* surgeon, David Samwell, who saw a man at Maui armed with 'two iron Skewers or Daggers', wrote in his journal that he and his companions supposed that these had come from ships that had previously touched at that island. 'But of this,' he added, 'we could get no clear information from the Indians'.[21] Several other officers expressed similar views.[22] But Cook himself was of the opinion that the iron seen among the Hawaiians was drift iron; and he thought 'the very great surprise they shewed at the sight of the ships and their total ignorance of fire arms' was proof that no European ships had visited the islands previously.[23]

For the time being, it was the opinion of Cook's officers that prevailed and gained currency. Thus, when the French explorer La Perouse visited Maui in 1786, he thought there were two factors that constituted 'new proofs of the communication which these islanders formerly had with Spaniards.' One was their familiarity with the art of bargaining; the other was their knowledge of iron, which, 'from their own confession,' he said, 'they did not acquire from the English.' La Perouse even produced a Spanish explorer, Juan Gaetan, as the discoverer of the Hawaiian chain. 'It appears certain that these islands were discovered for the first time by Gaetan, in 1542,' he said.*[24]

In 1798, an American seaman, Ebenezer Townsend, Jr, recorded further evidence in support of the Spanish discovery of the Hawaiian Islands. During a visit to Hawaii as supercargo of the sealing vessel *Neptune,* he wrote in his diary (which remained unpublished until 1888) that parts of a large European anchor had been found at Maui:

> It is very much doubted whether Capt. Cook was the first discoverer of these islands; it in fact appears pretty evident that he was not. . . . There is at Mowee the ring and part of the shank of an anchor of about seven hundred weight which was not long ago hooked up there, where there is no recollection of there ever having been a vessel, and from the appearance it must have been there a great many years. Mr. Young [a European resident since 1790] says they have a tradition that a couple of white men came on shore and remained there about one hundred and fifty years ago. They landed in a small vessel covered with skins and he had seen their descendants, which satisfied him of the truth of the story, and they were white.[25]

The LMS missionary William Ellis, who spent eighteen months in Hawaii in 1823-4 after eight years in the Society Islands, recorded three accounts of foreigners arriving in the Hawaiian Islands before Captain Cook. One concerned a solitary white man called Paao, who arrived in the time of Kahoukapu and became an important personage. He brought two idols or gods with him, which were added to the Hawaiian pantheon. Ellis was inclined to think that Paao might have been a Roman Catholic priest—'the only survivor of his party,' and that his two idols were an image and a crucifix.[26]

After Paao's death, his son Opiri was said to have acted as interpreter for a group of white men who landed somewhere on the south-west coast of Hawaii. These men lived in the mountains, and the Hawaiians treated them with great respect. They finally 'returned to their own country,' but no account was preserved of the kind of vessel in which they arrived or departed. In Ellis' view,

* Juan Gaetan was an Italian who sailed with Villalobos on his voyage from Mexico to the Philippines in 1542 (see chapter 4). He later gave details of the voyage to the Italian historian G. B. Ramusio, who published them in his *Delle Navigationi e Viaggi,* Venice, 1588. The Villalobos expedition did not go near the Hawaiian Islands; nor is there any reason to believe that Gaetan did so on any later voyage.—See Sharp 1960:66-8.

such people were possibly 'survivors of the crew of some Spanish ship wrecked in the neighbourhood, perhaps on the numerous reefs to the north-west.'[27]

> The third account [Ellis went on] is much more recent and precise, though the period at which it took place is uncertain.
>
> It states that . . . in the reign of Kahoukapu*, king at Kaavaroa, seven foreigners arrived at Kearake'kua bay, the spot where Captain Cook subsequently landed. They came in a painted boat, with an awning or canopy over the stern, but without mast or sails. They were all dressed; the colour of their clothes was white or yellow, and one of them wore a *pahi,*† long knife, the name by which they still call a sword, at his side, and had a feather in his hat. The natives received them kindly. They married native women, were made chiefs, proved themselves warriors, and ultimately became very powerful in the island of Hawaii, which, it is said, was for some time governed by them.[28]

Ellis also wrote of another party who were said to have arrived later at the same place. However, the accounts the islanders gave of them were 'not very distinct,' and he could not decide whether there were two separate landings or only two different accounts of the same event. He added that a chief of the island of Hawaii had told him of a tradition concerning a ship that had touched at Maui before Cook. But all the other chiefs had said they had no idea of a ship before those of Cook were seen off Kauai.[29]

In describing the Hawaiians generally, Ellis said they had 'open countenances' and features 'frequently resembling those of Europeans.' And in referring, in particular, to the foreigners who were reputed to have landed at Kealakekua Bay, and to have intermarried with the Hawaiians, he wrote:

> There are in the Sandwich Islands a number of persons distinguished by a lighter colour in the skin, and corresponding brown curly hair, called *ehu,* who are, by all the natives of the islands, considered as descendants of these foreigners, who acknowledge themselves to be such, and esteem their origin by no means dishonourable.[30]

Some of the stories that Ellis recorded were noted independently by Otto von Kotzebue, the Russian explorer, when he visited Hawaii in December 1824. Kotzebue's informant was Karemaku, 'the most distinguished and intelligent man in Hanaruro' (i.e. Honolulu). According to Kotzebue, the number of white men who had once come ashore at Kealakekua Bay was five, not seven as Ellis said. But in other respects the story that he learned was much the same. The white men were all given 'maidens of the highest rank' as their wives, and each was installed as governor of an island. Their descendants, Kotzebue was told, could still be distinguished by their 'whiter colour.' Kotzebue went on:

> The helmets and short mantles which Cook and King have described as worn by this people were introduced by these white strangers. At first, the kings only appeared in this costume; but in Cook's time it was common also among the Yeris [i.e. *alii* or chiefs]. Now that European fashions have quite

* The same chief mentioned in the tradition about Paao.
† Apparently an error for *pahoa.*

banished those of the original inhabitants, it is only preserved and shown to strangers as a relic of the past. The helmet, of wood covered with small red and yellow feathers, and adorned with a plume, perfectly resembles those of the chivalrous knights of yore; and the short mantle, also most ingeniously made with feathers to supply the want of woven stuff, forms a complete representation of the mantles worn by those ancient heroes: hence it is sufficiently evident that the white men who landed on O Wahi [Hawaii] were Europeans; and that we are therefore more nearly connected with, at least, a part of the inhabitants of the Sandwich Islands, than with the other South Sea islanders.

Kotzebue said that from the time of the first white king to Kamehameha (i.e. Kamehameha I who died in 1819), there had been 'seven successive reigns.' During this period, two vessels were said to have been wrecked on the coast of Hawaii, but tradition was not unanimous about what became of the crews. 'My informant, Karemaku, mentioned only one ship which was seen at a distance,' Kotzebue added, 'and although the iron anchors found at O Wahi [Hawaii] and at Muwe [Maui] prove that they must have been there, he could give no account of them.'[31]

Further information about the coming of white strangers to early Hawaii was published in 1838 by the Hawaiian historian David Malo. Like Ellis and Kotzebue, Malo fixed the spot where the strangers landed as being in Kealakekua Bay, but was more specific. He said their ship was wrecked on a point called the Pali of Keei. He wrote:

> In the time of Kealiiokaloa,* king of Hawaii and son of Umi, arrived a vessel at Hawaii. Konaliloha was the name of the vessel, and Kukunaloa was the name of the foreigner (white man) who commanded, or to whom belonged the vessel. His sister was also with him on the vessel.
>
> As they were sailing along, approaching the land, the vessel struck at the Pali of Keei, and was broken to pieces by the surf, and the foreigner Kukunaloa and his sister swam ashore and were saved, but the greater part of the crew perished perhaps; that is not well ascertained.
>
> And when they arrived ashore, they prostrated themselves on the beach, uncertain perhaps on account of their being strangers, and of the different kind of people whom they saw there, and being very fearful perhaps. A long time they remained prostrated on the shore, and hence the place was called Kulou, and is so called to this day.
>
> And when evening came, the people of the place took them to their house and entertained them, asking them if they were acquainted with the food set before them, to which they replied that they were; and afterwards, when breadfruit, *ohia,* and bananas were shown to them, they expressed a great desire to have them, pointing to the mountain as the place where to get them. The strangers cohabited with the Hawaiians and had children, and they became the ancestors of some of the Hawaiian people, and also of some chiefs.[32]

* Like the 'first white king' in Kotzebue's story, Kealiiokaloa flourished seven reigns before Kamehameha I—Fornander 1969:I:App. IX.

The traditions that Malo, Kotzebue and Ellis recorded about the Kealakekua Bay foreigners were widely known by the 1840s and were generally accepted as facts. Thus, when J. J. Jarves published his *History of the Sandwich or Hawaiian Islands* in 1843, he asserted that there was no 'reasonable doubt' that Europeans had visited Hawaii two centuries or more before Cook. 'The knowledge of such events has been perpetuated in numerous traditions which coincide with much collateral evidence,' he said. Jarves also mentioned La Perouse's statement about Juan Gaetan's discovery of Hawaii in 1842.[33] And before long, this, too, became part of Hawaii's lore, although the date of Gaetan's exploit was brought forward by thirteen years. 'There is little doubt,' wrote the Hawaiian historian W. D. Alexander in 1891, 'that the Sandwich islands were discovered by the Spanish navigator Juan Gaetano [sic] in 1555.'[34]

The Jarves-Alexander view on Hawaii's early contacts with Europeans prevailed among historians until 1916. Then a Swedish scholar, E. W. Dahlgren, upset all previous thinking on the subject with a solidly-researched monograph, *Were the Hawaiian Islands visited by the Spaniards before their Discovery by Captain Cook in 1778?* Having closely examined all evidence known to him, including everything discoverable on the Spanish galleons, Dahlgren concluded that: 'No historical fact proves, nor is there any sort of probability that the Hawaiian Islands were ever visited, or even seen by the Spaniards before . . . Captain Cook.'[35]

Over the next few years, an American ethnologist, J. F. G. Stokes, followed up Dahlgren's work with a series of papers in which he, too, discounted the possibility that the Spaniards may have anticipated Cook in his discovery of Hawaii.[36] Among the arguments that he and Dahlgren put forward were:

1. The Hawaiians' traditions were obscure and ambiguous and supplied no certain evidence that the foreigners mentioned in them were white men.[37]

2. Their genealogies were 'almost worthless' as historical testimony or as aids to fixing historical dates.[38]

3. The lighter skin colour of many Hawaiian families was 'undoubtedly due' to better food, freedom from bodily toil except martial sports, and constant attendance from servants, rather than to a mixture of European blood.[39]

4. Although the helmets of the ancient Hawaiians resembled those of the ancient Greeks, Etruscans and Romans, they did not resemble those worn by the Spaniards of the sixteenth century.[40]

5. All iron observed by Cook in Hawaii in 1778 had come as driftage.[41]

6. A piece of iron, which Cook's officers had thought was possibly the point of a European broadsword, was really a Japanese fish knife.[42]

7. There was 'little doubt' that the strange anchors mentioned by Kotzebue and Townsend had been 'stolen by natives and lost through coral cutting the cables' in post-Cook times.[43]

The arguments of Dahlgren and Stokes soon demolished the old belief in Spanish contact with Hawaii in pre-Cook times. The result was that it became unfashionable for local or Pacific historians to devote more than a passing reference to it. Thus, the Hawaiian historian Gerrit P. Judd wrote in 1961: 'At one time it was believed that Spanish voyagers of the Pacific chanced upon Hawaii on their regular trips between Panama [*sic*] and the Philippines. But in recent years the experts, who have sifted the evidence with care, have rejected this belief. At any rate, even if a stray Spanish vessel had encountered Hawaii, nothing came of it.'[44] Cook's erudite editor, J. C. Beaglehole, wrote in similar vein in 1967: 'It is hardly necessary to discuss the theory that [Cook] was not the first discoverer [of the Hawaiian Islands] . . . the scholarship of Dahlgren and the practical inquiries of Stokes seem to remove the matter beyond doubt.'[45]

In the light of the findings of Dahlgren and Stokes, and the respect with which their findings are held, it might seem presumptuous to revive the question of whether Hawaii did have contact with Europeans before Cook's time. Yet a glance at the main arguments of Dahlgren and Stokes will show that they were by no means conclusive. In fact, most of their arguments were little more than expressions of opinion, impossible to substantiate. Moreover, both Dahlgren and Stokes vitiated their conclusions by admitting, in the body of their writings, that European castaways may have settled in Hawaii in pre-Cook times. Thus, Dahlgren, after enumerating all the Spanish galleons known to have been lost in the Pacific, said: 'It is not incredible that one of these ships, or some other ships of which we have no knowledge, stranded on some rock or reef belonging to the Hawaiian group and that the shipwrecked men succeeded in reaching the inhabited islands in boats.'[46] Stokes, for his part, insisted that the iron seen among the Hawaiians in Cook's time was drift iron. Yet, he admitted that the Hawaiians might have acquired their knowledge of how to shape it from castaways.[47]

However, it is not so much the weaknesses and inconsistencies in the arguments of Dahlgren and Stokes that make it worthwhile to reconsider the possibility of European contact with Hawaii in pre-Cook times. It is the discovery of new evidence that cannot easily be brushed aside. The evidence comprises two non-Polynesian items found in the burial casket of a deified Hawaiian chief of pre-Cook times. The items are a piece of iron embedded in a wooden handle like a chisel and a length of woven cloth eight feet long by one wide. They were discovered by specialists at the Bishop Museum in the late 1950s.[48] But no word about them was published at the time because the specialists could not identify the material from which the cloth was made. Dr Emory, the museum's ethnologist, made several inconclusive attempts to do so. On 27 May 1957, for example, he wrote to Dr Junius Bird, a specialist in Peruvian archaeology at the American Museum of Natural History, New York:

> We have run into a real and significant problem which you could help us solve. In a casket of sennit braid, moulding the human form, and containing the bones of a deified chief who lived prior to the time of Captain Cook, was a loin cloth of the enclosed woven material. The Hawaiians, as you know probably, did not weave. . . . We are wondering if it is Mexican or South American. . . . There is no design or coloring of the material.

Bird eventually replied that the cloth, in his opinion, was not flax, jute, cotton or wool, that it was probably not linen, and was not of Peruvian manufacture. However, he thought it was possibly sailcloth* to which smudges of a reddish colour had been applied. He added that an examination of the web gave a thread count of 29 x 24 per square inch; and that if the cloth had been made in Mexico, it was *ixtil*.† An inquiry by Emory to a laboratory in Kew, England, proved even less rewarding, for there the experts stated that the material was too ancient to be identified, the elements in it having been destroyed. On the other hand, an inquiry in Japan revealed that the material was unlikely to have been of Japanese origin.

In the mid-1960s, Mr Francis B. Lothrop, an honorary trustee of the Peabody Museum at Salem, Massachusetts, made a new attempt to ascertain the identity of the cloth. Lothrop, a retired textiles manufacturer, soon ruled out the possibility of its being made of a bark fibre like that used by Indians on North America's North-West coast. He then turned to the suggestion that the material was possibly sailcloth, and began by examining four sailcloth-covered logbooks in the Peabody Museum. These were dated between 1783 and 1794, and yielded thread counts of 30 x 16, 31 x 26, 26 x 16 and 29 x 16. The logbook bindings were therefore in the same range as that of the Hawaiian cloth. Moreover, all had the same glossy appearance and, to Lothrop's practised eye, this suggested that the Hawaiian cloth was made of flax.

Later, the Peabody Museum obtained a small piece of sailcloth from the Swedish ship *Vasa* which sank near Stockholm in 1635. This, through having been under water for more than three centuries, was quite white. But otherwise, its appearance was remarkably similar to that from Hawaii. Furthermore, the thread count was 28 x 24—only one thread different from that of the Hawaiian cloth. Because of the language problem in communicating with Spanish museums, Lothrop did not pursue the question of whether the Spaniards were using a similar sailcloth in the sixteenth and seventeenth centuries. However, he wrote to the present writer in February 1972 that he had no doubt that the cloth was of Spanish origin, and that it had come from 'one of the galleons which never completed the trip from Manila to Acapulco.'[49]

Besides the apparent nature of the cloth itself, there are several reasons why Lothop's opinion seems likely to be correct:

1. The burial casket from which the cloth was obtained was once kept in a cave at Kaawaloa in Kealakekua Bay, where, according to the traditions recorded by Ellis, Kotzebue and Malo, a few white men once came ashore, were given wives, and became chiefs.[50]

2. The bones in the casket are thought to be those of an Hawaiian chief called Lono-i-ka-makahiki,[51] who is said to have been a nephew of Kealiiokaloa, the chief mentioned in Malo's tradition.[52]

3. Makahiki was the name of an ancient festival in which the Hawaiians

* i.e., canvas, an unbleached cloth made of hemp or flax.
† A fibre like henequen from which binder twine is made.

paraded an idol decorated with a length of tapa like a ship's sail. The idol was carved at the top of a long, mast-like pole, to which a cross-piece was attached like a ship's yard. The idol was called Lono-makua, meaning Father Lono.[53]

4. Captain Cook was named Lono after the god of the Makahiki festival, because of the 'resemblance the sails of his ship bore to the tapa of the god.'[54]

Lono-i-ka-makahiki is estimated to have flourished towards the end of the seventeenth century.[55] If this is correct, and if he was, indeed, a European castaway, then he is most likely to have come either from the lost galleon of 1693 or from that of 1705. In either case, he and his companions could not have left great numbers of descendants by Cook's time as there was only an interval of seven or eight decades. Nevertheless, whatever descendants there were should have been physically distinctive, just as the story of their ancestors' arrival should have been quite fresh on the lips of the Hawaiians when Ellis, Kotzebue and Malo recorded it. On the other hand, if the anchor at Maui that Townsend and Kotzebue mentioned was a relic of one of the lost galleons of the 1570s, then it would not be surprising if its origin had been forgotten by their time more than 200 years later. A band of European castaways might therefore have preceded the Kealakekua Bay foreigners by well over a century, and if they did, their descendants could easily have spread throughout the Hawaiian Islands by Ellis' time. The reason why many Hawaiians, in Ellis' view, had features 'resembling those of Europeans' could thus be explained. And so, too, could the widespread use of the Hawaiians' unusual daggers, capes and helmets.

Yet Dahlgren and Stokes do seem to have been right in asserting that the Hawaiian helmets look more like those of Greeks, Romans and Etruscans than those of Spain of the sixteenth and seventeenth centuries. On the other hand, any Spaniards cast away in the Hawaiian Islands might well have brought illustrated books with them containing pictures of helmeted Greeks, Romans or Etruscans, which could have served as models. On this point, it is of interest to note that among the treasures of the Peabody Museum is an early nineteenth century Japanese print depicting a two-masted Roman ship, undoubtedly copied from some nineteenth-century European book that found its way to Japan.[56] The Japanese print does not, therefore, constitute evidence of contact between Rome and Japan in Caesarian times. Nor is it proof that Roman ships were invented by the Japanese or built independently by them.

With this example in mind, it seems safe to conclude that, even though the Hawaiian-style helmets were not in vogue in Europe during the era of the Spanish galleons, they are more likely to have been of European origin than to have been invented in Hawaii. The same may be said of the Hawaiians' capes and daggers. It therefore seems likely that a close study of early Hawaiian literature and traditions might well reveal other culture items whose origin could be traced back to Europe. Indeed, this remark may equally be applied to the Caroline Islands, Gilbert Islands, New Zealand and all other islands where European castaway influence has been postulated in this book, but not explored in detail. . .

Epilogue

Polynesia has frequently been described as a unique laboratory for the study of cultural change. Those who have described it as such have felt confident in the belief that the only inhabitants of Polynesia in prehistoric times were Polynesians; that these people were of a common ethnic and cultural stock; that they originated in the area immediately west of the Polynesian Triangle; and that they spread throughout Polynesia from the Tonga-Samoa area.

The findings of this book suggest that the prehistory of Polynesia was much more complex. Besides being influenced by hitherto-unsuspected Europeans from the lost ships of the sixteenth and possibly later centuries, the role of South American Indians was apparently far more important than most specialists have been prepared to believe. These factors suggest, in turn, that immigrants from other places—Japan, China and North America, for example—might also have contributed to the genetic make-up and culture of some Polynesian islands in ancient times.

Certainly, Polynesia was *not* a laboratory sealed off for centuries from outside influences. To believe that it was is to fly in the face both of known evidence and probability, and to inhibit the solution of some of the outstanding problems of Pacific prehistory.

Epilogue

Acknowledgements

The active research for and writing of this book extended over some seven years, from about September 1967. However, most of the work was concentrated in the last five and a half years. Many people and institutions helped in the book's production, and it is a pleasure to record my indebtedness to them. Those named, of course, do not necessarily share all or any of the views expressed herein; nor do they bear any responsibility for any errors, omissions, or shortcomings.

From an academic point of view, I owe most to my friend and colleague Dr Niel Gunson, fellow in the Department of Pacific and Southeast Asian History, Research School of Pacific Studies, Australian National University, Canberra. Over innumerable sandwiches and cups of coffee in his book-filled room, he and I held innumerable discussions on the subject matter of *The Lost Caravel,* and I have greatly profited from his erudition on many subjects, particularly early Society Islands history and Polynesian genealogy. With a patience worthy of Job himself, Niel cheerfully tolerated almost daily progress reports on my researches for several years, and it is no exaggeration to say that virtually every seemingly significant discovery and new idea was first announced to or tested out on him. Later, as the book took shape, he again acted as a sounding board by reading my material. No writer ever had a more generous and knowledgeable critic and friend.

Another constant mentor and friend was not a person but a book—the monumental *Bibliographie de Tahiti et de la Polynésie française* compiled over many years by the doyen of Pacific bibliographers, Father Patrick O'Reilly (a Frenchman despite his name) and Edouard Reitman. To overlook or understate the value of the O'Reilly-Reitman opus in my researches would be a great injustice, for it was the starting point for countless discoveries and inquiries. Being a model of its kind, it was always a pleasure to use. Although *The Lost Caravel* might eventually have been written without it, the task would have taken immeasurably longer.

Of other friends, I am especially grateful to four people who read my manuscript in whole or substantial part and offered well-informed and much-appreciated criticism. First in point of time was Professor Harry Maude, then professorial fellow, Department of Pacific History, Research School of Pacific Studies, Australian National University, who read an early draft of my work and gently confirmed my own growing feeling that, in certain respects, I was not proceeding along the right path. Much later, he looked over many of the galley proofs. Two of my other critics are also members of the ANU—Professor Oskar Spate, formerly director of the Research School of Pacific Studies, and Dr Dorothy Shineberg, reader in Pacific History in the School of General Studies. The fourth is my long-time friend and former colleague, Mr Stuart Inder, editor of the *Pacific Islands Monthly,* Sydney.

Yet another whose criticism I greatly valued is Professor John Langridge, formerly professor of genetics at the Australian National University. Professor Langridge read all sections of my manuscript dealing with human heredity, made several corrections and suggestions, and helped me to reduce some highly technical information to comprehensible layman's terms. It was he who discovered the remarkable genetic similarity between the Basques and Easter Islanders described in chapter 20—after I had sought his assistance in interpreting the results of the recent histocompatibility tests on Easter Island. These tests, in turn, had been drawn to my attention by another good friend, Mr Grant McCall, who is currently writing a Ph.D. thesis on the modern Easter Islanders in the Department of Anthropology, Research School of Pacific Studies, ANU. By a coincidence, Grant had previously made an anthropological study of the Basques and had accumulated a substantial library on them. Some of the more recondite items of Basquology cited in my bibliography were generously lent to me by him. To him, also, I am indebted for many fruitful discussions both on the Basques and the Easter Islanders, and for his criticism of my twentieth chapter. Yet another helpful critic was Dr Darryl Tryon, an ANU linguist, who, among other things, cast an expert eye over chapter 15.

Many other present and former ANU friends contributed to my researches in various ways. To Professor John Mulvaney, professor of prehistory in the School of General Studies, I am grateful for some blunt, but fair-minded criticism in the early days of my researches—when I gave a seminar on 'European castaways in the Pacific before Captain Cook.' Some salutary lessons were also learned from others who attended that seminar, not the least of them being that man—particularly academic man—has an instinctive resistance to revolutionary ideas. Other ANU friends whose help I have particular reason to remember are: Drs Tom Dutton and Jacques Guy (Linguistics), Mr Michael Hoare (History), Mr Norman Douglas and Dr David Lewis (Pacific History), Dr Charles Price (Demography), and Mr Tissa Rajapatirana (South Asian and Buddhist Studies).

Of other allies in the production of *The Lost Caravel,* special mention must be made of Miss Aurora Natua, secretary of the Papeete Museum, Tahiti. As indicated in chapter 1, the book really had its genesis with her, for it was she who informed me of Captain Hervé Le Goaziou's recovery of two cannon from Amanu in 1969 and later put me in touch with him. To Captain Le Goaziou himself, I am especially grateful for his detailed account of how the cannon were recovered, plus the accompanying sketch map showing their location when found. This material is of primary historical importance, and I am honoured to have his generous permission to publish it.

Almost three dozen other friends or correspondents provided me with information that has been incorporated in this book or were otherwise particularly helpful. They are: Mrs Nola Arthur, assistant librarian, Auckland Institute and Museum; Mr A. G. Bagnall, formerly chief librarian, Alexander Turnbull Library, Wellington; Mr Jacques Boullaire (son-in-law of the late Captain François Hervé), of Paris; Dr Pierre Centlivres, assistant curator, Ethnography Department, Bernisches Historisches Museum, Berne; Mr Ron Conyers, industrial chemist, Royal Australian Mint, Canberra; Mr B. A. L. Cranstone, deputy keeper, Department of Ethnography, British Museum, London; Professor R. G. Crocombe, professor of Pacific studies, University of the South Pacific, Suva, Fiji; Dr Bengt Danielsson, of Tahiti; Dr R. K. Dell, director, National Museum of New Zealand, Wellington; Professor G. M. Dening, History Department, University of Melbourne; Dr Ernest M. Dodge, director, Peabody Museum, Salem, Massachusetts; Professor H. Epstein, Faculty of Agriculture, the Hebrew University of Jerusalem, Rehovot, Israel; Mr Clifford Gessler, of Berkeley, California; Dr Barry M. Gough, associate professor of history, Waterloo Lutheran University, Ontario, Canada; Professor Roger C. Green, professor of anthropology, University of Auckland; Dr Paul T. Heffron, Manuscript Division, Library of Congress, Washington; Father Francis X. Hezel, SJ, Micronesian Seminar, Truk, Caroline Islands; Dr Colin Jack-Hinton, director, Museum and Art Gallery of the Northern Territory, Darwin; Mr A. N. Kennard, formerly assistant master of the Armouries, Tower of London; Mrs C. Kelly, archivist, Royal Geographical Society, London; Dr Karl Erik Larsson, director, Etnografiska Museet, Stockholm; Mr Francis B. Lothrop, of Salem, Massachusetts; Dr A. T. Lucas, director, National Museum of Ireland, Dublin; Mr D. J. Lyon, Department of Ships, National Maritime Museum, Greenwich, England; Mrs B. McFadgen, ethnologist, National Museum of New Zealand, Wellington; Mr Ian Mackay, formerly secretary of the Heraldry and Genealogy Society of Canberra; Mrs Honor Maude, of Canberra; Archbishop Paul Mazé, of Tahiti; Dr Irmgard Moschner, Museum fur Volkerkunde, Vienna; Father J. M. Neyret, SM, of Iles Belep, New Caledonia; Dr Gifford B. Pinchot, of Upperco, Maryland; Mrs Judy Reed, librarian, Bernice P. Bishop Museum, Honolulu; Dr Saul H. Riesenberg, chairman, department of anthropology, Smithsonian Institution, Washington; Mrs Jane Roth, of Cambridge, England; Dr Ian Shine, The Thomas Hunt Morgan Institute of Genetics, Inc., Lexington, Kentucky; Dr J. R. Specht, assistant curator, anthropology, Australian Museum, Sydney; Mr S. Tuinaceva, archivist, Fiji National Archives, Suva, and the Hon. Ve'ehala, Governor of Haapai, Tonga.

To Mr John Lawrey, formerly Australian Ambassador to Spain, I am indebted for several photographs of Spanish subjects. In particular, I wish to thank him for obtaining a black and white print of Pablo de Uranga's painting of the departure of the Loaisa expedition for the Moluccas in 1525. A colour transparency of this impressive painting was subsequently obtained for me through the courtesy of Señor Salvador Barbera, second secretary of the Spanish Embassy in Canberra. I am indebted to the president of the Diputacion Provincial de Guipúzcoa in San Sebastian for permission to publish the photograph.

Other illustrations were made available to me by Messrs Boullaire, Danielsson, Epstein and Le Goaziou (mentioned above); by the Bishop Museum, Honolulu; the British Museum, London; the Dixson Library, Sydney; the National Library of Australia, Canberra; the National Museum of New Zealand, Wellington; the Metropolitan Museum of Art, New York; the Musée de la Marine, Paris; and the Corporation of Portsmouth, England. To all these individuals and institutions, I am grateful for permission to reproduce the illustrations provided.

To Mr John Collins, of Pacific Publications (Aust.) Pty Ltd, Sydney, I owe my very warm thanks for drawing the many maps that illustrate this book; and I have to thank Miss Anne Langridge, of Canberra, for her skill in redrawing the five caravels reproduced in chapter 2.

Last to be mentioned, but far from least, are three colloborators who lived with *The Lost Caravel* during all or much of its long gestation, who shared the author's enthusiasm for it, and who helped in its production in a variety of ways. One is Mrs Anvida Lamberts, who expertly typed various drafts of the manuscript and most of the correspondence concerning it. Another is Mrs Marta Langridge, who assisted with research into German-language documents and with the index. The third is my wife Iva, who devotedly tolerated and ministered to an often absent-minded partner, who helped to check typescripts and galley proofs, and who generally made the task of a spare-time author as easy and pleasant as such a task can be.

Canberra,

September 1974.

Appendices

APPENDIX A

Officers and men known to have sailed in the Loaisa expedition

Name	Provenance and other details	Authorities*
Crew of the flagship, 'Santa Maria de la Victoria'		
1 ALECHE, Andres de	Basque; witnessed Elcano's will; reached Moluccas	Markham, 17, 40; Oviedo, IV, 275
2 ANS (Maestre)	Presumably a Fleming; gunner; veteran of Magellan expedition; deserted to Portuguese in Moluccas	Markham, 40, 67; Navarrete, V, 383, 420
3 AÑASCO, Fernando de	Basque name; reached Moluccas	Oviedo IV, 288; Lopez-Mendizabal 290
4 ARGOTE, Roldan de	Fleming; of Bruges, Belgium; gunner; veteran of Magellan expedition; wounded in Moluccas	Markham, 16, 26, 40; Navarrete V, 295, 383
5 ARREVE, Joanes de	Basque; of Elcano family; ordinary seaman; died in Moluccas	Lalande 90
6 ARTUS, —	Fleming; gunner; deserted to Portuguese in Moluccas	Markham 40; Navarette V, 420
7 ATAN, Juan de	Probably Galician; ordinary seaman; reached Moluccas. (Atan is a village in La Coruña, Galicia)	Navarrete V, 288, Enciclopedia VI, 857
8 AYALA, Diego de	Basque name; seaman; reached Moluccas; remained in Malacca with two children he had by a native woman. (Ayala is in the Basque province of Alava)	Navarrete V, 308, 374; Oviedo IV, 274; Lopez-Mendizabal 343
9 BERMEJO, Antonio	Basque; witnessed Elcano's will; died at sea	Markham, 17, 40
10 BERMEJO, Rodrigo	Of Seville; pilot; died in Pacific	Markham, 40; Navarrete V, 369; Oviedo IV, 238
11 BUSTAMENTE, Fernando de	Of Merida, Extremadura; barber in Magellan expedition; treasurer of *Sancti Spiritus;* reached Moluccas in *Victoria;* poisoned on voyage home	Lalande 78; Markham, 25, 39; Navarrete V, 215, 375, 383, 407
12 CAMPO, Gonzales (or Gonzalo) de	?; became master-of-arms in Pacific	Markham, 40; Navarrete V, 407
13 CARQUIZANO, Andres de	Basque; son of Martin Iñiguez de Carquizano; page; died in Moluccas	Lalande 90

16	COBARRUBIAS (or COVARRUBIAS) Diego de	?; factor; died in Strait of Magellan	Lalande 79, 90; Markham, 17, 39; Navarrete V, 220, 265, 406
17	CUEVASRRUBIAS, Diego de	?; factor; died in Moluccas	Oviedo IV, 274, 304
18	DOMIGUEZ, Bartolomé	Galician; of La Coruña; man-at-arms	Lalande 79; Markham, 40; Navarrete V, 15; Oviedo IV, 198
19	ELCANO, Juan Sebastian	Basque; of Guetaria, Guipúzcoa; veteran of Magellan expedition; captain of *Sancti Spiritus;* transferred to *Victoria;* succeeded Loaisa as expedition commander; died in Pacific, 4 August, 1526	Lalande 78, 82; Markham, 39; Navarrete V, 219; Oviedo IV, 187
20	ELCANO, Martin Pérez	Basque; brother of Juan Sebastian; pilot of *Sancti Spiritus;* transferred to *Victoria;* died in Pacific	Lalande 90; Markham, 16, 40; Navarrete V, 407
21	ELORRIAGA (or Lor(r)iaga), Iñigo de	Basque name; boatswain; later master; died in Moluccas; heirs lived in Guipúzcoa. (Elorriaga is in Viscaya)	Lalande 89; Markham, 30, 51; Navarrete V, 408; Oviedo IV, 274; Patronato 39, Doc. 14; Indice, 59; Lopez-Mendizabal 594
22	GODOY, Francisco de	?; supernumerary; deserted to Portuguese in Moluccas	Markham, 67; Navarrete V, 420
23	GOIRI, Juan de	Basque name; ordinary seaman; died in Moluccas; heir lived at Bilbao, Viscaya	Lalande 87; Patronato 39, Doc. 4; Navarrete V, 329; Lopez-Mendizabal, 490
24	GOROSTIAGA, Andres de	Basque; witnessed Elcano's will; reached Moluccas	Markham, 40; Oviedo IV, 274
25	GUEVARA, Hernando de	Basque; witnessed Elcano's will	Markham, 17, 40
26	HUELVA, Juan de	Probably Andalusian; master; died on voyage to Moluccas. (Huelva is a town and province in Andalusia)	Lalande 90; Markham, 30; Navarrete V, 408
27	ISLARES, Martin de	Basque; of Laredo, Viscaya; seaman; reached Moluccas; returned to Spain	Oviedo IV, 236
28	LASALDE, Juan de	Negro; slave; cabin boy; also called Juan BLANCO	Lalande 85
29	LEON, Arias de	Probably Leonese; supernumerary; returned to Spain. (Leon is a province in north-west Spain)	Lalande 84
30	LEPARAZU, Hortuño de	Basque name; blacksmith; died in Moluccas; widow lived at Bilbao, Viscaya	Lalande 86; Patronato 38, Doc. 14

APPENDIX A

OFFICERS AND MEN KNOWN TO HAVE SAILED IN THE LOAISA EXPEDITION

Name	Provenance and other details	Authorities*
Crew of the flagship, 'Santa Maria de la Victoria' (continued)		
31 LEXUNDI, Juan Ruiz de	Basque name; seaman and blacksmith in *Sancti Spiritus;* transferred to *Victoria;* died at sea; daughters lived in Guipúzcoa	Lalande 89; Patronato 39, Doc. 13
32 LOAISA, Alvaro de	?; nephew of commander; accountant-general for a few days; died at sea	Markham, 39; Oviedo IV, 237; Navarrete V, 316
33 LOAISA, Garcia Jofre de	Of Ciudad Real; commander; died in Pacific, July 30, 1526	Lalande 78; Oviedo IV, 189; Markham, 50
34 LUZON, Luis de	?; treasurer; died at sea; father lived in Madrid	Lalande, 88; Markham, 39; Patronato 39, Doc. 7
35 MARINERO, Pablo	?; captured by Portuguese in Moluccas	Navarrete V, 293
36 MARRUECOS, Juan de (also called Juan de LEPE)	Probably Andalusian; seaman; transferred from *Sancti Spiritus*; returned to Spain from Moluccas. (Lepe, in the province of Ayamonte, is on the Gulf of Cadiz; Marruecos is Spanish for Morocco.)	Lalande, 81, 83; Navarrete V, 361-6; Indice, 86
37 MENA, Juan de	?; master-at-arms; died in Moluccas; heirs lived at Campillo, a common place name in Spain	Lalande, 86; Patronato 38, Doc. 16
38 MENCHACA, Juan de	Basque name; seaman and blacksmith; died in Moluccas; widow lived at Bilbao	Lalande, 86; Patronato 38, Doc. 15
39 MONTEMAYOR, Pedro de	?; seaman; reached Moluccas	Navarrete V, 335, 340, 426
40 ORO, Alfonso de	Galician; of La Coruña; shipwright	Navarrete V, 310
41 OSUNIGA, Juan de	Basque name; ordinary seaman; transferred from *Sancti Spiritus*	Navarrete V, 329; Lopez-Mendizabal, 660
42 OTINON, Gutierre	?; seaman; reached Moluccas	Oviedo IV, 274
43 PALACIOS, ——	?; seaman; deserted to Portuguese in Moluccas	Oviedo IV, 266.
44 PARIS, Francisco de	Greek; seaman; reached Moluccas and returned to Spain	Lalande, 82; Navarrete V, 368

47 PEREZ, Jorge	?; became pilot; died in Pacific	Navarrete V, 369-70
48 POYO (or PAYO), Macías de	Of Murcia; pilot; reached Moluccas and returned to Spain	Lalande, 82; Markham, 40; Patronato 37, Doc. 34; Navarrete V, 366-8, 390
49 RAIGADA, Pedro de	Galician; supernumerary; reached Moluccas	Navarrete V, 306, 428
50 RAMOS, Pedro	?; seaman; reached Moluccas	Oviedo IV, 274
51 REYNA, Antonio de la	?; seaman	Lalande, 81
52 RIO, Alonso del	?; servant of Loaisa; died in Moluccas; sister lived at Villaseca de la Gayra	Lalande, 88; Patronato 39, Doc. 6
53 RIOS, Alonso de (or de los)	?; man-at-arms; reached Moluccas	Markham, 40; Navarrete V, 168, 300, 308
54 SALAZAR, Toribio Alonso de	'Montañes', i.e. Asturian; originally accountant in the caravels; became commander of expedition; died in Marianas; his widow lived at Valladolid	Lalande, 88; Markham, 30, 39; Navarrete V, 277, 337, 367, 407-8; Patronato 39, Doc. 10; Oviedo IV, 238
55 SALINAS, Diego de	?; seaman; killed in Moluccas	Markham, 40; Navarrete V, 323, 414
56 SOLIER, Diego de	?; became agent-general; died in Goa	Lalande, 84; Markham, 40, 53; Navarrete V, 56, 228, 409
57 SOLIS, Alonso de	?; nominated treasurer of expedition	Markham, 39; Navarrete V, 215
58 SOMORROSTRO, Martin	?; seaman; killed in Moluccas	Navarrete V, 293; Oviedo IV, 278
59 SOTO, Francisco de	?; became accountant-general; reached Moluccas	Markham, 39, 53
60 SOTO, ——	?; ?; deserted to Portuguese in Moluccas; possibly same person as preceding	Oviedo IV, 266
61 TARRAGONA, Bachiller	?; man-at-arms; reached Moluccas	Markham, 40; Navarrete V, 303
62 TEJADA, Alonso de	?; named as accountant in the Moluccas; died at sea	Lalande, 79; Markham, 39; Oviedo IV, 237
63 TORRE, Fernando de la	Of Burgos; man-at-arms; became commander of expedition; reached Moluccas; returned to Spain	Lalande, 80; Markham, 30, 40, 124; Navarrete V, 241, 371, 414
64 TORRES, Juan de	?; principal chaplain; deserted to Portuguese in Moluccas and died there	Lalande, 86; Markham, 40; Navarrete V, 420

APPENDIX A

OFFICERS AND MEN KNOWN TO HAVE SAILED IN THE LOAISA EXPEDITION

Name	Provenance and other details	Authorities*
Crew of the flagship, 'Santa Maria de la Victoria' (continued)		
65 TUNION (or TAÑON), Gutierre(z) de	Asturian; supernumerary; transferred from *Sancti Spiritus*; died on voyage	Lalande 90; Markham, 39; Navarrete V, 407; Oviedo IV, 274, 285
66 URDANETA, Andres de	Basque; of Villafranca, Guipúzcoa; became accountant-general; reached Moluccas and returned to Spain	Lalande, 82; Markham, 16, 17, 39; Navarrete V, 382, 401; Patronato 37, Doc. 34
67 URIARTE, Martin de	Basque; pilot; reached Moluccas	Markham, 17, 40; Navarrete V, 241, 287
68 ZABAL Juanes de	Basque; witnessed Elcano's will	Markham, 17, 40
69 ——, Pablo	?; seaman; captured by Portuguese in Moluccas	Oviedo IV, 278
70 ——	Frenchman; ordinary seaman; reached Moluccas and remained there; married coloured woman	Navarrete V, 374
Crew of the 'Sancti Spiritus'		
71 ESTRELLA (or ESTELLA), Diego de	?; accountant; drowned in the Strait of Magellan	Markham, 40; Navarrete V, 14, 223
72 MUTIO, Esteban de	Basque name; nephew of Juan Sebastian Elcano; died on voyage	Lalande, 90; Lopez-Mendizabal, 629
Crew of 'Anunciada'		
73 SABUGAL, Diego de	Basque name; seaman; died in Strait of Magellan; son lived at Valmaseda, Viscaya	Lalande, 89; Patronato 40, Doc. 2; Indice, 161
74 VARA, Pedro de	Basque name; captain	Navarrete V, 219; Lalande, 78; Markham, 43; Lopez-Mendizabal, 737
Crew of 'San Gabriel'		

77 CASTRILLO, ——	?; seaman	Navarrete V, 230
78 CATORICO (or CATAN), Jorge de	?; seaman	Navarrete V, 314, 322
79 DAVILA (or de AVILA), Francisco	Of Madrid; supernumerary	Navarrete V, 225; Lalande, 80
80 ELCANO, Ochoa Martinez	Basque; brother of Juan Sebastian; boatswain; died during voyage	Lalande, 90
81 GALARRAGA, Martin de	Basque name; guard; transferred from *Sancti Spiritus*	Lalande, 85
82 GINOVES, Geronimo	Apparently Genoese; seaman. (Surname means Genoese)	Navarrete V, 314
83 GINOVES, Miguel	Apparently Genoese; seaman. (Surname means Genoese)	Navarrete V, 230
84 MORELOS, ——	?; seaman	Navarrete V, 230
85 NAPOLES, Alfonso de	Probably Neopolitan; seaman. (Surname means Naples)	Navarrete V, 314
86 NEGRO(N), Pascual de	?; seaman; Negron is in Valencia	Navarrete V, 314, Indice, 105
87 ORTIZ, Diego	Probably Basque; of Orue (which is in the Basque province of Alava); accountant	Navarrete V, 212; Lalande, 79; Markham, 40; Patronato 37, Doc. 15; Enciclopedia XL, 794
88 PILOLO (or PELOLA, or PILOLA), Juan de	Probably Basque; pilot; widow and son lived at Zumaya, Guipúzcoa	Lalande, 86; Patronato 38, Doc. 18; Navarrete V, 12, 226, 231; Indice, 172
89 RIOS, Alonso del	?; master; transferred from *Sancti Spiritus*	Navarrete V, 168
90 SALMERON, Gonzales de	?; treasurer; died at sea; widow lived at Madrid; Salmeron is in Guadalajara, north-east of Madrid	Lalande, 88; Patronato 39, Doc. 8; Navarrete V, 213
91 URTIAGA, Martin de	Basque; of Zumaya, Guipúzcoa; sailor and shipwright; returned to Spain	Lalande, 84
92 VILLAREAL, Sebastian	?; boatswain	Navarrete V, 229
93 VIZCAINO, Bartolomé	Presumably Basque; seaman; (Vizcaino means 'of the Basque province of Viscaya')	Navarrete V, 314
94 VIZCAINO, Machin	Presumably Basque; seaman. (See preceding item.)	Navarrete V, 314

APPENDIX A

OFFICERS AND MEN KNOWN TO HAVE SAILED IN THE LOAIŠA EXPEDITION

Name	Provenance and other details	Authorities*
Crew of the caravel 'Santa Maria del Parral'		
95 BENAVIDES, ——	?; pilot; killed by own crew near the Philippines	Markham, 30, 77
96 BENAVIDES, Juan (Francisco) de	?; treasurer; killed in the Philippines	Lalande, 90; Markham, 39; Navarrete V, 305; Oviedo IV, 287
97 CAMPO, Francisco del	?; seaman; mother and sons lived at Villa Diego, Burgos	Lalande, 89; Patronato 40, Doc. 1
98 ELCANO, Anton Martin	Basque; youngest brother of Juan Sebastian; assistant pilot	Markham, 16
99 MANRIQUE, Diego	Of Najera (south of the Basque province of Alava); ?; brother of Jorge Manrique; killed in the Philippines	Markham, 30; Navarrete V, 305; Indice, 103
100 MANRIQUE, Jorge	Of Najera; captain; killed in the Philippines	Markham, 30; Navarrete V, 219, 305; Indice, 103
101 OLAVE, Juan de	Probably Basque; seaman; Olave is in Basque province of Alava	Navarrete V, 307; Enciclopedia vol. 39, p. 961
102 OYO, Fernando del	?; seaman	Navarrete V, 307
103 PORTO, Sabastian de	Portuguese; seaman; rescued from the Philippines by Alvaro de Saavedra	Navarrete V, 303, 428
104 ROMAY, ——	Galician; seaman; rescued from the Philippines by Alvaro de Saavedra	Navarrete V, 304, 428; Oviedo IV, 287
105 SANCHEZ, ——	Galician; seaman; rescued from the Philippines by Alvaro de Saavedra	Navarrete V, 304, 428; Oviedo IV, 287
106 ——, Guillermo	Fleming; ?; reached Celebes and wrote letter from there	Oviedo IV, 287
Crew of caravel 'San Lesmes'		

108 ARREIZAGA (or ARYZAGA), Juan de	Basque; of Zumarraga, Guipúzcoa; chaplain; reached Mexico	Navarrete V, 223; Lalande, 79; Markham, 16, 40; Oviedo IV, 194
109 GUEVARA, Santiago de	Presumably Basque; brother-in-law of Juan Sebastian Elcano; cousin of Juan de Arreizaga; captain; reached Mexico	Markham, 16, 30, 90, 103; Navarrete V, 226
110 HIGUEROLA, Juan Perez de	?; seaman	Navarrete V, 29

Sailed in expedition, but name(s) of ship(s) unknown

111 CHINA, Tristan de la	Probably one of the four 'Malays' taken back to Spain in Magellan's *Victoria*. The name suggests a Chinese origin. A slave. Acted as interpreter**	Lalande, 85
112 GUEVARA, Martin Sanchez de	Basque; of Elcano family	Lalande, 90
113 RIO, Anton(io) del	Probably a Malay; slave; ordinary seaman	Lalande, 85, 90
114 SALAZAR, Juan de	?; goldsmith and lapidary; his widow lived at Valladolid	Lalande, 85
115 TARRAGO, Bartolomé Simon	?; accountant	Markham, 39
116 VICTORIA, Diego de	?; accountant	Markham, 40
117 VISCAYNO, Juan	Probably a Malay; slave; ordinary seaman. Surname means 'of the Basque province of Viscaya'.	Lalande, 85
118 ZEORAGA, Andres de	Basque; of Elcano family	Lalande, 90

* The dates of publication have been omitted from the bibliographical references. Those of individual authors are: Lalande 1966, Lopez-Mendizabal 1958, Markham 1911, Navarrete 1825-37, Oviedo 1945. For 'Enciclopedia' and 'Indice', see the entries in the bibliography beginning with those words. The key to such references as 'Patronato 39, Doc. 3', will be found in the bibliography under Archivo General de Indias.

** Of the four Malays, only three were embarked in the Loaisa expedition. The fourth was kept in Spain because he made so many inquiries about the value of spices in that country that the Spaniards feared he would ruin the market for them in the Moluccas—Oviedo IV, 189.

APPENDIX B

Collisions with coral reefs in the South Pacific, 1722-1809*

Date	Ship(s)	Particulars	Authorities
19 May 1722	*Africaansche Galei* (African Galley), 92 ft sailing ship. One of three vessels in the expedition of Jacob Roggeveen. Original crew: 31	Ran aground on reef at Takapoto Atoll, Tuamotu Archipelago, and stuck fast. All hands saved and accommodated in the other two vessels, one of whose sailors was drowned when thrown from a boat during the rescue operation.	Sharp 1970:13n, 20, 121-6
11 June 1770	HMS *Endeavour,* bark of 368 tons, Lieutenant James Cook. Complement at time of collision: 113	Ran aground on Great Barrier Reef, northeastern Australia. Cannon, ballast and other heavy articles thrown overboard. Ship heaved off reef by boats. Damage later repaired at Endeavour River. No lives lost.	Beaglehole 1955:343-9, 588-601
? 1788	*Boussole* and *Astrolabe,* frigates of 500 tons, under J. F. G. de Laperouse. Total complement on leaving Botany Bay: 201	Wrecked on reef at Vanikoro, near the Solomon Islands, after leaving Botany Bay, New South Wales, on 10 March 1788. None of crew returned to civilisation to tell the tale; but in 1827 and 1828 Captain Peter Dillon and Captain J. S. C. Dumont d'Urville respectively learned details from the Vanikorans and recovered relics of the *Astrolabe*. The natives stated that the ships were wrecked on a stormy night; that the *Boussole* sank quickly; and that the few survivors from her were killed when they got ashore. The *Astrolabe,* on the other hand, ran aground in fairly shallow water, and the crew had time to remove things from her and get ashore. D'Urville was told that 70 or 80 men survived. They built a small ship in which they sailed away after several 'moons'. They were not seen again. One of Dillon's officers saw a spot where the survivors had cut down trees. The wreck of the *Boussole* was discovered in 1962 in a deep, wedge-shaped chasm in the reef.	Milet-Mureau 1807; Dillon 1829:II:90-125; Dumont d'Urville 1830:V:8 and on; Langdon 1963b:17-21; Brossard 1964
25 Feb. 1792	*Matilda,* whaler, Captain Matthew Weatherhead. Complement at time of wreck: 29	Ran aground and stuck fast at Mururoa Atoll, Tuamotu Archipelago. No lives lost. Survivors sailed for Tahiti in four boats and reached it in about 10 days.	Lee 1920:40-1
29 Aug. 1792	HMS *Pandora,* 24-gun frigate, Captain Edward Edwards. Complement at time of wreck: 134	Ran aground on Great Barrier Reef, northeastern Australia. Beaten over reef into ten fathoms of water. Badly holed. Sank about eleven hours later. Two men crushed to death; 33 others either trapped in ship when she went down or drowned after jumping overboard. Ninety-nine survivors reached Timor in the frigate's	Thomson 1915:71-82

		[illegible] after the sails were hove aback. No loss of life. The violence of the blow 'beat in the copper [sheathing], deeply wounded the plank, and beat it to shivers.'	
Jan. 1800	*Argo,* schooner, ?	Wrecked on Mbukatatanoa Reef between Tonga and Fiji. Crew reached Tongatapu in boats. (Details vague).	Im Thurn 1925:xxii-xxiv, xlvi, 178n, 186
second half, 1800	*El Plumier,* William Reid, master. Crew on leaving Sydney on 20 January 1800: 13	Ran aground on reef at Koro Island, Fiji. Large part of keel carried away; and in less than half an hour she made seven feet of water. Driven off reef into deep water at high tide. Vessel repaired ashore. Later damaged on reef entering Mbua Bay and repaired again. No lives lost. The ship subsequently sailed to Guam.	Im Thurn 1925:xxvii-xl, 177-9
17 Aug. 1803	HMS *Porpoise,* Lieutenant Fowler, and *Cato,* 450-ton transport, John Park, master. Combined complement: 97	Both wrecked on Wreck Reef, 729 miles north-east of Sydney. Three lives lost, apparently in *Cato.* Fourteen survivors sailed to Sydney to get aid for the others, who lived on a small sandbank until rescued.	*SG,* 11 Sept. 1803, p. 4, 18 Sept. 1803, p. 2-3
20 May 1806	*Sydney,* 900-ton East Indiaman, Austin Forrest, master. Complement on leaving Sydney on 18 April 1806: 130	Wrecked on Sydney Shoal, south of the Admiralty Islands, New Guinea. All hands saved (Details vague).	*SG,* 15 Feb. 1807, p. 2
25 Aug. 1806	*Britannia,* whaler, Nathaniel Goodspeed, master. Crew at time of shipwreck: 24	Wrecked on Middleton or Elizabeth Reef in Coral Sea. Crew escaped in three boats, of which two reached Sydney. About eight men therefore appear to have been lost.	*SG,* 14 Sept. 1806, p. 3, 26 Oct. 1806, p. 2
20 June 1808	*Eliza,* brig, E. H. Correy, master	Wrecked on Mocea Reef, nine miles from Nairai Island, Fiji. One man lost who tried to swim from wreck. Others reached Nairai in boats.	Im Thurn 1925:96-7
10 Nov. 1809	*Hibernia,* 200-ton brig, William Campbell, master. Crew on later voyage: 33. Passengers on this voyage: 11	Ran aground in night on reef off the Macuata coast of Fiji. Refloated at high tide and sailed, leaking badly, to safety, where she was repaired. No lives lost.	Im Thurn 1925:120-1, 130-60, 206-7; Cumpston 1963:71

* The collisions listed above are of ships under way on the high seas. Ships that ran aground in working into or putting out of harbours are not included. Groundings of the latter kind were: the *Dolphin* (Tahiti, 1767), *Aguila* (Tahiti, 1772), *Resolution* (Tahiti, 1773) and *Sirius* (Norfolk Island, 1790). The *Norfolk,* which was driven ashore from her anchorage at Matavai Bay, Tahiti, in 1802, has also been omitted. There was no loss of life in any of these cases. Another omission is the brig *Union,* which was lost after leaving Sydney in 1804. There was a vague contemporary report that she was wrecked on Koro Island, Fiji, but nothing is known for certain about her fate.

APPENDIX C

Provenance of known members of Loaisa expedition

Ship	Basques, known and presumed	Galicians, known and presumed	Spaniards not identified as Basques or Galicians	Flemings, known and presumed	Other Europeans	Non-Europeans, known and presumed	TOTALS
S.M. de la Victoria	23	4	37	3	2	1	70
Sancti Spiritus	1		1				2
Anunciada	2						2
San Gabriel	7	1	9		3		20
S.M. del Parral	2	2	6	1	1		12
San Lesmes			1				1
Santiago	2		1				3
(Unknown)	2		3			3	8
TOTALS	39	7	58	4	6	4	118

Percentages: Basques, 33.05; Galicians, 5.9; Other Spaniards, 49.15; Flemings, 3.4; Other Europeans, 5.1; Non-Europeans, 3.4.

APPENDIX D

The peoples and culture of Tonga and Samoa

When the American anthropologist Louis R. Sullivan analysed the physical characteristics of some of the Polynesian peoples in the 1920s, he was emphatic on one point concerning the Tongans and Samoans. This was that they were *not* a people of Caucasian descent. They belonged, he thought, to what he called 'the brown division of the Yellow-Brown race'. 'The evidence for a Caucasian origin of the Samoans and Tongans is decidedly sparse and unconvincing,' he wrote. However, Sullivan admitted that the prevailing hair form of the Samoans and Tongans tended to 'depart somewhat' from that of most Yellow-Brown peoples in that it was not so stiff, straight and coarse as usual. He also thought the lack of projecting jaws and chin were two other features in which the two peoples varied from the Yellow-Brown norm. 'But,' he added, 'in skin color, eye color, the amount of conjunctival pigment, the elevation of the nasal bridge, the form and direction of the nostrils, nasal height, nasal breadth, nasal index, the thickness of the lips, the large faces reflected in the face height, face width and bigonial width, the Samoans and Tongans differ from the Caucasians and approach more nearly the norms of the brown division of the Yellow-Brown race.'

Sullivan's conclusions, which were based on a study of 215 randomly-selected Tongans and 93 Samoans,[1] corresponded closely with the rather less specific impressions of the early European explorers and missionaries. The only noteworthy difference was that two explorers did claim that, facially, some Tongans bore a resemblance to Europeans. On the other hand, none of the early visitors to Tonga and Samoa wrote of diverse racial types, variegated skin colours and occasional blondness as did those who visited Tahiti and the Society Islands. Moreover, several explorers, who visited both the western and eastern Pacific, stated categorically that no Tongans were similar in appearance to many of the Society Islands chiefs, the latter being much taller and generally fairer than the Tongan chiefs. The same could undoubtedly have been said of the Samoans, who were less visited by Europeans in the early days of exploration and so were less frequently described.

The first Europeans to have contact with the Tongans were the Dutch explorers Schouten and Le Maire. In 1616, they encountered a canoe to the eastward of Tonga whose occupants, according to Schouten, were red folk who smeared themselves with oil. Le Maire, on the other hand, described them as having 'a very yellow complexion'.[2]

In 1643, when Tasman visited Eua, Tongatapu, Nomuka and other islands in Tonga, neither he nor any of his companions described the Tongans in general. But Tasman said of three Eua islanders that they were of a brown colour and somewhat more than ordinary height.[3]

In 1767, when the *Dolphin* touched at the Tongan outliers of Tafahi and Niuatoputapu, her master, George Robertson, noted that their inhabitants were 'stout well bodyed men', tattooed on the legs and thighs like the Tahitians, but 'rather Blacker' than the copper-coloured Tahitians.[4]

The first European after Tasman to stay in either Tonga or Samoa for more than a few hours was Captain Cook. On his second voyage, in between visits to the Society Islands and New Zealand, he spent nearly a week at the islands of Eua and Tongatapu. At Eua, his companion George Forster described the first Tongan to board the *Resolution* as having black hair in short, frizzled curls, and a 'clear mahogany or chestnut brown' complexion—'like that of the common Taheitians.' Later, on a shore excursion at Eua, Forster noted that the islanders in general were from about five feet three to five feet ten; more muscular than the Tahitians; and different from them in appearance in that their faces were 'more oblong than round', their noses sharper and their lips thinner. The women were generally shorter than the men, 'but not so small as the lower class of women at Taheitee and the Society Isles.' Both sexes had a light chestnut-brown complexion, and there was no difference between that of the chiefs and the commoners. Indeed, Forster said, 'we recollected many individauls [in the Society Islands], especially of the principal families, to which none of these could be compared . . . That difference of colour and corpulence, by which we immediately distinguished the ranks of Taheitee, was not to be met with in this island.'[5]

Cook, himself, thought the skin colour of the people of Eua and Tongatapu was a 'lightish Copper', and 'more uniformly so' than in Tahiti or the leeward Society Islands. None of them was so fair, so tall or so well made as some of the Tahitians and their neighbours. On the other hand, none of the Tongans was so dark, small, or ill-shaped as others among those islanders. Generally, the Tongans' hair was black, but many put something on it to colour it red or blue.[6]

About three years later, Cook spent nearly twelve weeks in Tonga, during which he examined the Haapai group, and spent a further month at Tongatapu and five days at Eua. He did not alter his opinion about the Tongans' physical appearance, saying on this occasion that they were 'much darker' than the Tahitians although 'better limbed' and 'finer shaped'. He added: 'Their hair is of different colours, that is black, dark brown and flaxen, but not many of the latter except what is made so by art, for they have a method of staining it so that we frequently see different colours on the same head.'[7]

Two of Cook's officers were a little less sweeping than he was about the Tongans' complexions. But all used such expressions as 'deeper than the copper brown', 'dark copper' and 'lively brown' to describe their skin colour in general. Anderson, the surgeon, who used the first of these expressions, also stated that several men and women had a 'true olive complexion'. Some were even a great deal fairer—the fairest being corpulent chiefs who did not go out much in the sun. Anderson added that the Tongans' facial features were 'very various' and that it was 'scarcely possible to fix on any general likeness to characterize them by', except that a fullness about the point of the nose was very common. On the other hand, there were 'hundreds of truly European faces & many genuine Roman noses.'[8] Lieutenant King, for his part, noted that some of the principal Tongan women were fairer than the generality of Tongans. But he left no doubt on what he meant by this. 'Their colour,' he said, 'resembles that of the Mallays we saw at the Cape of Good hope.'[9]

The French naturalist Labillardiere, who was with the d'Entrecasteaux expedition when it called at Tongatapu in 1792, agreed with Anderson that many Tongans were like Europeans in facial features. But he did not remark on the colour of their skin or hair. He described a chief called Finau as being of middling stature, and very fat. 'Like the rest of the natives', Labillardière added, 'he had altogether the features of an European.'[10]

The first European to visit Samoa was the Dutch explorer Roggeveen, who said of some islanders who came off to his ships at the Manua group in 1722 that they were sturdy, robust and tattooed from the thighs downwards. His companion Cornelis Bouman wrote of the islanders as fat, sleek, lively fellows, of a brownish-red colour, with long black hair having a reddish shine. They reminded him of Indians he had seen in America.[11]

Some forty-six years later, Bougainville described some Samoans he saw as rather smaller than the Tahitians and not as good looking. One woman was positively ugly. Their hair was black, except in one instance where it was a reddish colour. 'I don't think these islanders are as gentle as our [Tahitians],' Bougainville wrote. 'Their features are more savage and they exhibit much distrust!' Pierre Caro, one of Bougainville's officers, thought the Samoans' hair was less curly than that of the Tahitians.[12]

In 1787, Bougainville's compatriot La Perouse described the complexion of the islanders of Manua as 'nearly that of the Algerines, or other people on the coast of Barbary.' The features of the men did not strike him as very agreeable, and those of the only two women he saw, 'had not a whit more delicacy.' Later, having also seen the islanders at the Samoan island of Tutuila and the Tongan island of Tongatapu (but not the Society Islanders), La Perouse wrote:

> To me it appears demonstrated that these different nations [of Samoa, Tonga and the Society Islands] are derived from Malay colonies, who conquered these islands at very remote periods . . . I am convinced that the race of woolly-haired men . . . [was vanquished and that they] intermingled with their conquerors; and hence originated that race of very black people, whose complexion still remains a few shades deeper than that of certain families in the country, who probably made it a point of honour not to contaminate their blood. These two very distinct races appeared striking to our eyes at the Navigators' Islands [i.e. Samoa], and I can ascribe to them no other origin. The descendants of the Malays have acquired in these islands a vigor, strength, height and stoutness, which they derived not from their ancestors; and for which they are unquestionably indebted to abundance of nutriment, the mildness of the climate, and the in-

This 'tongiaki' or Tongan double canoe was encountered off the Tonga islands in 1616 by the Schouten and Le Maire expedition. As may be seen, it differed considerably from the 'pahi' of the Society Islands and Tuamotus.

fluence of different physical causes, which have constantly been acting upon them for a long series of generations.*[13]

The Rev. J. B. Stair, an LMS missionary in Samoa from 1838 to 1845, described the complexion of the Samoans as brown, but said it was difficult to name a particular shade as there was a considerable variety. 'Mr. Heath [another missionary] speaks of them as of gipsy brown colour,' he said. 'An olive brown is also a term which correctly describes the complexion of numbers; others, again, are of a chocolate colour, or Vandyke brown, of the Tannese and other islanders of the Western Pacific.' Stair said the colour of the Samoans' eyes, as well as their hair, was usually black, except in a few cases of albinos. He added: 'The Samoans disliked the white colour of the Europeans, and often jocularly said to me, when alluding to my sunburnt appearance when much exposed, "Why, you are becoming as handsome as a Samoan".'[14]

Another early missionary in Samoa, the Rev. George Turner, did not entirely agree with La Perouse and Stair on the presence of very dark people in Samoa. He described the Samoans as of the 'prevailing light copper colour' of central and eastern Polynesia, and added: 'Hardly a vestige is to be seen among them of the crisped and woolly-haired dark-brown Papuans, or western Polynesian negroes.'[15]

On this last point, it is of interest to note that Sullivan could not decide whether Samoa had ever been inhabited by Melanesians, but he concluded that the amount of (obvious) Melanesian blood was small. 'This,' he said, 'may be due to the fact that the intermixture never took place on a very large scale in Samoa, or that if it did take place on a large scale it was so long ago that the Melanesian element is almost completely absorbed by the general Samoan population.' In Tonga, he went on, conditions were 'somewhat different' in that enough Melanesian blood was in evidence to alter noticeably the average physical type. '. . . without much doubt,' he added, 'there

---

* *If La Perouse had lived in later, more scientific times, he might have attributed the greater strength, height, etc., of Samoa's 'descendants of the Malays' to heterosis, or hybrid vigour, which is known to occur through the mating of people of diverse racial origins (see p. 55).*

is considerably more Melanesian blood in the general Tongan population than there is in the Samoan population.'[16]

Although all general descriptions indicate that, physically, there was little in common between the Tongan and Samoan chiefs and the light-skinned *hui arii* of the Society Islands, it would not be surprising if, over the centuries, an occasional Society Islands chief drifted to Samoa and made his home there. Drift voyages from the Society Islands to Samoa have occurred at least twice in the past century or so—once in 1862 and once in 1964.[17] So it may be assumed that they were of similar frequency in earlier times. Such voyages could explain the presence in Samoa in early times of anomalous cases of exceptionally Caucasian-looking islanders—one such individual being Lauaki Namulau'ulu Mamoe, a chief born in the 1840s. Lauaki is said to have been 'conspicuous among the Samoans for the fairness of his skin', and a photograph of him reveals him as virtually indistinguishable from Europeans.[18]

If ancestors of individuals such as Lauaki did, indeed, reach Samoa from the Society Islands, this, in turn, could explain how one small and possibly European cultural item happened to be in Samoa—and probably Tonga—in pre-contact times. The item is the netting needle—apparently the open-fork type—which Turner found in use among the women of the interior of Savaii some time after his arrival in Samoa in 1840. He described it as 'exactly the same in form as those in use in Europe' and said (his italics) that the women were amazed that his wife could 'handle a *Samoan* netting needle, and do Samoan work.'[19] Several decades earlier, Captain Cook had noted that the Tongans had fishing nets with meshes exactly like those of Europe.[20] So it could well be that they, in turn, had obtained the open-fork netting needle from Samoa, as they were in occasional canoe contact with those islands.[21] However, Buck, in his *Samoan Material Culture*, indicated that the open-fork netting needle was not anciently in use in Samoa, for he said that, according to Manuan authorities, the Samoan netting needle 'originally consisted of a stick about a foot long with a blunt point which was split.' He added, referring to an illustration of an open-fork needle, that 'the needles now in use [in Samoa] are similar to those in use in other parts of Polynesia.'[22]

Whatever the origin of the open-fork netting needle may have been in Samoa, and possibly Tonga, it seems to have been the only item of either material culture or folk culture that reminded early European visitors to those islands of items in their own culture. Thus neither the Tongans nor Samoans had sailing craft called, or similar to, the *pahi*, with its several seemingly European features.[23] And no evidence was ever gathered that they divided the horizon into four, eight or sixteen equal parts, and employed a 'star compass' on long voyages.[24] In fact, Turner said the Samoans were 'not noted among the Polynesians as enterprising navigators.' On the contrary, they were 'quite a domestic people' who rarely ventured out of sight of land.[25] The Tongans, on the other hand, did go on long voyages—particularly to Fiji for timber; and it is known that from about the end of the eighteenth century, they began to substitute the more serviceable and weatherly Fijian *ndrua* for the double-hulled *tongiaki* that had formerly been in use. It is quite likely, therefore, that the *tongiaki*, which was seen, described and pictured by Schouten, Tasman, Cook and Forster, was, in fact, also of Fijian origin, for nothing of consequence is known of Fijian sailing craft before the end of the eighteenth century.[26]

Certainly, much of the 'highly civilised' abstract knowledge that the early explorers and missionaries recorded in the Society Islands was never recorded in Tonga or Samoa. Nor did the Tongans or Samoans have entertainments like those of Raiatea which Banks, for example, described as closely resembling 'the Drama of an English stage dance'; nor the elaborate dresses like those that Europeans were wont to wear; nor the wind instrument called *hoe*, which a visitor to Raiatea compared to the European flageolet.[27] Finally, neither the Tongans nor the Samoans had religious beliefs remotely resembling some of the seemingly Biblical notions recorded in the Society Islands. In Western Polynesia, for example, the people had an evolutionary type of creation myth which told how human beings emerged from rocks or earth, either directly or through intermediate forms such as plants or maggots. Deities were spectators rather than creators—completely unlike Taaroa, the principal god of the Society Islands, who created man out of sand or red earth, and then made a woman for him from one of his ribs.[28]

The ethnologist Burrows listed no less than forty cultural traits (excluding some of those mentioned above) which distinguished Eastern Polynesia from the Tonga-Samoa area.[29] He tried to explain these in terms of differential diffusion from Melanesia and Micronesia, and local development and cultural loss within Polynesia itself.

APPENDIX E

The Biblical and Tuamotuan versions of creation

First three verses of Genesis in Authorised Version of Bible	*First three verses of Genesis in Tahitian Bible*	*Corresponding portion of Kio chant in Tuamotuan, as recorded by J. Frank Stimson*	*Stimson's translation of first portion of Kio chant*
1. In the beginning God created the heaven and the earth.	1. Hamani ihora te Atua i te ra'i e te fenua i te matamua ra.	(1) Ko Kio te tua matamua roa; na na i hakatupu, e na na i hakahope i te Ao katoga na roto i te mana o to na haga tuaturuturu.	(1) Kio was the first original god; it was he who created and brought to completion the whole universe by means of the magical powers and god-like attributes of his divine assistants.
2. And the earth was without form, and void and darkness was upon the face of the deep. And the Spirit of God moved upon the face of the waters.	2. Te vai ano noa ra te fenua aore e faufaa, e te pouri hoi i nia iho i te iriatai; e ua faaarepurepu ihora te Varua o te Atua i nia iho i te moana.	(2) E moe noa ana Kio-moe i roto i te Kore—ki te Po-tagotago ki te Po-rukiruki . . .	(2) Kio-the-sleeper slumbered immemorially in the Void—in the Night-of-utter blackness, in the Night of profound darkness, . . .
3. And God said, Let there be light: and there was light.	3. Ua parau ihora te Atua, Ei maramarama, ua maramarama ihora.	(3) Kua korero Kio-moe ki o na ga tua-turu-turu-noa, na ko atu ra, 'Na vai e hakamarumaru i te Po kia marumaru?' . . .—e kua oti ia.	(3) Kio-the-sleeper spoke to his merely divine assistants, saying, 'Who will cause the Night-realm to be infused with soft light that it be illuminated with the shaded glow of twilight?' . . .—and this was finished.

APPENDIX F

Evidence of a non-Polynesian language in eastern Polynesia

One of the most persistent assertions of Pacific scholars is that no language other than Polynesian was ever spoken on any Polynesian island in pre-European times. This notion seems to have originated in 1778 when Johann Reinhold Forster, Cook's erudite companion on his second voyage, brought out his *Observations made during a Voyage round the World*. In this, Forster published a comparative table of forty-six words and numerals that he had gathered in five widely-separated parts of Polynesia—the Society Islands, Tonga, Easter Island, New Zealand and the Marquesas. And he said that as many of the words were 'absolutely the same in all dialects' and as most of the others only differed in a few vowels and consonants, there was no doubt that all were descended from the 'same original stem'. Forster also claimed that the five dialects bore no resemblance to the languages of Mexico, Peru and Chile, and that the Pacific Islanders he had seen were unlike the people of those countries. On the other hand, there were linguistic and physical resemblances between the people of the Polynesian islands and the 'Indian or Asiatic northern isles,' and he therefore concluded that both the Polynesians and their language had originated in Asia.[1]

As other Polynesian dialects became known, and they, too, were seen to have numerous affinities with those that Forster described, Forster's view became a firm-fixed orthodoxy among Pacific scholars. It also came to be thought that such differences as existed between one dialect and another were merely due to differences of evolution—not to the influence of other languages from outside Polynesia. From this point, it was natural to infer that all Polynesians were of the same ethnic stock, although the studies of such physical anthropologists as L. R. Sullivan clearly demonstrated the contrary.[2] Moreover, the view became entrenched that, despite some obvious cultural differences, particularly between east and west, the culture of all Polynesians was basically the same.[3] In the circumstances no one took much notice of such isolated statements as were occasionally published that tended to suggest that long before the Polynesian-speaking people had reached the eastern Pacific from the west, another people, speaking a different language, had already established themselves there. As a result, many Pacific scholars have kept making Forsterian assertions that almost certainly have no foundation in fact. In the early 1970s, for example, a well-known Pacific historian wrote of the Polynesians as 'a relatively homogeneous group, culturally and linguistically',[4] while a specialist in Pacific pre-history referred to the problem of getting the 'linguistically and culturally homogeneous Polynesians' into the central Pacific 'without racial contamination'.[5] Another scholar, a professor of Oceanic languages, stated positively that 'within the Polynesian triangle only Polynesian languages were ever spoken,' and that 'despite repeated statements to the contrary, starting with Horatio Hale . . , there appears to be no evidence of a non-Polynesian element [in Tuamotuan]'.[6]

Contrary to the foregoing remarks, substantial evidence of a non-Polynesian language in the eastern Pacific can, it seems, be derived from three atolls in the Tuamotu Archipelago—Anaa, Reao and Napuka. Other evidence is also forthcoming from several other islands in that vicinity, including the easternmost outpost of Polynesia, Easter Island. Several factors suggest that the non-Polynesian language must have originated in South America many centuries ago. These are:

1. The geographical location of the islands where traces of the language still apparently exist, or did exist until recent years.

2. The fact that no trace of the language has been found in the dialects of Western Polynesia, but there are many apparent examples of it in that of Tahiti.

3. Easter Island, Napuka and Reao are all noted for massive stone structures—reminiscent of the stonework of Colombia, Ecuador, and Peru. (Anaa may also have had such structures at one time—before hurricanes and tidal waves destroyed them.)

4. The people of Reao and Napuka have

frequently been described as non-Polynesian in appearance, and they appear to answer descriptions of the *manahune,* or reputed original settlers of the Society Islands and elsewhere. Moreover, the Reao people and some of those of Anaa and Fangatau have been compared with American Indians.

The first reference in print to the existence of an anomalous language in Eastern Polynesia was in the introduction to an account of the voyage of the *Duff* published in 1799. The introduction bears no author's name. But it is known to be the work of the Rev. Samuel Greatheed, one of the leading lights of the London Missionary Society. Greatheed obtained some of his information from the then-unpublished journal of James Morrison of the *Bounty* (the linguistic section of which has since been lost), and from interviews with other seamen who had visited Tahiti. According to him, the island of Tupai, to the north of Bora Bora, was much-frequented by the speakers of a strange tongue who came from a 'low island to the eastward'. This island was called Papaa (i.e. the name formerly used by the Tahitians to describe the people of Anaa), and up to that time, Greatheed thought, it had 'not yet been seen' by Europeans. 'It is asserted,' he added, 'that their language is unintelligible to the natives of the Society isles; which leads to the supposition that some colony has been formed there of a different race from all the neighbouring islanders.'[7]

As chapter 15 has already revealed, the LMS missionary John Davies was the first person to record first-hand information about the Anaan tongue. This was in 1807 when four canoe-loads of Anaans were forced to land in Tahiti. Some of the information that Davies then gleaned was incorporated some twenty years later in a history he wrote of the LMS mission to Tahiti. He said in this that in pre-European times, the Anaans were 'the only strangers of a foreign speech' known to the Society Islanders, and that in the early days of the mission, few of them could understand Tahitian. In more recent times, he added, they had had so much contact with Tahiti that it seemed likely that their dialect would soon become obsolete.[8] Despite Davies' prediction, something of the distinctive Anaan dialect persisted for several more decades, and its peculiarities were duly noted by other linguists, notably Hale (1839) and Tregear (1891). Hale said that Anaan was made up of two distinct elements—one similar to Tahitian and one quite unlike it. The latter included numerous words that were 'usually original in a language, and very rarely introduced from abroad'. Tregear said among other things that Anaan was 'crossed' with many foreign words that were 'utterly strange to the Maori linguist'. Besides the numerals, the words for which Hale and Tregear recorded 'foreign' rather than Polynesian equivalents were: ashes (*tapurena*), bone (*keinga*), canoe (*aveke*), cloud (*paku*), to count (*kamoke*), dark (*ruki*), dog (*ngaeke*), egg (*touo*), fat (*paneke*), fault (*veke*), finger (*manemanea*), fire (*neki, korure, rotika*), fish (*paru*), fishhook (*tate*), to follow (*utari*), forest (*puka*), fruit (*teke*), girl (*manania*), good (*viru*), great (*toreu*), head (*pepenu*), heart (*upoupo*), heart of a tree (*nimo*), husband (*kaifa*), kidney (*pouru*), ladder (*kega*), large (*tuetue*), little (*korereka*), liver (*kerikeri*), man (*hakoi*), moon (*kavake*), mud (*niganiga*), oil (*mori*), rain (*toiti*), road (*keka*), salt (*toau*), sea (*takarari*), to see (*hipa*), slave (*titi*), to sleep (*piko*), smoke (*kaihora*), son (*makaro*), spirit (*mahoi, horohoro*), stone (*konao*), stupid (*kama*), sweat (*togari*), tongue (*maveu?*), tree (*mohoki*), water (*komo*), wind (*rohaki*), woman (*erire, morire*).[9]

Following the devastating hurricanes that struck Anaa in 1878 and 1906, the Tahitianisation of the language apparently continued apace, for J. Frank Stimson, who began studying that dialect in the 1920s, did not record several of the alien words that were included in the lists of Hale and Tregear; nor did he remark on any anomalies concerning it in the introduction to his posthumously-published Tuamotuan dictionary (The Hague, 1964).[10] On the other hand, Stimson's colleague K. P. Emory collected twenty plant names peculiar to Anaa before World War II—the greatest number for any atoll in the Tuamotus.[11]

The earliest evidence suggesting that a non-Polynesian language was once spoken on Easter Island is contained in the journal of Francisco de Agüera y Infanzon, an officer of the Spanish expedition to Easter Island of 1770. The journal was first published—in English—in 1909. It reveals that Agüera collected ninety-four Easter Island words, including the first ten numerals.[12] The numerals bear no resemblance to those in the island's Polynesian dialect of today, whereas most of the other words are clearly recognisable in present-day speech.[13] By contrast, when Captain Cook visited Easter Island in 1774, he recorded that the first islander to board his ship spoke in a language that was 'wholly unintelligible to all of us'—*except for the numerals,* which were like those of Tahiti.[14] The astronomer William Wales expressed a similar view—that the islanders in general had 'but few words common with Otaheite'.[15] Nevertheless, both J. R. Forster and Lieutenant Pickersgill recorded numerals that were almost identical to those of Tahiti of that time and of the Easter Island dialect of today. Forster also gathered thirty-six other words, most of which are recognisably Polynesian.[16] But he did not record whether he heard any words that were *not* intelligible to him.

Except for a brief (previously unpublished) comment by the English conchologist Hugh Cuming—who found at Easter Island in 1827 that a Tuamotuan he had with him could understand 'but a few words' of the local speech[17]—nothing else was recorded about the Easter Island language for almost a century. The information gathered up to 1774 is therefore an insubstantial base from which to draw conclusions. Nevertheless, several scholars have drawn conclusions. In the main, they have taken the view that the only language ever spoken on Easter Island was Polynesian. It therefore followed, in their view, that the Spaniard, Agüera, must have been in error in recording the numerals.[18] This, however, was not the view of the late Father Sebastian Englert, who lived on Easter Island for thirty-five years and made its culture his constant study. 'That some confusion of translation was involved seems unlikely,' he wrote, 'for those ten words have no known meaning whatever in the local speech [of today].' Father Englert also stated that the strange numerals may have belonged to the language of the Hanau Eepe, i.e. the reputed builders of Easter Island's huge statues and other stone structures. 'The Hanau Eepe appear to have spoken a language different from that of the [later-arriving] people of Hotu Matu'a . . ,' he wrote. 'It would seem reasonable that some influence of the language of the Hanua Eepe might have remained in modern speech . . . Perhaps some of the synonyms of today might be so explained.*[19]

An important point to be borne in mind about the language of Easter Island is that even in the past century or so it has been subject to some cataclysmic influences. In the first place, much must have been lost in the 1860s when the islanders were almost annihilated following the Peruvian slave raids and the subsequent smallpox epidemic. Secondly, the language became strongly influenced by Tahitian and Mangarevan in the years after 1864 as a result of the arrival on the island of Tahiti-oriented missionaries and teachers; the employment there of a number of Tahitians as ranchers; and the temporary migration of many islanders to Tahiti and Mangareva.[20] J. L. Palmer, a visitor to the island in 1869, wrote: 'Their language has so much altered that it is impossible to say what it was originally.'[21] Half a century later, another visitor, Professor J. Macmillan Brown, wrote: 'Tahitian . . . really penetrated into the heart of the language . . . It was inevitable that the native tongue should die out.'[22]

As no outsider other than Englert has ever made a thorough on-the-spot study of the Easter Island language, his opinions on that subject must be relied on much more heavily than would otherwise be desirable. However, there is other evidence that tends to support his views. On the one hand, the people of Easter Island were plainly of mixed origins when the first Europeans encountered them in 1722. Behrens, it will be recalled, recorded that some were 'brown like the Spaniards', while others were 'pretty black', 'quite white' or of a 'reddish complexion'.[23] These descriptions were 'still accurate' in 1914 when Mrs. Scoresby Routledge visited the island and found the people 'very conscious of the variations'. 'When we were collecting genealogies', she wrote, 'they were quite ready to give the colour of even remote relations.'[24]

Other likely support for Englert's views is to be found at Reao Atoll, one of Easter Island's nearest neighbours. On that atoll, the islanders were still speaking a strange dialect well into the present century; they were very dark and different physically from other Polynesians; and, as at Easter Island, their homeland was remarkable for numerous stone structures. In addition, there are two instances on record of Easter Islanders having drifted to Reao in canoes —once in the nineteenth century, and once in 1947-8.[25] These two events naturally suggest that the first inhabitants of Reao may have originated in Easter Island.

Reao, which lies some 1,200 miles to leeward of Easter Island, is remote from regular shipping lanes and was not discovered by Europeans until 1822.[26] Its inhabitants, who, it seems, formerly moved from time to time to neighbouring Pukarua, thirty miles north-westward, had virtually no contact with Europeans until the Catholic missionaries at Mangareva transported many of them to that island in the mid-1860s to be indoctrinated in the Catholic faith. On being repatriated about a year later, they were probably accompanied by Mangarevan catechists.[27] This contact with Mangareva apparently had a

---

* *If Hotu Matu'a and some of his followers were, indeed, of part-European descent, as is argued in chapter 20, then they could not have reached Easter Island before about the second half of the sixteenth century. In that case, the Hanau Eepe (according to carbon dates) must have been living on Easter Island for well over 1,000 years. During that time, they would undoubtedly have lost all immunity to even the mildest diseases from the outside world, and so, presumably, would have quickly been decimated by such ailments as Hotu Matu'a and his followers brought with them. Thus, the foundation would have been laid for the language and culture of a small group of invaders to become paramount.*

substantial effect on their language, for when the French scientist L. G. Seurat visited Reao at the turn of the twentieth century, he noted that the language was 'somewhat different' from that of the other Tuamotuan atolls, being 'closer to Mangarevan'.[28] The next person to comment in print on the Reao language was the French priest Hervé Audran, who claimed in 1918, after ten years in the Tuamotus, that a conversation among the Reao people was 'absolutely incomprehensible' to other Tuamotuans.[29] Stimson expressed similar views in the introduction to his Tuamotuan dictionary—views which supplemented his first impressions of the language in 1929 when he visited the atoll with Emory. In a report to the Bishop Museum at that time, Stimson emphasised that Reao had an extraordinary kinship system in which almost 200 terms were used. As this was more than three times as many as found in Tahitian, he found it difficult to avoid the inference of an intrusive non-Polynesian influence, although the words themselves were 'clearly of Polynesian linguistic stock'.[30] In his dictionary, Stimson went considerably further. The Reao dialect, he said, differed from other Tuamotuan dialects both structurally and semantically. Moreover, it was 'said to be intrusive in the Tuamotuan area', and old Tuamotuans claimed that neither they nor their immediate ancestors could understand it.

> The Reao dialect [Stimson went on] raises interesting problems both historically and morphologically. There are indications that it may be an extremely archaic form which has survived due to some unknown factor, perhaps isolation over a long period, and [is] not a congener of the other widespread and closely interrelated Polynesian speech groups. The language may contain an example of infix—a linguistic phenomenon not recorded, to my knowledge, east of Samoa and Tonga. There are traces of other anachronisms of grammatical process and morphological structure which should be verified independently. The kinship terms of Reao differ materially from those of the Tuamotus in certain respects, and are by far the most systematic and detailed of any recorded for the archipelago . . . Again, their counting method is the most systematic and complete of any I have recorded.

Stimson noted that the Reao people differed physically from most Polynesians in that they were short, stocky, very strong in the arms rather than the legs, and unusually dark in colour. Then he added a descriptive touch that is reminiscent of many of the statues of Easter Island. 'The [Reao] face has a vertically "compressed" appearance that is very distinctive,' he said.[31] Other visitors to Reao over the years also remarked on the distinctive features of the inhabitants. Captain F. W. Beechey who was there in 1826 thought the islanders were 'a very inferior race' compared with the Mangarevans. To him, they were 'more nearly allied in feature' to the people of Mangaia or New Caledonia —two places that he did not, in fact, know at first hand.[32] Edward Belcher, one of Beechey's officers, described the Reao people as 'sooty black in colour' and unlike any he had previously seen. They had rounder faces and less ferocity than usual.[33] In 1839, Commodore Wilkes wrote: 'Their colour was darker than that of our [North American] Indians, but their features resembled them. No tattooing was observed on the men . . . The hair . . . was long, black and straight.'[34] Captain W. L. Hudson, Wilkes' second-in-command, who did not go ashore, described the Reao people as being of a molasses or chestnut colour.[35] Emory, writing in 1929, thought the islanders were 'primitive' and 'readily distinguishable in a crowd of Tuamotuans'. 'Most of them,' he added, 'could be described as small, pug-faced, timid and non-Polynesian in appearance.'[36] Finally, there is the opinion of an American journalist, A. C. Rowland, who lived in Tahiti for many years and employed a Reao islander as a man-of-all-work in the early years of the century. Writing in 1943, Rowland claimed that the Reao people resembled South American Indians. 'I have never been in South America,' he said, 'but the physiognomy of the Reao people certainly resembles that of pictures I have seen of primitive natives of the South American interior.'[37] Rowland enlarged on the same subject in 1947 when he wrote:

> The more one studies the subject, the more one is persuaded that the islands of South-eastern Polynesia were inhabited by a colony of pre-Inca South Americans, long before the first Polynesians entered the Pacific from the west.
>
> Not the least of the evidence is the large vocabulary within the body of the language of this area, of which no trace nor relationship exists in the speech of Samoa, Tonga, Hawaii or Cook Islands.
>
> Then, too, the long-isolated far-eastern island, Reao—whose strange people have retained the physical characteristics of a non-Polynesian ancestry, whose massive stone platforms and arrangement of stone pillars correspond with those of Easter Island—presents convincing evidence of migration from the east.[38]

Rowland's statements on the stone remains of Reao were apparently based on those contained in Emory's monograph

Tuamotuan Stone Structures, published in 1934. In that work, Emory said that the *marae* ruins of Reao were more numerous and better preserved than those of any other atoll he had visited in the Tuamotus, and that they differed from those of the western atolls in many respects. On the other hand, they closely resembled those of Tatakoto Atoll, about 120 miles north-west of Reao, and also of Necker Island, Hawaii. 'It is easy to believe,' Emory went on, 'that the *maraes* of the eastern Tuamotus are survivals of the same culture which left the prehistoric *maraes* on Necker Island, and therefore that the Tatakoto and Reao *maraes* represent a form employed by the earliest settlers both in Hawaii and in southeastern Polynesia.' Emory also made the point that the 'great image platforms of Easter Island' followed a plan that could be construed as a magnification and elaboration of the Tuamotuan *marae*.[39] However, if he had not felt so certain that all prehistoric inhabitants of Polynesia had originated in the west, he might equally have stated that the Tatakoto and Reao *marae* could be viewed as degenerate forms of the Easter Island structures. On this point it is worth recalling Archbishop Paul Mazé's statement (p. 308) that the people of Reao and neighbouring Pukarua 'contrasted violently' in their physical appearance with those of Tatakoto in the 1920s. So it is scarcely likely that people so different could both have been directly descended from the builders of such similar stone structures.

Napuka, the third Tuamotuan island where strong traces of a seemingly non-Polynesian language have been recorded, is some 350 miles north-west of Reao. With its neighbour Tepoto, it is nearer to the Marquesas Islands than any other inhabited atoll. Probably the first European to notice anomalies in its language was Father Germain Fierens, who called there off and on for more than thirty years after his first visit in 1871. However, Fierens lost most of his papers in a notable hurricane of 1903,[40] and it was left to his colleague Father Audran to make the first comments about the language in print. Its peculiarities evidently impressed him, for he remarked in three separate articles that the Napukan tongue was completely different from other Tuamotuan dialects.[41] 'Both the Napukan and the Reao people could very well hold a conversation before another Tuamotuan in their own dialect without his understanding them,' he said on one occasion.[42] In another article, Audran listed the Napukan numerals from one to 100, and the names of the months, nights of the moon, winds, stars, and parts of a canoe. With four exceptions, the numerals were the same as the strange numerals recorded for Anaa by Davies, Hale and Tregear, and some of the other Napukan words were also similar or identical to their Anaan counterparts.[43]

In 1929, Stimson visited Napuka with Emory for ten days and gathered a list of 1,500 words.[44] In a report to the Bishop Museum, he said the language of Napuka appeared to show a certain linguistic affiliation with the Marquesas, and was linguistically extremely interesting in other ways. Many Napukan words indicated no apparent resemblance with other Polynesian dialects. 'Is it possible,' he wondered, 'that investigation may show some of these to be related to Melanesian or perhaps, even, to some mainland tongue? Certain of the Napukan words are also found in Easter Island; one of them is *maurikero*, in both languages the name of one of the nights of the moon . . .'[45]

In a similar report to the Bishop Museum, Emory remarked on the 'curious peculiarities of language, physical type and culture' to be found at Napuka. He also listed six words that Stimson had gathered to show the 'striking differences' between some Napukan words and those of 'standard Polynesian'. The words in question were those for canoe, leg, Tridacna, sand, to urinate and fire.[46] Two of them, sand and fire, were in the Anaan lists of Hale and Tregear.

Stimson wrote further about 'divergences' of the Napukan dialect in the introduction to his dictionary.[47] But the fullest account of it was given by the American journalist Clifford Gessler who visited Napuka for ten weeks with Emory in 1934. In his book *The Dangerous Islands*, Gessler acknowledged that much of what he knew of the language was derived from Emory, and he began by echoing what Davies had said of the Anaan tongue in 1807:

> The language situation [on Napuka] was very interesting inasmuch as many common objects are represented by three different words of identical meaning—suggesting remnants of three separate languages or dialects. Of three words signifying the same thing, one commonly is the Tahitian form; one is the general Polynesian form resembling the Hawaiian or the Maori; the third we were unable to relate, in most cases, to any known language. This third language, if language it be, is known by the natives as 'the root speech' (*te rekotumu*), a designation which may indicate its antiquity.[48]

Gessler went on to give several dozen examples of 'the root speech', some of which had been recorded for Anaa by Hale and Tregear. Further on in his book, in discussing the origins of the Polynesians, Gessler remarked that most Napukans seemed to be descended from an early wave of migrants. 'The evidence of this,' he said, 'is in their physical appearance, language and customs; the structure of their sacred places and the simplicity of their social organisation. Their culture evidently stems from the same period in Polynesian history as that which Hawaii-loa's supposed fifth-century migration took.' Gessler recalled that on one occasion, as he and Emory were discussing the *menehune* or early inhabitants of Hawaii, Emory glanced round the room at their Napukan friends and said: 'These are the *menehune*.' 'Indeed,' Gessler added, 'their lower stature, compared with many other Polynesians, and their compact though powerful build, suggest the physical differences exaggerated by Hawaiian legend into tales of a race of dwarfs.'[49]

Gessler's view of the distinctive appearance of the Napukans was shared by several earlier visitors to their island. In 1839, Commodore Wilkes described them as a 'peculiar' people—'totally distinct' from any others he saw in the Tuamotus, or, for that matter, anywhere else in Polynesia. They had strong, wiry beards and moustaches, and a 'different physiognomy'. At one end of the island, they were 'much darker' than at the other, some having hair 'inclined to frizzle'. Wilkes added: '[The islanders of the Tuamotus] are certainly not all from the same stock, and those of the Disappointment Group [i.e. Napuka and Tepoto] . . . in particular differ from the others. Since we have seen all the different Polynesian groups, these appear, however extraordinary it may be, to resemble the Feejee Islanders more than any other.'[50] Wilkes' colleague, Captain Hudson, had the impression that the Napukans he saw were two or three shades lighter than the Reao people, and that they had 'a strong Moorish cast of features'.[51] And yet another visitor, Major A. J. A. Douglas, who touched at Napuka in the early 1920s, thought the islanders resembled people he had seen on the coasts of southern India. 'The difference between these people and the Marquesans was very marked,' he added.[52]

Although Anaa, Napuka and Reao are the only islands of Eastern Polynesia where substantial evidence of an apparent non-Polynesian language has been recorded, there are at least four others where strong hints of such a language occur in the literature. These are Rapa and Raivavae in the Austral Group, and Fangatau and Hao in the Tuamotus.[53] Like the others, they are all far removed from the Society Islands and other high, volcanic groups; they are all noted for elaborate stone structures (including statues at Raivavae reminiscent of those of Easter Island); and on every island, people of a swarthy hue were reported by early European visitors.[54] (At Fangatau, a 'tall, rangy type with features suggesting certain tribes of American Indians' was also reported by Gessler.)[55]

Yet another language that shows every sign of being a hybrid is Tahitian. Paul Huguenin, it will be recalled (see chapter 14), was of the opinion that Tahitian was made up of two elements—one being a relic of the language spoken by the *manahune*, or original settlers of Tahiti, the other the language of the *raatira* and *arii* who conquered them. Huguenin cited a number of synonyms to support his view. These included: *toa, 'aito* (ironwood); *po, ru'i* (night); *ao, ra'i* (sky); *tai, miti, tua* (sea); *piti, rua* (two); and *'uru, maiore* (breadfruit).[56] Huguenin's list can apparently be considerably extended. A few further examples are: *'uo, teatea* (white); *mo'a, ra'a, tapu* (sacred); *'ava'e, marama* (moon); *ao, ata* (clouds); *ra, mahana* (sun); *anino, avae* (the foot); and *vai, pape* (water).[57]

There are several striking features about the Tahitian synonyms. First, they are invariably words for commonplace objects, materials or concepts. Second, the verbal equivalent of only one word of each pair or group can usually be found in Tongan and/or Samoan, but the other can generally be traced to the Tuamotus.[58] Moreover, some Tahitian words have no Tongan or Samoan equivalents at all, only Tuamotuan equivalents. An example of this is the word for 'black'—*'ere'ere* in Tahitian and *kerekere* in Tuamotuan; but *uliuli* or *uriuri* in the languages of Western Polynesia. Yet another noteworthy point is that the Tahitian form of any word with a Tuamotuan equivalent is almost invariably a corruption of the Tuamotuan word. Two examples are *'ava'e* and *'ere'ere*, where the *k*'s have been replaced by glottal stops.

These factors, in their turn, suggest that:

1. The Tuamotuan elements in Tahitian are as non-Polynesian as the strange elements in the dialects of Anaa, Reao and Napuka.

2. The Tuamotuan elements in Tahitian must have been brought to the Pacific by a people travelling from east to west, as the uncorrupted form of any word must be older linguistically than the corrupted form, and Tahiti is to the westward of the Tuamotus.

3. The only place east of the Tuamotus and Easter Island from which a non-Polynesian people is likely to have come is the west coast of South America.

4. The non-Polynesian people must have reached the Tuamotus-Tahiti area before the Polynesian speakers from the west, as the surviving relics of their speech are of a kind that are 'usually original in a language', to use Horatio Hale's expression.

The foregoing conclusions are in accord with the principles of a well-attested theory in linguistics called areal linguistics. This theory postulates that in any area where two languages or two forms of the same language are spoken, the older will survive longest in the most isolated parts of the area and (what may be the same thing) in those places that are farthest from its linguistic centre.[59] It is therefore in the nature of things that the alien element should still have been evident in such places as Napuka and Reao well into this century, as those islands are both isolated from all their neighbours and remote from Tahiti, the linguistic centre of Eastern Polynesia for the past 200 years. It was equally natural that Anaa should have begun to lose its distinctive dialect early in the nineteenth century, for once the Anaans established contact with Tahiti, they were constantly influenced by Tahitian speakers and books in the Tahitian language.

A further conclusion that may be drawn from the areal linguistics theory is that wherever an ancient language survives, the speakers of it must, of necessity, be of relatively pure descent from those who spoke it originally. It is therefore possible to deduce from the present-day appearance of the people of Napuka and Reao that wherever a non-Polynesian language was once spoken in the eastern Pacific, its speakers must have been much darker-skinned than most Polynesian speakers of later times.

That a non-Polynesian language was once widely spoken in the Tuamotus is evident from the fact that the people of that archipelago were, and are, invariably said to be darker, generally, than their neighbours in the Society Islands.[60] However, the Tuamotuans are plainly of mixed origins as their dialects are replete with words for various shades of skin colour. A few examples are: *kokere* (black-skinned), *tuhuamotu* (dark-brown—said of the Polynesian skin colour), *vakitau* (a race of white-skinned people), *angauru* (a member of a light, whitish, olive-skinned race; darker than *vakitau*).[61] In the Society Islands, the case for the former existence of a non-Polynesian language is supported by the fact that the early European visitors repeatedly described the *manahune*, or common people, as considerably darker than those of the chiefly class. The language of the *manahune* may, in fact, have still been spoken in Tahiti in historical times, for James Morrison recorded that some of the priests—who included people of the lowest class—chanted their hymns and prayers in an 'unknown tongue' (see p. 147). In the case of Easter Island, genetic evidence of the former existence of non-Polynesian speakers appears to have come down to modern times in the form of the 'pretty black' people described by Behrens and Mrs. Routledge. Finally, the swarthy people of Rapa and Raivavae, described elsewhere, provide the same kind of evidence for those islands.

Other factors that strongly support the notion of a non-Polynesian language in the eastern Pacific in former times are to be found in two of the principal food plants of the area when the first Europeans arrived. The two plants are the coconut and sweet potato.

The first of these was known in Tahiti —not by its pan-Polynesian name, *niu*— but under the name, *ha'ari*, a corruption of the Tuamotuan word, *hakari*.[62] This suggests that the first people to cultivate the coconut in Tahiti were not Polynesian speakers from the west, but non-Polynesian speakers from the east. So it may well be that the coconut of the eastern Pacific was not of Asiatic origin, as is usually supposed, but that it came from South America.

In the case of the sweet potato, it is noteworthy that when J. R. Forster gathered his list of forty-six basic Polynesian words in 1773-4, he recorded the word *kumara*, or something similar, for Easter Island, the Marquesas, the Society Islands and New Zealand. But he did not obtain any word for it in Tonga; nor did he or any of his companions list the sweet potato among the products of those islands. This, on the face of things, would seem to have been an omission, considering that a companion of Cook, on his third voyage, *did* mention it as a Tongan plant, as did several other European visitors to Tonga during the next thirty years.[63] However, the truth undoubtedly is that Cook himself took the sweet potato to Tonga in 1774; that the Tongans then acquired the Society Islands name for it; and that both the plant and the name were soon widely known. A present-day authority on Tongan language and tradition, the Hon. Ve'ehala, says there are two reasons for believing that the sweet potato is a very recent introduction to Tonga. One is that the vegetable has no place in traditional presentation ceremonies; the other is that there are no local names for the varieties of it.[64] The situation in Samoa provides further support for this notion, as statements by two early LMS missionaries make it clear that both the sweet potato and the word for it were unknown in those islands before the advent of Europeans.[65] Moreover, it was not recorded among the people of Futuna, to the northward of Tonga, when the Schouten and Le Maire expedition touched there in 1616; and it is still scarcely known either there or at neighbouring Wallis Island even today.[66] Finally, the word is not recorded in the first published dictionary (1907) of the language of Niue, which lies to the east of Tonga and to the south of Samoa.[67] All this shows that both the sweet potato and the name for it in Polynesia must have been brought to the Pacific from the east—not by way of the Polynesian heartland in the western Pacific. This, in fact, was the generally-accepted view of Pacific scholars for well over a century—until an American scholar, David Brand, suggested otherwise in a paper published in 1971. Brand pointed out that although the Chinchasuyo Indians of the Ecuadorian Andes used the word *cumar* for sweet potato, no word resembling *kumara* is or was used by the people of the coastal regions of Colombia, Ecuador or Peru, either now or in historical times. Brand therefore concluded that the Polynesian word *kumara* could not have been derived from any South American language. He was also inclined to think that the sweet potato reached Polynesia by way of Melanesia.[68]

Brand's view on the non-South American origin of the word *kumara* has since been accepted by at least two Pacific scholars.[69] But both they and he seem to have overlooked two important points. One is that the pre-history of the west coast of South America before the Spanish Conquest is extremely little known.[70] So it is quite possible that the Chinchasuyo Indians or some other people using the word *cumar/kumara* once lived on that coast—before some of their number set off for Polynesia, perhaps as many as 1,500 years ago, on what would almost certainly have been an involuntary voyage. Secondly, most of the languages of coastal Ecuador, not to mention those of coastal Colombia and Peru, have become extinct since the Conquest, and almost nothing is now known about them.[71] It is therefore too late now, probably, to determine whether any of them ever did have a word resembling *cumar* or *kumara*. Likewise, it may be too late to try to establish the origin of the other words in the dialects of the eastern Pacific that do not figure in those of the west. However, this should not be interpreted to mean that no attempt should be made to seek their origin. Nor should it be thought that this appendix gives anything more than a bare outline of the available literature concerning them. Many of the chants and traditions collected in the eastern Tuamotus by Stimson and Emory, for example, have never been adequately studied. Thus, as Stimson said in an introduction to his dictionary, an analysis of them could possibly yield 'a fairly accurate description of dialectical differences'.[72]

APPENDIX G

Light features among non-Europeans

White skin, red hair and blue eyes—three physical features that are especially associated with Europeans—are not, in fact, entirely confined to them. But with two exceptions, the combination of two or more of these light features seems to have been solely confined to the Caucasian peoples of Europe and North Africa until recent centuries. The two exceptions are albinos of dark-skinned ancestry and descendants of the Greek soldiers of Alexander the Great (356-323 BC), who penetrated to and settled in countries as far east as present-day Pakistan.[1]

White skin is found among the Ainu of Japan—who, according to a recent study, are *not* a Caucasian people as was once believed—and among the Japanese themselves.[2] Red hair is occasionally to be seen among people as dark as Negroes and the Melanesians of New Guinea.[3] And it has evidently been known in Polynesia since ancient times as two of the earliest European visitors to Samoa—where no miscegenation with 'pre-contact' Europeans is suspected—reported instances of it.[4] As for blue eyes, extremely rare cases of these are to be found among very dark-skinned, dark-haired, seemingly 'non-Greek' people in India and Sri Lanka (formerly Ceylon); and they are common among albinos of dark-skinned ancestry.

The geneticist R. R. Gates recorded seeing a man in Kandy, Sri Lanka, who had blue eyes with 'full dark skin colour and black wavy hair'. Other members of his family were 'in the same condition'. Gates concluded that the blue eyes, 'always recessive in other countries so far as known', were inherited in these cases as a dominant character.[5] I myself saw an Indian man of similar features at Savusavu, Fiji, in May 1972. His name was Bhagauti Prasad. He was the son of an indentured labourer brought to Fiji from near Calcutta some time before 1920. Prasad told me that his father had had blue eyes; his mother, a Fiji-born Indian, brown eyes. He, himself, had two sisters and one brother. One had blue eyes like himself; those of the others were 'brownish-blue'. Prasad was married to a brown-eyed Indian woman and had three children all of whom were brown-eyed. A notable feature of his own eyes was that the 'whites' were heavily pigmented, and were quite unlike those of blue-eyed Europeans.

The surgeon Frederick Debell Bennett, who visited the Society Islands in the 1830s, has left a record of the albino daughter of two dark-complexioned Tahitians. Her appearance prompted him to remark that 'the pink eyes, so usual with European albinos, do not appear to prevail in the albinos of the dark-skinned races of man'. He added that the Tahitian girl's eyes were blue and 'intolerant of light'.[6] I myself have seen similar eyes among albinos in Fiji.

The geneticists L. C. Dunn and Theodosius Dobzhansky state that among mankind as a whole, 'the usual coloration of the hair is black, of the eyes brown, and of the skin more or less brown'. They go on:

> It is only in Europe, and particularly across the northern part, from England, through Scandinavia and northern Germany to most of European Russia, that there is a large center of 'blondness'. From there these fair-skinned people have within the last few centuries spread all over the world. Southward and eastward from the northern countries the proportions of individuals with blue eyes, blond hair, and fair skin decrease and those with brown eyes, brown or black hair, and swarthy skin increase.[7]

Because the structure of the face cannot be readily measured or described, blanket statements on the facial structure of the various branches of the human race are not to be found in scientific literature. However, anyone who has visited India and the Arab countries will be well aware that the facial structure of many Arabs and Indians closely resembles that of Europeans, although the colour of their skin, hair and eyes is consistently much darker. It is therefore to the Arab or Indian world, apparently, that one must look for the origin of the 'hundreds of truly European faces & many genuine Roman noses'—but otherwise unEuropean features—that one of Cook's officers described in Tonga in the 1770s (see Appendix D). The ancestors of these Roman-nosed Tongans may have reached Tonga by way of the Malaysian archipelago, whence Arabs and Indians are believed to have traded before the tenth century.[8] This, however, is a matter for further investigation.

Notes and references

Notes and references

CHAPTER 1: The four cannon of Amanu

1. Five of the seventy-six islands are not atolls. One, Makatea, is of upraised coral. The other four were atolls originally but their lagoons have dried up. These are Nukutavake, Akiaki, Tepoto and Tikei.
2. For detailed accounts of the Tuamotu Archipelago generally, see Agassiz 1903 and Danielsson 1956.
3. Roggeveen did not use the term 'labyrinth' in his own journal, but one of his companions, Carl Friedrich Behrens, wrote: 'We named them the Labyrinth, because we were obliged to make many turnings before we could get out.'—Dalrymple 1771:101. The name has generally been attributed to Roggeveen.
4. Bougainville 1772:208.
5. Beaglehole 1961:195-6.
6. As the problem of determining longitude was not solved until the eighteenth century, the identity of some Pacific islands discovered by European explorers before that time is in doubt. However, Maude 1968:38-43 and Meinicke 1876:203 concluded independently that Magellan's first landfall in the Pacific was Pukapuka. Maude's arguments are particularly convincing. Audran 1917:53 thought San Pablo was 'probably' Pukapuka.
7. Captain Robert Fitz-Roy of HMS *Beagle* has long been considered the European discoverer of Taiaro and Kauehi, the last of the Tuamotuan atolls to be added to the published charts. See, for example, Findlay 1863: 457-8 and Sharp 1960:220. However, Kauehi was possibly known to European pearlers before Fitz-Roy's voyage.—Mauruc 1848:87-8.
8. A statement to this effect was made in NID. 1943-5:II:194. It is still true, although French naval hydrographers have made considerable improvements since World War II. For reports on recent hydrographic surveys in the Tuamotus, see *Annales Hydrographiques,* ser. 4, no. 2, p. 5-31; no. 5, p. 89-138; no. 8, p. 167-249; no. 12, p. 15-103; no. 13, p. 185-227.
9. British Admiralty chart no. 3664, 'Ile Hao', corrected to 24 Jan. 1964.
10. See US Hydrographic Office chart no. 5732. The name of the US Hydrographic Office was changed in 1962 to US Naval Oceanographic Office.
11. See, for example, US Naval Oceanographic Office chart no. H.O.77, 'Archipel des Tuamotus', 19th edition, 19 Nov. 1956, revised 19 Feb. 1968; and British Admiralty chart no. 992, 'Archipel des Tuamotus', 15 June 1955, with small corrections to 1962.
12. O'Reilly and Teissier 1962:211-3; Pinchot [1930]:487.
13. For information on the pearling industry, see chapter 15.
14. Duperrey 1827, pl. 3 and 1829:II:38.
15. Duperrey n.d.:23.
16. The *Mouette* is briefly described in *JOEFO,* 16 Sept. 1934. Ironically, she herself was wrecked in negotiating a pass at Amanu in mid-December 1934 and sank in fifteen fathoms.—Seligman 1947:225.
17. Pinchot [1930]:487. Hervé was a foundation member of the Société d'Etudes Océaniennes.—*BSEO,* 1917:1: 6.
18. Pinchot [1930]:486-7. Inquiries through Pinchot's son, Dr G. B. Pinchot of Upperco, Maryland, USA, have failed to reveal what became of the alien stones. Dr Pinchot, then a boy of eight, accompanied his parents on their Pacific cruise in 1929.
19. Russell 1935:149.
20. Robson 1935:173.
21. Subsequent editions of the *Pacific Islands Year Book* appeared in 1939, 1942, 1944, 1950, 1956, 1959, 1963, 1968 and 1972.
22. Langdon 1963a.
23. For a summary of theories on the origins of the Polynesians, see Heyerdahl 1952:4-8; Howard 1967.
24. Heyerdahl 1952:802, under the entry, 'Caucasian, Caucasoid, Caucasianlike', provides a key to many views on this subject. For other, more recent views, see, for example, Suggs 1960:25-37, and the introduction by Bengt Danielsson in Barrow 1967.
25. When I first read accounts of the Euro-

pean exploration of Polynesia in 1953-58 in researching my book on Tahiti (Langdon 1959), I was impressed by the theories of Thor Heyerdahl and wrote in the introduction (p. 4): 'The people of Tahiti are Polynesians. They seem to be descended from two, and possibly three, distinct races. No one is sure where they came from originally, but it seems possible that one race migrated from South America, one from what is now British Columbia, via Hawaii, and one from Melanesia. There had been a good deal of interbreeding before the Europeans arrived.'

26. For further details on the peregrinations of the Papeete Museum, see Jacquier 1967.

27. Langdon 1968.

28. *New Zealand Herald,* Wellington, 17 Feb. 1968:9.

29. Pers. comm., 25 Feb. 1959.

30. The museum was opened in 1969.—*PIM,* April 1969, p. 34-5.

31. For a biographical sketch of Darnois, see O'Reilly and Teissier 1962:109.

32. For clarity, I have altered the order of one sentence in the partial translation of Captain Le Goaziou's letter. A copy of the letter has been deposited in the Mitchell Library, Sydney.

33. As the sheathing of ships' bottoms with copper was not adopted until the latter part of the eighteenth century (see Carrington 1948:xxxi), Le Goaziou's assumption on this point is obviously correct. However, research has failed to establish the identity of the copper-sheathed wreck found by his divers. Ralph Varady, author of a book dealing partly with the Tuamotus, gave me a possible clue when I was in Tahiti in July 1969. He said that during a visit to Amanu in 1958 he had discovered a bell, partly buried in sand, while walking along the beach. The words 'Capiolani 1860' were crudely engraved on it. It had no clapper and had been dented on the outside through being struck with a hard object. Varady later suggested that the bell might have been used on Amanu for some years and then lost during a hurricane, possibly in 1903 or 1906. The only ship called *Capiolani* or *Kapiolani* that I have discovered in Pacific shipping records is the schooner *Kapiolani,* which made a voyage between Truk and the Mortlock Islands in 1887.—Bliss 1906:125. There was an Hawaiian chiefess called Kapiolani who died in 1841. Another of the same name was the consort of King Kalakaua in the 1880s.

34. The fourth cannon was possibly recovered by Hervé himself on a subsequent voyage to Amanu. There is a hint of this possibility in Gifford Pinchot's journal of the voyage described in Pinchot [1930], now in the Library of Congress, Washington. In an entry for 15 Oct. 1929, three days after Hervé had shown him the 'first' cannon in the Papeete Museum, Pinchot wrote: 'Hervé has promised, if we will come back to the Tuamotus, that he will give us one of the three cannon which remain at Amanu . . .' Pinchot did not return to the Tuamotus.

35. *Canberra Times,* 23 Sept. 1970.

36. Pers. comm., 30 Sept. 1970.

37. Mr Kennard's references are: ffoulkes 1937 and Hogg 1970. Parry 1964:133 says: 'All guns used in ships in the fifteenth century were of the forged or built-up type. In making such a gun, a number of long, thin bars of wrought iron were bound round a cylindrical core, heated in a forge and hammered into a tube open at both ends. Over the barrel so made, hoops of iron were slipped at white heat, and contracted on to the barrel by cooling, thus clamping the barrel more firmly together.'

38. Parry 1964:135-6 says that in the first two decades of the sixteenth century, a growing metallurgical industry, chiefly in Flanders and Germany, and later England, discovered ways of casting guns that were manageable enough for mounting in ships. However, sixteenth century blast furnaces could not easily produce enough iron in a sufficiently liquid state for the casting of large iron guns, and for about a century or more after 1520 most large guns, and all the best guns, were made of brass or gun-metal (usually an alloy of copper, tin, and zinc). For information on the development of the blast furnace in the sixteenth century, see Singer and others 1956:30-4, 62, 66, 70, 655.

39. Chiao-Min Hsieh 1967:87-95.

40. Beaglehole 1966:36-7, 39; NID 1943-5:I:244; Grattan 1963. A recent history that does devote a couple of pages to the Loaisa expedition is Brand 1967.

CHAPTER 2: The lost caravel

1. Boulnois 1966; Seligman 1939.

2. Woodcock 1966; Hourani 1951; Baker 1938.

3. For basic data on the voyages of Dias, Columbus and their immediate successors, I have made especial use of one of the earliest reference works—

compiled by a Portuguese, Antonio Galvão, and published in Lisbon in 1555. The most recent English edition is Galvano 1862.

4. Nowell 1945.
5. Galvano 1862:84-131.
6. For the antecedents of Magellan's voyage and the voyage itself, my main guide was Guillemard 1890, which is based on first-hand and other contemporary sources (see note 11 below). I also consulted Stanley of Alderley 1874; Nowell 1936; Zweig 1938; Nowell 1962; and Parry 1964:173-7.
7. Meinicke 1876:203; Audran 1917:53; Maude 1968:38-43.
8. Meinicke 1876:258-9; Maude 1968: 43-7.
9. The extract from Elcano's letter, as translated, is from Mitchell 1958:89. Mitchell's book, the only biography of Elcano in English, gives a useful summary of the immediate aftermath of the Magellan expedition. Blair and Robertson 1903-9:I:165-221 give a day-by-day account of the Badajoz-Elvas conference. Also consulted were Markham 1911:13-14; Nowell 1936: 326-8; Nunn 1934; and the article on Elcano in Spain's monumental *Enciclopedia Universal Ilustrada,* vol. 19, p. 496-8, cited hereafter as *Enciclopedia.*
10. Guillemard 1890:222n; Nunn 1934:628.
11. The extant original documents relating to this expedition to the Moluccas, commanded by Garcia Jofre de Loaisa, are housed in the Archivo General de Indias, Seville. An inventory of the documents in Portuguese by Maria de Lurdes Lalande was published in the *Boletim da Filmoteca Ultramarina Portuguesa,* no. 32, p. 78-91, Lisbon, 1966. Microfilm copies of them, on six reels numbered PMB 135-140 inclusive, are deposited in the Mitchell Library, Sydney; the National Library of Australia and the Library of the Australian National University, Canberra; the State Library of Victoria, Melbourne; the Alexander Turnbull Library, Wellington; and the University of Hawaii, Honolulu.

The first published account of the Loaisa expedition appeared in a 20-volume work by the Spanish historian Gonzalo Fernández de Oviedo y Valdés (1478-1557). This work, entitled *Historia General y Natural de las Indias, Islas y Tierra-Firme del Mar Oceano,* was published in Spain from 1535 to the year of Oviedo's death. It has been republished several times—the last in Asuncion, Paraguay, in 1945. The principal material on the Loaisa expedition in the 1945 edition is in vol. 4 and is cited in these notes as Oviedo IV. Oviedo obtained his information in an interview in Madrid in 1535 with a survivor of the expedition, Fray Juan de Arreizaga, and in interviews with two others, Andres de Urdaneta and Martin de Islares, in Santo Domingo, Hispaniola, in 1539—see Oviedo IV: 194, 236. Although Oviedo's Loaisa material contains some palpable errors, it is substantially correct where it can be checked against first-hand accounts. On some aspects of the Loaisa expedition it is the only authority. Some of Oviedo's material was incorporated into a work by a later Spanish historian, Antonio de Herrera y Tordesillas (1559-1625). Herrera also had access to official documents, some of which seem to have been lost. Herrera's work was entitled *Historia General de los Hechos de los Castellanos en las Islas, y Tierra firme del mar Oceano.* It appeared in Madrid in eight volumes from 1601 to 1615. The work is subdivided into *decadas, libros* and *capitulos* (decades, books and chapters), all of which are usually cited. However, as each decade fills one volume and is paginated separately, the citation Herrera III:273, for example, which is adopted hereafter, is sufficient to locate material in decade III (book 7, chapter 5), p. 273.

The writings on the Loaisa expedition of Oviedo and Herrera were used in the nineteenth century by another Spanish historian, Martin Fernández de Navarrete (1765-1844). From 1825 to 1837, Navarrete published a five-volume work, *Colección de los Viages y Descubrimientos que hicieron por mar los Españoles,* in which the most important and interesting of the extant documents relating to the early Spanish explorers were printed together with details gleaned from Oviedo and Herrera. Vol. 4 of Navarrete's work deals with the Magellan expedition, and vol. 5 with that of Loaisa. These are cited hereafter as Navarrete IV and Navarrete V.

Of the mass of published information on the Loaisa expedition in Spanish, only a small fraction has been translated into English. This appeared in a Hakluyt Society volume, *Early Voyages to the Strait of Magellan,* translated and edited by Sir Clements Markham and published in 1911. Because it is more accessible to English-speaking readers, Markham's work (cited as Markham 1911) has been used wherever possible. However, as the translation is sometimes at variance with the earliest or most authentic Spanish documents, details have been taken from the latter where appropriate. On all significant points, the most authentic Spanish documents are invariably cited.

12. Loaisa, a native of Ciudad Real, was a *comendador* (commander) of the Order of Rodas (Rhodes). He was a relative of a prelate, Garcia de Loaisa, who, in 1532, became the confessor of Emperor Charles V and subsequently Archbishop of Seville and president of the Council of the Indies. He is said to have exerted an exceptional influence on the Spain of his time. See *Enciclopedia* vol. 25, p. 787-8 and vol. 28, p. 2835.
13. Mitchell 1958:118 described this as 'the customary ingratitude of the Crown to its most famous navigators'.
14. Navarrete V:193-5; Mitchell 1958:117.
15. Guillemard 1890:137; 326-9. On p. 329, Guillemard said: 'The Biscayans [i.e. Basques], as was always the case on such expeditions, were largely represented'.
16. Oviedo IV:194; Navarrete V:3; and Markham 1911:30 give the total number of men. Those whose names have been found in the extant documents are listed in Appendix A with other pertinent details. See also Appendix B. For information on Basque surnames, see Lopez-Mendizabal 1958.
17. For a brief history of the Basque whaling industry, see Browne 1846:513. Gallop 1930:271 said Basque claims to the discovery of Newfoundland in 1372 could 'hardly be disputed'. Similar assertions are made in other reference books. However, Gandía 1942 could find no proof in extant documents, medallions, inscriptions, etc. of such an early Basque acquaintanceship with Newfoundland, although he concluded (p. 158) that Basque navigators were 'the most daring of the Middle Ages and the first to arrive on the coasts of Newfoundland before 1436.'
18. Mitchell 1958:119-22; *Enciclopedia* vol. 19, p. 498.
19. Mitchell 1958:122; Appendices A and B.
20. This summary is given in Navarrete IV:3. There are further details in Navarrete IV:12-22. However, Guillemard 1890:326 said: 'From the official lists, and from the casual occurrence of names in the numerous and lengthy *autos fiscales* connected with the expedition, we gather that at least 268 individuals embarked . . . It is more than probable that there were others who were neither entered in the ships' books nor the subject of casual mention, and it may be affirmed with tolerable certainty that between 270 and 280 persons manned the five ships . . .'
21. Oviedo IV:193-4; Navarrete V:3; Markham 1911:30. The *Santa Maria del Parral* and *San Lesmes* are described as caravels in numerous instances, e.g., Oviedo IV:194; Navarrete V:404; Markham 1911:46.
22. Parry 1964:80 and pl. 12.
23. Parry 1964:80-1; Nance 1913.
24. His name is spelt Hoces in some documents. The caravel appears to have been named after a canonized Spanish priest, noted for his work among the poor. He died in 1218, was buried in Burgos and is venerated on 28 January —*Enciclopedia* vol. 30, p. 189.
25. For the crew list of the *Victoria*, see Navarrete IV:19-21.
26. Herrera III:273. An inventory of items carried in Magellan's ships is published in Navarrete IV:162-88 and translated in Guillemard 1890:329-36.
27. The records are ambiguous on the armament carried in Magellan's ships. Navarrete IV:4, 167 (translated in Guillemard 1890:331) stated that the ships were provided with the weapons described. However, Navarrete added that this was 'besides the artillery they had' and that officials in Seville were ordered to provide them with 62 culverins, 10 falcons and 10 bombards. A possible explanation for the discrepancies is that the ships already had four culverins, three falcons, seven bombards and three *pasamuros,* so that the officials only provided what was lacking from their establishment. The fact that the ships carried cannon-balls of iron *and* stone shows that projectiles for artillery in Magellan's time were at a transitional stage. Extant documents on Portugese artillery up to the start of the sixteenth century mention only stone projectiles—Malheiro Dias 1923:43n.
28. The culverins (*bersos* in Spanish) are described in Navarrete V:4 as being of two quintals each. The OED defines a quintal as 100 or 112 lb and a culverin in the terms mentioned.
29. As artillery evolved, the various types of cannon varied in size, weight and bore from gun-founder to gun-founder and from one decade to another. Frequently it is difficult to establish what a particular type of cannon was like at a particular time. Except that they were large, no description of falcons at the time of Magellan's voyage has been found. However, the Elizabethan historian Raphael Holinshed (quoted in ffoulkes 1937:92) described a falcon of the year 1574 as being 800 lb in weight with a bore of 2½ in. I am indebted to Mr Ron Conyers, an industrial chemist at the Royal Australian Mint, Canberra, for calculating the approximate weight of the Amanu cannon from measurements provided by me. His estimate was 1,270 to 1,370 lb

(570-626 kg). One cannon has a bore of 9 cm; the other, 11 cm.

30. Goats, cats and dogs are apt to be the subject of casual mention in the journals of the early Pacific explorers rather than items in official inventories. No exhaustive search has been made for references to these animals. However, it can be stated, for example, that all three were carried by Quiros in 1605-6 (Markham 1904:201, 393); by Cook in 1772-5 (Beaglehole 1961:115n, 122, 169n, 296, 297, 411); by the Spanish expedition to Tahiti in 1774-5 (Beaglehole 1967:1371); and by Cook in 1776-80 (Beaglehole 1967:23-4, 83-4, 108n, 133n, 143, 288n, 1040 etc).
31. *Enciclopedia* vol. 43, p. 1062.
32. Oviedo IV:204-7, 222.
33. For the main details of Loaisa's voyage, I have followed the compilation in Navarrete V:5-190, which was based on first-hand accounts and on those of Oviedo and Herrera. The most useful first-hand account is that by Andres de Urdaneta in Navarrete V:401-439. It is translated in Markham 1911:41-89.
34. Herrera III:274-9; Markham 1911:31-8.
35. Navarrete V:225-33.
36. Oviedo IV:222.
37. Markham 1911:99n.
38. Navarrete V:268; Markham 1911:101.
39. Oviedo IV:218; Navarrete V:224; Markham 1911:102.
40. Navarrete V:176, 269; Markham 1911: 102.
41. Oviedo obtained the account of the pinnace from Arreizaga in Madrid in 1535—see note 11 and Oviedo IV:194.
42. Oviedo IV:222; Navarrete V:177; Markham 1911:102.
43. Herrera IV:9; Navarrete V:181; Markham 1911:107.
44. Original documents relating to the fitting out and voyage of these ships were published in Navarrete V:440-86.
45. The account of the expedition from this point onwards is mainly based on that of Urdaneta in Navarrete V:401-39 and Markham 1911:41-89.
46. The track of the *Santa Maria de la Victoria* has been plotted by Nunn 1934:616 and Brand 1967:116-17 from the daily positions of the pilot Martin de Uriarte, in Navarrete V:241-85.
47. Sharp 1960:12; Wallis 1953:96.
48. See note 44. A translation of an account of the *Florida's* voyage from Mexico and of her efforts to return there appears in Markham 1911:109-32.
49. Nowell 1936:335-6; Parry 1964:178; Blair and Robertson 1903-9:I:222-39.

CHAPTER 3: The laws of chance

1. A recent example of the human instinct to survive at sea even in the face of seemingly hopeless odds was provided, by my former colleague Dr David Lewis, author of *We, The Navigators* (Canberra, 1972), a book on Oceanic navigation techniques. On 22 November 1972, Lewis left Stewart Island off the southern tip of New Zealand in his 32 ft steel sloop *Ice Bird* in an attempt to become the first man to sail single-handed to Antarctica and then circumnavigate it. Five days from Stewart Island, his sloop rolled completely over in a tremendous storm and was badly damaged. By 7 December he, himself, was suffering frostbite on both hands and his feet were numb. On that day he wrote in his log: 'Chances of survival negligible but effort in spite of pain and discomfort. These last are very great. Must go on striving to survive as befits a man.' Next day he wrote: 'Surprising no fear at almost certainly having to die. A lot of disappointment though.' Although *Ice Bird* capsized a second time on 13 December, Lewis battled on and finally reached the United States base at Palmer, Antarctica, on 29 January 1973, nearly ten weeks after leaving Stewart Island.—Riseborough 1973.
2. Oviedo IV:222; Markham 1911:102.
3. Navarrete V:409; Markham 1911:53.
4. Navarrete V:272. Loaisa's ship reached the Tropic of Capricorn on 1 July 1526, five weeks after clearing the Strait of Magellan. Her course (see chapter 2, note 46) was more northerly and therefore more direct than that apparently taken by the *San Lesmes*. But the caravel was almost certainly a better sailer. Loaisa's ship reached the latitude of Amanu on 7 July.
5. Carrington 1948:110-33.
6. Visher 1925 and Giovanelli 1940 do not record any hurricanes in the Tuamotus outside this period.
7. Beaglehole 1955:343-69.
8. A ship that ran aground in the Tuamotus in seemingly similar, but less fortunate, circumstances was the British whaler *Matilda*. In 1792, she was wrecked on Mururoa Atoll, SSE of Hao, and became a total loss, although her entire crew was saved (see Appendix C). Thirty-four years later, the crew of HMS *Blossom* found many relics of her. These comprised two large anchors and

one small one, the strop and hook of a cat block, many small bits of iron, several copper bolts, some lead and copper sheets, a fish boiler, some staves, broken casks, broken iron hoops, a small cannon, two harpoons, a leaden pump, a hatch, part of the ship's keel and forefoot, and 'other pieces of the wreck.'—Beechey 1831:I:216-17; Peard 1973:108.

9. The two passes at Amanu can be negotiated by modern vessels of up to schooner size, and should therefore have been practicable for a caravel. However, neither pass is easy to negotiate. The northern one, Manavateikariki, is short and straight, but too narrow for comfort. The other, Hahameru, is also narrow, and is difficult to attempt without local knowledge—*Pacific Islands Pilot* 1959:99; *Annales Hydrographiques,* ser. 4, no. 13, p. 205.
10. Hao's pass, Kaki, was recently described as 'perfectly safe' apart from a few plainly visible coral patches—d'Anglejean Chatillon 1963-4: 29. The *Pacific Islands Pilot* 1957: 98 describes it as 'difficult under all conditions' but 'practicable for vessels of 15 ft draught.'
11. Markham 1904:199, 204.
12. See Shapiro 1930; Sullivan 1923; and the numerous descriptions of Eastern Polynesians in this book.
13. This is not a commonly held view at present. It is further elaborated in chapter 15 and Appendix F.
14. Danielsson 1956: 52-8 gives the fullest summary of the food available to the aboriginal Tuamotuans, but does not mention all the items listed here.
15. Rollin 1929:50; Heyerdahl 1952:63; Lewthwaite 1967:69; Titcomb 1969:33.
16. Both the Polynesian fowl and dog have been the subject of detailed studies, but little has been written about the Polynesian pig. Ball 1933 concluded that the Polynesian fowl was a domesticated variety of the jungle fowl; but Carter 1971:198 believes the Polynesians also had domestic strains of white fowl and some 'seemingly large Chinese mainland chickens, at least in the Marquesas.' The question is not pursued here as it is not relevant to this book. Regarding the Polynesian pig, the best description is that in Ellis 1831:I:72, who said it was small with long legs, a long nose, curly or almost woolly hair, and short, erect ears. Cook, in two oblique references, indicated that the pigs of both Tahiti and Tonga were small (Beaglehole 1967:973; Beaglehole 1961:262). And Forster 1778:188 stated that those of Tahiti were 'of the breed that we call Chinese.' New Zealand did not have pigs. The description of the Polynesian dog given in the text is derived from accounts which have been summarised or brought together in Titcomb 1969:48 and Luomala 1960a:191. Luomala 1960b:217 states that a scientist, L. J. Fitzinger, claimed in the 1860s that the Polynesian dog was descended from the pariah dogs of Asia. Support for this view is given by Epstein 1969:126, who describes the pariah dogs of South China as having long, slender jaws tapering to a pointed nose; small, V-shaped prick ears; thick, straight legs, usually a short, dense coat and short-haired tail. However, dogs with longer coats are occasionally seen, and these are distinguished by bushy tails. The eating of pariah dogs in China is an old custom, Epstein says.
17. This is the range of trees on most Tuamotuan atolls.—NID 1943-5:II:196; Danielsson 1956:34.
18. The well-known story of the *Bounty* mutineers provides an apposite example of what is likely to happen when a shipload of Europeans, with superior weapons and in some distress, is thrown among a Stone Age people with no previous contact with Europeans. Following the mutiny off one of the Tongan islands in April 1789, the *Bounty* mutineers sailed to Tubuai, an island some 300 miles south of Tahiti. They made their way ashore by force of arms and killed twelve natives who opposed their landing. Despite the islanders' hostility, the mutineers decided that Tubuai was a suitable place for a settlement, and after obtaining livestock from Tahiti (where they had previously spent six months), they returned to Tubuai. Having landed unopposed the second time, they began to build a fort for their own protection. However, some of the mutineers were subsequently ambushed by the islanders and stripped of their clothes, while others complained of the difficulty of getting women, although some did join the mutineers. When Fletcher Christian, the mutineers' leader, refused to head an armed party to get women by force, some of his men refused to work and broke into the spirit room to get grog. Meanwhile, several of the others, who had had no hand in the mutiny, plotted to steal one of the *Bounty's* boats and so escape from the island. Although Christian foiled them in this, all the ship's company finally agreed to leave the island. Sixty-six islanders were killed in another bloody encounter with the Englishmen before the *Bounty* got away.

Having returned to Tahiti, the *Bounty's* crew split into two parties. One, comprising sixteen men, including several non-mutineers, left the ship and took their belongings ashore; the other, comprising nine men, remained in the *Bounty* and left the island soon afterwards accompanied by twelve Tubuaian and Tahitian women and six men. Some of those who landed at Tahiti immediately went to live with native women, seemingly unconcerned about their own future. Others began to build a thirty-three foot schooner in which to sail to the East Indies. One man, who settled in the district of Taiarapu, contrived to become chief of that district; another married a chief's daughter. The boat-builders, headed by James Morrison, the *Bounty's* boatswain's mate, had to use considerable ingenuity to find substitutes for the tools and materials they lacked. They completed their schooner in eight months, and then began to make casks and to salt pork for their long projected voyage. Their labours were interrupted from time to time when the chief of the district in which they lived called on them, with their superior arms, to help him put down rebellions against his authority. Eighteen months after the mutineers landed in Tahiti, and before the boatbuilders could set out on their journey to the East Indies, a British warship arrived and captured them, along with the newly-built schooner. By that time, six children had been born to the mutineers and several of their wives were pregnant. The English sailors had thus made a significant contribution to Tahiti's genetic pool before being hustled off to stand trial in England.

Meanwhile, the mutineers who had remained in the *Bounty* sailed several thousand miles, first to the west, then to the east, in search of another island to settle on before they finally came upon uninhabited Pitcairn Island. There they landed their possessions, burned the *Bounty,* and established a second settlement. During the next ten years, bitter arguments—mainly over women—developed between the mutineers and the Polynesian men, and between some of the mutineers themselves. As a result, all the Polynesian men and all but two of the mutineers were killed. Despite this, the population of Pitcairn grew apace, for five of the mutineers had several children by their native wives, and most of the children began having offspring themselves as soon as they were old enough. Thirty-six years after the establishment of the Pitcairn settlement, the population of the island had increased from its original figure of twenty-seven adults to more than sixty; and after a lapse of sixty-six years, and with the addition of only three European men from the outside world, there was an Anglo-Polynesian population of 194.—Morrison 1935:45-124; Lee 1920: 44, 81, 96; Maude 1964:48-79; Maude 1968:20-34; Silverman 1967:92-3.

19. Audran 1931:318.

20. Gregory 1931:11; Gregory 1932:50; Stimson and Marshall 1964:485.

21. The minimum figures at the end of each generation (after adjustments to eliminate odd totals) would have been: 90, 135, 201, 300, 450, 675, 1,011, 1,515, 2,271, 3,405. The maximum figures would have been: 90, 270, 810, 2,430, 7,290, 21,870, 65,610, 196,830, 590,490, 1,771,470.

22. Information on the physical characteristics of Spaniards in this chapter is derived from the 58-volume Spanish encyclopedia, *Enciclopedia Universal Ilustrada* (cited as *Enciclopedia*). On skin colour, generally, this work (v.21, p. 410) says: 'In Europe the Spaniard is renowned for having well-pigmented skin (*cutis de color subido*), which is compared to cinnamon or the olive. However, in this matter people are just as mistaken as they are in other matters [relating to Spain].' A map (v.21, p. 411) showing the distribution of skin colour in Spain reveals that in all provinces along the Bay of Biscay, in nine out of twelve on the Mediterranean, and in several others, the percentage of people with swarthy skin (*cutis moreno*) does not exceed 47.2 per cent. Spain is, in fact, a very mixed country racially. Iberians from North Africa invaded it in the third millenium before Christ; later came Phoenecians, Celts, Carthaginians, Romans, Visigoths and Moors. The light-complexioned Celts and Visigoths made their greatest inroads in the northern part of the country. The other invaders, all of brown or tawny-white complexion, were more successful elsewhere. Hence today southern and south-eastern Spain is inhabited in general by people with brown eyes and hair and brunette complexions, while in the northern, north-eastern and central parts of the country, many people have light and light-mixed eyes and hair, and fair complexions. The Basques of the rugged north-eastern corner are descendants of some of the earliest immigrants in the Peninsula. They have retained their cultural identity throughout the various invasions.—NID 1941:185-7.

23. Scheinfeld 1950 (checked against a later, briefer work, Scheinfeld 1972) was my main guide for data on human genetics in this chapter. Several more technical works, noted below, were also used. Professor J. B. Langridge, then Professor of Genetics at the Australian National University, Canberra, kindly read an early draft of my genetics material and suggested several modi-

fications and the information on human genetics in the footnotes of this chapter. Scheinfeld 1950:78-86 gives a simple outline of the inheritance of skin colour.

24. Dunn and Dobzhansky 1952:59.

25. For the transmission of eye colour, see Scheinfeld 1950:64-72, 119; Carter 1970:90-4; Dunn and Dobzhansky 1952: 48; and Gates 1952:I:88-130. Hooton 1947:479 states that the far more heavily pigmented dark brown or black eyes of Mongoloids and Negroids (i.e. the probable ancestors of the people of Polynesia) are probably distinct genetically from the dark brown eyes of Europeans. Such heavily pigmented eyes, he says, are likely to be dominant in most cases over the mixed and light eyes of Europeans 'although perhaps incompletely so.'

26. At Rabi Island, Fiji, in May 1972, I had a first-hand opportunity to learn of the effects produced by a set of European genes in an overwhelmingly dark-skinned, black-haired, brown-eyed community. The Rabi Islanders, known as Banabans, have lived on Rabi since 1946. Their original home, Ocean Island or Banaba, is a small, isolated, harbourless spot, almost on the Equator in the Western Pacific. It is about 160 miles east of Nauru, its nearest neighbour, and 250 miles west of the Gilbert Islands. The Banabans are believed to be descended from a Melanesian people who intermarried with male invaders from Indonesia several centuries ago (Maude 1932:263-5). Until 1900 when rich phosphate deposits were discovered at Ocean Island, the Banabans had had little contact with Europeans or other outsiders, and few opportunities to visit other places and return home. They were thus an unusually homogenous people. However, after a British company began exploiting the phosphate deposits in 1901, some Banabans went abroad in the phosphate ships and intermingled with people of other races. One who did was a woman, name unknown, who went to Makatea, a phosphate island near Tahiti, several years before World War I. There she lived with a Frenchman by whom she had a son, Rui (Louis) Gil. A few months after the boy's birth, the parents separated and the mother returned to Ocean Island. She died in the following year (1914), leaving her son to be brought up by relatives. When I visited Rabi Island in May 1972, Gil was skipper of a fast launch that the Banabans used to link their island with other islands in the Fiji group. At first sight, he was not noticeably different from the generality of Banabans. But after his story became known to me and I studied him more carefully, it was evident that his skin was several shades lighter than that of his fellow islanders and that his eyes, although a deep brown, were not as dark. Some of his other features gave his face a distinctly European cast. Gil, who spoke only the local language, Gilbertese, told me through an interpreter that he had been twice married and that he had seven children by his second wife, a 'very dark' Banaban. One of his children was the only blue-eyed person on Rabi (whose total population in 1971 was 2,647). It was thus apparent that Gil's father was either blue-eyed or a carrier of blue-eye genes that were passed on through his son to his grandson. Gil described his seven children in these terms:

1. Meri, a girl, very fair skin with brown eyes; 2. Tokanikai, a girl, typically Banaban in colouration; 3. Taam, a boy, fair skin with dark brown eyes; 4. Tiro, a boy, dark; 5. Otintai, a boy, very fair skin with blue eyes and gingerish hair; 6. Roti, a girl, dark; and 7. Bwenaua, a girl, fair skin with brown eyes. Gil added that his first wife was a 'very fair-skinned,' black-haired, brown-eyed woman from Marakei, Gilbert Islands, and that he had had a daughter by her, Tute, who was 'very fair-skinned' with hazel eyes. Gil himself had a deformed foot, but this had obviously not hindered him from attaining an important position in his community which other, unhandicapped Banabans were apparently unable or less able to fill. A similarly interesting case was that of a man of Banaban-Japanese parentage who occupied an important accountancy post. Like Gil, he had been brought up as a Banaban and had not had any special opportunities. A Banaban leader, Tebuke Rotan, told me that in his view Gil and the part-Japanese owed their success to inherited qualities.

27. *Enciclopedia* v.21, p. 410 contains a map showing the distribution of *ojos garzos* in Spain. This work (p. 409) explains that although *garzo,* in its strict sense, means blue-eyed, it is used loosely in Spain to cover grey and green eyes, as well. (These are the next darkest colours in the pigmentation scale for eyes.) Marquer 1963:111, in an anthropological study of the Basques, found the following percentages of eye colour in Guipúzcoa: 5.2, blue; 17.7, grey; 42.0, green to light brown; 35.0, dark brown. In Viscaya province, the percentages were: 12.3, blue; 27.3, grey; 28.7, green to light brown; 31.5, dark brown.

28. See *Enciclopedia* v.21, p. 410 for the distribution of *cabellos rubios* in Spain. Like *garzo* the word *rubio* is used am-

biguously. It may signify red, reddish, ruddy, blonde, fair and golden (Peers 1959:689). So one can never be sure what a Spanish writer has in mind when he uses this word. Marquer 1963:110 in a survey of hair colour among 270 Guipúzcoan men found only 1.4 per cent with blond hair and 2.2 per cent with light chestnut hair. In a sampling of 73 Viscayans, there were no blonds and only 4.1 per cent with light chestnut hair. No such people were enumerated in the other two Basque provinces. However, Marquer's figures do not entirely square with statements by other authorities. Thus, Laxalt 1968:250, writing of 'The Land of the Ancient Basques,' says: 'Josep himself was blue-eyed and blond, as are so many Basques in the remote mountain villages.' Coon 1948:502 (quoting figures established by Collignon 1894) says that among *French* Basques about 16 per cent have light brown to blond hair, about 77 per cent brown, and only 7 per cent black. He adds: 'Among the Spanish Basques the incidence of blondism is somewhat lower, but Basques are still light compared to most other inhabitants of Spain.' NID 1941:190 states that the Galicians and Asturians are 'the only Spaniards among whom red hair is often noticeable.' Cooper 1957:137 describes the Galicians as 'quite different in appearance from other Spaniards and of Celtic origin, with witchcraft and superstition still deeply ingrained in many of the country-folk.'

29. Hooton 1947:472.
30. See Scheinfeld 1950:73-7, 120; Hooton 1947:473-4, 480-1; and Gates 1952:I: 88-130 for the inheritance of red hair and hair colour generally.
31. Scheinfeld 1950:87-113, 121-3 discusses the inheritance of the features mentioned in this paragraph. The final quotation is from Scheinfeld 1939:80.
32. See Scheinfeld 1950:262-79, 500-1, 516 for blood types; 502 for fingerprints; 365-8, 502 for vocal talent; and 330-51 for intelligence. Scheinfeld says scientists are not agreed on whether intelligence is due to heredity or environment, although many believe it is inherited.
33. On the examples of heterosis mentioned, see Shapiro 1929:33, 69; Scheinfeld 1950:515; and Hooton 1947:538 respectively.
34. *Enciclopedia* v.67, p. 171.
35. See note 16 above.
36. *Enciclopedia* v.63, p. 1062.
37. Winge 1950:55.
38. A breed of dog in which the prick-ear is known to have displaced the drop ear is the papillon, a dwarf spaniel. Cox 1965:79 writes: 'This breed is one of the comparatively large family of dwarf Spaniels, and as such has been known on the continent of Europe for several centuries past. We have ample evidence of this fact from the paintings of the old masters which have made almost a point of featuring these little dogs from as early as the thirteenth century. Most, if not all, of these early paintings, however, showed little spaniels with drop ears, whereas the features of the Papillon as we know it today is the wide flared ear, large and heavily fringed and set obliquely on the side of the skull . . . It is perhaps fortunate that the prick-eared variety has come to be accepted as the normal because unless this were so it would be difficult to justify the use of the French word for "butterfly"—papillon—as the name of the breed.' See also Winge 1950:41. Fiennes 1968:p1.20 reproduces a painting depicting a black and white spaniel with prick-ears.
39. McArthur 1967; Price 1963, 1964.
40. A vast literature could be cited on this very sensitive subject. A few samples must suffice. Silverman 1967:61-8 recalls that the *Bounty* mutineers on Pitcairn referred to the Polynesian men as 'blacks' and excluded them from land rights. Scheinfeld 1950:513, Herskovits 1928, and others have drawn attention to the social situation that has arisen in the United States because most American Negroes now carry some European genes due to miscegenation with Whites over the last three and a half centuries or so. Herskovits (p. 60) stated that the earliest freed slaves in the United States were those of mixed-blood, very often the light-coloured ones, and that the descendants of these have had the best chance to make their way in a civilization whose standards are 'essentially White standards.' In a survey of Negro communities, Herskovits (p. 60) found that the darker Negroes actually suffered discrimination by their own people. He also established (p. 61) that the 'lighter, less Negroid individuals' appeared to have a favoured position in their communities. The latter circumstance was 'not due to any inherent faculty conferred by the larger percentage of White blood.' Rather, it was a general reaction to the dominant patterns of behaviour . . . in a White civilization. This reaction had a biological effect—selective mating (p. 62). 'The dark man with a wife of light color,' Herskovits said (p. 64), 'finds many social and economic doors opened which would otherwise be closed to him; his lighter wife brings him the prestige he desires.' Herskovits (p. 64) quoted a Negro woman as saying: 'Of course a man wants to marry a lighter woman.

Doesn't he want his children to be lighter than he is, and doesn't he want to lift up the race?'

41. See footnote, p. 132.

42. For an account of the navigational knowledge of European seamen before the Loaisa expedition left Spain in 1525, see Taylor 1956:3-174. Taylor (pp. 7, 37) states that the idea of dividing the horizon into cardinal points arose in the Mediterranean in ancient times through giving names to the directions from which the various winds blew. '"Wind,"' she says, '. . . meant practically the same thing as "direction," and a wind was often named from the country from which it blew.' She goes on to say (p. 98) that in thirteenth century Italy, then the most powerful maritime nation in Europe, there were still only eight winds with individual names. These were Tramontane (N), Ostro (S), Levante (E), Ponente (W), Greco (NE), Sirocco (SE), Maestro (NW) and Libeccio (SW). However, from these eight winds, the names of the half-winds were derived, e.g. Tramontane-Greco (NNE). Then came quarter winds, e.g. Tramontane-quarter Greco (North by East); and finally eighth winds, e.g. Tramontane eighth Greco. 'It is clear that this refinement of the wind-rose could only have taken place after the discovery of the magnetic needle,' Taylor says. She adds that it was from Italy that 'the new methods spread over the Mediterranean basin.' Taylor states (p. 174) that in 1508 Queen Joanna (Juana) of Castille ordered all Spanish pilots to take instruction in the use of the quadrant and astrolabe—two instruments for taking sights and making positional calculations from the sun and stars. No person, the queen said, was to ship as a pilot until he had received a certificate of proficiency. This instruction was still in force when the Loaisa expedition departed. It may be assumed therefore that the men with pilots' 'tickets' in the *San Lesmes* would have been familiar with the Italian idea of quartering, requartering and then dividing the horizon into sixteen points, and that they would have been well-versed in the astronomical knowledge of the time.

43. For information on the Ptolemaic constellations and the additions made to them from Bayer's time onwards, see *Encyclopedia Britannica* 1963:VI:391-4.

44. More information on the astronomy of Ptolemy, Copernicus and Galileo appears on p. 189n.

45. Basque is a relic of a tongue spoken by some of the earliest inhabitants of the Iberian peninsula.—Bodmer 1945:342-3. Myhill 1966:38 says it is 'an agglutinative language, with strange word orders and extraordinary verbal constructions'. He goes on: 'To form phrases, or still more, to think in Basque, requires a different mental approach from that demanded by Indo-European languages.' Andrea Navagero, the Venetian ambassador to the court of Emperor Charles V, who visited the Basque provinces in May 1528, recorded that the Basque language was the strangest he had ever heard. 'It does not contain any Spanish words nor words from any other language,' he wrote. 'It does not have its own writing; for that reason to write it they [the Basques] learn Castilian and write with its letters. Thus most of the men know it [i.e. Castilian] but the women do not know it and speak only their native language.'—Fabié 1879:347. Oviedo IV:218 informs us that the priest Juan de Arreizaga spoke Basque when he tried to communicate with some Patagonians in the Strait of Magellan; and Mitchell 1958:149 states that the style of Elcano's will, which is among the extant documents of the Loaisa expedition, shows that neither he nor the Basque writer who drew it up were wholly at ease in Spanish, there being a confusion of genders and the incorrect use of articles.

46. Bodmer 1945:343 states that Portuguese is, in fact, derived from Galician. He adds that during the Moorish occupation which ended in 1492, the speech of the Iberian Peninsula was a mixture of dialects descended from Vulgar Latin. These were Castilian in the centre; Leonese, Aragonese and Asturian in the north; Catalan (resembling the Provençal of southern France) in the east and Galician in the west, including Portugal. Castilian was made the language of the Spanish court in 1253 and so became 'the pattern of correct Spanish.' There would thus have been some dialectical differences between any members of the Loaisa expedition who came from Leon, Aragon, Asturias and Catalonia. However, except in the case of Catalan, the differences, by then, were small. Catalan, which has remained a separate tongue, has not been mentioned in the text, as there is no evidence that anyone in the Loaisa expedition shipped from Catalonia, of which the chief centre is Barcelona. For fuller information on the languages of the Iberian Peninsula, see Entwistle 1962.

47. Pickering 1851: 286-7. Pickering pointed out that a single generation was 'sufficient to efface all knowledge of Africa' among the Negroes of the United States; and that the Negroes of Haiti and the Caribbean were two other groups that

had lost their own languages. A situation that seems to resemble that of the castaways closely is that of the Atlantic island of St Helena where 'very few traces' remain today of the Chinese and African languages even though hundreds of Chinese indentured labourers and Negro slaves were taken there 150 years ago and 'unleashed' among a long-established European population only one-quarter as numerous.—Shine 1969: 64; Shine 1970:16. The case of Pitcairn Island, where English became the language of the *Bounty* mutineers' descendants (although the mutineers' Polynesian wives never succeeded in learning it), cannot be taken as a parallel. In that case, Pitcairn was uninhabited when the mutineers settled on it, and so, linguistically, they had no competition except from their wives. That competition, however, was quite strong, as is evidenced by the fact that many Polynesian words and constructions found their way into the Pitcairnese speech.—Ross and Moverley 1964:136-88. See also Wurm 1954:266-8.

48. Banks 1963:275; Davies 1851:262; Stone 1964:42, 123.

49. Because churchmen thought the reading of the Bible in the vernacular could lead to errors of interpretation, it became a heresy to read the Bible in Spanish after the Spanish Inquisition was established towards the end of the fifteenth century. For this reason, it is highly improbable that anyone in the *San Lesmes* would have had a printed copy of any part of the Bible in that language. If they did, it could only have been an edition of the four Gospels and portion of the remainder of the New Testament, published in Madrid in 1512, because this was the only Biblical material to appear in Spanish before 1525 (*Enciclopedia,* v.68, p. 80). However, between 1514 and 1517 the great Complutensian Polyglot Bible was published at the newly established University of Alcalá, and it is possible that a copy of this, or part of it, would have been carried in each of the ships of Loaisa's fleet; or at least that there would have been a copy of the Bible in Latin. The Polyglot Bible appeared in six volumes. Vols I-IV contained the Old Testament in Greek, Latin, Hebrew and Chaldean; vol. V, the Greek and Latin texts of the New Testament; and vol. VI, a Hebrew-Chaldean vocabulary, an index of names and a Hebrew grammar. It was the first Polyglot Bible to be published in Europe (*Enciclopedia* v.68 p. 81; Green 1965:III:16-17). As Loaisa's instructions stated that if any religious were willing to remain voluntarily on any island discovered 'within the line' of Emperor Charles V, arrangements could be made for them to land, and as it was also stated that the sick should be confessed and should make declarations to the ship's writers (Markham 1911:33, 37), there is little doubt that each ship carried at least one priest and therefore a person capable of reading the Bible in one of the languages of the Polyglot version. Other educated men in the fleet could undoubtedly have done so too, as Latin was a common educational subject of the time and is closely related to Spanish. The first two verses of the Polyglot version in Latin placed side by side with those from a modern Spanish translation of the Bible (*La Santa Biblia* 1957:1) will demonstrate this:

LATIN	SPANISH
In pricipio	En el principio crió
creauit deus	Diós los cielos y la
celum & terra.	tierra. Y la tierra
Terra autem erat	estaba desordenada
inanis & vacua;	y vacía, y las
Et tenebre erant	tinieblas estaban
sup facie abyssi:	sobre la haz del
& spiritus dei	abismo, y el Espíritu
serebatut super	de Diós se movia
aquas.	sobre la haz de las
	aguas.

50. NID 1941:187-8.

51. Jensen 1970:217-52 discusses the invention of scripts in Africa and America following contact with literate outsiders. See Riesenberg and Kaneshiro 1960 for a similar development in the Caroline Islands.

52. Firth 1958:13 says: 'In greeting each other Englishmen shake hands; Frenchmen in exalted moments embrace and kiss on both cheeks; a polite Austrian salutes a lady's hand with his lips; and Polynesians press noses.'

CHAPTER 4: A gold ring, red hair and dogs of Castille

1. Crow 1948:71-103.
2. For accounts of the Grijalva expedition, see Galvano 1862:202-5; Wright 1945: 67-8; Sharp 1960:24-6; Brand 1967:122.
3. For the abortive Alvarado expedition, see Oviedo IV:236, V:10; Wright 1945:68-70. The Villalobos expedition is discussed at length in Gschaedler 1954. For briefer accounts, see Blair and Robertson 1903-9:II:47-73; Wright 1945:70-2; Sharp 1960:26-32; Brand 1967:122-3.

4. The voyages of Arellano and Legaspi are described in Gschaedler 1954; Blair and Robertson 1903-9:II:77-218; Wright 1945:73-7; Sharp 1960:33-9; Brand 1967:129-31.
5. For accounts of the galleon trade, see Dahlgren 1916 and Schurz 1939.
6. The background to the first Mendaña expedition is discussed in Jack-Hinton 1969:1-27; Amherst and Thomson 1901:i-x.
7. English translations of accounts of the first Mendaña expedition appear in Amherst and Thomson 1901. For summaries of the various accounts, see Beaglehole 1966: 42:55; Jack-Hinton 1969:28-67. For a calendar of the known documents on this and subsequent Spanish voyages to the South Pacific, see Kelly 1965.
8. For the aftermath of Mendaña's first expedition and the naming of the Solomon Islands, see Beaglehole 1966:56-8; Jack-Hinton 1969:79-84; 113-14.
9. The main details of the voyages of Drake and Cavendish are contained in Wycherley 1935:23-83. For Hawkins' voyage, see Williamson 1933. Their exploits generally and relevance in South Seas history are discussed in Beaglehole 1966:60-4.
10. Markham 1904:3-157 and Cummins 1971:97-105 contain English translations of Quiros' accounts of Mendaña's second voyage.
11. The background to the Quiros expedition is discussed in Markham 1904: xviii-xx, 161-81; Kelly 1966:2-30, 294-321.
12. There are six first-hand accounts of the Quiros expedition and one based on first-hand sources. All have been published in English and all but one in Spanish in the past 100 years. The works in which the first-hand accounts have appeared are: Justo Zaragoza's *Historia del Descubrimiento de las Regiones Austriales,* vols. 1 and 2, Madrid, 1876-80 (cited as Zaragoza I and Zaragoza II); Celsus Kelly's *Austrialia Franciscana,* vol. 1 Madrid, 1963 (cited as Kelly 1963); *The Voyages of Pedro Fernandez de Quiros, 1595-1606,* translated and edited by Sir Clements Markham, London, 1904 (cited as Markham 1904); *La Austrialia del Espiritu Santo,* translated and edited by Celsus Kelly, Cambridge, 1966 (cited as Kelly 1966); and *New Light on the Discovery of Australia,* edited by Henry N. Stevens, with annotated translations from the Spanish by George F. Barwick, London, 1930 (cited as Stevens 1930). The bibliographical details of the various accounts may be summarised as follows:

Author	*Spanish version*	*English version*
Pedro Fernandez de Quiros	Zaragoza I:192-402	Markham 1904:161-320
Gaspar Gonzalez de Leza	Zaragoza II:77-185	Markham 1904:321-403
Fray Martin de Munilla	Kelly 1963:19-106	Kelly 1966:137-270
Juan de Iturbe	——	Kelly 1966:273-93
Diego de Prado y Tovar	Stevens 1930:86-204	Stevens 1930:87-205
Luis Vaez de Torres	Stevens 1930:214-36	Stevens 1930:215-37; Markham 1904:455-66

The account based on first-hand sources is that of Fray Juan de Torquemada, first published in his *Monarquia Indiana,* vol. 1, Seville, 1615, pp. 809-29. It has been republished in Kelly 1963:107-46, and translated in Markham 1904:405-51. Kelly 1963:xxi-xxii remarks that the similarity or identity of passages in Torquemada's work with the accounts of Quiros and Munilla makes it clear that Torquemada had access to those accounts. However, there are also passages in Torquemada's account that are not found in the others, and these indicate that Torquemada also obtained information from other members of the expedition. Torquemada's account and the other six cited above have all been availed of in this chapter. On critical matters, both the Spanish and English versions are cited; otherwise only the English accounts are referred to. Markham's translations have been amended in two or three instances, where they were found to be inadequate or incomplete.
13. The background to Quiros' voyage is discussed in Kelly 1966:11-21.
14. For the identification of islands discovered by Quiros in the eastern Pacific, I have followed Maude 1959, which is reprinted in Maude 1968:35-83. Maude's identifications are accepted as the most likely in Kelly 1966:60-3, where those made by other writers are listed and discussed.
15. Maude 1968:68-9; Caillet 1884:135-8; and Sharp 1960:57-9 all agree that La Conversion de San Pablo was Hao. Markham and other writers of his time thought this landfall was Anaa—an untenable view in the light of documents now available.
16. Quiros' ships made contact with the islanders near the present-day site of Otepa village (see chapter 3, note 11). This is evident from statements in Kelly

1966:159 and Markham 1904:204, 336, 340, and from an examination of modern charts.

17. Markham 1904:198-9; Zaragoza I:250.
18. Markham 1904:199; Zaragoza I:250.
19. Markham 1904:416; Kelly 1963:114.
20. Kelly 1966:282. Torres described the complexion of the islanders as 'dusky' —Markham 1904:457.
21. Markham 1904:200; Kelly 1966:161.
22. The account of the old woman and her possessions is a composite one drawn from Markham 1904:200-1, 336, 420 and Kelly 1966:162. Quiros described her dog as *'un perro chico manchado'* (Zaragoza I:252), which is rendered as 'a little speckled dog' in Markham 1904:201. *'Manchado'* is the past participle of *'manchar'* meaning to stain, spot, daub, darken, speckle, etc. Leza stated that the dog was white—Zaragoza II:96; Markham 1904:337.
23. Markham 1904:337; Zaragoza II:96.
24. Markham 1904:201; Zaragoza I:253. Scholars who have puzzled over the old woman's emerald-studded gold ring and the cedar pole mentioned by Leza have suggested several explanations for their presence on Hao. Danielsson 1956:69 says: 'The most probable explanation is that the ring was part of some flotsam, which like the cedar pole had drifted with the south equatorial current from the South American coast. With our present knowledge of the force and constancy of this current, we may presume that wreckage can also occasionally have been washed ashore on other atolls of the Tuamotu group. During my repeated stays on Raroia it happened more than once that I found glass floats for fishing nets of Peruvian origin. The influence of such wreckage on the native culture cannot of course have been anything but very slight, but it must at least have made the natives conscious of the existence of other peoples and cultures at a very early date.' Sharp 1960:60 believed the ring and pole might have been 'relics, perhaps, of a vessel from Peru, not necessarily European, and not necessarily on a two-way voyage.' G. S. Parsonson (in Kelly 1966:163) believes the cedar pole 'might well have been carried to the Tuamotu by the South Equatorial Current.' He goes on: 'The presence of the ring is less easily accounted for. There are, however, several likely explanations. Chinese junks have on occasion been swept as far east as Hawaii and, if legend is to be trusted, might conceivably have been wrecked much further south on islands within the range of the great ocean-going Tuamotuan double canoe. In 1527, Alvaro de Saavedra lost two ships in a storm 1,000 leagues from New Spain. One of these is supposed to have been wrecked in the Hawaiian islands, but might well have come ashore in the Tuamotu. It is also feasible that such an object was left behind in the Marquesas in July-August 1595 during the course of Mendaña's visit to that group and that it was subsequently secured by some Tuamotuan navigator in the course of a trading expedition.'
25. Markham 1904:336; Zaragoza II:95. A galeot was a fast type of vessel, somewhat smaller than a galley, in which both oars and a single lateen sail were used. Generally, a galeot had seventeen oars, each stroked by one man—*Enciclopedia* vol. 25, p. 456-7.
26. Markham 1904:202; Zaragoza I:253. This is from the account of Quiros, who added that some locks of golden hair (*cabellos dorados*) fell from the crown to the middle of the chief's back, and that these were thought to be his wife's. See also notes 27 and 30.
27. Markham 1904:421; Kelly 1963:119. Torquemada used the ambiguous word *rubio* to describe the colour of the hair in the headdress. Munilla used it too—Kelly 1963:41. However, whereas Markham translates Torquemada's *rubio* as 'red', Kelly 1966:164-5 translates Munilla's as 'fair' and (in a footnote) 'blonde'. See also note 30 below, and note 28, chapter 3.
28. Markham 1904:340; Zaragoza II:100.
29. Markham 1904:204; Zaragoza I:256.
30. Markham 1904:340; Zaragoza II:99-100. Leza described the hair in the headdress as *'cabellos largos muy dorados como hilo de oro.'* Markham's translation of this, as quoted, is literally correct. The fact that Leza added that 'there could not be better in our Spain even if they were dyed' strongly suggests that the hairs were not dyed. This is significant, as the first pilot, Diego de Prado y Tovar, described the headdress as 'a cap of palm leaves and some red hairs of a woman which were dried in the sun, wherewith the said Quiros was very pleased' (*una montera de hojas de palmas y unos cabellos de muger rubios y curados al sol . . . .*) —Stevens 1930:102-3. Prado, it should be noted, consistently denigrated Quiros and his statement about the headdress has a derogatory tone. Besides contradicting Leza's on the issue of dyeing, it is the only one to claim that the headdress contained palm leaves rather than black feathers.
31. Kelly 1966:165; Kelly 1963:41.
32. Maude 1968:70.
33. For accounts of the expedition from Hao onwards, see Markham 1904:204-

320, 340-403; Kelly 1966:165-270, 282-93; Stevens 1930:102-205; 218-37.
34. Kelly 1965:225-313; Kelly 1966:105-15.

CHAPTER 5: 'Three Spanish dogs, very lean'

1. Sluiter 1933 deals at length with the Mahu expedition. This and the other early Dutch voyages are summarised in Buck 1953:11-16; Broek 1967.
2. No holograph accounts of the expedition of Schouten and Le Maire now appear to exist. But there are numerous published accounts. These are listed and discussed in Villiers 1906:xlvii-xlviii, 239-44, and Wallis 1953:542-7. All the published accounts appear to be based on a logbook of Aris Claesz, supercargo and purser of the *Hoorn*. The first, attributed to Schouten, is *Journal ofte Beschrijvinghe van de wonderlicke reyse . . . inde jaren 1615, 1616 en 1617,* Amsterdam, 1618. This account, with Le Maire's name substituted for Schouten's in the title, was republished in Leyden in 1619 as *De Australische Navigatien ontdeckt door Jacob Le Maire in de jaren 1615, 1616 en 1617.* (It has been translated into English in Villiers 1906:169-232). A third account, published in justice to the memory of Le Maire and claiming to be his authentic journal, appeared in Amsterdam in 1622. It contains many details not given in the earlier accounts. It is entitled *Spieghel der Australische Navigatie, door den wyt vermaerden ende cloeckmoedighen Zee-Heldt Jacob Le Maire*. The accounts of 1618 and 1622 are summarised in Dalrymple 1771:1-64. They have been republished in Engelbrecht and Herwerden 1945, who state that the 1622 account merits much greater confidence than those published earlier. Wallis speaks of it as being 'much more valuable' than the historian James Burney suggested.
3. For the identification of this and subsequent islands sighted by Schouten and Le Maire, see Sharp 1960:74; Buck 1953:14.
4. Dalrymple 1771:6.
5. The earliest use of the name Pukapuka that I have seen is in Caillet 1862:190.
6. Dalrymple 1771:7; Villiers 1906:192.
7. Dalrymple 1771:9-10.
8. Dalrymple 1771:8.
9. See note 2.
10. For Tasman's voyage, see Sharp 1968.
11. Dahlgren 1907.
12. Wycherley 1935.
13. Sharp 1960:88-90.
14. [Hall], [1605].
15. [Foigny], 1693.
16. [Nevile], 1668. This has been republished in Henderson 1930:225-35.
17. For the background to Roggeveen's voyage and Roggeveen's journal, see Sharp 1970.
18. Sharp 1970:125.
19. Bouman's journal has not been translated into English. It appears in Mulert 1911:52-183.
20. Behrens' book was first published in German as *Carl Friedrich Behrens Reise durch die Südlander und um die Welt . . . ,* Leipzig, 1737. It was republished with a somewhat different title in 1739. A paraphrase of it in French appeared in the same year under the title *Histoire de l'expedition de trois vaisseaux, envoyes par la Compagnie des Indes Occidentales . . . . ,* The Hague. An English summary of the French version appears in Dalrymple 1771:87-110. Dalrymple (p. 87) describes the book as 'a very poor performance, written with much ignorance, though with the parade of knowledge.' Sharp 1970:17 says Behrens' detectable inventions 'make his account of little value.' But on some points, it seems to have been more accurate than has been supposed.—See, for example, Appendix F, p. 306.
21. Dalrymple 1771:99.
22. Dalrymple 1771:104.
23. Dalrymple 1771:117. The anonymous chronicler's account, *Tweejarige Reyze rondom de Wereld,* was first published at Dordrecht in 1728.
24. Luomala 1960b:214.
25. Rollin 1929:50; Heyerdahl 1952:63; Lewthwaite 1967:69; Titcomb 1969:33.

CHAPTER 6: 'A thing most difficult to account for'

1. There have been many editions of Anson's voyage. One of the most accessible is Walter 1923. Anson's suggestions for establishing strategic settlements in the Atlantic and Pacific are outlined in Gallagher 1964:xxxvi-xxxviii.
2. For a discussion on the influence of Campbell and de Brosses, see Beaglehole 1955:lxxiv-lxxxiii.
3. Byron's journal of his voyage in the *Dolphin* and *Tamar* is published in Gallagher 1964.
4. For Byron's accounts of these islands, see Gallagher 1964:94-7.
5. Byron's account of Takaroa and its sister island Takapoto is in Gallagher 1964:98-103.
6. Gallagher 1964:104-5.

7. Gallagher 1964:lxvi discusses this point.
8. For an account of preparations for Wallis' voyage, see Carrington 1948: xix-xxiv.
9. Edited accounts of the voyages of both the *Dolphin* and *Swallow*, based mainly on the journals of Captains Wallis and Carteret, were published in Hawkesworth 1773:I:362-676. The journal of the *Dolphin's* master, George Robertson, appears in Carrington 1948; and Carteret's journal has been published in its entirety in (Helen) Wallis 1965. Carrington 1948:I states that Robertson's journal was 'obviously used by Hawkesworth', but this statement is open to question. What Hawkesworth does seem to have used is information compiled by Robertson and bearing his signature which was written in the back of the copy of Wallis' journal, now in the Public Record Office, London (Ad. 55/35). The information comprises 'Observations of Longitude, taken after Dr. Masculine's [sic] method . . .' on board the *Dolphin;* sailing directions for entering the ports used on the *Dolphin's* voyage; and 'A Description of all the islands discovered . . .' on the voyage. The 'Description' was undoubtedly written up from Robertson's journal as published by Carrington, but the wording in some passages is substantially different or in a different order, while many facts have been omitted and some added. This same observation applies to Hawkesworth's rendering of Wallis' journal. Therefore, wherever Wallis has been quoted in this chapter on critical matters, his journal has been used rather than Hawkesworth's printed version. The journal is cited as Wallis 1766-8. The material by Robertson contained therein is cited as Robertson 1766-8. The journals of other officers of the *Dolphin* are generally brief and uninformative, but two of them provide some useful information. These are the journals of Midshipmen Henry Ibbot and William Hambly, which are in the Public Record Office at Ad. 51/4542. Ibbot's journal has been partially printed in Corney II:458-60. Hambly's is cited as Hambly 1766-7.
10. Wallis 1965:I:120-74.
11. Carrington 1948:114.
12. Carrington 1948:116-17; Hawkesworth 1773:I:203-4. Pinaki is called Whitsun Island both in Wallis' original journal and Hawkesworth's narration. But Robertson recorded it as Whitsunday and it was usually shown as such on later maps.
13. Carrington 1948:118-20; Hawkesworth 1773:I:204-5.
14. Carrington 1948:120-2. Robertson's account of Nukutavake differs in several respects from that of Captain Wallis in Hawkesworth 1773:I:205-6 and Wallis 1766-8. Wallis' account says the islanders embarked in seven canoes (not four); that these were joined by two others (not one) at the western end of the island; and that each canoe had two masts. The last-named discrepancy is probably explained by the fact that Robertson was referring to a mast for each hull, as the concept of two hulls being joined together to form a single vessel was still strange at that time. I am indebted to the National Maritime Museum, Greenwich, England, for explaining that a topmast steering sail (an incorrect name for a studding sail) was triangular in shape.
15. Carrington 1948:123.
16. Hambly 1766-7: entry for 10 June 1767.
17. Carrington 1948:124.
18. Wallis 1766-8: entry for 9 June 1767.
19. Hawkesworth 1773:I:208; Carrington 1948:124-5.
20. Carrington 1948:126.
21. Hawkesworth 1773:I:212.
22. Carrington 1948:135.
23. Carrington 1948:137. For other references to handshaking, see Carrington 1948:160, 194, 213, 215, 227.
24. Carrington 1948:137-40.
25. Carrington 1948:148.
26. Carrington 1948:166.
27. Carrington 1948:177-8.
28. Carrington 1948:181-2, 222.
29. Carrington 1948:190.
30. Carrington 1948:224.
31. Carrington 1948:165, 179.
32. Carrington 1948:214. The cloth, as later voyagers learned, was called *tapa*.
33. Carrington 1948:215. For clarity, several amendments have been made to Robertson's punctuation in this and subsequent passages.
34. Carrington 1948:179.
35. Carrington 1948:223. Robertson took the three men to be brothers. None of the Englishmen had seen them before.
36. Carrington 1948:227-8; Robertson 1766-8: entry for 27 July 1767.
37. Carrington 1948:211.
38. Hawkesworth 1773:I:266-8; Wallis 1766-8:87-8.
39. Wallis 1766-8:87. Part of Wallis' description of the Tahitians' hair is ambiguous: '. . . some few don't tye it up, these generally have curled hair of different colours, black, brown, red and whitish or flaxen, especially the young boys and girls.' Hawkesworth 1773:I: 260, in editing Wallis' description, added a detail of his own: 'Their [the Tahitians'] hair in general is black, but in some it is brown, in some red, and

in others flaxen, which is remarkable, because the hair of all other natives of Asia, Africa, and America is black without a single exception. It is generally tied up . . . in the children of both sexes it is generally flaxen.'

40. Corney II:459.
41. Carrington 1948:227.
42. Carrington 1948:231-55, xxiv-xxv.
43. Corney II:457.

CHAPTER 7: Philibert de Commerson's forgotten theory

1. For the background to Bougainville's expedition, see Beaglehole 1966:214. Bougainville wrote an account of the expedition which was published in Paris in 1771. An English translation by J. R. Forster appeared in London in 1772. This, cited as Bougainville 1772, has been frequently used in this chapter, with a few minor changes in spelling and punctuation. Accounts of the voyage by several of Bougainville's companions have been published in France—usually in journals that cannot readily be consulted by English-speaking readers (see O'Reilly and Reitman 1967:34, 36-8 and Van der Sluis [1970]:139-41); and some are still in manuscript in various French repositories. However, details from both the published and unpublished accounts have been abstracted in Martin-Allanic 1964.
2. For the first part of the voyage, see Bougainville 1772:1-206.
3. Martin-Allanic 1964:643-4.
4. Bougainville 1772:205-6.
5. Bougainville 1772:206-8; Martin-Allanic 1964:644-5. For the identification of La Harpe as Hao, see Sharp 1960:115.
6. Bougainville 1772:208; Martin-Allanic 1964:646. Sharp 1960:115-16.
7. Martin-Allanic 1964:650. Vives used the words *'cheveux noirs et crépus'* to describe the hair of the man and children. On this point it should be noted that eighteenth century visitors to Tahiti and the surrounding islands frequently used the words *crisp* (English), *crépu* (French) and *crespo* (Spanish) or their derivatives to describe the islanders' hair; and in contemporary translations from one language to another the words were usually interchanged. It is difficult to know precisely what the original writers had in mind when they used these words. The English word *crisp* is now virtually obsolete in reference to hair, yet French/English and Spanish/English dictionaries almost invariably give it as their first definition of *crépu* and *crespo*. On the grounds that all three words are derived from the Latin *crispus*, meaning 'curled', and that the OED gives 'curly' as its first definition for 'crisp' hair, the practice adopted in this book is to substitute the word 'curly' for 'crisp' wherever it appears in a translation from French or Spanish. It should be noted, however, that *crisp*, *crépu* and *crespo* are also defined in various dictionaries as 'woolly', 'frizzy', 'crimped' and 'having curls or waves' etc.
8. Martin-Allanic 1964:650. Concerning the Tahitians' hair, Fesche wrote: *'Ils ont tours leurs cheveux crêpés.'*
9. Martin-Allanic 1964:652.
10. Bougainville 1772:217-19. Martin-Allanic 1964:655-6 gives the original French.
11. Martin-Allanic 1964:661-2.
12. Martin-Allanic 1964:663. For Forster's translations, see Bougainville 1772:222.
13. Bougainville 1772:228.
14. Martin-Allanic 1964:668. The Prince of Nassau-Siegen made a similar observation—Martin-Allanic 1964:670.
15. Bougainville 1772:250.
16. Bougainville 1772:242; Martin-Allanic 1964:668.
17. Bougainville 1772:244-5.
18. Bougainville 1772:248-9.
19. Bougainville 1772:256.
20. Bougainville 1772:250.
21. Bougainville 1772:254-5.
22. Bougainville 1772:246-7.
23. Martin-Allanic 1964:685.
24. Bougainville 1772:258.
25. Bougainville 1772:258-60.
26. Corney II:463. The companion was the surgeon-naturalist, Philibert de Commerson.
27. Bougainville 1772:260-1.
28. Bougainville 1772:270-1.
29. Bougainville 1772:271.
30. Bougainville 1772:241. Bougainville wrote his name 'Aotourou'.
31. Bougainville 1772:249, 253. Bougainville described Opoa—or Oopoa, as he wrote it—as 'an island near Tahiti'. It was, in fact, one of the nine districts of Raiatea. Cook anchored there on his first voyage in 1769.
32. Bougainville 1772:273-4.
33. Bougainville 1772:269.
34. Bougainville 1772:255-6.
35. O'Reilly and Reitman 1967:34 (item 280).
36. O'Reilly and Reitman 1967:42 (item 339).
37. Oliver 1909 was the first to publish Commerson's letter in an English-language work. It was subsequently published in Corney II:461-6.

CHAPTER 8: Traders in fine white dogs' hair

1. For the background to Cook's first voyage and its personnel, see Beaglehole 1955:civ-cxxxvii. That work contains Cook's journal of the voyage, as well as extracts from those of Robert Molyneux, master's mate; and W. B. Monkhouse, surgeon. Other published accounts of the voyage are Parkinson 1773, [Magra?] 1771 and Banks 1963.
2. Beaglehole 1955:69-70; Banks 1963: 224-5.
3. Beaglehole 1955:70-2; Banks 1963: 245-8.
4. Beaglehole 1955:72; Banks 1963:248.
5. Beaglehole 1955:85.
6. Parkinson 1773:21.
7. Banks 1963:266.
8. Beaglehole 1955:563.
9. Beaglehole 1955:117.
10. Banks 1963:292-3.
11. Beaglehole 1955:556-7. In a footnote (p. 557) on Molyneux's story, Beaglehole says: 'The story evidently combines two incidents of Roggeveen's voyage, the wreck of his *African Galley* on Takapoto, in May 1722, and his fatal brush with the people of Makatea in the following month.' Beaglehole's interpretation, however, seems erroneous, for Roggeveen lost no men at Makatea, so the islanders could scarcely have brought two white men's bodies from that place.
12. Beaglehole 1955:557.
13. Banks 1963:277.
14. Banks 1963:284-5.
15. Beaglehole 1955:108; Banks 1963:297.
16. For a discussion on this point, see Beaglehole 1955:cciv-ccviii.
17. Beaglehole 1955:123-4; Banks 1963: 334-5.
18. Beaglehole 1955:125; Banks 1963:335.
19. Beaglehole 1955:125-6; Banks 1963: 337-8.
20. Beaglehole 1955:126-7; Banks 1963: 349.
21. Beaglehole 1955:127; Banks 1963: 349-51.
22. Parkinson 1773:24.
23. Beaglehole 1955:129-31; Banks 1963: 364-5.
24. Beaglehole 1955:131; Banks 1963: 363-4.
25. Banks 1963:361.
26. Banks 1963:333.
27. Beaglehole 1955:153.
28. Banks 1963:315-16.
29. Banks 1963:316.
30. Beaglehole 1955:144.
31. Banks 1963:317.
32. Parkinson 1773:69.
33. Banks 1963:318n.
34. Beaglehole 1955:151. The term Society Islands was later extended to embrace Tahiti, Moorea, Maiao, Tetiaroa and Mehetia, and it is this extended meaning that the term has today. In this book, Cook's original meaning is adhered to until the end of chapter 13, where a page footnote indicates a change in usage.
35. Beaglehole 1955:153.
36. Banks described much of what he saw at Tahiti, Moorea, Huahine, Raiatea, Tahaa, etc. under a single, indiscriminate heading, 'Manners & customs of S. Sea Islands'—Banks 1963:333-86. In his only specific physical description of the Raiateans, he said: '. . . prettier children or better dressed we had no where seen.'—Banks 1963:324.
37. Banks 1963:372.
38. Beaglehole 1955:153; Banks 1963:318, 319, 324-5. For a sketch by Parkinson of a *fare no atua* at Huahine, see Beaglehole 1955:fig. 34. Sketches by Parkinson of Society Islands boat houses appear in Banks 1963, pl.17 and Parkinson 1773, pl.12.
39. Parkinson 1773:74. Banks 1963:368 described the boat houses (erroneously, it seems) as being in the form of a Gothic arch.
40. Beaglehole 1955:153-4, 154n.
41. Banks 1963:319-20, 364-8.
42. Beaglehole 1955:131.
43. Banks 1963:320, 365-6.
44. Banks 1963:366.
45. Banks 1963:325, 328; Beaglehole 1955:148-9. Parkinson's sketch of the women dancers (erroneously stated to be in Tahiti) is reproduced in Banks 1963:pl.12. See also Parkinson 1773: 74-5.
46. Beaglehole 1955:155.
47. Banks 1963:329-33.
48. Beaglehole 1955:282.
49. For a discussion on the probable authorship of this work, see Beaglehole 1955:cclvi-cclxiv.
50. [Magra?] 1771:43.
51. [Magra?] 1771:56.
52. Parkinson 1773:70n. and pl.11.
53. I am indebted for this information to Dr Ernest S. Dodge, director of the Peabody Museum, Salem, Massachusetts, who has made a special study of Cook ethnographical collections. Dr Dodge (pers. comm., 22 June 1971) states that of the thirteen Cook *taumi*, two each are in the British Museum; Gottingen Ethnographical Museum; and Ethnological and Archaeological Museum, Leningrad; and one each are

in the Ethnological Museum, Cambridge, England; National Museum of Ireland, Dublin; Australian Museum, Sydney; Dominion Museum, Wellington; Etnografiska Museet, Stockholm; Musée d'Histoire de Berne; and Museum für Völkerkunde, Vienna.

54. The first-named specimen—collector unknown—was received by the museum before 1821 and contains no European cloth. The other, received in 1809, does contain European cloth and is, presumably, of later manufacture.
55. When Mr B. A. L. Cranstone, deputy keeper, in the department of ethnography at the British Museum, wrote to me about *taumi* on 30 July 1971, his department with all its exhibits was being transferred to other buildings. Of five *taumi* that could then be examined, one was stated to be a Captain Cook piece; two were from Vancouver's voyage (1792); and the history of the others was unknown. The hair in the Cook piece was 5½ in. long and of silky texture.
56. Pers. comm., 5 and 21 July 1971, from Dr J. Specht, assistant curator, anthropology.
57. Pers. comm., 21 July 1971, from Dr A. T. Lucas, director.
58. Pers. comm., 13 July 1971, from Dr Pierre Cenlivres, assistant curator, ethnography department.
59. Pers. comm., 14 July 1971, from Mrs B. McFadgen, ethnologist.

CHAPTER 9: Blue eyes at Taiarapu

1. For the background to the Gonzalez expedition and English translations of accounts of it see Corney 1908.
2. Corney 1908:29-32.
3. English translations by Bolton Glanvill Corney of documents relating to this second Spanish expedition to the South Pacific are printed in vols 1 and 2 of *The Quest and Occupation of Tahiti by Emissaries of Spain* . . . published by the Hakluyt Society in 1913 and 1915. These are cited as Corney I and Corney II. For the king's instructions concerning the expedition and accompanying papers, see Corney I:224-8.
4. For Boenechea's journal of the voyage, see Corney I:285-345.
5. The viceroy's instructions are in Corney I:263-78.
6. Corney I:286-7; Corney II:32-4, 70-1.
7. Corney I:287-8; Corney II:34-6, 71.
8. Corney II:37.
9. Corney I:291.
10. Corney I:292.
11. Corney II:39. The word *uri* is written *curi* in the original manuscript, but Corney points out that the 'c' was undoubtedly a copyist's error for 'e'. The 'e' (or, correctly 'o') was the Tahitian article, which all the early European visitors to Tahiti mistakenly thought was part of each noun. A list of Tahitian words that the Spaniards later gathered has *euri* for 'nail' (see Corney II:14).
12. Corney I:294-6.
13. Corney II:41.
14. Corney II:73.
15. Corney I:319.
16. Corney I:317.
17. Corney I:329-30.
18. Corney I:336.
19. Corney II:79-80.
20. Corney II:82-3.
21. Corney II:55.
22. Corney I:358-9. In his report, Hervé described Tahiti as Amat's Island and Mehetia as San Cristobal—these being the names that Boenechea had bestowed on the two islands; and he wrote Orallatea for Raiatea. In addition, his measurements for the Raiatean canoe were given in terms of the *vara,* a Spanish measure equivalent to 32.875 inches. To avoid confusion, the names Tahiti, Mehetia and Raiatea have been substituted for those that Hervé used, and his measurements in *varas* have been translated into their approximate equivalents in feet.
23. Corney II:93.
24. Corney II:6.
25. Hassall 1964:26 says: '[Rupert Brooke inherited] his father's fair hair, blue eyes, and especially his skin. This was abnormally clear and smooth and at times transparent in appearance, so that the flesh seemed to shine through it, giving him an almost girlish complexion.' Brooke said in a letter from Tahiti to his mother: 'They call me Pupure here—it means "fair" in Tahitian—because I have fair hair.'—Keynes 1968:562.
26. Davies 1851:212, 214; Andrews 1944: 129; Stone 1964:89; Jaussen 1969:119. The last-named gives 'blond' as a definition for *pupure.*
27. Stimson and Marshall 1964:417.

CHAPTER 10: A problem for the learned

1. Cook's proposal was first recorded in a postscript to the journal of his first voyage—Beaglehole 1955:479.

2. Details of the personnel, etc. of Cook's second expedition together with Cook's journal of the voyage and extracts from the logbooks and journals of several of his companions are published in Beaglehole 1961. A journal kept by Johann Reinhold Forster, now in the Staatsbibliothek, Berlin, has never been published, but is being edited for publication by Mr Michael Hoare, of the Australian National University, Canberra. I am indebted to him for allowing me access to a microfilm copy of it and to his typewritten transcript. The journal is cited in these notes as J. R. Forster 1772-5. George Forster used it in compiling his narrative, *A Voyage Round the World in His Britannic Majesty's Sloop, 'Resolution'* . . . , 2 vols., London, 1777, after the Admiralty forbade his father to publish an account in opposition to Cook. In so doing, he appropriated some of his father's observations and published them as his own. However, it is evident that many of George Forster's observations were, indeed, his own, and that his published narrative was also based on a personal diary or notes, the whereabouts of which—if they still exist—is unknown. J. R. Forster made some use of his own journal, and many other extant notes, in writing his *Observations Made During a Voyage Round the World on Physical Geography, Natural History and Ethic Philosophy* . . . , London, 1778. In these notes the published works of the Forsters are cited as G. Forster 1777 and J. R. Forster 1778 respectively.
3. For Cook's account of the voyage to the expedition's arrival in Tahiti, see Beaglehole 1961:3-197.
4. Beaglehole 1961:201.
5. J. R. Forster 1772-5: entry for 17 Aug. 1773.
6. G. Forster 1777:I:257.
7. G. Forster 1777:I:258-60.
8. G. Forster 1777:I:304.
9. G. Forster 1777:I:304-5.
10. G. Forster 1777:I:308.
11. Beaglehole 1961:768.
12. Beaglehole 1961:769-70.
13. G. Forster 1777:I:378.
14. G. Forster 1777:I:380.
15. J. R. Forster 1772-5: entry for 6 Sept. 1773.
16. J. R. Forster 1772-5: entries for 9 and 10 Sept. 1773.
17. G. Forster 1777:I:393.
18. G. Forster 1777:I:393.
19. Beaglehole 1961:771.
20. G. Forster 1777:I:399.
21. G. Forster 1777:I:399-400.
22. Beaglehole 1961:224.
23. Beaglehole 1961:805.
24. G. Forster 1777:I:400-2.
25. J. R. Forster 1778:230 mentions the red-headed man, but not the blonde woman. They are both mentioned in J. R. Forster 1772-5: entry for 7 Oct. 1773, where the people of the islands seen up to that time are described.
26. G. Forster 1777:I:408.
27. G. Forster 1777:I:412.
28. For details of the voyage from Raiatea to Takaroa, see Beaglehole 1961: 239-377.
29. Beaglehole 1961:377.
30. George Forster's account of his visit to Takaroa is in G. Forster 1777:II: 39-43; his father's is in J. R. Forster 1772-5: entry for 18 April 1774.
31. G. Forster 1777:II:45.
32. Beaglehole 1961:385.
33. G. Forster 1777:II:62.
34. Beaglehole 1961:409. Cook's figure has since been regarded as a gross overestimate. For discussions on early population estimates for Tahiti, see Beaglehole 1955:clxxiv-clxxvii; Macarthur 1967:235-65.
35. G. Forster 1777:II:66.
36. G. Forster 1777:II:77-8.
37. G. Forster 1777:II:105-6.
38. G. Forster 1777:II:97.
39. Wales described the farce with great relish—Beaglehole 1961:842-3.
40. Beaglehole 1961:420 and n.
41. J. R. Forster 1772-5: entry for 4 June 1774.
42. For an account of the voyage from Raiatea to Spithead, see Beaglehole 1961:431-682.
43. Beaglehole 1961:clviii-clxiv discusses the production and present disposition of the graphic records of the expedition, including Hodges' paintings and drawings. See Smith 1969:45-7 for a discussion on Hodges' Tahitian landscapes. Smith does not comment on the portraits.

CHAPTER 11: The cross of Anaa and other oddities

1. Only a few of the original documents concerning the second Spanish expedition to Tahiti in 1774-5, and also the third in 1775-6, have been published in Spanish. English translations of the documents by Bolton Glanvill Corney appear in vols. 2 and 3 of *The Quest and Occupation of Tahiti by Emissaries of Spain* published by the Hakluyt Society in 1915 and 1919. These are cited as Corney II and Corney III.

2. Corney II:108.
3. Corney II:114n.
4. Corney II:112.
5. Corney II:114.
6. Corney II:116-17.
7. Corney II:230-3.
8. Corney II:233-5.
9. Corney II:209.
10. Cook's visits to Tahiti to that time were: 14 April-13 July 1769; 17-31 Aug. 1773; 22 April-14 May 1774.
11. Corney II:310-13.
12. Corney II:187-90.
13. Corney II:188n was in doubt as to whether Oaná and Tapuhoe were one and the same. Hitherto unpublished information gathered by the missionary John Davies in 1807—see chapter 15, n.21—make it clear that they were so.
14. For the identification of Maropua (i.e. Marupua) as Fangatau, see Stimson and Marshall 1964:290; Seurat 1904: 406; Brisson 1929:259.
15. Corney II:191-3.
16. Corney II:257-8. The words in brackets are Corney's.
17. Corney II:256-7.
18. Corney II:282.
19. Corney II:282-4.
20. Corney II: 284-7.
21. Corney II:356-7.
22. An English translation is published in Corney III. The original diary is in the library of the Royal Geographic Society, London, to whose librarian I am indebted for information in the next two notes.
23. Corney III:183. In the original, the words are: *'mui rubio aunque no de los más blancos.'*
24. Corney II:192-3. The words in the original describing Oviriau's appearance are: *'Tenia la tez [?]blanca, el pelo rubio y ensortijado, y ojos azules.'* It will be seen from this and the previous note that the ambiguous word *rubio* (see chapter 3, note 28) appears in both passages. But there is no ambiguity over the colour of Oviriau's eyes —these being *azules,* which can only mean 'blue.'
25. Corney II:397-422.
26. Corney II:471.

CHAPTER 12: The enigmatic 'Miss Poedoua'

1. For the background to Cook's third voyage, see Beaglehole 1967:xxix-lxviii. Besides Cook's journal, this work includes those of several of Cook's companions.
2. Clark 1940 tells the story of Omai's (or properly Mai's) sojourn in England. For a briefer account, see Langdon 1972:30-7.
3. Beaglehole 1961:949-50.
4. Beaglehole 1967:5.
5. Beaglehole 1967:78-81.
6. Beaglehole 1967:81-8. Anderson, see note 8 below, gave some slightly different details about the castaways.
7. Beaglehole 1967:87, note 3.
8. Beaglehole 1967:833-43, especially 840.
9. Beaglehole 1967:89-91.
10. Beaglehole 1967:184-5, 185 note 3, 969-71.
11. Beaglehole 1967:253.
12. Beaglehole 1967:1343.
13. Beaglehole 1967:1373.
14. Beaglehole 1967:232.
15. Beaglehole 1967:1067.
16. Beaglehole 1967:1070.
17. Beaglehole 1967:1074.
18. Beaglehole 1967:1390.
19. Reproduced in Beaglehole 1967:pl.30. The history of the Admiralty copy, like that of the others, is unknown. As they are all of ample proportions, they were probably painted after Webber returned to England from a smaller version done on the spot. There seems to be no contemporary reference to the execution of the original. But William Bligh, who accompanied Cook on his last voyage, and who visited Tahiti again in HMS *Bounty* in 1788-9, recorded in November 1788 that 'Poeedooah of Ulietea, the Lady who Mr Webber made a painting of,' was dead—Bligh 1937:385. Unless Bligh had seen the copy exhibited in the Royal Academy of Arts in 1785 (see note 22) this would suggest that the portrait done at Raiatea was a memorable one.
20. The National Library copy seems from photographs to be slightly inferior to the Admiralty version.
21. Reproduced, incorrectly captioned, as the 39th plate in Marau Taaroa:1971.
22. Graves 1906:186. Graves states that the painting was exhibited as 'Poedua, daughter of Oree, chief of Ulaietea, one of the Society Isles.' Webber exhibited seven others at the same time.
23. Beaglehole 1967:248, n. 3.
24. Smith 1969:93.

CHAPTER 13: Traditions 'like our books of the Old Testament'

1. Watts 1789:231-43, especially 239.
2. All observations made by Bligh during his voyage in the *Bounty* which are quoted in this chapter are from his log-

book—Bligh 1937—rather than from the edited account of his voyage published soon after his return to England —Bligh 1792. The latter was anonymously edited by James Burney, an officer in the *Adventure* on Cook's second voyage, with assistance from Joseph Banks who accompanied Cook on his first voyage. The edited account omits many of Bligh's observations made in Tahiti and interpolates ideas of both Burney and Banks—du Rietz 1962:115-25. The account of 1792 has been republished many times. One of the most accessible is in Mackaness 1938.

3. Bligh 1937:I:375; II:59-60.
4. Bligh 1937:I:385, 394, 396; II:77. 'Tatama auree' (esquire) is given as an additional rank in II:77.
5. Bligh 1937:I:385; II:45.
6. Bligh 1937:II:45-7.
7. Bligh 1937:I:386, 410, 416.
8. Bligh 1937:II:9.
9. Bligh 1937:II:14.
10. Bligh 1937:II:24.
11. Bligh 1937:II:24-5.
12. Both Bligh's logbook and Morrison's journal—Morrison 1935—were edited by Owen Rutter. In editing Morrison's work, Rutter used a transcript of the original journal in the Mitchell Library, Sydney, not the original itself. The transcript contains some errors and ignores most of Morrison's corrections and additions. However, it is sufficiently accurate to be quoted in most instances and is used here.
13. For some account of the history of Morrison's manuscript, see the note by Rolf du Rietz in Morrison 1966:ix-xiii. For accounts of the *Pandora's* visit to Tahiti, see Edwards and Hamilton, 1915.
14. The ethnographical data on Tubuai is from Morrison 1935:65-74.
15. Morrison 1935:176.
16. Morrison 1935:176-8.
17. Morrison 1935:103-6, 179.
18. Morrison 1935:180-1. Morrison was the only eighteenth century chronicler of Tahiti to mention the priests' 'unknown tongue'. However, on 1 January 1824, the LMS missionary J. M. Orsmond wrote in his journal that he had got two renowned priests of the old religion to give him 'several specimens of their original mode of prayers.' After describing these, he commented: 'I now see the nature of the services performed for Tahitian gods and who would have supposed it to be the oldest sister of popish ignorance.'—Orsmond 1824.
19. Morrison 1935:169.
20. Morrison 1935:170.
21. Morrison 1935:169-70.
22. Morrison 1935:171, 199-201, 204-5.
23. Morrison 1935:165-8.
24. The complex political situation in early Tahiti is discussed by C. W. Newbury in Davies 1961:xxxi-xxxviii.
25. Morrison 1935:100-1, 113, 116.
26. For a discussion on the custom of ***pi***, see White 1967:323-38. Other information on the subject, not cited by White, appears in Hale 1846:228-9; Lee 1920: 111-12; Morrison 1935:240; Vancouver 1801:I:316-19, 322-3.
27. Vancouver 1801:I:316-17.
28. Vancouver 1801:I:324, 328, 335-6.
29. Vancouver 1801:I:327, 337.
30. Lee 1920:40.
31. Lee 1920:42.
32. Lee 1920:1-45, 72-278.
33. [House] 1957.
34. Broughton 1804:26-8.

CHAPTER 14: The great white chiefs of Opoa

1. Wilson 1799:52-226.
2. Wilson 1799:181-215.
3. For accounts of the LMS mission to Tahiti, see Ellis 1831: II:1-438, III: 1-321; Ellis 1844; Lovett 1899; Davies 1961.
4. Maude 1968:178-232 gives an account of the pork trade.
5. The ships were: 1798—*Nautilus* (twice), *Sally, Cornwall;* 1799—*Betsy*, two Spanish prizes; 1800—*Eliza, Albion;* 1801—*Porpoise, Royal Admiral;* 1802—*Norfolk, Venus* (twice), *Nautilus* (twice), *Porpoise, Margaret;* 1803—*Unicorn, Margaret, Dart;* 1804—*Harrington* (twice), two Spanish prizes; 1805—*Alexander, Myrtle, Taber;* 1806—*Lucy, Hawkesbury, Britannia, Taber;* 1807—*Harrington, Elizabeth, General Wellesley* (twice), *Pegasus, Parramatta* (twice), *Seringapatam;* 1808—*Amethyst, Hero, Venus, Mercury, Perseverance*. The list has been compiled from LMS and other records.
6. Davies 1925:119-60 describes the exodus.
7. Davies 1961:x1vii-x1viii, 140-70.
8. Davies 1961:171-200.
9. Davies 1961:213-22.
10. For an outline of Orsmond's career, see Henry 1928:(IV)-(V); O'Reilly and Teissier 1962:345-7.
11. Ellis' career is outlined by Colin W. Newbury in Ellis 1972:I:7-19. See also O'Reilly and Teissier 1962:137; and Ellis 1873.
12. Ellis 1831:I:79-83.

13. Ellis 1831:I:84. Ellis added here that 'a fair complexion was not an object of admiration or desire.'
14. Ellis' statements are sometimes at variance. Thus, that of note 13 does not accord with that of note 15.
15. Ellis 1831:I:21. Davies 1851:202-3 defines *pori* as 'certain persons of both sexes, but chiefly women, who pampered their bodies to become fat and fair.'
16. Ellis 1831:I:110, 114.
17. Ellis 1831:I:115.
18. Ellis 1831:I:110, 323, 325.
19. Ellis 1831:I:110, 114.
20. Ellis 1831:I:110. Ellis was inclined to think that the word *ivi,* meaning both bone and widow, was the 'only aboriginal part of the story, as far as it respects the mother of the human race.' But, he added (p. 111): 'Should more careful and minute inquiry confirm the truth of their declaration, and prove that this account was in existence among them prior to their intercourse with Europeans, it will be the most remarkable and valuable oral tradition of the origin of the human race yet known.'
21. Ellis 1831:I:386-9.
22. Ellis 1831:I:106, 111, 229-47, especially 234; II:315-16; III:112.
23. Ellis 1831:I:342; III:394. Ellis occasionally retailed the same information in slightly different words. These two references provide the keys to two examples.
24. Ellis 1831:III:93-5. Ellis used the old spelling *bue,* rather than the modern *pue*. Davies 1851:207 defined *pue raatira* as 'the inferior chiefs collectively' and *hui arii* (p. 113) as 'the royal party or family.' He also gave *hui raatira* as a definition for 'the inferior chiefs collectively.'
25. Ellis 1831:III:98-101.
26. Ellis 1831:III:101-18.
27. Ellis 1831:I:85.
28. Ellis 1831:I:90.
29. Ellis 1831:I:91.
30. Ellis 1831:I:160, 164, 170; III:305.
31. Ellis 1831:I:141.
32. Gerstaecker 1853:II:171.
33. Ellis 1831:I:327-8. Henry 1928:545 supplies the detail about Maupiti and mentions two other Society Islands landmarks that bear Hiro's name. Handy 1930:94 and Emory 1933:156-7 mention yet others. None of the landmarks is on Tahiti.
34. Ellis 1831:I:200.
35. Henry 1928:537-52.
36. Henry 1928:247-9.
37. Bovis 1892:46-8, 53-4, 78. See also Montgomery 1840:26, 68-9.
38. Quatrefages [1866]:186, 195.
39. Nicholas 1892:20-9; Large 1904:133-44; Savage and Tamuera Te Rei 1907:1-2; Savage 1962:76-7.
40. Best 1922:111-21; Gudgeon 1903:120-1; Smith 1893:25-37. For other bibliographical references to Whiro in New Zealand tradition, see Tregear [1891]: 597, 625.
41. See, for example, Savage 1916:142n, 143n; Savage 1917:54n; Heyerdahl 1952:753; Lewthwaite 1973:225.
42. Ellis 1831:IV:431; Henry 1928:95, 98, 102, 115; Huguenin 1902: 17-18, 27-8; Chesneau 1928:93, 94; Handy 1930:15; Buck 1938:65-7.
43. Savage 1917:52-3. Nuiapu cannot be identified as a place on Borabora. However, the southernmost district on Tahaa is called Niua, and its chief bay is Apu. There may therefore be some confusion over the correct rendering and location of Nuiapu. The name of the *koutu-ariki* should, perhaps, be Niuapu (a shortened form of Niua Apu), and the locale of the legend not Vavau, but Kuporu (i.e. Tahaa). See Huguenin 1902:map facing p. 18; Emory 1933:156.
44. Davies 1961:xxxvi-xxxviii.
45. Henry 1928:128-31. The legend as published in *Ancient Tahiti* also states that after the building of the Taputapuatea *marae* at Taiarapu, the Oro priest's sister was 'kindly received at 'Uporu (Ha'apape) where she established a school for the aristocracy of Tahiti and taught them the folklore of the mother land, Ra'iatea.' This statement has not been included in the text of this book because it appears to contain two editorial errors, probably on the part of Teuira Henry, which make it false. The first is the identification of 'Uporu as Ha'apape (i.e. Point Venus). The second, probably a consequential error, is that the school at 'Uporu was for the 'aristocracy of Tahiti.' As is explained on p. 167, 'Uporu was the old name for Tahaa, Raiatea's sister island. In the early days of the Oro cult, that island rather than Tahiti is more likely to have been the site of a school for the aristocracy. Moreover, as Oro was the god of the *maro-ura* chiefs, it is almost certain that Oro was not introduced into the Ha'apape area of Tahiti until Te-tupaia, a high chiefess of Raiatea, married the Tahitian chief Teu (c. 1720-1802) and brought the *maro-ura* to the Pare district—see Henry 1928:249 and n. It should further be noted that 'Uporu is also identified as Ha'apape on pp. 74, 537 and 554 of *Ancient Tahiti,* but on p. 98 it is equated with Tahaa. No other writer appears to have identified 'Uporu as Ha'apape, and there seems no reason

to suppose that it should not be taken as the old name for Tahaa in every case.

46. Ellis 1831:III:250; Montgomery 1840: 28.

47. Lesson 1839:I:272. For information on the brief career of Pomare III, see O'Reilly and Teissier 1962:366-7.

48. Lesson 1839:I:289. Two inspectors of the London Missionary Society who visited the Society Islands about the same time as Lesson were under the impression that Aimata was only a half-sister of Pomare III—Montgomery 1840:28. This was not so. The two children were borne by Terito-o-te-rai, second daughter of Tamatoa III (sometimes called Tamatoa IV) of Raiatea. Terito was the younger sister of a woman to whom Pomare II had actually been betrothed.—Henry 1928:249; Davies 1961:137, 153n, Appendix I.

49. Lesson 1839:I:270.

50. Lesson 1839:I:365. See also pp. 321, 360-1.

51. Montgomery 1840:28; Nightingale 1835:120.

52. One such half-caste child was Nancy Connor, daughter of an Irish seaman from the whaler *Matilda* who settled in the Society Islands in 1792. Her story demonstrates how widely spread the genes of a single European sailor could become in a few generations. After being brought up by the LMS missionaries, Nancy married a Tahitian by whom she had a daughter, Maraea. Maraea became the wife of Thomas Bambridge, an ex-convict, who had served as an artisan-missionary in Tonga. This pair had 22 children, and it is from them that Tahiti's numerous and prominent Bambridge family of today is descended.—Gunson 1970:34, 44; O'Reilly and Teissier 1962:26-7.

53. Moerenhout 1837: II:247n. See also chapter 7 above, note 7.

54. Handy 1930:44.

55. Bennett 1840:I:104-5, 110, 136.

56. Bennett 1840:I:141.

57. Huguenin 1902:70-1, 70n.

58. Huguenin 1902:65-9. See also Appendix F.

59. Handy 1930:43.

60. Handy 1930:8.

61. Handy 1930:9-15, 67 summarises what he thought were *manahune* cultural traits.

62. Handy 1930:10.

63. Handy 1930:15.

64. Handy 1930:38.

65. Handy 1930:19-22, 35, 38.

66. Handy 1930:67 contains his summary of *arii* cultural traits. References to light skin also appear on pp. 44, 61.

67. Handy 1930:39-42.

68. Handy 1930:40.

69. Handy 1930:19.

70. Handy 1932:45, 63.

71. Handy 1930:6, 86.

72. Handy 1930:61. Handy based his opinion on a tradition apparently recorded by Orsmond in 1840 and published in Henry 1928:232.

73. Notably R. O. Piddington in Williamson 1939:201-301. See also Beaglehole 1955:clxxvii, n.3; Suggs 1960:135.

74. Hale 1846:124, 148.

75. See, for example, Suggs 1960:107, 137.

76. See chapter 3 above, note 42.

77. Dening 1962:138-53 lists several unintentional voyages by islanders from the Tuamotus to the islands to the west of them. Hornell 1945:183-5 describes the drift voyages of two derelict ships from the west coast of South America, through the Tuamotus, to the Society Islands.

78. Opoa, as Captain Cook noted in 1769, lies opposite the southernmost opening in the reef on Raiatea's eastern side.—Beaglehole 1955:145. The reef entrance is called Ava Mo'a (Sacred Entrance). For a view from the entrance, see *Pacific Islands Pilot* 1957:III:p1. facing 171.

79. *Collier's Encyclopedia* 1961:XIV:160.

80. Morrison 1935:73.

81. Buck 1952:37 suggests that the change from Hawaiki to Rangiatea (the original pronunciation of Raiatea) was taking place when the so-called great migration from Hawaiki to New Zealand occurred. He says the Ngati Ruanui tribe of Taranaki, whose ancestors came in the Aotea canoe, have a saying in which Rangiatea is mentioned. See also Tregear [1891]:394.

82. Handy 1930:6 quotes Marau as saying that fifteen years would approximate the average time elapsing between successive *arii* because the ruling *arii* was married as a boy. W. W. Gill, an early missionary in the Cook Islands, in referring to the length of time that should be allowed for a chief's reign, wrote: '. . . from what one knows of savage life, twenty-five years is too long a period.'—Gill [1876]:23. For discussions on the problems of dating Polynesian (usually Maori) history by the use of genealogies, see Biggs 1969; Fletcher 1930; Kelly 1940; Roberton 1956, 1957, 1958; Stokes 1930a.

83. Hornell 1945:169.

CHAPTER 15: Anaa: land of 'immense vessels like our ships'

1. The voyages through the Tuamotus of the *Aguila* and *Jupiter* (1774) and the *Aguila* (1775) are described in chapters 9 and 11. For an account of the *Pandora's* discovery of (South) Marutea and Tureia Atolls, see Edwards and Hamilton 1915:29-30. For Bligh's discovery of Tematangi Atoll in the *Providence* and *Assistant,* see Lee 1920: 34-5.
2. Wilson 1799:114-18.
3. Turnbull 1813:245-305; *SG,* 2 Oct. 1803.
4. Davies 1961:99-100; Davies 1807-8, entry for 21 Sept. 1807; Robarts 1974: 178-9. HRNZ:I:422-3.
5. Davies 1961:135; Im Thurn and Wharton 1925:125; Cumpston 1963:71.
6. Nott 1811; *SG,* 21 Sept. 1811; Cumpston 1963:70.
7. Between Campbell's voyage to Manihi in 1811 and the temporary cessation of the Tuamotus pearlshell trade in 1814, the following ships took part in it: *Trial* (1811); *Favourite* (1812); *Governor Macquarie, Daphne, James Hay* (1813); *Queen Charlotte, Governor Macquarie, Campbell Macquarie* (1814). For details of their voyages, see *SG,* 18, 25 May, 7, 21 Sept. 1811; 8, 25 May, 8 Sept., 13 Nov., 25 Dec. 1813; 1 Jan., 19 Feb., 18 June, 26 Nov. 1814; Nott 1811; Pomare II:1811; Nott 1813; Hendrike 1813; Bicknell 1816; Davies 1961:153, 156, 165-7, 169, 172-3, 180, 228; HRA, ser. 1:VIII:100; Moerenhout 1837:II: 457-8; Cumpston 1963:86, 88-9. The ships are variously described as having visited the 'Pearl Islands', 'Palmottoes', 'Paomottoes' and 'Paliseers.' The best clue to what was meant by those terms was given by Campbell after a voyage in the *James Hay*. He referred to the island of 'Hanna or Hannam' (i.e. Anaa) as 'considerably further to windward than any we have visited.'—*SG,* 1 Jan. 1814.
8. The extent of the Anaans' 'empire' and the method they used to preserve it will be partially gathered from evidence presented later in this chapter. See also Cuming 1827-8:22-3; Moerenhout 1837:II:371; [Lucett] 1851:260-1.
9. Davies 1961:208-9; Cumpston 1963: 100.
10. See chapter 8, note 4.
11. See chapter 8, note 51.
12. See chapter 9, note 8.
13. See chapter 11, note 4.
14. See chapter 11, note 13; Corney II:316.
15. Corney II:188-9.
16. Corney III:198.
17. Bligh 1937: II:45.
18. Morrison 1935:201.
19. Wilson and Elder 1803, entry for 19 July.
20. Youl, Davies and others 1806-7, entry for 22 July 1806.
21. Neither Danielsson 1956:40 nor Stimson and Marshall 1964: (end papers), include Anaa in the areas defined as Tapuhoe in their maps showing 'ancient divisions' and 'speech groups' respectively of the Tuamotus. These scholars place Anaa in a region of its own, Putahi or Parata. By contrast, Emory 1932:43 includes Anaa in the Central Tuamotus, but does not use the term Tapuhoe.
22. Davies 1961:270n states that the word *papaa* was used particularly to describe the 'Parata party', i.e. Anaans, before Wallis' time. See also note 76 below. Ottino 1965:15 says: 'Etymologically this term should signify "those with sunburnt shoulders"—i.e. *papa a*. It evidently refers to the first European navigators in the Pacific.' Davies 1851:1, 184, defines *papa* as shoulderblade, and *a* as an adjective meaning the opposite of 'raw', i.e. roasted, baked or boiled.
23. Parkinson 1773:56; Morrison 1935:146. Parkinson and Morrison were in Tahiti in 1769 and 1788-91 respectively. Morrison wrote that the Tahitians called the European shaddock *'Ooroo Papaa'* (i.e. *uru papaa*), which he translated as 'English bread.' *Uru* is Tahitian for breadfruit.
24. Davies 1807-8, entries for 19, 21, 23, 28 Sept. 1807.
25. *SG,* 1 Jan. 1814.
26. Maude 1968:199; Davies 1961:270n.
27. Davies 1813-14, entry for 29 Mar. 1813. Davies 1961:207-8, 271.
28. Cuming 1827-8:22. Ariipaea had apparently obtained his name by exchange with a Tahitian chief of that name. Cuming described him as about fifty years old, 'rather above the common height' and with a 'noble countenance.' He said Ariipaea had brought more than thirty islands under his subjection.
29. Davies 1961:209, 218, 247, 271; Ellis 1831:III:305-6; Cuming 1827-8:22-3; Montgomery 1840:16.
30. The pearling ships that operated out of Sydney, or took pearlshell to Sydney, in the second phase of the trade were: *Governor Macquarie, Dragon* (1822); *Governor Macquarie, Queen Charlotte* (1823); *Jupiter* (1824);

Brutus, Dragon, Snapper (1825), *Minerva, Sir George Osborne, Rolla* (1826). For details, see *Dragon* log-book, 1821-3; *SG,* 6 May, 17 June 1824; 10 Feb., 14 April, 28 Nov., 8, 19 Dec. 1825; 8, 22 Mar. 1826; 24 Feb., 10 Mar. 1827. Cumpston 1963: 136, 140, 145, 150, 153, 155; Davies 1961:290; Maude 1968:231; *Nautical Magazine* 1833:II:694.

31. Lesson 1839:I:253-5; Beechey 1831:I: 228-9, 237, 240, 245-6; Belcher 1825-7, entry for 13 Feb. 1826; Salas 1951:8; Peard 1973:112.
32. The first Valparaiso-based pearling ship was the schooner *El Terrible,* which sailed from there in December 1826—Salas 1951:8-10. The next was the *Discoverer*—Cuming 1827-8; then the *Volador*—Moerenhout 1837:I:11-19, 33-82, 102-34.
33. Salas 1951:8 lists maritime movements between Valparaiso and Oceania for the years 1825-37. For ships that called at Pitcairn Island in sailing to and from Valparaiso after 1837, see Lucas 1929: 102-45.
34. Beechey 1831:I:281-3; Moerenhout 1837:II:358-68; Fitz-Roy 1839:II:519, 530-3; [Lucett] 1851:I:305, 308; Danielsson 1956:83-4; Hanson 1970:31.
35. Bellingshausen 1945:225-94, especially 237-41, 244-5, 249, 255, 271-2. Bellingshausen sighted or examined twenty atolls: Manuhangi, Hao, Amanu, Fangatau, Takume, Raroia, Nihiru, Taenga, Makemo, Tuanake, Katiu, Tahanea, Faaite, Fakarava, Toau, Apataki, Niau, Kaukura, Tikehau and Matahiva.
36. Lesson 1839:I:230-4, 275.
37. Beechey 1831:220-5; Peard 1973:109-13, 118.
38. Beechey 1831:243; Peard 1973:112.
39. Peard 1973:117.
40. Moerenhout 1837:I:158-9, 176-96, especially 180.
41. Paris [1841]:136, p1.126. Paris stated that he did not see sails for the *pahi,* but he understood from the islanders' description of them that they were triangular.
42. Wilkes 1845:I:327, 345.
43. Wilkes 1845:I:326-7.
44. Hudson 1838-40:268; Wilkes 1845:I: 330.
45. Hudson 1838-40:268. Hudson, incorrectly, gave the Anaan spelling of coconut as *hiakari* and the Tahitian spelling as *niau.* Hale, however, was in error in stating that the Tahitian word for coconut was *niu.* In fact, the Tahitians were using *haari,* a derivative of the Anaan word, when the first explorers arrived.—Banks 1963:372; Corney II:7. But they used *niu* as the word for coconut palm.—Davies 1851: 155. *Niu* is given as the Fijian and pan-Polynesian word for coconut in Hale 1846:318, 407. It still has this meaning in Western Polynesia; but Stimson and Marshall 1964: 331 state that *niu,* meaning coconut tree, is now obsolete in the Tuamotus.
46. Hale 1846:143-6; 289.
47. Hale 1846:145-6 listed twenty-one Anaan words besides the numerals that had no cognates known to him in other Polynesian languages. Tregear [1891]: xxii listed forty-one such words besides the numerals, most of which did not duplicate Hale's list. Emory 1947a gives twenty plant names peculiar to Anaa, the greatest number for any atoll in the Tuamotus.
48. Tregear [1891]:xxii; Dyen 1966:4. See also Dyen 1965.
49. Ricardi 1844b.
50. For accounts of the Mormon mission to the Tuamotus, see Jenson 1914-17: V-VIII; Ellsworth 1959.
51. Laval 1851; Laval 1968:280; Terlyn 1900; Montiton 1855 describe the founding and early years of the Catholic mission in the Tuamotus. Brown 1960:215-51, 279-81 gives a highly-coloured account of his mission to Anaa and its aftermath. Caillot 1910: 278-81 gives the text of a convention drawn up in 1847 by Governor Lavaud of Tahiti which defined the area of the French protectorate as 'Tahiti-Moorea and its dependencies.' As the leading chiefs of Anaa and neighbouring atolls (which the Anaans had conquered) had acknowledged Pomare II as their supreme chief—see notes 28 and 29—the dependencies were deemed to include the whole of the Tuamotu Archipelago, except Mangareva, which had its own king. Mangareva had been under strong French Catholic influence since 1835.
52. The reason for the priests' failure to win converts has been inferred from the available evidence. The priests themselves published nothing about it. Caillet 1862:181 stated that Catholicism made little progress on Anaa until the State supported it. He did not say when this development occurred.
53. Montiton 1855:450-1.
54. French administration was extended to the Tuamotus in October 1853.—*Messager de Tahiti,* 16 July 1854.
55. Paiore is a somewhat mysterious figure. Despite his importance in Tuamotuan history, he is mentioned only a few times in published literature. The first reference to him is in December 1849 when he was described as one of two 'ringleaders of misrule' on Anaa who had been 'notorious in their subversion of order and contempt for the constituted laws.' The French at that time

sent a frigate to Anaa to arrest him and take him and the other ringleader to Tahiti 'to be dealt with.'—[Lucett] 1851:II:253. Whatever 'misdeeds' Paiore had been responsible for, the French apparently forgave him, and he, for his part, must have agreed to co-operate with them. Thus, when the French announced in July 1854 that they had extended their administration to the Tuamotus the previous October, Paiore was described as 'the regent,' who took orders from the Bureau Indigène (Department of Native Affairs).—*Messager de Tahiti,* 16 July 1854. In 1860, Paiore led an expedition to Fakahina Atoll in an attempt to bring it under the French administration. The expedition came to a bad end in that six of Paiore's men, who had acted provocatively towards the Fakahinans, were killed. The French sent a punitive expedition to the atoll in the following year; and, possibly as a matter of politics, Paiore was retired from his post. He later became chief of Kauehi Atoll.—Anonymous, 1934; Emory 1940b:573. It was at Kauehi that a French Protestant missionary, Thomas Arbousset, met him in 1864. Arbousset described him as 'a truly original nature' of no more than fifty years of age. 'No one can reproach him for lack of ability,' he said. 'As regent of the Tuamotus until recently, he has conducted his people with sure authority. Today the natives still have the highest respect for him.' Arbousset quoted a French government publication which described Paiore as 'one of those rare natives' who knew the islands well from the navigational point of view, and who could make use of charts. He also published a letter from Paiore in French in which Paiore expressed the wish that Arbousset should stay among the Tuamotuans as their minister—'minister of the true Gospel' as taught by the English missionaries. 'In these islands,' Paiore added, 'the Church of our Lord has become dormant.'—Arbousset 1867:315-21. Some nine years after Arbousset's encounter with him, Paiore acted as pilot and interpreter in the French hydrographic vessel *Vaudreuil* during a survey of the Tuamotus. An officer of the ship was impressed with the neatness of the houses and apparent industriousness of the people at Paiore's home island, Kauehi. —Pailhes 1875:268-9, 272.

56. O'Reilly and Teissier 1962:73.
57. *Annuaire . . . ,* 1863:94-5.
58. Henry 1928:347-9. A note on p. 347 says: 'Given in 1890 by X. Caillet, who received it from the chief and regent, Paiore.'
59. Emory 1939:2. Caillet's second term was from 29 Dec. 1869 to 11 April 1870. Paiore's drawing of 1869 is therefore likely to have been done before Caillet arrived.
60. A typical drawing of the Ptolemaic conception appears in Cunningham 1559:50.
61. Montiton 1874:339.
62. Christian 1910:opp. 194. Young 1919: opp. 211; Henry 1928:348. The drawing published by Christian was erroneously captioned: 'A piece of Rarotongan wood-carving representing the tradition of the stealing of fire from the Sun (Ra) by Maui, the Polynesian Prometheus. It is probably a rude copy of an ancient hieroglyphical record, either Cushite, Babylonian or Egyptian. Possibly the original was a parchment.'
63. Emory 1939; Emory 1940a; Emory 1940b; Emory 1943.
64. Young 1919:209 said: 'I am doubtful of the value of this drawing as I think the author was probably influenced by missionary teachings.'
65. Emory 1939:15 said: 'I believe that the Paiore charts are attempts to represent Tuamotuan conceptions graphically in emulation of illustrations in European books with which the western Tuamotuans were quite familiar when these charts were made.'
66. Apart from Montiton and the three Mormon missionaries, Grouard, Pratt and Brown, the only missionaries to serve on Anaa before 1869 were: Fathers Loubat, Fouqué and Bruno.
67. Arbousset 1867:317.
68. Arbousset 1867:308.
69. For bibliographical details of religious books published in Tahitian before 1869, see O'Reilly and Reitman 1967: 517-33.
70. Ricardi 1844b:2-3. Ricardi referred in his article to a god called Varoua-Kiro. The second part of the name may have been a mistake for Kiho because, among the French, the uvular 'r' and the aspirate are not far removed. If the name really was Kiho, this would be significant in the Emory-Stimson dispute described in chapter 16.
71. Green 1878; Stevenson n.d.:105; Teissier 1969:161-2, 208-10; Henry 1928:107; Ricardi 1844b:2; [Lucett] 1851:I:239; Teissier 1953:22.
72. Stimson 1933a:3; Emory and Ottino 1967:31-3; Robinson 1972:222-4.
73. Emory and Ottino 1967:34, 36-7, 54. Two Tangihia appear in a genealogy published by Emory and Ottino, who have taken one twelve generations before 1900 as the founder of the tribe. However, legends cited by them linking Tangihia with Te Kura appear to relate to one seventeen generations back.

74. Emory and Ottino 1967:39-40.

75. The information relating to string figures was kindly supplied by Mrs Honor Maude, of Canberra, who, in 1974, was preparing a monograph on Tuamotuan string figures in association with Emory.

76. Davies 1851:185 defined *papaa* as 'a foreigner, formerly applied to the inhabitants of the Paumotu islands before europeans visited them, but since to all foreigners; in some islands it is papalangy.'

77. Stimson and Marshall 1964:264. On Anaa, *kura* also means 'the first-born child of a personage of exalted rank, a high priest, or a renowned warrior-hero.'

78. A. Capell, a specialist in the languages of Melanesia, said in a review of *A Dictionary of Some Tuamotuan Dialects* . . . (Stimson and Marshall 1964) that the 'strange element' which Tregear had noted in Paumotuan 'still remains as something to be explained.'—Capell 1965-6:249. By contrast, a Maori-Polynesian linguist, Bruce Biggs, said in a review of the same work: 'It has become something of a linguistic folktale that there is a non-Polynesian element in Tuamotuan,' and he added that the dictionary provided no evidence of a sub-stratum or an intrusive element in the language.—Biggs 1965. See also Biggs 1966a. Stimson himself referred to intrusive elements in an introduction to the dictionary.—Stimson and Marshall 1964:23.

79. Between the *Kon-Tiki's* voyage and the end of 1973, ten rafts drifted from the coast of Peru and Ecuador to Polynesia. Of these, five continued to Australia. See Heyerdahl 1968:199 for a brief account of the first five voyages; Levison and others 1973:46, note 9 for citations on the first seven. The last three rafts were units of the Las Balsas expedition which reached Australia in late 1973. Hornell 1945:182-6 tells of two derelict European ships that drifted from off the South American coast to Polynesia. Heyerdahl and Skjolsvold 1956 and Heyerdahl 1968:122-32 cite historical and archaeological evidence to demonstrate that American Indians fished from balsa rafts between the Ecuadorian-Peruvian coast and the Galapagos Islands, 600 miles westward, and that they also visited the Galapagos. Lanning, a severe critic of Heyerdahl, says 'the claim for prehistoric visits to the [Galapagos] islands seems to be justified.' He adds: 'The apparent fact of prehistoric visits to the Galapagos does not, of course, prove that Ecuadorian sailors ever proceeded on out into Polynesia, but it considerably strengthens the possibility that they might have done so.'—Lanning 1970: 181.

80. McNab 1967:219 says, for example: 'There is no dispute today that the sweet potato (*Ipomoea batatas*) is of South American origin. If Vavilov's theory of plant origins is accepted then Yen's study of sources and numbers of varieties indicates a Peruvian centre for the domestication of the sweet potato.' However, like many scholars, McNab believes that Polynesians sailed to Peru and acquired the sweet potato there, not that Peruvians carried it to Polynesia. See Yen 1971a:12 for a discussion on 'the original transmission of the sweet potato from America to Polynesia;' also O'Brien 1972. Both Yen 1971b:337-8 and Brand 1971:363 conclude that there are powerful reasons for believing that there is no linguistic relationship between the Polynesian word *kumara* and the South American word *cumar*. Brand says 'nowhere on the Ecuadorian or Peruvian coast was there anyone cultivating [the sweet potato] using a name even remotely resembling *cumar* or *cumara*.' See, however, Appendix F.

81. Lanning 1970:182 describes the 'totora rush' of Easter Island as one of the 'most promising candidates' among plants to have been carried by human agency from South America to the Pacific. Heyerdahl 1952:439-46 discusses the question of the bottle gourd's existence in both South America and Polynesia in pre-European times. Several of the authorities he cites agree that the bottle gourd co-existed in the two areas but believe it was brought from South America by far-ranging Polynesians. For example, Emory 1942: 134 writes: '. . . as long as the gourd seems to stand as evidence that the Polynesians reached South America in early times, and the sweet potato as evidence that they returned, it will appear possible that some of the parallels between Polynesia and the coastal regions of the Americas are due to cultural borrowing.' Whitaker 1971 states that the bottle gourd is indigenous to tropical Africa, and that it may have been introduced to South America either from Africa or Polynesia by drift or human agency before about 3000 B.C. Green 1973:109 says the presence of the gourd in ancient archaeological deposits in Thailand and New Guinea, combined with evidence from the Americas, 'must rule out any Polynesian origin as a source for the plant in America.'

82. The similarity has been noted by

several writers, some of whom are cited in Heyerdahl 1952:386-9. See also Englert 1972:43.

83. Heyerdahl 1952:349-424 discusses this question at length with the aid of numerous illustrations.
84. Handy 1927:329 recognised this and suggested that 'some eastern Polynesians, probably Marquesans, borrowed the art of stone construction from the west coast of South America; and that within Polynesia the art spread from east to west.'
85. Emory 1934:65.
86. Dilated ears were described among the Easter Islanders by Roggeveen in 1722 (Sharp 1970:93, 96-7, 104) and by Beechey in 1825 (Beechey 1831:I:38); as known to the Marquesans by Tautain 1897—quoted by Heyerdahl 1952: 246; by Le Maire at Takapoto in 1616 (see p. 74); and by Bonacorsi at Raivavae in 1775 (see p. 131). All the islands concerned, except Takapoto, an atoll, are noted for their huge stone statues. See Heyerdahl 1952:pls. XXVI and XXVIII for portraits of 'long-eared' Peruvians.
87. Simmons and others 1955; Simmons 1965; Simmons 1968; Ferdon 1968: 98-9.
88. Heyerdahl 1968:34-6 lists the most important items of evidence, which, in his view, support the notion of American Indian influence in Polynesia. See also Heyerdahl 1952.
89. George Forster 1777:423-4 recorded that the first man to go aboard the *Resolution* when she anchored at the Tongan island of Eua in 1773 had black hair in short, frizzled curls, and that his skin colour was 'a clear mahogany or chestnut brown.' The OED defines mahogany as reddish-brown, and tawny as brownish-yellow or tan-coloured.
90. The Tuamotuan dictionary of Stimson and Marshall 1964 contains only 17 pages of words beginning with 'f' but 72 beginning with 'h'. The Tahitian dictionary of Davies 1851 has 28 pages of words beginning with 'f' and 29 pages beginning with 'h'.
91. Entwistle 1962:159-62.

CHAPTER 16: The 'remarkably European' people of Fangatau

1. *Pacific Islands Pilot* 1969:101; Stimson and Marshall 1964:290.
2. Audran 1926:86-9.
3. The tradition as published gives this name as Taharoa, presumably a misprint for Takaroa.
4. Corney II:189. Corney, tentatively but erroneously, identified Marupua as Marutea, an atoll in the central Tuamotus.
5. Bellingshausen 1945:I:232-4.
6. Kotzebue 1830:I:107-11.
7. Fitz-Roy 1839:II:519.
8. Fitz-Roy 1839:Appendix, chart 2.
9. Mauruc 1848:78-9. Neither Mauruc nor Ricardi (see next note) mentioned the name of the ship in which he visited Fangatau. But it is on record that the ship *Polynesiana,* A. Maurue [*sic*], touched at Pitcairn Island on 22 May 1838.—Lucas 1929:102.
10. Ricardi 1844a. Ricardi did not state that he was on board Mauruc's ship when he visited Fangatau; nor did Mauruc mention Ricardi in his account. However, several facts in the two accounts are identical; and Ricardi was described as 'M. Eugène, second a bord de la *Polynèsie,* capitaine Mauruque' in a letter written by Father Honoré Laval at Mangareva on 13 Dec. 1838—Laval 1968:189n.
11. [Lucett] 1851:I:249-57.
12. *Messager de Tahiti,* 12 Dec. 1858.
13. Caillet 1862:179.
14. Montiton 1873:280.
15. Fierens 1872:126-8.
16. Montiton 1873:279-84.
17. Terlyn 1900:191; Mouly 1954:90-4.
18. Montiton 1874.
19. Montiton 1874:342.
20. Montiton 1874:342-4.
21. Montiton 1874:354-6.
22. Montiton 1874:491-2.
23. For an account of Montiton's subsequent career, see Mouly 1954:90-118.
24. Terlyn 1900:192-3; Martin 1888.
25. Fierens 1874:383-4.
26. Martin 1888.
27. Bell 1883:745-6.
28. Seurat 1904:406.
29. Seurat 1905:302-6.
30. Bodin 1931:175.
31. MacQuarrie 1920:190-1.
32. Gregory 1930:10.
33. Gregory 1930:10-11, quoting a report by Harry L. Shapiro.
34. Gregory 1930:11-12, quoting a report by J. Frank Stimson.
35. Emory 1932:47.
36. Emory 1932:47-8.
37. Stimson 1933b. Montiton's articles are not mentioned in the bibliography of this or the next cited work. So Stimson seems not to have known of them at the time he wrote.
38. Stimson 1933a.
39. Stimson 1933b:3.
40. Stimson 1933b:3-5. 45-6.

41. Emory 1947b:6.
42. Emory 1939; Emory 1940a; Emory 1940b; Emory 1947b.
43. Emory 1947b:6.
44. Danielsson 1967:24.
45. Stimson and Marshall 1964:224.
46. Emory 1932:40.
47. Davies 1961:270n.
48. Emory 1939:22-3.
49. Emory 1940a:69.
50. As preceding.
51. Emory 1939:19-20.
52. The *Kon-Tiki* raft passed close to Fangatau after reaching the Tuamotus from Peru in 1947. Heyerdahl 1950: 171-84 describes how canoes from the atoll came off to try to tow the raft ashore.
53. Gessler 1935b:551-2; Gessler 1937: 225, 228.
54. Gessler 1935b:554; Gessler 1937:232.
55. Gessler 1935a:243.
56. Burrows 1933.
57. Burrows 1933:39-40.
58. Burrows 1933:97-8.

CHAPTER 17: Vahitahi: land of the Holy Trinity

1. For brief descriptions of the five islands, see NID 1943-5:III:214-5; *Pacific Islands Pilot* 1969:90-1.
2. See chapter 4, p. 66.
3. For the *Dolphin's* visit to the Vahitahi area, see chapter 6, p. 84-6.
4. See chapter 7, p. 94.
5. See chapter 8, p. 102.
6. Bayly 1824-42:I:entries for 9-10 Nov. 1825.
7. Beechey 1831:I:205-7.
8. Beechey 1831:I:208-9.
9. Belcher 1825-7:entry for 6 Jan. 1826.
10. Beechey 1831:I:209.
11. Beechey 1831:I:209-10.
12. Beechey 1831:I:210-12.
13. [Lucett] 1851:I:316-17, 329-30.
14. [Lucett] 1851:II:52-7.
15. *l'Océanie française,* 24 Nov., 1844.
16. Cloué 1870:75-6.
17. Fierens 1872:131.
18. Montiton 1873:284-5.
19. Montiton 1873:371-3.
20. Montiton 1873:374.
21. Fierens 1874:386.
22. Inferred from Mariot 1874:981.
23. Mariot 1874:979-82.
24. Fierens 1884:386-7, 389-90.
25. Townshend and Moore 1899-1900:65-6.
26. In Alexander 1902:766-7.
27. Alexander 1902:756-8.
28. Hermel 1911:563.
29. Hall and Nordhoff 1921:321-5. See also Nordman 1952:72.
30. Hamilton 1939:135. See also Langdon 1962.
31. O'Reilly and Teissier 1962:312-13.
32. Mazé 1933.
33. Emory 1932:48-9.
34. Stimson 1933a:3-6.
35. Stimson 1933a:7.
36. Stimson 1933a:89.
37. Stimson 1933a:88.
38. Williamson 1939:293-301.
39. Other editions appeared in 1847, 1863, 1878, 1884, 1898, 1920 and 1928.
40. Tregear [1891]:xvii-xviii lists some of the numerous differences. The most important are the lack of 'ng' and 'k' in Tahitian, both of which exist in the Tuamotuan dialects.
41. This was the situation until the twenty-first Ecumenical Council of the Vatican in 1962 when Pope John XXIII announced a relaxation in the Catholic Church's attitude towards non-Catholics and their works.
42. The photograph was reproduced in Stimson 1933a:p1.3.
43. Emory 1932:48-9. See also next note.
44. Hornell 1936:76-8.
45. Reproduced in Hornell 1936:86.
46. A perusal of Haddon and Hornell 1936-8 establishes this.
47. Gandía 1942:120 states that no historical study has yet been made of early Basque ships and their architecture, but indicates that extant records would not supply constructional details for the sixteenth century.
48. Nance 1913:266-9.
49. Clissold 1971:453.
50. Real Academía Española 1803.
51. Gessler 1937:237 and pl. opp. 240.
52. Emory 1947b:48-50. Emory added that in 1934 he was told on Nukutavake that the three gods named by Te Poa were called *kura atua.* This, in the light of what has been said about *kura* in chapter 15, may have been the old way of saying 'white men's gods.'

CHAPTER 18: Of far-flung islands and 'hauntingly Caucasian faces'

1. Mikhailov's sketch does not seem to have been published.
2. Bellingshausen 1945:223-4.
3. For information on the inheritance of blue eyes, see p. 50-1.
4. Caillot 1932a:25, 71-2.
5. Vancouver 1801:I:212.
6. Ellis 1831:III:375.
7. Davies 1961:279.
8. McArthur 1967:308.
9. Brown 1960:272.
10. Cumming 1827-8:125.
11. Wilson 1799:116-18.

12. Beechey 1831:I:186-7.
13. Belcher 1825-7: entry for 11 Jan. 1826.
14. Laval 1968:16.
15. Laval 1938:208.
16. Laval 1938:253, 295.
17. Huguenin 1902:53.
18. *Asiatic Journal,* 1823, vol. 16, p. 130.
19. Beechey 1831:I:199.
20. *ASC,* 1938, no. 434, p. 519.
21. Corney II:365; Montgomery 1840: 14-15; *Asiatic Journal,* 1823, vol. 16, p. 128; Lesson 1839:I:230.
22. Mauruc 1848:75-6.
23. Ricardi 1844a.
24. Montiton 1874:504.
25. Fierens 1872:128; Montiton 1873:286.
26. Fierens 1872:128-30.
27. Montiton 1873:288.
28. Montiton 1873:292.
29. Montiton 1874:491.
30. Montiton 1874:366.
31. Janeau 1906; Bodin 1931:175; O'Reilly and Teissier 1962:228.
32. Pers. comm., 15 July 1972.
33. Gregory 1935:66, quoting a report from Stimson.
34. Shapiro 1940:411, 412; Mourant and others 1958:9, 10.
35. Wilkes 1845:I:318-25; Fierens 1872:132.
36. Fierens 1872:131-5. Montiton had called at Napuka briefly in 1869.
37. Gessler 1937:24, 312.
38. Gregory 1930:11, quoting a report by Shapiro.
39. Gessler 1937:313.
40. Gessler 1937:20, 24.
41. Gessler 1937:25, 26. See also p. 193.
42. Gessler 1935a:243.
43. Bellingshausen 1945:235-6; Fitz-Roy 1839:II:516; Mauruc 1848:81-2; [Lucett] 1851:I:256-7, II:216-17; Ward 1966-7: VI:255; Kroepelien 1939; Danielsson 1956:90-1; Terlyn 1900:191.
44. Martin 1888.
45. Bell 1883:745.
46. Danielsson 1956:105.
47. Gerbault 1933:124.
48. Danielsson 1952: pl. opp. p. 49.
49. Danielsson 1952:96.
50. Danielsson 1956:37, Danielsson 1952: 98-100.
51. Danielsson 1956:41. Stimson and Marshall 1964:147 give 'hiva' as a Fangatau word meaning 'faraway, remote, distant.' 'Nui' is a pan-Polynesian word meaning 'big,' 'large,' 'great,' etc.
52. Caillot 1914:7-21 records Hao traditions concerning the creation, the deluge and one similar to the Tower of Babel. On p. 22-5, he records similar traditions from Makemo Atoll. The traditions evidently impressed him as Biblical, for he stressed on p. 16n and 25n that both the Hao and Makemo people claimed that the traditions existed before the arrival of Europeans. Caillot 1932b:40, 52-3 notes other similarities between Tuamotuan beliefs and those of classical antiquity or the Bible.
53. Gregory 1930:12, quoting a report from Stimson.

CHAPTER 19: New Zealand: last loitering place of Hiro

1. Bagnall and Petersen 1948:99, 408-9; Crawfurd 1867; *JPS,* 1930, vol. 39, p. 198; Thompson 1871:40-2.
2. *Connoisseur* 1906, vol. 15, p. 187-8; pers. comm., R. K. Dell, director, National Museum, Wellington, 11 April 1969.
3. In Spain, the morion was originally worn by foot soldiers, including arquebusiers. It was later adopted by cavalrymen because of its lightness, and it was apparently then that elegantly decorated examples of this type of headgear were made.—*Enciclopedia* vol. 36, p. 1165-6. Most examples in present-day museums appear to date from the morion's age of elegance. But a German war hat, of morion form, in the Wallace Collection, London, has been dated to about 1515-20.—Laking 1910:16. Magellan (see chapter 2) carried fifty arquebuses in his four ships, plus 100 corselets with their shoulder plates and helmets—presumably morions. It may therefore be assumed that proportionate quantities were taken in Loaisa's fleet.
4. Beaglehole 1939:viii.
5. Buck 1952:36, 40, 51-2; Hale 1846:146; Stimson and Marshall 1964:485; Tregear [1891]:21.
6. Kelly 1949:1-42. On p. 22, in a reference to Hiro, Kelly said: 'Toi, according to Tainui genealogies, is shown as the son of Whiro-te-tupua, which is in agreement with other tribes, but for some strange and unaccountable reason the Tainui genealogies have transported Whiro, Toi, and about four generations of their descendants from their rightful position and placed them far back in the misty past . . . When questioned, the present Tainui authorities explain this inconsistency by saying that there were several Toi. Their claim, however, . . . is not supported by other evidence, and their belief is but an example of the inconsistencies met with in Maori genealogies of this period.'
7. Biggs 1966b:451-2; Buck 1952:51-2, 55-6 summarises the *Tainui* and *Arawa* traditions.
8. For summaries of the principal canoe traditions, see Buck 1952:39-41, 46-61; Biggs 1966b:451-3; Tregear [1891]:20-2. Buck 1952:41 states: 'The accounts con-

cerning individual canoes vary a great deal in details, and it is natural that the second-hand accounts which have been diffused to other tribes should differ.' Biggs 1966:451 mentions the emphasis that the *Tainui* and *Arawa* people place on their ancestral canoes, and says it is typical of discovery and origin traditions that they are confused and contradictory. In this respect, it is noteworthy that the first Europeans to record the Maori canoe traditions—Hamlin 1842; Wilkes 1845:II:399; Hale 1846:146—all mentioned the *Tainui* and *Arawa* canoes and only two others. Hamlin added the *Matatua* and *Kurahaupo* canoes; while Wilkes and Hale added *Horouta* and *Takitimu,* the first of which is sometimes said to be merely another name for the second. The spellings of canoe names in this book are those now usually accepted, regardless of the orthography of the various chroniclers. But it should be noted that Hale wrote both *Tahi-nui* and *Tainui,* the first of which recalls the *Hotu-tahi-nui* associated with Hiro in a legend recorded by Stimson—see footnote, p. 160.

9. Tregear [1891]:606-7; Kelly 1949:63-4; Fraser 1966:120.
10. A replica of a sixteenth century map of Spain and Portugal in the author's possession is decorated with drawings of 'Hispani' (Spaniards), 'Biscale' (Biscayans or Basques), 'Lusitani' (Portuguese), etc. These are Latin words which were apparently used poetically in former times. Modern dictionaries still record Hispania, Hispano, etc. as poetic words for Spain, Spaniard, etc.
11. Hale 1846:146-7. Hamlin 1842:264 stated: 'It is not at all known, nor are the natives of the present generation able to guess, the number of generations supposed to have passed since the arrival of [the four canoes, *Tainui, Arawa, Kurahaupo* and *Matatua*] in the land. It is, however, generally admitted that the arrival of these canoes is of a recent date compared to that of the Mani [Maui?] family.'
12. Dieffenbach 1843:II:45-6, 48, 364. See also Williams 1844:32, 54, 98.
13. Dieffenbach 1843:II:47-8.
14. Dieffenbach 1843:II:7-10.
15. Crozet 1783:138. Crozet (p. 52) was of the opinion that the Maoris were of three racial types, the biggest being 'yellowish-white.'
16. Wright 1950:201.
17. Wright 1950:222.
18. Polack 1838:I:360-1.
19. Scherzer 1861-3:III:109-10.
20. Best 1924a:7.
21. Best 1952:2-3.
22. Brown 1907:32.
23. Acheson 1930:vii.
24. Smith 1893:29.
25. Davis 1876:13-14.
26. Smith 1913:vii.
27. Smith 1913:xi; Best 1924b:88.
28. Smith 1913:vii; xi.
29. Smith 1913:xiii.
30. Best 1924b; Buck 1952:526; Binney 1967:127-8. Io is barely mentioned in the three-volume *New Zealand Encyclopedia,* McLintock 1966.
31. Buck 1952:438, 535-6.

CHAPTER 20: A new key to an old Easter Island mystery

1. For the pro-South America view, see, for example, Heyerdahl 1952:211-15 and Heyerdahl 1968:183-98. For views on vanished archipelagoes and continents, see, for example, Brown 1924; Brown 1927:I:261-307; Spence 1933; and the discussion in Metraux 1957: 29-32. And for the pro-Polynesian view, see, for example, Buck 1938:222-38; Golson 1965; Emory 1972.
2. Englert 1972:39, 43. See also Lanning 1970; Handy 1927:329.
3. Dening 1962:142, 144; *PIM,* Aug. 1970, p. 25.
4. NID 1943-5:I:65.
5. For a fuller account of the *Aguila* and *Jupiter* at Raivavae, see chapter 11.
6. Tregear [1891]:393-4.
7. Davies 1961:273.
8. Davies 1961:274.
9. Montgomery 1840:167.
10. McArthur 1967:303-6.
11. *PIM,* Nov. 1938, p. 4, Dec. 1940, p. 35; Marshall 1962:15-27.
12. Marshall 1962:32. For a photograph of Mt Hiro, see *PIM,* May 1967, p. 96.
13. Marshall 1962:155.
14. Marshall 1962:155.
15. Marshall 1962:126, 127, 229, 231 for photographs of 'Uncle Bert', the son-in-law of Toari'i, Hapai and Tauira'i respectively.
15. Stimson and Marshall 1964:23.
16. Barthel had not consulted Stimson's work when his principal published work —Barthel 1958—appeared. This work is in German. Barthel's chief findings to that time are summarised in Suggs 1960:186-8.
17. Barthel 1971:1178-9.
18. Barthel 1971:1175, 1177-8. The 'repeated and interlinking' references to Huahine and Raiatea are *rongo-rongo* signs for the double-canoe, breast ornaments, dance paddle, breadfruit tree, pandanus and kava.
19. Barthel 1971:1171-2, 1178.
20. Barthel 1971:1169, 1173.

21. For literature on the problem of dating Polynesian events by genealogical data, see chapter 14, note 82.
22. Englert 1972:87-8. Most of the *ariki* lists contain about 30 names; one contains 57.
23. Heyerdahl 1952:206, 208. Heyerdahl used the longest *ariki* list.
24. Barthel does not indicate how he arrived at his figure.
25. Englert 1972:88. Englert took fifteen years as the average duration of a reign.
26. For the various traditions about Hotu Matu'a, see Metraux 1940:56-68.
27. A hint on how a system of hieroglyphs can develop is contained in the journal of J. L. Young, a well-educated trader who travelled extensively in the Pacific from 1870 until his death in 1929. The journal is in the Mitchell Library, Sydney. Describing a visit to Uvea (Wallis) Island in 1875, Young said he had met an American there called Smith who had lived on the island for thirty years and was 'a very good specimen of the genus, beachcomber.' Smith had arrived at the island as third mate in a whaler, had traded for various ship-owners, and could only read a newspaper with difficulty. 'I was favoured,' Young wrote, 'with a sight of the book in which he keeps his accounts in a species of hieroglyphics and shorthand of his own invention . . . When he wished to place on record that he had sold 1 yard of duck, he put down—1—and after the figure he placed a rough drawing which he intended to represent a duck!!'—Langdon, 1969:83.
28. For an account of the scripts of the world, see Jensen 1970.
29. Dalrymple 1771:94. The veracity of Behrens' account has been called in question (see p. 78). But on the matters mentioned here, his descriptions closely correspond to those of other visitors.
30. Sharp 1970:97,101.
31. Corney 1908:96.
32. Corney 1908:127.
33. Corney 1908:121, 126. The first netmaker on Easter Island is said to have been Tuu-ko-ihu, a companion of Hotu Matu'a. The needles used on the island were of the open fork type. See Metraux 1940:183-4.
34. Corney 1908:49,104.
35. Emory 1972:64 has suggested that *rongo-rongo* was developed on Easter Island 'in emulation of the European example'—*after* the Spanish visit of 1770.
36. Beaglehole 1961:820.
37. Beaglehole 1961:341.
38. Beaglehole 1961:351.
39. La Perouse 1807:II:1-27.
40. Lisiansky 1814:58.
41. Kotzebue 1821:18.
42. Beechey 1831:I:51-2.
43. Sharp 1970:96-7; Beaglehole 1961:355; Forster 1778:236. Metraux 1957:228, for example, stated that *all* Easter Islanders had long ears in the eighteenth and nineteenth centuries.
44. Lisiansky 1814:59.
45. Beechey 1831:I:52.
46. Beechey 1831:I:53; Sharp 1970:97.
47. Englert 1972:88-9.
48. Cook seems to have been the first to notice that the ears of the statues were 'unconscionably long'—Beaglehole 1961: 358. Englert 1972:95 says tradition has it that the Long Ears introduced the idea of building the great stone altars.
49. Englert 1972:108.
50. Ayres 1971:504.
51. Buck 1938:234.
52. Englert 1972:94.
53. Brown 1927:I:304-6 seems to have been the first to comment on this.
54. Metraux 1940:56-65; Englert 1972:46-9, 64.
55. Metraux 1957:125.
56. Metraux 1940:69-74; Englert 1972: 130-5.
57. Smith 1961:391.
58. Englert 1972:134.
59. Sharp 1970:97-8; Beaglehole 1961:341, 344-5, 357; La Perouse 1807:II:21; Du Petit-Thouars 1840-5:II:225; Palmer 1870:177.
60. Metraux 1957:46-7; Pinart 1878a:238 gives the 1877 figure as 111 and this has been widely quoted. However, Pinart 1878b gives 110. This is also the figure given in a Pinart manuscript in the Bancroft Library, University of California at Berkeley, according to information given me by Mr Grant McCall, Department of Anthropology, Research School of Pacific Studies, The Australian National University, Canberra.
61. Information from Mr McCall.
62. Eyraud 1864:172, 190-1.
63. For accounts of attempts to decipher the tablets, see Metraux 1957:183-207; Heyerdahl and Ferdon 1965:345-85.
64. Englert 1972:77-8.
65. Metraux 1957:190-1.
66. Englert 1972:79.
67. Routledge 1919:222, 224, 241-4, 278-9.
68. Routledge 1919:221.
69. Information from Mr McCall (see note 60). See also Meier 1970:138-42.
70. A copy of the photograph, contained in an album presented to Bishop Jaussen of Tahiti, is now in the archives of the Sacred Heart Fathers, Rome. The photograph was published in Knox 1889, probably its first appearance in a book. A sketch based on it appeared in Thomson 1889:461. Kaituoe is there described as 'Kaitae, nearest descendant of the last king of Easter Island' and

is said to have been eighty years old. Numerous editorial or typographical errors are to be found in Thompson's work. The figure '80' is clearly such an error.

71. Brown 1927:II:191.
72. For a full report on the survey, see Dausset and Colombani 1973. A second volume will contain more comprehensive analyses of the data.
73. Terasaki 1973:1.
74. Thorsby and others 1973:29; Dausset and others 1973:100; Dausset and Colombani 1973, especially p. 714 where the W29 of the map = W19.1.
75. Thorsby and others 1973:288-9.
76. Dausset and others 1973:99. These authors describe the Basques as a non-Caucasian people. This, in a strict sense, is reasonable in that the origin of the Basques is shrouded in mystery, and so it cannot be said that they are of the same race as other European peoples whose origin has been traced to the Caucasus. However, as the Basques have white skins and other physical features common to most Europeans, they are usually grouped with the Caucasians and they have been looked on as Caucasians throughout this book.

CHAPTER 21: The legion of lost ships

1. Ten of the lost ships are mentioned specifically in the body of the chapter. The other two were the Dutch vessels *Santa Maria* and *Hoop* of the expedition originally commanded by Jacob Mahu. With a third ship, *Liefde,* they left Valparaiso for Japan on 27 November 1599. The *Santa Maria* deserted at an island 'inhabited by man-eaters' in 16 deg. N latitude. The *Hoop* became separated from the *Liefde* in 28 deg N. Neither was seen again.—Sluiter 1933: 89-90.
2. Navarrete V:476-86; Markham 1911: 111-32. See also chapter 2.
3. Alvarado 1866:119; Gschaedler 1954: 53-4; Sharp 1960:28. Several authors have puzzled over the oddity of Villalobos' reception at Fais and Ulithi without ever putting forward the explanation offered here. See, for example, Hezel and del Valle 1972:27n.
4. Lessa 1962:337-8; Lessa 1966:5, 9-10 and pl. opp. p.x. See also Lessa and Lay 1953.
5. Cantova 1728:198-9.
6. The apparent genetic and cultural impact of the Ulithi and Fais castaways are dealt with more fully in Langdon (in press).
7. Markham 1904:112-13; Sharp 1960:54; Kelly 1965:153, 399-409.
8. Brown 1927:I:94-5; Kramer 1932:21-8, 213, 273-5, pls 4b, 6a, 6b, 6c, 19b. See also Langdon (in press).
9. Markham 1904:37-44; Kelly 1965:118.
10. Allen and Green 1972; Green 1973.
11. Grimble 1928:4.
12. Markham 1904: 225, 228, 493-4. See also Kelly 1966:184, 275, 377-8; Markham 1904:360-1.
13. In 1801, Captain Roger Simpson of the brig *Nautilus,* discovered the remains of 'a very large lower mast, next the keel' which led him to think that a large Spanish ship had been wrecked at Taumako a long time previously, as the timber was greatly decayed. In 1971 Roger Green found a single piece of pottery and some old iron during a 'dig' at Kakua on Taumako.—*Naval Chronicle* 1806, pers. comm. from Green, 17 July 1974.
14. For accounts of the galleon trade, see Blair and Robertson 1903-9; Dahlgren 1916; Schurz 1939.
15. Blair and Robertson 1903-9:III:29, 31, 44, XII:50, 77, XXVII:192, XXXV:44, XLII:286, 290, XLVII:75.
16. Blair and Robertson 1903-9:III:279, 282, XXXIV, 296.
17. Dahlgren 1916:44, 47, 98-9, 111; Blair and Robertson 1903-9:IV:91, 109; VII: 66; XV:54; XXVII:187; XLII:309; XLIV:142.
18. Beaglehole 1967:263-87.
19. Beaglehole 1967:473-542.
20. King 1785:137-8.
21. Beaglehole 1967:1151.
22. Beaglehole 1967:475n.
23. Beaglehole 1967:285-6.
24. Milet-Mureau 1807:I:121; II:41n-42n.
25. Townsend n.d.:17.
26. Ellis 1831:IV:392-3, 439-40.
27. Ellis 1831:IV:403-4, 437-8, 439.
28. Ellis 1831:IV:438.
29. Ellis 1831:IV:439.
30. Ellis 1831:IV:23, 438-9.
31. Kotzebue 1830:II:166-8.
32. Fornander 1969:II:106-7, quoting from a story by Malo published in *Moolelo Hawaii,* Lahaina, 1838.
33. Jarves 1843:88.
34. Alexander 1891:99.
35. Dahlgren 1916:213.
36. Stokes 1931; Stokes 1932; Stokes 1939.
37. Dahlgren 1916:141, 212.
38. Dahlgren 1916:143, 212.
39. Dahlgren 1916:213.
40. Stokes 1932:597; Stokes 1939:47; Dahlgren 1916:146-7.
41. Stokes 1931:12.
42. Stokes 1931:13.
43. Stokes 1939:92.
44. Judd 1967:30.
45. Beaglehole 1967:cxvi.
46. Dahlgren 1916:139.

47. Stokes 1931:9.
48. Summaries of reports and correspondence on the casket and its contents are filed in the Bishop Museum library under the heading 'Spanish problem.' The casket in which the cloth and iron were found was one of two which were opened at the time. The burial remains are reputed to be those of chiefs called Liloa and Lono-i-ka-makahiki. The remains were examined in 1958 by Charles E. Snow, who concluded that Liloa was a tall man of about 24 and of weak musculature; 'Lono' was a larger and much more powerful man of 40 to 45, possibly older. The cloth and iron came from the Liloa casket. However, tradition says that Liloa was a strong man who had a long reign, and Dr Emory told me verbally in July 1969 that the two caskets had apparently become mixed up during their various moves and that it was really in the 'Lono' casket that the cloth and iron were found. Stokes 1930b:63-73 gives an outline of the history of the caskets. He states that Liloa was estimated to have died in 1575 and that Lono-i-ka-makahiki was his great-grandson. The Liloa and 'Lono' caskets were probably in the Hale o Liloa, an ancient Hawaiian mausoleum at Waipio, Hawaii, when Ellis visited it in 1823. In 1830, the caskets were transferred to a cave in a cliff at Kaawaloa in Kealakekua Bay. In 1858, they were taken to Honolulu in a British warship and placed in the Royal tomb; and in 1865, they were put in coffins and moved to the Royal mausoleum. Since then they have been moved to the Bishop Museum where they now are.
49. With a letter dated 11 February 1972, Lothrop sent me copies of all his correspondence on the Hawaiian cloth—nineteen letters written between 15 May 1965 and 3 March 1966.
50. See note 48.
51. See note 48.
52. Fornander 1969:I:192 and II:64.
53. Malo 1951:144-5.
54. As preceding.
55. Stokes' date for the death of Liloa (see note 48).
56. Pers. comm. from Lothrop, 14 July 1972.

APPENDIX D: The peoples and culture of Tonga and Samoa

1. Sullivan 1921:3; 1922:28-9.
2. Villiers 1906:198; Dalrymple 1771:16, 18.
3. Sharp 1968:153.
4. Carrington 1948:251.
5. G. Forster 1777:I:423-4, 432-3.
6. Beaglehole 1961:267, 271.
7. Beaglehole 1967:I:166-7.
8. Beaglehole 1967:II:925-6.
9. Beaglehole 1967:II:1365.
10. Labillardiere 1800:II:98-9.
11. Sharp 1970:151; Mulert 1911:203.
12. Martin-Allanic 1964:699.
13. Milet-Mureau 1807:III:58, 106-7.
14. Stair 1897:58, 63.
15. Turner 1884:3.
16. Sullivan 1922:27.
17. Gill [1876]:22; Dening 1962:141; *PIM,* Aug. 1964, p. 7.
18 Davidson 1970:267; Davidson and Scarr 1970: pl. 10,
19. Turner 1884:168.
20. Beaglehole 1961:263.
21. Beaglehole 1967:957-8.
22. Buck 1930:470. Illustrations of three netting needles from the Society Islands in W. C. Handy 1927:110 all differ from the open-fork type illustrated in Buck 1930. See also Buck 1944:223.
23. A perusal of Hornell 1936 establishes this.
24. Lewis 1972:77 says 'unfortunately the Tongans have lost their names for the stars [to a very great extent].' But such evidence as there is on this subject suggests they did not have many names to forget. On the other hand, Lewis 1972:73 cites a Society Islands chant, recorded by J. M. Orsmond in 1818, which refers to the Pole Star (*Ana-ni'a*) as one of the 'Pillars of the Sky'. Lewis points out that Tahiti is too far south by 1,000 miles for the Pole Star to be seen, and concludes that the islanders' knowledge of it 'suggests that the range of Tahitian voyaging was once very wide.'
25. Turner 1884:166.
26. Hornell 1936:261-2, 265-73, 334.
27. For an account by the surgeon Anderson of the musical instruments of Tonga in 1777, see Beaglehole 1967:940-1. Anderson was not impressed by the Tongans' musical ability.
28. Burrows 1938:67-8.
29. Burrows 1938:88-90.

APPENDIX F: Evidence for a non-Polynesian language in Eastern Polynesia

1. Forster 1778:277, 280, 283.
2. Sullivan 1921, 1922, 1923.
3. As pointed out in Appendix D, note 29, Burrows 1938 demonstrated that there were significant cultural differences between Western and Eastern Polynesia and tried to explain these in terms of differential diffusion from Melanesia and Micronesia, and local development and cultural loss within Polynesia itself.

4. Maude 1971:4.
5. Golson 1972:20.
6. Biggs 1971:466, 498.
7. [Greatheed] 1799:xliii. For evidence of Greatheed's authorship, see, for example, Wilson 1799:273 and Greatheed's letter to Haweis of 7 Feb. 1797 in Haweis 1764-1820. For a note on Morrison's journal, see chapter 13, note 12. On the last page of the original journal, which has been cut, it is stated that a Tahitian vocabulary follows.
8. Davies 1961:270n.
9. Hale 1846:143-6; 289; Tregear [1891]: xxii.
10. Stimson's only comment was that Anaan resembled the dialects of both Tahiti and Fangatau—Stimson and Marshall 1964:23.
11. Emory 1947a:276 said: 'Anaa exhibits the greatest tendency to coin its own names, and Napuka and Reao come next.'
12. Corney 1908:109-10.
13. Englert 1972:94.
14. Beaglehole 1961:339n.
15. Beaglehole 1961:828.
16. Beaglehole 1961:360; Forster 1778: Appendix opp. 284.
17. Cuming 1827-8: entry for 15 Nov. 1827.
18. Emory 1972:61-2; Metraux 1936:190-1.
19. Englert 1972:94.
20. For details of this period of Easter Island history, see Metraux 1957:46-56.
21. Palmer 1870:109.
22. Brown 1924:283.
23. Dalrymple 1771:94.
24. Routledge 1919:221.
25. Seurat 1905:306; Jacquier 1948; Laguesse 1954.
26. The discoverer—not recognised as such in most reference books—was John Bell of the British merchant ship *Minerva*—*Asiatic Journal,* 1823, vol. 16, p. 130.
27. Laval 1968:350, 401-2, 473; Fierens 1874:385.
28. Seurat 1905:297.
29. Audran 1919b:36.
30. Gregory 1931:11, quoting a report from Stimson.
31. Stimson and Marshall 1964:23.
32. Beechey 1831:I:199.
33. Belcher 1825-7: entry for 19 Jan. 1826.
34. Wilkes 1845:I:314. Wilkes added that the Reao people 'spoke and understood the Tahitian dialect.'
35. Hudson 1838-40:242.
36. Emory 1932:49.
37. Rowland 1943.
38. Rowland 1947.
39. Emory 1934:21, 23.
40. Audran 1919a:35.
41. Audran 1918; 1919a; 1919b. See also Audran 1920; 1930.
42. Audran 1918:134.
43. Audran 1919b: 38-41.
44. Emory 1932:46.
45. Gregory 1930:12, quoting a report from Stimson.
46. Emory 1932:46.
47. Stimson and Marshall 1964:23.
48. Gessler 1937:314-16.
49. Gessler 1937:339.
50. Wilkes 1845:I:319, 321, 344.
51. Hudson 1838-40:256.
52. Douglas and Johnson 1926:165-6.
53. For Rapa, see Stokes 1955; for Raivavae and Fangatau, see Stimson and Marshall 1964:23, Audran 1919b:36, and the comments on the Fangatauan dialect in chapter 16; and for Hao, see [Lucett] 1851:I:329, Jones 1894; Audran 1920:43.
54. For information on the stone structures of Rapa and Raivavae, see Heyerdahl and Ferdon 1965:69-116; and for those of Fangatau and Hao, see Emory 1934: 39-49, 52-4. For accounts of swarthy inhabitants of all these islands, see the relevant chapters in this book.
55. Gessler 1937:337.
56. Huguenin 1902:35, 36, 65.
57. Davies 1851 draws attention to these synonyms in the body of his dictionary.
58. Of the synonyms given, the following (with the Tuamotuan versions in brackets) appear to have no congeners in the Western Polynesian dialects: *'aito* (*kaito*), *ru'i* (*ruki*), *tua* (*tua*), *rua* (*rua*), *mo'a* (*moa*), *'ava'e* (*kavake*), *ata* (*ata*), *pape* (*apape, papape*).
59. For a summary of areal linguistics, see Bonfanti 1968.
60. See, for example, Hale 1846:11; Caillot 1909:8.
61. The words are from Stimson and Marshall 1964.
62. For references, see chapter 15, note 45.
63. Dixon 1932:48.
64. Verbal communication from the Hon. Ve'ehala, Canberra, August 1974.
65. Newell 1911:70 states that *'umara* is an introduced word in Samoan, and Turner 1861:49 says the vegetable was introduced by Europeans and was an unimportant food. See also Dixon 1932: 49.
66. O'Reilly 1963:74-8; Barrau 1963:166.
67. Tregear and Smith 1907. McEwen 1970 gives *timala*, obviously a new word.
68. Brand 1971:359-63, 365.
69. Yen 1971b:337-8; Green 1973a:111.
70. See Steward 1963.
71. For information on the disappearance of languages in Ecuador, for example, see Murra 1963:792, 795, 797, 799, 801, 802, 803. Similar information for Colombia, Peru, Bolivia and Chile appears in the same volume, Steward 1963, which also reveals that existing Indian languages have not been deeply studied.
72. Stimson and Marshall 1964:22.

APPENDIX G: Light features among non-Europeans

1. For information on the Greeks in India, see Woodcock 1966.
2. Keane 1906:166-8; Omoto 1971-2.
3. Scheinfeld 1950:73; Hooton 1947:474. There are numerous field references on this.
4. See the statements by Bouman and Bougainville in Appendix D. It is possible, however, that the red colour in some cases was caused through the use of lime to destroy lice.—Wilkes 1845:II: 126.
5. Gates 1952:92.
6. Bennett 1840:I:158.
7. Dunn and Dobzhansky 1952:123-4.
8. Meilink-Roelofsz 1962:14.

Literature cited

This list includes all published and unpublished items cited in the notes, appendices and page footnotes. Unpublished items are preceded by an asterisk (*). Other abbreviations used, besides those in common use, are:

AAnth	*American Anthropologist,* Washington.
AHyd	*Annales Hydrographiques,* Paris,
AJCP mfm	Australian Joint Copying Project microfilm.
AJPH	*American Journal of Physical Anthropology,* Philadelphia.
APF	*Annales de la Propagation de la Foi,* Lyons.
ASC	*Annales des Sacrés-Coeurs,* Braine-le-Comte, Belgium.
BPBMB	Bernice Pauahi Bishop Museum Bulletin.
BPBMSP	Bernice Pauahi Bishop Museum special publication.
BSEO	*Bulletin de la Société des Etudes Océaniennes,* Papeete.
EL	Everyman's Library.
GHS	Geographical Handbook Series.
HRA	*Historical Records of Australia.*
HRNZ	*Historical Records of New Zealand.*
HS:I	Hakluyt Society, Series 1.
HS:II	Hakluyt Society, Series 2.
HSES	Hakluyt Society extra series.
JOEFO	*Journal Officiel des Etablissements Français de l'Océanie,* Papeete.
JPH	*Journal of Pacific History,* Canberra.
JPS	*Journal of the Polynesian Society,* New Plymouth, later Wellington.
JSO	*Journal de la Société des Océanistes,* Paris.
LMS	London Missionary Society.
MBPBM	Memoir of the Bernice Pauahi Bishop Museum.
MCath	*Missions Catholiques,* Lyons.
mfm PMB	Microfilm, Pacific Manuscripts Bureau, Canberra.
MPS	Memoir of the Polynesian Society.
NID	Naval Intelligence Division.
PAR, DABPBM	Pacific Anthropological Records, Department of Anthropology, Bernice Pauahi Bishop Museum.
PHHS	Papers of the Hawaiian Historical Society, Honolulu.
PIM	*Pacific Islands Monthly,* Sydney.
PRO Adm	Public Record Office, London, Admiralty Series.
RNAE	Reports of the Norwegian Archaeological Expedition to Easter Island and the East Pacific.
SDO	Société des Océanistes, Paris, publication.
SG	*Sydney Gazette.*
SSJ, LMS	South Sea Journals, London Missionary Society.
SSL, LMS	South Sea Letters, London Missionary Society.

Acheson, Frank O. V., 1930. *Plume of the Arawas,* Dunedin.

Agassiz, Alexander, 1903. *The Coral Reefs of the Tropical Pacific,* Cambridge, USA (Memoirs of the Museum of Comparative Zoology at Harvard College, vol. 28).

Alexander, A. B., 1902. 'Notes on the boats, apparatus, and fishing methods employed by the natives of the South Sea Islands . . .', *Report of the Commissioner for the year ending June 30, 1901,* US Commission of Fish and Fisheries, part 27, p. 743-829, Washington.

Alexander, W. D., 1891. *A Brief History of the Hawaiian People,* New York.

Allen, Jim, and Roger C. Green, 1972. 'Mendaña 1595 and the fate of the lost *almiranta*: an archaeological investigation', *JPH*, vol. 7, p. 73-91.

Alvarado, Garcia Descalante, 1866. 'Relación del viaje que hizo desde la Nueva-España á las islas del Poniente Ruy Lopez de Villalobos . . .', *Colección de documentos inéditos, relativos al descubrimiento, conquista y organización de las antiguas posesiones españolas en América y Oceania . . .*, Joaquin F. Pacheco and others, eds, ser. 1, vol. 5, Madrid.

Amherst of Hackney, Lord, and Basil Thomson, eds, 1901. *The Discovery of the Solomon Islands by Alvaro de Mendaña in 1568,* 2 vols, London (HS:II:7-8).

Andrews, Edmund, and Irene D. Andrews, 1944. *A Comparative Dictionary of the Tahitian Language,* Chicago.

Annales Hydrographiques, 1848-1968 (ser. 1, nos 1-41, 1848-1878; ser. 2, 1-36 1879-1916; ser. 3, nos 1-21, 1917-1949; ser. 4, 1950-1968), Paris.

Annuaire des Etablissements français de l'Océanie et du Protectorat des îles de la Société et dépendances pour l'année commune 1863, 1863, Papeete.

Anonymous, 1934. 'Arrestation des sauvages de Fakahina', *BSEO,* no. 52, p. 409-15.

Arbousset, Thomas, 1867. *Tahiti et les Iles Adjacentes . . .*, Paris.

* Archivo General de Indias, Seville. Documents relating to the expedition to the Moluccas of Garcia Jofre de Loaisa, 1525-38: Patronato 37, documents 11-38; patronato 38, documents 1-18, patronato 39, documents 1-14; patronato 40, documents 1-6.

Asiatic Journal, 1823. 'Extract from the ship "Minerva's" journal', vol. 16, p. 128-30.

Audran, Hervé, 1917. 'La mission des Tuamotu' *MCath.,* vol. 49, p. 53.

———, 1918. 'Napuka et ses habitants', *BSEO,* no. 3, p. 126-36.

———, 1919a. 'Notes sur le dialecte paumotu', *BSEO,* no. 5, p. 30-6.

———, 1919b. 'Etude linguistique du dialecte particular de Napuka', *BSEO,* no. 5, p. 36-41.

———, 1920. 'Traditions of and notes on the Paumotu (or Tuamotu) Islands' — part 6, *JPS,* vol. 29, p. 42-3.

———, 1926. 'Mapu Nui ou Mapu Teretere de Takume', *BSEO,* no. 14, p. 86-9.

———, 1927. 'Les Hiva', *BSEO,* no. 22, p. 317-18.

———, 1930. 'Linguistique comparative', *BSEO,* no. 35, p. 25.

Ayres, William S., 1971. 'Radiocarbon dates from Easter Island,' *JPS,* vol. 80, p. 497-504.

Bagnall, A. G. and G. C. Petersen, 1948. *William Colenso,* Wellington.

Baker, J. N. L., 1938. *Medieval Trade Routes,* London (Historical Association Pamphlet 111).

Ball, Stanley C., 1933. *Jungle Fowls from Pacific Islands,* Honolulu (BPBMB 108).

Banks, Joseph, 1963. *The 'Endeavour' Journal of Joseph Banks, 1768-1771,* J. C. Beaglehole, ed., 2nd edn, 2 vols, Sydney.

Barrau, Jacques, 1963. 'L'agriculture des Iles Wallis et Futuna', *JSO,* vol. 19, p. 157-71.

Barrow, T., 1967. *The Women of Polynesia,* Wellington.

Barthel, Thomas, 1958. *Grundelagen zur Entzifferung der Osterinselschrift,* Hamburg.

———, 1971. 'Pre-contact writing in Oceania', in Sebeok 1971:1165-86.

Bathurst, Charles, [1837]. *Notes on Nets; or the Quincunx Practically Considered,* London.

*Bayley, George, 1824-42. 'Journal of voyages to various parts of the world . . .', 2 vols. Ms. in Hocken Library, Dunedin.

Beaglehole, J. C., 1939. *The Discovery of New Zealand,* Wellington.

———, ed., 1955. *The Journals of Captain James Cook on his Voyages of Discovery: The Voyage of the 'Endeavour', 1768-1771,* Cambridge (HSES 34).

———, ed., 1961. *The Journals of Captain Cook on his Voyages of Discovery: The Voyage of the 'Resolution' and 'Adventure', 1772-1775,* Cambridge (HSES 35).

———, 1966. *The Exploration of the Pacific,* 3rd edn, London.

———, ed., 1967. *The Journals of Captain James Cook on his Voyages of Discovery: The Voyage of the 'Resolution' and 'Discovery', 1776-1780,* 2 vols, Cambridge (HSES 36).

Beechey, Frederick William, 1831. *Narrative of a Voyage to the Pacific and Beering's Strait . . .*, 2 vols, London.

*Belcher, Edward, 1825-7. 'Private journal, remarks, etc. [of a voyage in] HM ship *Blossom* on discovery during the years 1825, 6, 7, Captn F. W. Beechey, comr'. Ms. 129, Alexander Turnbull Library, Wellington.

Bell, J. C., 1883. 'Amongst the Pacific Islands', *Victorian Review,* vol. 8, p. 741-54, Melbourne.

Bellingshausen, Thaddeus von, 1945. *The Voyage of Captain Bellingshausen to the Antarctic Seas, 1819-1821,* Frank Debenham, ed., 2 vols, London (HS:II:91-2).

Bennett, Frederick Debell, 1840. *Narrative of a Whaling Voyage . . .*, 2 vols, London.

Best, Elsdon, 1922. 'The legend of Whiro', *JPS,* vol. 31, p. 111-21.

———, 1924a. *The Maori,* Wellington (MPS 5).

———, 1924b. *Maori Religion and Mythology,* Wellington (Dominion Museum Bulletin 10).

———, 1952. *The Maori as he was,* 3rd imp., Wellington (1st publ., 1924).

*Bicknell, Henry, 1816. Letter to directors, 13 Aug. 1816, SSL 2, LMS Archives (AJCP mfm M19).

Biggs, Bruce, 1965. Review of Stimson and Marshall 1964, in *JPS,* vol. 74, p. 377-8.

———, 1966a. Note re Dyen 1966, *JPS,* vol. 75, p. 4.

Biggs, Bruce, 1966b. 'Maori myths and traditions', in McLintock 1966:II:447-54.

———, 1969. *The Genealogical Records of the New Zealand Maori* (paper presented at World Conference on Records and Genealogical Seminar, Salt Lake City, 5-8 Aug., 1969).

———, 1971. 'The languages of Polynesia', in Sebeok 1971:466-505

Binney, Judith, 1967. 'The heritage of Isaiah: Thomas Kendall and Maori religion', *New Zealand Journal of History,* vol. 1, p. 124-47.

Blair, Emma H., and James A. Robertson, eds, 1903-9. *The Philippine Islands, 1493-1898,* 55 vols, Cleveland.

Blandford, P. W., 1961. *Netmaking,* 3rd edn, Glasgow.

Bligh, William, 1792. *A Voyage to the South Sea . . .,* London.

———, 1937. *The Log of the 'Bounty' . . .,* Owen Rutter, ed., 2 vols, London.

Bliss, Theodora Crosby, 1906, *Micronesia: Fifty Years in the Island World,* Boston.

Bodin, Henri, 1931. 'Quelques souvenirs des Tuamotu', *BSEO,* no. 40, p. 170-80.

Bodmer, Frederick, 1945. *The Loom of Language,* 3rd imp., London.

Bonfanti, Giuliano, 1968. 'Areal linguistics', *Collier's Encyclopedia,* vol. 2, p. 560-1.

Bougainville, Louis Antoine de, 1771. *Voyage autour du Monde . . .,* Paris.

———, 1772. *A Voyage Round the World . . .,* transl. from French by Johann Reinhold Forster, London.

Boulnois, L., 1966. *The Silk Road,* London.

Bovis, Edmond de, 1892. 'Etat de la société Tahitienne à la arrivée des Européens, *Annuaire de Tahiti pour 1892,* p. 41-96, Papeete (1st publ. in *Revue Coloniale,* Paris, 1855).

Brand, Donald D., 1967. 'Geographical exploration by the Spaniards', in Friis 1967:109-44.

———, 1971. 'The sweet potato: an exercise in methodology', in Riley and others 1971:343-65.

Brisson, Victor, 1929. 'Noms anciens de certaines îles [Tuamotu]', *BSEO,* no. 30, p. 258-9.

Broek, Jan O. M., 1967. 'Geographical exploration by the Dutch', in Friis 1967:151-69.

Brossard, Maurice de, 1964. *Rendez-vous avec Lapérouse à Vanikoro,* Paris.

Broughton, William Robert, 1804. *A Voyage of Discovery to the North Pacific Ocean . . .,* London.

Brown, J. Macmillan, 1907. *Maori and Polynesian,* London.

———, 1924. *The Riddle of the Pacific,* London.

———, 1927. *Peoples and Problems of the Pacific,* 2 vols, London.

Brown, James S., 1960. *Giant of the Lord,* Salt Lake City (1st publ. as *The Life of a Pioneer,* 1902).

Browne, J. Ross, 1846. *Etchings of a Whaling Cruise,* New York.

Buck, Peter H., 1930. *Samoan Material Culture* (BPBMB 75).

———, 1938. *Vikings of the Sunrise,* New York.

———, 1944. *Arts and Crafts of the Cook Islands,* Honolulu (BPBMB 179).

———, 1952. *The Coming of the Maori,* 2nd edn., reprint, Wellington.

———, 1953, *Explorers of the Pacific,* Honolulu (BPBMSP 43).

Bulletin de la Société des Etudes Océaniennes, 1917-to date, Papeete.

Burrows, Edwin G., 1933. *Native Music of the Tuamotus,* Honolulu (BPBMB 109).

———, 1938. *Western Polynesia: A Study in Cultural Differentiation,* Goteborg (Etnologiska Studier).

Caillet, Xavier, 1862. 'Iles Tuamotu', *AHyd.,* ser. 1, vol. 21, p. 176-99.

———, 1884. 'Iles découvertes par Pedro Fernández de Quiros', *JOEFO,* 29 May 1884, p. 135-8.

Caillot, A. C. Eugène, 1909. *Les Polynésiens Orientaux au Contact de la Civilisation,* Paris.

———, 1910. *Histoire de la Polynésie Orientale,* Paris.

———, 1914. *Mythes, Legends et Traditions des Polynésiens,* Paris.

———, 1932a. *Histoire de l'île Oparo ou Rapa,* Paris.

———, 1932b. *Histoire des Religions de l'Archipel Paumotu,* Paris.

Canberra Times, 1970. Canberra.

Cantova, Juan Antonio, 1728. Letter from Guam dated 20 Mar. 1722 in *Lettres Edifiantes et Curieuses,* collection 18, Paris.

Capell, A., 1965-6. Review of Stimson and Marshall 1964, in *Oceania,* vol. 36, p. 247-9.

Carrington, Hugh, ed., 1948. *The Discovery of Tahiti,* London (HS:II:98).

Carter, C. O., 1970. *Human Heredity,* Harmondsworth, England (Pelican Books).

Carter, George F., 1971. 'Pre-Columbian chickens in America' in Riley and others 1971:178-218.

Chesneau, Joseph, 1928. 'Histoire de Huahine et autres Iles Sous-le-Vent', *BSEO,* no. 26, p. 81-98.

Chiao-Min Hsieh, 1967. 'Geographical exploration by the Chinese', in Friis 1967:87-95.

Christian, Frederick William, 1910. *Eastern Pacific Lands,* London.

Clark, Thomas Blake, 1940. *Omai, First Polynesian Ambassador to England,* San Francisco.

Clissold, Peter, 1971. 'Galley beaks', *Mariner's Mirror,* vol. 57, p. 453.

Cloué, *Rear-admiral,* 1870. Information on Tuamotus obtained by Captain Marcq Saint-Hilaire, *AHyd.,* ser. 1, vol. 33, p. 74-85.

Collier's Encyclopedia, 1961. 20 vols, New York.

Collier's Encyclopedia, 1968. 24 vols, New York.

Collignon, R., 1894. 'Les Basques', *Memoires de la Société d'Anthropologie de Paris,* ser. 1, vol. 1, fascicule 4, Paris.

Connoisseur, 1906, vol. 15, p. 187-8, London.

Coon, Carleton Stevens, 1948. *The Races of Europe,* New York.

Cooper, Gordon, 1957. *Your Holiday in Spain and Portugal,* 3rd edn, London.

Corney, Bolton Glanvill, ed., 1908. *The voyage of captain Don Felipe Gonzalez . . . to Easter Island in 1770-1,* Cambridge (HS:II:13).

———, ed., 1913-19. *The Quest and Occupation of Tahiti by Emissaries of Spain during the Years 1772-1776,* 3 vols, London (HS:II:32, 36, 43). Cited as Corney I, II, III.

Cox, Major Harding, 1965. *Dogs of Today,* 4th edn rev. by Stanley Dangerfield, London.

Crawfurd, John, 1867. 'On an ancient Hindu sacrificial bell found in the northern island of the New Zealand group', *Transactions of the Ethnological Society,* vol. 5, p. 150-4, London.

Crow, John A., 1948. *The Epic of Latin America,* New York.

Crozet, Julien, 1783. *Nouveau Voyage à la Mer du Sud, commencé sous les ordres de M. Marion . . .,* Paris.

*Cuming, Hugh, 1827-8. 'Journal of a voyage from Valparaiso to the Society and the adjacent islands performed in the schooner *Discoverer,* Samuel Grimwood, master, in the years 1827 and 1828'. Ms. A1336, Mitchell Library, Sydney.

Cummins, J. S., ed., 1971. *Sucesos de las Islas Filipinas,* Cambridge (HS:II:140).

Cumpston, J. S., 1963. *Shipping Arrivals and Departures, Sydney, 1788-1825,* Canberra.

Cunningham, William, 1559. *The Cosmographical Glasse,* London (Reprint, Da Capo Press, Amsterdam, 1968).

Dahlgren, E. W., 1907. *Voyages Français à destination de la Mer du Sud avant Bougainville, 1695-1749,* Paris.

———, 1916. *Were the Hawaiian Islands Visited by the Spaniards before their Discovery by Captain Cook in 1778?* Stockholm.

Dalrymple, Alexander, 1771. *An Historical Collection of the Several Voyages and Discoveries in the South Pacific Ocean,* vol. 2, London.

d'Anglejean-Chatillon, Pierre, 1963-4. 'Rapport de la mission hydrographique en Polynésie française (1956-60)', *AHyd.,* ser. 4, vol. 12, p. 15-103.

Danielsson, Bengt, 1952. *The Happy Island,* London.

———, 1956. *Work and Life on Raroia,* London.

———, 1967. 'Ia Ora Keneti', in Highland and others 1967:1-36.

Dausset, Jean and Jacques Colombani, eds, 1973. *Histocompatibility Testing 1972,* Munksgaard, Copenhagen.

Dausset, Jean and others, 1973. 'Genetic structure and distribution of HL-A antigens in a Basque village', in Dausset and Colombani 1973:99-106.

Davidson, J. W., 1970. 'Lauaki Namulau'ulu Mamoe: a traditionalist in Samoan politics', in Davidson and Scarr 1970:267-99.

———, and Deryck Scarr, eds, 1970. *Pacific Islands Portraits,* Canberra.

*Davies, John, 1807-8. Public journal, 21 Aug. 1807-22 Nov. 1808, SSJ 31, LMS Archives (AJCP mfm M2).

*———, 1813-14. Journal, 25 Jan. 1813-20 Apr. 1814, SSJ 35, LMS Archives (AJCP mfm M3).

———, 1851. *A Tahitian and English Dictionary . . . and a Short Grammar of the Tahitian Dialect,* Papeete.

———, 1925. 'Journal of the missionaries put ashore from the *Hibernia* on an islet in the Fiji group in 1809', in Im Thurn and Wharton 1925:117-60.

———, 1961. *The History of the Tahitian Mission,* C. W. Newbury, ed., Cambridge (HS:II:116).

Davis, C. O., 1876. *The Life and Times of Patuone, the Celebrated Ngapuhi Chief,* Auckland.

Dening, G. M., 1962. 'The geographical knowledge of the Polynesians and the nature of inter-island contact', *JPS,* vol. 71, p. 102-53 and map.

Diamond, S., ed., 1960. *Culture in History,* Columbia University Press.

Dieffenbach, Ernest, 1843. *Travels in New Zealand,* 2 vols, London.

Dillon, Peter, 1829. *Narrative . . . of a Voyage in the South Seas,* 2 vols, London.

Dixon, Roland B., 1932. 'The problem of the sweet potato in Polynesia', *AAnth.,* vol. 34, p. 40-66.

Douglas, A. J. A., and P. H. Johnson, 1926. *The South Seas of To-day,* London.

* *Dragon* logbook, 1821-3, 'Logbook of the brig *Dragon,* 4 Oct. 1821-21 June 1823 of voyages from Sydney to Society Islands and Manila and back to the Derwent'. Ms. A2045, Mitchell Library, Sydney.

Dumont d'Urville, J. S. C., 1830. *Voyage de la Corvette 'l'Astrolabe',* 5 vols, Paris.

Dunn, L. C., and Theodosius Dobzhansky, 1952. *Heredity, Race and Society,* New York (New American Library).

Duperrey, Louis Isidore, n.d. *Mémoire sur les opérations géographiques faites dans . . . la 'Coquille' . . .,* Paris (reprinted from *Annales maritimes et coloniales,* 1828, part 2, vol. 1, p. 569-673).

———, 1827. *Voyage autour du Monde . . ., Atlas,* Paris.

Duperrey, Louis Isidore, 1829. *Voyage autour du Monde . . ., Hydrographie* [*et Physique*], Paris.

Du Petit-Thouars, Abel Aubert, 1840-5. *Voyage autour du Monde sur la frégate 'La Venus' (1836-39),* 4 vols, Paris.

Du Rietz, Rolf, 1962. 'Three letters from James Burney to Sir Joseph Banks', *Ethnos,* vol. 27, p. 115-25, Stockholm.

Dyen, Isidore, 1965. 'A lexicostatistical classification of the Austronesian languages'. *International Journal of American Linguistics,* Memoir 19, vol. 31.

———, 1966. Letter re Biggs 1965, in *JPS,* vol. 75, p. 4.

Edwards, Edward, and George Hamilton, 1915. *Voyage of H.M.S. 'Pandora' . . .,* Basil Thomson, ed., London.

Ellis, John Eimeo, 1873. *Life of William Ellis,* London.

Ellis, William, 1831. *Polynesian Researches,* 2nd edn, 4 vols, London.

———, 1844. *The History of the London Missionary Society,* London.

———, 1972. *A la Recherche de la Polynésie d'Autrefois,* transl. from English, with a preface by Colin W. Newbury, 2 vols, Paris (SDO 25).

Ellsworth, S. George, 1959. *Zion in Paradise: Early Mormons in the South Seas,* Logan, Utah.

Emory, Kenneth P., 1932. 'The Tuamotuan survey', in Gregory 1932:40-50.

———, 1933. *Stone Remains in the Society Islands,* Honolulu (BPBMB 116).

———, 1934 *Tuamotuan Stone Structures,* Honolulu (BPBMB 118).

———, 1939. 'The Tuamotuan creation charts by Paiore', *JPS,* vol. 48, p. 1-29.

———, 1940a. 'Tuamotuan concepts of creation', *JPS,* vol. 49, p. 69-136.

———, 1940b. 'A newly discovered illustration of Tuamotuan creation', *JPS,* vol. 49, p. 569-78.

———, 1942. 'Oceanian influence on American Indian culture: Nordenskiöld's view', *JPS,* vol. 51, p. 126-35.

———, 1943. 'Additional illustrations of Tuamotuan creation', *JPS,* vol. 52, p. 19-21.

———, 1947a. 'Tuamotuan plant names', *JPS,* vol. 56, p. 266-77.

———, 1947b. *Tuamotuan Religious Structures and Ceremonies,* Honolulu (BPBMB 191).

———, 1959. 'Origin of the Hawaiians', *JPS,* vol. 63, p. 29-35.

———, 1963. 'East Polynesian relationships: settlement patterns and time involved as indicated by vocabulary agreements' *JPS,* vol. 72, p. 78-100.

———, 1972. 'Easter Island's position in the prehistory of Polynesia', *JPS,* vol. 81, p. 57-69.

———, and Paul Ottino, 1967. 'Histoire ancienne de 'Ana'a, atoll des Tuamotu' *JSO,* vol. 23, p. 29-57.

Enciclopedia Universal Ilustrada, 1958. 70 vols, Madrid (with 10 vols of appendices and 15 supplementary vols, 1934-66). Cited as *Enciclopedia.*

Encyclopedia Britannica, 1963. 20 vols, Chicago.

Encyclopedia Britannica 1969. 24 vols, Chicago.

Engelbrecht, W. A., and P. J. van Herwerden, 1945. *De Ontdekkingreis van Jacob Le Maire en Willem Cornelisz Schouten in de jaaren 1615-1617 . . .,* 2 vols, 's-Gravenhage.

Englert, Sebastian, 1972. *Island at the Centre of the World,* William Mulloy, transl. and ed., London.

Entwistle, J., 1962. *The Spanish Language together with Portuguese, Catalan and Basque,* 2nd edn, London.

Epstein, H., 1969. *Domestic Animals of China,* Farnham Royal.

Eyraud, Eugène, 1864. Letter to Very Rev. Father Etienne Rouchouze, Dec. 1864, *APF,* vol. 38, p. 52-71, 124-38.

Fabié, Antonio Maria, ed. and transl, 1879. *Viajes por España . . .* [*incluyendo los*] *. . . de Andrés Navajero,* Madrid.

Ferdon, Edwin N., 1968. 'Polynesian origins', in Vayda 1968: 95-111 (reprinted from *Science,* 1963, vol. 141, p. 499-503).

ffoulkes, Charles, 1937. *The Gun-Founders of England,* Cambridge.

Fiennes, Richard and Alice, 1968. *The Natural History of the Dog,* London.

Fierens, Germain, 1872. Letter to Father Clair Fouqué, 28 June 1871, *APF,* vol. 44, p. 126-36.

———, 1874. Letter to Father Marcellin Bousquet, 26 Aug. 1873, *APF,* vol. 46, p. 383-7.

———, 1884. Letter to Father Rogatien Martin, 12 May 1884, *APF,* vol. 56, p. 383-93.

Findlay, A. G., 1863. *A Directory for the Navigation of the South Pacific Ocean,* 2nd edn, London.

Firth, Raymond, 1958. *Human Types,* New York (Mentor Books).

Fitz-Roy, Robert, 1839. *Narrative of the Surveying Voyages of His Majesty's Ships 'Adventure' and 'Beagle', between the years 1826 and 1836,* vol. 2 and appendix, London.

Fletcher, H. J., 1930. 'The use of genealogies for the purpose of dating Polynesian history', *JPS,* vol. 39, p. 189-94.

[Foigny, Gabriel de], 1693. *A New Discovery of Terra Incognita Australis, or the Southern World,* transl, by John Dunton, London.

Fornander, Abraham, 1969. *An Account of the Polynesian Race: Its Origins and Migrations,* 3 vols in one, Tokyo (reprint of 1880 edn).

Forster, George, 1777. *A Voyage Round the World in His Britannic Majesty's Sloop, 'Resolution' . . .,* 2 vols, London.

*Forster, Johann Reinhold, 1772-5. 'Journal of a journey from London to Plymouth and a voyage on board his Majesty's ship the 'Resolution', Captain Cook Commander . . .' Ms. in Staatsbibliothek Preussischer Kulturbesitz, Berlin.

———, 1778. *Observations Made During a Voyage Round the World on Physical Geography, Natural History and Ethic Philosophy . . .*, London.

Fraser, Bernard John, 1966. 'Hoturoa', in McLintock 1966:II:120.

Friis, Herman R., ed., 1967. *The Pacific Basin,* New York.

Gallagher, Robert E., ed., 1964. *Byron's Journal of his Circumnavigation, 1764-66,* Cambridge (HS:II:122).

Gallop, Rodney, 1930. *A Book of the Basques,* London.

Galvano, Antonió, 1862. *The Discoveries of the World, from their first original unto the Year of Our Lord, 1555,* London (HS:I:30).

Gandía, Enrique de, 1942. *Primitivos Navegantes Vascos,* Buenos Aires.

Gates, Reginald Ruggles, 1952. *Human Genetics,* 2 vols, New York.

Gerbault, Alain, 1933. *In Quest of the Sun,* London.

Gerstaecker, Friedrich Wilhelm, 1853. *Narrative of a Journey Round the World,* 3 vols, London.

Gessler, Clifford, 1935a. 'Napuka—Isle of Peace', *Asia,* vol. 35, p. 236-45, New York.

———, 1935b. ' "Aita Fanau" (There are no births)', *Asia,* vol. 35, p. 550-5, New York.

———, 1937. *The Dangerous Islands,* London (publ. as *The Road My Body Goes,* New York, 1937).

Gifford, Edward Winslow, 1923. *Tongan Place Names,* Honolulu (BPBMB 6).

Gill, W. Wyatt, [1876]. *Life in the Southern Isles . . .*, London.

Giovanelli, Joseph Louis, 1940. 'Les cyclones en Océanie française', *BSEO,* no. 68, p. 250-67.

Golson, Jack, 1965. 'Thor Heyerdahl and the prehistory of Easter Island', *Oceania,* vol. 36, p. 38-83.

———, 1972. 'The remarkable history of Indo-Pacific man', *JPH,* vol. 7, p. 5-25.

Grattan, H. C., 1963. *The Southwest Pacific to 1900,* Ann Arbor.

Graves, Algernon, comp., 1906. *The Royal Academy of Arts: A Complete Dictionary of Contributors and their Work from its Foundation in 1769 to 1904,* vol. 8, London.

[Greatheed, Samuel], 1799. 'Preliminary discourse', in Wilson 1799:i-lxxxviii.

Green, James Lampert, 1878. Report on cyclone, in *The Friend,* May 1878, p. 2, cited in Danielsson 1956:25-6.

Green, Otis H., 1965. *Spain and the Western Tradition,* 4 vols, Madison.

Green, Roger C., 1966. 'Linguistic subgroupings within Polynesia: the implications for pre-historic settlement', *JPS,* vol. 75, p. 6-38.

———, 1973a. Review of Riley and others 1971, in *JPS,* vol. 82, p. 108-12.

———, 1973b. 'The conquest of the conquistadors', *World Archaeology,* vol. 5, p. 14-31.

Green, Roger C., and M. Kelly, eds., 1970. *Studies in Oceanic Culture History,* vol. 1, Honolulu (PAR 11, DABPBM).

———, 1971. *Studies in Oceanic Culture History,* vol. 2, Honolulu (PAR 12, DABPBM).

Gregory, Herbert E., 1930. *Report of the Director for 1929,* Honolulu (BPBMB 78).

———, 1931. *Report of the Director for 1930,* Honolulu (BPBMB 82).

———, 1932. *Report of the Director for 1931,* Honolulu (BPBMB 94).

———, 1933. *Report of the Director for 1932,* Honolulu (BPBMB 106).

———, 1935. *Report of the Director for 1934,* Honolulu (BPBMB 133).

Grimble, Arthur, 1928. *Gilbert and Ellice Islands Colony Report for 1924-26,* London.

*Gschaedler, André, 1954. 'Mexico and the Pacific 1540-1565: The two voyages of Villalobos and Legaspi and the preparations made for them'. Ph.D. thesis, Columbia University.

Gudgeon, W. E., 1903. 'The whence of the Maori', part 3, *JPS,* vol. 12, p. 120-30.

Guillemard, F. H. H., 1890. *The Life of Ferdinand Magellan,* London.

Gunson, Niel, 1970. 'The deviations of a missionary family: the Henrys of Tahiti', in Davidson and Scarr 1970:31-54.

Haddon, A. C., and James Hornell, 1936-8. *Canoes of Oceania,* 3 vols, Honolulu (BPBMSP 27-9).

Hale, Horatio, 1846. *United States Exploring Expedition . . .: Ethnology and Philology,* Philadelphia (reprinted Ridgewood, NJ, 1968).

Hall, James Norman, and Charles Bernard Nordhoff, 1921. *Faery Lands of the South Seas,* New York.

[Hall, Joseph], [1605]. *Mundus Alter et Idem sive Terra Australis ante hac semper incognita longis itineribus peregrini Academici nuperrime lustrata,* [London?].

*Hambly, William, 1766-7. Journal, 23 June 1766-13 July 1767. PRO Adm 51/4542 (AJCP mfm 1560).

Hamilton, George, 1939. *The Treasure of the Tuamotus,* London.

Hamlin, James, 1842. 'On the mythology of the New Zealanders', *Tasmanian Journal of Natural Sciences, Agriculture, Statistics, &c.,* vol. 1, p. 254-64.

Handy, E. S. Craighill, 1923. *The Native Culture in the Marquesas,* Honolulu (BPBMB 9).

Handy, E. S. Craighill, 1927. *Polynesian Religion,* Honolulu (BPBMB 34).

———, 1930. *History and Culture of the Society Islands,* Honolulu (BPBMB 79).

———, 1932. *Houses, Boats and Fishing in the Society Islands,* Honolulu (BPBMB 90).

Handy, Willowdean Chatterson, 1927. *Handcrafts of the Society Islands,* Honolulu (BPBMB 42).

Hanson, F. Allan, 1970. *Rapan Lifeways,* Boston.

Harlan, Harry V., 1932. 'Early references to the white Indians of Panama', *Journal of Heredity,* vol. 23, p. 319-22.

*Hassall Papers. 2 vols. Ms. A859-60, Mitchell Library, Sydney.

Hassall, Christopher, 1964. *Rupert Brooke: A Biography,* London.

*Haweis, Thomas, 1764-1820. Letters to ... mostly concerning the sending of a mission to Tahiti. Ms. A3024, Mitchell Library, Sydney.

Hawkesworth, John, ed., 1773. *An Account of the Voyages . . . in the Southern Hemisphere . . . by Commodore Byron, Captain Wallis, Captain Carteret, and Captain Cook . . .,* 3 vols, London.

Henderson, Philip, ed., 1930. *Shorter Novels, Vol. 2, Jacobean and Restoration,* London (EL 841).

*Hendrike, Abraham, 1813. Deposition of Abraham Hendrike before Samuel Marsden, Sydney. Ms 55/35, no. 19, Hocken Library, Dunedin.

Henry, Teuira, 1928. *Ancient Tahiti* (BPBMB 48).

Hermel, Athanase, 1911. Letter to Father Marcellin Bousquet, 28 July 1911, *MCath.,* vol. 43, p. 549-52, 562-4.

Herrera y Tordesillas, Antonio de, 1601-15. *Historia General de los Hechos de los Castellanos en las Islas, y Tierra Firme del Mar Océano,* 8 vols, Madrid.

Herskovits, Melville J., 1928. *The American Negro: A Study in Racial Crossing,* New York.

Heyerdahl, Thor, 1950. *The Kon-Tiki Expedition,* London.

———, 1952. *American Indians in the Pacific,* London.

———, 1968. *Sea Routes to Polynesia,* London.

Heyerdahl, Thor, and Edwin Ferdon, eds, 1961. *Archaeology of Easter Island,* Stockholm (RNAE, vol. 1).

———, 1965. *Easter Island and the East Pacific: Miscellaneous Papers,* London (RNAE, vol. 2).

Heyerdahl, Thor, and A. Skjölsvold, 1956. *Archaeological Evidence of pre-Spanish visits to the Galápagos Islands,* Salt Lake City (Memoirs of the Society for American Archaeology, no. 12).

Hezel, Francis X., and Maria Teresa del Valle, 1972. 'Early European contact with the Western Carolines', *JPH,* vol. 7, p. 26-44.

Historical Records of Australia, 1914-25. Ser. I, 26 vols [Sydney].

Historical Records of New Zealand, 1908. 2 vols. Wellington.

Hogg, O. F. G., 1970. *Artillery: Its Origin, Heyday and Decline,* London.

Hooton, Earnest Albert, 1947. *Up From The Ape,* New York.

Hornell, James, 1936. 'The Canoes of Polynesia, Fiji and Micronesia', vol. 1 of Haddon and Hornell 1936-8.

———, 1945. 'Was there pre-Columbian contact between the peoples of Oceania and South America?' *JPS,* vol. 54, p. 167-91.

Hourani, George Fadlo, 1951. *Arab Seafaring in the Indian Ocean in Ancient and Early Medieval Times,* Princeton, NJ.

[House, William], 1957. *A Letter from the South Seas by a Voyager on the 'Daedalus',* John Earnshaw, ed., Cremorne, NSW.

Howard, Alan, 1967. 'Polynesian origins and migrations', in Highland and others 1967:45-101.

*Hudson, William L., 1838-40. Journal of the United States Exploring Expedition. Ms, American Museum of Natural History, New York (mfm PMB 146).

Huguenin, Paul, 1902. *Raiatea La Sacrée,* Neuchâtel, Switzerland (1st publ. in *Bulletin de la Société Neuchateloise de Géographie,* vol. 14, p. 1-247).

Im Thurn, Sir Everard, and Leonard C. Wharton, eds, 1925. *The Journal of William Lockerby . . .,* London (HS:II:52).

Indice Toponómico del Atlas Nacional de España, 1965. Madrid. (Presidencia del Gobierno, Instituto Geográfico y Catastral).

Jack-Hinton, Colin, 1969. *The Search for the Islands of Solomon, 1567-1838,* Oxford.

Jacquier, Henri, 1948. 'A la dérive de l'île de Pâques aux Tuamotu', *BSEO,* no. 83, p. 495-8.

———, 1967. 'Cinquantenaire de la Société d'Etudes Océaniennes', *BSEO,* nos 158-9, p. 716-9.

Janeau, Jules, 1906. 'Trois mois a Takoto', *ASC,* vol. 13, p. 345-7.

Jarves, J. J., 1843. *History of the Hawaiian or Sandwich Islands,* London.

Jaussen, Tepano, 1969. *Grammaire et Dictionnaire de la langue tahitienne,* 5th edn rev. by Archbishop Paul Mazé and Father H. Coppenrath, Paris (SDO 22).

Jensen, Hans, 1970. *Sign, Symbol and Script,* 3rd edn, transl. from German, London.

Jenson, Andrew, 1914-17. 'The Society Islands Mission [of the Church of Jesus Christ of Latter-Day Saints]', *The Utah Genealogical and Historical Magazine,* vol. 5, p. 1-12, 63-73, 108-20, 185-95; vol. 6, p. 39-47, 61-9, 131-6; vol. 7, p. 91-101, 112-21, 178-88; vol. 8, p. 30-8, 80-5.

Jones, Thomas, 1894. 'A ring of coral rock', *Deseret News,* vol. 50, p. 369, Salt Lake City.

Journal Officiel des Etablissements Français de l'Océanie, Jan. 1884-Aug. 1957, Papeete.

Judd, Gerrit P. IV, 1967. *Hawaii: An Informal History,* 4th printing, New York (1st edn, 1961).

Keane, A. H., 1908. *The World's Peoples,* London.

Kelly, Celsus, 1963. *Australia Franciscana,* vol. 1, Madrid.

———, 1965. *Calendar of Documents: Spanish Voyages in the South Pacific,* Madrid.

———, 1966. ed., *La Austrialia del Espiritu Santo,* 2 vols, Cambridge (HS:II: 126-7).

Kelly, Leslie G., 1940. 'Some problems in the study of Maori genealogies', *JPS,* vol. 49, p. 235-42.

———, 1949. *Tainui,* Wellington (MPS 25).

Keynes, Geoffrey, ed., 1968. *The Letters of Rupert Brooke,* London.

King, James, 1785. *A Voyage to the Pacific Ocean . . .,* vol. 3, London.

Knox, Thomas W[allace], 1889. *The Boy Travellers in Australasia: Adventures of two youths in a journey to the Sandwich, Marquesas, Society, Samoan and Feejee Islands . . .,* New York.

Kotzebue, Otto von, 1821. *Voyage of Discovery in the South Sea,* London.

———, 1830. *A New Voyage Round the World in the Years 1823, 24, 25 and 26,* 2 vols, London.

Krämer, Augustin, 1932. *Truk* (Ergebnisse der Südsee-Expedition, 1908-1910, G. Thilenius, ed., II:B:5, Ethnographie Micronesien), Hamburg.

Kroepelien, Bjarne, 1939. 'Pierre Felix Ribourt', *BSEO,* no. 65, p. 139-40.

Labillardière, Jacques Julien Houton de, 1800. *The Account of the Voyage in Search of La Perouse . . .,* 2 vols, London.

Laguesse, Janine, 1954. 'Migration polynésienne moderne', *BSEO,* no. 109, p. 354-7.

Laking, Guy Francis, 1910. *Catalogue of the European Armour and Arms in the Wallace Collection at Hertford House,* 4th edn, London.

Lalande, Maria de Lurdes, 1966. 'Archivo General de Indias de Sevilha: Patronato Real', *Boletim da Filmoteca Ultramarina Portuguesa,* vol. 11, p. 67-125, Lisbon.

Langdon, Robert, 1959. *Island of Love,* 1st edn, London.

———, 1962. 'Are those Pacific treasure stories more fancy than fact?' *PIM,* July 1962, p. 87-90.

———, 1963a. 'Little-known H-bomb atolls have a place in the hall of fame', *PIM,* May 1963, p. 69-72.

———, 1963b. 'The fate of La Pérouse', *Pix,* 23 Mar. 1963, p. 17-21, Sydney.

———, 1968. 'Were Europeans living in the eastern Pacific in the sixteenth century?' *PIM,* Jan. 1968, p. 61-9.

———, 1969. 'Vivid new light on the wild Pacific of Louis Becke's day', *PIM,* Mar. 1969, p. 81-9.

———, 1972. *Tahiti: Island of Love,* 4th edn, Sydney.

——— (in press). 'Of lobes and looms, white chiefs and gaping mummies'.

Lanning, Edward P., 1970. 'South America as a source for aspects of Oceanic cultures', in Green and Kelly 1970:175-82.

Large, J. T., 1904. 'The Aitutaki version of the story of Iro', *JPS,* vol. 12, p. 133-44.

La Santa Biblia, 1957. Buenos Aires (Sociedades Biblicas Unidas).

Laval, Honoré, 1851. Letter to Monseigneur de Calcédonie, *APF,* vol. 23, p. 392-9.

———, 1938. *Mangareva,* Paris.

———, 1968. *Mémoires pour servir à l'histoire de Mangareva, ère chretienne, 1834-1871,* C. W. Newbury and P. O'Reilly, eds, Paris (SDO 15).

Laxalt, Robert, 1968. 'Land of the ancient Basques', *National Geographic Magazine,* vol. 134, p. 240-77.

Lee, Ida, ed., 1920. *Captain Bligh's Second Voyage to the South Sea,* London.

Lessa, William A., 1962. 'An evaluation of early descriptions of Carolinian culture', *Ethnohistory,* vol. 9, p. 313-403.

———, 1966. *Ulithi: A Micronesian Design for Living,* New York.

———, and Tracy Lay, 1953. 'The somatology of Ulithi Atoll', *AJPA,* new ser., vol. 11, p. 405-12.

Lesson, René Primevère, 1839. *Voyage autour du Monde . . .sur la Corvette 'La Coquille',* 2 vols, Paris.

Levison, Michael and others, 1973. *The Settlement of Polynesia: A Computer Simulation,* Canberra.

Lewis, David, 1972. *We, The Navigators,* Canberra.

Lewthwaite, Gordon R., 1967. 'Geographical knowledge of the Pacific peoples', in Friis 1967:57-86.

———, 1973, Review of Lewis 1972, in *JPH,* vol. 8, p. 224-5.

Lisiansky, Urey, 1814. *A Voyage round the World . . .,* London.

l'Océanie française, no. 30, 24 Nov. 1844, Papeete, 'Iles découvertes dans les Pomotou par *l'Industriel'* (reprinted in *Revue de l'Orient,* Paris, 1845, vol. 8, p. 37-42).

Lopez-Mendizabal, Isaac, 1958. *Etimologías de Apellidos Vascos,* Buenos Aires.

Lovett, R., 1899. *The History of the London Missionary Society, 1795-1895,* 2 vols, London.

Lucas, Charles, ed., 1929. *The Pitcairn Island Register Book,* London.

[Lucett, Edward], 1851. *Rovings in the Pacific,* London.

Luomala, Katharine, 1960a. 'The native dog in the Polynesian system of values', in Diamond 1960:190-240.

———, 1960b. 'A history of the binomial classification of the Polynesian native dog', *Pacific Science,* vol. 14, p. 193-223, Honolulu.

McArthur, Norma, 1967. *Island Populations of the Pacific,* Canberra.

McEwen, J. M., 1970. *Niué Dictionary,* Wellington.

Mackaness, George, ed., 1938. *A Book of the 'Bounty' . . .,* London (EL 950).

McLintock, A. H., ed. 1966. *An Encyclopedia of New Zealand,* 3 vols, Wellington.

McNab, J. W., 1967. 'Sweet potatoes and settlement in the Pacific', *JPS,* vol. 76, p. 219-21.

MacQuarrie, Hector, 1920. *Tahiti Days,* New York.

[Magra, James?], 1771. *A Journal of a Voyage round the World . . . Undertaken in Pursuit of Natural Knowledge, at the Desire of the Royal Society . . .,* London.

Malheiro Dias, Carlos, ed., 1923. *Historia da Colonizacão Portuguesa do Brasil,* vol. 2, Porto (i.e. Oporto).

Malo, David, 1951. *Hawaiian Antiquities,* rev. edn, Honolulu (BPBMSP 2).

Marau Taaroa, 1971. *Mémoires de Marau Taaroa, Dernière Reine de Tahiti,* transl. from English, Paris (SDO 27).

Mariot, A., 1874. 'Notes sur les Tuamotous', *Revue Maritime et Coloniale,* vol. 43, p. 978-83.

Markham, Clements, ed., 1904. *The Voyages of Pedro Fernandez de Quiros, 1595-1606,* 2 vols, London (HS:II:14-15).

———, 1911. *Early Spanish Voyages to the Strait of Magellan,* London (HS:II:28).

Marquer, Paulette, 1963. 'Contribution à l'étude anthropologique du peuple Basque et au problème de ses origines raciales', *Bulletins et Mémoires de la Société d'Anthropologie de Paris,* ser. 2, vol. 4, p. 1-240.

Marshall, Donald Stanley, 1962. *Island of Passion (Ra'ivavae),* London (1st publ. New York, 1961).

Martin, Rogatien, 1888. Letter to Father Janvier Weiler, 9 Feb. 1888. *MCath.,* vol. 20, p. 243-4.

Martin-Allanic, Jean-Etienne, 1964. *Bougainville: navigateur et les découvertes de son temps,* 2 vols, Paris.

Maude, H. C., and H. E., 1932. 'The social organization of Banaba or Ocean Island', *JPS,* vol. 41, p. 262-301.

Maude, H. E., 1959. 'Spanish discoveries in the Central Pacific', *JPS,* vol. 68, p. 284-326.

———, 1964. 'The history of Pitcairn Island', in Ross and Moverley 1964:45-101.

———, 1968. *Of Islands and Men,* Melbourne.

———, 1971. 'Pacific history—past, present and future', *JPH,* vol. 6, p. 3-24.

Mauruc, Arnaud, 1848. 'Notes sur les îles de l'Archipel Dangereux', *Bulletin de la Société de Géographie,* ser. 3, vol. 9, p. 73-97, Paris.

Mazé, Paul, 1933. Letter to director, 6 Sept. 1932, *ASC,* no. 375, p. 6-11.

Meier, R. J., 1970. *The Easter Islander: A Study in Human Biology* (University Microfilms, Inc., Ann Arbor).

Meilink-Roelofsz, M. A. P., 1962. *Asian Trade and European Influence,* The Hague.

Meinicke, Carl, 1876. *Die Inseln des Stillen Ozeans,* vol. 2, Leipzig.

Merrill, Elmer Drew, 1954. *The Botany of Cook's Voyages,* Waltham, Mass.

Messager de Tahiti, 26 Sept. 1852-Dec. 1883 (vol. 1, no. 1-vol. 32, no. 52), Papeete.

Metraux, Alfred, 1936. 'Numerals from Easter Island', *Man,* vol. 36, p. 190-1.

———, 1940. *Ethnology of Easter Island,* Honolulu (BPBMB 160).

———, 1957. *Easter Island,* London.

Milet-Mureau, L. A., ed., 1807. *A Voyage Round the World Performed . . . by the 'Boussole' and 'Astrolabe' under the Command of J. F. G. de la Pérouse,* 3rd edn, transl. from French, 3 vols, London.

Mitchell, Mairin, 1958. *Elcano: The First Circumnavigator,* London.

Moerenhout, J.-A., 1837. *Voyages aux îles du Grand Ocean,* 2 vols, Paris (reprinted Paris, 1959).

Montgomery, James, comp. 1840. *Voyages and Travels round the World by the Rev. Daniel Tyerman and George Bennet, Esq. Deputed from the London Missionary Society to Visit Their Various Stations in the South Sea Islands* [*etc*] *. . . between the Years 1821 and 1829,* 2nd edn, London.

Montiton, Albert, 1855. Letter to his parents, 6 Apr. 1854, *APF,* vol. 27, p. 438-52.

———, 1873. Letter to Father Marcellin Bousquet, 4 Sept., 1872, *APF,* vol. 45, p. 275-95, 371-85.

———, 1874. 'Les Paumotus: traditions et coutûmes', *MCath.,* vol. 6, p. 339, 342-4, 354-6, 366-7, 378-9, 491-2, 497-8, 502-4.

Morrison, James, 1935. *The Journal of James Morrison . . .,* Owen Rutter, ed., London.

———, 1966. *Journal de James Morrison,* French transl. by Bertrand Jaunez, Paris (SDO 16).

Mouly, Delmas, 1954. *A travers les deserts d'Eau et de Corail,* Paris.

Mourant, A. E., and others, 1958. *The ABO Blood Groups: Comprehensive Tables and Maps of World Distribution,* Oxford.

Mulert, F. E., ed., 1911. *De Reis van Mr Jacob Roggeveen,* The Hague.

Murra, John, 1963. 'The historic tribes of Ecuador', in Steward, 1963:785-821.

Myhill, Henry, 1966. *The Spanish Pyrenees,* London.

Nance, R. Morton, 1913. 'Caravels', *Mariner's Mirror,* vol. 3, p. 265-71, London.

Naval Chronicle, 1806, vol. 17.

Naval Intelligence Division, 1941. *Spain and Portugal: Vol. 1: The Peninsula* [London]. (GHS, BR 502).

Naval Intelligence Division, 1943-5. *Pacific Islands,* 4 vols, [Cambridge]. (GHS, BR 519, 519A, 519B, 519C).

Navarrete, Martin Fernández de, 1825-37. *Colección de los Viages y Descubrimientos que hicieron por Mar los Españoles,* 5 vols, Madrid. Vols 4 and 5 cited as Navarrete IV and Navarrete V.

[Nevile, Henry], 1668. *The Isle of Pines, or A Late Discovery of a Fourth Island in Terra Australis Incognita,* London.

Newell, J. E., ed., 1911. *Pratt's Grammar and Dictionary of the Samoan Language,* 4th edn, Malua, Samoa (1st edn, 1862).

New Zealand Herald, 1968, Wellington.

Nicholas, Henry, 1892. 'Genealogies and historical notes from Rarotonga', *JPS,* vol. 1, p. 20-9, 65-75.

Nightingale, Thomas, 1835. *Oceanic Sketches,* London.

Nordman, Oscar, 1952. 'A voyage packed with incident', *PIM,* July 1952, p. 72-4.

*Nott, Henry, 1811. Letters to Rowland Hassall, 15 June, 15 July, 4 Nov, 1811, in Hassall Papers, vol. 2.

*———, 1813. Letter to Rowland Hassall, Feb. 1813, in Hassall Papers, vol. 2.

Nowell, Charles E., 1936. 'The Loaisa expedition and the ownership of the Moluccas', *Pacific Historical Review,* vol. 5, p. 325-36.

———, 1945. 'The treaty of Tordesillas and the diplomatic background of American history', in Ogden and Sluiter 1945:1-18.

———, ed., 1962. *Magellan's Voyage Around the World,* Evanston.

Nunn, George E., 1934. 'Magellan's route in the Pacific', *Geographical Review,* vol. 24, p. 615-33.

O'Brien, Patricia J., 1972. 'The sweet potato: its origin and dispersal', *AAnth.,* vol. 74. p. 342-65.

Ogden, A., and E. Sluiter, eds, 1945. *Greater America: Essays in Honor of Herbert Eugene Bolton,* Berkeley.

Oliver, S. Pasfield, 1909. *The Life of Philibert Commerson, D. M., Naturaliste du Roi,* London.

Omoto, Keiichi, 1971-2. 'Polymorphisms and genetic affinities of the Ainu of Hokkaido', *Human Biology in Oceania,* vol. 1, p. 278-88.

O'Reilly, Patrick, 1963. 'Le Maire et Schouten a Futuna en 1616', *JSO,* vol. 19, p. 55-80.

———, and Edouard Reitman, 1967. *Bibliographie de Tahiti et de la Polynésie française,* Paris (SDO 14).

O'Reilly, Patrick, and Raoul Teissier, 1962. *Tahitiens: Répertoire Bio-bibliographique de la Polynésie française,* Paris (SDO 10).

*Orsmond, John Muggridge, 1824. Journal, 1 Jan.-21 Feb. 1824, SSJ 74, LMS Archives (AJCP mfm M4).

Ottino, Paul, 1965. *La pêche au grand filet à Tahiti,* Paris (Cahiers ORSTOM — Sciences Humaines, vol. 2, no. 2).

Oviedo y Valdés, Gonzalo Fernández de, 1945. *Historia General y Natural de las Indias, Islas y Tierra-Firme del Mar Océano,* 14 vols, Asunción del Paraguay. Cited as Oviedo.

Pacific Islands Monthly, 1930-to date.

Pacific Islands Pilot, 1957. Vol. 3, 'The Eastern Groups . . .', 8th edn, London.

———, 1969. Vol. 3, 'The Eastern Groups . . .', 9th edn., Taunton.

Pailhes, A., 1875. 'Souvenirs du Pacifique', *Tour du Monde,* vol. 29, p. 241-72, Paris.

Palmer, J. Linton, 1870. 'A visit to Easter Island or Rapa Nui, in 1868', *Royal Geographical Society Journal,* vol. 40, p. 167-81, London.

Paris, Francis Edmond, [1841]. *Essai sur la Construction Navale des Peuples Extra-Europeens,* Paris.

Parkinson, Sydney, 1773. *A Journal of a Voyage to the South Seas . . .,* London.

Parry, J. H., 1964. *The Age of Reconnaissance,* New York (Mentor Books).

Pawley, Andrew, 1966. 'Polynesian languages: a subgrouping based on shared innovations in morphology', *JPS,* vol. 75, p. 39-64.

Peard, George, 1973. *To the Pacific and Arctic with Beechey,* Barry M. Gough, ed., Cambridge (HS:II:143).

Peers, Edgar Allison, ed., 1959. *Cassell's Spanish-English, English-Spanish Dictionary,* London.

Phillip, Arthur, 1789. *The Voyage of Governor Phillip to Botany Bay . . .,* London.

Pickering, Charles, 1851. *The Races of Man,* London.

Piddington, Ralph O., 1939. See Williamson 1939.

Pinart, Alphonse, 1878a. 'Voyage a l'île de Pâques' *Tour du Monde,* vol. 36, p. 225-40, Paris.

———, 1878b. 'Exploration de l'île de Pâques', *Bulletin de la Société Géographique,* ser. 6, vol. 6, p. 193-213, Paris.

Pinchot, Gifford, [1930]. *To the South Seas,* London.

Polack, J. S., 1838. *New Zealand: Being a Narrative of Travels and Adventures in the Country between 1831 and 1837,* 2 vols, London.

Pomare II, 1811. Letter to William Henry, 8 Nov. 1811, *Evangelical Magazine,* vol. 20, p. 281-2, July 1812.

Price, A. Grenfell, 1963. *The Western Invasions of the Pacific and its Continents,* Oxford.

Price, A. Grenfell, 1964. *The Importance of Disease in History,* Adelaide (George Adlington Syme oration).

Quatrefages, J. L. A. de, [1866]. *Les Polynésiens et Leurs Migrations,* Paris.

Real Academia Española, 1803. *Diccionario de la Lengua Castellana,* 4th edn, Madrid.

Ricardi, Eugène, 1844a. 'Les Pomotou', *l'Océanie française,* no. 26, 27 Oct. 1844, Papeete.

———, 1844b. 'Les Pomotou—L'île de la Chaine, Anaa', *l'Océanie française,* no. 27, 3 Nov. 1844, Papeete.

Riesenberg, Saul H., and Shigeru Kaneshiro, 1961. 'A Caroline Islands Script', *Anthropological Papers,* no. 60, Smithsonian Institution, Bureau of American Enthnology, Bulletin 173, Washington.

Riley, Carroll L., and others, eds, 1971. *Man Across the Sea,* Austin, Texas.

Riseborough, Don, 1973. 'Voyage of the "Ice Bird" ', *Canberra Times,* 24 Mar. 1973, p. 9.

Robarts, Edward, 1974. *The Marquesan Journal of . . . 1797-1824,* Greg Dening, ed., Canberra.

Roberton, J. B. W., 1956. 'Genealogies as a basis for Maori chronology', *JPS,* vol. 65, p. 45-54.

———, 1957. 'The role of tribal tradition in New Zealand prehistory', *JPS,* vol. 66, p. 249-63.

———, 1958. 'The significance of New Zealand tribal tradition', *JPS,* vol. 67, p. 39-57.

*Robertson, George, 1766-8. '. . . Observations of Longitude taken after Doctor Masculines [*sic*] method on board his majesty's ship *Dolphin* in her voyage in the years 1766, 1767, 1768 . . .', in Wallis 1766-8.

Robinson, W. A., 1972. *Return to the Sea,* London.

Robson, R. W., comp., 1935. *Pacific Islands Year Book,* 2nd edn, Sydney.

Rollin, Louis, 1929. *Les Iles Marquises,* Paris.

Ross, Alan S. C. and A. W. Moverly, 1964. *The Pitcairnese Language,* London.

Routledge, Catherine Scoresby, 1919. *The Mystery of Easter Island,* London.

Rowland, Alfred Cooper, 1943. 'How Polynesians came into the Pacific . . .', *PIM,* July 1943, inside front cover.

[Rowland, Alfred Cooper], 1947. 'Polynesians from Peru', *PIM,* Mar. 1947, p. 34.

Russell, Samuel 1935. *Tahiti and French Oceania,* Sydney.

Salas, Eugenio Pereira, 1951. 'Jacques Antoine Moerenhout y el comercio de perlas en Valparaiso', *Revista Chilena de Historia y Geografia,* no. 118, p. 5-21, Santiago.

Savage, Stephen, 1916. 'The period of Iro-Nui-Ma-Oata and Tangiia-Nui-Ariki' — part 1, *JPS,* vol. 25, p. 138-49.

———, 1917. 'The period of Iro-Nui-Ma-Oata and Tangiia-Nui-Ariki', parts 2-5, *JPS,* vol. 26, p. 10-18, 52-65.

———, 1962. *A Dictionary of the Maori Language of Rarotonga,* Wellington.

*Savage, Stephen, and Tamuera Te Rei, 1907. 'An ancient history of Tangiia, Rarotonga'. Ts. in Australian National University Library, Canberra.

Scheinfeld, Amram, 1939. *You and Heredity,* London.

———, 1950. *The New You and Heredity,* Philadelphia.

———, 1972. *Heredity in Humans,* Philadelphia.

Schenck, Earl, 1940. *Come Unto These Yellow Sands,* Indianapolis.

Scherzer, Karl, 1861-3. *Narrative of the Circumnavigation of the Globe by the Austrian frigate 'Novara' . . . in the years 1857, 1858, & 1859 . . .,* 3 vols, London.

Schurz, William Lytle, 1939. *The Manila Galleon,* New York.

Sebeok, Thomas A., ed., 1971. *Current Trends in Linguistics,* vol. 8, *Linguistics in Oceania,* The Hague.

Seligman, Adrian, 1947. *The Voyage of the 'Cap Pilar',* London.

Seligman, C. G., 1939. 'The Roman Orient and the Far East', *Report of the Smithsonian Institution for 1938:* 547-68, Washington.

Seurat, Leon Gaston, 1904. 'Observations sur quelques îles orientales de l'archipel Tuamotu', *JOEFO,* 15 Dec. 1904, p. 404-7.

———, 1905. 'Les engins de pêche des anciens Paumotu', *l'Anthropologie,* vol. 16, p. 295-307.

Shapiro, Harry L., 1929. *Descendants of the Mutineers of the 'Bounty',* Honolulu (MBPBM, vol. 11, no. 1).

———, 1930. *The Physical Characters of the Society Islanders,* Honolulu (MBPBM, vol. 11, no. 4).

———, 1940. 'The distribution of blood groups in Polynesia', *AJPA,* vol. 26, p. 409-16.

Sharp, Andrew, 1957. *Ancient Voyagers in the Pacific,* 2nd edn, Harmondsworth (Penguin Books).

———, 1960. *The Discovery of the Pacific Islands,* London.

———, 1963. *Ancient Voyagers in Polynesia,* Auckland.

———, ed., 1968. *The Voyages of Abel Janszoon Tasman,* Oxford.

———, ed., 1970. *The Journal of Jacob Roggeveen,* Oxford.

Shine, Ian, 1969. 'Hidden superstitions as a barrier between doctor and patient in an island culture', *Perspectives in Biology and Medicine,* vol. 12, p. 63-70.

———, 1970. *Serendipity in St Helena,* Oxford.

Silverman, David, 1967. *Pitcairn Island*, Cleveland.

Simmons, R. T., 1965. 'The blood group genetics of Easter Islanders (Pascuense) and other Polynesians' in Heyerdahl and Ferdon 1965:333-43.

———, 1968. 'Blood group genes in Polynesians and comparisons with other Pacific peoples' in Vayda 1968:45-62 (reprinted from *Oceania*, 1962, vol. 32, p. 198-210).

———, and others, 1952. 'A collaborative genetical survey in Marshall Islanders', *AJPA*, vol. 10, p. 31-54.

———, 1955. 'A blood group genetical survey in Cook Islanders, Polynesia, and comparisons with American Indians', *AJPA*, vol. 13, p. 667-90.

Singer, Charles, and others, eds, 1956. *A History of Technology*, vol. 2, 'From the Renaissance to the Industrial Revolution, c.1500-c.1750', Oxford.

*Sluiter, Engel, 1933. 'The voyage of Jacques Mahu and Simon de Cordes into the Pacific Ocean, 1598-1600'. MA thesis, University of California, Berkeley.

Smith, Bernard, 1969. *European Vision in the South Pacific*, paperback edn, Oxford.

Smith, Carlyle, 1961. 'The Poike Ditch', in Heyerdahl and Ferdon 1961:385-91.

Smith, S. Percy, 1893. 'The genealogy of the Pomare family of Tahiti from the papers of the Rev. J. M. Orsmond', *JPS*, vol. 2, p. 25-42.

———, ed., 1900. 'The *Aotea* canoe', *JPS*, vol. 9, p. 211-33.

———, ed., 1913. *The Lore of the Whare-wanaga; or teachings of the Maori College on religion, cosmogony and history*, New Plymouth, NZ (MPS 3).

———, 1921. *Hawaiki: The Original Home of the Maori*, 4th edn, Auckland.

Spence, Lewis, 1933. *The Problem of Lemuria, the sunken continent of the Pacific*, 3rd imp., London.

Stair, John B., 1897. *Old Samoa or Flotsam and Jetsam from the Pacific Ocean*, London.

Stanley of Alderney *Lord*, ed., 1874. *The First Voyage Round the World, by Magellan*, London (HS:I:52).

Stevens, Henry N., ed., 1930. *New Light on the Discovery of Australia*, London (HS:II:64).

Stevenson, Robert Louis, n.d. *In The South Seas*, London (EL 769).

Steward, Julian H., ed., 1963. *Handbook of South American Indians*, vol. 2, *The Andean Civilizations*, New York.

Stimson, J. Frank, 1933a. *Tuamotuan Religion*, Honolulu (BPBMB 103).

———, 1933b. *The Cult of Kiho-Tumu*, Honolulu (BPBMB 111).

———, 1957. *Songs and Tales of the Sea Kings*, Salem.

———, and Donald Stanley Marshall, 1964. *A Dictionary of Some Tuamotuan Dialects of the Polynesian Language*, The Hague.

Stokes, John F. G., 1930a. 'An evaluation of early genealogies used for Polynesian history', *JPS*, vol. 39, p. 1-42.

———, 1930b. 'Burial of King Keawe', *PHHS*, no. 17, p. 63-73.

———, 1931. 'Iron with the early Hawaiians', *PHHS*, no. 18, p. 6-14.

———, 1932. 'Spaniards and the sweet potato in Hawaii and Hawaiian-American contacts', *AAnth.*, vol. 34, p. 596-600.

———, 1939. 'Hawaii's discovery by Spaniards: theories traced and refuted', *PHHS*, no. 20, p. 38-113.

———, 1955. 'Language in Rapa', *JPS*, vol. 64, p. 315-40.

Stone, Thomas R., 1964. *A Revised Study Guide and Dictionary: The Tahitian Dialect of the Polynesian Language*, Papeete.

Suggs, Robert C., 1960. *The Island Civilizations of Polynesia*, New York (Mentor Books).

Sullivan, Louis R., 1921. *A contribution to Samoan somatology: based on field studies of E. W. Gifford and W. C. McKern*, Honolulu (MBPBM, vol. 8, no. 2).

———, 1922. *A contribution to Tongan somatology; based on field studies of E. W. Gifford and W. C. McKern*, Honolulu (MBPBM, vol. 8, no. 4).

———, 1923. *Marquesan somatology, with comparative notes on Samoa and Tonga; based on field studies of E. S. Craighill Handy and Willowdean C. Handy*, Honolulu (MBPBM, vol. 9, no. 2).

Sydney Gazette, 1803-27.

Tautain, Louis Frédéric, 1897. 'Notes sur les constructions et monuments des Marquises', *l'Anthropologie*, vol. 8, p. 538-58, 667-78, Paris.

Taylor, E. G. R., 1956. *The Haven-Finding Art: A History of Navigation from Odysseus to Captain Cook*, London.

Teissier, Raoul, 1953. 'Etude demographique sur les Etablissements français de l'Océanie . . .', *BSEO*, no. 102, p. 6-31.

———, 1969. 'Les cyclones en Polynésie française', *BSEO*, nos, 166-7, p. 152-235.

Terasaki, Paul, 1973. Preface to Dausset and Colombani 1973:1-2.

Terlyn, Vincent de Paul, 1900. 'La mission des Tuamotu ou Archipel Dangereux', *ASC*, new ser., vol. 7, p. 188-94.

Thompson, J. T., 1871. 'Ethnological considerations on the whence of the Maori', *Transactions of the New Zealand Institute*, vol. 4, p. 23-51, Wellington.

Thomson, Basil, 1915. See Edwards and Hamilton, 1915.

Thomson, William J., 1891. 'Te Pito te Henua, or Easter Island', *Annual Report of the . . . Smithsonian Institution . . . for the year ending June 30, 1889*: p. 447-552, Washington.

Thorsby, E. and others, 1973. 'HL-A, blood group and serum type polymorphism of natives on Easter Island', in Dausset and Colombani 1973:287-302.

Titcomb, Margaret, 1969. *Dog and Man in the Ancient Pacific . . .,* Honolulu (BPBMSP 59).

Torquemada, Juan de, 1615. *Monarquia Indiana,* vol. 1, Seville.

Townsend, Ebenezer, Jr, n.d. 'Extract from the diary of Ebenezer Townsend, Jr,' *Hawaiian Historical Society Reprints* no. 4, Honolulu (1st publ. 1888).

*Townshend, Charles H., and H. F. Moore, 1899-1900. 'Ethnographic notes on cruise of US Fisheries Commission steamer "Albatross" in the South Seas'. Ts. in Smithsonian Institution, Washington.

Tregear, Edward [1891]. *The Maori-Polynesian Comparative Dictionary,* Wellington.

———, and S. Percy Smith, 1907. *Vocabulary and Grammar of the Niué Dialect of the Polynesian Language,* Wellington.

Tudor, Judy, ed., 1972. *Pacific Islands Year Book,* 11th edn, Sydney.

Turnbull, John, 1813. *A Voyage Round the World . . .,* 2nd edn, London.

Turner, George, 1861. *Nineteen Years in Polynesia,* London.

———, 1884. *Samoa a Hundred Years Ago and Long Before,* London.

Vancouver, George, 1801. *A Voyage of Discovery to the North Pacific Ocean and Round the World . . .,* 6 vols, London.

Van der Sluis, Isaac, [1970]. *The Treponematosis of Tahiti,* Amsterdam.

Vayda, Andrew P., 1968. *Peoples and Cultures of the Pacific: An Anthropological Reader,* New York.

Villiers, J. A. J. de, ed., 1906. *East and West Indian Mirror,* London (HS:II:18).

Visher, Stephen Sargent, 1925. *Tropical Cyclones of the Pacific,* Honolulu (BPBMB 20).

Wafer, Lionel, 1934. *A New Voyage & Description of the Isthmus of America,* Oxford (HS:II:73).

*Wallis, Helen M., 1953. 'The exploration of the South Sea, 1519 to 1644: a study of the influence of physical factors with a reconstruction of the routes of the explorers: D. Phil. thesis, Oxford University.

———, ed., 1965. *Carteret's Voyage round the World, 1766-1769,* 2 vols, Cambridge (HS:II:124-5).

*Wallis, Samuel, 1766-8. Journal, 19 June 1766-13 May 1768, PRO Adm 55/35 (AJCP mfm 1579).

Walter, Richard, ed., 1923. *A Voyage Round the World in the Years 1740-4,* London (EL 510).

Ward, R. Gerard, ed., 1966-7. *American Activities in the Central Pacific, 1790-1870,* 8 vols, Ridgewood, NJ.

Watts, John, 1789. 'Lieutenant Watts' narrative of the return of *Lady Penrhyn* transport . . . ', in Phillip 1789:222-44.

Whitaker, Thomas W., 1971. 'Endemism and pre-Columbian migration of the bottle gourd, Lagenaria siceraria (Mol.) Standl', in Riley and others 1971:320-7.

White, Ralph, 1967. 'Onomastically induced word replacement in Tahitian', in Highland and others 1967:323-38.

Wilkes, Charles, 1845. *Narrative of the United States Exploring Expedition . . .,* 5 vols and atlas, London.

Williams, William, 1844. *A Dictionary of the New Zealand Language and a Concise Grammar,* Paihia, NZ.

Williamson, James A., ed., 1933. *The Observations of Sir Richard Hawkins,* London (Argonaut Press pub. 13).

Williamson, Robert W., 1939. *Essays in Polynesian Ethnology,* R. O. Piddington, ed. and contrib., Cambridge.

*Wilson, Charles, and James Elder, 1803. Journal of a tour of Taiarapu, 26 June-1 Aug. 1803, SSJ 14, LMS Archives (AJCP mfm Ml).

Wilson, William, comp., 1799. *A Missionary Voyage to the Southern Pacific Ocean . . .,* London.

Winge, Ojvind, 1950. *Inheritance in Dogs,* Ithaca, New York.

Woodcock, George, 1966. *The Greeks in India,* London.

Wright, Ione Stuessey, 1945. 'Early Spanish voyages from America to the Far East, 1527-1565', in Ogden and Sluiter 1945:59-78.

Wright, Olive, ed., 1950. *New Zealand 1826-1827 from the French of Dumont d'Urville,* Wellington.

Wurm, Stefan, 1954. 'The Indonesian element in Melanesia: a reply', *JPS,* vol. 63, p. 266-73.

Wycherley, George, 1935. *Buccaneers of the Pacific,* London (Neptune Library).

Yen, Douglas E., 1960. 'The sweet potato in the Pacific', *JPS,* vol. 69, p. 368-75.

———, 1971a. 'The development of agriculture in Oceania', in Green and Kelly 1971:1-12.

———, 1971b. 'Construction of the hypothesis for distribution of the sweet potato', in Riley and others 1971:328-42.

*Youl, John, and others, 1806-7. Missionaries' public journal, Tahiti, 8 Mar. 1806-11 Aug. 1807, SSJ 2, LMS Archives (AJCP mfm M2).

Young, J. L., 1919. 'The Paumotu conception of the heavens and of creation', *JPS,* vol. 28, p. 209-11.

Zaragoza, Justo, 1876-80. *Historia del Descubrimiento de las Regiones Australes,* 3 vols, Madrid.

Zweig, Stefan, 1938. *Magellan,* London.

Index

CORRIGENDA: On p. 108, line 16, for *plate 8* please read *plate 6;* on p. 145n, last line, for *chapter 19* read *chapter 18;* on p. 155, line 18, insert the word *southern* before *Europe;* on p. 245, line 2, for *p. 159* read *p. 160;* on p. 317, note 16, line 6, and note 19, line 2, for *Appendix B* read *Appendix C;* and on p. 318, note 8, line 8, for *Appendix C,* read *Appendix B.*

PACIFIC

AHE

TUAMOTU

MATAHIVA

TIKEHAU

RANGIROA

ARUTUA

KAUKURA

MAKATEA

NIA

TUPAI

SOCIETY ISLANDS

BORABORA

TAHAA

HUAHINE

RAIATEA

TETIAROA

MOOREA

TAHITI

MAIAO

MEHETIA

OCEA